Lecture Notes in Computer Science 11568

Commenced Publication in 1973
Founding and Former Series Editors:
Gerhard Goos, Juris Hartmanis, and Jan van Leeuwen

More information about this series at http://www.springer.com/series/7409

Masaaki Kurosu (Ed.)

Human-Computer Interaction

Design Practice in Contemporary Societies

Thematic Area, HCI 2019
Held as Part of the 21st HCI International Conference, HCII 2019
Orlando, FL, USA, July 26–31, 2019
Proceedings, Part III

 Springer

Editor
Masaaki Kurosu
The Open University of Japan
Chiba, Japan

ISSN 0302-9743   ISSN 1611-3349 (electronic)
Lecture Notes in Computer Science
ISBN 978-3-030-22635-0   ISBN 978-3-030-22636-7 (eBook)
https://doi.org/10.1007/978-3-030-22636-7

LNCS Sublibrary: SL3 – Information Systems and Applications, incl. Internet/Web, and HCI

This Springer imprint is published by the registered company Springer Nature Switzerland AG
The registered company address is: Gewerbestrasse 11, 6330 Cham, Switzerland

Foreword

The 21st International Conference on Human-Computer Interaction, HCI International 2019, was held in Orlando, FL, USA, during July 26–31, 2019. The event incorporated the 18 thematic areas and affiliated conferences listed on the following page.

A total of 5,029 individuals from academia, research institutes, industry, and governmental agencies from 73 countries submitted contributions, and 1,274 papers and 209 posters were included in the pre-conference proceedings. These contributions address the latest research and development efforts and highlight the human aspects of design and use of computing systems. The contributions thoroughly cover the entire field of human-computer interaction, addressing major advances in knowledge and effective use of computers in a variety of application areas. The volumes constituting the full set of the pre-conference proceedings are listed in the following pages.

This year the HCI International (HCII) conference introduced the new option of "late-breaking work." This applies both for papers and posters and the corresponding volume(s) of the proceedings will be published just after the conference. Full papers will be included in the *HCII 2019 Late-Breaking Work Papers Proceedings* volume of the proceedings to be published in the Springer LNCS series, while poster extended abstracts will be included as short papers in the HCII 2019 *Late-Breaking Work Poster Extended Abstracts* volume to be published in the Springer CCIS series.

I would like to thank the program board chairs and the members of the program boards of all thematic areas and affiliated conferences for their contribution to the highest scientific quality and the overall success of the HCI International 2019 conference.

This conference would not have been possible without the continuous and unwavering support and advice of the founder, Conference General Chair Emeritus and Conference Scientific Advisor Prof. Gavriel Salvendy. For his outstanding efforts, I would like to express my appreciation to the communications chair and editor of *HCI International News,* Dr. Abbas Moallem.

July 2019   Constantine Stephanidis

HCI International 2019 Thematic Areas and Affiliated Conferences

Thematic areas:

- HCI 2019: Human-Computer Interaction
- HIMI 2019: Human Interface and the Management of Information

Affiliated conferences:

- EPCE 2019: 16th International Conference on Engineering Psychology and Cognitive Ergonomics
- UAHCI 2019: 13th International Conference on Universal Access in Human-Computer Interaction
- VAMR 2019: 11th International Conference on Virtual, Augmented and Mixed Reality
- CCD 2019: 11th International Conference on Cross-Cultural Design
- SCSM 2019: 11th International Conference on Social Computing and Social Media
- AC 2019: 13th International Conference on Augmented Cognition
- DHM 2019: 10th International Conference on Digital Human Modeling and Applications in Health, Safety, Ergonomics and Risk Management
- DUXU 2019: 8th International Conference on Design, User Experience, and Usability
- DAPI 2019: 7th International Conference on Distributed, Ambient and Pervasive Interactions
- HCIBGO 2019: 6th International Conference on HCI in Business, Government and Organizations
- LCT 2019: 6th International Conference on Learning and Collaboration Technologies
- ITAP 2019: 5th International Conference on Human Aspects of IT for the Aged Population
- HCI-CPT 2019: First International Conference on HCI for Cybersecurity, Privacy and Trust
- HCI-Games 2019: First International Conference on HCI in Games
- MobiTAS 2019: First International Conference on HCI in Mobility, Transport, and Automotive Systems
- AIS 2019: First International Conference on Adaptive Instructional Systems

Pre-conference Proceedings Volumes Full List

1. LNCS 11566, Human-Computer Interaction: Perspectives on Design (Part I), edited by Masaaki Kurosu
2. LNCS 11567, Human-Computer Interaction: Recognition and Interaction Technologies (Part II), edited by Masaaki Kurosu
3. LNCS 11568, Human-Computer Interaction: Design Practice in Contemporary Societies (Part III), edited by Masaaki Kurosu
4. LNCS 11569, Human Interface and the Management of Information: Visual Information and Knowledge Management (Part I), edited by Sakae Yamamoto and Hirohiko Mori
5. LNCS 11570, Human Interface and the Management of Information: Information in Intelligent Systems (Part II), edited by Sakae Yamamoto and Hirohiko Mori
6. LNAI 11571, Engineering Psychology and Cognitive Ergonomics, edited by Don Harris
7. LNCS 11572, Universal Access in Human-Computer Interaction: Theory, Methods and Tools (Part I), edited by Margherita Antona and Constantine Stephanidis
8. LNCS 11573, Universal Access in Human-Computer Interaction: Multimodality and Assistive Environments (Part II), edited by Margherita Antona and Constantine Stephanidis
9. LNCS 11574, Virtual, Augmented and Mixed Reality: Multimodal Interaction (Part I), edited by Jessie Y. C. Chen and Gino Fragomeni
10. LNCS 11575, Virtual, Augmented and Mixed Reality: Applications and Case Studies (Part II), edited by Jessie Y. C. Chen and Gino Fragomeni
11. LNCS 11576, Cross-Cultural Design: Methods, Tools and User Experience (Part I), edited by P. L. Patrick Rau
12. LNCS 11577, Cross-Cultural Design: Culture and Society (Part II), edited by P. L. Patrick Rau
13. LNCS 11578, Social Computing and Social Media: Design, Human Behavior and Analytics (Part I), edited by Gabriele Meiselwitz
14. LNCS 11579, Social Computing and Social Media: Communication and Social Communities (Part II), edited by Gabriele Meiselwitz
15. LNAI 11580, Augmented Cognition, edited by Dylan D. Schmorrow and Cali M. Fidopiastis
16. LNCS 11581, Digital Human Modeling and Applications in Health, Safety, Ergonomics and Risk Management: Human Body and Motion (Part I), edited by Vincent G. Duffy

34. CCIS 1033, HCI International 2019 - Posters (Part II), edited by Constantine Stephanidis
35. CCIS 1034, HCI International 2019 - Posters (Part III), edited by Constantine Stephanidis

http://2019.hci.international/proceedings

Human-Computer Interaction Thematic Area (HCI 2019)

Program Board Chair(s): **Masaaki Kurosu,** *Japan*

- Jose Abdelnour-Nocera, UK
- Mark Apperley, New Zealand
- Kaveh Bazargan, France
- Simone Borsci, The Netherlands
- Kuohsiang Chen, P.R. China
- Stefano Federici, Italy
- Isabela Gasparini, Brazil
- Ayako Hashizume, Japan
- Wonil Hwang, Korea
- Mitsuhiko Karashima, Japan
- Shinichi Koyama, Japan
- Naoko Okuizumi, Japan
- Takanobu Omata, Japan
- Katsuhiko Onishi, Japan
- Philippe Palanque, France
- Alberto Raposo, Brazil
- Guangfeng Song, USA
- Hiroshi Ujita, Japan

The full list with the Program Board Chairs and the members of the Program Boards of all thematic areas and affiliated conferences is available online at:

http://www.hci.international/board-members-2019.php

HCI International 2020

The 22nd International Conference on Human-Computer Interaction, HCI International 2020, will be held jointly with the affiliated conferences in Copenhagen, Denmark, at the Bella Center Copenhagen, July 19–24, 2020. It will cover a broad spectrum of themes related to HCI, including theoretical issues, methods, tools, processes, and case studies in HCI design, as well as novel interaction techniques, interfaces, and applications. The proceedings will be published by Springer. More information will be available on the conference website: http://2020.hci.international/.

General Chair
Prof. Constantine Stephanidis
University of Crete and ICS-FORTH
Heraklion, Crete, Greece
E-mail: general_chair@hcii2020.org

http://2020.hci.international/

Contents – Part III

Design and Evaluation Case Studies

Design for Social Challenges

A Usability Evaluation of Diabetes Mobile Applications

Meng-Hsueh Hsieh[1], Yu-Ching Chen[2], and Chun-Heng Ho[1(✉)]

[1] Department of Industrial Design, National Cheng Kung University,
No. 1, University Road, Tainan, Taiwan (R.O.C.)
hoch@mail.ncku.edu.tw
[2] Department of Public Health, National Cheng Kung University,
No. 1, University Road, Tainan, Taiwan (R.O.C.)

Abstract. Technology has been demonstrated to have positive impact on diabetes self-care while usability of applications in diabetes self-care remains to be explored. Evidence-based study on usability is needed to justify the adoption of health information systems for diabetes. The aim of this study was to evaluate and compare the usability of three existing mobile applications for diabetes self-care. This study assessed the usability of the diabetes applications in terms of usability testing. A total of 30 participants (15 men and 15 women) with type 2 diabetes were enrolled in the usability evaluation. The participants had a mean age of 60.03 years (SD = 8.92). The participants were first time users of the three applications to be assessed. After completing a set of three task scenarios, participants evaluated the application with System Usability Scale (SUS). When operating the applications, participants were instructed to follow think-aloud protocol. The results showed that the mean SUS score of App 3 was significantly higher than scores of App 1 and App 2. No significant effect of gender on the SUS scores was found. Taken together, high SUS score, presented screenshots of the operation process, and pros identified by the participants during the think-aloud protocol serve as the proxy to design diabetes self-care applications attaining higher level of usability.

Keywords: Usability evaluation · Mobile health application ·
Diabetes self-care

1 Introduction

Usability evaluation enables researchers to identify problems of existing systems and products and provide insight for system improvement. Recognized as a key quality attribute of software, usability is defined as the degree to which a product can be effortlessly operated by users to accomplish particular objective with efficiency, effectiveness, and satisfaction (Harrati et al. 2016). In the domain of human-computer interaction, the usability of mobile applications has been highlighted since well-designed applications improves user experiences (Hoehle et al. 2016).

Meanwhile, with the prevalence of mobile devices, mobile health (mHealth) supporting medical care are becoming more common. Among the mobile applications, applications targeting diabetes self-care were developed. Diabetes, one of the chronic

© Springer Nature Switzerland AG 2019
M. Kurosu (Ed.): HCII 2019, LNCS 11568, pp. 3–15, 2019.
https://doi.org/10.1007/978-3-030-22636-7_1

illness, affect around 415 million people worldwide; based on estimation, 193 million people suffer from undiagnosed diabetes (Chatterjee et al. 2017). Moreover, study pointed out that diabetes is a main cause of hospitalization and in-hospital mortality (Li et al. 2018). Diabetes requires patients to monitor their own health condition. Poor glycemic control leads to complications including heart disease or stroke, visual impairment, hyperglycemic crisis causing death, and limb amputation (Fu et al. 2017). Based on a study of diabetes age from 3419 adults with T2DM, the mean ($\pm$ SD) age was 62.9 $\pm$ 12.5 years (Nanayakkara et al. 2018).

Despite the prevalence and the complications of diabetes, the conditions of patients can be alleviated by means of appropriate management. Diabetes self-care is essential to blood glucose levels control (Lin et al. 2017). According to studies, mobile applications assisting self-care has been found to be beneficial to diabetes patients. Mobile health applications could assist diabetes self-care through monitoring of blood glucose, weight, and dietary (Hoppe et al. 2017). Research found that diabetes applications were associated with improved glycemic control and have great potential to assist diabetes self-care (Fu et al. 2017).

Technology could assist diabetes self-care improvement while studies also pointed out the need for assessment of the experienced usability of users in the field of mobile health applications. Furthermore, the insufficiency of usability has been identified as one of the obstacles in the adoption of health information systems. Although the number of new healthcare applications greatly increased in the last few years, the usefulness of the applications is inconsistent (Rose et al. 2017). In addition, studies found that the prevailing obstacle in the adoption and operation of health information systems includes the ambiguous design and low usability (Khajouei et al. 2018). With the continuous growing number of patients suffering from diabetes and elderly patients, the usability of applications assisting diabetes self-care is especially important.

The objective of this study was to evaluate the usability of three existing diabetes self-care applications and explore the main pros and cons users pointed out during the operation of the applications. Usability evaluation study explores the problems of the system and assists designers in generating improved design solutions. Therefore, usability test, an effective and widely adopted method assessing the product by means of practical task scenario of product usage (Sonderegger et al. 2016) was utilized.

To collect more detailed information about the operation process of applications, participants followed think-aloud protocol. Think-aloud protocol has been widely applied to usability evaluation studies. With think-aloud data collection method, participants share their thoughts with the researcher (Verkuyl et al. 2018). Researchers conducting the usability testing of an electronic system utilized concurrent think-aloud moderating technique to encourage participants vocalize their thoughts during the test sessions (Aiyegbusi et al. 2018). Study showed that think-aloud protocol analysis and realistic simulations provided a presented a successful usability evaluation (Chrimes et al. 2014).

2 Methods

2.1 Participants

A total of 30 participants were enrolled in the usability evaluation of diabetes self-care mobile applications from a diabetes clinic. The basic criteria included a type 2 diabetes diagnosis, regular usage of smart phone, and normal vision.

The participants consisted of 15 women and 15 men between 41 and 78 years of age. Participants had a mean age of 60.03 years (SD = 8.92). Participants did not report any vision problems that interfered with mobile application operation. All participants had a type 2 diabetes diagnosis and the habit of using smart phones and tablet. The table below presents the participant demographics (Table 1).

Table 1. Participant demographics (n = 30).

Variable		n
Age	<65	20
	≧65	10
Gender	Male	15
	Female	15
Smart phone/tablet usage	Often (4–7 days per week)	28
	Occasional (1–≦3 days per week)	2
	Rarely (<1 day per week)	0
Education	Elementary school	2
	Middle school	4
	High school	7
	College	12
	Graduate school	5

2.2 Experimental Materials

The main experimental materials in this study included three different mobile applications for diabetes self-care, and a System Usability Scale (SUS). This study conducted the survey in a paper-based format. The three applications were actual products that could be downloaded for either iOS or Android systems from App Store or Google Play. For each app, the content was the same when operated in both systems. All three diabetes applications could present the entered blood glucose level in a graph view.

Since the study included elderly participants, mobile phone with larger screen was used to present the experimental stimuli. An iPhone 7 Plus with 5.5 in. (diagonal) widescreen LCD and 1,920 by 1,080 pixel resolution was adopted. The three applications were installed in the iPhone used in the experiment (Fig. 1).

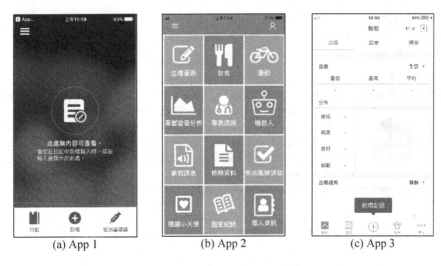

(a) App 1   (b) App 2   (c) App 3

Fig. 1. The interfaces of the three evaluated diabetes applications.

2.3 Experimental Task Scenarios Design

As a widely adopted and very effective method of usability evaluation, the purpose of usability test is to assess the product by constructing a practical product usage task scenario that involves prospective users (Sonderegger et al. 2016). Therefore, to design practical experimental tasks, this study conducted interviews at a diabetes clinic, one of the certified organizations of the National Diabetes Shared Care Network. Through the interview, 6 medical personnel including 2 diabetes dietitians and 4 diabetes educators (also registered nurses) identified the diabetes application functions most important and fundamental to diabetes patients' self-care. A feature list with 27 functions categorized from a study of 40 diabetes targeted applications (Hoppe et al. 2017) was provided to the personnel as the basis of important function identification. The selected functions became the basis of tasks scenario design for the usability evaluation.

The task scenarios included (1) Enter blood glucose value before breakfast into the application, (2) Enter blood glucose value after breakfast and enter food intake by adding a photo of the meal into the application, and (3) View the blood glucose measurement in a graph format.

Since the standard blood glucose value is different for before and after meal, entering the "before" or "after" meal in the record is important. For diabetes patients aiming for a target A1C of below 7%, blood glucose levels should mostly be under 130 mg/dl before meals and under 180 mg/dl after meals (Gebel 2011). For task one, a blood glucose value before meal was provided to the participant. For task two, a blood glucose value after meal was given. When using the applications, the picture of food consumed should be taken first. After finishing the meal, patients measure and put the glucose value with meal photo into the application. Therefore, a photo was provided in the album of the iPhone.

2.4   Procedures

The procedure of the experiment was as follows: All participants were informed about the purpose and experimental process. To reduce the stress of participants, the moderator highlighted that the purpose of the experiment was to evaluate the usability of the mobile applications instead of the performance of participants. Basic information was collected from the participants, including their age, frequency of using smart phone and tablet, and education backgrounds. Participants were asked to use think-aloud protocol as a strategy during the operation process.

Each task was printed on an A4-sized paper. Necessary information for task completion was provided below the task scenario description, including given blood glucose values of "before" or "after" breakfast information. For the task of entering food intake, a meal photo was prepared in the photo album of iPhone. During the operation, when the participants were not sure where to tap and asked for assistance, hint was provided. The moderator suggested an area, such as the upper or lower part of the screen, instead of directly pointing at the button. Following think-aloud protocol, the participants were asked to describe the issues that influenced the usability of the systems during the operation of mobile applications. After completing the three tasks, the participants finished the SUS subjective assessment to evaluate the overall usability of the applications. For each participant, the process of completing the three task scenarios and SUS was repeated to evaluate the three diabetes self-care applications.

3   Results and Discussion

3.1   Quantitative Results

The SUS (System Usability Scale) means of the three evaluated diabetes applications were first compared based on the scale matching the SUS scores, acceptability ranges, and grade scale. This study used repeated measures ANOVA to analyze the SUS scores of the three applications. The effect of gender on the SUS scores was analyzed with a t-test. The three diabetes applications were referred to as App 1, App 2, and App 3 in the results and discussion sections.

Developed by Brooke (1996), the ten-item SUS has been widely applied to usability studies. Researchers further established the five grade scales and six adjective ratings that correlates with the SUS score (Bangor et al. 2009) (see Fig. 2). Based on the means of SUS scores, in terms of acceptability ranges, App 1 ($M = 69.75$) and App 2 ($M = 65.42$) were "marginal" while App 3 ($M = 82.50$) was "acceptable." In terms of grade scale, App 1 and App 2 received a "D" scale while App 3 received a "B" scale.

There was a statistically significant difference between groups ($F(2,87) = 10.231$, $p < .001$). The results of the repeated measures analyses of variance revealed that the SUS scores of App 3 were significantly higher than that of App 1 and App 2. Post-hoc analysis using Scheffe indicated significant difference between the SUS scores of App 3 and App 1, as well as App 3 and App 2. The SUS scores did not differ significantly between App1 and App 2 (Tables 2 and 3).

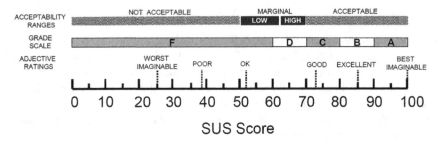

Fig. 2. A comparison of the average SUS score in relation to acceptability scores, grade scale, and adjective ratings (Bangor et al. 2009).

Table 2. SUS mean and standard deviation of the experimental data.

Application	M (SUS score)	SD	Scheffe post hoc test[a]
App 1	69.75	15.18	
App 2	65.42	17.23	
App 3	82.50	12.90	3 > 1, 3 > 2

[a]1 = App 1; 2 = App 2; 3 = App 3

Table 3. Multiple comparisons: SUS scores of the three applications.

(I) App no.	(J) App no.	Mean difference (I-J)	Std. error	Sig.
1	2	4.3333	3.9263	.546
	3	−12.7500*	3.9263	.007
2	1	−4.3333	3.9263	.546
	3	−17.0833*	3.9263	.000
3	1	12.7500*	3.9263	.007
	2	17.0833*	3.9263	.000

*The mean difference is significant at the 0.05 level.

Table 4. Independent sample t-test for gender effects on different apps

Application	Male		Female		t	p	F
	M	SD	M	SD			
App 1	67.50	16.39	72.00	14.05	−0.807	.426	0.060
App 2	64.17	14.19	66.67	20.26	−0.391	.698	1.608
App 3	78.67	11.87	86.33	13.12	−1.678	.104	0.347

An independent-sample t-test revealed no significant effect of gender on the SUS scores of the three applications, App 1: $t(28) = 0.807, p = 0.426$; App 2: $t(28) = 0.391$, $p = 0.698$; App 3: $t(28) = 1.678$, $p = 0.104$. For each application, both male and female participants gave similar evaluations to the usability (Table 4).

3.2   Qualitative Results

The following sections presents the usability issues identified by means of think-aloud protocol when the participants operated the applications to complete the assigned tasks. With the screenshots of the operation flow shown in the figures and description of the operation procedure, these findings could be a reference for diabetes application usability improvement and user interface (UI) design.

App 1. When opening App 1, the button entitled "Add a new record" at the bottom of the interface (see Fig. 3(a)) enabled the participants to understand its function. When entering blood glucose (see Fig. 3(b)), many participants were not sure where to tap even though the "Tap here" hint was shown in the text field next to the mg/dl. Below the mg/dl, another way of entering the blood glucose was using the slider, a horizontal track with a control. By tapping the plus and minus symbol on either end of the slider, the value could be adjusted. However, the function of the colorful slider was not clear to most of the participants.

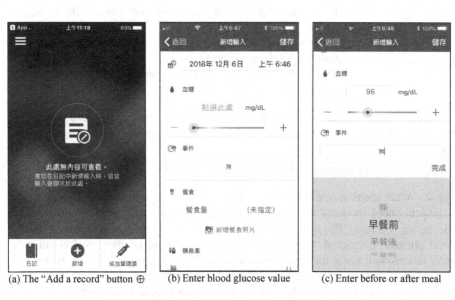

(a) The "Add a record" button ⊕   (b) Enter blood glucose value   (c) Enter before or after meal

Fig. 3. Operation flow screenshots of App 1.

At the section of entering the before or after meal timing, the title "Event" was not clear to participants (see Fig. 3(c)). After tapping the text field with rounded corners, a picker with a scrollable list was displayed. In addition, even if the participants overlooked the text field entering the before or after meal information, the blood glucose value record could still be saved. However, the information was critical to blood glucose self-care since before or after meal has different standards. Therefore, an error prevention mechanism to assist the correct procedure was required.

In App 1, the items for entering various information were placed on the same interface as a long form, including insulin amount, exercise, health condition, medicine taken, blood pressure, and body weight. However, participants found the interface complex and confusing with too much content. Instead, only the items most important to diabetes self-care should be displayed.

Except the "add a new record" button, the format of buttons in App 1 were ghost buttons, the button bordered by a thin line (see Fig. 3(b)). To participants, the buttons were difficult to find among the text on interface layout (Table 5).

Table 5. App 1 issues identified in think-aloud protocol.

App 1	Issue
Overall	Larger font size would be helpful to the operation
	Participants were not sure about where to tap next
	The dark background color made the text and interface unclear
Enter blood glucose value	The button entitled "Event" was not easily associated with before or after meal
	The function of the colorful bar and plus minus is not clear
	Even if the before or after meal information was not selected, the glucose record could still be saved
Enter food intake	The function of "take a photo" and "upload a photo" should be integrated in the same button
	As a frequently used function, the photo upload function should be moved to the upper part of the interface instead of locating at the very bottom
	The photo uploaded was not shown at the corresponding place
View graph of blood glucose	The view graph button was not easily found

App 2. When opening App 2, there were twelve buttons (see Fig. 1(b)). Therefore, the participants need to spend more time searching for the place to enter blood glucose. The button entitled "Physical measurement" was not immediately associated with blood glucose. Instead of "Physical measurement", before or after meal could be a better description. Since the first button includes the functions of entering blood glucose, blood pressure, heart beat, body weight measurement, the title of the button should be adjusted to include the above functions yet simple to understand.

According to participants, after entering the blood glucose entering section, the buttons on the top could not be noticed immediately since the green background color blended with the color on the top of the interface (see Fig. 4(b)). However, when the participants forgot to tap the before or after meal button, a reminder was provided by the application. The application prevented the users from going to the next section without recording before or after meal. The font size of the description above the buttons were too small. Participants with presbyopia had difficulty reading the description.

In addition, the transparent design of the "after breakfast" button was not clear enough. To several elderly participants, the color was too light to be noticed. Participants mentioned that both before and after meal font should be clearly displayed simultaneously while the underline could be used indicate the selected button. When

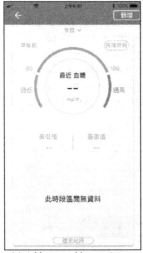

| (a) Add a record button (upper right corner) | (b) Enter blood glucose value | (c) Enter before or after meal by the buttons listed on the top |

Fig. 4. Operation flow screenshots of App 2.

the entered blood glucose value exceeds the standard level, App 2 provided an instant reminder to the users.

The formant of buttons in App 2 was ghost button bordered by a thin line, with transparent internal area consisting of plain text, as shown in the upper right corner of the figure. For the layout, important buttons were placed on the upper right corner, including the "add a new record" and "complete" buttons. Compared to App 3, Participants spent more time searching for buttons when using App 2 (Table 6).

Table 6. App 2 issues identified in think-aloud protocol.

App 2	Issue
Overall	Larger font size would be helpful to the operation
	Participants were not sure about where to tap
Enter blood glucose value	The menu page contains too many choices and buttons
	The button entitled "Physical Measurement" was not immediately associated with recording blood glucose
	The buttons on the top cannot be noticed immediately
	The before or after meal buttons should be clearly displayed
Enter food intake	The function of "uploading a photo" has a plus sign (+) without other indication; some participants found it hard to notice
	When entering the photo album, the latest photo was displayed on the very bottom of the list
View graph of blood glucose	The view graph button was not easily found

App 3. In App 3, participants found the "Next step" button useful because it provided guidance to the continuing process (see Fig. 5(a)). After entering the blood glucose value, the "Next step" button led users to the next section entering the before or after meal where eight buttons were clearly displayed, including before meal, after meal, before exercising, after exercising, fasting, before sleeping, midnight, or others (see Fig. 5(b)). Once a button was tapped, the following question "Which meal?" was presented below. With the question, four additional buttons were displayed, including breakfast, lunch, dinner, and dessert (see Fig. 5(c)).

(a) The filled button "Next Step"   (b) Before or after meal buttons   (c) breakfast, lunch, dinner, or dessert buttons at the bottom

Fig. 5. Operation flow screenshots of App 3.

The format of buttons in App 3 were filled button with rounded corners. The tapped buttons were colored while the other buttons remained unchanged. Compared to App 2, the areas of App3 buttons were twice larger than that of App 2 (Table 7).

Table 7. App 3 issues identified in think-aloud protocol.

App 3	Issue
Overall	Larger font size would be helpful to the operation
Enter blood glucose value	The button for adding a new record did not provide text description
Enter food intake	After selecting the meal photo, the "Complete" button was not easy to tap because the sensing area was not clear
View graph of blood glucose	The button entitled "Trend" was not easily associated with graph view and blood glucose value record

Comparison of the Applications. The major findings of the think-aloud protocol in this study were compared and discussed in the following points: First, "Guidance" was highlighted by the participants. Most participants found the guidance of App 3 helpful since they did not need to spend much time thinking about what to do next. With the "Next Step" filled button, the system directed users to the continuing procedure. In contrast, the other two applications did not provide clear guidance. In App 1 and App 2, various text fields for information inputting were displayed on an interface. Although participants could input information with random sequence, most of them found the user interface layout too complex.

Second, choices presented as buttons tend to help participants input information more efficiently. In App 1, all choices of before or after meal were integrated in the picker below the "Event" button. Therefore, the participants had to tap the "Event" button first in order to see the scrollable list with eleven choices including before breakfast, after breakfast, before lunch, after lunch, etc. In App 2, the choices of meal were displayed as six buttons, including fasting, breakfast, lunch, dinner, before sleep, and midnight. After tapping any of the six buttons, the submenu of before or after meal was displayed. App 3 presented all choices of the before or after meal at once with eight buttons, including before meal, after meal, before exercise, after exercise, fasting, before sleep, midnight, and others. Users did not need to tap the button to see the submenu. According to many participants, instead of using a picker, the choices should be presented as buttons for better usability.

Third, issue with interaction area was identified. During the observation, when the participants tried to tap a button but did not successfully hit the interaction area, they tend to give up and try tapping other buttons, especially in App 2, the application with the smallest buttons among the three applications. Therefore, the size and interaction area of the button could be extended for an improved usability. According to the research on elderly usage of interface, the surface of the interaction area should be extended instead of being limited to a small area (Castilla et al. 2018). For instance, the area of the buttons in App 3 were larger than that of the other two applications. To participants, larger buttons were easier to tap. Previous research on the effect of button size on performance and perceptions found that users generally had better performance with medium to large buttons when using touchscreen (Tao et al. 2018).

Consequently, error prevention was important to usability. For blood glucose monitoring, the before or after meal information is critical since the before or after meal has different standards. Inputting the record with before or after meal is mandatory. Therefore, the applications should assist the users in selecting before or after meal choices labeling the entered blood glucose value. For App 1, the before or after meal buttons could be skipped by mistake. In App 2, if the before or after meal buttons were not tapped, a reminder preventing users from saving the record appeared. However, many users could not find the "after meal" button due to its transparency. App 3 actively guided the participants to select before or after meal buttons during the information input process. Error prevention, one of the identified usability principles (Fung et al. 2016), should be highlighted in the design of diabetes applications.

In sum, based on the think-aloud protocol, participants mentioned that clear and simple user interface layout would increase the usability of the diabetes applications, especially to elderly users. Most importantly, "guidance" was frequently highlighted by participants. Applications for diabetes self-care should actively provide clear guidance that led to the following steps instead of displaying complex information on the interface. Font size and buttons should be larger for clear recognition, especially to users with presbyopia. If the usability of the applications were insufficient, the elderly users may give up using the applications.

4 Conclusion

This study evaluated and compared the usability of three existing diabetes self-care applications by means of usability survey, SUS. Based on the results of SUS, the usability of App 3 was significantly better than that of the other two applications. According to the independent t-test, gender did not have a significant effect on the SUS scores. Through think-aloud protocol, usability issues were identified in all three applications. Issues highlighted by elderly participants should be taken into consideration by designers since diabetes patients was composed largely of elderly people. With the quantitative scores, the qualitative results of think-aloud protocol, and the presented screenshots of the operation flow, the results could be applied to the interface design and usability improvement of diabetes self-care applications.

References

Aiyegbusi, O.L., et al.: Development and usability testing of an electronic patient-reported outcome measure (ePROM) system for patients with advanced chronic kidney disease. Comput. Biol. Med. **101**, 120–127 (2018)

Bangor, A., Kortum, P.T., Miller, J.T.: Determining what individual SUS scores mean: adding an adjective rating scale. J. Usability Stud. **4**(3), 114–123 (2009)

Brooke, J.: SUS: a quick and dirty usability scale. In: Jordan, P.W., Thomas, B., Weerdmesster, B.A., McClelland, I.L. (eds.) Usability Evaluation in Industry. Taylor and Francis, London (1996)

Castilla, D., et al.: Teaching digital literacy skills to the elderly using a social network with linear navigation: a case study in a rural area. Int. J. Hum. Comput. Stud. **118**, 24–37 (2018)

Chatterjee, S., Khunti, K., Davies, M.J.: Type 2 diabetes. Lancet **389**(10085), 2239–2251 (2017)

Chrimes, D., Kitos, N.R., Kushniruk, A., Mann, D.M.: Usability testing of avoiding diabetes thru action plan targeting (ADAPT) decision support for integrating care-based counseling of pre-diabetes in an electronic health record. Int. J. Med. Inf. **83**(9), 636–647 (2014)

Fu, H., McMahon, S.K., Gross, C.R., Adam, T.J., Wyman, J.F.: Usability and clinical efficacy of diabetes mobile applications for adults with type 2 diabetes: a systematic review. Diabetes Res. Clin. Pract. **131**, 70–81 (2017)

Fung, R.H.Y., Chiu, D.K.W., Ko, E.H.T., Ho, K.K.W., Lo, P.: Heuristic usability evaluation of University of Hong Kong libraries' mobile website. J. Acad. Librariansh. **42**(5), 581–594 (2016)

Gebel, E.: Back to Basics: Blood Glucose. http://www.diabetesforecastorg/2011/apr/back-to-basics-blood-glucose.html. Accessed 24 Jan 2019

Harrati, N., Bouchrika, I., Tari, A., Ladjailia, A.: Exploring user satisfaction for e-learning systems via usage-based metrics and system usability scale analysis. Comput. Hum. Behav. **61**, 463–471 (2016)

Hoehle, H., Aljafari, R., Venkatesh, V.: Leveraging Microsoft's mobile usability guidelines: conceptualizing and developing scales for mobile application usability. Int. J. Hum. Comput. Stud. **89**, 35–53 (2016)

Hoppe, C.D., Cade, J.E., Carter, M.: An evaluation of diabetes targeted apps for Android smartphone in relation to behaviour change techniques. J. Hum. Nutr. Diet. **30**(3), 326–338 (2017)

Khajouei, R., Hajesmaeel Gohari, S., Mirzaee, M.: Comparison of two heuristic evaluation methods for evaluating the usability of health information systems. J. Biomed. Inform. **80**, 37–42 (2018)

Lin, K., et al.: Effects of depression, diabetes distress, diabetes self-efficacy, and diabetes self-management on glycemic control among Chinese population with type 2 diabetes mellitus. Diabetes Res. Clin. Pract. **131**, 179–186 (2017)

Li, T.-C., et al.: Development and validation of prediction models for the risks of diabetes-related hospitalization and in-hospital mortality in patients with type 2 diabetes. Metabolism **85**, 38–47 (2018)

Nanayakkara, N., et al.: Age, age at diagnosis and diabetes duration are all associated with vascular complications in type 2 diabetes. J. Diabetes Complic. **32**(3), 279–290 (2018)

Rose, K.J., Petrut, C., L'Heveder, R., de Sabata, S.: IDF Europe's position on mobile applications in diabetes. Diabetes Res. Clin. Pract. **149**, 39–46 (2019)

Sonderegger, A., Schmutz, S., Sauer, J.: The influence of age in usability testing. Appl. Ergon. **52**, 291–300 (2016)

Tao, D., Yuan, J., Liu, S., Qu, X.: Effects of button design characteristics on performance and perceptions of touchscreen use. Int. J. Ind. Ergon. **64**, 59–68 (2018)

Verkuyl, M., Romaniuk, D., Mastrilli, P.: Virtual gaming simulation of a mental health assessment: a usability study. Nurse Educ. Pract. **31**, 83–87 (2018)

Comparative Review of Research on Health Information Technology in Biomedical Informatics and Human-Computer Interaction

Sunyoung Kim[✉]

Rutgers University, New Brunswick, NJ 08901, USA
sunyoung.kim@rutgers.edu

Abstract. This paper provides a comparative review of literature in Biomedical Informatics (BI) and Human-Computer Interaction (HCI) communities that conducted human-subject studies of health information technology (HIT) to understand the kinds of knowledge these two fields develop and disseminate. We systematically searched 8 databases to retrieve relevant articles published between 2007 and 2016. Articles involving human-subject studies of HIT were eligible for inclusion. Among 1,355 articles identified by the search strategy, 593 articles were selected for final analysis. Text mining techniques were used to cluster the selected articles into five themes, followed by a thematic analysis of randomly selected 3 articles per cluster through which a hierarchical taxonomy of research areas was created. The results illustrate that BI contributes mainly to generating knowledge associated with the use of HIT in clinical settings, while HCI focuses primarily on the design and evaluation of personal healthcare applications. We believe that better understanding and bringing together the strengths of each field's perspectives would yield results that are more generalizable and have greater potential impact in healthcare research.

Keywords: Health information technology · Human-computer interaction · Biomedical informatics

1 Introduction

Health information technology (HIT) has the enormous potential to transform healthcare practices by positively influencing quality, efficiency, and cost-effectiveness of healthcare [32]. However, these efforts have been made in several disjointed research communities, including but not limited to biomedical informatics (BI) and human-computer interaction (HCI). While these fields often pursue mutual goals of improving healthcare, they typically work in separation without established pathways for transfer of knowledge and expertise, as different fields have their own publication venues for disseminating research results that seldom overlap. Therefore, researchers and practitioners in different communities have suffered from lack of opportunities to interact with each other and develop a shared body of knowledge across communities [32].

Researchers in BI and HCI communities can greatly benefit from increased familiarity with the work of the other, as their strengths can complement each other. Furthermore, a shared understanding of the types of knowledge each community provides

© Springer Nature Switzerland AG 2019
M. Kurosu (Ed.): HCII 2019, LNCS 11568, pp. 16–32, 2019.
https://doi.org/10.1007/978-3-030-22636-7_2

could serve as a basis for cross-disciplinary collaborations that would lead to improved clinical outcomes and to new conceptual, generalizable knowledge. A key issue in developing a shared body of knowledge across different communities is to establish a common ground to understand differing research design, development, and evaluation practices and the inherently contrasting priorities and values of the different fields.

Efforts have been made to increase the interaction among different communities. These efforts have been in the form of workshops, seminars, and social events where researchers and practitioners get together to share and discuss methods, study designs, and findings within communities. A key outcome of these interactions was agreement about the need for greater collaboration among different research communities interested in the design, implementation, and use of HIT to transcend the mutual respect of one another's work [32].

While such effort promotes better understanding of each other's work, it does not provide for a systematic understanding of the differences and commonalities across different research communities. Thus, this study aims to contribute to existing efforts to advance shared understanding through a comparative analysis of published HIT articles in the BI and HCI communities. This paper identifies the distinct characteristics and contributions of HIT research in the fields of BI and HCI to shed light on the opportunities for integrating their perspectives, leveraging their complementary strengths, and developing better research practices for healthcare technology.

We conducted a comparative review of 593 articles from 8 publication venues in BI and HCI. We clustered these articles into five themes using text-mining techniques. Then, 3 articles from each cluster were randomly selected to conduct a thematic analysis through which a hierarchical taxonomy of research topics and contributions was created. The results illustrate that the primary focus of BI is on the clinical contexts that contribute to generating knowledge associated with the use of health information in clinical settings, while HCI focuses primarily on the everyday contexts that contribute to the design and evaluation of personal healthcare applications.

The contribution of this paper is to identify the kinds of knowledge that BI and HCI communities develop and disseminate systematically and comparatively. For people who are already working in the intersection of BI and HCI, there might be nothing much surprising about the findings. However, we believe that it is nonetheless useful to have this analysis done systematically. Furthermore, a categorization of research themes and methods in different communities can help researchers who are unfamiliar with the other community to easily comprehend and acknowledge similarities and differences. We believe that better understanding and bringing together the strengths of each research field's perspectives would yield results that are more generalizable and have greater potential impact in healthcare research.

2   Background

2.1   HIT Research in the HCI Community

HCI is the study of how people interact with computers and to what extent computers are or are not developed for successful interaction with human beings, spanning a number of disciplines, including computer science, design, psychology, ergonomics, etc. Among a wide range of application domains of HCI studies, healthcare has been one important area of inquiry. Thus, a large body of HCI research has been amassed to understand and enhance the relationships between humans and technology in the context of healthcare.

HCI researchers, however, have put relatively less effort in a systematic review of literature in healthcare. One exception is a comprehensive review by Fitzpatrick and Ellingsen that gives an overview of health-related research through review of literature published in the Journal and related conferences of Computer Supported Cooperative Work in the past 25 years (from 1986 to 2011) [12]. Their analysis illustrated a range of topics and solutions that the HCI community studied in healthcare, suggesting three areas for improvement: broadening the scope of study settings and perspectives, having a greater impact on larger-scale HIT projects, and adopting and adapting to traditional methods in clinical settings. While this review provided helpful insights on enhancing the impact of HCI research on healthcare, it did not investigate healthcare studies conducted in other fields.

2.2   HIT Research in the BI Community

BI is the interdisciplinary field that studies and pursues the effective uses of biomedical data, information, and knowledge for scientific inquiry, problem solving and decision making to improve human health. Like HCI, the work of BI spans a number of disciplines, including computer science, human factors, and medicine. The American Medical Informatics Association sees the goal of BI as "transforming health care through trusted science, education, and the practice of informatics".

BI literature references HCI literature, particularly in the context of usability and cognitive science. For example, in a textbook on informatics, Biomedical Informatics [36], the authors of a chapter on cognitive science and biomedical informatics defined HCI as a "multifaceted discipline devoted to the study and practice of usability". Usability aspect has been addressed within the BI community particularly within the context of electronic health records (EHRs) and patient safety. As part of the Health Information Technology for Economic and Clinical Health (HITECH) Act, enacted as part of the American Recovery and Reinvestment Act of 2009, the Office of the National Coordinator for Health Information Technology (ONC) funded four Strategic Health IT Advanced Research Projects (SHARP). One of these, SHARPC was to study "usability, workflow, and cognitive support issues of EHRs" [45]. One major product of the project was developing a framework for usability for EHRs resulting in a number of books..The authors of the first book, "Better EHR", emphasized that usability issues have not received attention in the BI until recently [45], and a follow-up, entitled "Inspired EHRs", focuses on design principles and usability aspects of EHR [7].

2.3   Current Efforts to Connect BI and HCI Communities

For years, efforts have been made to bring together researchers and practitioners working on HIT to foster conversation and promote deeper understandings and more profound connections between a range of relevant communities, including BI and HCI.

An increasing number of HCI researchers have published in both BI and HCI publication venues, playing key peer roles in connecting these disjointed communities. Also, HCI researchers are increasingly working closely with clinicians to conduct HIT research that embraces both the HCI concern for understanding the nuances of experience and to develop new conceptual understandings and systems, as well as a BI concern for measurable clinical impact and making more applied contributions. [6] is an example article which authors are from different domains to study an HIT problem using a range of methods, including observation, participatory design, and a randomized controlled trial.

Another form of effort has been made through workshops, seminars, and social events where people from different research communities meet and get to know each other. For example, the Workshop on Interactive Systems in Healthcare was enacted in 2010 to bring together researchers and practitioners in different communities to work together to improve the design, adoption, and use of health information technology. Another example is a series of CHI workshops that focused on understanding how the design of medical technology impacts its use in clinical settings [35], which yielded guidebooks on HCI fieldwork in healthcare [15]. To our knowledge, however, there has not been much effort to establish a comprehensive understanding of research articles published in these disjointed communities through a systematic, comparative literature review.

Table 1. Search of electronic resources.

Database for BI articles
Journal of Medical Internet Research (JMIR)
Journal of the American Medical Informatics Association (JAMIA)
Journal of Biomedical Informatics (JBI)
International Journal of Medical Informatics (IJMI)
Database for HCI articles
ACM conference on Human Factors in Computing Systems (CHI)
ACM conference on Computer-Supported Cooperative Work and Social Computing (CSCW)
ACM Conference on Pervasive and Ubiquitous Computing (Ubicomp)
International Conference on Human-Computer Interaction with Mobile Devices and Services (MobileHCI)

3 Methods

This study was carried out with reference to the PRISMA statement to aid transparent and complete reporting of the study [27]. A study protocol documenting keywords and eligibility criteria was produced in advance.

3.1   Search Strategy

To retrieve BI articles, we selected four relevant publication venues with the highest h5-index from the Medical Informatics category of Google Scholar. To retrieve HCI articles, we selected four relevant publication venues with a high h5-index from Human-Computer Interaction category of Google Scholar (See Table 1). Journals were retrieved to search BI articles, and conferences were retrieved to search HCI articles. These choices reflect the different publication proclivities: journal publications are predominant in the BI community, whereas the HCI community publishes high-quality papers to conferences due to the fast-evolving nature of technology.

We searched articles from aforementioned 8 databases using specific queries. We tried several iterations of combinations of different keywords to retrieve the most relevant but still widely inclusive set of search results. In the end, we determined the final set of BI keywords as technology, participant, patient, and usability (or user study), and HCI keywords as health, patient, participant, and clinical (or medical). We then found out the retrieved HCI articles included studies about wellbeing and persuasive technology for behavior change that are beyond the scope of traditional HIT research. Thus, we included extra keywords to exclude such articles, including wellness (or well-being, wellbeing) and persuasive in HCI keywords. Last, we selected the articles published within the last 10 years (2007 to 2016) to reflect recent publication trends in the fields. Consequently, the final search queries for each database are as following:

BI search query: ((technology AND participant AND patient AND (usability OR user study))) AND ("2007"[Date-Publication]: "2016"[Date-Publication])

HCI search query: ((health AND patient AND (clinical OR medical)) NOT ((wellness OR wellbeing OR well-being) AND persuasive)) AND ("2007"[Date-Publication]:"2016"[Date-Publication])

3.2   Eligibility Criteria

Any articles that reported human subject studies of HIT were eligible for inclusion. Human subject studies refer to systematic, scientific investigation that involves humans as research subjects, and HIT refers to information technology that captures, stores, manages or transmits information related to healthcare of individuals or the activities of organizations that work within the context of healthcare. The following criteria were used to exclude articles from consideration:

- An article that did not involve human subject studies
- An article with no section describing study methods
- Systematic review papers
- An article that is not a formal paper, such as workshop papers, extended abstracts, and letters

Table 2. Themes and randomly selected 3 sample publications for each theme.

Topic	Theme	Articles
BI	Technology and evaluation	Chan et al. [9]
		Goud et al. [17]
		Magrabi et al. [25]
	Web and usability	Atkinson et al. [4]
		Rabius et al. [31]
		Flynn et al. [13]
	Communication and management	Merrill et al. [26]
		Anderson et al. [3]
		Madathila et al. [24]
	Health information	Xue et al. [43]
		Jadhav et al. [20]
		Frost and Massagli [14]
	Behavior, activity and assessment	Chiu and Eysenbach [10]
		Veinot et al. [40]
		Cimperman et al. [11]
HCI	Device and application	Ananthanarayan et al. [2]
		Buttussi et al. [8]
		Larson et al. [23]
	Health document	Sarcevic [34]
		Park and Chen [29]
		Kientz et al. [21]
	App for disease and symptom	Rolland and Lee [33]
		Yun and Arriaga [44]
		Hailpern et al. [18]
	Sensor, game and exercise	Hernandez et al. [19]
		Alankus et al. [1]
		Balaam et al. [5]
	Display and screen	Piper and Hollan [30]
		Zadow et al. [41]
		Wilcox et al. [42]

3.3   Data Analysis

Text Mining for Document Clustering. The selected articles were clustered into themes using document-clustering techniques. Document clustering is to organize a large document collection into groups of related documents and to discern the most common general themes hidden within the corpus [22]. Using this method, we classified the selected articles into five themes that are not mutually exclusive.

More specifically, the latent structures within the identified articles were identified based on the similarity of article contents. First, a list of stop words was generated by NLTK to eliminate obvious non-technical words and was stemmed down into its root using the Snowball Stemmer. We then analyzed each article for text similarities of meaningful, content-related words using tf-idf vectorizer parameters. Cosine similarity was measured against the tf-idf matrix and used to generate a measure of similarity between articles. As a result, the mining process yielded more accuracy and reduced-noise in clusters. Five clusters were generated for each set of articles to represent major themes. Each cluster was indexed and sorted to identify the top 10 words nearest to the cluster centroid. This gives a good sense of the main topic of the cluster.

Thematic Analysis. We randomly selected 3 articles per cluster from the identified articles (see Table 2) to conduct an in-depth thematic analysis [39]. Two investigators analyzed the randomly sampled articles. Each investigator independently analyzed the complete content of the selected articles to identify the theme of the study, its human-subject study methods, and the relation between themes and methods. The analyses were then compared across investigators to develop an exhaustive set of sematic fields. We combined the clusters that emerged from text mining and the semantic themes identified from thematic analysis of the sampled articles, and gave a theme name for each cluster.

4   Results

The initial search yielded 1,023 BI articles and 332 HCI articles. Through a review of titles and abstracts of these articles, 607 BI articles and 97 HCI articles were selected for full-text relevance screening. The articles were then selected on the basis of pre-determined inclusion/exclusion criteria, resulting in a selection of 533 BI articles and 60 HCI articles that met all eligibility criteria. The selected articles were deemed to be

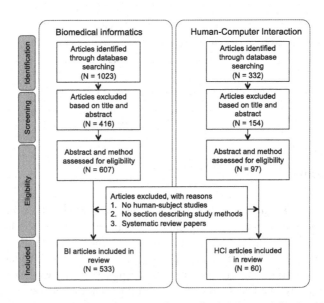

Fig. 1. PRISMA flowchart showing systematic search of review articles from BI and HCI.

of sufficient quality to contribute equally to the meta-analysis using text-mining and thematic analysis.

It was not surprising that over half of the initially identified BI articles met all eligibility criteria and only 20% of the initially identified HCI articles met all eligibility criteria, as the primary focus of BI encompasses healthcare, health information, and healthcare technology, while HCI articles study human factors and computing systems in a range of domains, one of which is healthcare. A Preferred Reporting Items for Systematic Reviews and Meta-Analyses (PRISMA) is presented in Fig. 1. In what follows, we describe the findings of our comparative analysis with emerged research themes with keywords in each theme.

4.1 BI Themes and Methods

Technology and Evaluation has emerged from the largest BI cluster (189 articles, 35%). Articles in this cluster investigated the use of HIT with an aim to improve the quality of HIT or enhance clinical outcomes through its use. Example research topics include evaluating the effectiveness of an e-prescribing system [25] or studying the effects of HIT in teaching patients with care strategies [9]. The major theme words identified via text-mining include technology, develop, implementing, design, data, information, evaluation, process, technological, and model, and the method terms include interviews, observations, and modeling. Controlled laboratory experiments and semi-structured interviews were identified as common methods used in this cluster.

Web and Usability emerged as a theme of the second cluster (111 articles, 21%). This theme pertains to studies that explore the current or potential use of web-based systems for various healthcare purposes. Example research topics include designing health promotion websites [4] or assessing the usability of Internet-based smoking cessation services [31]. Various qualitative data collection methods were used in this cluster, such as interview, focus group, and case study. The identified major theme words include web, participants, test, online, usability, significant, surveys, rates, measurement, and effective, and primary method terms identified are surveys and questionnaire.

Communication and Management emerged as a theme of the third cluster (91 articles, 17%). This theme represents studies to support healthcare communication or to improve the management of healthcare information in clinical contexts, such as investigating the current state of data management needs of biomedical researchers [3] or exploring ways to provide systematic support for public health information management [26]. Various qualitative data collection methods were mentioned in this cluster as well, such as interview, survey, and case study. The identified major theme words include health, information, management, participants, design, communication, providers, patient, managers, and data, and method terms include interviews, surveys, and coding.

Health Information emerged as a theme of the fourth cluster (81 articles, 15%). This theme is rather vague, as it could cover a wide range of healthcare studies. Example research topics include exploring older women's acceptance of mobile-based health information [43] or investigating social uses of online community to support health information exchange between patients [14]. Content analysis, interview, and survey were identified as primary methods of this cluster. The identified major theme words include patient, health, information, medical, clinical, record, electronic, participants, communication, and access, and method terms include interviews and coding.

Behavior, Activity and Assessment emerged as a theme of the last cluster (61 articles, 11%). The articles in this cluster focused on assessing human behaviors and activities relating to the use of HIT, such as studying family caregivers' use of electronic health services [10] or analyzing older adults' acceptance of telehealth services [11]. Various qualitative data collection methods, again, were identified as primary methods used in this cluster, such as interview, survey, and focus group. The identified major theme words include intervention, control, activity, effective, behavioral, significant, health, compared, assessing, and measurement, and method terms include controlled study and questionnaire.

4.2   HCI Themes and Methods

Device and Application emerged as a theme of the largest HCI cluster (21 articles, 35%). This theme covers a wide range of articles that study, implement, and deploy consumer health technologies, such as smartphone applications to support deaf people's communication in medical emergency situations [8] or to measure lung function [23]. Controlled laboratory experiments and semi-structured interviews were identified as primary methods used in this cluster. The identified major theme words include subjects, mobility, devices, sensors, clinicians, interfaces, treatment, application, scores, and families, and method terms include participants, subjects, information, data, and times.

Health Document emerged as a theme of the second cluster (19 articles, 32%). Articles in this cluster investigated ways to effectively adopt and adapt to electronic healthcare documents. Example research topics include examining the adaptation process of an EMR system in ED [28] or developing a new HIT system to improve the record-keeping process of children's early years for pediatricians and parents [21]. Observation and interview were identified as primary methods used in this cluster. The identified major theme words include nursing, team, ED, EMR, documented, clinicians, coordinates, doctors, hospital, and communications, and method terms include interviews, cases, and communication.

Application for Disease and Symptom emerged as a theme of the third cluster (7 articles, 11%). Specific diseases or health symptoms were prominent in this theme, such as aphasia [18] or pediatric asthma [44]. Controlled laboratory experiments and semi-structured interviews were identified as primary methods used in the sampled articles. The identified major theme words include chronic, pain, symptoms, health, variables, diseases, sharing, ill, searches, and diabetes, and method terms include interview and observations.

Sensor, Game, and Exercise emerged as a theme of the fourth cluster (7 articles, 11%). Articles that studied developing games or applications to promote relevant exercises for various health conditions, such as stroke rehabilitation [1] or cerebral palsy [19], were clustered in this theme. Participatory design and interview were identified as primary methods used in this cluster. The identified major theme words include games, exercise, home, session, controlled, motivation, motion, sensors, play, and movements, and method terms include data and logged.

Display and Screen emerged as a theme of the last cluster (6 articles, 10%). Articles in this theme described display-based systems to facilitate communication in various clinical contexts. Example research topics include an interactive display to support conversations between a deaf patient and a physician [30] or a patient-centric information display for inpatients [42]. Participatory design, wizard-of-OZ, observation, and interviews were identified as primary methods used in this cluster. The identified major theme words include images, simulates, interpreter, screen, safety, context, communications, table, and surfaces, and method terms include subjects, data, and times.

5 Results

Based on the analysis of the emergent themes and keywords, we propose taxonomy of two dimensional HIT research themes that categorize prevalent research topics and approaches to solving HIT-related problems in the BI and HCI communities (See Fig. 2). In what follows, we explain how we came up with this taxonomy, highlighting key differences in the communities.

5.1   Taxonomy of BI Themes

As mentioned before, we found that some themes encompass other themes (e.g., BI > health information), and other themes address particular aspects of healthcare and HIT (e.g., BI > Communication and Management). We also found that there is overlap between the themes in BI, which makes it hard to distinguish among different themes (e.g., BI > Technology and Evaluation vs., BI > Web and Usability), compared to HCI themes.

Health information is representative of other BI themes to encompass a wide range of research topics in healthcare and HIT. In fact, this theme is rather vague or too obvious, and thus could be applicable to any articles that studied HIT. However, this theme did not emerge in the HCI articles, which highlights one key difference in a focal point of research in BI and HCI communities. It means that health information is a basic or fundamental component of research in BI but not necessarily in HCI.

From the rest of the four BI themes, two perspectives have emerged. The first is a systems perspective that is to determine how HIT should function. Technology and Evaluation and Web and Usability are the themes focusing on the enhancement of experiences with health information from a systems perspectives, seeking ways to ensure or improve usability, effectiveness, and efficiency of HIT. These two themes are similar, as the term "technology" and "web" can be used interchangeably, as well as the term "evaluation" and "usability". The difference is that the articles in the Technology and Evaluation cluster investigated various forms of technical instruments (i.e., a tablet-based system, mobile apps) and evaluated them through diverse measures, while the articles in the Web and Usability cluster focus primarily on the usability aspect of online HIT systems (i.e., an e-prescription website).

The second perspective that emerged from BI themes is a users perspective that is to understand how users would operate HIT. Behavior, Activity and Assessment and Communication and Management are the themes to focus on enhancing experiences with health information from a user's perspective, seeking to understand human behaviors that might influence or be influenced by the use of HIT. The articles in Behavior, Activity and Assessment assessed human behaviors and activities to influence or to be influenced by the use of HIT in general, while the articles in Communication and Management explored how communication among multiple stakeholders in clinical contexts or health data management can be facilitated through the use of HIT.

Consequently, we developed a hierarchical taxonomy of the BI themes to account for different approaches to investigating various health information aspects of HIT. Health information is at the first level to encompass two approaches: a systems perspective and a users perspective. Technology and Evaluation and Web and Usability are categorized as the themes to study HIT from a system's perspective, and Behavior, Activity and Assessment and Communication and Management are categorized as the themes to study HIT from a user's perspective (See Fig. 2 top).

5.2   Taxonomy of HCI Themes

Compared to the BI themes, it was relatively easier to categorize HCI themes. We found it especially interesting that all the emerged HCI themes refer to different types of consumer health technologies used on an everyday bases by patients or in inpatient wards. That being said, Device and Application is representative of the rest of the HCI themes, investigating various types of consumer health technologies, including patients' access to health documents (Health Document), exergames (Sensor, Game, and Exercise), and displays for health communication and information (Display and Screen).

One reason HCI articles primarily focus on studying consumer health technology might be because it is not easy for researchers in the HCI community to access the clinical context without collaboration with clinicians. Another possible explanation might be because the proliferation of personal and mobile computing technologies has opened up opportunities for HCI researchers to explore novel ways to empower patients to manage their health concerns. The third possible explanation might be the different traditions of what is acceptable to be published in different venues. For example, it would be harder to get qualitative work published in a medical venue, and thus it is not surprising to see the pattern that many qualitative HIT studies are published in non-BI venues. Thus, there has been an argument among researchers in a medical community of accepting ethnographic work within BI [16]. Lastly, different research incentives and expectations from the different disciplines might have driven this pattern. For example, different funding resources have different expectations in terms of contribution types, study structure, and research methods (e.g., NIH vs. NSF), although this is only a US-centric perspective. Regardless of the reason, the trend was conspicuous that HCI articles primarily focused on the study and design of consumer health technologies.

There is one theme that does not refer to any specific type of consumer health technology: Application for Disease and Symptom. In fact, most HITs studied in HCI articles are deemed to be for diseases or symptoms. Thus, this theme is considered rather vague or too obvious, as Health Information in the BI themes. However, we found that the majority of HCI articles focused on the standpoint of patients to investigate casual healthcare practices, such as care plans, patient-provider communication, and patient access to health information. Meanwhile, articles in this cluster focused on managing specific symptoms or diseases, such as cancer, aphasia, or asthma. Thus, we took Application for Disease and Symptom into account as a sub-theme of Device and Application.

There was one exception in the type of HIT that is not consumer health technology: EMR (Electronic Medical Record). EMR is a digital version of the traditional paper-based medical record for an individual patient and is not consumer health technology. Interestingly, the term EMR emerged as one of the keywords in the Health Document cluster of the HCI articles, but nowhere in BI, even though EMR has been an important topic of research and widely studied in the BI community. This might be because of the way the themes are structured: BI themes are to explain different approaches to studying health information in relation to HIT so that a specific type of HIT did not emerge, whereas HCI themes are classified into different types of HITs, one of which is EMR.

Consequently, we came up with a hierarchical taxonomy of HCI themes to classify different types of HIT. Device and Application is at the first level and four subsequent types of HIT include: Health Document; Sensor, Game ad Exercise; Display and Screen; and Application for Disease and Symptom (See Fig. 2 bottom).

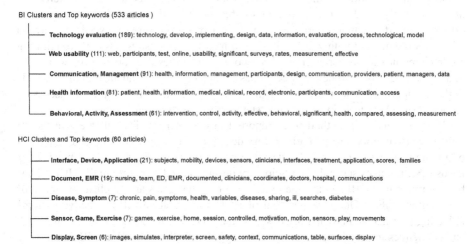

BI Clusters and Top keywords (533 articles)

— **Technology evaluation** (189): technology, develop, implementing, design, data, information, evaluation, process, technological, model

— **Web usability** (111): web, participants, test, online, usability, significant, surveys, rates, measurement, effective

— **Communication, Management** (91): health, information, management, participants, design, communication, providers, patient, managers, data

— **Health information** (81): patient, health, information, medical, clinical, record, electronic, participants, communication, access

— **Behavioral, Activity, Assessment** (61): intervention, control, activity, effective, behavioral, significant, health, compared, assessing, measurement

HCI Clusters and Top keywords (60 articles)

— **Interface, Device, Application** (21): subjects, mobility, devices, sensors, clinicians, interfaces, treatment, application, scores, families

— **Document, EMR** (19): nursing, team, ED, EMR, documented, clinicians, coordinates, doctors, hospital, communications

— **Disease, Symptom** (7): chronic, pain, symptoms, health, variables, diseases, sharing, ill, searches, diabetes

— **Sensor, Game, Exercise** (7): games, exercise, home, session, controlled, motivation, motion, sensors, play, movements

— **Display, Screen** (6): images, simulates, interpreter, screen, safety, context, communications, table, surfaces, display

Fig. 2. Hierarchical taxonomy of themes and keywords in BI and HCI articles

5.3   Methodologies Used in BI and HCI

Overall, methods used in the studies were similar across BI and HCI communities. Various qualitative methods were used in both communities, such as interview, observation, focus group, and case study, among which semi-structured interview was identified as the most popular method. Most sample articles in both communities conducted semi-structured interviews as a primarily data collection method, and data were analyzed employing a thematic analysis based on a grounded theory approach or other relevant qualitative analysis frameworks. This indicates a clear similarity between the BI and HCI communities in conducting HIT studies: researchers understand and solve problems through hearing directly from the current or potential users of HIT. The fact that the semi-structured interview is one popular method for data collection can be used as a starting point of mutual interest where researchers share practices and experiences, establish mutual understanding and appreciation, and engage in collective efforts to achieve a shared goal.

For quantitative methods, survey and controlled lab study were common across communities, but ways in which these methods were applied were quite different. First, we found a clear difference in conducting a survey: in the HCI articles a survey was commonly used as a supplement to qualitative methods to collect background or demographic information and answers to short-answer questions from a relatively small number of participants. For example, pre- or post-interview surveys were a common form, with an interview being a primary method for data collection. On the other hand, we identified several BI articles that used a survey as a primary method to collect a vast amount of quantitative data from a few hundred to thousands of subjects. Several BI articles conducted large-scale surveys and turned the results into quantitative analysis reports, which we did not find in the HCI articles. Second, a controlled lab study was also commonly used across communities, but we identified that the purposes were different: BI articles that reported on controlled lab studies were to investigate ways in which people interact with existing HIT or to measure an existing system's usability in a clinical context, whereas HCI articles reported on studies that ran experimental tasks in a lab setting to determine the effectiveness, efficiency and/or satisfaction of new HIT. Different approaches to the same method can be an interesting topic of discussion among researchers to help better understand and learn from each other.

We identified one method often reported in the HCI articles but rarely in the BI articles: participatory design. Participatory design is a method where the potential users of a system actively engage in the design process to ensure that the system meets their needs [28]. It makes sense that participatory design is used primarily in the HCI studies but not much in the BI studies due to different research goals and publication trends of these communities. One research goal of HCI is to create novel, interactive systems reflecting user needs. Participatory design can help better understand users, their needs, and challenges in the design of new technology. On the other hand, the BI community might be using participatory design relatively less, as technology design itself is seldom the focal point of the BI literature. (Apparently, participatory design has been used in the BI community – e.g., [37, 38], but none among the selected BI articles reported studies involving participatory design). This is a good example to demonstrate a significant difference between BI and HCI in the human-subject study of HIT. It can be a topic of interest for BI researchers to broaden their methodological approaches to studying HIT, since there is sheer volume of HCI studies that used participatory design to effectively identify and solve critical problems in HIT design and use. Furthermore, it can be an opportunity for HCI researchers to contribute to HIT research with their specialty and expertise when collaborating with BI researchers.

6 Limitations

We acknowledge that this study has limitations. First, this research included papers published only in the selected databases related to healthcare between 2007 and 2016. Therefore, there may be other relevant studies published in other publication venues that were not included in the systematic review in this paper. Also, the findings from our analysis may not capture a publication trend before 2007. Second, the number of articles selected in BI and HCI differs greatly due to their different primary foci of study, which may have influenced how the documents were clustered. However, such difference stems from the natural publication culture and circumstance, and thus the potential skewing in clustering may need to be considered as part of the trend. Last, we did not employ any theory or guidelines to evaluate the quality of each study we reviewed. Thus, all reviewed studies are assumed to be of the same quality.

7 Conclusion

This paper presents a comparative review of 593 articles in the BI and HCI publication venues that reported on human-subject studies of HIT. The primary goal of this paper is to advance shared understandings of the literature in the disjointed BI and HCI communities through a comparative analysis of published articles. Using text mining techniques, five themes emerged from each set of articles, and from these we created a hierarchical taxonomy of BI and HCI articles. The results illustrate that the BI community contributes mainly to generating knowledge associated with the use of health information in clinical settings, whereas the HCI community focuses primarily on the design and evaluation of personal healthcare applications. For people who are already working in the intersection of BI and HCI, there might be nothing surprising about the findings. However, we believe it is nonetheless useful to have this analysis done systematically. Furthermore, a categorization of research themes and methods in different communities can help researchers who are unfamiliar with the other community to easily comprehend and acknowledge similarities and differences.

This study contributes to existing efforts to increase familiarity across BI and HCI communities and promote collaboration more effectively and productively to achieve shared goals of enhancing healthcare. We believe that researchers would benefit from increased familiarity with the work done by the other. Bringing together the strengths of different communities, we will be able to yield results that are more generalizable and have greater potential impact in healthcare research.

References

1. Alankus, G., Lazar, A., May, M., Kelleher, C.: Towards customizable games for stroke rehabilitation. In: Proceedings of the SIGCHI Conference on Human Factors in Computing Systems, pp. 2113–2122. ACM (2010)
2. Ananthanarayan, S., Sheh, M., Chien, A., Profita, H., Siek, K.: Pt Viz: towards a wearable device for visualizing knee rehabilitation exercises. In: Proceedings of the SIGCHI Conference on Human Factors in Computing Systems, pp. 1247–1250. ACM (2013)
3. Anderson, N.R., et al.: Issues in biomedical research data management and analysis: needs and barriers. J. Am. Med. Inf. Assoc. **14**(4), 478–488 (2007)
4. Atkinson, N.L., Saperstein, S.L., Desmond, S.M., Gold, R.S., Billing, A.S., Tian, J.: Rural eHealth nutrition education for limited-income families: an iterative and user-centered design approach. J. Med. Internet Res. **11**(2), e21 (2009)
5. Balaam, M., et al.: Motivating mobility: designing for lived motivation in stroke rehabilitation. In: Proceedings of the SIGCHI Conference on Human Factors in Computing Systems, pp. 3073–3082. ACM (2011)
6. Bardram, J.E., Frost, M., Szántó, K., Faurholt-Jepsen, M., Vinberg, M., Kessing, L.V.: Designing mobile health technology for bipolar disorder: a field trial of the monarca system. In: Proceedings of the SIGCHI Conference on Human Factors in Computing Systems, pp. 2627–2636. ACM (2013)
7. Belden, J., et al.: Inspired EHRs: Designing for Clinicians. https://inspiredEHRs.org
8. Buttussi, F., Chittaro, L., Carchietti, E., Coppo, M.: Using mobile devices to support communication between emergency medical responders and deaf people. In: Proceedings of the 12th International Conference on Human Computer Interaction with Mobile Devices and Services, pp. 7–16. ACM (2010)
9. Chan, H.-Y., Dai, Y.-T., Hou, I.-C.: Evaluation of a tablet-based instruction of breathing technique in patients with COPD. Int. J. Med. Inf. **94**, 263–270 (2016)
10. Chiu, T.M.L., Eysenbach, G.: Theorizing the health service usage behavior of family caregivers: a qualitative study of an internet-based intervention. Int. J. Med. Inf. **80**(11), 754–764 (2011)
11. Cimperman, M., Brenčič, M.M., Trkman, P.: Analyzing older users' home telehealth services acceptance behavior—applying an Extended UTAUT model. Int. J. Med. Inf. **90**, 22–31 (2016)
12. Fitzpatrick, G., Ellingsen, G.: A review of 25 years of CSCW research in healthcare: contributions, challenges and future agendas. Comput. Support. Coop. Work (CSCW) **22**(4–6), 609–665 (2013)
13. Flynn, D., Gregory, P., Makki, H., Gabbay, M.: Expectations and experiences of eHealth in primary care: a qualitative practice-based investigation. Int. J. Med. Inf. **78**(9), 588–604 (2009)
14. Frost, J.H., Massagli, M.P.: Social uses of personal health information within Patients-LikeMe, an online patient community: what can happen when patients have access to one another's data. J. Med. Internet Res. **10**(3), e15 (2008)
15. Furniss, D., Randell, R., OKane, A.A., Taneva, S., Mentis, H., Blandford, A.: Fieldwork for healthcare: guidance for investigating human factors in computing systems. Synth. Lect. Assistive Rehabil. Health-Preserving Technol. **3**(2), 1–146 (2014)
16. Greenhalgh, T., Swinglehurst, D.: Studying technology use as social practice: the untapped potential of ethnography. BMC Med. **9**(1), 45 (2011)

17. Goud, R., et al.: The effect of computerized decision support on barriers to guideline implementation: a qualitative study in outpatient cardiac rehabilitation. Int. J. Med. Inf. **79** (6), 430–437 (2010)

18. Hailpern, J., Danilevsky, M., Harris, A., Karahalios, K., Dell, G., Hengst, J.: ACES: promoting empathy towards aphasia through language distortion emulation software. In: Proceedings of the SIGCHI Conference on Human Factors in Computing Systems, pp. 609–618. ACM (2011)

19. Hernandez, H.A., et al.: Design of an exergaming station for children with cerebral palsy. In: Proceedings of the SIGCHI Conference on Human Factors in Computing Systems, pp. 2619–2628. ACM (2012)

20. Jadhav, A., et al.: Comparative analysis of online health queries originating from personal computers and smart devices on a consumer health information portal. J. Med. Internet Res. **16**(7), e160 (2014)

21. Kientz, J.A.: Understanding parent-pediatrician interactions for the design of health technologies. In: Proceedings of the 1st ACM International Health Informatics Symposium, pp. 230–239. ACM (2010)

22. Kim, H.-J., Lee, S.-G.: A semi-supervised document clustering technique for information organization. In: Proceedings of the Ninth International Conference on Information and Knowledge Management, pp. 30–37. ACM (2000)

23. Larson, E.C., Goel, M., Boriello, G., Heltshe, S., Rosenfeld, M., Patel, S.N.: SpiroSmart: using a microphone to measure lung function on a mobile phone. In: Proceedings of the 2012 ACM Conference on Ubiquitous Computing, pp. 280–289. ACM (2012)

24. Madathil, K.C., et al.: An investigation of the efficacy of electronic consenting interfaces of research permissions management system in a hospital setting. Int. J. Med. Inf. **82**(9), 854–863 (2013)

25. Magrabi, F., Li, S.Y.W., Day, R.O., Coiera, E.: Errors and electronic prescribing: a controlled laboratory study to examine task complexity and interruption effects. J. Am. Med. Inf. Assoc. **17**(5), 575–583 (2010)

26. Merrill, J., Bakken, S., Rockoff, M., Gebbie, K., Carley, K.M.: Description of a method to support public health information management: organizational network analysis. J. Biomed. Inform. **40**(4), 422–428 (2007)

27. Moher, D., Liberati, A., Tetzlaff, J., Altman, D.G., Prisma Group: Preferred reporting items for systematic reviews and meta-analyses: the PRISMA statement. PLoS Med. **6**(7), e1000097 (2009)

28. Muller, M.J., Kuhn, S.: Participatory design. Commun. ACM **36**(6), 24–28 (1993)

29. Park, S.Y., Chen, Y.: Adaptation as design: learning from an EMR deployment study. In: Proceedings of the SIGCHI Conference on Human Factors in Computing Systems, pp. 2097–2106. ACM (2012)

30. Piper, A.M., Hollan, J.D.: Supporting medical conversations between deaf and hearing individuals with tabletop displays. In: Proceedings of the 2008 ACM Conference on Computer Supported Cooperative Work, pp. 147–156. ACM (2008)

31. Rabius, V., Pike, K.J., Wiatrek, D., McAlister, A.: Comparing internet assistance for smoking cessation: 13-month follow-up of a six-arm randomized controlled trial. J. Med. Internet Res. **10**(5), e45 (2008)

32. Reddy, M., Mamykina, L., Parker, A.G.: Designing interactive systems in healthcare: a report on WISH 2011. Interactions **19**(1), 24–27 (2012)

33. Rolland, B., Lee, C.P.: Beyond trust and reliability: reusing data in collaborative cancer epidemiology research. In: Proceedings of the 2013 Conference on Computer Supported Cooperative Work, pp. 435–444. ACM (2013)

34. Sarcevic, A.: Who's scribing?: documenting patient encounter during trauma resuscitation. In: Proceedings of the SIGCHI Conference on Human Factors in Computing Systems, pp. 1899–1908. ACM (2010)

35. Sellen, K., Furniss, D., Chen, Y., Taneva, S., O'Kane, A.A., Blandford, A.: Workshop abstract: HCI research in healthcare: using theory from evidence to practice. In: CHI'14 Extended Abstracts on Human Factors in Computing Systems, pp. 87–90. ACM (2014)

36. Shortliffe, E.H., Cimino, J.J.: Biomedical Informatics: Computer Applications in Health Care and Biomedicine. Springer, London (2013). https://doi.org/10.1007/978-1-4471-4474-8

37. Sjöberg, C., Timpka, T.: Participatory design of information systems in health care. J. Am. Med. Inf. Assoc. 5(2), 177–183 (1998)

38. Sullivan, F.: What is health informatics? J. Health Serv. Res. Policy 6(4), 251–254 (2001). (1), 45 (2008)

39. Thomas, J., Harden, A.: Methods for the thematic synthesis of qualitative research in systematic reviews. BMC Med. Res. Methodol. 8(1), 45 (2008)

40. Veinot, T.C., Campbell, T.R., Kruger, D.J., Grodzinski, A.: A question of trust: user-centered design requirements for an informatics intervention to promote the sexual health of African-American youth. J. Am. Med. Inform. Assoc. 20(4), 758–765 (2013)

41. Von Zadow, U., Buron, S., Harms, T., Behringer, F., Sostmann, K., Dachselt, R.: SimMed: combining simulation and interactive tabletops for medical education. In: Proceedings of the SIGCHI Conference on Human Factors in Computing Systems, pp. 1469–1478. ACM (2013)

42. Wilcox, L., Morris, D., Tan, D., Gatewood, J.: Designing patient-centric information displays for hospitals. In: Proceedings of the SIGCHI Conference on Human Factors in Computing Systems, pp. 2123–2132. ACM (2010)

43. Xue, L., et al.: An exploratory study of ageing women's perception on access to health informatics via a mobile phone-based intervention. Int. J. Med. Inf. 81(9), 637–648 (2012)

44. Yun, T.-J., Arriaga, R.I.: A text message a day keeps the pulmonologist away. In: Proceedings of the SIGCHI Conference on Human Factors in Computing Systems, pp. 1769–1778. ACM (2013)

45. Zhang, J., Walji, M.: Better EHR: usability, workflow and cognitive support in electronic health records. National Center for Cognitive Informatics and Decision Making in Healthcare (2014)

The Clothing Design for the Elderly Care

Hsiu-Ching Lu[1,2(✉)], Fong-Gong Wu[1], Wen-Yu Yang[1],
and Adam Book[1]

[1] Department of Industrial Design, National Cheng Kung University,
Tainan, Taiwan
emily0937218810@gmail.com
[2] Department of Styling and Cosmetology, Tainan University of Technology,
Tainan, Taiwan

Abstract. The physiological functions of the elderly will gradually degenerate with age, and their daily life will require special care as well. With the aging population around the globe, the elderly population has increased gradually, and the care of the elderly is getting more and more attention. More and more elderly people are living in nursing homes to acquire convenient care. By observing the care for elderly people, we can find that although the elderly can receive full care in nursing homes, they can also be exposed to occupational injuries.

Therefore, this study aims to explore and analyze the care-giving procedures to improve the care efficiency and quality of caregivers for the elderly living in nursing homes, and to reduce the pressure of care-giving, thus enhancing the autonomy of the elderly. By re-examining the methods of care for the elderly, we will start from improving the dressing problems encountered by the elderly and aim at improving the self-care of the elderly and reducing the work injuries suffered by the caregivers, thus improving the quality of life of the elderly and contributing to the issue of aging population around the globe in the future.

Keywords: Occupant injury · Elderly clothing · Ergonomics design · Nursing home dressing

1 Introduction

1.1 Background

In the global aging society, the care of the elderly has received more and more attention. However, domestic care personnel often suffer occupational injuries due to insufficient manpower and long working hours. Therefore, the main purpose of this study is to analyze the interaction between the care personnel and the elderly living in the nursing home, find the main causes of pain and injuries suffered by care personnel in the clothes-changing process through analysis and observation of the dressing procedure, and identify the inability of the elderly to perform dressing independently due to physiological deterioration. Taking the deterioration of the physiological function among the elderly as the starting point, this study attempts to understand the relationship between the physiological and psychological changes, the dressing process

© Springer Nature Switzerland AG 2019
M. Kurosu (Ed.): HCII 2019, LNCS 11568, pp. 33–46, 2019.
https://doi.org/10.1007/978-3-030-22636-7_3

and the care personnel and identify design parameters for the elderly care clothing from the interaction between the elderly and care personnel in the clothes-changing process.

According to 2010 Population and Housing Censuses by Directorate General of Budget Accounting and Statistics under the Executive Yuan, there are about 475,000 people who need the long-term care in Taiwan, of which the elderly account for 65.4%, but only half of them live together with their children. As population aging and childlessness have slightly reduced the traditional family function as a caregiver, the family type in Taiwan is moving towards becoming the nuclear family. The average number of family members is about 3, but it requires 2 to 3 or more people to provide care assistance for the more proper care. It is foreseeable that the long-term care has become an indispensable option in the future [1]. According to the national population statistics information published by Directorate General of Budget Accounting and Statistics under the Executive Yuan, the ratio of people aged 65 and over in long-term care and nursing institutions is 1.6%. The growth of institutional care has slowed down as the long-term care service is becoming more and more solid with the development of home and community care. According to the statistics of the Ministry of Health and Welfare, there were 1,048 long-term care and nursing institutions in Taiwan by the end of June 2014, including 1,023 long-term care institutions and 25 nursing institutions which could accommodate 58,000 people, showing a decrease by 1.7% compared to those numbers in 2009. The actual number of people institutionalized was 44,000, accounting for 1.6% of the population over 65 years old in Taiwan. In 2012, while the utilization rate of institutions taking care of senior citizens stricken by dementia reached about 90%, the utilization rate of other institutions was only about 60% to 70%.

1.2 Research Questions

Human aging has a significant degenerative effect on physiological functions. When the physiological functions of elderly are degenerating owing to normal aging with diseases striking at the same time, the human body function can be significantly degraded. When the body functions degenerate, the activity and performance of the physiological system will deteriorate. For example, the hearing and visual functions deteriorate, soft tissues (skins and blood vessels) become less elastic, or the cardiopulmonary function, physical strength and muscle strength decline. Physiological deterioration and mobility disorder may even cause disability in the elderly. The elderly encounter a variety of age-related physical changes from clothes-changing, including a weakened sense of balance, dizziness and joint degeneration [2]. With the gradual loss of the basic life skills and autonomy, many of the actions in the life of the elderly will be hindered and restricted. Either at home or in care institutions, aging will undoubtedly seriously affect their quality of life. Under the more serious circumstances, the daily activities of the elderly may even depend on the care personnel completely. The elderly show a clear dependence on the care personnel for clothes-changing. As of 1999, the Centers for Disease Control and Prevention (CDC) reported that only 13% of the elderly livings in nursing homes were able to take care of themselves in clothing-changing, and the number among the elderly who could take care of themselves in clothing-changing was declining [3]. 91% of the elderly dementia patients with the Alzheimer's disease need to rely on others to complete the act of clothes-changing.

Although the aging disorder does not make the elderly lose their autonomy in clothes-changing completely, they rely on others for assistance. Therefore, caring for the disabled elderly people will definitely cost a relatively large amount of manpower and money. Social costs for medical care, general care and social welfare can also pose a heavy burden.

Studies have shown that more than half of caregivers have problems with their shoulders, elbows, wrists and suffer from neck pains owing to their work [4]. As the elderly receive the long-term care, they can gradually lose their autonomy and heavily rely on the help of caregivers. Therefore, research shows that the issues concerning dressing have a negative impact on the elderly. The inability to dress on one's own and loss of autonomy have seriously affected the quality of life of the elderly [5]. Exploring the problems in the elderly clothes-changing, we find that the clothes worn by the elderly are tailored for the general public, but as the bones change from aging, shoulders and chests will shrink, so the clothes will become loose and unfit, and besides issues like loss of warmth and poor spirits, the existing design of clothes can also cause the problem of inconvenience in clothes-changing among the elderly. Based on the above viewpoints, it is of great value and contribution to explore the effects of physiological deterioration on clothes-changing and care personnel, find the best solution, and design a more comprehensive elderly care suit from the perspective of human factors.

2   Literature Review

2.1   The Influence of Clothes-Changing Care on Care Personnel

In addition to inconvenience in clothes-changing among the elderly, care personnel that assist the elderly clothes-changing can suffer great impacts as well. In general, a care worker usually needs to care for a number of elderly people at the same time. According to a study by Cohen-Mansfield et al. [6], a care worker may spend 4–9 min assisting an elder in clothes-changing. And the number of the elderly that the nursing home needs to care for is even larger. It can be seen that the clothes-changing care has virtually increased the workload of the care personnel and put pressure on the care personnel. In addition, due to long hours of work, excessive loads for handling, long-term repetitive movements, improper force applied, and poor posture can also lead to occupational injuries among the care personnel. According to a French study on musculoskeletal disorders among health care workers in 2014, among more than 2,000 participants, nearly half of them had neck pain and relevant problems [4]. In addition to neck pain, back pain is another pain often encountered by health care workers. From the record of compensation claimed by health care workers, it was found that the back injury is one of the top five occupational injuries in the nursing profession. Many studies between 1988 and 1990 even found that vertical and lateral movement were the main causes of serious injuries among the care personnel. Moving those being cared for has been identified to cause excessive stress on the spine [7]. According to a report in 2013 [8] even pointed out this high prevalence of such illness among female health care workers. The report showed that the smaller body size of women on average was the reason why there was a high percentage of back pain among female health care workers, and moving patients could cause a greater physical impact. Therefore, the care personnel need to take into account the physical state of the elderly and efficiently complete the clothes-changing procedure when assisting the elderly clothes-changing. The care personnel have to assist the elderly clothes-changing in a stressful environment over a long time, which often causes muscle strain, soreness, posture damage and similar issues owing to improper force applied. Accumulation of the harm over the long term can cause a great harm to the care personnel. So, how to alleviate the pain and damage suffered by the care personnel from long-term assistance is an important question that must not be ignored.

2.2 Injuries of the Care Personnel

The care personnel must work in a high-pressure work environment for a long time, and the pressure on the psychological and physical levels is not to be underestimated. Interviews with care personnel working in the nursing home revealed that assisting the elderly bathing was the most difficult task in the care work, followed by assisting the elderly clothes-changing. The care personnel have suffered a lot of occupational injuries as they must avoid the strain and injuries on the hands and wrists of the elderly from direct use of force while assisting the elderly clothes-changing. Exploring the occupational injuries suffered by care personnel in the process of assisting the elderly clothes-changing, it is not difficult to find that many injuries are caused by the movement of hands, shoulders, the back and the waist during the clothes-changing process when they try to move the elderly, thus causing damage to their intervertebral disc (L5/S1). However, long-term accumulation of the harm has made more than half of the care personnel suffer from the neck pain, and the problems of waist injury and back pain are also very common. According to research, nearly 30% of the care personnel suffer from the lower back pain, which is even more serious among the more petite women.

2.3 Considerations for the New Elderly Care Clothing

In addition to conforming to the wearer's physical conditions, the elderly clothing should be designed to keep warmth and optimal comfort throughout the body. It is best that the elderly avoid excessive and extreme muscle movements while wearing the clothes. At present, most studies on Care Clothing aim to explore the influence of clothing materials and heat dissipation on the elderly, but few studies have been done for improvement to the elderly clothes-changing. In addition, on the market, most clothes-changing accessories are designed to assist the elderly clothes-changing on their own, such as: sock wearing frames, sock wearing slips, clothes-changing rods, etc. But such accessories are not that convenient in our daily life as they rarely take into account the actions of the elderly. This study will propose an improvement solution based on the interaction between the care personnel and the elderly clothes-changing. It will conduct research and discussion on how to reduce the difficulties faced by both parties and how to directly improve the clothing to facilitate clothes-wearing. Finally, it will propose a new design for the elderly care clothing. It is hoped that the improvement to the Care Clothing design can reduce difficulties in the elderly clothes-changing and improve the efficiency of care.

Clothes-changing can take lots of time for both the elderly and the care personnel, so it can also impose a great burden on both parties. Therefore, in this research, it is hoped that through further understanding of the key factors influencing the clothes-changing and the entire changing process, we can design the new elderly care clothing, so that during the clothing-changing process, with the help of the care personnel, the autonomy of the elderly can be enhanced, and the chances of damage from clothes-changing to the elderly, such as the body pain and injuries from involuntary movement, can be reduced. From the perspective of the care personnel, the new design can also reduce the occupational burden on the bodies of the care personnel in the process of assisting the elderly clothes-changing, and increase the efficiency of the clothes-changing at the same time.

2.4　The Existing Elderly Clothing Designs and Textures

Clothes are meant to maintain the dignity of the wearer and make them feel comfortable [9]. At present, except for the clothing brought from the home, the clothing worn by the elderly in the nursing home is provided by the nursing home. However, the clothes provided by the nursing home are not designed for the elderly, so the elderly can face a certain degree of difficulty in clothes-changing on their own and they need help from the care personnel. In the process, the dignity and confidence of the elderly can be impacted. On the other hand, since the clothes are not designed for the care personnel, the care personnel are often injured while assisting the clothes-changing process (Table 1).

Table 1. Observation of the elderly clothing

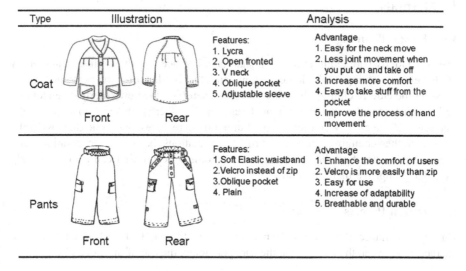

Type	Illustration		Analysis
Coat	Front	Rear	Features: 1. Lycra 2. Open fronted 3. V neck 4. Oblique pocket 5. Adjustable sleeve	Advantage 1. Easy for the neck move 2. Less joint movement when you put on and take off 3. Increase more comfort 4. Easy to take stuff from the pocket 5. Improve the process of hand movement
Pants	Front	Rear	Features: 1. Soft Elastic waistband 2. Velcro instead of zip 3. Oblique pocket 4. Plain	Advantage 1. Enhance the comfort of users 2. Velcro is more easily than zip 3. Easy for use 4. Increase of adaptability 5. Breathable and durable

2.5   Advice for the Study on the Elderly Care Clothing

Existing research on the Elderly Care Clothing shows that the design of the Elderly Care Clothing varies according to the different changes from biological aging among males and females. Studies have shown [4] that explored the clothing for elderly women in nursing homes and rendered suggestions for improvement on such clothing. These suggestions include (1) Corrections to the size and fitness: smaller and wider clothes, large-area cuts to cope with changes. (2) Material requirements: soft and light materials with a smooth backside, easy to organize, no need for ironing, distinct, soft colors; materials with appropriate elasticity. (3) Functional requirements: extra-loose style, the beauty of the clothes when the wearer is in the sitting state, good warmth and good ventilation. (4) Easy to put on and take off: coat style, large opening or front opening, extra loose, deep-cut armholes and wide sleeves on the back, elastic materials, the front opening that can be closed with just one hand, no need to pull onto the head to wear clothes, no need to demand for the strength and precision while opening and closing the clothes with the hands and no big action required in the clothes-changing.

The water content in the body of an elderly male can decrease from 80% in infancy to 50–60%, and after 65 years old, EMG function of the elderly can significantly degenerate, and the sensitivity to external stimuli can be reduced [10]. The size of the clothes and the appropriate correction: The back area should be increased, because the body can lean forward. The height can be reduced because the water in the cartilage tissue of the spine can be reduced as well. The height can be reduced by 2.5 cm every 5 years after the age of 50, and after the age of 75, the height can reduced by 5 cm every 5 years. The fabric of the shoulder part should be reduced; the size around the pelvis should be increased; the fabric of the front piece will be adjusted: the ratio between the width and the depth of the chest will be reduced. Material requirements: Soft fabrics are preferred.

3   Methods

3.1   Design Planning

The new elderly care clothing research shall take into account the decline in autonomy of the elderly owing to biological aging and the burden of care personnel while assisting the elderly clothes-changing process. Therefore, the new elderly care clothing design must consider the physiological state of the elderly, and aim to improve the autonomy of the elderly and reduce the burden on care personnel while they assist the elderly clothes-changing process. Through evaluations based on observations and interviews, we can find the new elderly care clothing design that can effectively help the elderly improve their autonomy.

3.2   Design Process

Through Literature Review and Expert Interview, this study mainly focuses on the interaction between the elderly and the care personnel, the use of the elderly body parts, the autonomy of the elderly, and the injury rate among health care workers to propose the new care clothing design (Fig. 1).

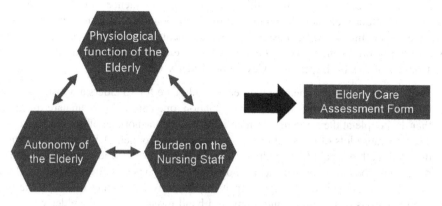

Fig. 1. Architectural diagram

3.3   Autonomy of the Elderly-the Elderly Clothes-Changing Quality and Habit Observation Interview

Through observation of the elderly in this interview, the inconvenience and habits of the elderly in the dressing process were discussed to provide a reference for the future development of the new elderly care clothing. The items for observation include the actual dressing conditions among the elderly, clothes-changing habits and physical phenomena, and interactions of the wearer and care personnel with the clothing. This study uses the most direct way to understand and analyze the use conditions, clothes-changing habits and personal preferences. The interview was conducted with the generally healthy elderly, and preliminary interviews were conducted with 10 elders. The interview questions included the family life, health status, clothes-changing habits, normal wear, cold-weather wear, laundry ways, exercise habits, preferred ways to open and close the clothes, and operations of the shoes and zippers, as shown by the elderly clothes-changing operations in Fig. 2.

Fig. 2. The elderly clothes-changing operations

3.4   Physiological Function of the Elderly-Expert Interview

This study has conducted 3 Expert Interviews to inquire about the daily work conditions of the care personnel, the difficulties and inconveniences in the process of assisting the elderly clothes-changing, and the injuries and pains caused by the work. And the Expert Interviews also asked for improvements and suggestions that could be used in the future as the basis for developing the new elderly care clothing.

Content of the 1st Expert Interview about Elderly Care:

- The law stipulates that one care worker can only care for 15 elders at most, but with the insufficient manpower in the actual situation, one care worker can care for more than 15 people at the same time, which indicates that a shortage of human resources can also cause lots of physical burden on the care personnel. Daily routines include dressing, bathing, pain testing, dispensing medications, etc., and dressing is usually done on the bed, as is for wheelchair-bound patients. Experts believe that the Velcro fastener is designed for the caregiver, as it is rapidly convenient to use, while the use of buttons can promote autonomy and hand movement for the elderly.

Content of the 2nd Expert Interview about Elderly Care:

- A nurse can take care of 44 to 56 elders, and there can be 6 care workers subordinate to the nurse to be in charge of 7 to 10 elders each. Common illnesses among care personnel include the knee and hand arthritis, and their clothing can cause their bodies to suffer from temperature loss, poor blood circulation and dry skin. The elderly need to do exercise in their daily activities, such as the detailed movement of the hands or the stretching of the limbs, but they also must avoid falls or cramps during exercise.

Meanwhile, time and efficiency are also some other important matters that must be considered. As care personnel needs to care for several elders that suffer from muscle losses and slow motions at the same time, it often adds up the difficulty in wearing clothes and takes a lot of time for them to do so, which often affects their breakfast time in the care center. So, improvements need to be made to make the care personnel more effectively assist the elderly clothes-changing process and reduce the burden and time pressure as well. Experts suggest the physiological conditions of the elderly and some mechanisms for warmth-keeping should be taken into account.

Content of the 3rd Expert Interview about Elderly Care:

- When the care personnel take care of the elderly, the prolonged lifting and use of the hands while helping the elderly wear the clothes can easily cause a pain in the shoulder blade, and they may also suffer from a waist injury from the act of moving the elderly. When the care personnel are helping the elderly wear the clothes, the elderly will be asked to raise their arms so as to help them to put on their clothes. If any limb is injured, the clothes shall be put on the injured limb first, so that the elderly that can still move can buckle up the buttons on their own. Meanwhile, the zipper may be too small for the elderly to wear the clothes. The elderly clothing shall be able to open from the front, and it shall be flexible with large buttons to avoid damage caused by the large angle of the stretching arm. The Velcro fastener will be suitable for the elderly, but it can be accidentally pulled open when the elderly are lifting arms or moving around.

From the 3 Expert Interviews, it is known that: (1) the care personnel do need efficiently effective dressing solutions. (2) The elderly are less mobile and they require an easier way to change clothes. (3) The elderly clothing must be able to keep warmth and fit the physiological conditions of the elderly (Table 2).

Table 2. Table of the interview content

The influence of elder	1. Action show
	2. Keep warm
	3. Degenerative joint
	4. Degree in bed
	5. Do some easy actions
The influence of care attendant	1. Time-consuming
	2. Joint disease
	3. Lack of manpower
Notes	1. Velcro is convenience but danger
	2. Big buckle can improve hand movement
	3. Clothes need more elasticity
	4. Open fronted can avoid hand-lift
	5. It's not suitable for elder cause the zip is too tiny

Through the advice provided by this Expert Interview, we can learn about the deficiencies in the existing Elderly Clothing to enhance the autonomy among the elderly and help avoid harms to the care personnel when they are assisting the elderly clothes-changing process. As the Literature Review has clearly defined the direction of this study, the Expert Interview also provides a preliminary understanding of the current needs of the elderly and the care personnel for the Elderly Clothing and the way to increase their autonomy. And from the preliminary interviews, we can learn that the elderly clothing must enhance the autonomy of the elderly and reduce injuries suffered by the care personnel while assisting the clothes-changing process, so that we can revise subjects of this study, formulate experiment details in this study, and establish the basis and references for the design of the new elderly care clothing.

3.5   Burden on the Nursing Staff-Data Collection and User Observation

Through the Expert Interview, we can understand that in the process of assisting the elderly clothes-changing, the care personnel will try to let the elderly perform some simple actions to achieve the effect of rehabilitation, such as: lifting the legs, lifting the waist, etc. In the process of dressing, the care personnel will dress the injured limb first before dressing the normal limbs. In the process of undressing, it is quite the opposite of dressing; the normal limbs will be undressed first before the injured limb can be dressed, mainly to avoid movement of the injured limb and/or unnecessary harms.

In the choice of the clothes style, the upper outer garment of the front open type is preferred, but considering that the winter weather is relatively cold, and the front open type has a poor warming effect, the loose (larger by 2 scales) and elastic general sweater can be a better choice. And the pants with the elastic band is preferred. In the choice of clothing materials, the breathable, elastic fabric with a low coefficient of friction, such as the cotton fabric, is a better choice, and materials like the denim shall be avoided (Fig. 3).

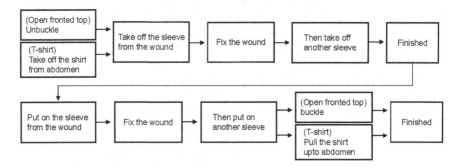

Fig. 3. Steps in the clothes-changing process under observation

Field observation shows that the caregiver uses Rescue Anne during practice and as a prop in the caregiver license exam. The angle of the elbow in this process of changing clothes is not possible for the elderly with arthritis. There is much needed to be improved (Fig. 4).

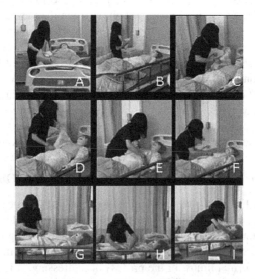

Fig. 4. The procedure of dressing CPR Annie (A to I)

Figure 5 shows how the caregiver dresses the elderly. In picture A and B, the caregiver uses rescue Anne as a prop in simulation. In Picture C and D, the caregiver dresses a real person. You can see the difference in the angle of the elbow.

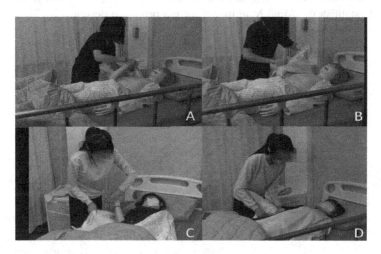

Fig. 5. The procedure of dressing CPR Annie (the top part) and patients (the bottom part)

3.6   The Focus Group Methodology

The implementation process is for the designer with the relevant background to elaborate the current situation of dressing among the elderly, in hope to:

- address the reduced flexibility of the elderly, simplify the clothes-changing methods and increase autonomy of the elderly.
- reduce repeated damage to the care personnel in the process of assisting the elderly clothes-changing (Fig. 6).

Fig. 6. Discussion in the focus group

3.7   Design Simulation After Concept Comparison

Through On-Site Observation, Expert Interview and Literature Review, parameters to be considered can be established for the new elderly care clothing to develop a systematic evaluation scale for relevant needs, design model development recommendations, and establish the Mind Map model for the proposed design (Fig. 7).

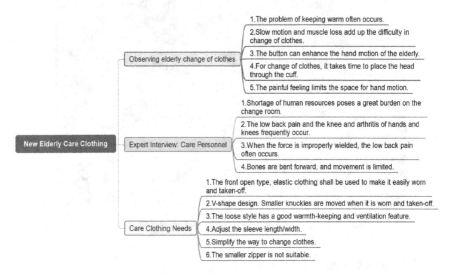

Fig. 7. Mind map of the new elderly care clothing

Introduction We will discuss the feasibility of each scheme and figure out the weights of each part based on their respective importance, such as: easiness to put on/take off the clothes, the cuff width, the front opening design and the button design, in order to conduct the objective conception and design based on relevant needs, evaluate all ideas, and use the ideas with higher scores to make drawings.

The design of the cuff style: The clothes-changing process often creates difficulties in making the hand pass through the cuff, so adding a zipper to the cuff can assist dressing and make it complete faster (Figs. 8 and 9).

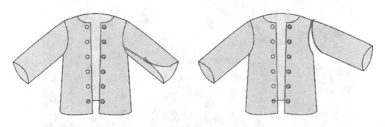

Fig. 8. Cuff design A   **Fig. 9.** Cuff design B

(1) Two-Section Cuff Design: The elderly can autonomously find the cuff for clothes-changing. As the cuff can be detached, the elderly can take it off or put it on autonomously for more ventilation and warmth (Fig. 10).

Fig. 10. Cuff design C

(2) Automatic Alignment: The design of the large neck opening can assist put-on or take-off of the clothes. The adjustment of the cuff can make the process of clothes-changing faster. The front buckle has a magnet in the middle to assist the clothing alignment, and the different styles of the buttons can help the elders get used to it and avoid mistakes (Fig. 11).

Fig. 11. Automatic alignment

4 Conclusion

From the interview, it is known that the elderly have indeed faced much inconvenience in clothes-changing. Therefore, we can further discuss relevant inconveniences and observe relevant advantages of preferable clothing among the elderly. The new elderly care clothing design in this study aims to enhance the autonomy of the elderly. By exploring the decline in the physiological function, the care personnel can understand the harms suffered by the elderly during the clothes-changing process and develop the new elderly care clothing to immediately provide external assistance, as this can not only increase the autonomy of the elderly in the clothes-changing process, but also reduce the harm suffered by the care personnel in the process of assisting the elderly clothes-changing.

References

1. Summary Analysis and General Report on 2010 Population and Housing Censuses, "Permanent Resident Population.pdf" (2012)
2. Rosenblad-Wallin, E., Karlsson, M.: Clothing for the elderly at home and in nursing homes. J. Consum. Stud. Home Econ. **10**(4), 343–356 (1986)
3. Squillace, M.R., Remsburg, R.E., Bercovitz, A., Rosenoff, E., Branden, L.: An introduction to the National Nursing Assistant Survey. Vital and health statistics. Ser. 1, Programs and collection procedures, no. 44, pp. 1–54 (2007)
4. Pelissier, C., et al.: Occupational risk factors for upper-limb and neck musculoskeletal disorder among health-care staff in nursing homes for the elderly in France. Ind. Health **52** (4), 334–346 (2014)
5. Mann, W.C., Kimble, C., Justiss, M.D., Casson, E., Tomita, M., Wu, S.S.: Problems with dressing in the frail elderly. Am. J. Occup. Ther. **59**(4), 398–408 (2005)
6. Cohen-Mansfield, J., Creedon, M.A., Malone, T., Parpura-Gill, A., Dakheel-Ali, M., Heasly, C.: Dressing of cognitively impaired nursing home residents: description and analysis. Gerontologist **46**(1), 89–96 (2006)
7. Owen, B.D., Keene, K., Olson, S.: An ergonomic approach to reducing back/shoulder stress in hospital nursing personnel: a five year follow up. Int. J. Nurs. Stud. **39**(3), 295–302 (2002)
8. Rasmussen, C.D.N., Holtermann, A., Mortensen, O.S., Søgaard, K., Jørgensen, M.B.: Prevention of low back pain and its consequences among nurses' aides in elderly care: a stepped-wedge multi-faceted cluster-randomized controlled trial. BMC Public Health **13**(1), 1088 (2013)
9. Yang, W.-Y., Wu, F.-G., Book, A.: A new elderly clothing design reduces nurse aides' occupational injury in nursing homes. In: Duffy, V.G., Lightner, N. (eds.) Advances in Human Factors and Ergonomics in Healthcare. AISC, vol. 482, pp. 49–59. Springer, Cham (2017). https://doi.org/10.1007/978-3-319-41652-6_5
10. Çivitci, Ş.: An ergonomic garment design for elderly Turkish men. Appl. Ergon. **35**(3), 243–251 (2004)

Designing Inclusive User Experience for Impaired People. An Rtd Driven Proposal for Albanian Urban Spaces

Valerio Perna[1], Ledian Bregasi[2(✉)], Saimir Kristo[2], and Keti Hoxha[2]

[1] INNOVATION_Factory Unit (IF) | Research Center of Architecture, Engineering, and Design, Faculty of Architecture and Design (FAD), Universiteti POLIS Tiranë, Rr. Bylis 12, Autostrada Tiranë-Durrës, Km 5, Tirana, Albania
valerio_perna@universitetipolis.edu.al

[2] Faculty of Architecture and Design (FAD), Universiteti POLIS Tiranë, Rr. Bylis 12, Autostrada Tiranë-Durrës, Km 5, Tirana, Albania
{ledian_bregasi, saimir_kristo, keti_hoxha}@universitetipolis.edu.al

Abstract. A significant percentage of the studies regarding the user experience of urban spaces does not take into account a segment of the population characterized by people with physical and communication impairment. Even though HCI is a current major field of interest in design, disability - and consequently accessibility - is still a localized and understudied field of opportunity for contemporary research. Most of the solution proposed by architects - and designers - tend to refer to a generic type of user and, even though claiming to be inclusive, they primarily engage able-bodied people. In the last decades, design and HCI have moved beyond the workplace and have begun to tackle increasingly wicked and particular problems affecting the everyday lives of people. The result of this significant shift materialized into a playful, bottom-up and human-centered way to design the urban space.

The research for this contribution is rooted in a Research Through Design (RtD) approach (Zimmerman et al. 2007, 2010), where design is used to raise awareness and to generate design knowledge on disability and accessibility issues. This paper aims for proposing catalytic interventions for public space where interactive technologies are used to create a bridge between different typologies of users. Moreover, this paper is speculative also for the authors themselves. The identified operative categories will set the sparkle for the deployment of a design cell where to gather quantitative/qualitative data to understand better the spatial needs of impaired people, and to offer them a better and more inclusive design experience.

Keywords: Impairment · Architecture · HCI

© Springer Nature Switzerland AG 2019
M. Kurosu (Ed.): HCII 2019, LNCS 11568, pp. 47–69, 2019.
https://doi.org/10.1007/978-3-030-22636-7_4

1 Between Umwelt and HCI. Designing for Inclusive Environments

A high percentage of the world population deals every day with multiple severe problems related to disability and impairment. With these words, - even though the right use of them according to specific situations has been long discussed in medicine (Jones 2001) - we refer to a broad field of disadvantages in which a different perception of public spaces - and private as well - leads to a continuous struggle for these people to adapt to the so-called able-bodied people. Visual, hearing and brain damages related, impairments are just some generic definition of a whole specter of issues that affect almost 15% of the human beings (WHO 2011). What is interesting to point out is that, in 2001, the World Health Organization, published a work with the aim of integrating different kinds of disabilities; this framework - the International Classification of Functioning Disability and Health (ICF) for adults (2001) and for children and youth (2007) - has been adopted by many international countries and is useful to tackle the problems related to disability in a holistic way rather than to focus on many single fragments of a much bigger system. In this framework, impairment is used as an umbrella to include not only bodily problems but also activity limitations, or participation restrictions that relate to a health condition.

Even though people with disability are always defined also 'disadvantaged', we believe that disability is not an issue to solve in any way, but a general point to be taken in account by the design community, which deserves a much better understanding and needs for a new way of problem-solving. What we argue for is to have more care regarding impaired people - especially when it comes to design spaces that claim themselves to be 'inclusive' -, and our contribution will not just shape as a design solution from an external perspective, but it will also serve to ourselves to develop a more nuanced awareness regarding the topic itself and to start a better communication with all the others stakeholders involved in this kind of researches. For this reason, ample attention to address the notion of 'user experience' has been given to people with a different way of interacting, and perceiving, the spaces they are experiencing, that are rarely used as a point of departure for design speculation.

Moreover, one of our main interesting lies in defining how these people's mental structure is modified by the environment they are forced to live and relate with. According to von Uexküll (1957), every living being creates it's on Umwelt - a subjective world or an interpretation of it - characterized by the way the subject interacts with the space that surrounds him. Even though these studies are more related to the biological world - and the differences between the sensorial apparatus of men and animal - our objective is to create a 'parallelism' and use this specific 'ecological thinking' to trigger new speculations regarding people's behavior - and experiences - of the external world (Fig. 1).

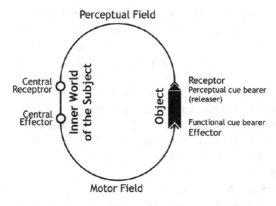

Fig. 1. Uexküll's model of the functional cycle.

Indeed, every human being, through the dualism perception-interaction, shapes his own Umwelt in the form of a singular and peculiar world, where there's no need to distinguish the individuality that generates from the external situation. This leads to a whole system of possibilities regarding the different layers that can be created, and projected, on reality. We can assume then that there is an isomorphic dependance between the perception that we have of the space itself and the categories of it that we (can) activate. Nevertheless, what is interesting in our case of von Uexkull studies is that every single living creature - from monocellular to the most complex ones - creates its own mental representation of the world from the way it interacts with it. The more the sensory organs are developed, the more the Umwelt will be extensive and stratified, and the Bauplan - the reality construction plane - is specific to the individuality perceiving the space. The union of Umwelt and Bauplan creates what is known as the perceptive bubble, a specific tonality of perception that unifies external and the interior one of the subject.

The fundamental characteristic of the Umwelt does not lie primarily in the extent of the sensorial apparatus instead in a very original way of constructing the world for every one of us. Human beings enter in connection only with something that can send stimuli which are strong enough to overcome the barrier of the senses and to generate a proactive reaction able to define proxemic behavior (Hall 1966).

It is clear at this point that designing the user experience for impaired people it's not just a matter of quantitative guidelines, but primarily a question of which kind of informative systems we want to relate to their perception, and the precise way of interaction we want to foster to model the amount of invisible information of which the world is filled with (Saggio 2013, 2015). If we shift then our interest from quantitative to qualitative solutions, we can reshape the concept of space itself taking into intangible account criteria that are currently forgotten or neglected. Using a thematic analysis mindset (Braun and Clarke 2012) we want to identify clusters of meaningful data that can be used not only to describe a precise phenomenon, but also to become prescriptive quality guidelines to identify design patterns that can used - site-specifically - to address issues of how to shape a better user experience in public spaces for not able-bodied people.

Furthermore, in the last decades, advanced technologies like the Internet of Things (IoT), sensors and networked information infrastructures have facilitated the diffusion of digital and intelligent features in the urban environment. The use of these technologies can help to develop completely innovative views on to deal with complex and emergent behaviors in the urban fabric and generative more inclusive dynamics; indeed, their implementation can help in modeling different kinds of informative layers and make them tangible also for people that generally don't perceive it. In fact, through the use of interactive technologies, we can foster a new way of understanding urban spaces and think about design practices that could be fully inclusive and where term inclusion does not refer to a later solution for spaces that are originally meant to be for non-disabled people.

Deaking and Alwaer (2011) underline how this passage is valid in the ever-growing attention towards the role of sensors and actuators embedded in physical and the appearance of ubiquitous and disappearing computers. Indeed since the 2000s, 'Smart City' has been used as a label to environments where clusters of Big Data, through the use of sensors and actuators, help to monitor and organize the activity of visitors or simple citizens (Nijholt 2017). What we want to reflect upon is a more comprehensive use of the ideas of "smart" and "intelligence" to tackle different aspects not taken into account when referring to Smart Cities. There are some other elements of the smartness in contemporary cities which is not only related to efficiency and management; for example, daily life activities which are undertaken without any specific purpose but just for fun, leisure and social interaction among citizens. Going beyond the idea of smartness and intelligence only related to economy and services can produce new insights on how we need smart technology to allow residents to reconfigure city services and to make a city livable and fully inclusive for different kinds of users.

The use of these tools and their deployment as an urban catalyst in public spaces will be useful to us in two ways: to help conceptualize what we actually miss in the understanding of impairment, and how these new features we add can be used as operative categories to enhance better design practices for the many professionals - and stakeholders - involved in such this topic. Since we are currently dealing with academic and design education under different perspectives, we found interesting to address this issue using a heterogeneous field of knowledge and speculative thinking. To create a common ground to develop our contribution the topic of user experience, we decided to filter our research under the shared lens of Research Through Design and Playful Smart Technologies, as tools to raise awareness and to generate design knowledge on disability and - user experience related - accessibility issues.

1.1   RtD and Urban Play. Behavioral Playful Approach for Better Urban Spaces

RtD is one of the many methodologies and epistemologies that are leveraged in the broader field of design research and has to do with the use of design practice as a form of scientific inquiry (Zimmerman et al. 2007, 2010; Stappers and Giaccardi 2013). The act of designing it's itself a form on theoretical speculation which is implemented in practical problem-solving procedures. Moreover, the act of concretely making something that can be identified as a research instrument (Koyré 1967) fosters a particular cognitive activity that can be used to make people aware of tacit values and latent needs. Since many countries in the world - like Albania - are still missing specific guidelines regarding essential accessibility for impaired people, we aim for starting a debate on what accessibility for urban spaces should - and might - be within the implementation of digital technologies and smart tools. It's important to point out how cities - and public spaces as well - have always been a place to gather social interaction and experiences according to specific categories of users. According to Oldenburgh (2001) the spaces in which we live in are divided into three main categories: First Places (our home environment) which are the more private and intimate one, where the sensorial stimulation is decided and oriented by ourselves; Second Places (the work environment), where the Umwelt we build has to relate also with other people one to guarantee a sustainable level of interaction which is actually filtered through work and productive dynamics; and finally Third Places, where the citizens are allowed to spend their free time and freely interact with humans and the external environment. These are the spaces that we are currently interested in developing more inclusively, taking into account a specific portion of the population which is actually suffering for a 'user experience' which is not - in any way - flexible to their needs, but forces this category of users to find themselves a modality to interface with them (Fig. 2).

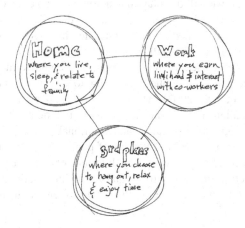

Fig. 2. Diagram representing the 'spaces' described by Oldenburg and their interrelation.

These are the spaces where play happens, specific designed urban sites where citizens are allowed to spend their free time and interact with others. The Third Wave of HCI (Bødker 2006) is currently dealing with the idea of materializing a new playful, bottom-up and human-centered way to design the urban space. These designers start their creative speculation basing on the assumption that mobile technologies are ubiquitous, and not confined anymore in workplaces or desktop solutions. If the Second Wave was more interested in groups working with a collection of applications - within a specific set of well-established communities of practice and situated situations, the Third one uses contexts and application types that are broadened and mixed through different media. Moreover, through the use of digital technologies, new elements of human life are included in human-computer interaction such as culture, experiences, and emotions (Norman 2002). However, Norman, didn't move to a cognitivist mindset - that sees emotions as a simple add-on to cognition itself - and we are more interested in focusing the theoretical works where the later does not have a secondary role (Boehner et al. 2005) but are interpreted as the result of the interaction among different actors rather a solipsistic way of engaging the world.

According to this view, we propose a design strategy where psychological categories can be used a strong-concepts (Höök and Löwgren 2012; Stolterman and Wiberg 2010) and how these concepts can be shaped into concrete prototypes (Hobye and Löwgren 2011; Löwgren 2007, 2009, 2013) to be used for raising awareness and sparking discussions. An essential feature in the research that we present is that we shifted from the typical architects' top-driven design approach, where solutions are always typified to an average user rather than a heterogeneous set of them, towards a bottom-up technology driven one where different fields are interrelated on common research ground. Rooting in an Action-Research approach (Foth and Brynskov 2016; Hayes 2011, 2014) our aim is for joining together - in an innovative way - a medic/psychological perspective on introversion and prescriptive design practises, to reach an "intermediate knowledge" and "strong concepts" midway entities uniting theories, research methods and prototypes.

To achieve this goal, we will use playful technologies and embedded smartness as a way to develop a new sense of engagement regarding disability issues and to foster the idea that the use of cross-field media can be translated in changes - both relational and physical - in our environment. We will briefly define what we mean for games in this paper, and how they can be used to create an emotional empowerment processes in the different agents perceiving the public space and to develop a horizontal sense of 'appropriation' for them (Dix 2007), where with the latter we refer to the capacity - operating another parallelism with the design and HCI field - to foster a sense of belonging that leads people to physically - and emotionally - use the space they live in. Since we are dealing with a specific category of people, we will underline how their appropriation is connected to the way they live and experience social dynamics in public spaces. But, before moving to the actual Albanian situation, let's briefly define what a 'game' is and how they can be used to raise awareness on such a delicate topic such as disability.

1.2   Play Is? Raise Awareness Through the Use of Playful Intelligent Tools

'Games' and 'play' have always been an important part of humans growth and behavior through the centuries (Huizinga [1938] 2008). Even though many studies have been conducted in the last century - leading to the development of a specific discipline called Game Studies - the definition of terms such as play, playfulness, and playability are still blurry, and we are currently facing a substantial overlap between definitions and explanations. What we are sure, is that play does not relate only to child's play (Bateson and Martin 2013) but also to grown-up actors that can gather and interact under through playful social dynamics. According to their six categories of play, for our speculation, we want to focus on the sixth which is the more open to further development and implementation in a broader range of study: playful play. With the latter, we intend an activity accompanied by a particularly positive mood state in which the individual is more inclined to behave (and, in the case of humans, think) spontaneously and flexibly (Bateson and Martin 2013). Furthermore, we can assume that the implementation of games technologies in urban fabric can push our cities to develop another of intelligence and be more playful rather than smart (Perna 2018). This opens up a new range of possibility because, through their deployment, we can achieve the goal of motivating motivate citizens to appropriate the physical space they live to discover new paths, write new stories and co-create new perspectives for tomorrow, and reaching at the same a better awareness regarding impairment that we can highlight in design strategies (Grønbæk et al. 2012).

At this point, we will briefly illustrate three different games where a specific disability (visual impairment) is used as meaningful system of mechanics and dynamics to gather research questions and to engage people with playful categories as scenario, empathy, relatedness, participation, agency, etc. (Schouten et al. 2018).

- **Beyond Eyes:** BE it's a progressive (Juul 2005) storytelling game where the player acts a young blind girl in her daily life. Besides the fancy graphics and the lovely character illustrations, the game wants to foster a profound reflection on how every single regular action can become a considerable obstacles in life a ten years old girl. The interesting thing is that disability is not seen as a hindrance for Rae, but as a way to appropriate the world she lives in to discover a whole new range of possibilities within her interaction with she doesn't see but is perceived;
- **Screencheat:** it's a multiplayer FPS (First Person Shooter) where everyone is blind. The disability is represented through the metaphor of invisibility. Each player is not able to see his opponents but can only hear them moving. The easiest way to win the game is don't make a single step and wait for the opponents to come your way. Even in this case, this strategy is seen as a positive behavior, and it wants to make player reflect on how sometimes blind people do not freely act in public space due to the difficulty of interacting with non-disabled people due to their handicap. Space, in this way, becomes a dark prison where you can perceive the others but put a 'visual barrier' between you and them;
- **Perception:** the last of the examples presented is a horror game where the main character has to deal with a paranormal entity that she cannot harm with traditional weapons but with intangible powers. Even though Cassie is blind, she uses echolocation (an orientation system based on sounds) to show the path in front of her. The game wants to raise awareness about how scary can be the external world for people that they don't sight as the main sensor to quickly get a representation of it. Furthermore, it stresses the importance of digital technologies to empower impaired people since Cassie's main helpful tool is her smartphone from which she can acquire sound information and tips (Fig. 3).

Fig. 3. Screenshot from the game *Beyond Eyes*. The image points out the relational – and discovering – system that the protagonist Rea develops to overcome her impairment.

2 Objectives and Contribution

After presenting the reader our specific field of knowledge, and the different inter-disciplinary theoretical frameworks and tools we use to address the particular topic of designing a better inclusive user experience for impaired people, we enter the more design-oriented part of this paper. What we want to point out, before going ahead with our research, is that from the get-go we didn't want to present disability as a topic to solve - there are other kinds of professional figures that can activate critical thinking in regards to this - but a broad range of opportunities for designers to rethink concepts such as inclusiveness, democratic user experience, and engaging public spaces in contemporary cities. For this reason, our objectives are threefold: on the side, to sparkle a wider dialogue to include not only architects but experts coming from different fields, to facilitate a lateral design thinking phase that could link to more effective and long-term applications; on the other hand we aim for proposing catalytic interventions for public space where interactive technologies can be used to create a bridge between different typologies of users and to foster communication can help in the creation of diverse and overlapping frameworks of action: architectural, social, education, and economic ones. As we do so, we aim to contribute to an inclusive design agenda to architects, and HCI designers in specific, through the development of a more nuanced shared vocabulary.

3 Vision from Tirana. From Socialism to Emergent Complexity

To synthetically describe the urban development in Tirana during the early '90s, it is important to introduce the term "Shock Therapy". Jeffrey Sachs invented the term and it consists of a neoliberal economic doctrine, evolved from Milton Friedman's "Shock Policy" approach. After the collapse of the socialist system in Albania, and following this doctrine, the presence of the state in the public and economic affair was drastically reduced. This was followed by the practically total elimination of state subsidies and large-scale privatization of public assets. What was collapsing in the early '90s in the eastern block was the "System". For this reason, the resulting changes that shocked Tirana and Albania need to be understood following a systematic approach.

Up to that moment, the development of the city had been guided by a robust deterministic approach. The ruling party and the state apparatus intended to organize the territory and the whole society by drafting five-years plans, organizing in this way every detail of the social and economic activity in the country. The strong deterministic approach was directly reflected in city planning and urban design. The party was planning and building a new city for the modern man of socialism. A system striving for equality used the standardization as a tool for city planning. This city was thought for similar people, doing similar jobs, having similar salaries and at the end living similar lives. The homogeneous use zones and the housing standards created cities that where a reflection of the mechanistic understanding of reality. In this kind of system, a higher authority –the Party- was the custodian of the higher truth and the guardian of equality.

The housing block resulting from this way of conceiving the city where highly standardized and showed very little specialization or variation of the activities. The main difference in these blocks was the size of the apartments that was a direct correlation to the number of members of the dwelling family. An additional factor that influenced the very low specialization of different parts of the city was the total absence of private land property. During communism, the entire land of the country was owned by the state. For this reason, the land value was uniform, and consequently, the market did not influence the density of the city. In these conditions, the city growth was a direct consequence and function of the natural growth of the population.

After the moment of the collapse, the new system of reference introduced an entirely new paradigm. It reduced the presence and control of the authority in the territory, and the same idea of planning was questioned and refused. The expansion of Tirana at this moment was characterized by rapid and uncontrolled development. Large portions of the inhabitants of Albania left the most peripheral areas of the country that without the state subsidies were unable to compete in a free market. The authorities were unable to respond to the needs of the migrating fluxes and the private housing market was inexistent. In these conditions, a large number of abusive buildings, self-constructed by the inhabitants started to appear in the peripheries of Tirana. At the same time, the more consolidated areas of the city started to become characterized by abusively added volumes to the existing housing blocks (Fig. 4).

The function of these combined volumes varies very much from case to case. In most of the, examples, they consist of attached rooms for the members of the family. In other cases, especially in the lower floors, the added volume hosted embryonic economic activities like primitive shops or bars.

The abusively built houses and added volumes, where able to convert a very strictly design city to a more complex organism that was able to adapt to the new socio-economical system in a relatively fast way. This new city was able to specialize more and diversify the offered services. One of the most exciting features of this city was that a central authority did not guide the majority of the decision-making process. The development was guided by the interaction of the single agents present in the territory.

Fig. 4. Abusively added volume in Tirana

This interaction, which sometimes resulted in conflicts and in other cases brought collaboration between the inhabitants, was able to convert a highly standardized and mechanical city into a complex system that faced new and unpredictable challenges without the presence of controlling authority. This new kind of town was able to be reactive, flexible and competitive, even though in many cases unjust and unfair.

The extreme difference between the two city models in Tirana allows us to make some considerations on the questions of rules and order in urban development. The over-regulation of a complex system, such as the case of a city, can erase some unpredictable features of a system, eliminating in this way the possibility of the spontaneous emergence of novelty. On the other hand, complex and chaotic systems show a high degree of adaptability, very useful in the cases of uncertain future conditions. Small-scale interactions of the agents can result in the emergence of a higher level of large-scale behavior in the city. The information exchanged by the agents can be considered a measure of order in the town. The grass rooted decision-making system proved to be an effective way for problem-solving in a city that could not be controlled by higher authority.

4   Understanding Albania. A Brief Overview

To have a deeper understanding of the situation of public space in Albania, it is also interesting to relate the evolution of the city itself with the general events that characterized the recent history of the country. After centuries of isolation and suppression by one of the harshest communist dictatorships, Albania has made great efforts in opening up towards modernization and freedom. Although the country faces many similar difficulties like its neighbors, the way it deals with them does not show many similarities. Looking for original solutions, to respond to its problems and to create a new identity, Albania's capital has become a place where rational and bizarre elements co-exist, generating a character that is not permanent but always about to change.

A mosaic-like portrait of Tirana – a city that provokes architects to dare more and at the same time blocks them in front of its monumental ruins.

Once known for their strict government-controlled spatial planning, many former communist cities in the Western Balkans have been transformed by feverish uncontrolled urban growth. After 30 years of transition, the Western Balkans peninsula is still looking for a way to create new cultures of spatial planning in a region where not only residents but even architects and urban planners may feel excluded from spatial developments.

Tirana is situated in the middle of a significant European transit corridor connecting Southern Europe to the Near East and closely connected geographically and economically to the nearby harbor city Durrës. It is the primary driver of the country's economic and cultural development, continuously growing into a super-regional metropolis. This article is looking at Albania's evolutionary process, focusing on the capital's ambitions while evolving into Greater Tirana[1] and trying to become a competitive metropolis in the Balkans. It's an attempt to understand the generative points that lead to this innovative and experimental 'island' in a territorial 'sea' of ex-communist countries that are denying to the change and staying hidden in the shadow of the past.

Initiated as an organic city in the 17th century, Tirana oscillated several times between spontaneity and organized planning[2]. It is a city not easily shaped through plans: a blurred and fragmented situation created by the continuous interaction between organic development and planning decisions. However, it has all undergone unbelievable changes offering a unique perspective for urban planning and development with enormous energy within.

During the authoritarian regime of Enver Hoxha [1944 to 1985], significant shifts occurred in the structure of the city. Architecture and urban planning were called to influence the creation of a new social reality. A massive erasure of historical areas and religious centers was executed to free the space for the construction of low-cost housing areas as a new social model becoming an 'excellent' example of a city designed by demolition. An example imposed by its authoritarian communist leader, experiencing one of the most severe communist systems in the entire Eastern European block, suffering for more than 40 years negation of the freedom of speech, leaving out social participation and, abusing with the 'collective' approach.

In 1990 Albania started on the new and challenging road of transition, but rather in a very chaotic manner and even with severe setbacks such as the 1997 social unrest caused by the collapse of the fraudulent pyramid schemes. After a massive rural exodus occurred in the same years the city of Tirana was confronted with the phenomenon of extensive informal building activity resulting in vast areas of uncontrolled urban sprawl which placed at great risk the quality of urban life for the whole city (Fig. 5).

With its actual population of nearly one million inhabitants, Tirana is four times the size it used to be 20 years ago and amounts to more than one-quarter of the country's entire population. Almost 60% of Albania's population is living in an urban

---

[1] Tirana Municipality (2006).

[2] Kristo (2004).

Fig. 5. The destruction of Enver Hoxha's statue by thousands of Albanian citizens. A central image of the 'fall of the dictator'. 1991

Fig. 6. The informal settlement of Bathore in Tirana. One of the most problematic and non-inclusive areas of the whole municipality. 2015

surrounding. The transition from socialism to capitalism had a direct impact on the social, economic and spatial structures of the city. Tirana's urban space has transformed rapidly, towards two different directions: On one side lies the transformation of the city center and the main road axes where commerce, offices, and entertainment have been introduced. New housing complexes have been constructed in these central areas, too. On the other side, since the early 1990s, an informal extension of the city's borders, firstly by small-scale housing and later by large-scale housing, was gradually developed without planning, social and technical infrastructure or provision for public spaces, leading to the creation of a poor urban environment, with no apparent intention to be integrated with their existing surrounding context. At the same time, informal development processes have also taken place within the existing urban fabric, occupying former public land and blocking passages by erecting small, medium or even large-scale constructions. These large-scale housing and commercial complexes were implemented in the periphery of the city by the private sector and had undergone a recent series of actions to legalize them and understand that they are part of the urban reality and have to be integrated into the future urban development plans (Fig. 6).

The municipality tried to regain public control with several beautification campaigns in the 2000s and serious of international competitions inviting several star architects to create a new image for the city. Streets, parks, and riverfronts were cleared of illegal kiosks and thousands of trees were planted, ready to welcome visionary ideas from West.

A lot of attention on an international level was drawn to Tirana by the attempt of its former Mayor, Edi Rama, in 2001 to reinvent the city's identity. As an artist he cleaned up the very scruffy avenues with a radical facelift that through interventions on the major public spaces and by upgrading the public infrastructure attempted to construct a new image and a new identity for the city center, regenerating the city by attracting new activities and investments, as part of the vision of Greater Tirana and 'Durana'. Representing nowadays one of the most vibrant cities in Albania, Tirana can be considered as a planning laboratory of architectural and spatial experimentation.

The study 'Strategic Planning for Greater Tirana', conducted in 2001 by Tirana's Municipality, showed a massive population expansion in the metropolitan region embracing Tirana and Durres, a harbor city just 30 km away, creating a chaotic situation. Today the area is accommodating one-third of the Albanian population. This pattern of exceptional growth in economically important capitals has been typical of post-communist regimes[3]. A majority of domestic and foreign enterprises are located in and around the Tirana-Durres Corridor (World Bank 2007[4]). It is one of the main circulation axes of Albania that connects the two biggest cities in the country and again connects them both to the airport. It has become an economic corridor that brings large revenue to the country. Now the need to improve the urban condition along this area has been identified. The concept of 'Durana' also investigated in the publication "DURANA Albania's New Sustainable Image" is used as a tool to think about the metropolitan region on a bigger scale: Tirana and Durres as one city; an eventual fusion of two cities in a new metropolis with a green heart in between.

The Urban Catalyst Theory provides a brand new direction for incremental urban renewal. Countries with rapid urban development and increasing needs to rethinking their spatial and urban development strategies. In this case, a series of interviews were organized with different academics, architects, urban planners, sociologists and anthropologists to understand their overview related to the catalytic role of urban

---

[3] Nedović-Budić, Zorica, Urban Studies, 2001, Vol. 30. No. 6. pp. 899–905.

[4] World Bank. 2007. Doing business 2008, Eastern Europe. [report] Available at: http://www. doingbusiness.org/Documents/RegionalReports/DB2008_RP_Eastern_Europe.pdf, last accessed 2009/12/18.

strategies that can be undertaken in the development of our cities. These experts are professionals acknowledged in their fields internationally with valuable experience on the Albanian territory and way of progress, providing their input on this topic. In these sections, there are their answers and opinions in the above question.

It is a common denominator from the above interviews between the selected experts that the role of architecture and architects must not be isolated from the multitude of layered developments in the urban sphere. The architect should act interdisciplinary to analyze all the levels on a city operates, and be an active part of not only design making but also decision-making. The above discussions highlight the importance of developing new strategies, which don't act solely in singular operations focused in an architectural level but understand the city as a living organism where every action should provide positive reactions.

There is an apparent attempt from the Albanian government to address more attention on the importance of urban public space. This concern is taken into account as part of the national governmental strategy of "Urban Rebirth". This strategy aims to revitalize all major city centers in Albania and renew public squares, historical areas and other buildings of significant importance. It can be considered as a necessary strategy in improving public space qualities in Albania, but there are no evidences of a catalytic approach since most examples consider the development of singular elements, which act alone. In this case, they are not able to penetrate in the deep layering of the urban complexity in order to provide sustainable urban solutions generating economy. In this framework, most of the examples are only able to intervene superficially, considered actions on city beautification than urban renewal and regeneration. This section will focus on strategies that can be considered furthermore, improving the existing interventions.

Building comprehensive, reliable, pragmatic, and gainful urban communities are maybe the best test confronting humankind today, and there are no simple arrangements. A vital piece of the riddle, however, lies comfortable heart of the world's urban zones: its open spaces. Here are 5 different ways you can help fortify the social texture of your locale and kick off monetary advancement by making and supporting solid open spaces.

4.1   Enhance the Human Scale in Public Space

Placemaking depends on a straightforward rule: if you plan urban communities for autos and traffic, you will get vehicles and traffic. If you plan for individuals and spots, you will get individuals and places.

Increased traffic and the addition of supporting road infrastructure are not measures to avoid the intensive flow of automobiles in the city, which as a result create an unfriendly environment for pedestrians in the city. It is crucial that catalytic actions to provide urban development and in particular near the city center must take in account the human factor. Future development should provide the necessary infrastructure in terms of public transportation, space for pedestrians and bicyclists and drivers acting as the primary catalyst for urban regeneration and growth.

Several examples across the world such as the Metrocable in Medellin, Colombia, river and boat transportation in cities such as Delft, the Netherlands but also Gjakova and Prizren, Kosovo have created successful pedestrian public spaces, which enhance street life contributing to social cohesion.

4.2 Transform Public Space as a Destination

An urban oasis and park serves as a buffer zone for the city, especially for citizens living in dense urban areas. It is often not only an area of leisure and recreation but also a gathering point for the city creating a new dimension away from the heavily trafficked roads. Depending on the activities and accessibility in such areas they can result in successful public spaces, but also if all measures to ensure safety and maintenance are not taken it can lead into an undesirable place to visit. A positive example, in this case, is the one of Santiago, Chile and the Las Condes Plazas as a former prosperous area of inter-modality after a desolated area full of muggers and crime.

Actions were taken from the local and central government, investing in the development of retail spaces but also the urban regeneration of the adjacent public spaces also creating new ones to enhance the general character of that area. This action required a coordinated effort from the authorities and cannot be conceived as an act of direct economic investment but as an action of strategically planned and executed urban development.

The main ingredient of this action was the inclusion of the local community and integration in all the processes of this initiative. In this case, the sense of ownership was actively transmitted to the community acting as the main actor and catalyst on this urban development process.

4.3 Develop Local Economies

The recent phenomena of urban development created a chaotic structure not only in terms of cityscape but also the local economy. Even Though private initiative was one of the main driving forces growing the Albanian economy, the conditions were in many cases informal. Examples that initiate from industry till small scale initiatives and local markets in the city centers are still part of informal schemes either in terms of economic operation but also in the infrastructure on which they operate.

Various reasons in addition to the lack of governmental control but also lack of public and private investment to implement a qualitative infrastructure for commercial facilities were the main aspects for the above phenomenon.

A successful strategy to reactive urban centers and in particular historical urban centers in different cities in Albania initiated with the restoration of different historical bazaars/markets in cities such as; Kruja, Korca, Tirana, Shkodra, Gjirokastra, etc. This initiative showcased successful results not only as part of a facade operation strategy and city beautification but because of their short and long term impact in the local economy.

Their development should focus on the creation of a sustainable economy within the communities to catalyze social cohesion. Areas as such for the small scale cities of the Albanian territory became reference points in the city, and as a result, they quickly become touristic viewpoints attracting visitors from nearby cities or foreign tourists from abroad. In this case, they are able to provide much more from what they were designed for in the beginning, but in the end, they can serve as true catalysts for sustainable urban development.

4.4 Empower Public Space Through Design

The use of design is fundamental in the implementation of any urban development project. What makes a design strategy or solution successful is its ability to empower the value and quality of public space increasingly through its implementation.

The effects of poorly designed public spaces can be easily identified among many case studies of public spaces, and as quickly we can observe the difference between design solutions conceptualized as catalytic actions for an urban space.

In this framework, a holistic approach is required not only to understand the problems of the context of intervention but also the tools that are being offered to implement any possible idea or proposal. Both the combination of the above characteristics will provide us with examples of public spaces, which are not thought as single entities but they are conceptualized as agents of urban catalysis, being able to affect their surrounding context positively and generate development by triggering the local economy and enhancing urban quality for the communities.

4.5 Create a Comprehensive Public Space Agenda

It is vital for the future development of public space to understand the need of including two typologies of approach. "top-down" and "bottom-up" approaches are necessary not only to include all levels of decision-making but also to provide the sense of ownership to all actors and interested parties.

All actions that need to be overtaken in the successful development of a new intervention for the city require strong collaboration along the above parties.

Catalytic urban development cannot occur through isolated and sporadic actions but through a comprehensive urban agenda that takes in account a broader vision for the city and operates with the use of all necessary tools that are required to provide an effective and efficient result.

Including all parties since the beginning of this process would provide a full view of the issues in an inclusive way that must be addressed to improve life quality in a city and through coordination to attack all the problems strategically. The actions that would be overtaken would not only work in the aesthetic, functional and design level but their impact will contribute with a focus in the social and economic layers of the city.

5 Disability. One Definition, a Broad Spectrum of Meanings

After dealing specifically with Albanian situations, let us briefly introduce some practices that can be taken into account when dealing with accessibility and user experiences problems for impaired people. The proposed analysis will focus on two different directions to address this topic: the first one based on traditional/analog solutions; the second one on the implementation of digital technologies that can empower the first category and the user.

Furthermore, according to WHO (World Health Organization) around 15% of the world's population lives with a form of disability. As the age of life expectancy is increasing, along with it the figures are expected to increase. The leading causes of these increasing numbers are numerous, such as the outgrowth of new diseases that cause impairment, increasing life span, malnutrition in young ages, the prevalence of health conditions, etc.

Disability is seen in many forms and can be categorized as above:

- **Physical** which can be visible and nonvisible and can include: **mobility problems** and **limited use of limbs**;
- **Sensory** limitations such as **hearing difficulties** or deafness and **vision difficulties** or blindness;
- **Neurological disabilities** which may lead to physical disabilities;
- **Cognitive limitations**, which include some developmental and intellectual disabilities;
- **Psychiatric restrictions** in which are included mental illnesses that follow with sensorial and cognitive limitations.

Approximately most of the individuals will experience a sort of disability, which may be temporary but may become even permanent, so it should be seen as a state that can affect anyone in different forms. The UN Declaration of the Rights of Disabled Persons with Disabilities (2008) declares that disabled persons should be respected and treated equally. This means that they should have the right to access and use all the public services along with enabling them to be self-reliant and independent. Although in legislation accessibility is obligatory, there is lack of physical availability in urban and building environments, especially in developing countries. In Albania according to the regulatory for using spaces by impaired people 2018, it is mentioned the necessity of the urban and architectural solutions that provide accessibility for people with disabilities to provide service for all individuals. In a few public buildings, there is seen an effort for providing accessibility to individuals with mobility difficulties, although in the open spaces there is a lack of solutions for providing a safe circulation for these individuals. There are two major problems in urban spaces in Albania concerning the aspect of orientation and access for people with different types of impairment. Firstly, the movement is interrupted by physical barriers and secondly, orientation difficulty.

The urban spaces in the cities of Albania are impossible for independent circulation and inappropriate for assisted circulation. The most problematic areas in the urban environment in Tirana are the crossroads, which are the most dangerous areas for all users. The height of the pedestrian walkways is a barrier, and furthermore, there is not enough distance for multiple pedestrians, especially for those with mobility disabilities. The most important aspect is the condition of not having a clear definition of what passage is for pedestrians, what is the bicycle lane and the one for vehicles. This mixture of modality typologies is become a barrier even for those not impaired. An effort is made in pedestrian walkways for those that have visual disabilities, where the orientation line is implemented which it has visible problematics: firstly, the height of the texture differentiation is not appropriate and secondly, these lines lead the person into dangerous areas, such as to the bicycle lane, where the user is not informed. The most common phenomena is the presence of bars even in the public areas or positioning of the tree in the middle of the pedestrian space. The zebra crossing not only that do not have a change in texture and material but are most of the time not visual, becoming a source of accident and confusion quickly. There is no auditory traffic light for the visually impaired to be informed. Most of the walkways and streets are not in good condition, becoming a barrier for everyone. All of these aspects clearly show that it is impossible for people with disabilities to circulate and orient themselves in the urban environment.

Another problematic aspect is the impossibility to access public buildings, especially for those with mobility issues. Most of the buildings are designed with stairs but do not have ramps. Guidance with Braille text is not available, and the hand railing in stairs is missing. There have been some efforts to make these spaces accessible but not in an appropriate way. Ramps are of an inappropriate slope or even with a slippery material, not functioning as a facility but a barrier. When ramps are present for accessing the building from the outside, the inside is inaccessible. Such accessibility problems are present even in educational buildings and offices, which excludes to these persons the possibility to be educated and work. Public transport is another problem for people suffering from disabilities. There is no clear definition of pedestrian areas, no presence of ramps and furthermore, the public transport vehicles are inappropriate for being accessible.

As a result, they are obligated to move in the city with the assistance of a person, and as a result, they are depended to others and not to themselves. The dependency to others to use urban spaces and public services leads to depression or other psychological difficulties linked to the fact that they do not feel self-reliant, so it remains the central aspect to take into consideration. The loss of independence is not only in performing their everyday life activities but also regarding their cultural and leisure activities. Cities that continue to have barriers of different types are cities of "gaps" and extremely uneconomic, apart from being controversial cities from the social and human aspect. Urban sociologists argue that not eliminating the architectural barriers is a negative issue that impact the entire collective[5]. Inclusive Design seeks to provide to people with disabilities equality in using public spaces and services, eliminating obstacles, maximizing the accessibility to use equally and independently environments, and involving these people in the community. It is the architects' responsibility to promote these qualities in urban and architectural spaces. An inclusive approach through providing better accessibility for the impaired consequently will provide accessibility for all the users. We all benefit from an inclusive environment designed following the principles of inclusive design, which are as follow:

1. Design should create spaces for promoting the creation of sustainable communities;
2. Inclusive design identifies the barriers that lead to exclusion and creates spaces taking into consideration the diversity of people;
3. It provides flexibility in use, to adapt and inspire users;
4. An inclusive design does not require all the people's need but avoids exclusiveness but offers solutions from which everyone can benefit

---

[5] Parchi per tutti – fruibilità per un'utenza ampliata. Accessibilità e fruibilità delle strutture e dei servizi da parte di un'utenza ampliata alle persone con disabilità, agli anziani, ai bambini: Linee Guida per gli enti di gestione dei Parchi nazionali Italiani, ACLI, 2003.

"Inclusive design doesn't mean you're designing one thing for all people. You're designing a diversity of ways to participate so that everyone has a sense of belonging[6]"

Inclusiveness should be seen in two dimensions. Firstly, in recognizing the diversity and the "special demands" required to provide social inclusiveness in a non-restrained way. Secondly, if solutions are to be universal, they not only should meet the requirement of the group in question but also to improve the general environment for all citizens. In the second dimension, errors can be easily made. By applying ideal technical solutions might lead to the creation of an inclusive environment for the impaired person but exclusive for the rest of the society. Some of these solutions instead of providing equality for all might stress differences among individuals.

Public spaces should shape following these principles:

- More **focused** on the **pedestrians**;
- The **boundaries** between the road dedicated to pedestrians, vehicles, and bicycles must be well **defined** and **continuous**;
- The character of the public spaces should **provide social interaction** and involvement even for the person with any accessibility impairment.
- **Recognizable spaces** for the blind along with the presence of recognizable elements;
- **Repetition of the landmarks** to provide a secure mental state by making the individuals comfortable by recognizing these elements consistently. If an environment is predictable, it simplifies the navigation process.
- **Presence of comfort cones:** providing several areas dedicated to the visually impaired. These areas serve as resting spots and orientations spots in the city. This can be a space designed in different colors, materials, street furniture appropriate for these users. These areas may be present in spots that are more crowded in people and traffic, mainly between crossing and decision points. This area should be clearly defined and should provide the understanding when the user is inside or outside of it.
- **Destinations** should be all **accessible:** continuous and uninterrupted routes should provide a connection with all the targets in the city. This system may translate in a good network of trails using grid patterns.
- **Non-visual landmarks:** change in surface, which can be understood by the touch with the cane and feet. The changes in the surface can be seen in various forms: A curb, a slope, a change in material. The sound of traffic informs the person when he is approaching a side street, and the traffic density sound gives him the information of the direction he is taking. Green spaces are an important factor not only for the state of well-being but can be orientation elements visually and through smell;
- **Route guidance:** clear guidance provided by continuous guiding lines or tactile paving. Crossing place Striking landmarks should make the areas recognizable when it begins and when the other side is reached. The transition from pedestrian zone to the beginning of the crossing should be felt by feet and long cane through the changes in materials and the presence of the marks. Drivers should also be

---

[6] Inclusive Design leader Susan Goltsman.

Fig. 7. Different systems through address impaired people issues through route guidance

assertive of these areas where the speed should be lower. Change in material and color can be a signal of this area. When another guidance is missing tactile pavement should be used which should be detected by foot and cane. Obstacles should not interrupt this type of pavement, and the contrast between color texture and luminance should be detectable. This pavement should be located 60 cm at least from the curb road delimitation and obstacles (Fig. 7);

- **Auditable differences.** Special sound tiles or rubber tiles
- **Decorative use** of materials, color and contrast differences leads to confusion. These differences should be made uniformly. Route guidance line is linear and continuous and is composed of several elements.

Due to the increasing speed of city life, blind individuals cannot rely only on visual signage and landmarks in a city. It is vital to implement technologies to provide to them the use of these spaces. Various new smart tools can be implemented in the urbanscapes - such as GPS Wayfinding Apps - which inform the user for the location of the bus stations, shopping centers or even other public buildings and spaces. These applications can be linked to small transmitters, which can be placed in buildings or other notable spots, and the user is informed through the mobiles devices through auditory information. These transmitters are called beacons and can be positioned indoor and outdoor spaces. This technology is applied in Poland, Warsaw. With the changes in technology, various solutions can be found to ease the accessibility in the urban areas for the visually impaired. These solutions are essential to improve their life quality and future. Most of the people that later became visually impaired are afraid of using the urban environments not only alone but even assisted. This comes from the uncertainty in perception when vision is missing and because urbanscapes are the spaces where echolocation becomes even more complicated, because there is auditory information. Through providing them an urban system dedicated to them, they feel more secure to face with the outside world which offers them the possibility to use the services and interact with the built and urban environment. Therefore, social interaction is made possible, where they are capable of sharing their experiences with others. Through social interaction, they gain their individuality, feel included to the community and trespassing the psychological barrier created because of the lack of the appropriate infrastructure. Moreover, these solutions are a key factor for exploring more about their sensorial system capability, gaining more confidence in navigating in several typologies of spaces.

6   Conclusion and Further Discussion

After pointing out our interest concerning the topic of disability in Albania – and the related user experiences practices – let us finish this paper with a critical reflection regarding our work until now. From the get-go, we did not want to frame the selected topic from a narrow perspective, but we aimed to sparkle a broader dialogue to include not only architects but also experts coming from different fields, to facilitate a lateral design-thinking phase that could link to more effective and long-term applications. Working on accessibility in architecture and design has genuinely been a curiosity-driven initiative from one of us who is currently dealing with this topic within its doctoral research. With this in our minds, we wanted to detach from generic solutions that claim to be fully inclusive, to focus our attention on a specific segment on the society with different problems and needs, and to use lateral thinking in design to better understand disability ourselves. For this reason, through studies of psychology and neurosciences, we proposed some 'strong-concepts' (Höök and Löwgren 2012) and elaborated them to shape our design process following a process inspired by Action Research (Hayes 2011).

In sum, our approach to this work is "non-solutionist". We believe that disability is not an issue per se to solve in any way, but a widespread point to be taken in account by the design community, which deserves a much better understanding and needs for a new way of problem-solving. What we wanted to foster it is a lateral thinking based way of dealing with this topic that could avoid top-down driven solution to focus more on a bottom-up and horizontal approach tailored on the users. With this in mind, our future objectives are three-fold: On the one hand, we aim for developing a shared nuanced vocabulary between architects and HCI designers to tackle multiple issues regarding user experience for impaired people in urban spaces, and helping other designers to benefit significantly from having more speculative design methodologies at hand. On the other hand, we want to propose catalytic interventions for public space where interactive technologies can be used to create a bridge between different typologies of users and to foster communication can help in the creation of diverse and overlapping frameworks of action: architectural, social, education, and economic ones. As we do so, we aim to contribute to an inclusive design agenda to architects, and HCI designers in specific. Moreover, this paper is speculative also for ourselves; the operative categories we identify will set the sparkle for the deployment of a design cell where to gather quantitative and qualitative data to understand better the spatial needs of impaired people, and to offer them a better and more inclusive design experience. The team will develop the latter as an interactive environment that could be used to gather quantitative and qualitative data, that will be further analyzed to understand deeper the needs and requirements when it comes to design accessible spaces for impaired people.

Since we believe that disability issues are not just a matter of quantitative outcomes, that usually leads to a misconception – and simplification – concerning this topic, we aim for focusing our attention on a more in-depth and more meaningful data analysis that could identify a significant cluster that can orientate the research on practical implemented solutions. The deployment phase will see a heterogeneous group of users

– either able-bodied or disabled – dealing with the interactive inner environment of the cell that will simulate a specific disability condition. A series of the survey will be conducted before and after the experiment, to document not only their physical reaction to the simulation but also the changes in their awareness regarding impaired people condition and issues. With this deployment, we hope to define some behavioral patterns that can work as a middle point where the expectations of both kinds of users are satisfied to establish some design categories to trigger the whole designers community to start new debates regarding the notion of user experience for impaired people in Albanian – and not only – public spaces.

References

Bateson, P., Martin, P.: Play, Playfulness, Creativity and Innovation. Cambridge University Press, Cambridge (2013)

Bødker, S.: When second wave HCI meets third wave challenges. In: Proceedings of the 4th Nordic Conference on Human-Computer Interaction: Changing Roles (NordiCHI 2006), pp. 1–8 (2006)

Boehner, K., DePaula, R., Dourish, P., Sengers, P.: Affect: from information to interaction. In: Proceedings of the 4th Decennial Conference on Critical Computing: Between Sense and Sensibility, Aarhus, Denmark, 20–24 August 2005 (2005)

Braun, V., Clark, V.: Thematic analysis. In: Cooper, H. (Editor-in-Chief) APA Handbook of Research Methods in Psychology. Research Designs, vol. 2 (2012)

Deakin, M., Alwaer, H.: From intelligent to smart cities. Intell. Build. Int. 3(3), 140–152 (2011)

Kristo, F.: History of Tirana as a city till 1920, vol. 1, p. 17. Toena Publications, Tirana (2004)

Dix, A.: Designing for appropriation. In: Proceedings of the 21st British HCI Group Annual Conference on People and Computers: HCI… but not as we know it-vol. 2, pp. 27–30. British Computer Society, London (2007). Author, F.: Article title. Journal 2(5), 99–110 (2016)

Schouten, B.A.M., Ferri, G., Hansen, B.N., van Heerden, A.: Design Concepts for Empowerment through Urban Play (2018, in press)

Foth, M., Brynskov, M.: Participatory action research for civic engagement. In: Gordon, E., Mihailidis, P. (eds.) Civic Media: Technology, Design, Practises. MIT Press, Cambridge (2016)

Grønbæk, K., Kortbek, K.J., Møller, C., Nielsen, J., Stenfeldt, L.: Designing playful interactive installations for urban environments – the SwingScape experience. In: Nijholt, A., Romão, T., Reidsma, D. (eds.) ACE 2012. LNCS, vol. 7624, pp. 230–245. Springer, Heidelberg (2012). https://doi.org/10.1007/978-3-642-34292-9_16

Hall, E.T.: The Hidden Dimension. Doubleday, Garden City (1966)

Hayes, G.R.: The relationship of action research to human-computer interaction. ACM Trans. Comput.-Hum. Interact. 18(3), 15:1–15:20 (2011)

Hayes, G.R.: Knowing by doing: action research as an approach to HCI. In: Olson, J.S., Kellogg, W.A. (eds.) Ways of Knowing in HCI, pp. 49–68. Springer, New York (2014). https://doi.org/10.1007/978-1-4939-0378-8_3

Hobye, M., Löwgren, J.: Touching a stranger: designing for engaging experience in embodied interaction. Int. J. Des. 5, 3 (2011)

Höök, K., Löwgren, J.: Strong concepts: intermediate-level knowledge in interaction design research. ACM Trans. Comput.-Hum. Interact. 19(3), 23:1–23:18 (2012)

Jones, R.B.: Impairment, disability and handicap—old fashioned concepts? J. Med. Ethics **27**, 377–379 (2001)

Juul, J.: Half-Real: Video Games Between Real Rules and Fictional Worlds. MIT Press, Cambridge (2005)

Koyré, A.V.: Dal mondo del pressappoco all'universo della precisione. Einaudi, Torino ([1950] 1967)

Huizinga, J.: Homo Ludens. Einaudi, Torino (2008)

Löwgren, J.: Pliability as an experiential quality: exploring the aesthetics of interaction design. Artifact **1**(2), 85–95 (2007)

Löwgren, J.: Toward an articulation of interaction esthetics. New Rev. Hypermedia Multimedia **15**(2), 129–146 (2009)

Löwgren, J.: Annotated portfolios and other forms of intermediate-level knowledge. Interactions **20**(1), 30–34 (2013)

Nijholt, A.: Playable Cities: The City as a Digital Playground. Springer, New York (2017)

Norman, D.A.: Emotion and design: attractive things work better. Interactions Mag. **ix**(4), 36–42 (2002)

Oldenburg, R.: Celebrating the Third Place: Inspiring Stories about the "Great Good Places" at the Heart of Our Communities. Marlowe & Company, New York (2001)

Perna, V.: From smart cities to playable cities. Towards playful intelligence in the urban environment. Archi-Doct | e-J. Dissem. Doctoral Res. Archit. (11), 52–63 (2018)

Saggio, A.: The IT Revolution in Architecture. Thoughts on a Paradigm Shift. Lulu.com, Raleigh (2013)

Saggio, A.: Perché rappresentare l'invisibile? Information Technology, spazio dell'informazione e nuove sfide per il progetto e la rappresentazione Information Technology, information space and new challenges for design and representation. Disegnare, Idee, Immagini 50 (2015)

Stappers, P., Giaccardi, E.: Research Through Design. In: The Encyclopedia of Human-Computer Interaction, 2nd edn (2013)

Stolterman, E., Wiberg, M.: Concept-driven interaction design research. Hum.-Comput. Interact. **25**(2), 95–118 (2010)

Tirana Municipality: Greater Tirana Project, October 2006

von Uexküll, J.: A stroll through the worlds of animals and men: a picture book of invisible worlds. In: Instinctive Behavior: The Development of a Modern Concept, edited and translated by C. H. Schiller. International Universities Press, New York (1957)

World Health Organization: Report on disability (2011)

Zimmerman, J., Forlizzi, J., Evenson, S.: Research through design as a method for interaction design research in HCI. In: CHI '07 Proceedings of the SIGCHI Conference on Human Factors in Computing Systems. ACM, New York (2007)

Zimmerman, J., Forlizzi, J., Evenson, S.: An analysis and critique of research through design: towards a formalization of a research approach. In: DIS '10 Proceedings of the 8th ACM Conference on Designing Interactive Systems, pp. 310–319. ACM, New York (2010)

Exploring Methods and Guidelines for Child-Computer Interaction Research with Refugee Children

Rabail Tahir[(⊠)] and Alf Inge Wang

Norwegian University of Science and Technology, Trondheim, Norway
{rabail.tahir,alf.inge.wang}@ntnu.no

Abstract. There exist many guidelines and methods on how to do Child-Computer Interaction (CCI) research, but very few focusing specifically on refugee children with a challenging background. The complex situations and multiple changes refugee children undergo, including community, culture, schooling, friendships, language, war, displacement, physical violence and even identity, makes them different from children who are not refugees. They suffer learning disabilities, mental health issues, poor physical health, trust issues and overall developmental disabilities. As there are a large number of refugee children in the world, who are displaced and out of school, it is important to help these children using available technology and assess the effectiveness of the use of technology. This paper presents a literature study on available research guidelines and methods for CCI. The literature has been reviewed for guidelines and evaluation methods, starting from more general research with children, moving to more specific research with refugee children, and finally to identify gaps, present common grounds and directions for research with this specific population. The results from 55 articles reveal that although guidelines and methods for research with children can be used for refugee children, special attention and additional guidelines are needed to address specific needs of this group. Further, the review reveals a lack of CCI research and research methods for refugee children and most adapted/new children-friendly research methods are not fully employed in research with refugee children. The results of this review could serve as a starting point for researchers entering the CCI field to work with refugee children.

Keywords: Research methods · Research guidelines · Evaluation ·
Refugee children · Child-Computer Interaction

1 Introduction

With the emergence of Child-Computer Interaction (CCI) initiative, researchers have highly acknowledged the importance of children's viewpoint in research. Evaluation of children-friendly products also requires adapted research methods and guidelines due to the difference in children's skills, nature and complexities [1]. United Nations Convention on the Rights of the Child (UNCRC) states: "All Children and Young People who can form their own views, have a right to express those views freely in all

© Springer Nature Switzerland AG 2019
M. Kurosu (Ed.): HCII 2019, LNCS 11568, pp. 70–89, 2019.
https://doi.org/10.1007/978-3-030-22636-7_5

matters affecting them, with the views of the child being given due weight in accordance with their age and maturity" [2]. In psychology, research with children is considered more complex compared to adults, since researchers must carefully plan the data collection process to avoid additional stress, time and effort [3]. Many researchers see the need for distinguishing between research with adults and research with children which introduce additional issues [48]. Further, this research study investigates how research with refugee children distinguish itself in characteristics and context from research with children in general. More specifically, this study investigates if there are special areas you have to take into account when conducting Child-Computer Interaction research with refugee children. Our research goal is to investigate whether research guidelines and methods for refugee children must be different considering the extraordinary circumstances of this vulnerable population. The increasing number of refugees has intensified the interest of research within this population, and a need for new knowledge and understanding of this particular group [6]. This extension of research involves uncovering unique requirements relevant to the design of research protocols and ethics. Therefore, there must be particular attention on methodological and ethical dimensions in research with refugee children [7]. Some researchers have reported that refugee children suffer from high rates of mental health issues such as psychological disturbance, stress, anxiety, and learning difficulties [49–51]. Furthermore, the barriers they encounter, such as diverse traumatic experiences, different languages, parent separation, socio-economic issues, identity issues, and cultural shock, add to the special needs making them different from children without the same experiences [52]. The question here is whether these barriers and special issues infuse the need for additional guidelines and research methods for refugee children. This paper aim to address this failing by exploring guidelines and methods for CCI research, and examining, in a structured process, how it differs from research with refugee children, and by highlighting areas where future work might be required.

The literature study presented in this paper emphasized on how CCI research is carried out focusing on methods and guidelines, and we were especially interested in research where refugee children were involved. Owing to the fact that CCI began with work driven from interest in childrens' technology use within education, further extending to involvement in design and evaluation process [70] and also for this specific group (refugees) there has been a great focus on educational technology which can help these children where many do not have access to school or at least do not have an opportunity to learn to read and write their own mother tongue [21, 36, 39]. This meant that in addition to searching for literature on Human-Computer Interaction (HCI) and Child-Computer Interaction (CCI), the study also included research on educational technology including educational games. Moreover, as there is limited work on evaluation of CCI involving refugee children, this study also include literature from social science research and evaluation studies with refugee children to compile a list of guidelines and methods used with this population. The results of this review could serve as a starting point for many novice researchers in CCI community to conduct research with refugee children. The remaining paper is structured as follows: Sect. 2 describes the background, Sect. 3 explains the methodology used for the review, Sect. 4 illustrate the results with respect to research methods and guidelines, Sect. 5 presents discussion and limitations, and finally Sect. 6 concludes the paper.

2 Background

An increasing interest for children as users of technology has led to efforts to understand these users' impact on the methodology and how this influence evaluation (in terms of guidelines) where children participate [9]. This section introduces a background on research with children, specifically refugee children.

2.1 Research with Children

Samantha [71] investigated seven methodological issues to explain problems in research with children and claim that it is different because children are inherently different from adults. Other researchers highlighted the issues of verbalization and gender differences in children [1, 29]. Research with children is considered more complex as compared to adults owing to the strict requirements regarding ethical principles and preparation of environment etc. Although involvement of children in the design and evaluation process of a product is highly encouraged [4], the opinion of young children is difficult to collect and different methods have been explored for this challenging task and many new/adapted methods are devised [3, 5, 25, 26, 29].

Many researchers address research involving children with specific focus on guidelines and methods [22–28]. According to Read and Mathilde [70], CCI is a research area within HCI that grew from work mainly driven from interest in the use of educational technology with children and involving them in design and evaluation process. Druin proposed a framework for understanding the children's role in the design and evaluation process of learning technologies [10]. Jenkinson presented the shortcoming of traditional methods to measure the effectiveness of educational technology, identifying a need for more fine-grained research studies taking a flexible approach [18]. Appropriate evaluation methods are required to conduct evaluation with children [22]. Sim and Zaman proposed a method impact assessment framework that can be used by the CCI community as a critical lens for assessing evaluation methods with children [24]. Several researchers highlight methods and guidelines for usability research with children [9, 11–14]. However, research on educational game evaluation goes beyond just usability and includes constructs such as learning, flow and game factors [15]. Playing games is one of the most natural forms of learning. Children learn to talk by playing with sounds, and even learn strategic and collaborative thinking by playing games [20]. Prensky revealed that combining games with educational goals could not only trigger learning motivation but also offer interactive learning opportunities [19], which makes them relevant and important in CCI research.

2.2 Research with Refugee Children

According to the 2016 UNHCR report, the estimated number of refugees is 21 million, and half of them are less than 18 years old [7]. In recent years, refugee children who have faced experiences of war and violence have been the subject of a number of research studies [16]. The special circumstances of this group demand extra emphasis on research ethics and more careful selection of research methods [7].

What Makes Refugee Children Different? The definition of a refugee is: "A person who has been forced to leave his or her country to escape war, persecution, and natural disaster" [40]. As refugees end up in another country than their own, they face cultural challenges in addition to other problems [40]. Research shows long-lasting effects of pre- and post-displacement risk-factors on refugee children and their caregivers [7]. A number of challenges are associated with the displacement of refugee children such as experiences of trauma in the past, several overlapping transitions, and unfamiliar social setup [7, 40]. Most refugee children have interrupted education, and during their displacement they experience multiple language transitions which affect their learning, their wellbeing, and overall development. Further, many refugee children have experienced psychological and physical violence, threats of harm, separation or disappearance of family members, and have been under combat fire. Moreover, settlement and relocation produce additional stress in their lives, when these families have to compromise their needs in new environments with minimal social support facing experiences such as poverty, food insecurity, accusation, stress and discrimination [7]. These complex situations and multiple changes refugee children undergo, including community, culture, schooling, friendships, language and even identity, makes them different from children who are not refugees [7, 40].

The Role of Human-Computer Interaction (HCI) in Refugee Context? The HCI community has started to give attention to the refugee crisis leading to several initiatives developing technologies to aid refugee and assist them in their camps, and in their new relocated countries and communities [36]. Some of these contributions include: Deana and Rebecca's work to aid refugee resettlement processes by utilizing asynchronous interactive voice response and setting a translator as a mediator sharing same culture and language as the refugee [37]. Jennifer and her colleagues used field communication tags to help guide refugees through the city by providing information in their preferred language [38]. Some studies highlight that the use of smart phones is common among refugees [36]. A few technology applications have been developed to help refugees, such as "Refugee Info" to help refugees overcome the language difficulties; "Refugees Welcome" which connects refugees looking for accommodation to landlords, and "Hababy" which helps refugees find health services in Europe. However, there is very limited number of HCI studies focusing on research methods and guidelines for the context of refugee children. Reem and her colleagues identified some key deficiencies regarding the role of the HCI community in refugee context and emphasized the need to adapt HCI research methods and guidelines [36]. Most studies within HCI focusing where refugee children are involved are within educational technology and game-based learning and are described in the following section.

Educational Technology and Evaluation with Refugee Children. Some educational technology research projects have been launched for refugee children displaced by conflict, but most of these projects are in initial stages or under development, and little research has yet been published [8]. Two projects with some initial evaluation results include "Learning Sudan" - a computer game that is custom-built and offers supplementary mathematics learning opportunities to out-of-school children in Sudan [21, 36], and "EduApp4Syria" that introduces innovative smartphone educational games to improve Arabic literacy skills for Syrian children [39]. Despite the evident motivational appeal of learning technology and its effectiveness, little evaluation research has been conducted regarding the use of educational games with refugee children [8, 21]. George and his collogues developed and evaluated a reusable process for the design and evaluation of educational technology for war-affected displaced children [73]. However, most of the evaluation research conducted with refugee children comes from social science researchers exploring the complex humanitarian and political aspects in which these children live, exploring areas to improve their wellbeing, research on education of refugee children and their social and cognitive development [7]. Although it is highly emphasized that methodological dimensions and ethical engagement is crucial in research with refugee children and is identified as a challenging process [7], it has not been sufficiently addressed so far in the CCI community. To the best of our knowledge, no comprehensive research guidelines and methods have been proposed for refugee children by researchers in this field.

3   Methodology

In this study, we performed a systematic review initially with the aim of identifying and compiling research methods and guidelines for educational games evaluation with refugee children. As little CCI research is available for this specific population within the area of interest and also otherwise, we approached this research objective by investigating the extent to which research with refugee children can be regarded as similar, or different from research with children who are not refugees in terms of research methods and guidelines. The research questions include: RQ1 What evaluation methods are used for conducting research with children in CCI and how do they compare to research methods used with refugee children?; RQ2 What guidelines are used for conducting research with children in CCI and how do they compare to guidelines for research with refugee children?; and RQ3 Are there specific guidelines and methods for the refugee context in addition to those generally used with children in CCI?

The methodological approach followed the steps mentioned in [53]. The literature search was performed in five digital databases (Google scholar, ACM Digital Library, Science Direct, IEEE Xplore, and Springer Link) for conference papers, journal papers and published reports in the period from December 2017 to January 2018. The search strings used for the literature search included the keywords: "research guidelines", "children", "child computer interaction", "human computer interaction", "refugee children", "evaluation", "research methods", "evaluation methods", "educational", and "games". The keywords educational and games were included as we knew there were relevant CCI studies that focused specifically on these areas. Search strings were constructed using the keywords (including synonyms) based on the following criteria: (1) Methods for research with children in CCI or educational game evaluation, (2) Guidelines for research with children in CCI or educational game evaluation, (3) Methods for research with refugee children in CCI or game evaluation, (4) Guidelines for research with refugee children in CCI or educational game evaluation, (5) Methods for research with refugee children in general, and (6) Guidelines for research with children or refugee children in general. Search strings were modified and adapted for the specific syntax of each selected data source.

The article selection process included three cycles: First, an initial search using search strings to examine titles and keywords. Second, the abstracts of the papers were read for relevance, all irrelevant papers were rejected, and duplications were removed, which resulted in 129 articles. Third, the articles were filtered using inclusion/exclusion criteria resulting in 52 articles selected for this review. For an article to be included, it had to focus on one of the six criteria described above and written in the English language. The articles were also excluded if full text was not available. Since almost a year was passed until publication, the search was performed again in same five digital databases following same procedure in December 2018 to add any new relevant articles published during this year. After completing the cycles of selection process, 3 new articles were added, resulting in 55 primary studies for this review.

To ensure the quality of reviewed studies, only the articles providing sufficient information on guidelines and methods were considered. After assessing the quality of the relevant papers, data was extracted from each article and organized using a spreadsheet. The information included methods and guidelines for children/refugee children concerning RQ1 and RQ2. For RQ3, data from first two questions was further analyzed for differences to highlight specific methods/guidelines for refugee children.

4   Results

This section presents the results from reviewing 55 articles. 36 papers focused on children, and 19 papers focused on refugee children. The selected articles are listed in Table 1. We focused on the approach of investigating the extent to which research with refugee children can be regarded as similar, or different from research with children who are not refugees. After extracting data for methods (RQ1) and guidelines (RQ2) for children and refugee children separately from selected articles (see Table 1), the data was initially grouped into two main categories to initiate comparison: similarity in research methods/guidelines (methods/guidelines that were found common or similar in both corpus of literatures on research with children and refugee children) and difference in research methods/guidelines (methods/guidelines that were found uncommon or different for each corpus of literature on children vs refugee children). The main findings for each research question are summarized in the following subsections.

Table 1. Selected articles

Category	Research papers
Children methods and guidelines	[1–5, 9–13, 17, 22–35, 47, 54–58, 67–69, 74, 75]
Refugee children methods and guidelines	[7, 16, 21, 40–46, 59–66, 73]

4.1   RQ1: Research Methods with Children vs. Refugee Children

This section highlights the methods used in research with children in general as well as research methods used with refugee children. Table 2 provides a summary of methods and recommendation for use. According to the results of this literature review, three categories emerged from the content of data collected for RQ1 using inductive approach during analysis. The categories are: Preferred methods (explicitly mentioned as preferred for each target group), General methods (normally used with any user group regardless of differences), and Specific methods (used or adapted with focus on each target group). Preferred and general methods used with children with and without refugee background were mostly same and come under the category of similarity in research methods, whereas specific methods are different for children and refugee children and come under the category of difference in research methods. Furthermore, recommendations for use of each method with children or refugee children were categorized into 4 categories based on type of results provided by the selected articles regarding method usage. These categories are listed under Table 2.

Similarity in Research Methods Used with Children and Refugee Children in Reviewed Literature. First, in the category "preferred methods" for both children with or without refugee background; the methods found were the mixed method approach, the participatory method and the observation method using an observation form/checklist. However, our study found that details regarding how the methods are used with refugee children slightly differ on areas such as flexibility and the special needs of refugee group (for details see Sects. 4.2 and 4.3). Furthermore, visual methods are specifically preferred for research with refugee children, as their refugee experiences can make them silent and less expressive, and these techniques help them to speak [60]. Second, there are some "general methods" which are reportedly used with any user group including children with or without refugee background. Further, there are some recommendation found in literature for their use with children. E.g. although questionnaires are used with children, research has found that this method is not recommended as an effective child-friendly method. Quasi-experimental methods are mostly used with children for educational game evaluation employing a mixed methods approach [30, 32, 33]. However, for refugee children specifically, there is a lack in research focusing on applicability or effectiveness of employing these research methods.

Difference in Research Methods Used with Children and Refugee Children in Reviewed Literature. Third, the review results also highlighted some "specific methods" in research with children both with and without refugee background. For children these include think-aloud protocol, co-discovery, active intervention and most of the specific methods for children (see Table 2) are new/adapted methods for research with children: for example, adapted survey techniques (fun sorter, smileyometer, again-again, tangible interface), interview techniques such as contextual laddering (adapted from laddering technique), and techniques such as constructive interaction, peer tutoring and video diary. The specific methods found in literature with refugee children mostly include: clinical evaluations, case study, individual in-depth interviews and self-reports, which typically come from the social science research where focus was more on the social aspects and behaviors rather than the effectiveness of the methods used.

There is a lack of research in CCI community for this specific area. Also, there are very few new/adapted research methods for this specific group of refugee children. The review highlighted only three methods: communicative focus groups, social network mapping with group debriefing and self-report with pictorial questionnaire, which were adapted specifically for solving issues concerning research with refugee children [46].

Table 2. Research methods with children and refugee children

Children			Refugee children		
Research methods	Used w/children	Ref.	Research methods	Used w/refugee children	Ref.
Similarity in research methods used with children and refugee children in reviewed literature					
Preferred methods with children in CCI			*Preferred methods with refugee children*		
Mixed method/multi-methods	Yes	[4, 5, 13, 22, 23, 54, 55, 74]	Mixed method	Yes	[16, 21, 42, 45, 46, 61]
Participatory techniques	Yes	[26, 28, 34, 57, 58]	Participatory method	Yes	[7, 43, 46, 60, 63, 64]
Observation using checklist/observation form	Yes	[22, 55, 74]	Observation with observation form	Yes	[45]
			Visual methods	*Yes*	[46, 60, 63, 64, 73]
General methods with children in CCI			*General methods with refugee children*		
Interview (*structured*)	Yes	[12, 27, 29]	Interview (*general/semi structured*)	Yes	[16, 41, 42, 44, 45]
Experiment/quasi-experimental methods: pre-test and post/test with/without experimental and control groups	Yes	[13, 30–33]	Quasi-experimental methods: pre-post-test with/without experimental and control groups	Yes	[16, 21, 42, 66]
Observation	Yes	[4, 13, 29, 33]	Observation	Yes!	[21, 44, 46]
Questionnaire	No	[2, 13, 25, 27, 74]	Questionnaire	Yes!	[16, 42, 45]
User field test	Yes	[23, 27, 56]	User field test	Yes!	[21, 45]
Data log	Yes	[5]	Logged data	Yes!	[21]
Difference in research methods used with children and refugee children in reviewed literature					
Specific methods with children in CCI			*Specific methods with refugee children*		
Think-aloud method	Yes*	[1, 9, 12, 13, 22, 23, 29, 55]	Communicative focus groups	Yes	[46]
Video recording	Yes	[5, 13, 22, 23, 27, 74]	Social network mapping with group debriefing	Yes	[46]

(*continued*)

Table 2. (*continued*)

Children			Refugee children		
Research methods	Used w/children	Ref.	Research methods	Used w/refugee children	Ref.
Smileyometer	Yes*	[25, 27, 29, 33, 55]	Self-report with pictorial questionnaire	Yes	[42]
Drawings	Yes*	[17, 23, 28, 29, 74]	Sticky note activity	Yes	[73]
Again - Again	Yes	[25, 29, 55]	Case reports	Yes!	[16, 44]
User laboratory test	Yes	[13, 27, 56]	Wellbeing survey/computerized surveys	Yes	[42, 46]
Photographs	Yes	[47, 67]	Clinical evaluations	Yes!	[16, 44]
Peer tutoring	Yes	[23, 69]	Oral test	Yes!	[21]
Contextual laddering	Yes	[4, 22]	Individual in-depth interviews	Yes!	[46]
Fun sorter	Yes	[25, 29]	Self-reports	Yes!	[16, 44]
Active intervention	Yes*	[1, 22]			
Constructive interaction	Yes*	[13, 23]			
Tangible survey/tangible interface	Yes	[5, 23, 75]			
Video diary	Yes*	[57]			
Picture cards method	Yes	[68]			
Structured/unstructured checklist	Yes	[2]			

* *is used with methods that fall under the subcategory (preferred, specific, general) but does not comply with the main category (similarity, difference).*
Yes: *used & recommended for children,* **Yes*:** *used with children but doubt/disagreement among researchers if recommended or not,* **Yes!:** *used with children but article does not mention whether it was effective or not.* **No:** *used with children but ineffective and thus not recommended.*

4.2 RQ2: Guidelines for Research with Children vs. Refugee Children

To a lesser or greater extent, participation in the research does influence the participants. Likewise, the research methods and the research process itself has the potential to influence the phenomenon being studied [46]. This section presents the guidelines for conducting research with children in general and specifically for refugee children. Also, for RQ2, three categories emerged from the content of data extracted for guidelines, using inductive approach during analysis. These categories are: ethical, practical and methodological. Table 3 provides a summary of these guidelines. Ethical category comprises of guidelines that focus on "ethical complexities linked with research while protecting research participants and reducing potential harms"; Practical category encompass guidelines focusing on "developing the research processes that maximize the benefits"; and methodological category contain guidelines which focuses on "adapting research methods to enhance their relevance to the specific circumstances of participants' and heighten their engagement in research."

Similarity in Research Guidelines Used with Children and Refugee Children in Reviewed Literature. The results show that some guidelines appear in both for research with children in general and in refugee context and can be considered as general guidelines for conducting research (in children context). However, deeper analysis reveals that the specific refugee context makes the application of these general guidelines different for this specific group. To illustrate this, consider the issue of obtaining consent from parents which becomes more difficult for refugee children; where the extraordinary circumstances such as separation from parents and their unaccompanied status can make parental consent impossible and further raises issues of obtaining consent from caretakers or social workers responsible, depending on local laws [65]. Similarly, for ensuring confidentiality of data collected from research participants in the case of refugee children, special attention must be paid to the ethnic culture and context, as things considered confidential in the west are public knowledge in many tight-knit communities and cultures and vice versa which might confuse the participants rather than comforting them. For example, in refugee context where many participants are not familiar with the research protocol, sometimes research respondents spontaneously reveal the adverse incidents, such as exploitation, self-harm and abuse which are normal experiences for refugees, in these cases researcher must make clear the limits of confidentiality, especially when researchers have a duty to report based on disciplinary norms [72]. Another example is of collecting video recording, where some conservative refugee societies have reservations and therefore should be further ensured of the opportunity to request destruction of videos in which they appeared [72]. In the same way, obtaining a written signed confidentiality agreement which is normal in western culture might be different in refugee context as in some cultures signing a document is considered dangerous matter and should be avoided [40]. Although the general guidelines look the same, refugee context induce additional details to implementation.

Difference in Research Guidelines Used with Children and Refugee Children in Reviewed Literature. The results of our literature review also brought forth specific guidelines for research with children and refugee children (see Table 3). Difference in specific guidelines for research with children with and without refugee background highlight that needs of refugee children are different from children with normal background. For example, in refugee context wellbeing, trust and respect becomes more of a concern than just emphasizing on fun or creativity. Instead of just focusing on simple language and limited writing you must focus on additional issues of language barriers, low literacy rates and gaining access. Furthermore, the review also highlighted that specific guidelines for research with refugee children are more focused on ethical category, which is also reflected in practical guidelines being more directed on translating the ethical reflections into practice in the research process. In contrast, specific guidelines with children in CCI have strong emphasis on methodological category in addition to ethical and practical. Whereas, no specific methodological guidelines are found in literature reviewed of refugee children that underline the lack of methodology guidelines for research with refugee children which is in accordance with the results of Sect. 4.1 (subheading difference in research methods) emphasizing the need for adapted methods for this specific group (refugee children).

4.3   RQ3: Specific Methods or Guidelines for Refugee Children

According to the review, although participatory, mixed method and observation with checklist are preferred methods generally with children with or without refugee background. However, details on using these methods with refugee children differ with focus on guidelines. Participatory and visual methods are particularly focused by many researchers as useful for refugee context in addressing the issues of power, vulnerability, ethics and language by following guidelines (Table 3) in research process [60]. The visual methods found useful for refugee children included photovoice, fotonovela, digital storytelling and quilting [60, 64]. The specific methods for refugee children were mostly found to be the general methods used in social science research with any user group such as case reports, laboratory evaluations and in-depth interviews. Most articles did not provide any details on usefulness of the employed method, which illustrate the lack of research on effectiveness of methods for research with refugee children. Unfortunately, review results did not highlight many new/adapted methods developed for refugee children, which emphasizes the need of methodology research for this specific user group. However, *communicative focus groups, social network mapping with group debriefing* and *self-report with pictorial questionnaire* are three specific methods found in the reviewed literature adapted specifically for the context of research with refugee children [46]. The fact that despite there are not many adapted/new methods for this specific group, the methods developed/adapted for children in general are also not yet fully employed for research with refugee children. Future research is required to explore their effectiveness for this specific group. The review highlighted only two methods: sticky note activity that used smiley faces and visual methods including photographs that were employed for refugee children considering their effectiveness as the children friendly methods.

The results highlight that there are some differences in research guidelines for children with and without refugee background (see "specific guidelines" in Table 3). The majority of the differences comes from specific ethical and practical guidelines pertaining to refugee paradigm. For refugee children there is a need for additional guidelines that take into account issues such as language barriers, culture, diverse background (illiteracy or mental health issues), refugee status (more vulnerable due to separation from family), relocation, and gaining access and reaching out to refugee communities. This review did not highlight any specific methodological guidelines for refugee children, which is in line with the results from Sect. 4.1. However, the reason for this as deduced from current review, is more inclined towards the scarcity of research in this area than concluding that no additional methodological guidelines or adapted/new methods are needed for refugee children. Most of the studies conducted with refugee children focused on the intervention results sidelining the effectiveness or outcome of methods used for research, and to a greater extent using general research methods without much discussion about method selection or their perceived impact.

Table 3. Guidelines for research with children and refugee children

Guidelines with children		Ref.	Guidelines with refugee children	Ref.
Similarity in research guidelines used with children and refugee children in reviewed literature				
General guidelines				
Ethical	Obtain consent from children and parents	[2, 26, 34, 35, 48, 57, 58]	Provide complete explanation and obtain informed consent from both children and parents or caretaker	[40, 46, 65, 73]
	Confidentiality	[2, 35, 57, 58]	Confidentiality (with respect to ethnic culture)	[40, 46, 62, 65]
	Impact of research on child/protection from harm	[2, 26, 35, 48, 58]	Protection from harm and distress	[40, 46, 62, 65]
	Build rapport	[26, 28, 48, 57]	Build trust: show interest, empathy and care	[7, 40, 46, 60, 64, 73]
Practical	Present and discuss results with children/not inflicting researchers' own perceptions	[2, 26, 28, 48]	Involve children to help researchers to interpret the findings	[64, 65]
			Feedback the research results	[62, 65]
Methodological	Conduct a pilot study	[21, 24]	Conduct a pilot study	[46, 60]
	Use appropriate methods and tools (age, language, content, gender, capability etc.)	[2, 25, 28, 48]	Use/modify methods and tools appropriate for them instead of universal standard: using standardized research instruments may be invalid when applied to different cultural groups	[40, 46, 62, 65]
	Use participatory approach	[34, 48]	Use collaborative and participatory research approaches	[46, 59, 62, 65]
	Use more than one evaluation methods	[23, 48]	Use mixed methods to engage young people with refugee background	[46, 61]
Difference in research guidelines used with children and refugee children in reviewed literature				
Specific guidelines				
Ethical	Cater children interest and allow them to be creative	[2, 26, 28, 34]	*Ethical* Contribute to their wellbeing: research should add value to the lives of refugee children	[7, 46, 62]
	Payment or gift/reward*	[26, 57, 58]	Don't misinform them or make promises that cannot be kept	[7]
Practical	Provide assistance	[2, 25]	Work with them, not on them: treat them with respect and not just as a source of data	[7, 46]
	Make it Fun	[25, 57]	Recognize, learn and accept their diverse backgrounds (culture, religion, education, experiences etc.)	[40, 59, 60, 62, 64, 73]

(continued)

Table 3. (*continued*)

Guidelines with children		Ref.	Guidelines with refugee children		Ref.
	Be nice	[2, 25]		Use oral consent if written form is difficult to obtain (considering certain reservations (distrust) or illiteracy)	[40, 46, 60, 62, 64]
	Limit the writing	[2, 25]		Get approval of all procedures by ethics committee to ensure sensitivity	[46, 62, 65]
	Create an open and informal atmosphere	[2, 25]	Practical	Consider context and surrounding conditions of refugees	[59, 60, 73]
Methodological	Keep it short	[2, 25, 26]		Debriefing session with children and as well as caretakers after research	[62]
	Use simple language	[2, 25, 28, 57]		Thinking carefully about overall design of the research process for it to be ethical and sensitive to refugee context (research material, approach, schedule, children involvement etc.)	[64, 65, 73]
	Research context and setting (open, stress-free, child friendly environment)	[2, 28, 48, 57]		Recognize language barriers and need for a translators/interpreter	[40, 46, 62, 64, 65]
	Work in small groups	[26, 34, 57]		Flexible rather than tightly defined approach: expand the concept of 'ethical research' by applying both the relational and procedural ethical frameworks. For example, oral consent if written is not possible	[7, 59, 65]
				Ways of gaining access to refugee communities and children (collaborating with trusted members and leaders of host community)	[59, 73]

5 Discussion and Limitations

According to the review, there are several issues highlighted in CCI that demanded for new/adapted methods for research with children such as verbalization, skills, nature, gender differences, attention span, cognitive load etc. These issues were the driving force for methodology research which not only justified the need for new/adapted methods with children but also made sense to prioritize certain methods over the others. For example, researchers found that think aloud method worked only with children who can verbalize making it a difficult method to apply with children as not many children are naturally talkative [23]. Therefore, many researchers focused on active intervention method and found it effective to elicit verbal comments from children and consequently decided to combine the think-aloud method and the active intervention method which solved this issue to some extend [1]. However, another issue with children is that they are more inclined to answer what they feel adults like to hear in order to please them. This explained the reason for preferring a multi-method/mixed method approach by some researchers when working with children [54], e.g. using observation or recording children' s facial expressions and behaviors in addition to other methods used. Often nonverbal communication reveals more information than the verbal communication [1]. While some other researcher advocated the use of participatory or collaborative methods to solve this issue [23] e.g. using drawing intervention method which is considered to elicit extra information as children are involved in doing an activity that they were familiar with and in a large group, so they are more relaxed and feel less conscious when talking; or using Peer Tutoring method which require little input from the researcher and children are engaged in teaching their friends or helping them to carry out the tasks and therefore less conscious about their answers. The same rationale is true regarding the need for changes/adaptations in research guidelines in conducting research with children. For example, the issue of short attention span for children demanded for the short sessions [2, 25, 26] and the issue that children have not attained the legal right to consent required adaption in research guidelines and justified the need for the new guideline of obtaining consent from parents which has now become a standard in research with children [2, 26, 34, 35, 48, 57, 58].

Similarly, concluding from the above discussion where issues were seen as the driving force for changes and adaptations in research with children. The issues in research with refugee children as describe in this paper (Sect. 2.2) goes far beyond the general issues in research with children as a user group [52]. They have faced experiences of war and violence, dislocation, poverty, stress, discrimination, language barrier, loss of family members, difference in culture etc. These special circumstances result in learning disability, mental health issues, insecurity, distrust, physical health issues, access issues etc. Therefore, these children must be represented as special target group as compared to the general user group of children because it is impossible to ignore these specific issues and unavoidable to control their impact on conducting research with refugee children. Consequently, the above discussion implies that this group demand additional emphasis on research guidelines and ethics, and more careful selection of research methods. The prior is also depicted in the results of this review (see Table 3). For example, the issues of low literacy, distrust and dislocation in refugee context demanded adaption in research guidelines which require more flexible approach of obtaining oral consent [41], approaching them through trusted member of their community to build trust and in case of unaccompanied or separated children, it is required to gain access to local authority social worker or other officials responsible for the child in accordance with the law [65]. However, regarding research methods little has been contributed by researchers in reviewed literature but the need for such effort is highlighted by many [46, 60] which shows a lack of research in this area and a potential direction for future work for CCI community. Some researchers have highlighted the importance of visual and participatory methods in research with refugee children which to some extent solve the issues of trust, language, power and vulnerability [60]. Also, it is argued that in the context of refugee children most of the methodological challenges can be resolved by ethical reflexivity that further supports the results of this review where more focus is on ethical guidelines in research with refugee children [46]. To illustrate this, we mention the example of an adapted research method for refugee children where ethical reflexivity led the adaptation. For example, inclusion of group debriefing with hypothetical example of a social network circle with some gaps (that depicts the case of most participants) in social network mapping method solved the issues of trust and normalizing refugee experiences (missing parents or family members). However, further research is required by focusing on the effectiveness of different research methods when used with ethical reflexivity in refugee context to validate this argument. Conversely, sometimes you cannot solely rely on ethical reflexivity to guide adaptation because methodological approach is essential to solve a particular issue. To illustrate this, we give an example of another adapted research method for refugee children known as communicative focus group. Here focus group method (which resulted in simplistic responses) is adapted to solve the issues of eliciting complex experiences of refugees and addressing ethical risk of inflicting harm (through symbolic violence) by incorporating methodological approach of critical communicative methodology (CCM) and using visual prompts to stimulate discussion on issues of interest [46]. Therefore, we need further research and innovative methods in CCI to conduct research with this specific population of refugee children.

The review also highlighted that research with children focused mostly on design and evaluation of products such as educational games, prototypes, educational toys or children experiences and the constructs/aspects used for research were fun, ease to use, usability, likability, experience, attractive to use. Whereas for refugee children, research focused more on evaluation and effects of interventions, creative programs, psychosocial treatments and just recently on educational games. The constructs/aspects mostly used in research with refugee children included emotional distress, behavioral problems, learning, knowledge acquisition, wellbeing, settlement experience, perceived difficulty, cooperation, psychosocial wellbeing, mental health care, enjoyment and motivation. This difference in research focus and constructs/aspects is also depicted in the specific methods used with children and refugee children. Where most of the specific methods used with refugee children came from social science.

One of the limitations of this study could be the choice of databases and search strings used for selecting articles. Although we included articles from social science research on refugee children, we might have missed some important work and including other databases and different keywords might result in additional papers.

6 Conclusion

This paper has addressed challenges related to research methods and guidelines for CCI research with children with or without refugee background. Our literature study resulted in three identified categories of research methods: Preferred, General and Specific methods. To a large extent the methods used in research with children with and without refugee background are similar for preferred and general methods, with more variation found for specific methods (RQ1). For research guidelines we found two categories general (similar) and specific (different) guidelines. Our review also showed that even for general guidelines there are some differences in details for research with refugee children that must take additional issues into account (RQ2). Further, guidelines were introduced in the three groups ethical, practical, and methodological. Our study revealed the need to adapt guidelines for research with specific emphasis on the context of refugee children (RQ3). This need comes from specific issues such as language barrier, culture, war traumas, mental health issues, separation, and socio-economic conditions due to relocation of this population. Thus, there is a need to take into account additional ethical, practical and methodological parameters when conducting CCI research with refugee children to make sure the results of introducing technology includes a good understanding of its users. Unfortunately, only three new or adapted research methods were found in review specifically for refugee children, but there are some preferred and specific methods used with this population which we have highlighted and can guide researchers.

The review also highlighted some gaps in current literature: Firstly, there is a lack of research on new/adapted research methods for refugee children and/or effectiveness of general research methods when used in this context. Secondly, most children-friendly research methods are not fully employed in research with refugee children, and existing evaluation methods that work well with children might need to be adopted or tailored before they can be used with refugee children. Thirdly, there is a gap in literature regarding focus on methodological guidelines for the specific group of refugee children which is in line with the scarcity of research on effectiveness of methods for research with this user group. However, this study presents a starting-point to guide researchers and evaluators in the CCI community in conducting research with the specific population of refugee children and, methods and guidelines identified in this review for working with refugee children might be helpful to guide the adaption of the research process.

References

1. Zaman, B., Geerts, D.: Gender differences in children's creative game play. Young People and New Technologies, Northampton (2005)
2. Shaw, C., Brady, L.-M., Davey, C.: Guidelines for research with children and young people. National Children's Bureau Research Centre, London (2011)
3. Lanna, L.C.: How to collect audiovisual data in a research with very young children. Digit. Educ. Rev. **24**, 43–52 (2013)

4. Zaman, B.: Introducing contextual laddering to evaluate the likeability of games with children. Cogn. Technol. Work **10**(2), 107–117 (2008)
5. Gallacher, S., Golsteijn, C., Rogers, Y., Capra, L., Eustace, S.: SmallTalk: using tangible interactions to gather feedback from children. ACM (2016)
6. UNHCR: Missing out. Refugee education in crisis (2016)
7. Kaukko, M., Dunwoodie, K., Riggs, E.: Rethinking the ethical and methodological dimensions of research with refugee children. ZEP: Zeitschrift für Internationale Bildungs-forschung und Entwicklungspädagogik **40**(1), 16 (2017)
8. Lewis, K., Thacker, S.: ICT and the education of refugees: a stocktaking of innovative approaches in the MENA region (English). World Bank Education, Technology and Innovation: Systems Approach for Better Education Results (SABER)-ICT Technical Paper Series; no. 17. World Bank Group, Washington, D.C. (2016)
9. Markopoulos, P., Bekker, M.: How to Compare Usability Testing Methods with Children Participants. Shaker Publisher, Herzogenrath (2002)
10. Druin, A.: The role of children in the design of new technology. Behav. Inf. Technol. **21**(1), 1–25 (2002)
11. Hanna, L., Risden, K., Alexander, K.: Guidelines for usability testing with children. Interactions **4**(5), 9–14 (1997)
12. Vermeeren, A.P.O.S., Bekker, M.M., Van Kesteren, I.E.H., de Ridder, H.: Experiences with structured interviewing of children during usability tests. British Computer Society (2007)
13. Als, B.S., Jensen, J.J., Skov, M.B.: Exploring verbalization and collaboration of constructive interaction with children. In: Costabile, M.F., Paternò, F. (eds.) INTERACT 2005. LNCS, vol. 3585, pp. 443–456. Springer, Heidelberg (2005). https://doi.org/10.1007/11555261_37
14. Tahir, R., Arif, F.: A measurement model based on usability metrics for mobile learning user interface for children. Int. J. E-Learn. Educ. Technol. Digit. Media **1**(1), 16–31 (2015)
15. Tahir, R., Inge Wang, A.: State of the art in game based learning: dimensions for evaluating educational games. In: European Conference on Games Based Learning, pp. 641–650. Academic Conferences International Limited (2017)
16. Möhlen, H., Parzer, P., Resch, F., Brunner, R.: Psychosocial support for war-traumatized child and adolescent refugees: evaluation of a short-term treatment program. Aust. N. Z. J. Psychiatry **39**(1–2), 81–87 (2005)
17. Light, R.: Accessing the inner world of children: the use of student drawings in research on children's experiences of game sense. In: Proceedings for the Asia Pacific Conference on Teaching Sport and Physical Education for Understanding, pp. 72–83. University of Sydney, Sydney (2006)
18. Jenkinson, J.: Measuring the effectiveness of educational technology: what are we attempting to measure? Electron. J. E-Learn. **7**(3), 273–280 (2009)
19. Prensky, M.: Digital game-based learning. Comput. Entertain. (CIE) **1**(1), 21 (2003)
20. Sung, H.-Y., Hwang, G.-J.: A collaborative game-based learning approach to improving students' learning performance in science courses. Comput. Educ. **63**, 43–51 (2013)
21. Stubbé, H., Badri, A., Telford, R., van der Hulst, A., van Joolingen, W.: E-Learning Sudan, formal learning for out-of-school children. Electron. J. E-Learn. **14**(2), 136–149 (2016)
22. Zaman, B.: Evaluating games with children. In: Proceedings of Interact 2005 Workshop on Child Computer Interaction: Methodological Research (2005)
23. Xu, D.: Design and evaluation of tangible interfaces for primary school children. In: Proceedings of the 6th International Conference on Interaction Design and Children, pp. 209–212. ACM (2007)
24. Sim, G., Zaman, B., Horton, M.: A method impact assessment framework for user experience evaluations with children. In: Proceedings of the 31st British Computer Society Human Computer Interaction Conference, p. 82. BCS Learning & Development Ltd. (2017)

25. Read, J.C., MacFarlane, S.: Using the fun toolkit and other survey methods to gather opinions in child computer interaction. In: Proceedings of the 2006 Conference on Interaction Design and Children, pp. 81–88. ACM (2006)
26. Gielen, M.A.: Exploring the child's mind-contextmapping research with children. Digit. Creat. **19**(3), 174–184 (2008)
27. Razak, F.H.A., Hafit, H., Sedi, N., Zubaidi, N.A., Haron, H.: Usability testing with children: laboratory vs field studies. In: 2010 International Conference on User Science and Engineering (i-USEr), pp. 104–109. IEEE (2010)
28. Barendregt, W., Bekker, T.: Exploring the potential of the drawing intervention method for design and evaluation by young children. In: CHI 2013 Extended Abstracts on Human Factors in Computing Systems. ACM (2013)
29. Yusoff, M.Y., Landoni, M., Ruthven, I.: Assessing fun: young children as evaluators of interactive systems. In: Proceedings of the Workshop on Accessible Search Systems Held at the 33rd Annual International ACM SIGIR Conference on Research and Development in Information Retrieval, New York, USA (2010)
30. Hung, C.-M., Huang, I., Hwang, G.-J.: Effects of digital game-based learning on students' self-efficacy, motivation, anxiety, and achievements in learning mathematics. J. Comput. Educ. **1**(2–3), 151–166 (2014)
31. Herodotou, C.: Young children and tablets: a systematic review of effects on learning and development. J. Comput. Assist. Learn. **34**(1), 1–9 (2018)
32. Bragg, L.A.: Testing the effectiveness of mathematical games as a pedagogical tool for children's learning. Int. J. Sci. Math. Educ. **10**(6), 1445–1467 (2012)
33. Sim, G., MacFarlane, S., Horton, M.: Evaluating usability, fun and learning in educational software for children. In: EdMedia: World Conference on Educational Media and Technology, pp. 1180–1187. Association for the Advancement of Computing in Education (AACE) (2005)
34. Thomas, N., O'kane, C.: The ethics of participatory research with children. Child. Soc. **12** (5), 336–348 (1998)
35. Neill, S.J.: Research with children: a critical review of the guidelines. J. Child Health Care **9** (1), 46–58 (2005)
36. Talhouk, R., Ahmed, S.I., Wulf, V., Crivellaro, C., Vlachokyriakos, V., Olivier, P.: Refugees and HCI SIG: the role of HCI in responding to the refugee crisis. In: Proceedings of the 2016 CHI Conference Extended Abstracts on Human Factors in Computing Systems, pp. 1073–1076. ACM (2016)
37. Brown, D., Grinter, R.E.: Designing for transient use: a human-in-the-loop translation platform for refugees. In: Proceedings of the 2016 CHI Conference on Human Factors in Computing Systems, pp. 321–330. ACM (2016)
38. Baranoff, J.R., Gonzales, I., Liu, J., Yang, H., Zheng, J.: Lantern: empowering refugees through community-generated guidance using near field communication. In: Proceedings of the 33rd Annual ACM Conference Extended Abstracts on Human Factors in Computing Systems, pp. 7–12. ACM (2015)
39. Norad Innovation Competition: EduApp4Syria (2017). https://www.norad.no/eduapp4syria. Accessed 2 Dec 2017
40. Kabranian-Melkonian, S.: Ethical concerns with refugee research. J. Hum. Behav. Soc. Environ. **25**(7), 714–722 (2015)
41. Candappa, M., Ahmad, M.: Education and Schooling for Asylum-Seeking and Refugee Students in Scotland: An Exploratory Study. The Scottish Government, Edinburgh (2007)
42. Rousseau, C., Drapeau, A., Lacroix, L., Bagilishya, D., Heusch, N.: Evaluation of a classroom program of creative expression workshops for refugee and immigrant children. J. Child Psychol. Psychiatry **46**(2), 180–185 (2005)

43. Fisher, K.E., Yefimova, K., Yafi, E.: Future's butterflies: co-designing ICT wayfaring technology with refugee Syrian youth. In: Proceedings of the 15th International Conference on Interaction Design and Children, pp. 25–36. ACM (2016)

44. Jordans, M.J.D., Tol, W.A., Komproe, I.H., De Jong, J.V.T.M.: Systematic review of evidence and treatment approaches: psychosocial and mental health care for children in war. Child Adolesc. Mental Health **14**(1), 2–14 (2009)

45. Stubbé, H., Badri, A., Telford, R., Oosterbeek, S., van der Hulst, A.: Formative evaluation of a mathematics game for out-of-school children in Sudan. In: Cai, Y., Goei, S.L., Trooster, W. (eds.) Simulation and Serious Games for Education. GMSE, pp. 61–79. Springer, Singapore (2017). https://doi.org/10.1007/978-981-10-0861-0_5

46. Block, K., Warr, D., Gibbs, L., Riggs, E.: Addressing ethical and methodological challenges in research with refugee-background young people: reflections from the field. J. Refug. Stud. **26**(1), 69–87 (2012)

47. Einarsdottir, J.: Playschool in pictures: children's photographs as a research method. Early Child Dev. Care **175**(6), 523–541 (2005)

48. Morrow, V., Richards, M.: The ethics of social research with children: an overview. Child. Soc. **10**(2), 90–105 (1996)

49. Fazel, M., Stein, A.: The mental health of refugee children. Arch. Dis. Child. **5**, 366–370 (2002)

50. Rousseau, C.: The mental health of refugee children. Transcult. Psychiatr. Res. Rev. **32**(3), 299–331 (1995)

51. Fazel, M., Stein, A.: Mental health of refugee children: comparative study. BMJ **327**(7407), 134 (2003)

52. Strekalova, E., Hoot, J.L.: What is special about special needs of refugee children? Guidelines for teachers. Multicult. Educ. **16**(1), 21–24 (2008)

53. Kitchenham, B., Pearl Brereton, O., Budgen, D., Turner, M., Bailey, J., Linkman, S.: Systematic literature reviews in software engineering – a systematic literature review. Inf. Softw. Technol. **51**(1), 7–15 (2009)

54. Obrist, M., Förster, F., Wurhofer, D., Tscheligi, M., Hofstätter, J.: Evaluating first experiences with an educational computer game: a multi-method approach. IxD&A **11**, 26–36 (2011)

55. Sim, G., Read, J.C., Horton, M.: Practical and ethical concerns in usability testing with children, games user research: a case study approach, p. 1 (2016)

56. Dimitracopoulou, A.: Learning environments and usability: appropriateness and complementarity of evaluation methods. In: Proceedings of 8th Conference on Informatics, Towards the Information Society, pp. 545–554 (2001)

57. Iivari, N., Kinnula, M., Kuure, L., Molin-Juustila, T.: Video diary as a means for data gathering with children-encountering identities in the making. Int. J. Hum.-Comput. Stud. **72**(5), 507–521 (2014)

58. Powell, M.A., Fitzgerald, R.M., Taylor, N., Graham, A.: International literature review: ethical issues in undertaking research with children and young people, for the Childwatch International Research Network. Southern Cross University, Centre for Children and Young People, Lismore/University of Otago, Centre for Research on Children and Families, Dunedin (2012)

59. White, A., Tyrrell, N.: Research with children seeking asylum in Ireland: reflecting on silences and hushed voices. In: Skelton, T., Evans, R., Holt, L. (eds.) Methodological Approaches, pp. 179–197. Springer, Singapore (2017). https://doi.org/10.1007/978-981-287-020-9_5

60. Due, C., Riggs, D.W., Augoustinos, M.: Research with children of migrant and refugee backgrounds: a review of child-centered research methods. Child Indic. Res. 7(1), 209–227 (2014)
61. Boeije, H., Slagt, M., van Wesel, F.: The contribution of mixed methods research to the field of childhood trauma: a narrative review focused on data integration. J. Mix. Methods Res. 7 (4), 347–369 (2013)
62. Thomas, S., Byford, S.: Research with unaccompanied children seeking asylum. BMJ Br. Med. J. 327(7428), 1400 (2003)
63. Su-Ann, O.: Photofriend: creating visual ethnography with refugee children. Area 44(3), 282–288 (2012)
64. Vecchio, L., Dhillon, K.K., Ulmer, J.B.: Visual methodologies for research with refugee youth. Intercult. Educ. 28(2), 131–142 (2017)
65. Hopkins, P.: Ethical issues in research with unaccompanied asylum-seeking children. Child. Geogr. 6(1), 37–48 (2008)
66. Sirin, S., Plass, J.L., Homer, B.D., Vatanartiran, S., Tsai, T.: Digital game-based education for Syrian refugee children: project hope. Vulnerable Child. Youth Stud. 13(1), 7–18 (2018)
67. Jones, S., Hall, L., Hall, M.: The photograph as a cultural arbitrator in the design of virtual learning environments for children and young people. In: Proceedings of the 2011 International Conference on Electronic Visualisation and the Arts, pp. 258–265. BCS Learning & Development Ltd. (2011)
68. Barendregt, W., Bekker, M.M.: Development and evaluation of the picture cards method. In: Proceedings of Interact 2005, Tenth International Conference on Human Computer Interaction (2005)
69. Höysniemi, J., Hämäläinen, P., Turkki, L.: Using peer tutoring in evaluating the usability of a physically interactive computer game with children. Interact. Comput. 15(2), 203–225 (2003)
70. Read, J.C., Bekker, M.M.: The nature of child computer interaction. In: Proceedings of the 25th BCS Conference on Human-Computer Interaction, pp. 163–170. British Computer Society (2011)
71. Punch, S.: Research with children: the same or different from research with adults? Childhood 9(3), 321–341 (2002)
72. Clark-Kazak, C.: Ethical considerations: research with people in situations of forced migration. Refuge: Canada's J. Refugees/Refuge: revue canadienne sur les réfugiés 33(2), 11–17 (2017)
73. Alain, G., Coughlan, T., Adams, A., Yanacopulos, H.: A process for co-designing educational technology systems for refugee children. In: Proceedings of the 32nd International BCS Human Computer Interaction Conference (HCI 2018), Belfast, UK, 4–6 July 2018
74. Fleck, S., Baraudon, C., Frey, J., Lainé, T., Hachet, M.: Teegi's so cute! Assessing the pedagogical potential of an interactive tangible interface for schoolchildren. In: IDC 2018-17th Interaction Design and Children Conference (2018)
75. Veytizou, J., Bertolo, D., Baraudon, C., Olry, A., Fleck, S.: Could a tangible interface help a child to weigh his/her opinion on usability? In: 30eme conférence francophone sur l'interaction homme-machine, p. 8 (2018)

A Review of the Gaps and Opportunities of Nudity and Skin Detection Algorithmic Research for the Purpose of Combating Adolescent Sexting Behaviors

Muhammad Uzair Tariq$^{(\boxtimes)}$, Afsaneh Razi$^{(\boxtimes)}$,
Karla Badillo-Urquiola$^{(\boxtimes)}$, and Pamela Wisniewski$^{(\boxtimes)}$

University of Central Florida, Orlando, FL, USA
uzairtq@gmail.com, {afsaneh.razi,
kcurquiola10}@knights.ucf.edu, pamwis@ucf.edu

Abstract. We present a comprehensive literature review of algorithmic or computational approaches to detect nudity and/or skin that could be used as a means of preventing adolescent sexting behaviors. We identified 45 peer-reviewed articles that summarize the state-of-the-art in this field to show research gaps and opportunities for future research. We found several important gaps in the literature. For instance, most of the work related to the detection of nudity and/or skin has been done at the software level only; and while numerous algorithms exist in this space, they all operate on already digitized images. Therefore, researchers should consider addressing nudity detection at the hardware level to prevent digitization of these images before they cause harm. In addition, most of the literature we reviewed focused on the computational aspects of detection without further exploring what interventions may be appropriate once detection has occurred. Hence, they do not meaningfully address risk mitigation strategies that would be effective for tackling the problem of adolescent sexting behaviors. Therefore, computational researchers who focus on nudity and/or skin detection need to engage with Human-Computer Interaction (HCI) researchers to determine how to translate their research into actionable solutions for adolescent online safety.

Keywords: Computer vision · Nudity detection · Skin detection · Sexting · Adolescent online safety

1 Introduction

According to a recent survey by Pew Research Center, nearly 95% of adolescents have access to the internet and almost half (45%) of them are constantly online [1]. The internet provides great advantages, such as information sharing. Yet, it also introduces numerous problems dealing with accessing and sharing of explicit content, including sexting, cyberbullying, and child pornography [2]. Prolific sharing, combined with the permanence of digitally captured nudity, is particularly problematic for minors. While the dissemination of child pornography is a crime punishable by law [3], such

© Springer Nature Switzerland AG 2019
M. Kurosu (Ed.): HCII 2019, LNCS 11568, pp. 90–108, 2019.
https://doi.org/10.1007/978-3-030-22636-7_6

momentary mistakes could also cause physical harm and prolonged psychological problems for adolescents, including sexual predation, emotional trauma, cyberbullying, and even suicidal behaviors [4].

It is estimated that about 15% of teens on Snapchat report having received sexually explicit photos. In addition, 4% of cellphone-owning teens, ages 12–17, report having sent sexually suggestive, nude, or nearly nude images of themselves to someone else via text messaging [5]. Sexting behaviors make adolescents vulnerable to a number of offline risks, such as bullying [2] and sexual predation [6]. These types of teen sexting behaviors can be perpetuated by mobile technologies and by several direct messaging applications available on smartphone devices, such as Kik, Snapchat, and AskFM [7]. Unfortunately, such activities often fall under the jurisdiction of child pornography laws. Child pornography is illegal, and the federal law states the following: "A picture of a naked child may constitute illegal child pornography if it is sufficiently sexually suggestive. Additionally, the age of consent for sexual activity in a given state is irrelevant; any depiction of a minor under 18 years of age engaging in sexually explicit conduct is illegal" [3]. So, while sexting behaviors may seem innocent and exploratory to teens, in reality, they can have severe negative consequences.

Solutions have been proposed to approach the problem of adolescent sexting within the overlapping boundaries of various disciplines. For example, this topic has been studied within computer science [8], psychology [9], communications [10], and digital forensics [2]. Overall, very few actionable solutions have been proposed, but the core focus of computer science research has been on the accurate detection of nudity and/or skin as a means of prevention. Computational researchers have used different methods of machine learning, which we synthesize in this paper. Specifically, we investigated the following research questions in topic of nudity and/or skin detection:

- **RQ1:** *What characteristics are common among existing research on nudity and/or skin dominance detection?*
- **RQ2:** *What algorithmic approaches have been used in this literature?*
- **RQ3:** *What research or user studies have been conducted to translate this research into real-world interventions for adolescent online safety?*

We present a comprehensive literature review of algorithmic and computational approaches to detect nudity and/or skin that could be used as a means of preventing teen sexting behaviors to answer these research questions. Our main findings are that most research related to nudity detection has been studied after such images have been captured (RQ1), so there is a need to prevent capturing such images at first place. General solutions for nudity detection should be applicable on mobile platforms. Also, visual features in images should consider detecting the age range of the subject to protect adolescents and minorities from engaging in this behavior (RQ2). Finally, more risk mitigation solutions should be proposed in addition to risk detection and user-centered design should be incorporated to address the problem (RQ3).

2 Background Literature

Prior to conducting our literature review, we searched for existing review papers in this space. We identified two survey papers that categorized different nudity detection approaches. Ries et al. [11] categorized visual adult image recognition approaches to three main groups: skin-color, shape, and local feature-based approaches. They reported that color-based and shape-based approaches seemed more robust than only color-based approaches because they result in more true positive rates and less false positives rates. Shayan et al. [8] conducted a literature review on different approaches for adult image filtering techniques and pornographic image recognition. They have categorized adult image filtering techniques including keyword-based methods, IP-based blacklist methods, and visual content-based methods. They used the same three categories for pornographic image recognition approaches as Ries et al. [11]. They argued that a quantitative comparison of these approaches is not possible because of the lack of a standard dataset and definition for this field.

While these literature review papers categorized the different approaches for pornography and adult image detection, as well as some of the challenges in implementing these approaches, they did not specifically address the intersection of adolescent's online safety and machine learning for nudity and/or skin detection approaches. We argue that more human-centered approaches are needed if we are to implement such solutions in real-world situations. Therefore, we took on a more human-centric perspective for conducting our literature review on adolescent online safety and nudity detection algorithms.

Over the last decade, academic and industry researchers have tried to address the dissemination of child pornographic images indirectly through exploring various nudity and skin detection techniques. To track down illicit photos of minors, for instance, Facebook, Twitter, and Bing have worked closely with organizations such as the National Center for Missing and Exploited Children's Child Victim Identification Program [12], by designing detection and mitigation solutions. Yet, the approaches taken across academic and industry research have had their limitations. The solutions mainly focus on preventing the dissemination of child pornographic images, not proactively protecting teens before the damage has been done. As such, there is a need for more effective and teen-centered approaches to tackle the problem at the source to prevent the creation and dissemination of such imagery.

Therefore, we report key trends and potential gaps in the field of nudity and/or skin detection as it relates to the problem of adolescent sexting behaviors to bring the attention of the research community to this matter. Our research contributions include the following:

1. A synthesis of 45 peer-reviewed articles from computational literature related to nudity and/or skin detection.
2. Identification of potential gaps in the literature on computational nudity and/or skin detection techniques as it relates to adolescent sexting behaviors.
3. Recommendations for future research related to nudity and/or skin detection for the purpose of adolescent online safety.

3 Methods

We performed a comprehensive review of the nudity detection literature and identified 45 peer-reviewed articles that summarize state-of-the-art approaches. We used a grounded approach to qualitatively code the articles. We created a codebook, added codes as we read each paper, and iteratively refined the codebook throughout the coding process. Below is the description of how the systematic literature search was conducted and how the literature was synthesized.

3.1 Literature Search

We searched for articles involving adolescent sexting behaviors from mobile smartphones (both through photos and video imagery), through various libraries and databases including IEEE Xplore Digital Library, ACM Digital Library, and Springer-link to ensure comprehensive coverage of the existing literature. For this review, we focused on nudity detection using the following search terms: "teen nudity," "adolescent nudity," "nudity detection," "skin detection," "explicit content," and "censored nudity." We used all the mentioned resources to come up with an initial set of articles that mainly focus on the detection of nudity and explicit content. We then walked through the citations from the initial set of articles to identify additional articles that were relevant to include in our data set. We also used Google Scholar to conduct a wider search to ensure we were inclusive to multidisciplinary peer-reviewed articles.

We used the following inclusion criteria to evaluate if an article was relevant to our review: (1) The study was a peer-reviewed published work, (2) The study was published after 2008, and (3) The study must suggest a technique to detect nudity and/or skin that could potentially be used for the purpose of mitigating adolescent sexting behaviors. Articles that did not meet all three criteria were considered irrelevant and were not included in our review.

3.2 Data Analysis Approach

We identified 45 relevant articles that met the inclusion criteria mentioned above. The first author then coded them based on the dimensions found in Table 1. A grounded coding approach was used to code the articles, and the codes were iteratively updated as new codes emerged. We mapped the coded dimensions to our three high-level research questions presented in the introduction of our paper. For example, pre or post capture type (whether the algorithm ran in real-time or on a post-digitized image) and the type of media being processed (e.g., image, video, etc.) aligned with our RQ1 on the characteristics that were common to this type of research. For RQ2, we coded for the algorithmic approach used in the respective studies. For RQ3, we used a more user-centered lens to determine whether and how the research incorporated risk mitigation strategies or user studies to apply the research findings to real-world settings. The coded dimensions, their descriptions, and the corresponding codes can be found in Table 1.

Table 1. Final codebook

RQs	Dimension	Description (codes)
RQ1	Capture type	The technique detects nudity before or after capturing/digitization of image (PRE, POST)
	Media type	The technique mentioned is applicable to images, videos, both or none (IMAGE, VIDEO, GEN)
	Nudity class	The technique detects the nudity only when the subject is completely nude, private parts are naked, or it's only non-nude sexually suggestive, or other general approaches to consider nudity (COMP, PP, NN_SUGG, GEN)
	Nudity type	The technique specifically detects nudity of teens (under 18), or general nudity (TEEN, GENERIC)
	Platform type	The technique provides a solution as general software or as mobile apps and services (GEN, MOBILE)
RQ2	Detection type	The approach is for nudity detection (NUDITY) or skin detection (SKIN)
	Detection approach	The implementation makes use of machine learning techniques, computer vision or natural language processing (ML, CV, NLP)
RQ3	User study	Is the article based on a survey where a certain population is studied (YES, NO)
	Risk mitigation approach	The article suggests an implementation of blocking or the reporting of the detected content (BLOCK, REPORT)

4 Results

We present the key findings from our literature review in this section. We organize and present the results by our code dimensions. We first present the results by capture and media type, followed by nudity class and type, platform type, detection type and approach, and finally by user studies and risk mitigation.

4.1 Capture and Media Type

The code "PRE" in Table 1 for "Capture type" means that the detection of nudity happens even before the image is digitized in standard RGB matrix form. All 45 articles which we reviewed, all of them focused on post-digital capture imagery (i.e., "POST"), as opposed to pre-digital capture (i.e., "PRE"). This means that a digitized, nude image had to exist in order for the nudity detection approaches to be effective. Most of the computational academic work related to the detection of nudity has been designed to increase the accuracy and efficiency of detecting nudity [13–21], but they all operate on the already-digitally-stored instances of nudity.

Already-digitally stored images and videos can be classified very accurately through sophisticated techniques like extraction of low and high-level features [22]. This requires large processing time and space. However, when these techniques are used in real-time, it is crucial to follow time deadlines and memory constraints [23]. This indicates that detecting nudity live or in real-time applications like Skype is challenging and reliance on low-level features is more appropriate in these cases. The post-capture digital media analyzed in the reviewed articles included images (66% of articles), videos (25% of articles), text (11% of articles), and mixed media (i.e., "GEN", 23% of articles). The articles that analyzed images mostly used visual learning techniques, like feature extraction, to classify the nude or non-nude image.

Deselaers [24] proposed a method for detecting adult nudity in videos based on a bag-of-visual-features representation for frames. Kovac et al. [25] provided a method for detecting skin color based on RGB color space. Lin et al. [26] used a Support Vector Machine (SVM), which has learning skills in the image detection of human nudity. PhotoDNA [27] is one of the most popular and latest technological solutions for detecting digital nudity by analyzing digital imagery and metadata compared to a database of known images developed by Microsoft.

Though some articles [14, 16–18, 20, 24] focused on detection of explicit content in videos, few made use of the temporal correlations inside video data. Behrad et al. [15] utilized different novel features for obscene video content recognition including spatial, spatiotemporal, and motion-based features, using 3D skin volume method. Khan et al. [28] used the Viola-Jones object detection framework that works on real-time data to detect skin. Polastro et al. [20] considered the contribution of the percentage of explicit frames while classifying the video as pornographic. Hence, their techniques could also be applied to single frames that is the same as detecting nudity in images. Apart from these three papers, all who indicated their focus on video did not actually implement a technique that made use of distinctive video properties.

Text, in most cases, was analyzed on the metadata attached to the image or video under consideration. Some of the articles that we studied focused on combining already available techniques to come up with the nudity filtering system. Wijesinghe et al. [29] proposed improvement in a Parental Control and Filtering System by combining techniques like site restrictions, denial of access to web proxy servers, identification of images containing nudity, and control over uploads of images of people. We coded these articles as "GEN" (general) for media type.

4.2   Nudity Class and Type

We categorized the types of nudity detected in three classes as per their level of explicitness. We found that 40.1% of the articles proposed a method that would only detect nudity if the image was completely nude. These techniques relied more on skin detection percentage rather than region-based feature extraction, or they used some hardcoded high-level feature assumption like the use of a navel recognizing process [30]. A little over 7% of the articles presented a solution that would detect exposed private parts of one's body even if the body was mostly covered; they focused more on high and low-level feature extraction (e.g., Santos et al. [31]). Four of the articles had such a complex way of extracting features that they could almost be classified as using contextual learning for nudity. Therefore, they could detect if a naked body image was sexual or non-sexual, like in the case of a breastfeeding mother. Sevimli et al. [32] made use of 4 descriptors (feature extraction methods) to classify images in 5 classes of nudity: normal images (class 1), swimming suit images (class 2), topless images (class 3), nude images (class 4), and sexual activity images (class 5).

Most (70.5%) of the articles focused on general (primarily adult) nudity detection, as opposed to specifically detecting the nudity of a minor. In the 29.5% of articles that focused on teen nudity detection, age and nudity were separately. To determine age, very few made use of the image itself; rather they used additional information like text from metadata or information entered directly by the uploader of the image. Articles that propose a solution to general nudity detection in terms of age mostly make use of two very general steps: skin detection and pornography detection [33, 34]. For detecting teen nudity, the third step, 'age detection' is added. Polastro et al. [35] makes it clear that there are some intrinsic characteristics that need to be considered to distinguish child nudity from adult nudity. For example, most of the child sexual content does not contain explicit sex scenes and the motion (in a video) can be distinguished from an adult porn scene. Also, the sound can be distinguished since it is different or sometimes absent in the case of child porn video. Figure 1 depicts the number of articles for methods specific for teens and general methods and their nudity class.

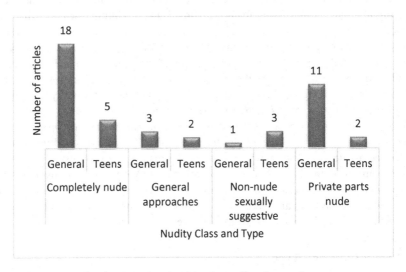

Fig. 1. Number of articles by nudity class and type

4.3   Platform Type

Even though mobile social networking and dating apps are a major platform for sexting [36], only 5% of the articles focused on detecting nude content specifically via mobile devices. While the software-based detection techniques that most of the researchers presented were general enough to be used via mobile platforms, none were tested to see if the mobile processor had the adequate processing power for the detection task. Two of the articles present a third-party mobile-application to detect explicit content. Lin et al. [37] presented an app that detects skin and classifies it, and for further detection of nudity, the app would conduct a user poll.

Amato et al. [38] presents an application that is more of a background service, an interceptor that detects nudity or other explicit content being received through MMS and Bluetooth messaging on mobile devices based on the Symbian™ operating systems. Once intercepted, the images are analyzed by the component of the system that automatically classifies images with explicit sexual content. Apart from these two articles, all others provide a general solution that can be implemented at a different level of abstraction of the operating systems, depending on the authority. For instance, solutions could be implemented by the Internet Service Provider at the network level to provide information to law enforcement agencies or by an application that is controlled by parents of the device.

4.4 Detection Type and Approach

In order to detect nude scenes, detection of different kinds of contextual and visual features in an image are necessary. In reviewing the literature, skin was one of the important features for CV nudity detection techniques [39, 40]. Islam et al. [41] stated that "Nudity and pornography have a direct link with human skin. In fact, no pornography can exist without exposure of human skin. Apart from pornography, a wide range of image processing applications exist, where skin detection is playing a crucial role. Using color as a detection cue has long being recognized as a robust feature and has become a popular choice in human skin detection techniques. Human skin has a characteristic color which is easily distinguishable from the colors of other objects."

Nine of the papers [23, 28, 32, 34, 41–46] implemented skin detection as a part of the procedure to detect nudity. Islam et al. [41] used a Wavelet transform that involves recursive filtering and sub-sampling. It has discriminating ability in texture analysis that facilitates capturing subtle differences between child and adult skin texture. Bhoyar [23] proposed a three-layer feedforward neural network used for skin color classification with three neurons in the input layer, five neurons in the hidden layer and two neurons in the output layer. The two neurons in the output layer represent skin class and non-skin class. Povar et al. [42] and Kelly et al. [43] used clustering in color space (s) to filter skin tone. Sevimli et al. [32] used a method based on inferring pixels on statistical skin and non-skin models which are represented and trained with Gaussian Mixture Models. Vijayendar et al. [47] proposed a method to filter adult images in websites; they use MFC(Most Frequent Color) where face detection is not possible. Selamat et al. [48] used modified fuzzy rules to improve skin detection. Choudhury et al. [49] proposed a skin tone detection filter that can identify images with a large skin color count that are pornographic in nature. Dewantono et al. [50] proposed nudity detection and localization in images and videos using a skin filtering method based on a Bayes rule, a novel histogram back projection of skin samples, and a SVM. Siqueira et al. [34] constructed color histograms through both the skin and non-skin groups of RGB images; they applied a certain threshold on the histograms to classify pixels into groups. Khan et al. [28] used adaptive skin color modeling where pixels that are most likely non-skin are discarded from a detected region of pixels and the region is then extracted for further processing. Liu et al. [44] proposes to detect pornographic images in a two-stage scheme; the first step employs a Content-Based Image Retrieval technique (CBIR) to determine whether the image has a human in it. The second step is a skin color model established to analyze the skin-like pixels and identify the presence of pornographic content.

Soysal et al. [51] proposed a concept detection system (one of the concepts is nudity detection) using generalized visual and audio concept detection modules. Adnan et al. [16] analyzed low-level features for their suitability in pornography detection; they found that in order for pornography detection systems to be accurate, not only do low-level features need to be considered, but high-level features should also be incorporated. Esposito et al. [52] proposed a nudity detection classifier based on both body geometric properties and global features. Eleuterio et al. [53] improved child pornography video detection algorithms by proposing an adaptive sampling approach.

Westlake et al. [54] tackled the dissemination of online child sexual exploitation (CE) using a different approach; they investigated the communities that are created around public websites involved in the distribution of child sexual exploitation material. One criterion of identifying a website as CE-related was that it contained one of a set of known images from Royal Canadian Mounted Police (RCMP) database using a hash value. Girgis et al. [55] proposed a pornography detection and filtering system for images in web pages using skin recognition. In addition, CBIR methods can be used for nudity detection filters [56].

From a computational perspective, most articles (86.4%) employed methods from the field of Computer Vision (CV) [50, 52, 57–61]. Only 9% of the articles proposed Natural Language Processing (NLP) techniques. A few papers presented pure CV solutions without any learning aspect; for example, Ivan et al. [62] used the RSOR algorithm that performed recognition and selection of the largest region in a segmented image. Some articles (e.g., Polastro et al. [63]) used mixed techniques from ML, CV, and NLP to come up with a comprehensive technique to detect nudity. Vanhove et al. [14] presented a solution that used Picture Analysis, Text Analysis, and Audio/Video analysis for social network monitoring. More detailed categorizations of different pornography and adult image detection methods could be found in Ries et al. and Shayan et al. articles [8, 11].

4.5   User Studies and Risk Mitigation Strategies

A common theme among the nudity detection approaches was that they came from a purely computational perspective and failed to incorporate any aspects of user-centered design or needs analysis. None of the articles included formative or summative user evaluations of the solutions developed. For instance, an online article [64] talks about parental control software and briefly mentions mitigation approaches that require a user study, which can consider different mitigation approaches to the problem depending on the relation or trust between parents and children. In terms of risk mitigation strategies after nudity detection has occurred, the article set was also lacking. About 22.7% of the articles suggested naïve approaches, such as blocking the explicit content or reporting it. In another 27%, the articles suggested that their solutions could be used by law enforcement agencies, security companies, or parents. None of the articles suggested any kind of design that would directly engage teen users in a way to address the root of the risky behavior. In summary, the majority of the articles focused on risk detection over risk mitigation.

Table 2 summarizes all articles with the research issues that they tried to address. Most of the articles proposed nudity and/or skin detection systems without embedding them in any particular context or application. Though some of the papers proposed parental control apps and/or filtering systems, other articles proposed cataloging tools and/or retrieval systems. These systems could be used by different agencies, such as police investigation departments. There were no cases were the articles proposed that the technologies were suited for use in applications targeted for teen users.

Table 2. Source articles and their intended purpose

Topic/purpose	Sources
Skin detection	Islam et al., 2011 [41]; Bhoyar et al., 2010 [23]; Siqueira et al., 2013 [34]; Selamat et al., 2009 [48]; Santos et al., 2015 [46], Kelly et al., 2008 [43]
Nudity detection	Flores et al., 2011 [62]; Santos et al., 2012 [31], Polastro et al., 2012 [35]; Soysal et al., 2013 [51]; Behrad et al., 2012 [15]; Adnan et al., 2016 [16]; Esposito et al., 2013 [52]; Sevimli et al., 2010 [32]; Uke et al., 2012 [17]; Silva et al., 2014 [18]; Lin et al., 2012 [37]; Ras et al., 2016 [61]; Platzer et al., 2014 [33]; Eleuterio et al., 2010 [63]; Polastro et al., 2012 [20]; Dewantono et al., 2014 [50]; Deselaers et al., 2008 [24]; Wang et al., 2009a [65]; Wang et al., 2009b [30]; Lopes et al.,2009 [21]; Ap-apid, 2009 [45]; Liu et al., 2009 [44]; Eleuterio et al., 2012 [53]; Lopes et al., 2009 [66]; Steel et al., 2012 [60]; Polastro et al., 2010 [63]
Parental control and/or filtering system	Wijesinghe et al., 2012 [29]; Ahuja et al., 2015 [29]; Lienhart et al., 2009 [57]; Vijayendar et al., 2009 [47]; Amato et al., 2009 [38]; Khan et al., 2008 [28]; Girgis et al., 2010 [55]; Vanhove et al., 2013 [14]; Choudhury et al., 2008 [49]
Cataloguing tool and/or retrieval system	Povar et al., 2011 [42]; Grega et al., 2011 [67]; Patil et al., 2013 [22]; Sidhu et al., 2015 [56]

5   Discussion

Our review indicated potential gaps in the literature that can inform new research directions. In this section, we summarize our major findings and identify the gaps and opportunities for future research on nudity and/or skin detection for the purpose of mitigating risks associated with adolescent sexting behaviors.

5.1   Summary of Findings

Most research related to the detection of nudity and/or skin has been studied at the software-level on already digitized images. A problem with this approach is that it implies that the naked image of a minor must already be digitized in order for the algorithm to work. This raises a crucial need for a more effective approach that addresses the problem at the source to prevent the creation and dissemination of such imagery in the first place. Skin detection at the pre-digitization level might ensure privacy and, in the future, can be combined with detection of other spatial and/or temporal features in nude scenes to prevent the digitization of such images at all.

We also found limited research related to the detection of nudity and/or skin detection within the context of mobile devices. Since most teens use mobile devices as their primary means for going online [1], more research in this area is warranted. Researchers should focus on addressing the limitations of processing power and memory to apply their general solutions to the nudity and/or skin detection problem within mobile platforms.

Another limitation we found within the articles was that very few researchers contextualized their algorithmic solutions to children and teens. Many of the studies did not use teen data sets to train the nudity and/or skin detection algorithms, nor did they validate ground truth based on adolescents. Additionally, many of the algorithms themselves are often generic and not optimized for adolescent data. The algorithms are typically developed outside of the context of how they would need to be used for adolescent sexting risk detection. Therefore, researchers should consider conducting studies with teen datasets. These studies can help determine the level of nudity that constitutes risks for teens to determine thresholds that could establish a ground truth in nudity and/or skin detection for adolescent online safety.

Finally, we found that articles focus more on risk detection, rather than risk mitigation. Future research should shift the focus to more proactive solutions by incorporating aspects of user-centered design or developing formative and summative user evaluations of the solutions. This would allow for the design and development of interventions that would directly engage teen users in a way to actively manage their online behavior and address the root of the risky behavior.

We further discuss these gaps in the following sections.

5.2   The Need to Detect Nudity and/or Skin Before Digital Capture

To our knowledge, there is no peer-reviewed literature that deals with the issue of handling teen sexting behaviors before they have already been digitally captured via a nude image or video. Skin detection at the pre-digitization level has the advantage of privacy, and in the future, it can be combined with detection of other spatial and/or temporal features in nude scenes to prevent teen sexting. The literature presents techniques that detect nudity and/or skin in digitized images or frames of videos. Unfortunately, by this point, the damage has already potentially been done. The image or video could have already reached a multitude of individuals and platforms. Also, there is no method of knowing whether the image or video was saved, allowing for the possibility of it to re-surface in the future. Therefore, a mechanism to detect nudity and/or skin at the pre-digitization level can be more useful. Two major potential benefits of pre-digitization detection include the following:

(1) **Security:** The British Broadcasting Corporation (BBC) reported that once an Apple iPhone, iPod Touch, or iPad owner grants permission for an application to access location information from their device, the application can potentially copy their photo library [33]. Also, in several high-profile examples, celebrity photos

have been leaked onto the Internet after their phones were hacked. By detecting nudity and/or skin before an image or video is captured, the probabilities of these types of risks taking place can be reduced.

(2) **Real-time detection:** At the heart of almost all techniques provided in the literature is a basic step of feature extraction. So far, there has been more emphasis on accuracy of classification of nude images which improves by extracting both low and high-level features. This requires considerable processing time and space, whereas, dealing with only low-level features will require less processing time and that would help to detect nudity and/or skin in real time with a compromise on accuracy. However, nudity detection in live or real-time video applications, like Skype, could be possible.

For example, Tariq et al. [68] developed a low-powered sensor as a proof-of-concept for detecting skin before an image is captured. They were able to detect skin dominance with 83.7% accuracy. Future research should build upon this work and investigate how to develop even more effective methods of detecting nudity and/or skin at the pre-digitization level.

5.3   The Need to Develop Risk Detection Solutions for Mobile Platforms

Most articles we reviewed made use of machine learning, on the features from images and videos. Classifying them accurately requires adequate memory and processing time, which likely requires high-processing power on a centralized server. This implies that the image would first need to be sent to the centralized server before the algorithms could be applied to detect skin or nudity.

Research has shown that teens are increasingly becoming more mobile with their online access [1]. Yet, the articles we found do not specify the application of these general methods to mobile platforms, because of the limited memory and processing power of the mobile device. Amato et al. [38] mentions that "classifiers can recognize and discriminate between harmless and offensive multimedia contents (in a mobile device). However, the complexity of such systems discourages from implementing and running them on small mobile devices." On the other hand, every device has the connectivity capabilities necessary for sending and receiving a relatively rich amount of information which gives software developers the liberty to do extensive calculations at the server side. However, interruption in connectivity could be a problem especially when dealing with real time detection. For general risk detection solutions to be effective, they must be able to be applied within the appropriate context (in this case mobile devices). Therefore, researchers should consider investigating approaches for incorporating risk detection into mobile platforms.

5.4   The Need to Contextualize Risk Detection Algorithms to Adolescent Sexting Behaviors

Most of the articles that we studied propose nudity and/or skin detection methods irrespective of the subject's age. General solutions typically make use of textual data attached with the image to identify the age of the subject. However, visual learning techniques could be used to detect visual features that could identify the age range of the subjects, whether they are a child or a teen [35]. Further, contextual learning could be used to detect images that are sexually suggestive, as almost all the detection techniques mentioned above simply detect complete nudity or the private areas of a human body. These proposed methods could help prevent false positives [63], for example, correctly identifying a semi-nude sexual image of a child versus incorrectly identifying a child playing at the beach in their bathing suit. Both examples may have the same amount of nudity, but the human context would indicate whether it is an appropriate image or not.

Additionally, as far as adolescent online risk is concerned, there has not been a study to understand what level of nudity actually constitutes risks for teens. For instance, a bathroom selfie in a towel may exhibit less skin, but the suggestiveness of the context would make it riskier. As such, detecting nudity in binary terms may not adequately serve to mitigate risks. More studies should focus on understanding the thresholds used to determine ground truth in nudity detection. As discussed earlier, there was also no article, to our knowledge, that suggested a design that would directly engage teen users in a way to address the root of the risky behavior. In short, most articles focused on risk detection over risk mitigation, failing to incorporate any aspects of user-centered design or a formative/summative user evaluation of the solutions developed [69]. The detriment of this gap is made evident in existing research on the limitations of parental control applications [70, 71], which implement many of the risk detection methods discussed in this paper. Parent-focused interventions that increase parental control through restriction and monitoring may not be as effective as teen-centric solutions that empower teens to make better online decision [70–72]. Researchers should focus their efforts on designing more teen-centric risk detection algorithms that take into consideration the unique characteristics of teens.

5.5   The Need for Human-Centered Machine Learning Research

Almost all the reviewed articles were algorithms and/or systems developed by engineers and computer scientists, who did not take into consideration users' interpretations of results which might be different from their personal interpretations of results. Most of the reviewed papers used metrics such as accuracy, recall, precision, and F1 score to evaluate the performance of algorithms, but they did not incorporate any human-centered evaluation based on the perceptions of actual users. The algorithmic systems for nudity and/or skin detection need to benefit human-centered designs, approaches, and evaluations, to devise and improve the systems for adolescents to meet their specific characteristics. To meet this objective, researchers should involve adolescents and their parents to help them design and evaluate their systems [71, 73–75].

Researchers should take into consideration how machine learning algorithms may unintentionally be influenced by biases [76]. Human-centered machine learning takes this into account by considering the goals and capabilities of humans and having them help with the design and evaluation of these algorithms and systems [77]. Baumer [78] proposed a human-centered algorithm design which requires the design process for algorithmically based systems to incorporate human and social interpretations. He provided theoretical, participatory, and speculative strategies for these types of designs.

As machine learning systems are being used in more real-word systems, it is important that they are useful to people. That's where human-centered approaches could help improve human experiences in development of new machine learning technologies.

5.6 Limitations and Future Research

In the future, researchers should take the necessary steps towards a more cohesive solution for providing risk mitigation after detection. If it were possible to detect risky online behaviors (e.g., a teen taking a nude photo or streaming video while unclothed) using a teen's internet-connected device (e.g., mobile smartphone, tablet, or laptop), then we would be able to mitigate these risks in more meaningful ways. Unfortunately, nudity detection poses additional risks to teens, as a high-fidelity digitized nude image of a minor (possibly transmitted to a server for additional processing) already negates our goal of preserving the privacy of minors. Therefore, an integral part of this long-term goal of detecting nudity prior to digital capture is a sensor that integrates directly with a mobile application to decouple skin detection (performed by the sensor) from risk mitigation strategies (managed by the application layer), so that parents can customize how to handle problematic behavior based on the age and unique needs of their teen. Whether risk mitigation comes in the form of blocking digital transmission, notifying parents, or nudging teens to make better choices, detection without mitigation cannot serve to effectively protect teens.

6 Conclusion

In this paper, we synthesized past research on nudity and/or skin detection for the purpose of combatting adolescent sexting behaviors. Our review uncovers potential gaps in the literature that can inform new research directions. This work contributed the first literature review of nudity and/or skin detection with the focus of solutions customized for adolescents. The key points that future researchers should consider include the following: (1) To design nudity detection solutions at the pre-digitization levels to ensure privacy. (2) To provide solutions that are applicable on mobile platforms. (3) To conduct studies to understand specific characteristics of adolescent sexting. By designing solutions for nudity detection focusing on adolescents as end users, researchers will be able to provide more effective solutions for combating adolescent sexting behaviors.

Acknowledgements. This research was supported by the William T. Grant Foundation under grant number #187941 and the U.S. National Science Foundation under grant number #IIP-1827700. Any opinion, findings, and conclusions or recommendations expressed in this material are those of the authors and do not necessarily reflect the views of the research sponsors.

References

1. Teens, Social Media & Technology 2018—Pew Research Center (2018). http://www.pewinternet.org/2018/05/31/teens-social-media-technology-2018/
2. Lievens, E.: Bullying and sexting in social networks: protecting minors from criminal acts or empowering minors to cope with risky behaviour? Int. J. Law Crime Justice **42**, 251–270 (2014). https://doi.org/10.1016/j.ijlcj.2014.02.001
3. Citizen's Guide To U.S. Federal Law On Child Pornography. https://www.justice.gov/criminal-ceos/citizens-guide-us-federal-law-child-pornography
4. Drouin, M., Ross, J., Tobin, E.: Sexting: a new, digital vehicle for intimate partner aggression? Comput. Hum. Behav. **50**, 197–204 (2015). https://doi.org/10.1016/j.chb.2015.04.001
5. Teens and Sexting—Pew Research Center (2009). http://www.pewinternet.org/2009/12/15/teens-and-sexting/
6. Ngejane, C.H., Mabuza-Hocquet, G., Eloff, J.H.P., Lefophane, S.: Mitigating online sexual grooming cybercrime on social media using machine learning: a desktop survey. In: 2018 International Conference on Advances in Big Data, Computing and Data Communication Systems (icABCD), pp. 1–6 (2018)
7. Snapchat sexting and the predators of Kik: The apps your children need to stay away from—Daily Telegraph. https://www.dailytelegraph.com.au/news/snapchat-sexting-and-the-predators-of-kik-the-apps-your-children-need-to-stay-away-from/news-story/ad63dc7962ff4098b0785d2671f5c89c
8. Shayan, J., Abdullah, S.M., Karamizadeh, S.: An overview of objectionable image detection. In: 2015 International Symposium on Technology Management and Emerging Technologies (ISTMET), pp. 396–400 (2015)
9. Lee, S.-J., Chae, Y.-G.: Balancing participation and risks in children's Internet use: the role of internet literacy and parental mediation. Cyberpsychol. Behav. Soc. Netw. **15**, 257–262 (2012). https://doi.org/10.1089/cyber.2011.0552
10. Byrne, S., Katz, S.J., Lee, T., Linz, D., McIlrath, M.: Peers, predators, and porn: predicting parental underestimation of children's risky online experiences. J. Comput.-Mediat. Commun. **19**, 215–231 (2014). https://doi.org/10.1111/jcc4.12040
11. Ries, C.X., Lienhart, R.: A survey on visual adult image recognition. Multimed Tools Appl. **69**, 661–688 (2014). https://doi.org/10.1007/s11042-012-1132-y
12. PhotoDNA Lets Google, FB and Others Hunt Down Child Pornography Without Looking at Your Photos. https://petapixel.com/2014/08/08/photodna-lets-google-facebook-others-hunt-down-child-pornography-without-looking-at-your-photos/
13. Raverkar, S.D., Nagori, M.: Classification of YouTube metadata using shark algorithm. Int. J. Comput. Appl. **132**, 18–21 (2015)
14. Vanhove, T., Leroux, P., Wauters, T., Turck, F.D.: Towards the design of a platform for abuse detection in OSNs using Multimedial data analysis, p. 4 (2013)
15. Behrad, A., Salehpour, M., Ghaderian, M., Saiedi, M., Barati, M.N.: Content-based obscene video recognition by combining 3D spatiotemporal and motion-based features. J Image Video Proc. **2012**, 23 (2012). https://doi.org/10.1186/1687-5281-2012-23
16. Adnan, A., Nawaz, M.: RGB and hue color in pornography detection. Information Technology: New Generations. AISC, vol. 448, pp. 1041–1050. Springer, Cham (2016). https://doi.org/10.1007/978-3-319-32467-8_90
17. Uke, N.J., Thool, D.R.C.: Detecting pornography on web to prevent child abuse – a computer vision approach. Int. J. Sci. Eng. Res. **3**, 3 (2012)

18. Silva, P.M., Polastro, M.D.: An overview of NuDetective forensic tool and its usage to combat child pornography in Brazil. Presented at the XLIII Jornadas Argentinas de Informática e Investigación Operativa (43JAIIO)-VI Workshop de Seguridad Informática (Buenos Aires, 2014) (2014)

19. Eleuterio, P., Polastro, M.: Identification of high-resolution images of child and adolescent pornography at crime scenes. Int. J. Forensic Comput. Sci., 49–59 (2010). https://doi.org/10.5769/j201001006

20. Polastro, M., Eleuterio, P.: Quick identification of child pornography in digital videos. Int. J. Forensice Comput. Sci. **7**, 21–32 (2012). https://doi.org/10.5769/J201202002

21. Lopes, A.P., de Avila, S.E., Peixoto, A.N., Oliveira, R.S., Coelho, M.D., Araújo, A.D.: Nude detection in video using bag-of-visual-features. In: 2009 XXII Brazilian Symposium on Computer Graphics and Image Processing, pp. 224–231 (2009)

22. Patil, S.T., Chavan, N.A.: Image cataloguing tool using descriptor for forensic application. Int. J. Comput. Appl. **975**, 8887 (2013)

23. Bhoyar, K.K., Kakde, O.G.: Skin color detection model using neural networks and its performance evaluation. J. Comput. Sci. **6**, 963–968 (2010)

24. Deselaers, T., Pimenidis, L., Ney, H.: Bag-of-visual-words models for adult image classification and filtering. In: 2008 19th International Conference on Pattern Recognition, pp. 1–4 (2008)

25. Kovac, J., Peer, P., Solina, F.: Human skin color clustering for face detection. In: The IEEE Region 8 EUROCON 2003. Computer as a Tool, pp. 144–148, vol. 2 (2003)

26. Lin, Y.-C., Tseng, H.-W., Fuh, C.-S.: Pornography detection using support vector machine, p. 8 (2003)

27. PhotoDNA—Microsoft. https://www.microsoft.com/en-us/photodna

28. Khan, R., Stöttinger, J., Kampel, M.: An adaptive multiple model approach for fast content-based skin detection in on-line videos. In: Proceedings of the 1st ACM Workshop on Analysis and Retrieval of Events/Actions and Workflows in Video Streams, pp. 89–96. ACM, New York (2008)

29. Wijesinghe, S., Wijewardana, V.O., Karunarathna, Y.D.D., Ridmal, H.S.: Parental Control and Filtering System (2013)

30. Wang, X., Hu, C., Yao, S.: An adult image recognizing algorithm based on naked body detection. In: 2009 ISECS International Colloquium on Computing, Communication, Control, and Management, pp. 197–200 (2009)

31. Santos, C., dos Santos, E.M., Souto, E.: Nudity detection based on image zoning. In: 2012 11th International Conference on Information Science, Signal Processing and their Applications (ISSPA), pp. 1098–1103 (2012)

32. Sevimli, H., et al.: Adult image content classification using global features and skin region detection. In: Gelenbe, E., Lent, R., Sakellari, G., Sacan, A., Toroslu, H., Yazici, A. (eds.) Computer and Information Sciences, pp. 253–258. Springer, Netherlands (2010). https://doi.org/10.1007/978-90-481-9794-1_49

33. Platzer, C., Stuetz, M., Lindorfer, M.: Skin sheriff: a machine learning solution for detecting explicit images. In: Proceedings of the 2nd International Workshop on Security and forensics in Communication Systems - SFCS 2014, pp. 45–56. ACM Press, Kyoto (2014)

34. de Siqueira, F.R., Schwartz, W.R., Pedrini, H.: Adaptive Detection of Human Skin in Color Images. 5

35. de Castro Polastro, M., da Silva Eleuterio, P.M.: A statistical approach for identifying videos of child pornography at crime scenes. In: 2012 Seventh International Conference on Availability, Reliability and Security, pp. 604–612 (2012)

36. Apps to improve your sext life - NY Daily News. http://www.nydailynews.com/news/national/9-apps-improve-sext-life-article-1.2465165

37. Lin, Y., Wu, Y.: Machine learning application on detecting nudity in images. Presented at the (2012)
38. Amato, G., Bolettieri, P., Costa, G., la Torre, F., Martinelli, F.: Detection of images with adult content for parental control on mobile devices? In: Proceedings of the 6th International Conference on Mobile Technology, Application & Systems, pp. 35:1–35:5. ACM, New York (2009)
39. Smola - Introduction to Machine Learning.pdf. https://alex.smola.org/teaching/cmu2013-10-701/slides/3_Instance_Based.pdf
40. A Hierarchical Method for Nude Image Filtering– 《Journal of Computer Aided Design & Computer Graphics》2002年05期. http://en.cnki.com.cn/Article_en/CJFDTOTAL-JSJF200205004.htm
41. Islam, M., Watters, P.A., Yearwood, J.: Real-time detection of children's skin on social networking sites using Markov random field modelling. Inf. Secur. Tech. Rep. **16**, 51–58 (2011). https://doi.org/10.1016/j.istr.2011.09.004
42. Povar, D., Vidyadharan, D.S., Thomas, K.L.: Digital image evidence detection based on skin tone filtering technique. In: Abraham, A., Lloret Mauri, J., Buford, J.F., Suzuki, J., Thampi, S.M. (eds.) ACC 2011. CCIS, vol. 190, pp. 544–551. Springer, Heidelberg (2011). https://doi.org/10.1007/978-3-642-22709-7_53
43. Kelly, W., Donnellan, A., Molloy, D.: Screening for objectionable images: a review of skin detection techniques. In: 2008 International Machine Vision and Image Processing Conference, pp. 151–158 (2008)
44. Liu, B., Su, J., Lu, Z., Li, Z.: Pornographic images detection based on CBIR and skin analysis. In: 2008 Fourth International Conference on Semantics, Knowledge and Grid, pp. 487–488 (2008)
45. Ap-apid, R.: Image-based pornography detection. Presented at the January 1 (2008)
46. Santos, A., Pedrini, H.: Human skin segmentation improved by saliency detection. In: Azzopardi, G., Petkov, N. (eds.) CAIP 2015. LNCS, vol. 9257, pp. 146–157. Springer, Cham (2015). https://doi.org/10.1007/978-3-319-23117-4_13
47. Vijayendar G.: Integrated approach to block adult images in websites. In: 2009 International Conference on Computer Technology and Development, pp. 421–425 (2009)
48. Selamat, A., Maarof, M.A., Chin, T.Y.: Fuzzy mamdani inference system skin detection. In: 2009 Ninth International Conference on Hybrid Intelligent Systems, pp. 57–62 (2009)
49. Choudhury, A., Rogers, M., Gillam, B., Watson, K.: A novel skin tone detection algorithm for contraband image analysis. In: 2008 Third International Workshop on Systematic Approaches to Digital Forensic Engineering, pp. 3–9 (2008)
50. Dewantono, S., Supriana, I.: Development of a real-time nudity censorship system on images. In: 2014 2nd International Conference on Information and Communication Technology (ICoICT), pp. 30–35 (2014)
51. Soysal, M., et al.: Multimodal concept detection in broadcast media: KavTan. Multimedia Tools Appl. **72**, 2787–2832 (2014). https://doi.org/10.1007/s11042-013-1564-z
52. Esposito, L.G., Sansone, C.: A multiple classifier approach for detecting naked human bodies in images. In: Petrosino, A. (ed.) ICIAP 2013. LNCS, vol. 8157, pp. 389–398. Springer, Heidelberg (2013). https://doi.org/10.1007/978-3-642-41184-7_40
53. Eleuterio, P., Polastro, M.: An adaptive sampling strategy for automatic detection of child pornographic videos. In: Proceedings of the Seventh International Conference on Forensic Computer Science, pp. 12–19. Abeat (2012)
54. Westlake, B.G., Bouchard, M.: Liking and hyperlinking: community detection in online child sexual exploitation networks. Soc. Sci. Res. **59**, 23–36 (2016). https://doi.org/10.1016/j.ssresearch.2016.04.010

55. Girgis, M.R., Mahmoud, T.M., Abd-El-Hafeez, T.: A new effective system for filtering pornography images from web pages and PDF files. IJWA **2**, 13 (2010)
56. Sidhu, S., Saxena, J.: Content Based Image Retrieval A Review, 5 (2015)
57. Lienhart, R., Hauke, R.: Filtering adult image content with topic models. In: Proceedings of the 2009 IEEE International Conference on Multimedia and Expo, pp. 1472–1475. IEEE Press, Piscataway (2009)
58. Nude image detection based on SVM. https://www.researchgate.net/publication/224586727_Nude_image_detection_based_on_SVM
59. Ahuja, C., Baghel, A.S., Singh, G.: Detection of nude images on large scale using Hadoop. In: 2015 2nd International Conference on Computing for Sustainable Global Development (INDIACom), pp. 849–853 (2015)
60. Steel, C.M.S.: The mask-SIFT cascading classifier for pornography detection. In: World Congress on Internet Security (WorldCIS-2012), pp. 139–142 (2012)
61. Ras, L.T., Barfeh, D.P.Y.: Nudity prohibition system. LPU-Laguna J. Eng. Comput. Stud. **3** (2016)
62. Flores, P.I.T., Guillén, L.E.C., Prieto, O.A.N.: Approach of RSOR algorithm using HSV color model for nude detection in digital images. Comput. Inf. Sci. **4**, 29. https://doi.org/10.5539/cis.v4n4p29
63. de_Castro Polastro, M., da Silva Eleuterio, P.M.: NuDetective: a forensic tool to help combat child pornography through automatic nudity detection. In: 2010 Workshops on Database and Expert Systems Applications, pp. 349–353 (2010)
64. Discipline for Defiant Teens and Preteens. http://www.myoutofcontrolteen.com/
65. Xin-Lu, W., Xiao-juan, L., Xiao-bo, L.: Nude image detection based on SVM. In: 2009 International Conference on Computational Intelligence and Natural Computing, pp. 178–181 (2009)
66. Lopes, A., Avila, S., Peixoto, A., Oliveira, R., Araujo, A.: A Bag-of-features Approach based on Hue-SIFT Descriptor for Nude Detection. 5
67. Grega, M., Bryk, D., Napora, M.: INACT—INDECT advanced image cataloguing tool. Multimed Tools Appl. **68**, 95–110 (2014). https://doi.org/10.1007/s11042-012-1164-3
68. Tariq, M.U., Ghosh, A.K., Badillo-Urquiola, K., Jha, A., Koppal, S., Wisniewski, P.J.: Designing light filters to detect skin using a low-powered sensor. In: SoutheastCon 2018, pp. 1–8 (2018)
69. Pinter, A., Wisniewski, P., Xu, H., Rosson, M.B., Carroll, J.M.: Adolescent online safety: moving beyond formative evaluations to designing solutions for the future. In: the 16th Interactive Design and Children Conference, Stanford, CA (2017)
70. Ghosh, A.K., Badillo-Urquiola, K., Rosson, M.B., Xu, H., Carroll, J.M., Wisniewski, P.J.: A matter of control or safety?: Examining Parental use of technical monitoring apps on teens' mobile devices. In: Proceedings of the 2018 CHI Conference on Human Factors in Computing Systems, pp. 194:1–194:14. ACM, New York (2018)
71. Ghosh, A., Badillo-Urquiola, K., Guha, S., LaViola, J., Wisniewski, P.: Safety vs. surveillance: what children have to say about mobile apps for parental control. In: Proceedings of the 2018 CHI Conference on Human Factors in Computing Systems (2018)
72. Wisniewski, P., et al.: Resilience mitigates the negative effects of adolescent internet addiction and online risk exposure. In: Proceedings of the 33rd Annual ACM Conference on Human Factors in Computing Systems, pp. 4029–4038. ACM, New York (2015)
73. Badillo-Urquiola, K., Smriti, D., McNally, B., Bonsignore, E., Golub, E., Wisniewski, P.: Co-designing with children to address "stranger danger" on Musical.ly. Presented at the SOUPS, The Fourteenth Symposium on Usable Privacy and Security (2018)

74. Wisniewski, P., Xu, H., Rosson, M.B., Perkins, D.F., Carroll, J.M.: Dear diary: teens reflect on their weekly online risk experiences. In: Proceedings of the 2016 CHI Conference on Human Factors in Computing Systems, pp. 3919–3930. ACM (2016)

75. Wisniewski, P., Xu, H., Rosson, M.B., Carroll, J.M.: Parents just don't understand: why teens don't talk to parents about their online risk experiences. In: Proceedings of the 2017 ACM Conference on Computer Supported Cooperative Work and Social Computing, pp. 523–540. ACM (2017)

76. Barocas, S., Selbst, A.D.: Big data's disparate impact. Calif. L. Rev. **104**, 671 (2016)

77. Fiebrink, R., Gillies, M.: Introduction to the special issue on human-centered machine learning. ACM Trans. Interact. Intell. Syst. **8**, 7:1–7:7 (2018). https://doi.org/10.1145/3205942

78. Baumer, E.P.: Toward human-centered algorithm design. Big Data Soc. **4**, (2017). https://doi.org/10.1177/2053951717718854

ADAPT- The Approach to Accessible and Affordable Housing Solutions for People with Disability and Aging in Place

Shu-Wen Tzeng[(⊠)]

School of Industrial and Graphic Design, Auburn University,
Auburn, AL 36849, USA
szt0004@auburn.edu

Abstract. Studies conducted by US federal and state government agencies, NGOs, and advocates for independent living attest to the need for accessible housing for people with significant disabilities and for those aging in place. According to AARP, by 2030 more than 20% of the population of the United States will be age 65 or older and 87% of adults age 65+ want to stay in their current home and community as they age. Unfortunately, staying in home to many people with mobility or physical impairment presents both logistical and financial challenges. In 2017, Auburn University's College of Architecture, Design and Construction (CADC) proposed to collaborate with HUD in the development of housing solutions for people with disabilities and those seeking to age in place and was granted a 3-year project from the federal government. This paper will illustrate the team's approach to comprehensive housing solutions that are both accessible and affordable for people with disability and aging in place.

Keywords: APP design · Accessible and affordable housing solutions ·
Design approach

1 Introduction

Studies conducted by US federal and state government agencies, NGOs, and advocates for independent living attest to the need for accessible housing for people with significant disabilities and for those aging in place. In the United States, escalating health care costs are exacerbated by dramatic increase in the number of people with disability and chronic illness in the over-65 population [1].

The Medicare Current Beneficiary Study (2015) indicates that 74% of Medicare beneficiaries reported living with two or more chronic conditions including heart disease, hypertension, diabetes, arthritis, osteoporosis, pulmonary disease, stroke, Alzheimer's, Parkinson's and cancers [2]. The cost of institutional care for our aging population is escalating beyond our collective capability to pay. Nationally, the annual private pay costs for nursing home services average 241% of an older person's annual income [3]. This population is projected to soar to 73 million by 2030, an increase of 33 million in just two decades with nearly 70% needing some form of long-term care. Cost of care plus increasing demand is leading to a health care and insurance crisis.

© Springer Nature Switzerland AG 2019
M. Kurosu (Ed.): HCII 2019, LNCS 11568, pp. 109–117, 2019.
https://doi.org/10.1007/978-3-030-22636-7_7

Prolonging our ability to live independently with home-based care is the optimal solution and what people want.

According to AARP (2014), by 2030 more than 20% of the population of the United States will be age 65 or older and 87% of adults age 65+ want to stay in their current home and community as they age. Among people age 50 to 64, 71% of people want to age in place [4]. Unfortunately, staying in home presents both logistical and financial challenges to many people in current and future society.

Federal guidelines define housing as "affordable" if total costs, including rent, utilities, insurance and taxes, don't exceed 30% of a renter's or owner's household incomes. According to Harvard's Joint Center for Hosing Studies (2014), a third of adults aged 50 and over in the US are still paying approximately 50% of their income for housing that may or may not meet their needs [5]. To remain at home, affordable options that accommodate the challenges of aging and disability must be made available and be exposed to people in need.

In 2017, Auburn University's College of Architecture, Design and Construction (CADC) proposed to collaborate with HUD (Department of Housing & Urban Development) in the development of housing solutions for people with disabilities and those seeking to age in place and was granted a 3-year project from the federal government. This paper will illustrate the team's approach to comprehensive housing solutions that are both accessible and affordable for people with disability and aging in place.

2 The Team

The CADC at Auburn University houses three schools with professors from Architecture, Industrial Design, and Building Science. In addition to the internal collaboration, the CADC partners with Auburn's Center for Disability Research and Policy Studies to offer an interdisciplinary team of architects, designers, construction professionals, smart home technologists, people with disabilities, and disability research and policy specialists. Auburn also has secured participation agreements for Advisory Council members from Habitat for Humanity, AARP, Volunteers of America, Alabama Institute of Deaf and Blind, Alabama Home Builders Association, and individuals with disabilities who have been actively engaged in policy issues, advocacy, and home adaptation.

The team contains the essential elements in it unified structure to provide a highly experienced and qualified cross-disciplinary team capable of addressing all kinds of challenges mentioned above.

3 The Goal and Final Deliverables

The overarching goal is to enhance the capacity for independent living among people with disabilities and those seeking to age in place through new and existing home design solutions.

To achieve this goal, we need to generate design guidelines and recommendations that do not just meet individual needs but also are easily accessible and understandable. Therefore, the final deliverables for this project will include (1) design guidelines and recommendations for accessible and affordable housing that later can be delivered to the individuals in need, (2) A mobile application (app) that allows users to find and share recommendations and tips needed for creating an accessible and affordable living environment.

4 The Approach

A systematic approach is required for the team to extract, analyze, learn, create, and synthesize to ensure the feasibility of our design solutions. The entire project is divided into 4 major phases in which each has a specific goal and can be related to others in a seamless way. These 4 phases are (1) Research, (2) Concept Ideation, (3) Solution Testing, and (4) Application (Fig. 1).

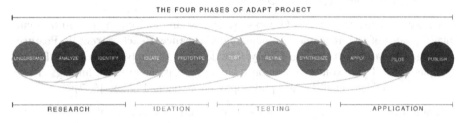

Fig. 1. The 4 phases of ADAPT project

The team identified a group of experts and practitioners to provide guidance to the project, and advisory panel. The team would convene the advisory panel a given number of times throughout the duration of the project to share research findings to date, identify challenges and best practices, and provide guidance to the next phase of project development. From the meeting with the experts, the team was able to finalize the Final Management and work plan (FMWP) and begin project activity.

4.1   Phase One_ Research

In the research phase, the team was divided into 5 working groups each with a specific task:

1. The New Housing Design Working Group researched on best practices, challenges and recommendations.
2. The Redesign of Existing Home Working Group researched on best practices, challenges and recommendations.
3. The Focus Group Working Group identified potential participants and conduced a Focus Group session to collect information on specific needs of those with mobility issues and those with significant visual impairments.
4. Policy Analysis Working Group researched on best practices, challenges and recommendations.
5. Implementation Strategies Working Group researched on best practices, challenges and recommendations

Working groups convened multiple times to complete their recommendations for presentation to the full group at the second Advisory Panel meeting.

Focus Group Working Group conducted a survey at the Focus Group session by utilizing a checklist. This checklist detailed some of the requirements found in the ADA Standards for Accessible Design (Standards). The ADA Accessibility Guidelines (ADAAG), when adopted by DOJ, became the Standards. However, individual homes are not required to be accessible, therefore this checklist was used for the Focus Group participants to identify accessibility problems and solutions in their existing homes.

This checklist was structured based on the four priorities recommended for planning readily achievable barrier removal projects:

Priority 1: Accessible approach and **entrance**.
Priority 2: Access to main living spaces: **kitchen, bedroom, living room**.
Priority 3: Access to **bathroom**.
Priority 4: **Any other measures** necessary.

The key findings from Focus Group session were summarized and categorized into 7 major groups of recommendations including: **Clearance, Reach, Strength, Posture, Lighting, Climate Control, and Safety**. The demand for applying Universal Design principles in all design solutions were also emphasized in the research findings. The 7 key principles of Universal Design philosophy are explained below [6, 7]:

1. **Equability** of design suggests that the item is useful and marketable to people with diverse abilities. Provisions for privacy, security, and safety should be equally available to all users.
2. **Flexibility** of design assumes that the design accommodates a wide range of individual preferences and abilities.
3. Designs are **Simple and Intuitive** if procedures to use the item are easy to understand, regardless of the user's experience, knowledge, language skills, or current concentration level.
4. **Perceptibility** requires that the design communicates necessary information effectively to the user, regardless of ambient conditions or the user's sensory abilities. This is accomplished through the implementation of multiple modes (pictorial, verbal, tactile) for presentation of essential information.
5. **Tolerance** for error means that the design minimizes hazards and the adverse consequences of accidental or unintended actions.
6. Designs that require **Low Physical Effort** can be used efficiently and comfortably with minimal fatigue.
7. **Proportionality** assumes that appropriate size and space is provided for approach, reach, manipulation, and use regardless of user's body size, posture, or mobility.

These 7 key principles of Universal Design philosophy should be applied to the designs of both housing solutions and mobile application.

All working groups reported their findings from research to the full team and the advisory panel. The feedback and comments from the meeting were used to development an implement plan to guide what will refine the parameters of the design activity.

4.2   Phase Two_ Concept Ideation

In the design phase, the New Housing Design Working Group and the Redesign of Existing Home Working Group created high quality, technically appropriate illustrations and drawings to illustrate the critical design and planning issues relevant to new and existing construction. All preliminary designs were documented in orthographic drawings, renderings, diagrams and cost analysis. Two examples of preliminary housing design are shown in Figs. 2 and 3.

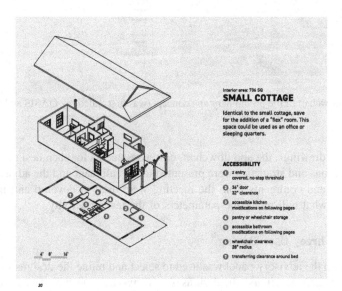

Fig. 2. Accessible layout for a 736 SQ small cottage

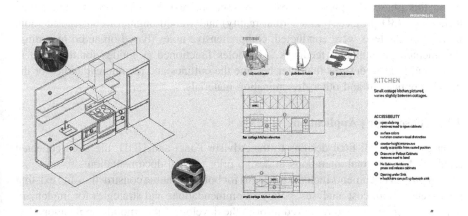

Fig. 3. Accessible layout for kitchen renovation

The app design considerations and general outline on app content were also generated in this phase and presented in a flowchart as shown in Fig. 4.

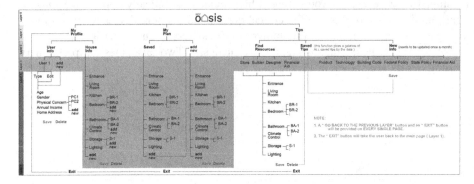

Fig. 4. The flowchart of the preliminary app concept (was first called my OASIS and changed to ADAPT later)

All design drawings, the app flowchart, cost assessments for each design and policy recommendations and strategies were presented to the full team and the advisory panel. The feedback and comments from the meeting were used to develop and implement plan to guide what will refine the parameters of the testing activity.

4.3   Phase Three_ User Testing

Feedback from the advisory panel was used to select and refine the designs to be prototyped and tested. Once defined, the designs were converted to testable formats to include immersion technology and constructed prototypes. Users to participate in the testing process were identified and scheduled for testing sessions. Note that all photographs taken during the testing process can't be disclosed due to HIPPA's privacy policy.

In this phase, designs were tested by users in two different formats: immersion technology (3D projection and virtual reality) and walkthroughs of constructed room prototypes. As tests were conducted, comprehensive notes (based on audio recording) documented participants' feedback. The notes functioned as guides for the team to refine and finalize designs that later became the outlines and recommendations for the mobile application and other dissemination materials.

4.4   Phase Four_ Application

After presenting all final designs to the Advisor Panel and HUD, the team collected feedback for any final alterations in design prior to final documentation.

All project documents including designs for both new home construction and existing home renovation, cost analyses, policy recommendations and strategies for implementation were collected and reviewed prior to the development of mobile application.

In this phase, the app outline was refined and simplified based on the 7 key principles of Universal Design philosophy. The 7 major groups of recommendations

(Clearance, Reach, Strength, Posture, Lighting, Climate Control, and Safety) are now converted into 3 essential categories: Mobility, Visibility, Safety. Tips including Financial Aid, State/Federal Programs, Building Professional, Assistive Products, Videos, and New Technology are provided as part of recommendations. All recommendations will be customized based on the information provided in the House Profile function where resident profile and house location are stored. The refined app structure is presented in a flowchart as shown in Fig. 5.

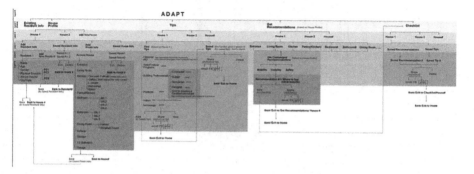

Fig. 5. The refined flowchart of ADAPT mobile application

To ensure that ADAPT app is easy to understand and intuitive to use, all design recommendations are presented in illustrations with great color/value contrast, scalability and color-coding that can be associated with a specific category of recommendations (Figs. 6 and 7).

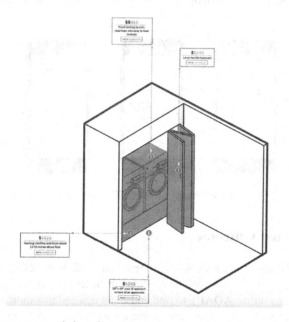

Fig. 6. Mobility recommendations for a laundry room designed for residents in wheelchair

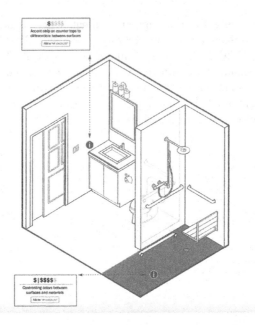

Fig. 7. Visibility recommendations for a bathroom designed for aged residents

The initial GUI concept features function icons comprising both symbol and text and utilizes grid system to ensure all graphic elements are easy to see and absorb. ALL functions on the homepage are hidden but can be easily accessed through the swiping gesture (to the right). A few examples of the ADAPT pages are presented in Fig. 8.

Fig. 8. Examples of ADAPT's page designs

5   The Expected Outcome

Although ADAPT app is still a work in progress and needs to be tested, the team hopes that this app is able to offer a One-Stop-Shop for accessible and affordable housing solutions. Users can utilize ADAPT to find and share tips and recommendations needed for creating an accessible and affordable living environment. What's even better is that people with disabilities or those seeking to age in place in the US can better utilize the resources provided by the government for making their house more affordable, accessible, and enjoyable.

References

1. Kennedy, J., Erb, C.: Prescription noncompliance due to cost among adults with disabilities in the United States. Am. J. Public Health **92**(7), 1120–1124 (2002)
2. The Medicare Current Beneficiary Study. https://mcbs.norc.org
3. Reinhard, S.C., Kassner, E., Houser, A., Mollica, R.: Raising Expectations- A State Scorecard on Long-Term Services and Supports for Older Adults, People with Physical Disabilities, and Family Caregivers (2011)
4. AARP PPI: What is Livable? Community Preferences of Older Adults (2014)
5. Chapter 6 - Housing Challenges: The State of The Nation's Housing 2014 (2014). http://www.jchs.harvard.edu/research-areas/reports/state-nations-housing-2014
6. Imrie, R.: Universalism, universal design and equitable access to the built environment. Disabil. Rehabil. **34**(10), 873–882 (2012). https://doi.org/10.3109/09638288.2011.624250
7. Mace, R.L.: Universal design in housing. Assist. Technol. **10**(1), 21–28 (1998). https://doi.org/10.1080/10400435.1998.10131957

Towards a Multi-modal Transportation Scenario: An Analysis About Elderly Needs

Valentina Volpi[1], Antonio Opromolla[1],
Giovanni Andrea Parente[1,2(✉)], and Carlo Maria Medaglia[1]

[1] Link Campus University, Via del Casale di San Pio V 44, 00165 Rome, Italy
{v.volpi,a.opromolla,g.parente,c.medaglia}@unilink.it
[2] CoRiS Sapienza University of Rome, Via Salaria 113, 00198 Rome, Italy

Abstract. For the elderly the use of public transportation services represents a central need, not only from an economic point of view, especially for the most disadvantages social classes, but also from a social perspective, since it creates social relations. However the elderly have several needs in their travel experience, deriving mainly from their psychophysical problems. In this scenario, to improve the travel experience of the elderly it is necessary to adopt an inclusive design approach, in which the different categories of people are considered as a resource for a more accommodating design.

In this paper, the authors present a research on the design of multi-modal transport services with a focus on the interactions of the elderly with the digital services provided by the transport companies. Starting from the analysis of academic studies in this specific field, the authors present the results of an empirical survey. It has been conducted with the aim to identify the elderly needs, to define the elements that can improve their travel experience and to define those characteristics that allow to create more usable, accessible and sustainable interactive services. From this survey different types of needs emerge. They can be considered as requirements and consequent system features for potential digital services based on the elderly needs.

Keywords: Public transport services · Elderly · Inclusive design approach

1 Introduction

The present study is part of a larger research about the smart city suitability to elderly needs, especially in the use of public transport services.

More specifically, it constitutes the following step of a previous study [1] oriented to examine the design of public transport services fitting different user categories, with a focus on the interactions between elderly and digital services. Starting from that theoric analysis, the authors have conducted an empirical research about elderly needs in public transport by referring to a larger travel experience scenario.

As emerged by the previous study, better services can be implemented by adopting inclusive design approaches. In particular, thanks to the adoption of inclusive design processes, the different categories of people are considered as a resource for a more accommodating design and the designers are encouraged to realize solutions that really

© Springer Nature Switzerland AG 2019
M. Kurosu (Ed.): HCII 2019, LNCS 11568, pp. 118–129, 2019.
https://doi.org/10.1007/978-3-030-22636-7_8

are easy to use for all citizens. In this way, taking into account the user experience of elderly for creating transport services suited for all can bring effective benefits even for the others travellers, as they can experience the same problems as permanent or temporary issues at some point in their life.

Moreover, it is due to consider that there are different physical or digital impediments that can arise during the various phases of the interaction between people and transport services that can cause the social exclusion of the most vulnerable groups in terms of access to the services available within the city. For example, the difficulty in using digital devices, or in hearing and understanding audio infomobility announcement, but also in transporting heavy or bulky objects (such as a suitcase or a stroller), etc. Then, it is important to include the needs of different segments of the population in the design of services, so as to reduce social inequalities in terms of access to those services. Indeed, in this way the whole society can benefit of a more vibrant and varied urban environment made liveable and accessible thanks to effective, efficient and pleasant city services.

Starting from this premise, the empirical study presented into this paper puts a particular focus on the elderly needs in public transportation services, as it appears fundamental in order to assure a better quality of life for the entire city. This becomes especially evident if considering the shift of city transportation services towards a multi-modal and "mobility as a service" (MaaS) scenario [2]. According to the insights derived from the previous theoric study, the issues to consider in designing an adequate travel experience for elderly are the usability and accessibility of digital services, the active involvement of the elderly in the design process, the focus on the whole travel experience (not only on a single step of it) and on the design of solutions that fit different users needs, without stigmatizing or discriminating anyone. Starting from these insights, in this paper the authors present the results of the empirical study about elderly needs in public transport services within a multi-modal transportation scenario. The study has directly involved elderly during the design process, in order to create more usable, accessible and sustainable travel experiences.

In detail, in the first section the authors describe the main factors that influence the elderly use of mobility services, especially of the public transport services. In the second one they identify the elderly needs related to the travel context by gathering them from the academic studies on the topic. In the third section they describe the methodological approach and the main results of the empirical survey. Then, the effects on the design of a multi-modal transportation solution suiting a wide range of travellers, included elderly, are discussed in section four. Finally, in the conclusion the authors state further steps for the creation of inclusive travel services.

2 Elderly Needs in the Use of Transport Services

With ageing, older people change their mobility habits. In fact, the use of public transportation services becomes a fundamental way for participating in social activities and for maintaining relationships, especially for the most disadvantaged social classes [3]. However, elderly make fewer trips than other categories of travellers, as by retiring they have less need to move daily. Moreover, since their needs change, they are led to change their usual means of transport, too.

These aspects are confirmed by the research conducted by ISTAT, i.e. the Italian National Institute of Statistic, in the 65–74 age group [4]. From these data emerge how, with ageing, the people's preferences towards the use of trains and buses increase, even if they use them sporadically during the year. These data also suggest that elderly people do a more occasional use of means of transport, especially of the suburban ones compared to the urban ones. In this sense, elderly people are less familiar with the exploration of unknown places. So, it can be assumed that they need more information for organizing a trip and for effectively moving towards their destinations. In details, the data collected by ISTAT in 2017 showed that the 55.4% of people belonging to the 65–74 age group is satisfied of the trains services and the 51.4% of the buses services. On the other hand, the main factors that cause the dissatisfaction of elderly people are the cleanliness, especially for the trains (only the 38.6% is satisfied) and the lack of comfort during waiting times at stops, especially for buses (only the 45.4% is satisfied). In effect, these two factors can be both connected to the need of elderly for comfort during the travel, that seems to have an important impact on the use of public transport means. In this sense, also the delivery of more and better information can help to make the travel more comfortable, as it permit to the elderly people to better orient them-selves and feel more safe.

As a consequence, by improving this aspect, it will be easier for elderly to reach their destinations and access to different transport services. In the end, this leads to an overall improvement of the whole travel experience.

3   Related Works

Most of the elderly needs derives from their psychophysical problems and the resulting restricted mobility. But there are specific issues that influence their behaviours in the different contexts of their life. In details, the main academic research areas about mobility for the elderly concern essentially two aspects: on the one hand the factors, especially the critical conditions, that influence the behaviour of the elderly, and on the other hand the interactive systems properly suiting the elderly's informative needs. Both these research lines are interested in the role of technology as a means to simplify the elderly experience with the public transport. This is evident especially for the second one. Regarding the first one, the focus is mainly on the categorization of the variables that influence the elderly behaviours. For example, Sungyop e Ulfarsson [5] propose a model consisting of five groups of variables: personal, family, neighborhood, travel, information. With the same purpose, Haustein [6] identifies some subcategories of this age group, proposing a segmentation based on living condition, level of dis-ability, financial resources, and social relationships. In details, from each of these subcategory he derives specific needs that characterize the different target groups. The main aim of these researchers is often to highlight the critical aspects of the public transport system that reduce the user-friendliness of the means and disincentive their use. In this regard, Holley-Moore and Creighton [7] draw the attention to the excessive number of tickets that the elderly must preserve in the multimodal journeys. In effect, also the features of the means of transport often are not suited to the the physical condition of elderly travellers. In this sense, Broome, McKenna, Fleming and Worrall [8] point out how the unsuitability of a bus can penalize elderly people having health problems or disability. In details, they identify three specific variables from which it is possible to find specific disadvantages that combine the decline of people's psychophysical abilities with the inappropriateness of the bus: personal factors that concern the specific traveller, contextual factors that include the aim to be achieved, and the relational factors that put in connection the personal issues with the surrounding environment.

Consistent with all these matters, the second aforementioned research area refer to the informative needs which affect the elderly experience with the public means of transport. Most of the studies in this field consider this specific category of needs in respect of the different stages of a trip. For instance, Farag and Lyon [9] analyze the various information needs related to the planning of the travel. According to their study, the seniors research information especially through a face-to-face interaction. Indeed, the use of connected devices is not so frequent in the trip planning, because most of the elderly is not at ease with the use of technologies. In fact, their most recurring interaction in this sense is requesting assistance through the customer support telephone number. It is also because the direct interaction with a human operator reassured the elderly people, despite the difficulties to correctly listen to the information (since hearing problems) and to memorize it. With reference to the information about the departure times of the means of transport, Farag and Lyon [9] highlight how the consultation of printed timetables can result easier for elderly, even if doubts remain about their accuracy. Such information is especially needed to consent to the elderly to better orienting themselves in unknown urban spaces, where significant cognitive accessibility problems are likely to emerge. In this sense, giving them recurring feedback about the compliance with the planned itinerary can reduce their anxiety while travelling [10].

Technologies located on board or near the bus stop greatly affect the elderly travel experience. Holley-Moore and Creighton [7] underline the importance of having information systems on board. They pay particular attention to the benefits of visual and acoustic information, especially for those who have orientation and sensory problems.

However, in order to be effectively useful, technological devices on board must be designed by putting special attention to meet the elderly travellers' needs, especially if these devices are the only available information source. In this regard, according to the Universal Design approach [11], elements such as volume of the sensors, display dimensions, physical characteristics of the devices, etc. should take into account elderly needs, in order not to cause them troubles. In fact, as stated by Hjorthol [12], the difficulties they could encounter can provoke fear and nervousness moments, produced by the lower perception of control over the context, especially when they are on board. At this regard, Bekiaris, Panou and Mousadakou [13] conducted a study which emphasizes the importance to consider the aspects related to the accessibility of these systems. These authors affirm that in designing digital devices, such as interactive totems or electronic information panels, more and more attention needs to be given to several elements: lighting, weight, physical conformation of the device, interface (color, text character, etc.), sound and tactile feedbacks, voice users interaction, and location.

Also Waara and Stahl [14] conducted an analysis on these aspects, focusing on the informational needs of elderly before the trip. Among them, they report, for example, the need to receive information regarding the cost of the trip, the possibility to choose the seats and to select paths with a few sections on foot.

Finally, the state of the art shows that in the design of technological solutions, elderly needs must be considered both at the software (the usability of the interface) and hardware level (the device shape). Moreover, the provided considerations confirm that taking into consideration the needs of the elderly can also improve the user experience of all users.

4 The Empirical Survey

The aim of our empirical study was to focus on specific elderly needs in public transport services. This paragraph shows the methodological approach we followed and the main outcomes of the conducted study.

4.1 Methodological Approach

The empirical study was carried out through qualitative interviews. This choice is justified by the importance to explore in depth thoughts and needs of the respondents. In particular, we carried out seven interviews to participants with the following characteristics:

- aged over 65;
- having a middle/high school diploma;
- moving on short-medium distances at least once every three months, mainly to take part in specific events;
- having low familiarity with technologies.

One moderator and one observer took part in each interview. The latter consists in five sections:

- an introduction showing the aim of the research;
- shift habits analysis, focusing on motivations and frequence of moving;
- travel related aspects analysis, focusing on the services during the different stages of the travel;
- technologies employed during the different stages;
- identification of the main user needs.

The next paragraph, which summarizes the main outcomes of the empirical survey, will reflects this organization.

4.2   Survey Outcomes

This paragraph will focus on the most important elements emerged from the survey. It should not be considered as an exhaustive content, since specific and particular elements are not completely investigated. Its aim is to give a general overview on behaviours and approaches of elderly in the investigated fields related to the multi-modal transportation scenario. It has to be considered strictly connected to the discussion section, in which indications on how these results influence the design of technical solutions are identified.

Shift Habits

The economic convenience, the calm moving, and the exhaustiveness of information are the most important elements influencing the choice of the transportation means by the elderly.

Generally, elderly move towards known destinations (related to administrative practices or linked to leisure activities), making mainly short or medium-distance trips. They use public means of transportation, with a multi-modal scheme: the motivation is not only related to economic issues, but also to the possibility to carry out other activities during the trip. Individual means represent an alternative marginally taken into consideration, due to the concern for parking the car and for the possible lack of orientation. Moreover, none of the participants use sharing and sustainable means (e.g.: car sharing, bike sharing, bicycle, etc.). Finally, the choice to take a walking path depends on the physical problems of the participants: in the best cases, they also travel half a kilometer (even enjoying the offered view).

The most frequently perceived problems during the trip are not only the ones related to the infrastructure (also connected to their physical condition, e.g.: the lack of comfortable seats), but also those related to the waiting times for public transport. These problems are considered more serious if satisfactory information on the arrival of the vehicles lacking or it is not updated.

During the trip planning, elderly find information through web channels (mainly on the website of the structure they will be visiting, but also on the websites of transport companies or through "cross-cutting" tools such as Google Maps) and paper tools (e.g.: paper maps). In case of long distance journeys, they prefer to rely on specialized agencies. However, during the trip they do not prefer acquire information from digital tools but by having a face to face contact (e.g.: with the crew or other passengers), which represents the main reference for the older passengers.

Travel Habits

In case of touristic journeys, information required by elderly does not refer only to the transportation means, but also to accommodation facilities and the specific points of interest to visit. Generally they are helped by travel agencies, which support them in searching and booking trip and structures and which provide them informative material and tickets. These activities are integrated with an autonomous research activity, which aims at evaluating the booked facilities, by going to the websites of the facilities or using evaluation services provided by other users (even if they do not have a high trust in other people).

Some people are totally autonomous in choosing and booking these services: they rely on the web channels, very often completing the reservation by making a phone call to the structures or by sending them an e-mail.

Before starting the journey, people find information related to the points of interest to be visited. In order to complete this task, they use paper guides, often integrated with information from travel websites and blogs, and pin information on a personal agenda or on a map. Usually the itinerary is not strictly defined, even if they think when and how to visit the various points of interest.

None of the participants shares photos, experiences, evaluations on the carried out trip after its conclusion; they simply save their materials on personal devices.

Use of Digital Technologies
The use of technologies by the elderly depends on the age: the greater the age, the lower their use. Generally, the use of digital technologies is more frequent during the trip planning phase, whereas during the trip the use of personal or non-personal digital technologies is low.

In the trip planning phase, elderly use desktop computers in order to find useful information, combining it with the material provided by travel agencies.

During the trip, elderly use devices available on their path (for example electronic displays and auditory technologies). People who own a mobile device, use it, for example to access mobile applications to orientate in the space, to get information on the points of interest or for entertainment goals.

Considering the payment methods, on the one hand, the older passengers declare to buy tickets only at the physical retailers, on the other hand the less elderly passengers take more various behaviours. In particular in case of short or medium distances, they buy tickets at the physical retailers near the place of departure; on the contrary in case of long distances (and probably of more than one ticket) the action is entrusted to another subject, by asking to a travel agency of a relative who will make the purchase online. So, generally elderly are not familiar with the online payment systems and a general distrust towards these systems emerges.

Finally, at the end of the trip most part of the respondents do not use digital tools, except for photo storage technologies (operation for which, the help of other people is required).

User Needs
During the trip planning, elderly would appreciate information related to the timing of the vehicles (e.g.: delays, arrival times, etc.) and unforeseen events (e.g.: strikes, traffic, works in progress, accidents, etc.) in order to better plan the itinerary and the departure time. For this reason, they would need to receive push notifications, to better deal with the journey (e.g.: a system that signals the stop to go down, the real time crowding of the means of transport, alternative routes, etc.). The older people need to know in advance the routes to be covered on foot, in order to better organize their moving.

The possibility to have a unique ticket which comprises all the means of transport is a central point since it give the elderly a perception of more security and control on the journey experience.

In the move phase, the elderly mainly need services that support their orientation towards the destination and that give the real time and updated information (for example explaining the motivation of possible delays). The face to face contact with the on board staff is a central need of the elderly, so it is important to design services that require people as an important touchpoint for this particular people category.

5 Discussion of Results

On the basis of the survey outcomes, different kind of needs have been identified and converted into possible requirements and consequent system features for potential digital services. In this section some of these features identified as part of a design process addressed to the creation of an adequate travel experience for elderly are presented and discussed. The following is not an exhaustive list of all the possible features of a multi-modal solution for public transport suiting elderly needs. In fact, the ultimate aim of this paper is to highlight how the identified requirements can be integrated in an inclusive technical solution suiting a wide range of travellers, including elderly, for creating a better user experience with public transport in a multi-modal scenario.

In effect, most of the identified features meeting the elderly needs are suited also for other types of travellers, such as frequent-business travellers, occasional travellers, commuters, etc., regardless their age or psychophysical condition. Indeed, according to the previous study conducted by the authors [1], in the design of digital solutions there are some principles that should be considered in order to sustain the inclusiveness of the interactive system. They can be summarized into four kinds of objectives to fulfill in the design of a multi-modal travel solution: (1) Minimization of the effort in the different phases of the travel; (2) Personalization of the travel experience, with the aim of accommodating the different needs of the targets; (3) Implementation of a clear communication that allows travellers to easily understand all the steps of the interaction with the online and offline services delivered in the multi-modal transportation scenario; (4) Creation of a seamless travel experience, extended to multiple transport services and multiple information channels.

So, these general objectives are matched with the specific needs emerged by the empirical survey in order to identify an inclusive solution. In detail, in the following examples the focus is on the features that can be implemented on an interactive system supporting the information retrieval before, during and after the travel.

Minimization of the Effort in the Different Phases of the Travel   •
Before starting a new trip, there are several technical solutions that can minimize the effort required to reach a given destination.

In order to easily obtain the needed information and quickly visualize only the most interesting travel options, the user should be able to memorize (automatically or manually) on the interactive system the most frequent or preferred travel habits, i.e. the stops or routes taken more frequently. As this feature is tailored on the user habits and preferences, it is strictly connected also with the personalization of the travel experience. In general, it is possible to minimize the effort required to the traveller by increasing the amount of useful information in possession of the user in advance to the travel. This permit the user to adapt the itinerary to his or her requirements. For example, especially for elderly people having physical problems related to age, knowing if the itinerary include a long walking or stairs is important in order to find the path accessible with the minimum effort.

More broadly, in any moment, the interactive system can also facilitate the traveller in the retrieval of useful information by suggesting points and services of interest directly or indirectly related to the travel, also on the basis of the context of the trip, that the user can add to his or her itinerary. A close feature concerns the sending of alerts (i.e. notifications and reminders) by the system about the scheduled travel agenda to allowing the traveller to relax and, simultaneously, be ready to act in time when requested, without missing anything about the travel, e.g. the right bus stop.

Lastly, the interactive system should offer as much support as possible during the most critical phases of the travel experience, for example during the purchase of tickets or the localisation of the requested bus stop. Moreover, in order to increase the inclusiveness of the solution, the use of simplified and intuitive interfaces, requiring only very needed information, should be preferred. This and other features addressed to assist the traveller during the journey make possible to avoid too stressful situations. This aspect is especially important when dealing with elderly or fragile people in general, as too risky situations might lead to the exclusion of these categories of travellers.

Personalization of the Travel Experience
In order to accommodate the travel options to the specific needs of the traveller, a technical solution should acquire and return to the user some essential information characterizing him or her experience. It is fundamental for this kind of services that the user can select the different options consistently with the personal wishes and the travel habits.

By integrating the personalization objective with the minimization of the effort, the system should also consider the most used or preferred travel options, i.e. the most used means of transport or bus stops, in order to return personalised itinerary and to visualize only the most interesting information. Generally the user can set specific parameters or filters to research and choose the more appropriate travel conditions. A very important parameter to consider when designing a solution suiting elderly need is the economic one, for example the possible discounts, promotions or economic facilitation applicable to a specific travel.

Other identified features are the possibility to view and combine the different transport modalities according to the user preferences and the possibility to select and reserve specific seats on the different means of transport.

The personalization of the solution can be the result of a set of parameters configured by the user or the consequence of the acquisition of data by the system, e.g. about the most frequent uses of the interactive system by the user. In any case, the user should be able to define the level of personalization of the system and which data he or her wants to share with it.

Implementation of a Clear Communication

In order to avoid disorientation and facilitate the interaction with multiple online and offline services occurring during the travel experience, the traveller should have plenty of information in advance of the travel. For example, given specific spatial and temporal travel options (data/time and place of departure and arrival), the user should know: the itinerary to follow with the scheduled times; the means of transport and their on-board equipment (especially in the case of facilities for people with special needs, such as the presence of ramps or reserved seats or automatic doors); the location of transport hubs and the modality to safely access to the different transport services (e.g. validity of tickets, approved operators, facilities for people with special needs, health care services, safe location of self-service ticket kiosks, etc.); the total amount to be paid for the whole travel on the basis of the different fare types, along with the related payment options: the presence of architectural barriers and the related indications on alternative paths.

Another important requirement is the delivery in advance to the travel of information about permanent or temporary change of course or restrictions to the ordinary circulation of vehicles or service operations. Indeed, especially in the case of elderly or travellers with a limited knowledge of the surrounding context, it is better to avoid unexpected changes of plans. For this reason, the traveller needs also real-time informations, e.g. about the regularity of the service, and updates on his or her scheduled travel agenda.

As mentioned previously, by having a clear picture of the whole travel thanks to the possession of information clearly explaining all the different steps of the services, the user is able to minimize the efforts required during the travel.

Creation of a Seamless Travel Experience

Before, during and after the travel, it can be useful, especially for elderly to have a unique virtual space where to collect all the different elements concerning a specific travel, i.e. transport tickets, service cards, etc. Similarly, the traveller should have the possibility to integrate the useful information coming from his or her other accounts on a single platform.

In order to create a seamless experience, the interactive system should allow the user to find information about the location and the available services of the touchpoint diffused on the territory, such as ticket offices or interactive totems. Regarding this aspect of the user experience, the traveller should be able to interact with the multimodal-transportation services through different channels and devices, depending on the context, Moreover, the system should warn the user about the effective state of each touchpoint (e.g. opening times, presence of front office employees, etc.), in order to avoid to the user a worthless waste of time.

In conjunction with the minimization of the effort in the different phases of the travel, the personalization of the travel experience, and the implementation of a clear communication, this last objective permits to create a travel experience perceived as a whole. Indeed, the traveller can continuously interact with the different elements of the travel, before, during and after, moving from one place to another within a multi-modal transportation scenario as a seamless travel.

6   Conclusion

In this paper, the authors have discussed as the adoption of an inclusive design approach allows the creation of transportation services accessible to all categories of users, included the elderly. Further works aiming at reaching this purpose, should consider the application of research methodologies based on co-design. The latter are already been applied in the mobility field [15], since they allow to better understand needs and perceptions of users, involving them in creating solutions which they can use. In particular, the co-design process requires that designers, professional experts and potential users work together in creating a service which meets real needs and desires, by reducing the gap between designer objectives and user requirements. In fact, this represents an important weakness in the design process, since designers take often for granted some elements if the user point of view is not adequately taken into account.

The central aspect in co-design practice is adopting an iterative approach, by planning spaces and moments of interaction among these different stakeholders, that ensures a permanent user engagement and inclusion, also by continuously adapting the service features to the evolution of needs. This consideration is particularly true if we consider the peculiarity of the elderly, characterized by elements that rapidly evolve over time.

In the future works, the authors propose to apply co-design methodologies with the elderly that use multi-modal means of transportation. In fact, it is important making elderly aware of the potential of the application of this approach in improving their lives. In order to do that it is necessary to provide adequate explanations. A design model like this will increase the engagement and empathy of the elderly in expressing needs and ideas regarding their use of public transport.

References

1. Grimaldi, R., Opromolla, A., Parente, G.A., Sciarretta, E., Volpi, V.: Rethinking public transport services for the elderly through a transgenerational design approach. In: Zhou, J., Salvendy, G. (eds.) ITAP 2016. LNCS, vol. 9755, pp. 395–406. Springer, Cham (2016). https://doi.org/10.1007/978-3-319-39949-2_38
2. Sochor, J., Strömberg, H., Karlsson, I.M.: Implementing mobility as a service: challenges in integrating user, commercial, and societal perspectives. Transp. Res. Rec.: J. Transp. Res. Board **2536**, 1–9 (2015)
3. Mollenkopf, H., Marcellini, F., Ruoppila, I., Flaschenträger, P., Gagliardi, C., Spazzafumo, L.: Outdoor mobility and social relationships of elderly people. Arch. Gerontol. Geriatr. **24** (3), 295–310 (1997)
4. Istituto Nazionale di Statistica (ISTAT). Censimento popolazione istat (2016)
5. Sungyop, K., Ulfarsson, G.: Travel mode choice of the elderly: effects of personal, household, neighborhood, and trip characteristics. Transp. Res. Rec.: J. Transp. Res. Board **1894**, 117–126 (2004)
6. Haustein, S.: Mobility behavior of the elderly: an attitude-based segmentation approach for a heterogeneous target group. Transportation **39**(6), 1079–1103 (2012)

7. Holley-Moore, G., Creighton, H.: The Future of Transport in an Ageing Society. Age UK, London (2015)
8. Broome, K., McKenna, K., Fleming, J., Worrall, L.: Bus use and older people: a literature review applying the person–environment–occupation model in macro practice. Scand. J. Occup. Ther. **16**(1), 3–12 (2009)
9. Farag, S., Lyons, G.: What affects use of pretrip public transport information? Empirical results of a qualitative study. Transp. Res. Rec.: J. Transp. Res. Board **2069**, 85–92 (2008)
10. Fobker, S., Grotz, R.: Everyday mobility of elderly people in different urban settings: the example of the city of Bonn. Germany Urban Stud. **43**(1), 99–118 (2006)
11. Demirbilek, O., Demirkan, H.: Universal product design involving elderly users: a participatory design model. Appl. Ergon. **35**(4), 361–370 (2004)
12. Hjorthol, R.: Transport resources, mobility and unmet transport needs in old age. Ageing Soc. **33**(7), 1190–1211 (2013)
13. Bekiaris, E., Panou, M., Mousadakou, A.: Elderly and disabled travelers needs in infomobility services. In: Stephanidis, C. (ed.) UAHCI 2007. LNCS, vol. 4554, pp. 853–860. Springer, Heidelberg (2007). https://doi.org/10.1007/978-3-540-73279-2_95
14. Waara, N., Stahl, A.: The need of information in public transport: elderly and disabled people's pre-journey travel information requirements. In: 10th International Conference on Mobility and Transport for Elderly and Disabled People, Japan Society of Civil Engineers Transportation Research Board (2004)
15. Gebauer, H., Johnson, M., Enquist, B.: Value co-creation as a determinant of success in public transport services: a study of the Swiss federal railway operator (SBB). Manag. Serv. Qual.: Int. J. **20**(6), 511–530 (2014)

Monetize This? Marketized-Commons Platforms, New Opportunities and Challenges for Collective Action

Denise Wilkins[1]([✉]), Bashar Nuseibeh[2,3], and Mark Levine[1,4]

[1] University of Exeter, Exeter, Devon, UK
d.j.wilkins@exeter.ac.uk
[2] The Open University, Milton Keynes, Bucks, UK
[3] Lero - The Irish Software Research Centre, University of Limerick, Limerick, Ireland
[4] Lancaster University, Lancaster, Lancs, UK

Abstract. In this paper we argue that recent developments in peer-to-peer platforms, including those underpinned by distributed-ledger technology (or blockchains), represent a new model for organizing collective action, which we term the "marketized-commons" model. Drawing on social psychological and economic theory, we compare this concept to established modes of organizing collective action. We also consider the marketized-commons model in relation to other peer-to-peer economies. We consider why individuals might be motivated to create and use platforms underpinned by the marketized-commons model, as well as how it might be counterproductive for cooperation, collaboration, participation and social goals. Finally, we recommend implications for those interested in designing peer-to-peer platforms to support collective action. Ultimately, we argue that to develop effective platforms in this context designers need to look beyond the financial considerations of individual platform users. Rather, they also need a concern for social psychological principles and processes, specifically how groups work and operate in these settings.

Keywords: Collective action · Peer-to-peer · Social identity approach

1 Introduction

Digital technology has enabled greater connections between individuals. The Internet allows individuals to connect to, and cooperate with, known and unknown others. In particular, recent years have seen the rise of peer-to-peer (P2P) platforms, which enable users to interact with one another directly for the production and exchange of goods. For example, 'peer-to-peer markets', such as eBay and Airbnb, enable individuals and small organizations to connect with unknown others to exchange goods and services for money [1]. These platforms empower individuals against established structures, which is often referred to as the disruptive potential of connecting individuals. In contrast 'commons-based peer production' platforms enable volunteers to come together for collective enterprise. Platforms like Wikipedia, Pirate Bay and

M. Kurosu (Ed.): HCII 2019, LNCS 11568, pp. 130–147, 2019.
https://doi.org/10.1007/978-3-030-22636-7_9

NASA's ClickWorkers allow users to cooperate to produce knowledge or goods for others without the need for market pricing to structure their efforts [2]. Here, we are interested in a third variant of P2P platform, which we term 'marketized-commons' platforms. Marketized-commons platforms attempt to incentivize collaborative efforts through market principles. In order to advance ideals that are perceived to be beneficial for society ('the common good'), developers are creating P2P platforms that enable collective action participation to bought and sold between platform users. Here, we define collective action as: "action taken by a group (either directly or on its behalf through an organization) in pursuit of members' perceived shared interests" [3]. So, by collective action participation we mean activities like the production of renewable electricity by those who wish to avert catastrophic climate change. Accordingly, there are P2P platforms that enable users to produce and trade renewable electricity with others [4]. Similarly, Slock.it's hypothetical SweepTheStreets platform enables a group of neighborhood residents who want their streets cleaned to hire other residents from the same neighborhood to clean the streets [5].

We argue that this third type of P2P platform represents a new model for organizing collective action, we call this model the marketized-commons model. What is novel about these platforms is that they involve turning collective action participation into a commodity. Households have traditionally produced renewable electricity as a means of reducing CO_2 to fight against climate change [6–8]. Similarly, communities have traditionally achieved the clean street outcome of SweepTheStreets through voluntary work (e.g., seattlecleanstreet.org). Thus, these new platforms 'marketize' collective action participation; they transform it to a market-based economy. In this way, marketized-commons platforms are enabling individuals to come together to create a market where there previously was none. Consequently, they transform the very notion of collective action by allowing market forces to become a basis for its organization [9]. However, how can we ensure that marketized-commons platforms support collaboration, cooperation and user aims to advance the common good?

In the present paper, our objective is twofold: First we will introduce the marketized-commons model that underpins these platforms, outlining its importance for the HCI community; and second we will describe how social science can help designers create marketized-commons platforms that support users' goals. Beyond technical infrastructure, there may be skepticism about what is new, different or interesting about different types of P2P platform. Rather than simply a novel technical artifact, we argue that marketized-commons platforms are interesting because they create new opportunities for different types of social relations, and enable new motivations for contributing to the common good. In particular, they create a market-based structure for motivating, organizing and enacting collective action participation. We are interested in understanding how these market-based platforms work: how they enable collaboration, coordinate effort, and advance users' goals. We suggest that in order to address these questions we first need to recognize the model of organization that underpins these platforms; we outline this model and use it as a basis to engage with further questions about marketized-commons platforms.

We propose that to fully understand how these platforms work, we need to consider the relationship between the collective and the self, and how design choices affect this relationship. We suggest that the social identity approach is a fruitful framework for this aim. The social identity approach is a social psychological framework grounded in the principle that in certain contexts an individual's subjective sense of self is defined and experienced as something that is 'collective' and identical to a group of other people [10]. This premise stands in contrast to popular conceptions of the self as something that is innately individual and personal. Likewise, it goes further than conventional understandings of a social self that might be public and perceived by others, or have social elements that have been adopted from social groups [10]. Given HCI's focus on the interface between humans and computers, and the increasing attention in HCI on P2P platforms, the marketized-commons model brings together HCI's core interests with a number of social psychological and social structural concerns. In particular, it leads us to reflect on how the HCI community might benefit by a closer consideration of the relationship between the collective and the self.

We begin in Sect. 2 by reviewing existing research that examines collective action and the potential role of technology in supporting participation. In Sect. 3 we move on to explore 'P2P' as a concept, and detail different types of P2P platforms that are already recognized in existing research. In Sect. 4 we identify and introduce a novel concept, which is the 'marketized-commons' model and outline its distinguishing features. We then move on to explore the social psychological and social structural assumptions underlying the marketized-commons model and consider how these present a challenge to platform designers. In Sect. 5 we introduce the social identity approach. Finally in Sect. 6 we consider implications for designers and make design recommendations for marketized-commons platforms.

2   Why Collective Action?

How can we encourage individuals to take action to uphold the common good? Social scientists have frequently grappled with the problem of cooperation. Evidence suggests that it is difficult to get individuals to pursue collective – rather than individual – goals when self-interest and joint-interest do not align [11–13]. Although there are different types of cooperation, here we are particularly concerned with collective action. Given that the benefits obtained by collective action are equally available to all regardless of an individual's contribution (i.e. a public good; such as clean air, women's rights, National Health Service), and that participation in collective action is costly (e.g., time, associated financial costs), individuals can personally benefit by not participating in collective action and instead relying on the contribution of others [14, 15]. Unsurprisingly, a classic question in social science is what makes collective action possible [15–18].

Traditional solutions to the problem of cooperation in collective action include private ownership of the commons resource, community mobilization, and institutions for collective action [17, 18]. However, these solutions are not without fault. For example private owners can restrict access to a resource and thereby prevent it from collapsing, but private ownership isn't applicable to moveable resources (e.g., fish, water, clear air; [18]). Similarly, Community mobilization relies on groups to work together to foster cooperation, but the organization of groups can be time consuming and expensive [16]. While institutions for collective action encourage participation by providing sanctions for unwanted behavior and/or selective incentives for desired actions, but incentive provision is expensive to implement and unreliable incentive provision encourages free-riding [18]. Accordingly, there has been great interest in creating alternative mechanisms to facilitate collective action participation; ICTs represent an alternative set of tools.

Although facilitating collective action is clearly a socially-relevant topic, and a number of papers examine the intersection of collective action and ICTs, it may not be apparent why HCI researchers should be concerned with designing to support collective action participation. Societies have invariably relied on tools to support participation in collective action. Traditional devices, such as institutions for collective action and private ownership, have historically been used for organizing, motivating and coordinating collective action to achieve a shared goal [7]. Thus, collective action participation encompasses challenges that are central to HCI, like facilitating collaboration and coordinating action. Moreover, when tools for supporting collective action participation are embodied in technology, the design of this technology is fundamental for its efficacy [19].

Accordingly, research in HCI and CSCW has considered how digital technology can support collective action. Existing work has examined the role of technology in facilitating collective action, as well as implications for technology design [20–24]. Scholars have typically been concerned with the ways that technology can reduce the costs associated with organizing and participating in collective action. For example, many social media platforms enable users to share photos about key issues and events, which can enforce transparency and thereby establish the legitimacy of involved actors and organizations [25]. Similarly, the increased availability of one-to-many communication afforded by email, SMS and social media can lower the costs of organizing action as it can freely promote campaigns to global audiences and be utilized to create bottom-up definitions of movement issues [24, 26, 27].

In addition to examining existing platforms, developers have created new systems to support collective action. Dynamo was created to help crowd workers pitch ideas for action, which are voted on by others, with action taken upon winning ideas [22]. WeDo was designed to support end-to-end collective action by enabling the creation of high-level missions, it allows users to create ideas for missions and vote on how to achieve them [28]. Similarly, Catalyst utilizes activation thresholds to coordinate collective action events [29]. Taken together, this research indicates that digital technology can create new opportunities for communication and action that can be employed to facilitate collective action participation. It also emphasizes the role of the HCI community in designing and critically evaluating platforms for collective action.

Nevertheless, although a large body of research examines computer-supported collective action, and many different tools are designed to facilitate cooperation, less HCI research has critically examined or made explicit the models of organization that underpin such platforms. In particular, research is yet to consider how different models of organizing collective action – when instantiated in technology – can shape users' motives for participating in collective action and thereby influence key processes; such as coordinating effort, enabling collaboration, shared sense-making and participation, as well as the actualization of users' aims to advance the common good. Here we define and examine a new model for organizing collective action that is emerging in technology development: the marketized-commons model. This model suggests that by treating collective action participation as a commodity, and trading it through P2P platforms, we can create better motivation for participating in collective action. This model represents a marked distinction from those underpinning the types of collective action technologies previously examined in HCI. However, while these platforms present many new and exciting opportunities, they also introduce novel challenges that we will proceed to outline. This creates an opportunity for the HCI community take an engaged role in shaping the success of marketized-commons platforms, we describe how attending to users' collective and group-level motivations can provide direction for such endeavors.

An examination of marketized-commons platforms – and the organizing model that forms a basis for participation in these platforms – could also shed light on central concerns in HCI and CSCW such as awareness, cooperative sense-making, coordination and motivation. Although HCI has a longstanding record of engaging with psychology, less work has built upon social psychological research that examines group processes and the relationship between the collective and the self. Here we draw on the social identity approach, a social psychological framework that seeks to explain how group memberships shape cognitions and behavior. Before providing a more detailed outline of the social identity approach, we introduce the marketized-commons model and existing research that examines P2P platforms for collaboration and exchange.

3   Crowdsourcing and Peer-to-Peer Platforms

Societal shifts and advances in digital technology have seen the rise of crowdsourcing and P2P platforms. Enabled by digital technology, these ways of interacting are concerned with facilitating cooperation among individuals and groups. 'P2P' does not refer to a specific technology nor initiative, and there is debate around its precise definition. However, it typically describes a series of ideas and tools that allow decentralized distributed computing and direct transfer of data between individuals, without a centralized infrastructure [30, 31]. Likewise, rather than a specific set of technologies, crowdsourcing describes a paradigm that outsources jobs, which are normally performed by individuals, to an unspecific group of others [32, 33]. Researchers working in HCI and CSCW have examined crowdsourcing and P2P platforms in a number of distinct settings and have typically asked how design can motivate and sustain participation and collaboration [19, 33, 34].

Although a variety of different P2P and crowdsourcing platforms have been designed, one way to explore the similarities and differences in these platforms is by considering their social aims and outcomes. In particular, researchers examining the intersection of ICTs and society have identified P2P markets and commons-based peer production as two distinct types of P2P platform that are concerned with actualizing different types of good. P2P markets enable individuals to exchange goods and services for money. Exemplified by platforms such as eBay, Uber and Airbnb, they help buyers and sellers find each other and engage in trustworthy transactions [1]. Thus, P2P markets are primarily concerned with 'private goods', which are benefits that can be withheld from an individual, and use of the good prevents its use by others (e.g., food, clothing, most purchasable goods; [3]). In contrast, commons-based peer production aims to facilitate the production of public goods. As a specific instance of crowd-sourcing, commons-based peer production allows individuals to collaborate through collective action to produce a public good without the need for market pricing or managing hierarchy to coordinate individuals' efforts; examples of platforms include Wikipedia, Pirate Bay and ClickWorkers [2]. In sum, whereas P2P markets exist to facilitate cooperation in financial transactions and market exchange, commons-based peer production is intended to organise collaboration among volunteers for the pro-duction of freely available goods [1, 2].

Nevertheless, while P2P markets and commons-based peer production exist as distinct modes for facilitating cooperation, we suggest that there is a new and emerging trend for hybrid marketized-commons platforms. These are decentralized networks, which operate on a P2P basis, for the production and trade of collective action par-ticipation. Marketized-commons platforms represent a new way to support cooperation in collective action. Specifically, subject to the laws of supply and demand, individuals operating within a decentralized network can buy and sell collective action participa-tion. Thus, the marketized-commons model suggests that by marketizing collective action participation we can better motivate individuals to participate in collective action. It implies that financial incentives, paid by users, can facilitate collaboration and encourage others to contribute to the common good. In the following section we outline the marketized-commons model describing both social and technical factors, we give examples of real-world and hypothetical platforms, and discuss the opportunities and challenges associated with this model.

4   The Marketized-Commons Model

Marketized-commons platforms enable groups of individuals to collaborate to produce a good, and other users to pay for these collaboration efforts. However, what is interesting about these platforms is that rather than producing and trading goods that society has traditionally recognized as commodities, they are concerned with the production of public goods. Moreover, in contrast to commons-based peer production, which relies on volunteers, marketized-commons platforms involve turning collective action participation into a commodity. Specifically, they are underpinned by an implicit model that assumes: (1) individuals are able to incentivize others financially to engage in collective action; and (2) by treating collective action participation as a commodity it is possible to advance the production of public goods. Thus, they are an attempt to marketize collective action participation as a way to motivate users to engage in col-lective action and thereby produce public goods.

Several real and hypothetical examples of marketized-commons platforms exist. P2P energy trading projects are some of the most frequent real-world instances [35–37]. As already outlined, within P2P energy platforms users are involved as both producers/sellers of renewable electricity (e.g., through solar panels installed on their houses) and as buyers through purchasing renewable electricity credits from other users [38]. SweepTheStreets is a further example, and one that we have already mentioned. It is a hypothetical network of neighborhood residents who want their streets cleaned and can hire other residents of the neighborhood to clean the streets [5]. Within an activism context, Demoscoin and ACT are under development [39, 40]. Demoscoin is designed to be paid to the early participants of social movements, funded by those who are sympathetic to the cause. Similarly, the ACT platform enables activists to submit funding proposals that aim to advance the common good, in turn other users are able to buy ACT tokens and vote to decide which proposals receive funding. Although these platforms have different aims and exist in different contexts, each involves a transformation of the very notion of collective action as platform developers expect users to incentivize the participation of others financially. Moreover, blockchain technology underpins each platform.

Blockchains are an emerging technology that platform developers have recently applied to a collective action context. Publicized as a technology that has the potential to change the way that businesses are conducted and regulated, a blockchain is a distributed database that collects transaction records into groups (blocks) and stores them with reference to the previous block [38]. There are certain characteristics of blockchains that enable new opportunities for collective action in particular. For example, a 'smart contract' is: "a piece of code (running inside a blockchain platform) that represents and enforces the protocol and any terms of a contract agreed upon by the contractual parties" [38]. They enable low-level housekeeping tasks (e.g., keeping records, providing information, contacting members, allocating resources) and governance rules (e.g., who should receive rewards and when) to be formalized, automated and enforced through software [41], which reduces the resources needed to for organizing collective action [9]. Nevertheless, marketized-commons platforms also present new challenges. In the following subsection, we begin by considering why developers may be interested in the marketized-commons as a model for organizing collective action. We then move on to consider specific challenges that the model presents to a collective action context with a particular focus on questioning the social psychological and structural assumptions that underpin the model.

4.1   Challenges

There may be several reasons why platform developers, policy makers and industry perceive marketized-commons platforms to be beneficial. Particularly because they provide new economic and business models. Global recession and increased economic austerity in the United States and Europe means that many governments have less money for public spending [42]. This means that there are limited subsidies to offset the financial costs of the production of public goods [43–45]. There is also an associated upsurge of neoliberal ideation, including privatization and increased individual responsibility for welfare, which calls for reduced state intervention in social and economic affairs [46–48]. Thus, the desire for a marketized-commons structure may represent a changing social norm; specifically, society expects individuals to take responsibility for their own individual welfare, rather than relying on governments and taxpayer-funded schemes for producing public goods. Nevertheless, although marketized-commons platforms have the potential to be beneficial on a number of levels, existing literature indicates that the model that underpins these platforms may suboptimal in the long-term. In particular, social psychological and structural conditions may create an environment that constrains cooperation and equality goals.

Motivation. There are a number of psychological assumptions implicit within the marketized-commons model. Firstly, it implies that cost-benefit calculations are the primary consideration in collective action decisions – that individuals are intuitive economists and will only participate in collective action when participation provides distinct and tangible benefits for the self. Although this assumption is consistent with early economic models of collective action [15], recent social psychological literature indicates that the proposed prominence of cost-benefit calculations in an oversimplification. Importantly, it suggests that other motives, which are independent to economic considerations, are at least equally involved in the mobilization process [49]. Research indicates that there are a variety of intrinsic psychological motivations that can stimulate contribution to the common good. For example, feelings of injustice, identification with the group and the belief that one's efforts can make a difference are fundamental motivators of collective action participation [50]. However, the marketized-commons model deemphasizes these intrinsic pathways. Moreover, there is evidence to suggest that compared to other motives financial incentives are generally poor drivers of collective action participation [51]. Thus, a focus on financial incentives at the expense of intrinsic drivers of participation could make marketized-commons platforms suboptimal for stimulating participation.

Sustaining Participation. However, going further than this, there is also evidence to indicate that the use of financial incentives to facilitate collective action can be counterproductive to user aims in the long-term. First of all, financial incentives for collective action participation can change how individuals perceive collective action and erode other motives for participation, which can have unintended effects on collective action [52–57]. For example, a focus on financial incentives can attract participants who don't feel committed to the cause, have reduced willingness to give their time and are less inclined to engage in activities organized by the group [51]. Similarly, if the incentive is reduced or removed it can be difficult to sustain behavior [58]. Not only this, but there is evidence to demonstrate the negative effects of financial incentives on collective action can spill-over to other domains and undermine engagement in other prosocial actions that are not financially attractive [58]. Consequently, a marketized-commons platform that relies on financial incentives may be detrimental for sustained participation by eroding intrinsic psychological motivations for engagement.

Collaboration. Moving on from the question of whether financial incentives – in and of themselves – can adequately motivate participation, the P2P incentive model also provides its own unique challenges. Given that the marketized-commons model expects users to incentivize the participation of others, there may be a tension between self-interest and acting in the benefit of the group, which may be detrimental for cooperation and collaboration [18]. Specifically, buyers who use the platform may be primarily motivated to pay the lowest price, while sellers want to achieve the highest price. Thus, it may become difficult to achieve a satisfactory financial arrangement for both parties and the financial incentive for collaboration may be weak. Although this issue is not unique to a marketized-commons and could happen in any market, within a public goods context it could present novel consequences in that individuals are not sufficiently motivated to contribute to a public good and the good is not created.

Moreover, when considering the broader concept of the common good, there may be circumstances where a component of the common good involves wide-ranging support, in other words cooperation with those who are not users of the platform. As in the case of P2P renewable electricity networks, where the price paid for electricity not only needs to incentivize individuals to produce renewable electricity, but it also needs to encompass national public goods, such as maintenance of the national electric grid, social obligations to those who are in fuel poverty, and future renewable electricity production [59]. If users are primarily looking to trade collective action participation at a price that benefits themselves these public goods could be eroded, as fewer resources are available for their production [60]. In sum, the tension between individual welfare and collective welfare may come to the forefront in a platform that relies on market pricing to create the conditions necessary for users to incentivize others to collaborate.

Justice. Although we outlined several psychological assumptions implicit within the marketized-commons model, we also need to consider structural and societal-level conditions. Specifically the way that design choices might influence for poverty, access and social exclusion. To begin with, it is relevant to consider how power inequalities operate in these markets and how a marketized-commons model can contribute to the meaningful distribution of important goods [61]. Take for example the production of renewable electricity, there are a number of structural barriers to renewable energy production. Buying renewable generation equipment involves substantial financial costs. Moreover, due to housing restrictions, it is unlikely that property owners will permit individuals in private rented, social housing or temporary accommodation to install – and/or receive the benefits of – renewable generation equipment. On the other side of the coin, in Slock.it's description of SweepTheStreets, finically advantaged users might opt to 'buy out' of community responsibilities. Specifically, they might choose to pay others so that they do not have to do the work that the community needs to produce the public good. Thus, marketized-commons platforms have the potential to reproduce existing inequalities in power, tangible resources and status.

The second consideration is whether participation and decision making in a blockchain-enabled marketized-commons can ever be truly inclusive. A large body of literature has documented and examined a digital divide across a variety of contexts, which is social and economic inequality in the access, use and impact of digital technology [62]. Although research is yet to examine whether a digital divide exists in regards to blockchain technology, existing literature provides evidence for disparities based on age, income, education, and geographic location for various other technologies [63–65]. A blockchain-enabled platform might exclude older people, people on low incomes or people with fewer years of formal education if platform developers to not design communications, training and the platforms themselves to be inclusive across demographic categories. Moreover, the algorithm mechanism that enables distributed consensus presents novel challenges for inclusion. Specifically because consensus in blockchains rely on the use of full nodes [66]. As there is substantial financial cost and technological expertise required to become a node there are likely to be systematic disparities in decision-making power. Only certain types of people will be able to afford – and understand how – to become a node. Thus, there is a risk that marketized-commons platforms reproduce structural inequalities in decision-making power.

In sum, in addition to the psychological assumptions underpinning a marketized-commons model, there are a number of assumptions about who can access technology and attention, which platform developers need to consider. This is important because of the public goods context in general, but also because of the specific social issues contexts (e.g., climate change, activism) where platform developers are applying the marketized-commons model. Although these present key challenges to developers of marketized-commons platforms, we argue that designers can build better platforms by attending to the social psychological concerns of platforms users; in particular the relationship between the self and the collective. Social psychological research has long recognized the importance of intrinsic motives and subjective appraisals in motivating collective action participation. In particular, research within the social identity approach has found that group identities and group processes are integral to cooperation, collaboration, and participation, and that groups can be harnessed as a resource to motivate collective contribution to the common good [67, 68]. Thus, knowing why groups are important and how they operate, as well as understanding the contexts in which individuals experience a sense of collective self, can help developers design platforms that are more effective for advancing HCI and CSCW's core concerns, as well as addressing key social issues. In the follow sections we outline how the social identity approach can provide an effective framework for these aims.

5 The Social Identity Approach

The social identity approach is a social psychological framework that incorporates social identity theory [69, 70] and self-categorization theory [71]. It suggests that people's motivations, cognitions and behavior can be understood by examining group memberships and recognizing the existence of a collective self. The framework understands the self as existing on a continuum from personal (I) to social (we). It suggests that in addition to personal identity, individuals also have a range of social identities available to them that are collective in nature and drawn from their membership of social and psychological groups [72, 73]. These different levels of the self are functionally antagonistic, so as social identity becomes more salient personal identity decreases in salience [74].

The social identity approach argues that the content of social identities – their norms and values – will direct behavior [75, 76]. So, when a social identity is salient an individual will act in accordance with its content. Importantly, the social context is said to play a fundamental role in determining the salience of a social identity, and as a consequence behavior: social identity becomes salient when an individual categorizes themself with similar others in an intergroup context [10, 71]. Moreover, the social identity approach argues that social behavior also exists on a continuum: interpersonal behavior will occur when a personal identity is salient, whereas social identity makes intergroup behavior possible [73].

Applied to the present context, it is social identities that make group cooperation, group collaboration and collective action possible. A large amount of social psychological literature has examined how group-level processes – including social identification, social identity salience, norms, affect and efficacy – are integral to promoting cooperation through collective action [49, 50, 77–82]. Moreover, a growing body of research indicates that designers can encourage collaboration and collective action participation by implementing social identity principles into platform design. The social identity approach has begun to examine how digital technology affects cooperation and participation within groups. Findings indicate that different platforms offer different identity signals and opportunities for action that affect collective action participation [83]. Here we are particularly interested in three distinct ways that ICTs affect collective action.

Firstly, group-level communication and interaction have been found to play a fundamental role in computer-supported collective action. Specifically, opportunities for interaction can contribute to the building of shared social identity, group identification and norms for action [81, 84, 85]. For example, when users are able to interact via social media and express their group identities this increases their identification with their group and in turn promotes cooperation [86]. Second, research indicates that digital platforms can contain cues to identity that enhance (or diminish) the salience of group identities, which has implications for social influence, attraction, group cohesiveness and participation [87–89]. For example, Chan [90] found that the visual anonymity provided by email can promote donations to a collective cause by increasing the salience of group norms and reducing perceptions of differences within the group. In contrast, there are also affordances for action that can inhibit important outcomes, such as sustained participation. For example, when platforms enable users to participate in low-threshold and low-impact collective action, users have reduced willingness to participate further due to the feeling of having already made a satisfactory contribution to the group [91]. However, notwithstanding the negative effect on sustained participation, this finding also indicates more general principles: (1) users are concerned about and value group-level rewards for participation; and (2) digital platforms can offer opportunities for action that achieve those rewards. Taken together, these findings indicate that designers of marketized-commons platforms can facilitate cooperation, collaboration and participation by embracing social psychological principles and processes, and implementing them into the design of their platforms. We will draw on this research in Sect. 6 to make specific recommendations for designers.

6   Implications for Designers

How can we design to support cooperation, collaboration, participation and contribution to the common good? One way of exploring this question is to consider how individuals need to be able to interact with each other in order to experience a sense of collective self. We have argued that marketized-commons platforms bring new complexity to the ways in which individuals interact with each other and as a result motivation, sustained participation and collaboration. In contrast to traditional tools that were designed to support cooperation and relied on intrinsic motivations or third-parties (i.e. social movement organizations, private companies, institutions for collective action), the marketized-commons model assumes that a P2P market can provide sufficient motivation. Furthermore, we have suggested this model risks ignoring alternative pathways to cooperation and consequently may have the potential to undermine boarder goals; existing research indicates that a focus on financial incentives can erode intrinsic motives for collaboration and participation, even in other domains of engagement.

Taken together this suggests that platform designers should not solely rely on financial incentives to stimulate participation within marketized-commons platforms. Instead our analysis indicates that that developers can support user aims by attending to users' social psychological concerns. Moreover, research within the social identity approach implies that developers need to establish how users' social identities can be nurtured, supported and receive appropriate value within their platforms. Thus, we suggest that important outcomes can be obtained by supporting group-level communication, representations and rewards. This suggestion extends existing recommendations in CSCW, which tend to center around interpersonal relations and individual-level concerns. Building on the social identity approach and existing CSCW research, we suggest three recommendations that designers can employ when creating P2P platforms for collective action participation.

First, *support varying levels of contact and exchange between platform users*. Existing HCI research indicates that users have a variety of motives for participating in P2P platforms. In accordance with the marketized-commons model, instrumental motives have been identified as a key concern. Specifically, users want to receive goods and payment at an increased level of personal convenience. However, these papers also demonstrates that users also have social motives for engaging with these platforms [92–96]. Accordingly, there are many design recommendations for balancing users' instrumental and social goals, however these recommendations generally center on building interpersonal relationships [95, 97]. In contrast, the social identity approach implies that developers should also create opportunities that enable users to develop psychological connections to their group and group-based norms for cooperation. As already outlined in Sect. 5, opportunities for group-level communication and interaction can play a key role in this respect [81, 84–86]. An example of this might be 'group-level exchange', in which marketized-commons platforms offer users the possibility to engage as members of relevant social identities. For example, in the case of a 'local community identity' for users of a renewable energy trading platform. Users would have the opportunity to first form, and then interact within, a local community group. These interactions would be based around shared local community identity with other group members. The products of interaction (e.g., group-based norms, community identification, community pride, social cohesion) are designed to improve the welfare of this imagined community as a whole.

Similarly, we advocate a social identity approach to how information is presented to the user. Developers of marketized-commons platforms should *consider how social identity-enhancing features can be incorporated into the platform interface*. Existing HCI research highlights that how information is presented within P2P platforms is fundamental for promoting cooperation. In particular, representations of users that provide a sense of being with another ('social presence') facilitates trust, perceived reciprocity and sharing behavior [98]. Accordingly, recommendations for practice tend to focus on creating opportunities that allow users to present information about their personal identities. At the same time, there is also the acknowledgement that providing this type of information can accentuate users' privacy concerns [97–99]. Research within the social identity tradition implies that opportunities to provide 'depersonalized' information could represent an alternative solution. Specifically, it indicates that opportunities to highlight characteristics that are prototypical of the group and present oneself as a homogenous group member will promote cooperation between users and collaboration for the common good [83]. Designers need to evaluate whether opportunities to display social identity-enhancing representations and markers can be built into P2P platforms. To incorporate 'group-level features' marketized-commons platforms could allow our exchange group could co-produce and display shared and depersonalized values. In the renewable energy context shared values for a local community identity might center on local and cooperative-owned wind turbines, or the local farmers market as a model of local sustainability and control.

Finally, we suggest that developers of marketized-commons platforms should *incorporate social identity values as part of the platform's reward system.* Specifically they should provide opportunities for rewards at a collective-level as a means to motivate collective action participation. Although there are existing recommendations to provide opportunities for social and financial rewards in P2P platforms [100, 101], these recommendations tend to prioritize benefits for individuals rather than benefits for the group. As outlined in Sect. 5, group-level benefits can provide an important motivation for engaging in computer-supported collective action [91]. These 'group-level products' could be financial or psychological in nature. For example, our local community group could be given the opportunity to divert profit into products that have collective benefit, like a community swimming pool (that is run using renewable technology). Similarly, psychological benefit might be increased group reputation in the eyes of other community groups that are based in other locations.

7 Conclusion

The marketized-commons model gives researchers and developers a new way to think about organizing and motivating CSCW. In particular, it invites us to reconceptualize our notion of collective action and to explore new possibilities for supporting cooperation and collaboration for the common good. At the same time, social psychological research provides a way to guide the development of marketized-commons platforms. It suggests that by attending to users' social identities – and providing opportunities to value, nurture and build these identities – we can support users in obtaining their collective goals. After all, motivation for collective action participation doesn't have to be financial it can be psychological, and psychological motivations can operate on the group-level as well as the individual-level. HCI researchers and designers need to explore ways that digital technology can be used to support and harness these group-based motivations for the common good.

Acknowledgements. Supported, in part, by Science Foundation Ireland grant 13/RC/2094, and Engineering and Physical Sciences Research Council grant EP/P031838/1.

References

1. Einav, L., Farronato, C., Levin, J.: Peer-to-peer markets. Ann. Rev. Econ. **8**, 615–635 (2016)
2. Benkler, Y., Nissenbaum, H.: Commons-based peer production and virtue. J. Polit. Philos. **14**, 394–419 (2006)
3. Scott, J., Marshall, G. (eds.): A Dictionary of Sociology. Oxford University Press, Oxford, New York (2005)
4. Morstyn, T., Farrell, N., Darby, S.J., McCulloch, M.D.: Using peer-to-peer energy-trading platforms to incentivize prosumers to form federated power plants. Nat. Energy **3**, 94–101 (2018)
5. Tual, S.: On DAO Contractors and Curators. https://blog.slock.it/on-contractors-and-curators-2fb9238b2553#.dyd2r1zeb
6. Caird, S., Roy, R., Herring, H.: Improving the energy performance of UK households: results from surveys of consumer adoption and use of low- and zero-carbon technologies. Energ. Effi. **1**, 149 (2008)
7. Ostrom, E.: Polycentric systems for coping with collective action and global environmental change. Glob. Environ. Change **20**, 550–557 (2010)
8. Palm, J., Tengvard, M.: Motives for and barriers to household adoption of small-scale production of electricity: examples from Sweden. Sustain.: Sci. Pract. Policy **7**, 6–15 (2011)
9. Greenfield, A.: Radical Technologies: The Design of Everyday Life. Verso, London, New York (2018)
10. Turner, J.C., Oakes, P.J., Haslam, S.A., McGarty, C.: Self and collective: cognition and social context. Pers. Soc. Psychol. Bull. **20**, 454–463 (1994)
11. Rapoport, A.: Prisoner's Dilemma—recollections and observations. In: Rapoport, A. (ed.) Game Theory as a Theory of a Conflict Resolution, pp. 17–34. Springer, Netherlands, Dordrecht (1974). https://doi.org/10.1007/978-94-010-2161-6_2
12. Rapoport, A.: Prisoner's Dilemma. In: Eatwell, J., Milgate, M., Newman, P. (eds.) Game Theory, pp. 199–204. Palgrave Macmillan, London (1989)
13. Rapoport, A., Chammah, A.M., Orwant, C.J.: Prisoner's Dilemma: A Study in Conflict and Cooperation. University of Michigan Press (1965)
14. Oliver, P.E., Marwell, G.: The paradox of group size in collective action: a theory of the critical mass. II. Am. Sociol. Rev. **53**, 1 (1988)
15. Olson, M.: The Logic of Collective Action: Public Goods and the Theory of Groups. Harvard University Press, Cambridge (1971)
16. McCarthy, J.D., Zald, M.N.: Resource mobilization and social movements: a partial theory. Am. J. Sociol. **82**, 1212–1241 (1977)
17. North, D.C.: Institutions, Institutional Change, and Economic Performance. Cambridge University Press, Cambridge, New York (1990)
18. Ostrom, E.: Governing the Commons: The Evolution of Institutions for Collective Action. Cambridge University Press, Cambridge, New York (1990)
19. Lampinen, A., Brown, B.: Market design for HCI: successes and failures of peer-to-peer exchange platforms. In: Proceedings of the 2017 CHI Conference on Human Factors in Computing Systems, pp. 4331–4343. ACM, New York (2017)

20. Li, H., Dombrowski, L., Brady, E.: Working toward empowering a community: how immigrant-focused nonprofit organizations use twitter during political conflicts. In: Proceedings of the 2018 ACM Conference on Supporting Groupwork - GROUP 2018, pp. 335–346. ACM Press, Sanibel Island (2018)

21. Ruiz-Correa, S., et al.: SenseCityVity: mobile crowdsourcing, urban awareness, and collective action in Mexico. IEEE Pervasive Comput. **16**, 44–53 (2017)

22. Salehi, N., et al.: We are dynamo: overcoming stalling and friction in collective action for crowd workers. In: Proceedings of the 33rd Annual ACM Conference on Human Factors in Computing Systems - CHI 2015, pp. 1621–1630. ACM Press, Seoul (2015)

23. Starbird, K., Palen, L.: "Voluntweeters": self-organizing by digital volunteers in times of crisis. In: Proceedings of the 2011 Annual Conference on Human Factors in Computing Systems - CHI 2011, p. 1071. ACM Press, Vancouver (2011)

24. Wulf, V., et al.: Fighting against the wall: social media use by political activists in a Palestinian village. In: Proceedings of the SIGCHI Conference on Human Factors in Computing Systems - CHI 2013, p. 1979. ACM Press, Paris (2013)

25. Zheng, Y., Yu, A.: Affordances of social media in collective action: the case of Free Lunch for Children in China: affordances of social media in collective action. Inf. Syst. J. **26**, 289–313 (2016)

26. Dimond, J.P., Dye, M., Larose, D., Bruckman, A.S.: Hollaback!: the role of storytelling online in a social movement organization. In: Proceedings of the 2013 Conference on Computer Supported Cooperative Work - CSCW 2013, p. 477. ACM Press, San Antonio (2013)

27. Hou, Y., Lampe, C.: Social media effectiveness for public engagement: example of small nonprofits. In: Proceedings of the 33rd Annual ACM Conference on Human Factors in Computing Systems - CHI 2015, pp. 3107–3116. ACM Press, Seoul (2015)

28. Zhang, H., et al.: WeDo: end-to-end computer supported collective action, p. 4 (2016)

29. Cheng, J., Bernstein, M.: Catalyst: triggering collective action with thresholds. In: Proceedings of the 17th ACM Conference on Computer Supported Cooperative Work & Social Computing - CSCW 2014, pp. 1211–1221. ACM Press, Baltimore (2014)

30. Mauthe, A., Hutchison, D.: Peer-to-peer computing: systems, concepts and characteristics. PIK - Praxis der Informationsverarbeitung und Kommunikation **26**, 60–64 (2003)

31. Saroiu, S., Gummadi, P.K., Gribble, S.D.: Measurement study of peer-to-peer file sharing systems. Presented at the Electronic Imaging 2002, San Jose, CA, 10 December 2001

32. Howe, J.: Crowdsourcing: Why the Power of the Crowd Is Driving the Future of Business. Crown Business, New York (2009)

33. Pan, Y., Blevis, E.: A survey of crowdsourcing as a means of collaboration and the implications of crowdsourcing for interaction design. In: 2011 International Conference on Collaboration Technologies and Systems (CTS), pp. 397–403 (2011)

34. Massung, E., Coyle, D., Cater, K.F., Jay, M., Preist, C.: Using crowdsourcing to support pro-environmental community activism. In: Proceedings of the SIGCHI Conference on Human Factors in Computing Systems, pp. 371–380. ACM, New York (2013)

35. Brooklyn Microgrid. https://www.brooklyn.energy

36. Electron | Blockchain Systems for The Energy Sector. http://www.electron.org.uk/

37. SunContract Team: SunContract. https://suncontract.org/

38. Chitchyan, R., Murkin, J.: Review of Blockchain Technology and its Expectations: Case of the Energy Sector. arXiv:1803.03567 [cs] (2018)

39. Brown, F.: DAOACT testnet launch (2018). https://medium.com/daoact/daoact-testnet-launch-a1e871a25f4a

40. White, M.: Demoscoin. https://www.micahmwhite.com/new-tactics/demoscoin

41. Jentzsch, C.: Decentralized autonomous organization to automate governance (2016). https://download.slock.it/public/DAO/WhitePaper.pdf

42. Kitson, M., Martin, R., Tyler, P.: The geographies of austerity. Camb. J. Regions Econ. Soc. **4**, 289–302 (2011)
43. Ifanti, A.A., Argyriou, A.A., Kalofonou, F.H., Kalofonos, H.P.: Financial crisis and austerity measures in Greece: their impact on health promotion policies and public health care. Health Policy **113**, 8–12 (2013)
44. Karanikolos, M., et al.: Financial crisis, austerity, and health in Europe. Lancet **381**, 1323–1331 (2013)
45. Ridge, T.: 'We are all in this together'? The hidden costs of poverty, recession and austerity policies on Britain's poorest children. Child. Soc. **27**, 406–417 (2013)
46. Aalbers, M.B.: Neoliberalism is dead ... long live neoliberalism! Int. J. Urban Reg. Res. **37**, 1083–1090 (2013)
47. England, G.I., Meegana, R., Kennettb, P., Jonesa, G., Croftb, J.: Global economic crisis, austerity and neoliberal urban (2013)
48. Power, A.: Personalisation and austerity in the crosshairs: government perspectives on the remaking of adult social care. J. Soc. Policy **43**, 829–846 (2014)
49. van Zomeren, M., Leach, C.W., Spears, R.: Protesters as "passionate economists": a dynamic dual pathway model of approach coping with collective disadvantage. Pers. Soc. Psychol. Rev. **16**, 180–199 (2012)
50. van Zomeren, M., Postmes, T., Spears, R.: Toward an integrative social identity model of collective action: a quantitative research synthesis of three socio-psychological perspectives. Psychol. Bull. **134**, 504–535 (2008)
51. Knoke, D.: Incentives in collective action organizations. Am. Sociol. Rev. **53**, 311–329 (1988)
52. Ariely, D., Bracha, A., Meier, S.: Doing good or doing well? Image motivation and monetary incentives in behaving prosocially. Am. Econ. Rev. **99**, 544–555 (2009)
53. Frey, B.S.: Not Just for the Money: An Economic Theory of Personal Motivation. Edward Elgar Pub., Cheltenham, Brookfield (1997)
54. Frey, B.S., Oberholzer-Gee, F.: The cost of price incentives: an empirical analysis of motivation crowding-out. Am. Econ. Rev. **87**, 746–755 (1997)
55. Gneezy, U., Meier, S., Rey-Biel, P.: When and why incentives (don't) work to modify behavior. J. Econ. Perspect. **25**, 191–210 (2011)
56. Meier, S.: Do subsidies increase charitable giving in the long run? Matching donations in a field experiment. J. Eur. Econ. Assoc. **5**, 1203–1222 (2007)
57. Thøgersen, J.: Monetary incentives and environmental concern. Effects of a differentiated garbage fee. J. Consum. Policy **17**, 407–442 (1994)
58. Bolderdijk, J.W., Steg, L.: Promoting sustainable consumption: the risks of using financial incentives. In: Reisch, L., Thøgersen, J. (eds.) Handbook of Research on Sustainable Consumption, pp. 328–342. Edward Elgar Publishing (2015)
59. Breakdown of an electricity bill. https://www.ofgem.gov.uk/data-portal/breakdown-electricity-bill
60. Bray, R., Woodman, B., Connor, P.: Policy and Regulatory Barriers to Local Energy Markets in Great Britain, p. 103 (2018)
61. Fuchs, C.: Social Media: a Critical Introduction. SAGE, Los Angeles (2014)
62. Helsper, E.J., van Deursen, A.J.A.M.: The third-level digital divide: who benefits most from being online? In: Communication and Information Technologies Annual, pp. 29–52. Emerald Group Publishing Limited (2015)
63. Salemink, K., Strijker, D., Bosworth, G.: Rural development in the digital age: a systematic literature review on unequal ICT availability, adoption, and use in rural areas. J. Rural Stud. **54**, 360–371 (2017)

64. Scheerder, A., van Deursen, A., van Dijk, J.: Determinants of Internet skills, uses and outcomes. A systematic review of the second- and third-level digital divide. Telematics Inform. **34**, 1607–1624 (2017)
65. van Deursen, A.J., van Dijk, J.A.: The digital divide shifts to differences in usage. New Media Soc. **16**, 507–526 (2014)
66. Zyskind, G., Nathan, O., Pentland, A.: "Sandy": decentralizing privacy: using blockchain to protect personal data. In: 2015 IEEE Security and Privacy Workshops, pp. 180–184. IEEE, San Jose (2015)
67. Cremer, D.D., Vugt, M.V.: Social identification effects in social dilemmas: a transformation of motives. Eur. J. Soc. Psychol. **29**, 871–893 (1999)
68. Dawes, R.M., Messick, D.M.: Social Dilemmas. Int. J. Psychol. **35**, 111–116 (2000)
69. Tajfel, H.: Social psychology of intergroup relations. Annu. Rev. Psychol. **33**, 1–39 (1982)
70. Tajfel, H.: Differentiation Between Social Groups: Studies in the Social Psychology of Intergroup Relations. Academic Press (for) European Association of Experimental Social Psychology, London (etc.) (1978)
71. Turner, J.C., Hogg, M.A., Oakes, P.J., Reicher, S.D., Wetherell, M.S.: Rediscovering the Social Group: A Self-categorization Theory. Basil Blackwell, Cambridge (1987)
72. Brown, R.J., Turner, J.C.: Interpersonal and intergroup behavior. In: Turner, J.C., Giles, H. (eds.) Intergroup Behavior, pp. 33–65. Chicago Press, Chicago (1981)
73. Turner, J.C.: Towards a cognitive redefinition of the social group. In: Tajfel, H. (ed.) Social Identity and Intergroup Relations, pp. 15–40. Cambridge University Press, Cambridge (1982)
74. Turner, J.: Social categorization and the self-concept: a social cognitive theory of group behavior. In: Lawler, E.J. (ed.) Advances in Group Processes: Theory and Research, pp. 77–122. JAI, Greenwich (1985)
75. Abrams, D., Wetherell, M., Cochrane, S., Hogg, M.A., Turner, J.C.: Knowing what to think by knowing who you are: self-categorization and the nature of norm formation, conformity and group polarization. Br. J. Soc. Psychol. **29**(Pt 2), 97–119 (1990)
76. Hopkins, N., Reicher, S.: Social movement rhetoric and the social psychology of collective action: a case study of anti-abortion mobilization. Hum. Relat. **50**, 261–286 (1997)
77. Bliuc, A.-M., McGarty, C., Reynolds, K., Muntele, D.: Opinion-based group membership as a predictor of commitment to political action. Eur. J. Soc. Psychol. **37**, 19–32 (2007)
78. Klandermans, B.: How group identification helps to overcome the dilemma of collective action. Am. Behav. Sci. **45**, 887–900 (2002)
79. Lalonde, R.N., Silverman, R.A.: Behavioral preferences in response to social injustice: the effects of group permeability and social identity salience. J. Pers. Soc. Psychol. **66**, 78–85 (1994)
80. Louis, W.R., Amiot, C.E., Thomas, E.F., Blackwood, L.: The "activist identity" and activism across domains: a multiple identities analysis: activism across multiple domains. J. Soc. Issues **72**, 242–263 (2016)
81. McGarty, C., Thomas, E.F., Lala, G., Smith, L.G.E., Bliuc, A.-M.: New technologies, new identities, and the growth of mass opposition in the arab spring. Polit. Psychol. **35**, 725–740 (2014)
82. Smith, L.G.E., Thomas, E.F., McGarty, C.: "We must be the change we want to see in the world": integrating norms and identities through social interaction. Polit. Psychol. **36**, 543–557 (2015)
83. Spears, R., Postmes, T.: Collective action online: extensions and applications of the SIDE model. In: Sundar, S.S. (ed.) The Handbook of the Psychology of Communication Technology, pp. 23–46. Wiley, Oxford (2015)

84. Postmes, T., Spears, R., Lea, M.: The formation of group norms in computer-mediated communication. Hum. Commun. Res. **26**, 341–371 (2000)
85. Smith, L.G.E., Gavin, J., Sharp, E.: Social identity formation during the emergence of the occupy movement: social identity formation during Occupy Wall Street. Eur. J. Soc. Psychol. **45**, 818–832 (2015)
86. Kende, A., van Zomeren, M., Ujhelyi, A., Lantos, N.A.: The social affirmation use of social media as a motivator of collective action. J. Appl. Soc. Psychol. **46**, 453–469 (2016)
87. Lea, M., Spears, R., Watt, S.E.: Visibility and anonymity effects on attraction and group cohesiveness. Eur. J. Soc. Psychol. **37**, 761–773 (2007)
88. Postmes, T., Spears, R., Lea, M.: Breaching or building social boundaries?: SIDE-effects of computer-mediated communication. Commun. Res. **25**, 689–715 (1998)
89. Postmes, T., Spears, R., Sakhel, K., de Groot, D.: Social influence in computer-mediated communication: the effects of anonymity on group behavior. Pers. Soc. Psychol. Bull. **27**, 1243–1254 (2001)
90. Chan, M.: The impact of email on collective action: a field application of the SIDE model. New Media Soc. **12**, 1313–1330 (2010)
91. Schumann, S., Klein, O.: Substitute or stepping stone? Assessing the impact of low-threshold online collective actions on offline participation. Eur. J. Soc. Psychol. **45**, 308–322 (2015)
92. Bellotti, V., Ambard, A., Turner, D., Gossmann, C., Demkova, K., Carroll, J.M.: A muddle of models of motivation for using peer-to-peer economy systems. In: Proceedings of the 33rd Annual ACM Conference on Human Factors in Computing Systems, pp. 1085–1094. ACM, New York (2015)
93. Glöss, M., McGregor, M., Brown, B.: Designing for labour: uber and the on-demand mobile workforce. In: Proceedings of the 2016 CHI Conference on Human Factors in Computing Systems, pp. 1632–1643. ACM, New York (2016)
94. Hawlitschek, F., Teubner, T., Gimpel, H.: Understanding the sharing economy – drivers and impediments for participation in peer-to-peer rental. In: 2016 49th Hawaii International Conference on System Sciences (HICSS), pp. 4782–4791 (2016)
95. Lampinen, A., Cheshire, C.: Hosting via Airbnb: motivations and financial assurances in monetized network hospitality. In: Proceedings of the 2016 CHI Conference on Human Factors in Computing Systems, pp. 1669–1680. ACM, New York (2016)
96. Tussyadiah, I.P.: Factors of satisfaction and intention to use peer-to-peer accommodation. Int. J. Hosp. Manag. **55**, 70–80 (2016)
97. Jung, J., Yoon, S., Kim, S., Park, S., Lee, K.-P., Lee, U.: Social or financial goals?: comparative analysis of user behaviors in Couchsurfing and Airbnb. In: Proceedings of the 2016 CHI Conference Extended Abstracts on Human Factors in Computing Systems, pp. 2857–2863. ACM, New York (2016)
98. Teubner, T., Adam, M.T.P., Camacho, S., Hassanein, K.: Understanding Resource Sharing in C2C Platforms: The Role of Picture Humanization. ACIS (2014)
99. Cho, S., Park, C., Kim, J.: Leveraging consumption intention with identity information on sharing economy platforms. J. Comput. Inf. Syst. **59**, 1–10 (2017)
100. Antoniadis, P., Grand, B.L.: Incentives for resource sharing in self-organized communities: from economics to social psychology. In: 2007 2nd International Conference on Digital Information Management, pp. 756–761 (2007)
101. Gerber, E.M., Hui, J.S., Kuo, P.-Y.: Crowdfunding: why people are motivated to post and fund projects on crowdfunding platforms. In: Proceedings of the International Workshop on Design, Influence, and Social Technologies, p. 10. ACM, New York (2012)

PiChat: Smartphone Application to Expand the Social Network for the Elderly

Ting-Hui Wu[1(✉)], Bing-Cheng Zhu[1(✉)], Elizabeth Wianto[1,2(✉)],
Shan-Wen Shih[1(✉)], Yang-Cheng Lin[1,3(✉)],
and Chien-Hsu Chen[1,3(✉)]

[1] National Cheng Kung University, No. 1 University Road,
Tainan 70101, Taiwan, R.O.C.
tinghui06@gmail.com
[2] University Kristen Maranatha, Jl. Surya Sumantri MPH no. 65,
Bandung 40164, Indonesia
[3] Hierarchical Green-Energy Materials (Hi-GEM) Research Center,
National Cheng Kung University, Tainan, Taiwan, R.O.C.

Abstract. The success in medical and multidisciplinary research has resulted in the longevity in human age. Longevity in human age has caused an increase in the elderly population, and this condition becomes a new phenomenon. The scientific and medical research focusing on the elderly becomes one of the biggest concerns, and cross-disciplinary cooperation to promote the health of the elderly is a global issue. However, many factors are affecting the physical and mental health of the elderly. The reduction in a social circle after retirement is a common problem for the elderly. Smaller social circle makes the elderly isolate and can cause loneliness. In order to reduce the problem, this study proposed a smartphone application called PiChat. This application manages to pair similar photos uploaded to help the elderly found new acquaintance and guidance of the conversation topic to begin. However, emphasizing the ease of use and considering the deterioration of the visual ability of the elderly, this application will lead the elderly to create a new social circle gradually. The preliminary test showed that this application is feasible to anticipate social circle reduction for the baby boomer's elderly.

Keywords: Social network · Quality of life · Interaction design · Old age

1 Introduction

The success in medical and multidisciplinary research has resulted in the longevity in human age. Longevity in human age has caused an increase in the elderly population, and this condition becomes a new phenomenon. With the longer lifespan, the proportion of the society become aged. Aged society has its own problem, and this issue should anticipate seriously especially in Taiwan. Specifically, Taiwan is most likely will progress to super-aged society from aged society with only take seven years [1].

© Springer Nature Switzerland AG 2019
M. Kurosu (Ed.): HCII 2019, LNCS 11568, pp. 148–158, 2019.
https://doi.org/10.1007/978-3-030-22636-7_10

Research has shown that several potential problems for aging society are loneliness, social isolation and the decrease of physical activities which directly affect the health and quality of life of the elderly and can lead to increased cost in health care [2–5].

Social circle reduction could happen for elderly since they lose the opportunity to meet colleague on a daily basis in their retirement period, the gradually decreasing physical strength due to their physically aged, and also their grown-up children are too busy to accompany. According to research by Marcelino et al., Information Communication Technology (ICT) can allow people to interact without being limited by time and space. Therefore, if this technology can be used in the elderly, there will be an effective way to overcome their loneliness or reduction in the social circle. Unfortunately, due to the lack of technological skills, it is often difficult for older people to operate applications on smartphones and tablets [5]. However, the elderly could improve their technical skills, and this already proven by the training about direct navigation and social network systems in the context of digital literacy in the study conducted by Castilla et al. [6].

Research regarding skill improvement on elderly shows that, they are not refused to learn. Elderly are also comfortable with technology and still eager to learn. This finding indicates that the new medium is not the barrier as long as the stimulus, engagement, and the introduction provides the information needed by the older adults [7]. The momentum to use the new medium with technology have hope now since the new generation of older adults is the baby boomers who have a different profile than the current generation of older adults. Other research shows that the percentage of this new generation of older adults in Taiwan have experience with computers and internet four to five times than the current generation of older adults, so the popularity of mobile phones and household broadband internet connection has reduced the technological barriers of the new generation of older people [8].

A study done by Takahashi et al. showed that the decreasing of the social circle and non-active physical activities could anticipate by using ICT. They designed a group walking program using smartphone application that can detect synchronized beacon had set before in several public facilities. In order to increase the motivation of the participants during the group walking, this application also implemented gamification such as points, badges, and rankings [9]. There are two interesting points found in this study. The first is this ICT based design can gather elderly lives in community-dwelling that are relatively isolate in their home, and the second is similar hobby or interest is the trigger for elderly to being friendly through group walking.

The previous study was emphasizing on how to increase the social circle and to create new friends, but they can't ensure that this new acquaintance have a common interest and also there are no proposed topic to begin the conversation. However, the study confirms that similar hobby is the desirable quality to make a friend. Therefore, this study tries to enhance this opportunity to upload a favorable image to verify that they have the same interest or value. Image recognition's similarity chose in this study to help to create a common topic to begin the conversation.

The purpose of this research is to solve the problem of decreasing the social circle of the elderly with the technology that familiar with them. By uploading a favorable image, the elderly could find the others with similar interest. The pair with similar interest will be more natural to have a common topic and become friends. In order to do this research, we conducted a semi-structured interview with the target users to collect information. The purpose of this interview is to obtain a preliminary insight from the potential user. The second step was to build a possible prototype, focusing on the suitable user interface design and simple workflow for the elderly. The third step was to test the prototype to the potential target user with the stress on ease of use and usability of the application.

2 Research Objective

The initial goal of this research was to design and develop applications on smartphones, providing a platform for the elderly to expand the new social network with common interests and help them to meet new people.

3 Theoretical Background

3.1 Loneliness and Social Isolation

Retired people are gradually decreasing their social network due to the limited physical function are shallowing their daily activities. The impact of longevity and aging population is more people to live alone and causing social isolation [3]. Loneliness and social isolation directly affect the health and quality of life of the elderly and also increase the cost of health care [4]. The systematic literature review provided by Khosravi and Ghapanchi [10] identified eight targeted issues, that are: dependent life, the risk of falls, chronic disease, dementia, social isolation, depression, poor health, and poor drug treatment. In this systematic review, from 2000 to 2015, at least 34 studies tried to solve the social isolation or loneliness of older people proves that this issue should get serious attention.

The conclusion in the same systematic review [4] stated that the concepts of loneliness and social isolation are often used interchangeably in literature and practice, but the precise definitions are not identical. If social isolation refers to the objective and quantitative degree of network size and frequency of contacts, then loneliness is a subjective sense of isolation and satisfaction with the frequency of connections, dis-satisfied intimacy, and social needs. Both of these are related to the lack of social needs [4, 11], which could lead to their physical and mental health.

3.2 Opportunities for ICT

In recent years, ICT helped many aspects of the lives of older people in innovative and effective ways. Some research reported that assistive technology has a positive impact on improving the lives of older people [3, 10].

A systematic review of the literature provided by Khosravi and Ghapanchi [10] identified six ICT clusters: (1) universal ICT, (2) robotics, (3) telemedicine, (4) sensor technology, and (5) drug therapy manage apps, and (6) video games. The technologies that have been applied to alleviate social isolation are: (1) ICT, (2) video games,

(3) support chat rooms, (4) remote care (5) 3D virtual environments, (6) robots, (7) Social networking sites, (8) personal reminders and social management systems [4].

The systematic review of the information indicates that loneliness and social isolation will lead to a reduction in the social circle of the elderly and for a new generation of elderly who are familiar with the technology, such problems will have a better chance to solve. This premise argued by the Calouste Gulbenkian Foundation, which recommended to support the elderly to get online and increasing awareness in the public sector for the issue to adapt technology-based service that will help the problem. [3].

3.3 Interest and Social Network

A study shows that from a social point of view, the principle of homogeneity constitutes various types of connections, and people are more likely to be close to people who are similar to themselves, so people with similar interests are more likely to become friends [12].

In the real-world environment, it is difficult to find friends with similar interests and background personality, but in the online world, because of the vast number of users, it is not hard to find friends with similar interests [13].

The interesting map is a network map built by people's common interests. Pinterest is an example of the interest map website. By 2012, it has become the third largest social networking site in the United States.

Some studies have investigated online dating, and the reason for online dating is because of the loading factors of new friends who can find similar interests up to 0.77. One of the main reasons to motivate people to search for online friends is that users can use the Internet to find Friends who are willing to share their interests [14].

4   Method

In order to solve the reduction of social circle problem in the elderly, this study designed by qualitative approach base on the elderly insight—the steps of the study consist of three steps.

First, the preliminary information gathered using semi-structured interview to the target users regarding: (1) the usage of smartphone for them, (2) the daily activities after retired or in their daily lives, (3) the opinion regarding social circle reduction in their late-life phase; (4) the idea about getting new social circle, (5) the ability to obtain or make picture using their smartphone.

Second, the team proposed several possible application concepts using the consideration of the information gathered from the target users and the limitations of the elderly derived from literature reviews.

Third, the team building application prototyping using Python programming language and tested to the elderly for the application refinement.

4.1   Semi Structured Interview

Semi-structured interview conducted to several elderly in Tainan, Taiwan, so the team have a better understanding of the elderly concern. The inclusions criteria for the respondents were: (1) 65 years old or above, (2) using a smartphone in their daily lives, (3) retired, (4) fluent in the Chinese language, and (5) considered healthy as they still performed exercises in their ages.

There were six main questions asked as follows: (1) Loneliness in older adults, (2) Activities in everyday life, (3) the idea of getting new friends, (4) the frequency using smartphone in daily life, (5) the idea to get permanent gallery for their favorite photos, (6) the idea about getting new friend which have same interest.

In the investigation, eight older adults (4 men and four women), with an average age of 68 years old were used as participants. From the interview, here is the insight gathered:

(1) Most elderly didn't feel lonely, but they feel that there were not many things to do, so they feel bored. This situation is overcome by finding activities to fill their spare times,
(2) Most elderly choose to plant, take photos, read books, at home or nearby. It is seldom for them to meet their friend because of one or another reason,
(3) Most elderly find to get new friends or acquaintances were interesting,
(4) Most elderly used their mobile phones every day, usually using communication application, such as Facebook and Line,
(5) Most older adults were excited to get the idea of having permanent photos of the picture they took because they do not feel fluent in managing their photos,
(6) Most elderly preferred to have new friends with the same preference as they believed it would make them easier to share the same topic interest.
(7) Most elderly would like to see more photos considerably same interest as theirs. The owners of the similar photos are preferable to become their new acquaintance online since their limited 'real' friend might not have similar interest.

In conclusions, most of the elderly with mobile phones use it every day and are willing to make new friends, especially with the one with the same interests. The reason why the elderly isn't having as many friends as they before are because of the limitation of the activities, and the limitation of the topic to begin the conversation. Furthermore, respondents positively thought that it is feasible to meet new people with photos. With this opportunity, they enthusiastic to help people with the same area of interest and fascinate by the pictures take or get in the process.

After the pension, the elderly's situation is a bit different, if previously they usually travel and chat with the old friend, then in this period they rarely have the opportunity to meet the others.

4.2   Application Concept

Based on the conclusions of semi-structured interviews and literature reviews, it is found that the daily activities of the elderly are mostly concentrated in sports, family, cooking, and traveling. The common activities while doing their daily activities is to use photo records, and most elderly people also like to share photos. Therefore, this study proposes a mobile app called PiChat, which provides opportunities for the elderly to anticipating the social circle with photos. The elderly can upload their favorite and most interesting pictures every day, and the system will calculate the same interest with the similarity of the images. Using the real-time similarity calculation, the paired user will know the most similar person and having the opportunities to connect. By using this method, the elderly will be geographically restricted, and similar pictures in the application are more natural for them to begin the topic to converse.

PiChat's user interface designed as simple as possible, to avoid a complicated operation. Every page in the display has one primary function to prevent the elderly from confusing. Regarding the limitation of the elderly's vision, green color chose as the dominant color. In addition, PiChat also considering the cyber-crime issue, so to connect or pair user, there are gradual steps to open the information provided by the elderly. Figure 1 shows the PiChat's user interface and the main consideration for the elderly vision limitation and ease of use.

(1)   (2)   (3)

Fig. 1. Loading page, registered and login page of PiChat (left to right: (1) green as main color; (2) one-page single function; (3) step-by-step/progressive connection (Color figure online)

For the first connection, each other could only praise or comment the uploaded photos. The default setting for people to directly connect is three times. That means on four-times paired, the two connected people could start a chat to each other. This default setting could customize by the elderly, so they will comfortably expand their social circle.

The key features in PiChat are:

(1) Photo albums with the most favorite photos (assuming the elderly only upload their best or favorite photos).
(2) Pairing older people who have the same photos and interests.
(3) Interactive topics and patterns with other elderly.
(4) The current application design will progressively open the connection between the paired elderly, but the setting can be adjusted manually. The adjustment features implemented to make sure that the elderly feel comfortable while expanding their social circle.

4.3   How to Use PiChat

Considering the features of older people and making them easy to use, the application interface is designed to be as simple as possible and requires minimal login steps. With PiChat, the elderly can add new friends and chat with them every day, they can collect pictures they like, and the system helps them make a unique photo album. Figure 2 shows the workflow of PiChat.

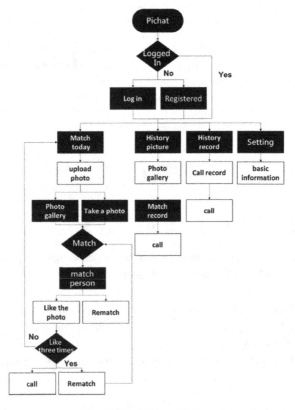

Fig. 2. Workflow of PiChat

(1) After the user install the application, they need to input the necessary information, such as: name, gender, age, uploading a photo, et cetera (for first time only). This stage is called account registration. If the user is already registered, the user can choose 'log in'.

(2) In the 'Today Matching' screen, the user can select a favorite photo and upload it. The user can select it from the photo library or take a photo directly. After uploading, the system will automatically match them to other users. The picture is matched for the first time. The user can press the other party's photo to like it. The preset of two parties are paired and pressed three times or more to choose whether to connect with the other party.

(3) The historical photo page allows the user to view previously uploaded images, as well as matching similar images and their owners. To contact other photo owners again, press the button to connect.

(4) The history page allows the user to see all the calls and pairing records, or the user can choose to contact again.

(5) On the setting page, the user can change the basic information, pair it several times before contacting (Figs. 3, 4 and 5).

Registered   Match Today

Fig. 3. Interface design of PiChat (registered and match today pages)

Take a Photo   Match Person

Fig. 4. Interface design of PiChat (take a photo and match person)

Photo Gallery   History Record

Fig. 5. Interface design of PiChat (photo gallery and history record)

4.4   Calculating Picture Similarities

The main algorithm in PiChat is to calculate the similarity in the uploaded image. PiChat designed with Python programming language. Python chooses as the programming language because of the modest and easy to use syntax. Python was integrated with Open CV to emphasize the readability and uses standard keywords. The integration between Open CV and Python provides a common infrastructure for computer vision application and accelerate machine learning used in commercial products. Open CV-Python also able to focus on real-time image processing. Among of all features, color features are the most commonly used in the image recognition, so this application selected colors as the identification method, with the following steps:

(1)   Convert the picture to a probability density function.
(2)   Using the calcHist() method in open CV.
(3)   Calculate the consistency of all histograms.

Color data in images can use histograms to represent color histograms that are very effective for many practical uses because they can shrink and change views steadily. Open CV-Python has an essential technique to conduct simple histogram checking. To create a histogram, a clustering algorithm, the k-means, is used. The k-means clustering algorithm collects n data points into clusters with the most recent mean. The average of each group is called the "centroid" or "center." In general, the k-mean was applied to isolate the cluster of the first n data points. Data points within a particular cluster are considered "more comparable," and data points to each other indicate locations with different clusters.

4.5   Preliminary Evaluation

PiChat's prototype was evaluated through the expertise of the committee's experts with results are as follows:

(1)   This application should be more comprehensive in considering how to avoid cybercrime, and the process of pairing users should be more cautious.
(2)   The image is a way to link the interests of two people primarily.
(3)   Adding other data and information of the elderly, so the mode of connecting the two highs may not necessarily be through the picture.

5   Conclusion and Suggestion

After retirement, the elderly most likely will have a smaller social circle. Due to factors such as single life, declining physical function and a limited range of activities, the social circle will gradually decrease, which leads to problems such as boredom. Issues such as boredom in everyday lives will take effect on the health of the elderly and cause further problem. The health and quality of life of the elderly, also the ability to use smartphones by the baby-boomers elderly open the opportunity to overcome the social circle reduction of the elderly. This premise is the background for this research to create a smartphone application called PiChat to increase the possibility of expanding the social circle of the elderly. However, the design must consider the ease of use, the possible technology, and the danger regarding the cyber-crime issue. PiChat's prototype will be refine with an addition to pairing with photos, collectible photos, location and other information at the same time, increasing the matching conditions, so that the matched elderly people have higher accuracy in similar living circles.

References

1. Lin, Y.Y., Huang, C.S.: Aging in Taiwan: building a society for active aging and aging in place. Gerontologist **56**(2), 176–183 (2016)
2. Bilbao, A., Almeida, A., Lopez-de-Ipina, D.: Promotion of active ageing combining sensor and social network data. J. Biomed. Inform. **64**, 108–115 (2016)
3. Independent Age., Older People, Technology and Community: The Potential of Technology to Help Older People Renew or Develop Social Contacts and to Actively Engage in Their Communities. Independent Age, United Kingdom (2010)
4. Khosravi, P., Rezvani, A., Wiewiora, A.: The impact of technology on older adults' social isolation. J. Comput. Hum. Behav. **63**, 594–603 (2016)
5. Marcelino, I., Laza, R., Pereira, A.: SSN: senior social network for improving quality of life. Int. J. Distrib. Sens. Netw. **12**(7), 2150734 (2016)
6. Castilla, D., et al.: Teaching digital literacy skills to the elderly using a social network with linear navigation: a case study in a rural area. Int. J. Hum Comput Stud. **118**, 24–37 (2018)
7. Istance, D.: Learning in retirement and old age: an agenda for the 21st century. Eur. J. Educ. **50**(2), 225–238 (2015)
8. Hsu, Y.L. et al.: Profile of the "Aging Boomers" in Taiwan, pp. 1–2. Gerontechnology Research Center. Yuan Ze University, Taoyuan City (2012)
9. Takahashi, M., et al.: Mobile walking game and group-walking program to enhance going out for older adults. In: Proceedings of the 2016 ACM International Joint Conference on Pervasive and Ubiquitous Computing, UbiComp 2016 (UBICOMP/ISWC 2016), 12–16 September 2016, pp. 1372–1380. Heidelberg (2016)
10. Khosravia, P., Ghapanchi, A.H.: Investigating the effectiveness of technologies applied to assist seniors: a systematic literature review. J. Int. J. Med. Inform. **85**, 17–26 (2016)
11. Hung, J.Y., Lu, K.S.: Research on the healthy lifestyle model: active ageing, and loneliness of senior learners. Educ. Gerontol. **40**(5), 353–362 (2014)
12. McPherson, M., Smith-Lovin, L., Cook, M.J.: Annual review of sociology. Annu. Rev. **27**, 415–444 (2001)
13. Bonebrake, K.: college students' internet use, relationship formation, and personality correlates. Cyber Psychol. Behav. **5**(6), 551–557 (2002). Department of Psychology. Elon University, Elon, North Carolina
14. Zhang, Y.T.: Motivations of online relationships and associations with personality, loneliness, social anxiety and self-disclosure (thesis). Graduate Institute of Information Management (2018)

Design of Human-Computer Interaction Products for the User with "Mood Disorder"

Tingyu Yang and Qian Ji[✉]

Industrial Design Department, School of Mechanical Science and Engineering,
Huazhong University of Science and Technology, Wuhan 430074, Hubei, China
{TingyuYang,QianJi}@hust.edu.cn

Abstract. With the rapid development of society, people are facing increasing social pressure. Excessive pressure not only promotes production, but also has a lot of adverse effects on people's psychology. One of them is feeling depressed. In view of this social phenomenon, this paper proposes a design scheme, which help people to alleviate their own bad emotions and have a good attitude towards life. The questionnaire are based on related theory and the analysis of similar competing goods, which analyzing the user's psychological preferences, mining the user behavior pain points, finally designed a human-computer interaction intelligent products - 'LOVE HUG' and "DI LUO" APP, the intelligent products can through their own characteristics for the interaction with users, achieve the goal of relieve the user of undesirable mood.

Keywords: Human-computer interaction · Product design ·
User with mood disorder

1 Social Background

With the accelerating pace of life, people are generally under increasing pressure. This is how the term "mood disorder" appears. "Mood disorder" is what we call depression conventionally [1]. In today's life, study and work, people tend to face a lot of situations that trigger depression. If such situations last long, it will easily develop into "Depressive Disorder". How to relieve people's psychological pressure and give vent to their emotions in modern society is pressing issue. By setting the immersive human-computer interaction mode, the product can interact with the user through the interface interaction and achieve a more perfect user experience for the user.

2 Theoretical Background: Concept and Significance of Human-Computer Interaction

Through the collection and analysis of the existing human-computer interaction theories, the design guidance related to the design have been obtained.

M. Kurosu (Ed.): HCII 2019, LNCS 11568, pp. 159–173, 2019.
https://doi.org/10.1007/978-3-030-22636-7_11

2.1   Interaction Design Guidelines: Interactive Design Criteria

- Ethical, harmless, improve the human condition. For users with mood disorders, it can improve the users' condition and alleviate their emotions.
- Intentional, that is, it can help users with 'Mood Disorders' to realize the needs of self-awareness and self-acceptance.
- Pragmatic, that is, to achieve the expected goals after the product is designed.
- Elegant, the simplest complete scheme, with the appropriate accommodation and emotions.

2.2   General Design Principles

The principle of equal use, and the principle of fairness. As a product designed for all people, everyone can use it as equally as possible. In the use of the product, it is not targeted at a certain group of people but for all people. It is suitable for all people who suffer from short-term or long-term psychological trauma, and it can be used to comfort the body and mind when they are in bad mood.

The Principle of Simplicity and Intuition. The product can be understood and used regardless of the user's experience. "Fool-style" design allows people to quickly understand usage and achieve the best user experience.

The size and space should be suitable for use. There should be space for the product when it is idle. In the process of using the product, taking into account different users' stature and other problems, the space within the customers' line of sight should be increased as much as possible.

2.3   Maslow's User Demand Theory

In Maslow's Demand Theory, people have five levels of needs, including physiological needs, security needs, social needs, esteem needs, and self-actualization needs. The product meets the second level of needs, which means that the pursuit of security mechanism of the applicable population is satisfied while meeting their physiological needs. The third level of needs is the needs for emotions and belongings. Everyone wants to be cared and loved. The emotional needs are more delicate and sensitive than the physiological needs. The fourth level of needs is the needs for esteem and self-actualization. User with "mood disorders" mostly need the second and third levels of needs. Emotionally, they have more delicate emotions than ordinary people and are more sensitive to the surrounding environment. Therefore, in product design, great attention shall be paid to the product's sense of protection, feeling of social affection and care as well as understanding of the true mind of the design object [2].

3   Related APP Interface Analysis: Xinchao APP

Xinchao APP was launched in May 2015. After three years of development, it has provided services for 6 million users. which ranks high among all mental health products. it's similar with the design of following APP. By analyzing the similar APP to seek out the advantages and disadvantages, getting a conclusion to guide the next step of the design. Xinchao decompression APP is a main stress relief app. The most attractive module and the most important module of this APP are to test the users' psychological pressure and give corresponding relief guidance. Analyze its index bar, decompression evaluation module, and decompression guidance module.

The interface of the decompression evaluation module is as follows: Click pressure index on the first interface to carry out pressure measurement. First select the corresponding picture for the users' recent status. Then the app will open the camera to identify the user's face and measure the user's real-time heart rate and breathing. Next the user's pressure value will be obtained based on the comprehensive data. Table 1 gives a summary of the interface [3].

Table 1. Shows the summary of the interface.

Decompression evaluation option	Select the description picture	Perform facial scanning	Test the pressure value

Guidance module interface: After the pressure test is completed, the user can select the guidance module for psychological relaxation according to their needs. Table 2 gives four parts of the decompression modules.

Table 2. Shows four parts of the decompression modules.

Music decompression guidance module	Relaxation guidance module	Meditation guidance module	Sleep guidance module
Music Take best	Fast relaxation and guidance - deep relaxation and guidance of powerful male voice a - deep relaxation and	I meditation from the guide - rich male voice) meditation from the guide Pro male voice	Deep sleep guide - deep sleep guide with deep male voice -- gentle female voice complete sleep

Index bar interface: The index includes the information of the entire interface. The index bar can basically identify the contents covered by the whole application. In the DI LUO APP, users can intuitively identify the module classification: home, decompression, discovery, and mine. Table 3 gives the other parts of the decompression modules.

Table 3. Shows the other parts of the decompression modules.

Home	Decompression	Discovery	Mine

Analyze the interface, function and structure features of xinchao decompression APP. Table 4 gives the analysis of Xinchao APP.

Table 4. Shows the analysis of Xinchao APP.

	Spine decompression
Advantages	Interface: The interface uses monochrome cool colors and white with low lightness. The interface is simple Function: The theme is clear Structure: The basic structure is simple, and the structure framework is clear
Disadvantages	There are many redundant modules in the structure framework. For example, it is found that the settings of modules are more redundant than other modules. The framework module should be streamlined in later application upgrades

Conclusion of APP Research Analysis. Through the analysis of similar apps, a conclusion is drawn. In APP interface design, the hierarchy should follow the humanized design theory and conform to the user experience. Meanwhile, the APP module framework should be simplified to simplify the interface as much as possible. Interface colors should be low saturation, high brightness cool colors, such as light blue, light green, or low saturation, low brightness colors, such as dark blue, dark green.

4 Questionnaire Survey

The purpose of the questionnaire survey is to understand the different psychological preferences of the current population and summarize people's general psychological needs and preferences by setting color perception questions and social needs questions. So as to get a good command of user psychological. The randomness of the questionnaire is large, so the final result is only for reference. The questionnaire questions are universal. The total number of respondents is 206. Table 5 shows the questionnaire survey [4].

Overall analysis of the questionnaire: A total of 206 questionnaires were collected, with a wide age distribution and diverse populations. Today's society is developing rapidly, and the age range of social pressure population is mainly 27–35 years old. This age group is a group with high social work output, heavy social burden and great pressure. 80% of the respondents said that they would feel depressed in their daily work and life [5]. Most of them tend to get simple language comfort when they are depressed. They also need physical comfort. In physical comfort, it is head touching and hugging that makes the respondents feel more comfortable. When feeling down, 70% of the respondents said that they liked to share their feelings with others and hoped to get professional guidance to ease their mood. Through the analysis, the design of the APP should be attention to the users' needs. Meanwhile, the conclusions obtained from the questionnaire will be applied in the following interface design [6].

Table 5. Shows the questionnaire survey.

Questions	Chart	Analysis of Questionnaire Questions
Q1. How old are you? (see Fig. 1).	Fig. 1. The age of the respondents.	Wide age distribution, avoiding age limitations. Most of the respondents are between the ages of 27 and 35. This age group is in the stage of social work and has relatively high pressure, making them an important research group of our product design
Q2. Have you felt depressed in your daily life? (see Fig. 2).	Fig. 2. The proportion of the respondents who have felt depressed in daily life.	81% of the people said that they felt depressed in their daily lives in the questionnaire, indicating that depression is a common phenomenon in our lives. Great attention shall be paid to this common phenomenon, and how to relieve emotional stress shall be stressed

(*continued*)

Table 5. (*continued*)

Questions	Chart	Analysis of Questionnaire Questions
Q3. What do you usually do to ease your mood when you feel depressed? (see Fig. 3).	 **Fig. 3.** The different choice of the respondents. Choices include singing, watch movies, and so on.	There were 102 votes for listening to music in the poll, followed by dancing, singing and sleeping. It can be seen from the results that music can ease people's mood
Q4. How do you want people around you to comfort you when you are depressed? (see Fig. 4).	 **Fig. 4.** The actions include appetite comfort. physical comfort and so on.	Verbal comfort topped the poll, followed by self-comfort, appetite comfort and physical comfort
Q5. What language do you think can play a good comforting role? (see Fig. 5).	 **Fig. 5.** The different choice of respondents.	There were 114 votes for simple oral comfort, indicating that most people can get psychological satisfaction through the simple oral comfort from the people around them

(*continued*)

Table 5. (*continued*)

Questions	Chart	Analysis of Questionnaire Questions
Q6. What body language do you think makes you feel more comfortable? (see Fig. 6).	Fig. 6. The proportion of the users choice.	Head touching and hugging are regarded as a comforting body language in the poll. It is worth noting that what makes people feel comfortable in body language is touching
Q7. Which color do you prefer to accept when you are unhappy? (see Fig. 7).	Fig. 7. The proportion of the users choice.	42% of the respondents chose picture seven, but 20% of the respondents chose picture one, indicating that while in a low mood, people prefer to see calm, quiet and elegant colors with low saturation and high brightness. By comparing the color options, the respondents prefer the cool color system
Q8. When you're feeling down, do you like interacting with people who are feeling the same way? (see Fig. 8).	Fig. 8. The proportion of the users choice. There are two choices: like or dislike.	About 70% of the respondents said in the questionnaire that they liked interacting with people who had the same mood when they were depressed. Therefore, attention shall be paid to this demand in product design

Table 5. (*continued*)

Questions	Chart	Analysis of Questionnaire Questions
Q9. What pictures do you like to look at when you are unhappy? (see Fig. 9).	 **Fig. 9.** The proportion of the users choice, including the picture of the scenery, the cute animals and so on.	About 30% of respondents said that they were more inclined to look at pictures of landscapes when feeling down. Landscape elements can be added in product design to make users feel more calm and natural
Q10. When you are in a low mood, do you want a professional to ease your mood? (see Fig. 10).	 **Fig. 10.** The proportion of the users choice. The choices include need and no need.	About 70% of respondents hope to get professional guidance when they are depressed. A module for professional guidance can be added in the product

5 Human-Computer Interaction Product Design

After theoretical analysis, relevant product analysis and questionnaire survey, relevant conclusions will be applied in the product design process.

5.1 Product Features

Target group: people with low mood (not limited to people with depression, but also those with low mood due to various reasons in daily life.

Name: The product is named 'LOVE HUG', which means hug users with love.

Product positioning: The product could sense the changes in human emotions with a sensor and give people comfort by simulating human body movements. At the same time, it will adjust its own temperature according to the external temperature. At the same time, connect to the mobile app, divert people's attention and give encouragement through the APP, or consult professionals or communicate with others in the app to ease their emotions.

Entity product intention: close, stable, care, a sense of security.

Virtual product intention: natural, soft, fresh, caring.

Sketch. Select five objects for line extraction. Including Human Arm, Seal, Panda, Love shape and Cat. (see Fig. 11).

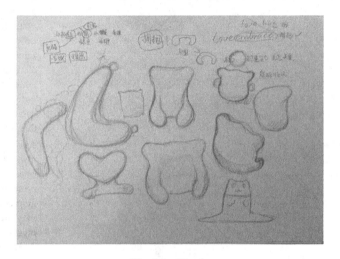

Fig. 11. Sketch.

Image Selection of Product Sketch. The images were summarized through the image questionnaire survey. (see Fig. 12). Table 6 shows the selection of sketch.

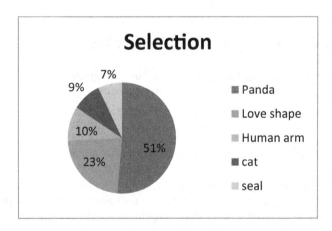

Fig. 12. Questionnaire survey about the selection.

Table 6. Shows the selection of sketch.

Product bionic object	Product expression image	Screening
Human arm	Safe, close, warm	Fail
Seal	Lively, cute, flexible	Fail
Panda	Steady, cute, close	Pass
Love shape	Love, closeness, harmlessness, dedication	Fail
Cat	Cute, close, harmless, lively	Fail

The panda is a lovely animal, it could bring user a sense of security. Other images are not completely consistent with our initial product positioning. So we finally chose the panda shape as the bionic object of the product.

Rendering of Physical Product Model. (see Fig. 13).

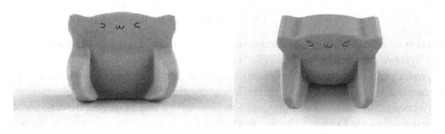

Fig. 13. The appearance of the model.

The product gives users a feeling of closeness and cuteness.

Home Use Scene. (see Fig. 14).

Fig. 14. The using scene of the model.

The product has a widely applicability can be applied in multiple scenarios, It can be used as an ordinary pillow at work. It can automatically detect the mood of users and provide timely interactive feedback. It can also be used as emotional support at home.

Design Description. This product is designed to relieve stress for people who are in a bad mood. The external modeling is like a panda, adopting the cute panda modeling and simplifying the lines. The main materials of the product are organic textile materials such as cloth weaving. The inner bracket is made of carbon fiber, which can reduce the weight of the product. The color abandons the traditional black, white and gray of the panda, and adopts the sunny spring colors (green and blue cool color with low saturation).

When the user hugs the product, there is a soft robot sensor inside the product, which can sense the user's heart rate. The soft robot technology is a new type of robot technology, is widely used in the intelligent medical treatment and grasping field. Body temperature and other signs and transmit the data to the mobile phone APP. The APP will analyze and respond to the data. At the same time, the product will close the "feet" to wrap the user and simulate the hug, so that the user can feel comfort and relieved [8].

5.2   Virtual Mobile APP-DI LUO- a Mobile APP with Smart Emotions

Intention of product name: The product name is taken from "DI LUO" which refers to users in a low mood. The homophonic "DI LUO" is used in the hope that the APP and the product can dissolve and eliminate people's negative emotions like flowing water, and create a more healthy and positive living environment for people.

According to the results of the questionnaire survey and Maslow's demand theory, the first level of the Demand Theory, there are six modules at the first level in the APP: Mood record, Mood monitoring, Equipment link, Professional communication, Personal settings, Message to remind. (see Fig. 15). There are three parts following the Mood record, such as music, the scenery and encouraging words. User could chose to click on the music button to listen to music so as to click on the scenery button to see the beautiful world.

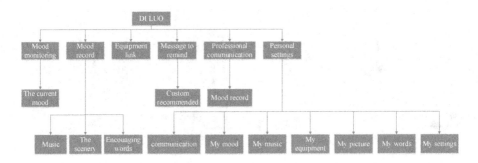

Fig. 15. The first level of the APP.

Table 7. Shows the introduction of the interface.

	The initial interface of the APP has three weather states, which represent three moods. Through the dynamic effect of running water, it is hoped to give users a feeling that their emotions are being dissipated.
	After entering the APP, there will be an interface to display "one day, one wisdom", which will encourage each user to face life with an optimistic and happy.
	Connecting the device with the product LOVE HUG Bluetooth can intelligently process the information transmitted by the product and make timely response, such as playing soothing music to relax the user. The APP satisfies the users' second level of needs, that is, self-satisfaction. When the user is in a bad mood, LOVE HUG pillow will feel the user's mood and visualize the mood on the mobile terminal to help the user understand the current mood. There are three sub-levels under the mood level: music, landscape, and spiritual discourse. In the music module, users can select soothing or heartening music according to their needs. In the landscape module, users can see the customs of various cities in the world, broaden the horizon and find the beauty of the world. In the spiritual discourse module, users can see various motivational words and stories that can help quickly revive the spirit.

At the same time, users can record their mood. The mood record mainly records the time and reason of their bad mood.

Users can add encouraging words or interesting events or pictures in life to each record, so that they can intuitively see every psychological change, thus encouraging them to be positive in their future lives.

Professional communication is set for users' third level of needs. 70% of respondents hope to receive professional guidance when they feel depressed. Through professional manual communication, there will be professionals who will provide targeted solutions when the users are in bad mood. Notification.

Users can quickly contact his own spiritual advisor after entering the APP, and receive relevant recommendations collected by the APP according to the users' preferences.

Personal settings are set to meet the users' personality needs. Users can find their own information records in the personal settings.

The whole interfaces are concise and clear, which are easily for user to understand, have a better User Experience. The overall color of interface is mazarine, compared with light color, Blue gives a more peaceful visual experience, for the user with 'Mood Disorder', it can make user feel better when they are dysphoric. Table 7 shows the selection of sketch.

6 Conclusion

With the accelerated development of society, the emergence of "mood disorder" is inevitable. "LOVE HUG" and "DI LUO" can accompany people at any time just like friends and mentors. By relieving the mood in a timely and effective manner through human-computer interaction, it can bring users a wonderful day!

Acknowledgements. Supported by National Natural Science Foundation of China (Grant No: 51708236). Supported by Seed Foundation of Huazhong University of Science and Technology (Grant No:2016YXMS273).

References

1. Zhang, Z., Zou, J., Ding, J., Song, Z., Cheng, G., Wang, X., Guo, L.: Research status of soft robot driver [J]. Robot **40**(05), 648–659 (2008)
2. Wang, C., Liu, Y.: The importance of color in product design. Architect. Cult. **08**, 182 (2018)
3. Wenjin, H., Wang, C.: Research on color design of household medical products. Popular Lit. Art **15**, 48 (2018)
4. Yu, Q.: Research on Japanese general design. Packag. Eng. **38**(24), 245–247 (2017)
5. Xu, Y.: Discussion on the development and practical thinking of general design. Art Technol. **30**(11), 254–287 (2017)
6. Wang, C.: Design of robot embedded sensing and human-computer interaction technology. Nanjing university of science and technology (2017)
7. Fan, J., Tian, F., Yi, D., Liu, Z., Dai, G.: Some thoughts on human-computer interaction in the era of intelligence. Chin. Sci. Inf. Sc. **48**(04), 361–375 (2008)
8. Norman, D.A.: Natural user interfaces are not natural. Interactions **17**(3), 6–10 (2010)

Design for Culture and Entertainement

Multiple Representations of the UI, Score and Scale for Musical Performance System and Score DB

Sachiko Deguchi(⊠)

Kindai University, Higashi-Hiroshima, Hiroshima 739-2116, Japan
deguchi@hiro.kindai.ac.jp

Abstract. This paper describes the development and evaluation of the UIs and scores of musical performance system. The aim of this research is to provide a musical tool for elderly people and caregivers. Another aim of this research is to use the performance system and score database to conserve some non-Western music genres. The UIs are designed on a tablet PC, which look like keyboards. Four UIs with scores are evaluated by young people and elderly people: plain keyboard with staff notation score, and keyboards of note name/number/color representation with scores of the same representation. The results of the experiment indicate that the number representation would be useful to most people and the note name/color representations would be useful to some people. This system also have a UI of koto music which is one genre of Japanese traditional music. This system can be used for the explanation of the difference between the temperament and scale of koto music and those of Western music. Scores for musical performance system and scores of koto music are also discussed. This research provides a system to add melody and rhythm using score DB to the lyric input by a user. This system can also explain the melisma of koto songs and asynchronicity of the rhythms of voice part and koto part.

Keywords: Musical performance · Score database · Koto music · Staff notation · Numbered notation · Color representation

1 Introduction

In the field of music therapy, music listening and/or singing are commonly taking place [1–3]. However, it is difficult to use a musical instrument with staff notation scores. The objective of this research is to provide a musical performance system and score database to improve the quality of life of the people (especially elderly people) who have difficulty with using staff notation scores for performance [4]. Many musical performance system have been proposed and evaluated in the field of Computer Music [5–8], however, it is difficult for elderly people without musical experience to use these systems.

Today, Western music is accepted worldwide; however, the temperament and the scale of music are simplified, e.g., Twelve-tone equal temperament and the Major/Minor scales are commonly used. Another objective of this research is to use the performance system and score database to conserve some non-Western music genres. Koto music is discussed in this research.

© Springer Nature Switzerland AG 2019
M. Kurosu (Ed.): HCII 2019, LNCS 11568, pp. 177–191, 2019.
https://doi.org/10.1007/978-3-030-22636-7_12

2 UI and Score for Musical Performance

2.1 Representation of UI

This research has developed a musical performance system on tablet PCs. This system has several user interfaces: UI-1: UI like keyboard instrument, UI-2: UI with note names on keyboard, UI-3: UI with numbers on keyboard, UI-4: UI with colors on keyboard, and UI-5: Different layout of UI-3 (vertical keyboard). Figure 1 shows UI-1, Fig. 2 shows UI-2, Fig. 3 shows UI-3 and Fig. 4 shows UI-4.

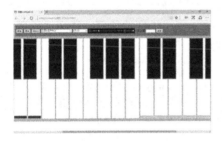

Fig. 1. UI-1: plain keyboard

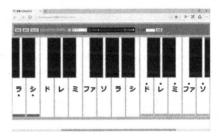

Fig. 2. UI-2: keyboard with note names

Fig. 3. UI-3: keyboard with numbers

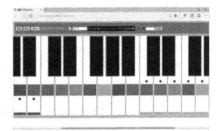

Fig. 4. UI-4: keyboard with colors (Color figure online)

Fig. 5. UI of previous version

In UI-2, note names are written in Japanese. In UI-3, numbers: 1 to 7 represent notes: C, D, E, F, G, A and B. In UI-4, colors: red, orange, yellow, green, light blue, blue and violet represent notes: C to A. Note names, numbers, or colors with an upper/lower dot mean the pitches are one octave higher/lower.

In our previous research [4], we designed three layered keyboard as Fig. 5; however, we redesigned one layered keyboard (normal keyboard) with scrolling function because some people mentioned about the layout of keyboard in the questionnaire of previous experiment. We also decided to eliminate the UI with shapes on keyboard because the result of previous experiment showed that shapes were not recognizable as musical notation.

This system provides sound sources of piano (C2 to C7) and koto (C2 to C7) in WAVE data format. Our previous system provided sound sources of piano and organ. These sounds were generated by additive synthesis. This system can read a musical score from score database which was developed in previous research, and a user can listen to the melody before performance. This system can also record user's performance to support practice and improvisation. This system has a metronome function so that a user can play the system rhythmically.

This system was implemented by HTML, CSS and JavaScript, and it is working without perceptible time delay on Windows tablet PCs.

2.2 Representation of Score

Each user interface needs different score form: UI-1: staff notation, UI-2: note name representation, UI-3: number representation, UI-4: color representation, and UI-5: same as UI-3. Note names are written in some staff notation scores today for the beginners. Numbered notation is common in Japanese traditional music and some genres of non-Western music in the world.

The scores for UI-2, UI-3 and UI-4 are generated from musical score database (DB) which was developed by this research in Humdrum format [9]. We have extended the system to generate scores from MusicXML format data [10]. This system can display two types of scores. Type 1 scores specify the durations as the lengths of space and Type 2 scores specify the durations by using symbols as Western music. Type 1 scores are designed based on the notation of Ikuta school koto scores [11], while type 2 scores are designed based on the notation of Yamada school koto scores [12]. Figure 6 shows Type 1 score of number representation, Fig. 7 shows Type 1 score of color representation, and Fig. 8 shows Type 2 score of number representation. In these scores, Lyrics are written below note names, numbers or colors.

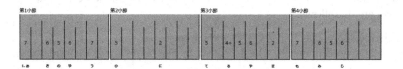

Fig. 6. Type 1 score of number representation

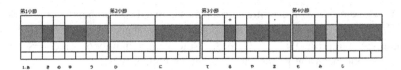

Fig. 7. Type 1 score of color representation

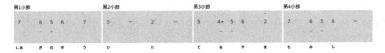

Fig. 8. Type 2 score of number representation

2.3 Experiment on UI and Score

The experiments of previous research [4] showed that UI-2 (note name) was easy to play the system and that UI-3 (number) was easy to play and sing at the same time. It also showed that UI-4 (color) could be useful. The 16 examinees of the previous experiments were college students.

Methods. In this research, UIs are improved and UI-1, UI-2, UI-3 and UI-4 are evaluated by elderly people and young people as follows.

– Examinees:
   32 young people of age 20–24 (24 people without experience of keyboard instruments, and 8 people with experience), students of Engineering School, 1 female and 31 male.
   27 elderly people of age 60–79 (21 people* without experience of keyboard instruments, and 6 people** with experience), people who live near our University, all female. * age 60–64: 3 people, 65–69: 5, 70–74: 10, and 75–79: 3. ** 60–64: 1, 65–69: 2 and 70–74: 3.
– Songs used for the experiment: Sakura for UI-1, Haruno-ogawa for UI-2, Yuyake-koyake for UI-3, Mushinokoe for UI-4.
– Date: November, 2018 for elderly people, December, 2018 for young people.
– Condition before the experiment: The examinees did not practice the system.
– Condition during the experiment: First, the examinees played the system using each UI and score. Next, the examinees played and sang using each UI and score.

The examinees answered the questions by rating 4, 3, 2 or 1 (4:positive, 3:mildly positive, 2:mildly negative, 1:negative) for each UI and its score after using them. Questions are as follows.

Q1: Is the score easy?   Q2: Is the UI easy?
Q3: Is it easy to play?   Q4: Is it easy to play and sing at the same time?

Results and Discussion. The results of the experiments are as follows.

People Without Musical Experience. The mean values of questions for four UIs and scores answered by young people (24 people without experience of keyboard instruments) are shown in Table 1, and those answered by elderly people (21 people without experience) are shown in Table 3. Table 1 indicates that UI-2 and its score (note name representation), UI-3 and its score (number representation) and UI-4 and its score (color representation) might be easier to recognize and to use than UI-1 and its score (staff notation) for the people who are not familiar with musical performance. While, Table 3 indicates that UI-2, UI-3 and UI-4 might be easier to use than UI-1, however all UIs and scores may be almost the same to recognize.

Paired sample t-test was used for the comparison of the mean values of each question for two UIs. UI-1 and UI-2, UI-1 and UI-3, UI-1 and UI-4, UI-2 and UI-3, UI-2 and UI-4, and UI-3 and UI-4 are compared. In the experiment of 24 young people, the degrees of freedom is 23, and the critical value for significance level of 0.05 (two-tailed test) is 2.07. T-ratios of those comparisons are shown in Table 2. Table 2 shows that there is a significant difference between the mean values of UI-1 and UI-2/UI-3/UI-4 in Q3. This indicates that UI-2, UI-3 and UI-4 would be easier than UI-1 to play the system. Table 2 also shows that there is a significant difference between the mean values of UI-1/UI-2 and UI-3/UI-4 in Q4. This indicates that UI-3 and UI-4 would be easier than UI-1 and UI-2 to play and sing at the same time. The experiment of previous research showed the same result for UI-1, UI-2 and UI-3, and we confirmed that the number representation would useful to play and sing at the same time. Since the sequence of numbers (1, 2, 3 ... 7) is acquired by everyone, the spatial recognition of the number sequence on keyboard should be easy for most people. On the other hand, the experiment of this research showed that the color representation would be also useful to sing and play at the same time. In this system, the layout of colors on keyboard is based on the spectrum, so the spatial recognition of the color sequence might be easy for some people.

Table 1. Mean values of evaluation of UI-1/2/3/4 by young people without experience

	UI-1	UI-2	UI-3	UI-4
Q1	1.88	3.13	3.21	2.79
Q2	2.63	3.29	3.25	3.08
Q3	2.00	3.00	3.17	2.83
Q4	2.13	2.21	3.00	3.13

Table 2. T-ratios of t-test for UI-1/2/3/4 by young people without experience

	UI-1 vs. UI-2	UI-1 vs. UI-3	UI-1 vs. UI-4	UI-2 vs. UI-3	UI-2 vs. UI-4	UI-3 vs. UI-4
Q1	-6.19	-5.78	-3.82	-0.53	1.78	2.85
Q2	-4.00	-3.50	-2.30	0.37	1.31	1.28
Q3	-4.44	-5.67	-2.97	-1.16	0.61	1.40
Q4	-0.40	-3.60	-3.81	-5.38	-3.94	-0.65

Paired sample t-test was also used in the experiment of 21 elderly people. The degrees of freedom is 20, and the critical value for significance level of 0.05 (two-tailed test) is 2.09. T-ratios of UIs' comparisons are shown in Table 4. The result indicates that UI-2 and UI-3 would be easier than UI-1 to play the system. It also indicates that UI-3 would be easier than UI-1 to play and sing at the same time, however, it cannot indicate that UI-3 would be easier than UI-2 to play and sing at the same time. Note names would conflict with songs when young people use UI-2 and its score to play and sing at the same time; however, elderly people could sing without reading the lyric because they knew the songs (old Japanese songs) better than young people.

Table 3. Mean values of evaluation of UI-1/2/3/4 by elderly people without experience

	UI-1	UI-2	UI-3	UI-4
Q1	3.29	3.71	3.48	2.90
Q2	3.00	3.43	3.62	3.33
Q3	2.62	3.52	3.43	3.00
Q4	2.52	2.86	3.19	3.00

Table 4. T-ratios of t-test for UI-1/2/3/4 by elderly people without experience

	UI-1 vs. UI-2	UI-1 vs. UI-3	UI-1 vs. UI-4	UI-2 vs. UI-3	UI-2 vs. UI-4	UI-3 vs. UI-4
Q1	-2.12	-0.81	1.56	1.56	4.25	2.68
Q2	-2.01	-3.08	-1.50	-1.07	0.44	1.67
Q3	-3.40	-3.30	-1.36	0.49	2.45	2.01
Q4	-1.78	-3.16	-1.75	-1.38	-0.48	0.94

People with Musical Experience. The mean values of questions for four UIs and scores answered by 8 young people with experience of keyboard instruments are shown in Table 5. Table 5 indicates that UI-1 and its score (staff notation) would be useful for these people. Paired sample t-test was used for the comparison of the mean values of Q4 for UI-1 and UI-3. The critical value for significance level of 0.05 (two-tailed test) is 2.36, and t ratio is 1.93, therefore, this data cannot show the difference because the data is small.

The mean values of Q4 for UI-1 answered by 8 young people with musical experience (3.13 in Table 5) and 24 young people without experience (2.13 in Table 1) are compared using Welch's t-test. The critical value for significance level of 0.05 (two-tailed test) is 2.20 and t ratio is 2.24, therefore, this data can show the difference. UI-1 and its score (staff notation) would be useful for the people with experience of keyboard instruments. The mean values of questions for four UIs and scores answered by 6 elderly people with experience of keyboard instruments are not analyzed because the data is too small.

Table 5. Mean values of evaluation of UI-1/2/3/4 by young people with experience

	UI-1	UI-2	UI-3	UI-4
Q1	3.75	3.13	3.38	2.25
Q2	3.63	3.63	3.38	2.88
Q3	3.00	3.50	3.25	2.38
Q4	3.13	2.13	2.50	2.63

About the Performance. The mean values of Q3 and Q4 in Tables 1 and 3 for four UIs are also compared using paired sample t-test. In the experiment by 24 young people without experience of keyboard instruments, the degrees of freedom is 23 and the critical value for significance level of 0.05 (two-tailed test) is 2.07. T-ratios of the comparisons of mean values of Q3 and Q4 (in Table 1) are shown in Table 6. Tables 1 and 6 indicate that UI-2 (note name) would be easy to play but difficult to play and sing, and that UI-4 (color) would be difficult to play but easy to play and sing. In the experiment by 21 elderly people without experience, the degrees of freedom is 20 and the critical value for significance level of 0.05 (two-tailed test) is 2.09. T-ratios of the comparisons of mean values of Q3 and Q4 (in Table 3) are shown in Table 7. Tables 3 and 7 indicate that UI-2 would be easy to play but difficult to play and sing.

Table 6. T-ratios of t-test of Q3 and Q4 by young people without experience

	UI-1	UI-2	UI-3	UI-4
Q3 vs. Q4	−1.00	4.16	1.70	−2.29

Table 7. T-ratios of t-test of Q3 and Q4 by elderly people without experience

	UI-1	UI-2	UI-3	UI-4
Q3 vs. Q4	0.62	3.84	1.56	0.00

Choice of One UI and Score. The examinees also answered the question: Which UI and score do you choose to play and sing? The numbers of people who chose each UI and score are as follows.

(1) 24 young people without experience of keyboard instruments
     staff notation: 2, note name: 4, number: 8, color: 10
(2) 21 elderly people without experience of keyboard instruments
     staff notation: 5, note name: 7, number: 4, color: 5
(3) 8 young people with experience of keyboard instruments
     staff notation: 4, note name: 2, number: 0, color: 2
(4) 6 elderly people with experience of keyboard instruments
     staff notation: 2, note name: 0, number: 3, color: 1

Conclusion of the Experiment. The analysis of results shows that number representation would be useful to play and sing at the same time for the people who are not familiar with musical performance. The analysis also shows that note name/color representation would be useful for some people. The analysis shows that staff notation would be difficult for the people without musical experience; however, some of them prefer staff notation to other representations. On the other hand, staff notation would be useful for the people with musical experience; however, some of them prefer note name, number or color representation. Therefore, we decided to provide these four UIs and scores in our system.

3   Temperament, Scale and UI for Non-Western Music

This research added some functions to our system to conserve non-Western music genres. In this research we discuss koto music (one genre of Japanese traditional music) as non-Western music.

3.1   Temperament and Scale

Temperament. Koto music uses Pythagorean tuning system. In koto music, the tuning system had been strictly defined; however people today often use 12-tone equal temperament. Therefore, our system provides 12-tone equal temperament and Pythagorean system so that users can choose one of them.

   The temperament of koto music was defined in the author's research in 2001 [13]. We extracted the intervals between two notes sequentially from the koto score data, and found that the semitones and whole tones were restricted. We defined the interval used for the semitone as "x" and the interval not used for the semitone as "y". The sequence of these intervals (x and y) was determined as shown in Fig. 9. We calculated the frequency-ratios of tones: x = 256/243, y = 2187/2048, xy = 9/8. Figure 9 shows that the interval between D and D# is 256/243 (semitone), D and E is 9/8 (whole tone), D and G is 4/3 (perfect fourth), D and A is 3/2 (perfect fifth), and D and D' is 2 (one octave).

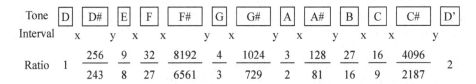

Fig. 9. The temperament of koto music

Scale. Users of this system can also study the scales other than the Major or Minor scales. Seven different scales are theoretically possible, and it is said that six different scales were used in medieval music. Koto music uses a scale which is different from Major or Minor scales. Our system provides an explanation about five scales: the Major, Minor, Japanese court music (Ryo and Ritsu) [14, 15], and koto music so that users can know the difference. The sequence of intervals (semitones and whole tones) is as follows, where "s" is semitone and "w" is whole tone.

Major: w w s w w w s
Minor: w s w w s w w
Japanese court music (Ryo): w w s w w s w
Japanese court music (Ritsu): w s w w w s w
Japanese traditional music (Miyako-bushi): s ww w s ww
   (Miyako-bushi is basically a pentatonic, where "ww" is a major third.)
koto music: s w w w s w w

In Major and Minor scales, there are keynotes. If the scale is Major and the keynote is C, it is called C Major. There are 15 keynotes in Major and Minor scales. In koto music, there are also keynotes. Since the intervals (frequency-ratios) of two sequential tones are not uniform (256/243 or 2187/2048), there are six keynotes theoretically. The author analyzed the frequency of each note appeared in koto score data because tunings cannot specify the keynotes, and found the five keynotes. We call them koto-modes as follows [16].

D koto-mode: D D# F G A A# C D' (mostly used in Hira-choshi tuning)
G koto-mode: G G# A# C D D# F G' (mostly used in Kumoi-choshi tuning)
A koto-mode: A A# C D E F G A'
C koto-mode: C C# D# F G G# A# C'
E koto-mode: E F G A B C D E'

3.2   Representation of UI

Our system provides the UI for koto music as Fig. 10, which is similar to UI-5 (vertical version of UI-3: number representation), with string numbers on the keyboard. Koto has 13 strings and each string is numbered: 1, 2 … 10, To, I, Kin (To, I and Kin are written in Chinese characters, and represent 11, 12 and 13). There is already a koto performance system (iKoto) on iPad [17], which has a UI that looks like a real koto with 13 strings. Since the aim of our system is the explanation about the difference between koto music and Western music, we developed the UI as keyboard.

Fig. 10. The UI of koto music for explanation

The UI of Fig. 10 is for D koto-mode (Hira-choshi tuning). The uses could play this system using koto scores, however, there are several restrictions in this version. Basically, users cannot use left-hand playing techniques, e.g., "Tsuyo-oshi" (pushing the string to make a pitch whole tone higher) can be replaced by playing the key marked as tsuyo-oshi (black triangle mark in Fig. 10) and "Yuri" (vibrato) cannot be played. Users cannot use normal right-hand playing techniques either, e.g., "Sha" (playing 2 tones at almost the same time) can be replaced by chord using multi-touch.

4 Score DB

4.1 Songs for Musical Performance

Score DB. We have been working on the DB of public domain songs. We have encoded 17 Japanese Children's songs and 10 English Children's songs in Humdrum format. We are now converting them to MusicXML format. We would like to add more songs to DB, however, we can't use most pieces of popular music because of the copyright. On the other hand, there are huge resources of Classical music pieces (mainly instrumental music) and there are some sites which provide free DBs.

Adding Rhythm and Melody to a Lyric. We have been developing the following system: When a user input a lyric to the system, the system adds melody and rhythm to the lyric using Classical music pieces. There are some systems which generate melody and rhythm to a lyric [18], however, our approach is reusing huge resources of Classical music. In this system, the rhythm (sequence of durations) is determined by the number of syllables and the parameters specified by the user. First, we developed the system for haiku (Japanese seventeen syllable poem). Since haiku has 5 syllables, 7 syllables and 5 syllables, we developed the system using rhythmic patterns of 5 notes and 7 notes, then we revised the system using algorithm to generate rhythms for 5 notes and 7 notes. Our system generates rhythms in four-four time. Examples of the rhythm for 5 notes are (quarter, quarter, 8th, 8th, quarter), (quarter, 8th, 16th, 16th, half), and so on, and examples of the rhythm for 7 notes are (8th, 8th, quarter, 8th, 8th, 8th, 8th), (quarter, 8th, 8th, 16th, 16th, 8th, quarter), and so on. On the other hand, the melody (sequence of pitches) is cut from the original piece and the starting point is specified by the user. Figure 11 shows the system which adds rhythm and melody to haiku.

In this research, we revised the system to generate rhythms for any numbers of notes to adapt the system for general poems. We made a DB of rhythmic patterns from score DB of Classical music in order to retrieve the rhythmic patterns for the numbers of syllables input by a user. For example, if a user inputs a poem: 6 syllables, 8 syllables and 7 syllables, the system retrieves rhythmic patterns for 6 notes, 8 notes and 7 notes. We used the score DB of Mozart's string quartets, which was developed by CCAHR, Stanford University [19].

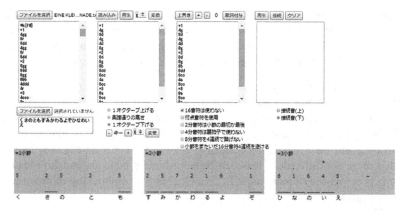

Fig. 11. The system for adding rhythm and melody to the lyric

Questionnaire. We have asked examinees who attended the experiment for the evaluation of UIs and scores. The questions and the numbers of answers are as follows.

(1) Do you want to use the system which adds melody to Haiku?

> Young people: Yes 13, No 19
> Elderly people: Yes 11, No 16

(2) Which is easy to write: Haiku? or Poem?

> Young people: Haiku 10, Poem 22
> Elderly people: Haiku 12, Poem 15

4.2   DB for Non-Western Music

We are interested in conserving non-Western music genres using musical performance system and score DB. Today, koto songs are not common even among the people who play the koto. People prefer instrumental koto music. There are two main problems in koto songs.

(1) There are variations of the melody of voice part because koto music had been an oral tradition. Koto songs have melisma mostly in each syllable, and the variations appear in the melisma.

(2) The rhythms of koto part and voice part are different (not synchronizing) as other genres of Japanese traditional music.

This system explain these problems using examples of koto scores.

Koto Scores. We have score data of the koto part and voice part of following songs: Sumiyoshi (1792 tones in koto part), Sakuragari (1724 tones), Enoshima (1413 tones), Kogo (1463 tones), Yuya (1503 tones), Shikinonagame (1627 tones). Two versions notated by Nakanoshima [20] and Ito [21] were encoded. Figure 12 shows examples of score data files. The koto scores are notated using string numbers. In the score data of Nakanoshima's Voice part, "51 1/8 11 # ke" means "bar 51, 8th note, string 11 with #, syllable ke". The tuning defines the pitch of each string, e.g., Hira-choshi tuning defines the pitches of the 1st to 13th strings as follows: D4 G3 A3 A#3 D4 D#4 G4 A4 A#4 D5 D#5 G5 A5, where middle C is C4. The pitches are converted from string numbers into MIDI note numbers, where middle C is 60, and a semitone is 1.

Melisma. Figure 13 shows examples of melismas in the voice part of Nakanoshima score and Ito score. In Fig. 13, the first pitch of each syllable is notated in MIDI note number and the melisma is notated by relative pitches. In Nakanoshima score of Fig. 12, the melisma of syllable "ke" is "11# 10 11## 11# 8", so it is converted to "76 74 77 76 69", and then it is represented as "76: −2 3 −1 −7" in Fig. 13. Figure 13 shows that there are differences between Nakanoshima's melisma and Ito's melisma. A melisma is composed of patterns, e.g., "−1−2 2" is the combination of down pattern (−1) and vibration (−2 2).

The differences of melismas are classified as follows [22].

- The first pitches of the melisma are different.
- The last patterns of the melisma are different or additional patterns are attached to the end of melisma.
- The middle patterns of the melisma are different or additional patterns are attached to the middle of melisma.

[Nakanoshima Voice Part]
49 1/4 -; 49 1/8 0; 49 1/8 10 uu; 50 1/8 -; 50 3/8 11 # ti; 51 3/8 -; 51 1/8 11 # ke; 52 1/8 -; 52 1/4 10 e; 52 1/8 11 ## e; 53 1/8 11 # e; 53 1/8 8 e; 53 1/8 10 mu; 53 1/8 11 # u;

[Ito Voice Part]
48 1/4 -; 48 1/8 10 o; 48 1/8 10 uu; 49 1/8 -; 49 3/8 11 # ti; 50 1/4 -; 50 1/8 10 i; 50 1/8 11 # ke; 51 1/8 -; 51 1/4 10 e; 51 1/8 11 ## e; 52 1/8 11 # e; 52 1/8 9 e; 52 1/8 10 mu; 52 1/8 11 # u;

[Nakanoshima Koto Part]
49 1/2 11 #; 50 1/4 11 # v; 50 1/4 0; 51 1/4 13; 51 1/4 11 #; 52 1/4 10; 52 1/4 12; 53 1/2 11 #;

Fig. 12. An example of koto score data file

[Nakanoshima's Melismas]	[Ito's Melismas]
uu 74 :	uu 74 :
ti 76 :	ti 76 : -2
ke 76 : -2 3 -1 -7	ke 76 : -2 3 -1 -6
mu 74 : 2 -2 -4 -1 -2	mu 74 : 2 -2 -4 -1 -2
ri 69 :	ri 69 : 1 -1 -2 2

Fig. 13. Examples of melisma

Rhythm. Figure 14 shows an example of the correspondence between koto part and voice part. Usually, the melody and rhythm of both parts are not synchronizing. The asynchronicity of rhythm is especially difficult for the people who are not familiar with Japanese traditional music. In the 50th bar of Fig. 14, string 11 with # (pushing the string to make a pitch semitone higher) is plucked at the beginning of the bar, and the syllable "ti" is pronounced in pitch 11# (the same pitch as the koto part) after 8th note from the beginning of the bar. Usually, the voice part follows the koto part; however, the voice part sometimes precedes the koto part.

[Nakanoshima Koto Part]	[Nakanoshima Voice Part]
49 1/2 11 #	49 1/4 -
	49 1/8 0
	49 1/8 10 uu
50 1/4 11 # v	50 1/8 -
50 1/4 0	50 3/8 11 # ti
51 1/4 13	51 3/8 -
51 1/4 11 #	51 1/8 11 # ke
52 1/4 10	52 1/8 -
52 1/4 12	52 1/4 10 e
	52 1/8 11 ## e

Fig. 14. An example of rhythms of koto part and voice part

5 Conclusions and Future Work

5.1 Conclusions

Musical Performance System and Scores. This research provides musical performance system and score display system. The performance system and display system have several representations of UI and score for the people who are not familiar with musical performance. The UIs are redesigned and developed on a tablet PC, which look like keyboards with note names/numbers/colors on the keys. Scores are notated by note names/numbers/colors.

Four UIs and scores are evaluated in the experiment: a plain keyboard and staff notation score, and keyboards of note name/number/color representation and scores of the same representation. Examinees are 32 young people (24 people without experience of keyboard instruments, and 8 people with experience) and 27 elderly people (21 people without experience of keyboard instruments, and 6 people with experience). The mean values of each question for two UIs are compared by t-test. The results of the experiment indicate that the number representation would be useful to most people and the note name/color representations would be useful to some people.

Public domain score DB is used to display scores in several representations. Score DB of Classical music is used to add the melody and rhythm to the lyric input by a user of this system.

System for Non-Western Music and Scores. This performance system also has a UI of koto music and it can be used to conserve koto music which is one genre of Japanese traditional music. This system explains the difference between the temperament and scale of koto music and those of Western music.

A koto score DB is used to conserve koto music along with the performance system. This system explains the melisma of koto songs and asynchronicity of the rhythms of voice part and koto part.

5.2   Future Work

Future work includes following problems. We have to improve the system on score DB for musical performance, which adds melody and rhythm to the lyric input by a user. DB of rhythmic patterns and the method to retrieve the melody from score DB should be enhanced. Also, the system should be evaluated by users.

We have to add some functions to the system for koto music, e.g., playing techniques. The explanation of melisma and rhythm of koto songs should be improved. Our system explains the difference between scales, so we are planning to do an experiment to know if people can recognize the difference. The analysis of asynchronicity of the rhythms will be challenging research.

Acknowledgments. The author would like to thank A. Sasaki, M. Aiga, T. Yamada, K. Nakashima and R. Shinohara for their contribution to the system development.

References

1. Groene, R.W.: Effectiveness of music therapy 1:1 intervention with individuals having senile dementia of the Alzheimer's type. J. Music Ther. **30**(3), 138–157 (1993)
2. Raglio, A., et al.: Efficacy of music therapy in the treatment of behavioral and psychiatric symptoms of dementia. Alzheimer Dis. Assoc. Disord. **22**(2), 158–162 (2008)
3. Satoh, M., et al.: Music therapy using singing training improves psychomotor speed in patients with Alzheimer's disease: a neuropsychological and fMRI study. Dement. Geriatr. Cogn. Disord. Extra **5**(3), 296–308 (2015)
4. Deguchi, S.: A study on the UI of musical performance system and score representation. In: AAAI 2018 Spring Symposium Series Technical Report, pp. 207–211 (2018)
5. Zbyszynski, M., et al.: Ten years of tablet musical inter-faces at CNMAT. In: Proceedings of the International Conference on New Interfaces for Musical Expression, pp. 100–105. NIME (2007)
6. Hochenbaum, J., et al.: Designing expressive musical interfaces for tabletop surfaces. In: Proceedings of the International Conference on NIME, pp. 315–318. NIME (2010)
7. Oh, J., et al.: Evolving the Mobile Phone Orchestra. In: Proceedings of the International Conference on New Interfaces for Musical Expression, pp. 82–87. NIME (2010)
8. Brown, D., Nash, C., Mitchell, T.: A user experience review of music interaction evaluations. In: Proceedings of the International Conference on NIME, pp. 370–375. NIME (2017)

9. Huron, D.: Humdrum Toolkit. https://csml.som.ohio-state.edu/Humdrum/. Accessed 10 Jan 2019
10. MusicXML. https://www.musicxml.com/. Accessed 10 Jan 2019
11. Miyagi, M.: Rokudan no Shirabe. Koto Score of Ikuta School, Hogakusha, Tokyo (2005)
12. Nakanoshima, K.: Rokudan no Shirabe. Koto Score of Yamada School, Hogakusha, Tokyo (2008)
13. Deguchi, S., Shirai, K.: An analysis of the temperament and the scale of koto music based on the scores. Transact. IPSJ **42**(3), 642–649 (2001)
14. Hirano, K., et al. (ed.): Nihon Ongaku Daijiten. Heibonsha, Tokyo (1989, In Japanese)
15. Toyo Ongaku Gakkai (ed.): Nihon no Onkai. Ongaku-no-tomo-sha, Tokyo (1982, In Japanese)
16. Deguchi, S., Selfridge-Field, E., Shirai, K.: The temperament, scale and mode of koto music. In: Proceedings of International Congress of Musicological Society of Japan 2002, pp. 434–438 (2002)
17. iKoto. http://www.gclue.com/. Accessed 10 Jan 2019
18. Sagayama, S.: ORPHEUS. http://www.orpheus-music.org/v3/. Accessed 10 Jan 2019
19. CCARH: Kern Scores. http://kern.ccarh.org/. Accessed 18 Jan 2019
20. Nakanoshima, K.: Koto Score of Yamada School, No. 1481, 1455, 1486, 1457, 1488, 1459, 1201, Hogakusha, Tokyo (1991–1997)
21. Ito, S.: Koto Score of Yamada School with Sangen Score, No. Ro-23, 10, 48, 39, 40, 62, 3, Hakushindo, Tokyo (1988–1998)
22. Deguchi, S., Shirai, K.: An analysis of melismatic patterns in koto songs. Comput. Musicol. **14**, 159–170 (2006)

Enhancing Cultural Engagement: A Heuristic Evaluation of World Cultural Heritage Websites

Yu-Hsiu Hung[1($\boxtimes$)], Yun-Lun Huang[1], and Chi-Wen Hsieh[2]

[1] Department of Industrial Design, National Cheng Kung University,
Tainan, Taiwan
{idhfhung, P36061061}@mail.ncku.edu.tw
[2] Telexpress, No. 45, Dongxing Road, Xinyi District, Taipei City, Taiwan
chiwendou@gmail.com

Abstract. Tourists usually visit cultural heritage websites before they travel to the actual sites. The design of the websites thus influences how an individual expect from the historical sites. This study aimed to investigate current cultural heritage websites and to identify the missing features/information that could potentially impact viewers' cultural engagement. A heuristic evaluation was conducted with eight subject matter experts (each having more than two years of cultural product/web design experiences) on ten world cultural heritage websites (e.g., the official ones for *Tower of London, Taj Mahal*, and *Statue of Liberty*, etc.). For the purpose of the evaluation, the goals of cultural web applications (proposed by the Minerva Working Group 5) were provided to the experts. Ratings and design recommendations were collected and analyzed. Results showed numerous misalignments with the goals that made the websites unable to effectively deliver cultural values to viewers. This paper provides insight and contributes to cultural heritage web design.

Keywords: Heuristic evaluation · Cultural engagement · Cultural heritage

1 Introduction

People in old days get information about historical sites through travel books, TV programs, or word of mouth. Nowadays, as Internet technologies advance, people obtain these information through social forums, blogs, or cultural websites. Thus, websites were developed that attempt to provide tourists with an overview of (1) the culture, the lifestyle of the people living in the geographical areas, the history of the people, their art, architecture, and religion(s), as well as (2) the services that engage tourists with the culture, such as location/parking information, events, schedule planning, [1]. However, the interfaces/information of the current cultural heritage websites do not necessarily allow tourists to get a good understanding of the culture and connect people to local places, objects, and events.

An effective and user-friendly cultural website should not only ensure the quality of delivered culture [2], but also propagate knowledge and provide learning sources and scientific research, etc. [3]. However, what current cultural heritage websites

© Springer Nature Switzerland AG 2019
M. Kurosu (Ed.): HCII 2019, LNCS 11568, pp. 192–202, 2019.
https://doi.org/10.1007/978-3-030-22636-7_13

communicate are simply factual information (e.g., direction to the place/site, the history of the place and/or the architecture, and tickets booking, etc.), in other words, filling visitors with facts. The websites are not designed to help visitors come to an understanding of 'hidden truths.' For example, visitors might want to know, while visiting the heritage site, how to get immersed into the cultural aspects of the heritage, as well as how to explore the value of the heritage and how to relate this value to them in their real life.

In the literature, the quality issues of cultural websites had been studied extensively. Di Blas, Guermand, Orsini, and Paolini [4] developed a framework, called "*MiLE*," to evaluate the quality and usability of museum websites. The framework broke the features and the contents of a museum website into three groups of constituents: (1) site presentation, (2) museum presentation, and (3) virtual museum. The framework divided tourists' concerns into three types of tasks: (a) Practical (a tourist wants to gather useful information), (b) Operational (a tourist wants to do something) and (c) Cognitive (a tourist wishes to learn something). In Di Blas et al.'s framework, twelve criteria for inspecting an intended website were proposed: *Efficiency, Authority, Currency, Consistency, Structure effectiveness, Accessibility, Completeness, Richness, Clarity, Conciseness, Multimediality, Multilinguisticity*. In a similar vein, Davoli, Mazzoni, and Corradini [5] looked at the quality of cultural websites from the perspectives of usability and technical performance. In their study, six quantitative linguistic indices were used: *Basic functionality, Advanced functionality, Usability, Accessibility, Efficiency, and Maintainability and Compliance*.

In fact, according to Minerva Working Group [3], users' perceptions of a cultural website are determined not only by the cultural content it offers, but also by the history of the institution it represents, by its mission, by its functional organization and by its internal and external relations. Caffo and Hagedorn-Saupe [2] shared the same viewpoint of Minerva Working Group [3]. They asserted that a good quality cultural website must be transparent, content-effective, updated at an appropriate level, accessible to all users, user-centred, responsive, multi-linguality, being interoperable within cultural networks, managed to respect legal issues such as IPR and privacy, and finally preserved for the long-term use. The above studies indicated that the quality of a cultural website should not be viewed simply on its usability-related attributes (e.g., esthetics, functionality, efficiency, effectiveness, etc.). Tourists' cultural needs and engagements were not seriously considered for increasing the satisfaction and enjoyment of visiting the heritage sites [4].

The purpose of cultural heritages is mainly about delivering cultural values, as well as provoking thoughts and awareness of the significance of culture. Thus, this study aimed at investigating current cultural heritage websites, as well as identifying the missing features/information that could impact viewers' perceptions and expectations of an intended culture. For the purpose of the evaluation, the quality goals for cultural websites [6] were used. The following research question guided the design of the experiment in this study: "*What are the misalignments with the quality goals that made the websites unable to effectively deliver cultural values to viewers?*" This study is important as it provides insight and contributes to cultural heritage web design.

2   Literature Review

2.1   The Definition and Importance of Cultural Entity

Different countries and races have their own unique culture. However, the formation of culture takes time, which makes it a fairly abstract subject [7]. Conversely, if cultural elements (language, symbol, religion, artifact, object, and social norm) are not adequately preserved, culture could disappear quickly. Thus, organizations/institutions/ societies for the conservation of cultural and scientific heritage started to draw public attentions. These organizations/institutions/societies, according to Minerva Group 5 [6], are called cultural entities who conserve tangible and intangible cultural knowledge and value. They generate and propagate knowledge to influence the value and the way of thinking among people in real world [2].

Museums or historical heritages are cultural entities that are having greater impacts. In one hand, they contain rich cultural elements. On the other hand, their numbers of visitors are increasing across these years [4]. Take the number of visitors of the Louvre Museum for instance, the number has grown exponentially, averagely increasing two hundred thousand visitors per year [8].

As web applications have become a major channel that tourists used to understand cultural entities, improving the design of cultural web applications has become a vital issue [9, 10] for designers.

2.2   The Quality Framework for Cultural Web Applications

The quality of cultural websites is important to ensure cultural contents are delivered to users. However, quality is a broad, generic and a subjective concept. In reality, the most comprehensive framework to assess the quality of cultural web applications was proposed by the Minerva Working Group 5 [6].

Minerva is a network of European Union member states' ministries (started from 2002) working together as a national representatives group in building an information society for all European citizens that reflects the wealth of European cultural creation and heritage. One of the main goals of the network was to support cultural institutions all over Europe as they were in charge of preserving and exploiting heritage and played an important role in delivering the best services to European citizens.

As high-quality websites allow European citizens to discover, to explore and to benefit from online material representing the diversity of European culture, the Minerva group defined and published twelve goals (satisfying both the goals of cultural institutions and their users) to promote the quality of cultural websites. The goals are in the following:

(1) **Presentation of the identity of the cultural entity:** A high-quality website should demonstrate the constitutional elements that contributed to forming the unique features of a cultural entity.

(2) **Transparency on the activities of the cultural entity:** A high-quality website should show activities (including programmes, projects, funding, procedures, realization phases, and/or results) that achieve the mission of a cultural entity.

(3) **Transparency on the mission of the cultural web application**: A high-quality website should show an obvious purpose or mission by stating the subject of the website, the most important content on the site, and the organization responsible for maintaining the site, and optionally the target audience.

(4) **Efficiency in the sector networks:** A high-quality website must collaborate and coordinate with other similar online cultural entities. Each site activates a section which, via links to parallel available resources (those with the same objectives), puts information, databases, and references into common use. The co-ordination is based on co-operative participation (i.e. between equals and aimed at achieving a common objective). This principle broadens the focus of quality beyond the individual website, by considering how it can interface with other cultural websites and with entities, such as cultural portals, which are higher and lower in the information hierarchy.

(5) **Presentation of standards and regulations of the sector**: A high-quality website must have updated references to the basic regulations in the cultural sector and on the mission of the cultural entity, with the added value of an institutional picture of the cultural activity.

(6) **Spreading of cultural content:** A high-quality website must spread cultural content for the purpose of promoting culture growth. The spreading must be managed to respect legal issues (such as intellectual property rights and privacy) and clearly state the terms and conditions on which the website and its contents may be used.

(7) **Support of cultural tourism**: A high-quality website must provide services of information in tourism activities that aim to sustain the territorial values of the cultural heritage.

(8) **Offer of educational services**: A high-quality website must exploit the cultural heritage by providing multimedia and interactive didactic support to demonstrate how and when the cultural heritage gained its significance in the history. Didactic web services (such as e-magazines for diffusion of news and comments) between similar or related sites can be created to encourage connections between cultural heritage and the territory.

(9) **Offer of services of scientific research**: A high-quality website should provide researchers with consulting scientific documentation and the access to reports, library catalogues, archive inventories, and/or museum catalogues.

(10) **Offer of services to specialists in the sector:** A high-quality website should offer services to specialists in their sectors of cultural and scientific heritages. The services can be supplied on demand or through various enrolments.

(11) **Offer of services of reservation and acquisition of goods:** A high-quality website must be accessible to all users (despite of their disabilities), regarding navigation, content, interactive elements, digital resources, and acquisition of goods, etc.

(12) **Promotion of web communities in the sector:** A high-quality website must establish strategies for reaching various user categories in the culture sector through interactive tools/media on the website. User comments and feedback are expected to be collected, analyzed, and monitored continuously to enhance the quality of the services and to promote the influence of the cultural entity in its web communities.

The above goals form the quality framework for assessing cultural web applications. We believed that this quality framework could be used to predict tourists' engagements with an intended culture. In fact, similar framework could be easily found in the literature. Although they are not as comprehensive as the one Minerva proposed, they were proved to be valid [4, 5]. What drew the attention of this research was that the adoption rates of these cultural design framework had been low-evidenced by the fact that cultural websites did not effectively deliver the missions/values of cultural heritages, causing bad user experiences in terms of cultural engagement. Thus, the research questions that were not particularly answered were: "What is wrong with the design of the current cultural heritage websites?", and "what caused tourists' misperceptions of the missions/values of the cultural heritages?" The following explains our research method for answering these research questions.

3 Method

3.1 Participants

A heuristic evaluation [11, 12] was conducted with eight subject matter experts (each having cultural product/web design experiences) (SMEs) on the levels of cultural engagement of 10 world heritage websites. Our number of experts satisfied Nielsen's [13] evaluation requirements that suggested that five experts were able to identify 80% of the problems of a website. The twelve quality goals for cultural websites (developed by the Minerva Working Group 5) were given to the experts. The rating score ranged from 0 to 5, 0 being not at all satisfied with the quality principle, and 5 being extremely satisfied with the quality principle. Each of the experts evaluated the websites individually without communications. Ratings and design recommendations were collected and analyzed by researchers of this study.

3.2 Materials

The website assessments were conducted using a personal laptop. The ten selected world cultural heritage websites (determined by the popularity and the number of visitors stated on the websites) included: (1) *Tower of London* (https://www.hrp.org.uk/tower-of-london/), (2) *Taj Mahal* (https://www.tajmahal.gov.in/), (3) *Emperor Qin Shi Huang's Mausoleum Site Museum* (http://www.bmy.com.cn/2015new/index.htm), (4) *Leaning Tower of Pisa* (http://www.towerofpisa.org/), (5) *Palace and Park of Versailles* (http://en.chateauversailles.fr/discover/estate/palace), (6) *Itsukushima Shinto Shrine* (http://www.en.itsukushimajinja.jp/), (7) *Acropolis of Athens* (http://www.acropolisofathens.gr/aoa/), (8) *Statue of Liberty* (https://www.nps.gov/stli/index.htm), (9) *The Great Wall* (http://www.great-wallofchina.com/), and (10) *Hagia Sophia Museum* (https://ayasofyamuzesi.gov.tr/en). Each SME was given a standardized form for performing the website assessments. The form included Minerva's goals for cultural websites and their definitions. Along with each principle was a space for entering the rating score, the explanations for the score, and the design comments.

3.3 Procedure

Before the evaluation started, the researcher explained the purpose of the experiment and obtained the consents from the participants. The researchers then gave the assessment forms to the participants. Participants were told to take their time and that they could ask any questions about the form and the experiment.

After being familiarizing with the content of the form, participants were shown the list of ten world cultural heritage websites and asked to perform the assessments. Participants were asked to use as much time as they want to look at, in every website, the design, the features, the functions, the information, the layout, etc. Participants were asked to rate how well the website design satisfied the requirements of each of the Minerva's goals. Participants were also asked to provide the explanations for their ratings, the comments, and the design recommendations for the websites.

In the experiment, every participant performed his/her assessments individually without communications and discussions. No time restrictions were put on the website assessments.

4 Results

The aim of the study was to investigate current cultural heritage websites and to identify the missing features/information and bad designs that caused misunderstanding and misinterpretations of an intended culture. The descriptive statistics of the ratings of the eight SMEs were shown in Table 1. From Table 1, the mean ratings for the websites were very different, ranging from 1.11 to 4.05.

Table 1 also shows that fifty percent of the websites received ratings above the average (2.5) of the 6-point rating scale. The website that received the highest mean rating was "*Tower of London*", with the rating of 4.05. The website that received the lowest mean rating was "*Itsukushima Shinto Shrine*" with the rating of 1.11.

Table 2 describes how well the websites engage tourists with culture from the viewpoint of each quality principle. From Table 2, we can see that only five goals were satisfied (with the mean ratings $\geq$ 2.5) by the design of the cultural heritage websites. Particularly, "Goal #1: Presentation of the identity of the cultural entity" was mostly addressed, with the rating of 3.8. "Goal #5: Presentation of standards and regulations of the sector," "Goal #12: Promotion of web communities in the sector," and "Goal #9: Offer of services of scientific research," were least addressed, with the rating of only 1.73, 1.65, and 1.55, respectively.

Table 1. Descriptive statistics for the ratings of the ten cultural heritage websites

No.	Cultural heritage website	Mean	SD
1	Tower of London	4.05	1.12
2	Palace and Park of Versailles	3.43	1.48
3	Statue of Liberty	2.97	1.67
4	Leaning Tower of Pisa	2.74	1.76
5	Emperor Qin Shi Huang's Mausoleum Site Museum	2.64	1.79
6	Hagia Sophia Museum	2.20	1.69
7	Acropolis of Athens	1.96	1.55
8	Taj Mahal	1.82	1.42
9	The Great Wall	1.68	1.52
10	Itsukushima Shinto Shrine	1.11	1.38

Note: Range of rating score: 0 to 5; 0 represents "not at all satisfied with the quality principle;" 5 represents "extremely satisfied with the quality principle."

Table 2. Descriptive statistics: how-well the cultural websites satisfied the quality goals

	Quality goals for cultural websites	Mean	SD
Goal #1	Presentation of the identity of the cultural entity	3.80	1.00
Goal #6	Spreading of cultural content	3.24	1.13
Goal #3	Transparency on the mission of the cultural web application	3.00	1.34
Goal #2	Transparency on the activities of the cultural entity	2.96	1.78
Goal #8	Offer of educational services	2.50	1.85
Goal #4	Efficiency in the sector networks	2.46	1.75
Goal #7	Support of cultural tourism	2.24	1.73
Goal #10	Offer of services to specialists in the sector	2.24	1.83
Goal #11	Offer of services of reservation and acquisition of goods	2.14	1.81
Goal #5	Presentation of standards and regulations of the sector	1.73	1.66
Goal #12	Promotion of web communities in the sector	1.65	1.59
Goal #9	Offer of services of scientific research	1.55	1.86

Note: Range of rating score: 0 to 5; 0 represents "not at all satisfied with the quality principle;" 5 represents "extremely satisfied with the quality principle."

5   Discussion and Design Recommendations

The descriptive statistics of the heuristic evaluation suggested that the design of the cultural heritage websites was diverse in engaging tourists with culture.

To explore how each cultural website addressed each of the quality goals, Table 3 was constructed. From Table 3, we can see that only one website addressed Goal #5, only two websites addressed Goal #12, only three websites addressed Goal #7, Goal #9, and Goal #11, and only four websites addressed Goal #10. These results explained the low mean rating scores of some cultural websites in Table 1. In fact, the SMEs commented in the experiment that these cultural heritage websites did not (1) present information on the standards and regulations of their intended culture; (2) provide good amounts of information services in tourism activities; (3) provide enough supports and services for scientific research and specialist activities; (4) offer tourists a convenient channel to purchase goods and reserve services; (5) aggressively promote culture to other web communities/user groups. These comments answered the research question regarding the websites' misalignments with the quality goals proposed by the Minerva Working Group 5.

Table 3. The average ratings for the cultural heritage websites in satisfying the quality goals

	W1	W2	W3	W4	W5	W6	W7	W8	W9	W10	Number of websites addresses the goal
Goal #1	4.8	3.3	3.9	4.5	4.3	3.5	3.4	3.9	2.8	3.9	10
Goal #2	4.9	1.3	3.4	4.0	4.5	0.8	0.9	3.5	2.4	4.1	6
Goal #3	3.9	1.6	3.8	4.3	3.8	1.8	3.1	3.4	2.1	2.8	7
Goal #4	4.5	2.6	1.0	3.5	2.0	0.0	2.9	3.0	2.6	2.3	6
Goal #5	3.5	2.0	0.8	1.3	1.9	1.1	1.9	2.4	1.8	0.8	1
Goal #6	3.9	2.3	3.1	3.8	4.5	2.3	2.5	4.4	2.6	3.1	8
Goal #7	4.0	2.4	1.9	2.4	3.6	1.5	1.0	3.1	1.5	1.0	3
Goal #8	4.8	0.6	3.5	3.1	2.8	1.1	2.6	4.3	1.0	1.3	6
Goal #9	3.4	0.6	3.5	0.4	3.4	0.3	1.9	0.5	0.6	1.0	3
Goal #10	3.4	1.6	3.4	1.3	3.9	0.5	2.4	2.5	1.3	2.3	4
Goal #11	4.8	1.8	1.9	2.6	4.0	0.4	0.8	2.4	1.1	1.8	3
Goal #12	3.0	1.9	1.6	1.9	2.6	0.3	0.3	2.4	0.4	2.3	2
Number of Goals Satisfied	12	2	7	7	10	1	5	8	3	4	

Note: The cell that contains a fill color denotes satisfaction with the quality goal (the rating score≧2.5); **W1:** *Towel of London*; **W2:** *Taj Mahal*; **W3:** *Emperor Qin Shi Huang*; **W4:** *Leaning Tower of Pisa*; **W5:** *Palace and Park of Versailles*; **W6:** *Itsukushima Shinto Shrine*; **W7:** *Acropolis of Athens*; **W8:** *Statue of Liberty*; **W9:** *The Great Wall*; **W10:** *Hagia Sophia Museum*

Table 3 also shows how well each website satisfied the overall quality framework. From Table 3, we can see that only three websites (W1: *Towel of London*, W5: *Palace and Park of Versailles*, and W8: *Statue of Liberty*) were able to satisfy over 60% of the goals (≧8 goals) in the quality framework. The website design of W6: *Itsukushima Shinto Shrine* only satisfied one of the goals (Goal #1) in the quality framework.

By looking at the highest rating scores of the goals and their corresponding websites, we summarized the design comments made by the SMEs in the following. These could be used as design strategies for enhancing cultural engagements with tourists.

(1) With regards to Goal #1, cultural heritage websites could clearly state their identity using a short and concise sentence along with the iconic image of the heritage on the landing page. On the landing page, it is important as well to

embed images and information related with key cultural DNAs (including symbols, behaviors, objects, norms, and values, etc.) [14] of intended culture, allowing visitors virtually interacting with the heritage in the first place.

(2) With regards to Goal #2, cultural heritage websites could present events and activities either all on the landing page or with a clearly identifiable link/tab on the landing page. Information about the events and activities could use differing media (e.g., text, image, or animation) to engage with viewer attention.

(3) With regards to Goal #3, cultural heritage websites should clearly state their missions, responsibilities, and objectives using either clear/concrete/concise sentences or a numbered list of items. These information should be placed either in the landing page or with a clearly identifiable link/tab on the landing page.

(4) With regards to Goal #4, cultural heritage websites could use an easily identifiable link/tab showing that they maintain good relationships and actively collaborate with other (nearby/related) cultural entities in preserving and creating shared cultural values.

(5) With regards to Goal #5, cultural heritage websites should show updated and direct links/references to the standards/regulations related with cultural preservation.

(6) With regards to Goal #6, the information shown in cultural heritage websites should be written in simple and easily-understood language and respect legal issues (such as intellectual property rights and privacy) and clearly state the terms and conditions on which the website and its contents may be used.

(7) With regards to Goal #7, cultural heritage websites should provide touring services/information and/or links to other local cultural spots that tourists can benefit when/after visiting the cultural heritage.

(8) With regards to Goal #8, cultural heritage websites should provide the didactic services (e.g., showing historical events chronically) that engage tourists with intended culture. The services should be tailored to satisfy differing customer needs (e.g., the elderly/people with disabilities, etc.) and be delivered with interactive multimedia/games.

(9) With regards to Goal #9 and #10, cultural heritage websites should show the services (in details) that they provide particularly to researchers/specialists in the cultural sector. Some digital archival records such as books/magazines/reports could be made online available to a vast community of researchers.

(10) With regards to Goal #11, cultural heritage websites could place links that can be easily seen in the landing page to guide visitors to the shopping/ticket/space and service booking pages. These pages should present information (e.g., tickets, rooms, gifts, books/publications, or collections, etc.) in a nice order and with high quality images and item descriptions. Payments should be made flexibly and easily.

(11) With regards to Goal #12, cultural heritage websites could leverage the power of social media (e.g., using Facebook, Twitter, or Instagram applications and call-to-action buttons, etc.) to promote the explicit/implicit cultural values to differing social groups locally or internationally and to obtain feedback from their visitors for enhancing the quality of the provided services.

6 Conclusions

The purpose of the study was to assess well-known world cultural heritage websites and to identify the missing features/information that could impact viewers' cultural engagement. Heuristic evaluation was conducted with eight SMEs using the Minerva's quality framework for cultural web applications. Results of the study showed that the mean ratings for the ten cultural websites were diverse (ranging from 1.1 to 4.05), which suggested that current cultural heritage websites could not consistently and effectively arouse viewers' cultural engagement.

Our evaluation also found that only five out of ten websites received ratings above 2.5 (the average of the 6-point rating scale); only three websites (W1: *Towel of London*, W5: *Palace and Park of Versailles*, and W8: *Statue of Liberty*) were able to satisfy over 60% of the goals (≥ 8 goals) in the quality framework.

The SMEs commented that, in general, cultural heritage websites did not (1) provide information on the standards and regulations of intended culture; (2) provide sufficient information on services in tourism activities; (3) provide information on the services for scientific research and specialist activities; (4) offer tourists an easily identifiable channel to purchase goods and reserve services; (5) put efforts in promoting culture to other community users.

This study also made twelve practical design recommendations for cultural heritage websites. It was our hope that the outcomes provide insight in the field of designing cultural heritage web. This study is limited by the number of evaluated cultural heritage websites and by the use of SMEs for identifying design problems. To enhance the validity of the research outcomes, more cultural websites should be included and surveys should be distributed to real end users for the evaluation.

References

1. Mich, L., Franch, M., Marzani, P.: Guidelines for excellence in the web sites of tourist destinations: a study of the regional tourist boards in the alps. In: IADIS International Conference e-Society (2004)
2. Caffo, R., Hagedorn-Saupe, M.: Handbook on Cultural Web User Interaction. Mi-nerva EC Working Group Quality, Accessibility and Usability (2008)
3. Minerva Working Group: Quality Principles for Cultural Websites: a Handbook (2005)
4. Di Blas, N., Guermand, M.P., Orsini, C., Paolini, P.: Evaluating the Features of Museum Websites: (The Bologna Report) (2002)
5. Davoli, P., Mazzoni, F., Corradini, E.: Quality assesment of cultural web sites with fuzzy operators. J. Comput. Inf. Syst. **46**(1), 44–57 (2005)
6. Minerva Working Group 5: Handbook for Quality in Cultural Web Sites Improving Quality for Citizens (2003). http://www.minervaeurope.org/publications/qualitycriteria1_2draft/qualitypdf1103.pdf. Accessed 1 Feb 2019
7. Smith, A., Dunckley, L., French, T., Minocha, S., Chang, Y.: A process model for developing usable cross-cultural websites. Interact. Comput. **16**(1), 63–91 (2004)
8. The Musée du Louvre. http://presse.louvre.fr/10-2-million-visitors-to-the-louvre-in-2018/. Accessed 3 Jan 2019

9. Cunliffe, D., Kritou, E., Tudhope, D.: Usability evaluation for museum web sites. Mus. Manage. Curatorship **19**(3), 229–252 (2001)

10. Marty, P., Twidale, M.: Lost in gallery space: a conceptual framework for analyzing the usability flaws of museum Web sites. First Monday, 9(9) (2004)

11. Nielsen, J., Molich, R.: Heuristic evaluation of user interfaces. In: Proceedings of the SIGCHI Conference on Human Factors in Computing Systems, pp. 249–256. ACM, March 1990

12. Nielsen, J.: Finding usability problems through heuristic evaluation. In: Proceedings of the SIGCHI Conference on Human Factors in Computing Systems, pp. 373–380. ACM, June 1992

13. Nielsen, J.: Why you only need to test with 5 users, 2000. Jakob Nielsen's Alertbox (2012). www.useitcom/alertbox/20000319.html

14. Hung, Y.H., Lee, W.T., Goh, Y.S.: Integration of characteristics of culture into product design: a perspective from symbolic interactions. In: Proceedings of the 15th International Conference on Human-Computer Interaction. Las Vegas, United States (2013)

Development of an Embodied Group Entrainmacent Response System to Express Interaction-Activated Communication

Yutaka Ishii[✉] and Tomio Watanabe

Okayama Prefectural University, Kuboki 111, Soja, Okayama, Japan
{ishii,watanabe}@cse.oka-pu.ac.jp

Abstract. In situations that demand audience participation, such as lectures and speeches, the sense of unity of the communication place is created by mutual interactions between the performer and audience. Therefore, the speaker's willingness to talk increases with the increase in the responses of the listeners, thus strengthening the interaction. We have developed a speech-driven embodied entrainment toy robot called Pekoppa that generates communicative motions and actions such as nods for entrained interactions from speech rhythm based only on voice input. In this research, we developed a system that activates the interaction by changing the embodied response by nodding from multiple toy robots based on speech inputs. Moreover, we confirmed the effectiveness of the system by sensory evaluation and behavior analysis through experiments on 24 participants.

Keywords: Embodied communication · Group entrainment · Audience characters

1 Introduction

In scenes with audience participation, such as lectures and speeches, the sense of unity of the communication place depends on the mutual interactions between the performer and audience. Visualizing the excitement of the audience is considered important for effective communication. Sejima has defined the state in which embodied interactions, such as body motions and voice responses, are activated as "interaction-activated communication", and the effectiveness of this estimation model has been confirmed by the heat conduction equation using speakers' voice inputs [1].

In contrast, group communication is formed by a gradual gathering of people around the speaker that causes excitement. Therefore, the speaker's willingness to talk depends on the number of listeners, who gradually form a group and activate the interaction.

In this research, we developed a system that activates interaction through changes in the embodied response by nodding using multiple objects based on speech inputs. We confirmed the effectiveness of the system by evaluation experiments.

© Springer Nature Switzerland AG 2019
M. Kurosu (Ed.): HCII 2019, LNCS 11568, pp. 203–211, 2019.
https://doi.org/10.1007/978-3-030-22636-7_14

2 Related Work

Watanabe et al. developed a speech-driven embodied interactive actor called Inter-Actor, with functions of both speaker and listener, for activating human interaction and communication by generating expressive actions and motions that are coherently related to speech inputs [2]. Giannopulu et al. has reported that minimalistic artificial environments, such as toy robots, could be considered as the root of neuronal organization and reorganization with the potential to improve brain activity in children with autism [3]. Moreover, they analyzed nonverbal and verbal information associated with the heart rate and emotional feeling in ASD and neurotypical children respectively. As a result, analogies of heart rate between ASD and neurotypical children were expressed when the human was the 'passive' actor and the robot was the 'active' actor; disanalogies were observed when the human was the 'active' actor [4].

Regarding the collective communication research by robot, Karatas et al. proposed driving agents called NAMIDA (Navigational Multiparty based Intelligent Driving Agents) as three friendly interfaces those sit on the dashboard inside a car [5]. Rubenstein et al. proposed an open-source, low cost robot called Kilobot that designed to make testing collective algorithms on hundreds or thousands of robots [6].

3 Overview of an Embodied Group Entrainment Response System

3.1 Concept

In a one-to-many dialogue situation such as a speech or an over-the-counter sale, the presence of the audience greatly affects the activation of the interaction. Active involvement of audiences influences the interaction with other audiences and motivates the speaker's utterances. In this research, we propose a communication support system showing activation of interaction by an increase in the audience objects. A communication effect is obtained by group entrainment using a response model based only on the speech input (Fig. 1).

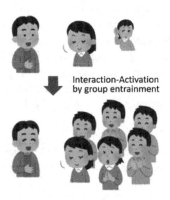

Fig. 1. Concept.

3.2   Interaction Model

A listener's interaction model includes a nodding reaction model that estimates the nodding timing from a speech ON-OFF pattern and a body reaction model linked to the nodding reaction model (Fig. 2). A hierarchy model consisting of two stages, macro and micro, predicts the timing of the nodding. The macro stage estimates whether a nodding response exists in a duration unit that consists of a talkspurt episode $T(i)$ and the subsequent silence episode $S(i)$ with a hangover value of 4/30 s. The estimator $M_u(i)$ is a moving-average (MA) model, expressed as the weighted sum of unit speech activity R (i) in (1) and (2). When $M_u(i)$ exceeds the threshold value, the nodding $M(i)$ is also an MA model, estimated as the weighted sum of the binary speech signal $V(i)$ in (3). The body movements are related to the speech input at a timing over the body threshold. The body threshold is set lower than that of the nodding prediction of the MA model that is expressed as the weighted sum of the binary speech signal to nodding.

$$M_u(i) = \sum_{j=1}^{J} a(j)R(i-j) + u(i) \tag{1}$$

$$R(i) = \frac{T(i)}{T(i) + S(i)} \tag{2}$$

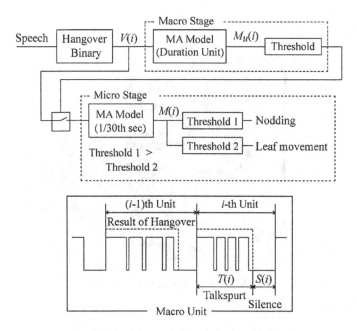

Fig. 2. Listener's interaction model.

$a(j)$: linear prediction coefficient
$T(i)$: talkspurt duration in the i-th duration unit
$S(i)$: silence duration in the i-th duration unit
$u(i)$: noise

$$M(i) = \sum_{k=1}^{K} b(j)V(i-j) + w(i) \tag{3}$$

$b(j)$: linear prediction coefficient
$V(i)$: voice
$w(i)$: noise

3.3 Development of System Prototype

System Prototype Using LED. In this research, we developed a prototype system based on the concept of light emission by an LED (Fig. 3). Based on the listener interaction model, the listeners group is represented by the blinking LED corresponding to the speaker's voice input. However, a few test users opined that an LED is difficult to recognize as an independent object, and it seems like a product of art on the panel (Fig. 4).

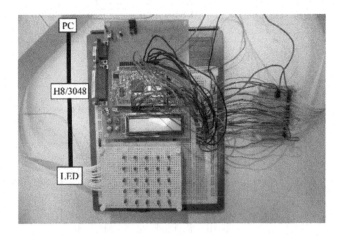

Fig. 3. System prototype using LED.

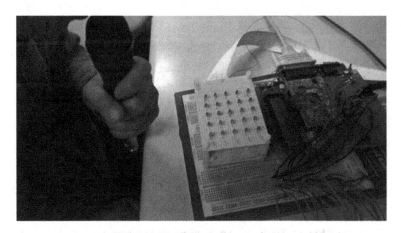

Fig. 4. Example of a using scene.

System Construction Using Bilobed Plant Toys. To express the increase in the number of independent objects reacting to the speaker, we assumed a situation in which toy plants that perform large interaction actions against human speech are spread. Based on a model predicting nodding from the voice of the interlocutor, 25 of the bilobed plant toys (Fig. 5 Pekoppa: SegaToys 2008) that perform nodding reactions automatically are placed on a 700 mm square plate. They are arranged in 5 rows on the board and express the group (Fig. 6). Vocal utterance is captured by the microphone input on the PC and the timing estimation result of the nodding start is transmitted from the PC to the H8/3048 micro-computer by serial communication. The H8 microcomputer individually controls the behavior of the plant-type toy, so that any toy can nod and react at the timing of the nod starting. Interaction activation based on population entrainment can thus be considered by expressing increase of listener individual freely.

Fig. 5. Pekoppa: a bilobed plant toy.

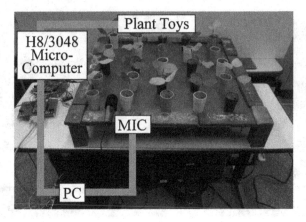

Fig. 6. System prototype using bilobed plant toys.

4 System Evaluation Experiment

4.1 Experimental Setup

We conducted an evaluation experiment to examine the motivation of the speaker's utterance. Experiments were conducted in a three-mode comparison. These are Mode A in which all the plant type toys nod from the beginning of the nodding timing, Mode B in which the plant type toys nod in a row by side frequency (Fig. 7), and Mode C in which the number of plant type toys nods increases from one to semicircular. (Figure 8). Each participant was presented with the three modes in a random order to eliminate any ordering effect. Experiment participants were 24 male/female students aged 18 to 24 years.

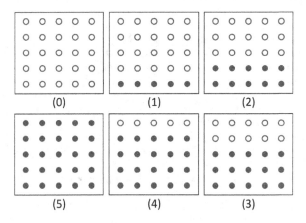

Fig. 7. Increasing pattern in Mode B.

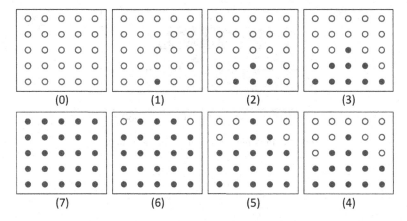

Fig. 8. Increasing pattern in Mode C.

At first, the participants were introduced to the three operational modes and the differences between them while using the system. Next, the subjects were instructed to perform a pairwise comparison of each mode for an overall evaluation. Since three comparisons were required, the experiment was conducted three (= 3C2) times. Then, the questionnaire was examined using a-3 (not at all) to 3 (extremely) bipolar rating scale. The subjects evaluated the three modes in terms of six items—preference, enjoyment, ease of talking, comfortableness, interaction-activation, and usability. Finally, we conducted a free utterance experiment to stop the utterance when the participants thought that it was sufficient. The upper limit of speech time was set to 300 s.

4.2   Result

The results of the paired comparison for the three modes are shown in Table 1. Figure 9 shows the calculated results of the evaluation provided in Table 1, based on the Bradley–Terry model given in Eq. (4). Mode C in which the number of plant-type toys' nods increase from one to semicircular was evaluated most affirmatively, with Mode A and Mode B following the order.

Table 1. Result of the paired comparison.

	A	B	C	Total
A		13	11	24
B	11		10	21
C	13	14		27

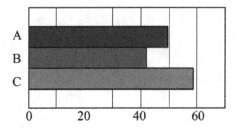

Fig. 9. Preference strength π for each mode.

$$P_{ij} = \frac{\pi_i}{(\pi_i + \pi_j)}$$
$$\sum_i \pi_i = const.(= 100) \tag{4}$$

(π_i: intensity of i, P_{ij}: probability of judgement that i is better than j.)

Figure 10 shows the result of the sensory evaluation in the experiment. Significant differences between each of the three modes were obtained by administering Friedman's test. Significant differences were also obtained by administering the Wilcoxon's rank test for multiple comparisons. As a result, a significant level of 5% was obtained for the "Interaction-Activation" factors between Modes A and C. The plant type toy that responds to the speaker's voice seemed to come closer to the experiment participant, and the speaker gradually felt the interaction activation.

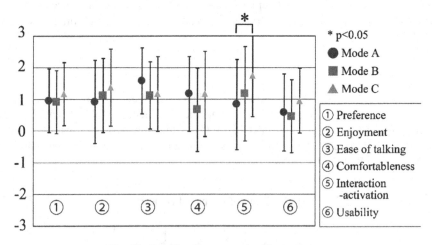

Fig. 10. Results of seven point bipolar rating.

Further, the result of the free conversation experiment was that it was spoken for a long time in Mode A and Mode C in comparison with Mode B (Fig. 11). In Mode B, in the free description section of the questionnaire to the experiment participants, there were opinions that increasing the number of mechanical and monotonous instruments felt unnatural. It may be caused by the fact that the way the audiences gathered is not natural. From the results, it is concluded that not only does the response increase but the reaction that excites the speaker also increases, leading to the motivation from the speaker's utterance.

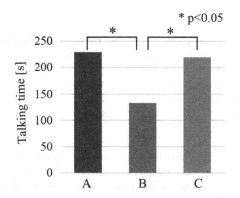

Fig. 11. Talking time of participants in each mode.

5 Conclusion

In this research, we have developed a system that presents the activation of interaction through a change in the embodied response by nodding of multiple objects based on speech input. We confirmed the effectiveness of the system by the evaluation experiment.

Acknowledgments. This work was supported by JSPS KAKENHI Grant Number 16K00278.

References

1. Sejima, Y., Watanabe, T., Jindai, M.: Estimation model of interaction-activated communication based on the heat conduction equation. Journal of Advanced Mechanical Design, Systems, and Manufacturing **10**(9), 1–11 (2016). Paper No. 15-00548
2. Watanabe, T., Okubo, M., Nakashige, M., Danbara, R.: InterActor: speech-driven embodied interactive actor. Int. J. Hum. Comput. Inter. **17**(1), 43–60 (2004)
3. Giannopulu, I., Montrrynaud, V., Watanabe, T.: Minimalistic toy robot to analyze a scenery of speaker-listener condition in autism. Cogn. Process. Springer **17**(2), 195–203 (2016)
4. Giannopulu, I., Terada, K., Watanabe, T.: Communication using robots: a perception-action scenario in moderate ASD. J. Exp. Theor. Artif. Intell. (2018). https://doi.org/10.1080/0952813x.2018.1430865
5. Karatas, N., Yoshikawa, S., De Silva, P.R.S., Okada, M.: NAMIDA: multiparty conversation based driving agents in futuristic vehicle. In: Kurosu, M. (ed.) HCI 2015. LNCS, vol. 9171, pp. 198–207. Springer, Cham (2015). https://doi.org/10.1007/978-3-319-21006-3_20
6. Rubensteina, M., Ahlera, C., Hoffa, N., Cabrerab, A., Nagpala, R.: Kilobot: A low cost robot with scalable operations designed for collective behaviors. Robot. Auton. Syst. (2013). https://doi.org/10.1016/j.robot.2013.08.006

Typography in Interactive Poetry: Gestures and Their Contributions to Reading Multiplicities

Karine Itao Palos[✉], Gisela Belluzzo de Campos,
and Andréa Catrópa da Silva

Anhembi Morumbi University, São Paulo, Brazil
karineipa@hotmail.com, giselabelluzzo@uol.com.br,
andreacatropa@gmail.com

Abstract. This study investigates the ways in which visual poems have expanded their creation and interpretation possibilities in digital environments. A significant poetic contribution of these media is the possibility of physical interferences by the reader, thus transforming the reader into an interactor. Another fundamental element for the materialization of electronic poetry (or e-poetry) is typography. Contrary to what occurs on paper, it is possible to interact, deform and transform the types that constitute poems in digital interfaces, which brings the novelty of inserting gestures as creative poetry potentialities. In order to explore these hypotheses, this article comprises two stages. In the first, we will establish a relation between the following poems: *lygia fingers* (1953), *dias dias dias* (1953), *Poemóbile vivavaia* (1974) and *cripto-cardiograma* (2003), all by Augusto de Campos, and the theory raised by Plaza [1] concering the degrees of interpretation that influence interactivity. In the second stage, we will discuss the subjectivity of implicit gestures in digital poetry, based on two works: *Segundo Soneto Meio Barroco* (2000), by Alckmar Luiz dos Santos and Gilbertto Prado, and *Between Page and Screen* (2012), by Amaranth Borsuk and Brad Bouse.

Keywords: Visual poetry · e-poetry · Typography · Design · Gesture and digital interaction

1 Introduction

The contribution of poetic structure experimentation to the development of typography is perceptible by observing the use of this graphic element throughout the twentieth century. This contribution is mainly associated with visual poetry, which, according to Menezes [2] (p. 14, our translation) "[…] refers to a poetic phenomenon of the twentieth century, which is the cross-linking of languages in direct consequence of the visual scenario of great cities and mass media."

It was also in the twentieth century that typography was able to reach a large part of the masses, since, although the advent of the printing press in the west dates from 1456, its democratic ratification was the result of the late nineteenth-century industrial progress, which disseminated basic education and access to printed content.

© Springer Nature Switzerland AG 2019
M. Kurosu (Ed.): HCII 2019, LNCS 11568, pp. 212–227, 2019.
https://doi.org/10.1007/978-3-030-22636-7_15

This industrial fervor, along with the freshness provided by recent photographic inspiration, reverberated in the arts and literature, and paved the way for design to consolidate itself as an area of knowledge. Influenced by this technological and social enthusiasm, the poets of that period began to experience word materiality in page spaces.

Visual poems often disregard grammatical syntax in favor of word exploration as a visual resource, accentuating the material perception of letters and syllables by typographical experimentation, as well as the breaking down of the linear paradigm. These visual studies 'exploded' off-line and out-of-text typography.

At the end of the twentieth century, by virtue of the democratization of personal computers, we entered the digital age and, since then, with the consolidation and multiplication of digital platforms, new supports are evident, leading to poetry stratification. Neitzel and Bridon [3] (p. 121, our translation) point out that visual poetry represents a new path for poetic texts "[...] the union of words with the exploration of spaces, non-linearity, syntactic disorganization and, with this new aesthetic, electronic poetry was created".

Digital or electronic poetry (also known as e-poetry) paved the way for further discussions concerning reader interaction with poems. We begin from the premise that the typographic form influences its visuality and the way we interpret poems, and that is also acts as a graphic element that allows the reader to establish different poem interpretations by inserting his/her own gestural subjectivities as he/she interacts with the poem.

Thus, this article aims to investigate the relation between four elements: the poem; the reader or the interactor; typography and digital devices. To understand the correlation between these elements, we begin with a reference research on interaction, gesture and typography, then applying this research to visual poems and e-poetry, such as: *lygia fingers (1953), dias dias dias (1953), Poemóbile vivavaia (1974), criptocardiograma (2003), Segundo Soneto Meio Barroco* (2000) and *Between Page and Screen* (2012).

2   Typography and Gestures in Poetry

Digital poems can present interactive forms with relative ease. This interaction allows for the inclusion of the reader through gestural performances, where such movements provide new interpretations, since they insert all the subjectivities associated with gestures.

Flusser [4, 5] discusses gestures as a way of modeling abstract thinking. Since gestures include the individual subjectivities of each person, the intention of the gesture is imprecise and its actual intention is not possible to determine, as it may occur both consciously or unconsciously. According to Hall [6], among all human senses, the sensations experienced by touch are the most personal, and this characteristic is then reflected in its subjectivity.

McCullough [7] (p. 01) reports that "By pointing, by pushing and pulling, by picking up tools, we act as conduits through which we extend our will to the world. They also serve as conduits in the other direction: hands bring us knowledge of the world. " For the author, gestures contribute both in humans being able to carry out their work and modifying the world around them, but also as a way of understanding this world.

Typography, on the other hand, can be defined as a set of visible symbols, containing orthographic and paragraphic characters [8]. This assembly can have its design conceived either by hand or by machine. However, it is essential that the character be prefabricated in a mechanical medium, independent of whether it is analog or digital, such as a typographical press, a printer or a prefabricated graphic on a computer [9].

The presence of the gesture within the typographic universe is not as evident as in calligraphy and lettering because, the hand movement in these forms of writing is perceptible in the strokes and drawings that make up the letter traces. It is important to emphasize that, although these handwritings are not considered typographies, both models, according to Esteves [10] (p. 23, our translation) "[...] have always served as a reference for the conception of typographic forms".

Currently, due to the ease that digital media provide for the design of typographic forms, almost eliminating the technical limitations found in previous methods, typographic fonts are not uncommon and are based on lettering and calligraphy, reinforcing the importance of gestural procedures even today.

The typographic element has always been associated and confined to a static and, often linear, surface. Gesticulation occurs when pressing keyboard characters, either on a typewriter or using a text editor on the computer. Nevertheless, this gesture is not as expressive or subjective as the gesture of drawing with a pen, because the movement is mechanized.

In the typography used by designers, the gesture is not directly related to the final form of the letters. However, its applicability in the digital scope opens the possibility that this letter requires the gesture of the interactor after it is finished. It is important to understand how the gesture is present within the ephemeral context of electronic media.

Typography thrives in virtual environments not only as a form of content presentation, but also as an interactive object. The gesture is present in these virtual and participative environments, since, it allows for a more intuitive contact with the device as it is a primitive sense.

3 The Relation Between Degrees of Interpretation and the Work of Augusto de Campos

The ephemeral qualities of digital devices allow the reader to be inserted within poems through means of a wide range of interfaces that have expanded alongside the evolving technology used in electronic devices. These qualities foster discussions about user or reader interactions with the work. It is worth emphasizing that such discussions are not unique to the digital scene, since, even before the first computers, interaction signs between poems and reader were already noted.

In this sense, in the 1990s, Plaza [1] (p. 09, our translation) observed "... a shift from the restorative functions (the artist's poetics) to the functions of receptor sensibility (aesthetic) [...] ", this transition was characterized by a mixture of poetic genres. According to Plaza, three degrees of interpretation related interaction levels are noted:

first-degree opening, second-degree opening and third-degree opening. For a better understanding of these degrees of interpretation, we relate them to Augusto de Campos' works. His works were chosen to exemplify Plaza's degrees of interpretation [1], as this poet, whose theoretical and creative trajectory, according to Antonio [11], is permeated by poetry, the arts and technologies, and has experimented with all three degrees of interpretation.

Augusto de Campos was considered one of the forerunners of concrete poetry in Brazil in the 1950s. He is also one of the authors of the concrete poetry manifesto, in which we find the following passage:

> concrete poetry: tension of words-things in space-time. dynamic structure: multiplicity of concomitant movements. also in music - by definition, an art of time - space intervenes [...]; in the visual - spatial arts, by definition - time intervenes [...]. [12] (p. 89, our translation)

Due to the fact that concrete poetry has explored the graphic visuality of the word and typography, it fits in the proposed discussion of the presence of typography in interactive poetry.

3.1   First-Degree Opening

Let us turn our attention again to Plaza's [1] observations concerning degrees of interpretation. The first degree of interpretation is related to a passive participation of the reader or the spectator regarding the work of art, since he/she is only the view, with its subjectivities, that interferes in the work interpretation, i.e. because it is not a physical opening, the reader does not externalize his/her participation in the poem.

This means that the poet leaves room in his/her work so that the reader may insert his subjectivities to complete the work, without physically altering it, by means of interpretation ambiguities.

We observe these characteristics in several Augusto de Campos works, two of them visually similar: *dias dias dias* and *lygia fingers* (see Fig. 1), both published in 1953. According to Antonio [11], both poems explored the spacings within the white sheet. The colors applied to the linguistic symbols allow the reader to establish new relations between word meanings.

A single typography was used in both poems, the *sans serif* font named *Futura*. According to Menezes [2], this source was the most applied during the first phase of the concrete poetic movement, since it presents a clean design with both geometric and "rational" forms. Thus, typography was used along with several colors in *lygia fingers* and *dias dias dias*. The colors, typography and page layout are graphic elements explored in these poems in order to encourage the reader to make his/her own poetic journey within these works. These possibilities of reading path choices guaranteed the permutational characteristic of the works.

According to Plaza [1] (p. 12, our translation), interchangeability is implicit in the concrete movement work, as "the concrete poet sees the word in itself as a magnetic field of possibilities." The open matrix of many concrete poems permits several reading paths, both horizontal and vertical, allowing for the combinatorial and permutational [...] ". This feature still belongs to the first degree of interpretation.

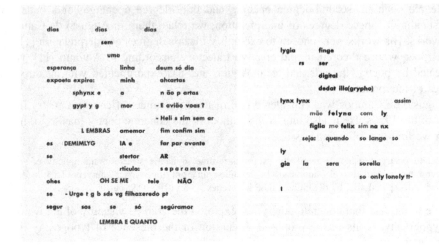

Fig. 1. *dias dias dias* and *lygia fingers*. Source: revistamododeusar.blogspot.com.br/2009/01/a ugusto-de-campos.html?-view = magazine, last accessed 2018/12/01.

In this sense, element interchangeability and support and typography characteristics provide new user interpretations for those elements, and the opening of new possibilities of interpretation is the first step towards interaction.

3.2   Second-Degree Opening

Contrary to the previous degree, in which contact occurs only through the possibility of different interpretations, the second degree of interpretation results in interactions through the insertion of the interactor's body in the work, i.e. the reader physically participates in the work. Aquinas [13] (p. 93, our translation) reports that in this context "the dimension of action is, therefore, essential to participatory art by overcoming the binary opposition between the activity and passivity of the platonic spectator".

Thus, paraphrasing Plaza [1], there is a dramatic confrontation between the artistic environment and the spectator, because the work of art is not closed in itself nor is it open only to interpretation ambiguity.

The work of art is dematerialized when human participation is added, i.e. it only materializes at the moment of physical contact with the spectator.

This degree of openness brings the possibility of the spectator to be inserted within the work, acting actively, as an interactor. It should be noted that this interactor does not interact directly with the poem typography, but with the surface to which it is confined to, as typography is a graphic element with strictly visual characteristics.

The work by Julio Plaza and Augusto de Campos, *Poemóbiles*, was first published in 1974, comprising 12 poems grouped in book format.

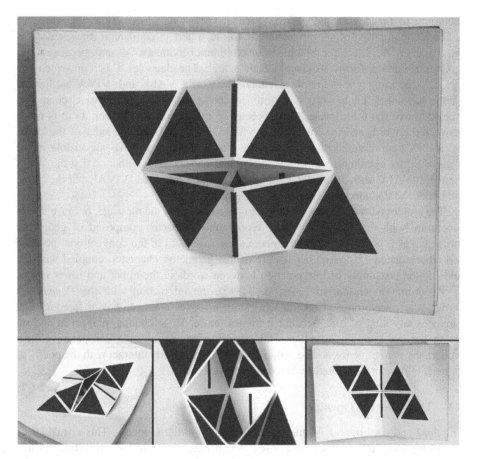

Fig. 2. *Poemóbile vivavaia.* Source: CAMPOS, A., PLAZA, J.: Poemóbiles. Brasiliense, São Paulo (1974).

The *Poemóbiles* are like pop-ups, mounted from two printed, overlapping and half-folded pages. The top sheet receives extra folds and geometric cuts, allowing the shape to 'jump' from the paper when folded, resulting in a three-dimensional effect. The 12 poems share these characteristics, with differential linguistic and typographical content, as well as differential cutout formats and top-sheet folds.

By allowing reader participation, the poems must be opened so they can be read and interpreted. The opening angle and relative spatial position of the reader in front of the poem influence his/her perception of the work. According to Gasparetti (p. 90, our translation) "in it, we clearly see that the physicality of self-interpenetration inter-penetrates the poem, presenting itself as a physical body, in such a way that the poem only exists because the book exists as an object. " This physicality makes the poem happen and the participation of the viewer becomes intrinsic to the work.

One of the *Poemóbiles* is the *vivavaia* (see Fig. 2). In this work, all elements are printed in red, comprising two words "VAIA" and "VIVA", both interspersed according to the degree the page is opened. Observing *vivavaia's* typography, we notice it is composed of simple geometric forms, a perfect equilateral triangle used as the character 'A'. The same triangle is inverted and becomes a 'V' and, because it has no internal counter-forms, its visual weight is high. The character 'I' is represented as a rectangle the same size as the other letters. The words 'VAIA' and 'VIVA' are located on the top sheet. Each word is positioned above the other, with the 'I' characters aligned above the fold, located in the center of the page. In this sheet, a cut is noted between the words and the folds, and the folds are aligned with the sides of the letters 'A' and 'V', represented by triangles. The words 'IVA' and 'VAI' are visible in the lower sheet by opening the top sheet, positioned one above the other so that the 'V' of the word 'VAIA' above completes the 'IVA', forming the word 'VIVA', and the 'A' of the upper 'VIVA' alongside the 'VAI', originates 'VAIA'.

The employed typography in the poem *vivavaia* drives the message, because it is in synchrony with the sheet folds. The typographic character composed of geometric forms makes it possible to read the poem's message both in the conventional position and when rotated 180°. Another feature of this geometric character, coupled with the folds, is the possibility of interpolation between words in the upper and lower layers.

According to Gasparetti [14] (pp. 94–95), the interaction with the *Poemóbiles* allows "the play proposed by the work and provokes a movement of freedom that surpasses any kind of rule, because it invites the reader to change, play, read and re-create the work in an articulate and performative way [...]". We perceive how typography can influence and be influenced by how the users interact with the poem, as its readability can be altered by interactor movement.

3.3   Third-Degree Opening

The third and final degree of interpretation occurs in digital media. This virtual space allows for real time dynamic responses, which open the way for interaction. In this sense, Plaza [1], when focusing on the work of art, ends up sketching a meaning for digital space interaction, which could easily be assigned to digital poems or e-poems:

> An interactive work of art is a latent space susceptible to all sonic, visual and textual extensions. The scheduled scenario can be modified in real time or depending on the response of the operators. Interactivity is not only a technical and functional convenience; it involves the spectator physically, psychologically and sensibly in a transformation practice. [1] (p. 20, our translation).

The author recognizes the insertion of an active agent such as a computer program. The relationship between person and machine changes the pattern of traditional communication. The dynamic active agent characteristics transform the way people relate to objects and amongst themselves.

Another author who describes the relationship between humans and digital inter-action is the communication teacher Primo [15]. To Primo, digital space interactions can be divided into two niches: the first, characterized by 'mutual interactions', and the second, by 'reactive interactions'. The difference between both categories is given by the ability of both interacting parties to be influenced by each other.

'Reactive interaction' can be observed in most computer systems that make use of multimedia resources. Multimedia features include buttons, hypermidiatic links, menus, animations and graphics, and give feedback to the poem reader. When system interactions occur through these graphical elements, the system is reactive, since all animations, substitutions and word explosions were previously planned by the programmer who conceived of the program, and respond to interactor perturbations.

As Primo [15] (p. 114, our translation) postulates, 'mutual interactions' are characterized by the mutual influence between all those involved in communication, and are characteristic of human communication, due to the fact that our individual subjectivities are added to the conversation when we communicate with other people.

In this case, the purpose of the interaction is not defined; it is malleable and independent of prior planning. Thus, although computers have evolved to the point of having sensors capable of interpreting the world and human beings, this interpretation is the result of parameters established in their matrix code.

According to Antonio [11], the associations between poetry, multimedia and hypermedia allow the development of interactive poems. Interactive poems also allow reader users to interfere in poem structure by building new narratives for themselves. In this way, the digital poems that will be listed in this article can be classified within 'reactive interactions'.

Let us return to the work of Augusto de Campos by observing the poem *criptocardiograma* (see Fig. 3), from 2003. This poem is composed of a heart formed by several pictograms. These hearts are accompanied by a red stripe located on the left side of the screen, with several characters arranged in alphabetical order superimposed on this stripe. Existing pictograms represent love or love relationships, such as hearts, daggers, flowers and dice (love game).

A corresponding character exists for each pictogram in the poem and, to interact with the application, the interactor must drag the characters and position them above one of the pictograms. If the character corresponds to the pictogram, the graphic symbol is replaced by the verbal symbol and a pulsating sound is triggered. As equivalences are discovered, the poem is 'decrypted' and verses are formed.

After all the characters are discovered, the poem verses are visible and an animation and a sound are created, both similar to a beating heart. The poem verses mention the word heart, represented in several languages.

The poem interaction occurs through the gesture of dragging the character through the screen making the multimedia elements mediators between the interactor and the program. The poem, however, is only capable of performing what has been specified in its array code, and if the user wants to perform any operation that does not conform to this specification, he/she will not obtain any results.

However, despite displaying this predetermined characteristic, the digital space allows for the possibility of significant interactions due to its ephemeral quality. This ephemerality enables the materialization of any graphic format in real time and allows for different readings of the poem itself.

The ephemerality of computer images allows for gesture and physical interactions in digital space interactions but, unlike manipulation with physical objects, digital interaction occurs indirectly, through interfaces and a mediator.

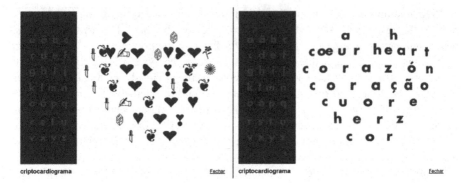

Fig. 3. *criptocardiograma.*   Source: http://www2.uol.com.br/augustodecampos/criptocardio grama.htm, last accessed 2018/12/02 (Color figure online).

4 Digital and Gestural Poetry

Digital media allows for the dynamic union between textual and imagery elements. This characteristic permits the manipulation of typographic elements that are materialized on the screen, which, in turn, comprises a new way of interpreting poems, because, besides the inscription of the reader's view, this environment inserts gestures into the work. On this issue, Santos [16] reports:

> Habituating this space of various visualities, the reader can then witness and perceive the installation of the verbal in/as images. We have, in this case, the confrontation of a space of perceptions (not only visual) to which the reader's body and even gestures are called and exposed to the gesturality of words. In this way, it is the very visibility that opens (itself) (in) spaces and times for the verbal, allowing to inscribe a semantization in each image movement, in each icon displacement, in every reader interaction with the keyboard and mouse. [16] (p. 82, our translation).

In this way, the author considers interaction and multimedia as resources that allow new organizations of meaning. Interactive poems designed to accept and include user input are also available. Often, this type of poem is conceived and only comes to fruition when it receives user interference. As Antonio [11] postulates, when interacting, the reader has the potential to be a co-author of the work.

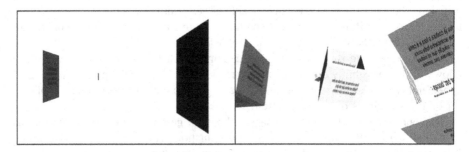

Fig. 4. *Segundo Soneto Meio Barroco.* Source: SANTOS, A., PRADO, G.: *Segundo Soneto Meio Barroco.* Brasiliense, São Paulo (2000).

According to Santos [16] (p. 82, our translation), the confrontation of the perception space occurs in digital space. This space is not only visual, but also counts on the gestural interferences of the reader. "In this way, it is the very visibility that (opens) spaces and times for the verbal, allowing for the inscription of a semantization in each image movement, in each icon displacement [...]". This movement occurs throughout the reader's interaction with the digital interfaces.

It is obvious that typography is an element of great importance in digital poems since, in addition to adding graphical and visual contours to the text, as noted during the avant-gardes of the twentieth century, it allows for poem materialization, in a way that favors word interactions.

This interaction clearly occupies the third degree of interpretation, since it is favored by electronic and digital media, but also covers both the first and second degrees proposed by Plaza [1]. In the case of typography present in digital poetry, the second degree of interpretation appears even more proprietarily, because digital environments allow for reader actions to directly influence typographic characters, and not only the support to which the letters areconfined. To clarify such concepts, we will observe two poems: *Segundo Soneto Meio Barroco* (2000) and *Between Page and Screen* (2012).

4.1 Segundo Soneto Meio Barroco

The poem *Segundo Soneto Meio Barroco* (see Fig. 4) was published in 2000 by Alckmar Luiz dos Santos and Gilbertto Prado. This work was developed in Virtual Reality Modeling Language (VRML). It is a digital poem that allows the reader to move between stanzas by means of the simulation of a three-dimensional environment.

The poem consists of four stanzas, each attached to a cube. Each of the four cubes has five closed sides, while the sixth is open, so that the five inner sides are visible, with the same stanza attached to each side (see Fig. 5). In three of the five faces, the poem obeys the conventional sense of reading in the West, with lines written from left to right. In the other two, however, the text is inverted: written from right to left.

On the outside of the cube, the same stanza is also visible on each side and its senses follow the opposite of the inner facets, i.e., if the inner face of the text is inverted, it will be in the usual position on the outer side. When the cube is manipulated using the mouse, another stanza of the same poem is heard, repeated every time the reader interacts with the object.

The poem also allows the interactor to move between the four cubes that appear to be at different distances, simulating the depth of the physical environments. This movement is performed through the keyboard arrows (◄▲▼►).

The typography used in this poem is a *sans serif* with bitmap characteristics. However, despite being interactive, it still behaves as if it were attached to a support, because it is fixed to the faces of the cube and the interaction occurs with the object.

4.2 Between Page and Screen

The book *Between Page and Screen* (see Fig. 6), created by artists Amaranth Borsuk and Brad Bouse was originally published in 2012. This work does not resemble a digital book or e-paper. Instead, it is a hybrid graphic project, which lies on the frontier

Fig. 5. Verses of the *Segundo Soneto Meio Barroco*. Source: SANTOS, A., PRADO, G.: *Segundo Soneto Meio Barroco*. Brasiliense, São Paulo (2000).

between the physical and digital. According to Borsuk and Bouse [17], the poem themes correspond to a series of enigmatic letters between two lovers struggling to map their relationship between the screen or the page.

The project consists of a physical book and a web application. The format is an 18 × 18 cm book and finishes as a booklet, comprising 22 pages. Inside are 16 engravings, slightly different from each other, measuring 4 × 4 cm, one centered on each page. All resemble a bar code known as a QR code. The web application is located on the website www.betwenpageandscreen.com. According to the authors, the project uses *ActionScript* as the base source code.

To interact with the work, it is necessary to have a camera attached to the device. The operation occurs through image capture, where the interactor must position the picture in front of the device camera. As the images are processed by the system, it recognizes the implicit code in the picture. The recognition of this QR code, in turn,

Fig. 6. *Between Page and Screen* book images. Source: https://www.betweenpageand screen.-com/, last accessed 2018/12/01.

causes small texts to appear on the screen, which intertwine with the projected image of the interactor. Although it is a virtual object, the sensation is of holding the text with your hands (see Fig. 6). According to Borsuk and Bouse [17], Between Page and Screen is a "[…] augmented reality project only accessible to the reader who has both the physical object and the device necessary to read".

Fig. 7. Interaction with the sixth poem of the book *Between Page and Screen*. Source: https://www.betweenpageandscreen.com/, last accessed 2018/12/01.

Most of the poems present themselves as a block of text, not necessarily rectangular, as certain poems present forms other than rectangles, such as the shape of a pig. Even if it is a text block, the reader can manipulate it. As the angle of the printed image changes, the virtual text changes position, similar to what happens when we observe a hologram. Thus, two QR codes of this book were chosen for observation and description.

The first is the sixth poem (see Fig. 7), without considering the cover poem. In it, besides the movement generated by the manipulation of the angle of the QR code, an implicit movement added by the system is noted. This movement occurs in order to simulate a 'horizontal' 3D rotation and, as the angle changes, the circular motion accompanies it. The poem is composed of a parallelepiped with a word arranged vertically on each side, containing four letters: 'POLE', 'PALE' 'PAWL' and 'PEEL', who revolve around the base of the parallelepiped.

The second highlighted poem is the eleventh (see Fig. 8), which, unlike the others in this book, is initially composed of a single word that changes in a certain space of time, forming new words. The words are: 'A', 'PAGAN', 'AGENT', 'PET', 'GEANT', 'PEAT', 'PANT', 'GENT', 'EAT', 'GEAN', 'PEA', 'AN', 'AGE', 'GANT', 'GET', 'GEAT', 'PENT', 'PAGE', 'PEN', 'A', 'PAEAN', 'PAGEANT' and 'PAN'. Like other poems, it can also change its angle according to manipulation of the printed figure.

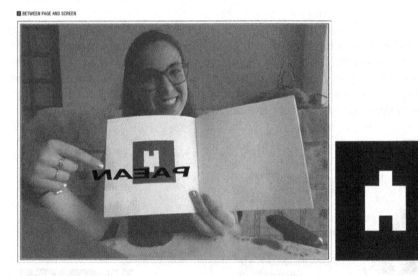

Fig. 8. Interaction with the eleventh poem of the book *Between Page and Screen*. Source: https://www.betweenpageandscreen.com/, last accessed 2018/12/01.

The typograpies present in the project is subject to changes relative to the presented angles, since they may be altered by simulating a top view or a mirrored character, for example. A *sans serif* font with similar characteristics to the grotesque or neo-grotesque category is employed in all examined poems. One of the most apparent aspects of this type of source is the use of heavy strokes.

5 Discussion

In the first part of this article, we discuss the question of the degrees of interpretation elaborated by Plaza [1]. To elucidate the author's concepts, we chose four poems by Augusto de Campos. The poems *days days days* and *lygia fingers* comprise the first degree, both presenting typographically similar characteristics. They present colors and spacings that allow for interpretation multiplicities, both due to the graphic aspects implicit in the poems and the interchangeability proposed by the word divisions.

These characteristics can be observed in Menezes's reflection [2] (p. 31, our translation) on the two poems: "[...] language is broken by fragmented words, a mixture of sounds from different languages, mainly sounds that resemble African or indigenous languages." According to the author, this type of poem was the most radical at the time.

Concerning the second degree of interpretation, we presented *vivavaia*, belonging to the work *Poemóbiles*, where the question of support materiality is noted. This materiality implies in reading possibilities, as the piece opens or unfolds for the reader, displaying hidden words. In this sense, the entire poem allows for new experiments.

Although the typography present in *vivavaia* is fixed to the support, this support allows for manipulation, thanks to its pop-up characteristics. Due to the typographic spectator character being exposed as basic geometric forms (triangles and rectangles), the word can be rotated and still preserve its verbal meaning. Such structure manipulations allow for great interpretation variability.

In the third and last degree of interpretation, the poem chosen to transcend the concepts elaborated by Plaza [1] was *criptocardiograma*. This poem was concretized in the digital space, where it is clear that the interaction occurs with the character and not with the support, as noted in *vivavaia*. The ability to drag the letters around with the mouse and swap them with the pictograms is an intrinsic feature of the digital space.

In the second part of the article, we delve into electronic and digital poetry, with the intention of better understanding how poetry is favored by reader's action, present as gestures, and observe how the use of typography occurs in this scenario. Two poems were selected for these observations, *Segundo Soneto Meio Barroco* and *Between Page and Screen*.

In *Segundo Soneto Meio Barroco* the authors used the stanzas attached to the cubes, and the interaction with the cubes also approaches the manipulation of the physical object. The typography presents itself in a conservative manner, because it is confined to the verses that compose the stanzas.

The interactions presented in the poem represent 'reactive interactions', since they are provided by multimedia resources and the reader can only relate to the system in a previously planned manner, both by rotating the cube using the mouse and traversing the 3D environment using the keyboard.

In *Between Page and Screen*, the interaction does not only occur in the digital media, since the poem is printed in code and must be scanned to reveal its message. Instead of a mouse, keyboard, or piece of hardware, this interaction is carried out through an unconventional object for virtual environments, i.e. a physical book, and its manipulation allows the reader to explore the text from a variety of angles as he/she manipulates the book. Although it is a differentiated interface, this form of interaction fits into 'reactive interactions'.

Typographical interaction in this project occurs not only through visual simulation, but also through the gestural sensation of typographic characters, since it is possible to manipulate the typographic object with the book, distorting the angle, as long as the on-screen program recognizes the symbol printed on the pages.

Thus, typography in the digital poem space may contain aspects that enable interactions with the reader-interactor, graphic, visual and gestural. In this sense, the action does not occur in function of the support, but as a function of the character itself.

6   Final Considerations

It is clear that the third degree of interpretation incorporates the first two, as the presence of the first two in e-poetry is evident. When we observe the employed typography, we perceive that it allows for differential interpretations through visual qualities, and also conclude that this characteristic was very well explored by the visual poets of the twentieth century.

Digital and interactive poems incorporate the second degree of interpretation much more proprietarily than paper, due to their polyvalent qualities and interface flexibility that can be added to digital environments, contributing to reader experiences.

Thus, digital environments open the possibility of interacting in different ways, as observed in the projects presented herein: interactions take place both in *Segundo Soneto Meio Barroco* and *Between Page and Screen* through a personal computer and are carried out mainly by hand - in the former, using the mouse and keyboard, and the latter, by means of a book.

It is evident that this type of computer interaction allows for physical interactions with the poems, that digital poems contemplate the other degrees of interpretation suggested by Plaza [1] and that gestures, being subjective, interfere in the ways we interpret poems.

As observed in the projects presented herein, digital poetry or e-poetry opens the possibility of the existence of a gestural relationship between the reader-interactor and typography, without the latter having to be attached to the support. In fact, this interaction is a differentiated form of language that allows us to add movement and include the reader's participation in the work, enabling new meanings for the millennial art of poetry.

References

1. Plaza, J.: Arte e interatividade: autor-obra-re-cepção. ARS (São Paulo) 1(2), 09–29 (2003). São Paulo
2. Menezes, P.: Roteiro de leitura: poesia concreta e visual. Editora Ática, São Paulo (1998)
3. Neitzel, A., Bridon, J.: Poesia digital: reflexões em curso. Literatura y Lingüística, n. 27, pp. 111–134 (2012)
4. Flusser, V.: Gestos: fenomenología y comuni-cacíon. Herder, Barcelona (1994)

5. Flusser, V.: Gestos, 1ª edn. Anna Blu-me, São Paulo (2014)
6. Hall, E.: La dimension oculta: En-foque antropológico del uso del espacio. Instituto de Estudios de Administracion Local, Madrid (1973)
7. McCullough, M.: Abstracting Craft: The Practiced Digital Hand. MIT Press, Massachusetts (1998)
8. Farias, P.: Tipografia digital. O impac-to das novas tecnologias. 4a (edn.) Edi-tora 2AB, Rio de Janeiro (2013)
9. Noordzij, G.: O Traço: teoria da escrita. Editora Blucher, São Paulo (2013)
10. Esteves, R.: O design brasileiro de tipos di-gitais: a configuração de um campo profissional. Blucher, São Paulo (2010)
11. Antonio, J.: Poesia digital: teoria, histó-ria e Antologias. CD-ROM. Editora Navegar, São Paulo (2010)
12. Campos, A., Pignatari, D., Campos, H.: Plano-piloto para poesia concreta. In: Bandeira J., Barros L.(Orgs). Poesia concreta: o projeto verbivocovisual, pp. 89–92. Editora Artemeios, São Paulo (2008)
13. Aquino, R.: Arte participativa, mediação cul-tural e praticas colaborativas: perspectivas para uma curadoria expandida. REPERTÓRIO 19(27), 90–103 (2016)
14. Gasparetti, A.: Poemóbiles: leituras em jogo [master's thesis]. Pontifícia Universidade Católica de São Paulo, São Paulo (SP) (2012)
15. Primo, A.: Interação mediada por computador: comunicação, cibercultura, cognição. Editora Sulina, Porto Ale-gre (2007)
16. Santos, A.: Leituras de nós no cibe-respaço e literature. Itaú Cultural, São Paulo (2003)
17. Borsuk, A., Bouse, B.: Between Page and Screen. www.be-tweenpageandscreen.com/about. Accessed 12 Nov 2018

Impact Analysis of Order of Presentation on Champion Book Selection in Bibliobattle

Hirofumi Masui$^{(\boxtimes)}$, Yumiko Kaigawa, Namiko Mitoma, and Tadahiro Taniguchi

Ritsumeikan University, 1-1-1, Noji-higashi, Kusatsu, Shiga, Japan
masui.hirofumi@em.ci.ritsumei.ac.jp

Abstract. This paper analyzes the degree of influence of the presentation order on the voting behavior of participants in the book review game, Bibliobattle, and examines ways to reduce this influence. We collected and analyzed the data of Bibliobattle games that were spontaneously conducted in various places, and this method was applied to research other communication-field mechanism designs. We classified the results of approximately 800 Bibliobattle games collected from the Internet by the order of presentation. Subsequently, we compared the number of Champion Book awards secured by the first and second, and last and last but one in the presentations when compared to others in the presentation order. Consequently, the possibility of the first and second presenters acquiring a Champion Book award has a detrimental effect on the other presenters in the order. Conversely, the possibility of the last and second-last presenters acquiring a Champion Book award is advantageous for the other presenters in the order. We considered the possibility that the response order effect influences voting in the Bibliobattle game. Then, by performing the voting process in the reverse order of the presentation, we examined ways to reduce the influence of the response order effect.

Keywords: Bibliobattle · Response order effect · Communication-field mechanism design

1 Introduction

There are numerous approaches to create communication games and revitalize it by using a voting process to select winners and losers. Bibliobattle is a good example of such a communication game. Bibliobattle is a popular social book-review game, especially in Japan, which encourages sharing of interesting books [1].

The important element of Bibliobattle is deciding a Champion Book by voting [2]. McGonigal defined four elements of the game, i.e., goals, rules, feedback

© Springer Nature Switzerland AG 2019
M. Kurosu (Ed.): HCII 2019, LNCS 11568, pp. 228–238, 2019.
https://doi.org/10.1007/978-3-030-22636-7_16

system, and voluntary participation [3]. The goal of Bibliobattle is to be chosen from numerous participants and to win a Champion Book award. This mechanism encourages people to present books that participants are interested in at the Bibliobattle. Therefore, the process of deciding the Champion Book must be fair and appropriate.

However, the response order effect has been recognized in cognitive science [4]. The response order effect is the effect wherein the response result changes corresponding to the difference in the order of presentation of a subject to be measured in the experiment or investigation. There are two types of effects: primacy effects (in which response choices presented early were most likely to be selected) and recency effects (in which response choices presented last were more likely to be selected). In Bibliobattle, each presentation is delivered individually. Consequently, the response order effect might have a certain influence on the decision.

However, no studies have provided any evidence on the response order effect in Bibliobattle. Therefore, in this study we investigated the response order effect in Bibliobattle by gathering information about results of approximately 800 Bibliobattle games and presented a statistical analysis of the response order effect in the selection process of Bibliobattle.

2   Backgrounds

2.1   Bibliobattle

The Bibliobattle is a communication field for knowledge sharing through book reviews. The Bibliobattle game was initially proposed as a social interaction field

Fig. 1. Bibliobattle at a university

design facilitated by book reviews [1]. Subsequently, this game became popular with not only related researchers but also with people in various fields. Figure 1 shows Bibliobattle conducted in a class at a university.

According to a survey conducted by the Committee of Bibliobattle, this game has already been organized in 247 universities and 284 public libraries in Japan. Bibliobattle has become popular all over the world including American bookstores, Korean television programs, reading education programs in the Solomon Islands[1].

The Committee of Bibliobattle has defined the official rules for Bibliobattle[2]. Figure 2 illustrates the official rules.

1. Come together with a favorite or an interesting book.
2. Introduce your favorite book for 5 minutes, one by one.
3. After each presentation, talk about the book for 23 minutes with all participants.
4. After all presentations, select the "Champion Book" by the votes of all participants, both audience and presenters. The criterion is, a book, which you want to read the most. The book with the most votes is called the "Champion Book."

Fig. 2. Bibliobattle: official rules

Empirical research on Bibliobattle has been conducted on areas such as the influence of the Bibliobattle field on introduction, the influence on the setting of the time limit, and the evaluation when considering it as a recommendation system [1,5,6].

2.2   Response Order Effect

The response order effect is an effect that changes the measurement/response result marginally or significantly depending on the difference in the order of presenting the subject to be measured in the experiment or investigation [7]. It is primarily known as knowledge in the field of research and cognitive science [8]. Here, we will mainly describe the recency effect and the primary effect which are assumed to have influenced the voting of Bibliobattle.

First, there are two types of option lists. The first list is the case where individual choices constitute an independent meaning. They can arbitrarily rearrange the options. The second is a choice list whose order is meaningful. For example, "1. I like it 2. I like it to a certain extent 3. I dislike it to a certain extent 4. I dislike it." The order in which the choices are presented is either in descending or ascending. The selection of books available for voting in the Bibliobattle is an example of the first list and the response order effect that will be described subsequently also occurs mainly when using the first list.

---

[1]   http://www.bibliobattle.jp/pu-ji-zhuang-kuang-deta.
[2]   http://en.bibliobattle.jp/rule-of-bibliobattle.

The case where an item is selected because it was placed at the beginning of the list is called the primary effect, and the case where an item is selected because it was presented at the end of the list is referred to as a recency effect. The primary effects are likely to occur in the case of surveys that utilize visual media such as postal mail surveillance reporting and interview surveys using option cards that are referenced by the respondents. Further, in the case of an interview survey without selection cards or a survey based only on auditory evaluations such as telephone surveys, the recency effect tends to occur.

The process of occurrence of such a tendency is explained primarily by two factors, memory limitation and cognitive elaboration [9,10]. The factor of memory limitation is related to the cases where a long choice list is used, especially in an auditory investigation. For respondents, choices presented from the beginning of the list to the middle stage may be difficult to remember when they are finally queried for answers. Therefore, the options presented at the end are easier to choose. This is one of the causes of the recency effect.

However, even when short and concise choice lists are used in an auditory survey, the nearest effect occurs. This effect cannot be explained by only the factor of memory limitation. Further, in a visual investigation, a primary effect is demonstrated. This also cannot be explained by the factor of memory limitation. This is because as the options are constantly being presented in a visual investigation, the respondents are not required to memorize a considerable quantity of data.

The second factor is cognitive elaboration. When choices with equal probability are compared with each other, it becomes easier to select the option examined in detail by the respondents. In the visual survey, we assume that the respondents will consider a choice based on the order of presentation. Then, for the choices presented later, the analysis is more likely to be influenced by the information from the options presented earlier. Therefore, if we compare the options exhibiting the same degree of probability, the option presented earlier becomes easier to choose. Conversely, in the auditory survey, the examination time for each option is limited by the pace at which the investigator reads. Moreover, the investigator usually takes time to wait for a response only after reading all the options. Therefore, the review time of the last option tends to be longer than other options. Owing to this and the memory limitation factors mentioned above, it is observed that the auditory survey is likely to be influenced by the recency effect.

2.3 Communication-Field Mechanism Design

The communication-field mechanism design is a new approach to technically understand the communication field between humans. Bibliobattle is one good example of a communication-field mechanism. The definition of communication-field is presented as follows; as a result of participants acting to maximize their utility, building a mechanism to fulfill the purpose by making fruitful communication.

Taniguchi classifies the approach of revitalizing community and organizational communication and creating intellectual creation into three categories: space design, facilitation, and communication-field mechanism design.

The design of space is an approach to create a space to communicate, such as creating a resting room inside a company or setting up an in-house social network service. However, if we just create a space, we cannot induce the behavior and communication of the people participating in it; therefore, sometimes such spaces will be quiet.

Facilitation focuses on the involvement and remarks of participants in the communication field and the method to control the whole communication field. The facilitator does not participate in the discussion and only supports activities from a neutral position. However, this approach is based on the existence of a facilitator, and the quality of the conference depends significantly on the ability of the facilitator.

The mechanism of the communication-field refers to the design of the institution that controls the field. Specifically, in many cases, it refers to rules when communication is a segment of the games. Communication-field mechanism design tries to promote intellectual activities by creating a liberal environment for communication. Even though the facilitator is not skillful, the designed mechanism is aimed to be available to everyone. In Bibliobattle, for example, a moderator does not need special skills. This contributes significantly to the popularity of Bibliobattle.

3   Materials and Methods

We gathered data on Bibliobattle under the following conditions from the Internet.

1. We obtained information about Bibliobattle from Google Alert, Twitter, and the Committee of Bibliobattle group page on Facebook. We searched for the term "Bibliobattle" in Japanese and English on these websites.
2. We gathered data that included the number of presenters and the order of presentations in Bibliobattle from January 2011 to September 2016.
3. We excluded the data when there were multiple Champion Books or the number of presenters was less than or equal to two.
4. This survey was conducted around October 2016.

There were 797 data elements satisfying these conditions. Table 1 lists the number of acquisitions of Champion Book award per list containing the presentation order.

This survey is significant importance. Generally, it is challenging to conduct experiments for examining the mechanism design of communication in various studies because they require a lot of time and labor. However, Bibliobattle is a communication field that is already popular throughout Japan. Many people in various places use the same rules to communicate. As these games are not conducted as experiments, the specific situation in every game varies. However, it is considerably useful to collect these data to analyze the tendency of a communication mechanism. This is because significant time and labor required for the data collection can be reduced. We believe that this research method also provides knowledge for the research on other designs of communication mechanism having similar properties.

Table 1. Number of Champion Book acquisitions for each presentation order in the sequence

Presentation order	Number of presenters							
	3	4	5	6	7	8	9	Total
1	25	59	39	24	5	0	0	152
2	24	58	37	25	9	0	1	154
3	26	77	55	22	12	4	0	196
4	—	66	56	27	6	3	1	159
5	—	—	56	37	4	0	0	97
6	—	—	—	26	4	2	0	32
7	—	—	—	—	2	1	0	3
8	—	—	—	—	—	2	1	3
9	—	—	—	—	—	—	1	1
Total	75	260	243	161	42	12	4	797

4 Results

4.1 Test Methods

We used the data of Bibliobattle with 4, 5, and 6 presenters because they contained sufficient number of data (664 data) for analysis. We conducted a chi-square test (significance level: 5%) considering each of the following conditions.

1. The Champion Book acquisitions by the first presenter and the presenter other than the first presenter.
2. The Champion Book acquisitions by the final presenter and the presenter other than the final presenter.
3. The Champion Book acquisitions by the first and second presenters and the presenters other than the first and second presenters.
4. The Champion Book acquisitions by the last and last but one presenters and the presenters other than the last and last but one presenters.

4.2   Test Results

Table 2 lists the test results.

Considering conditions 1 and 2, there was no significant difference in the number of Champion Book acquisitions ($p = 0.109$, 0.231).

Under condition 3, the Champion Book acquisitions by the first and second presenters were significantly less than those of presenters other than the first and second presenters ($p = 4.94 \times 10^{-3}$).

Under conditions 4, the Champion Book acquisitions by the second and last presenters from the end were significantly more than those of presenters other than the last and last but one presenters ($p = 3.63 \times 10^{-4}$).

Table 2. Results of examination of the number of champions when the total presenters were 4, 5, and 6

Bibliobattle with 4, 5, 6 presenters					
Presenter order	Champion Book acquisitions	Champion Book not acquired	Chi-square value	p-value	Significant difference
First	122	542	2.567	0.109	n.s.
Other than first	542	2,015			
Last	148	516	1.433	0.231	n.s.
Other than last	516	2,041			
First and second	242	1,086	7.899	4.95×10^{-3}	**
Other than first and second	422	1,471			
Last and last but one	318	1,010	15.321	3.63×10^{-4}	**
Other than last and second last	346	1,547			

n.s. : No significant difference , * : p <0.05 , ** : p <0.01

5   Discussion

5.1   Interpretation of Results

The above results suggest the following while considering the Bibliobattle with 4, 5, and 6 presenters:

1. The possibility of acquiring a Champion Book for the first and last presenters is neither advantageous nor disadvantageous compared to other orders.
2. The possibility of acquiring a Champion Book for the first and second presenters has a disadvantageous tendency compared to other orders.
3. The possibility of acquiring a Champion Book for the last and last but one presenters is an advantageous tendency compared to the other orders.

These trends indicate that the voting in Bibliobattle is similar to an auditory investigation with a long choice list, indicating that there is a possibility that the recency effect may have occurred. However, in Bibliobattle, unlike auditory investigation, the options (book titles) are often presented after publication, or participants present it in memos. Therefore, effect of the memory limitation factor is weakened, and it is considered that the option that was presented at the end was not necessarily advantageous as compared to other presentation orders. Further, as the options are presented visually, the time to review the books presented at the beginning is longer. Therefore, we consider that the effect of the cognitive elaboration mentioned earlier has a primacy effect, and the result is that the first introduced book is not necessarily in a disadvantageous position when compared to the other presentation orders.

Based on this interpretation, we considered two points. Firstly, we only revealed the trends mentioned above, and the cause of these trends is not necessarily the response order effect. This research collected and analyzed the results of Bibliobattle simultaneously performed in various parts of Japan. Detailed conditions such as presence/absence of ice-breaker sessions, voting system, method for deciding the order, were not uniform across the venues where Bibliobattle was conducted. To understand the influence of the response order effect on the possibility of acquiring Champion Books according to the presentation order in Bibliobattle, it is necessary to conduct experiments uniformly across all venues.

Secondly, the players accustomed to Bibliobattle, generally choose the order of presentation that is closest to the end. This implies a trend of the last and last but one in the order being advantageous. Thus, it is impossible to exclude the possibility that presenters at Bibliobattle feel that it is advantageous to be closer to the end of the order of presentation and expect that the second half will be likely to be chosen. However, Bibliobattle is a game in which victory/defeat significantly depends on the "participant's preference of books", which implies that the factors cannot be predicted by players. Thus, having a lot of experience as a presenter does not imply that it is easy to acquire Champion Books. Therefore, even if experienced players tend to choose the latter half of the order for presentation, we think that the influence is small.

5.2   Consideration on Methods to Reduce the Influence of Response Order Effect

Although its strength is unknown, it is considered that the response order effect influences the decision of awarding the Champion Book of Bibliobattle. Here, we consider two ways to weaken its effect in Bibliobattle.

The first suggestion is to decide presenting options after placing the books in a position that can be seen by all the participants. Alternately, the titles of the book can be displayed in a visible position. Consequently, the influence of the recency effect caused by the memory limitation factor can be reduced. However, as this method has already been adopted empirically by many organizers, it can be observed that this method does not exert a big influence on the tendency discussed in this paper.

Secondly, we considered changing the procedure of voting. According to the official rule of Bibliobattle, the procedure of voting is decided by the organizer. Therefore, there are various voting methods, such as raising hands, pointing fingers, and ballot sheets. However, voting by hands is frequently used in many Bibliobattle. In this method, the chief speaker reads out the title name in the order of presentation, and the participants raise their hands to vote for the book that they want to read the most. We considered the possibility of reducing the response order effect of the presentation order by voting in the reverse order of presentations. To verify the second method, we conducted experiments on Bibliobattle with 4, 5, and 6 presenters. The number of games conducted was 26, and the total number of presenters was 119. Table 3 lists the number of acquisitions of Champion Books per presentation order when voting was conducted in the reverse order.

Table 3. Number of Champion Book acquisitions per order of presentation in reverse order of voting

Presentation order	Number of presenters			
	4	5	6	Total
1	2	1	0	3
2	6	1	0	7
3	2	1	1	4
4	4	3	1	8
5	—	3	0	3
6	—	—	1	1
Total	14	9	3	26

As with the previous test, we performed a chi-square test (significance level 5%) considering the following four conditions.

1. The Champion Book acquisitions by the first presenter and the presenter other than the first presenter.
2. The Champion Book acquisitions by the final presenter and the presenter other than the final presenter.
3. The Champion Book acquisitions by the first and second presenters and the presenters other than the first and second presenters.

4. The Champion Book acquisitions by the last and second-last presenters and the presenters other than the last and second-last presenters.

Table 4 shows the results of the test.

Table 4. Results of examination of the number of champions from a total of 4, 5, and 6 presenters in reverse order of voting

Bibliobattle with 4, 5, 6 presenters

Presenter order	Champion Book acquisitions	Champion Book not acquired	Chi-square value	p-value	Significant difference
First	3	23	2.071	0.150	n.s.
Other than first	23	70			
Last	8	18	1.550	0.231	n.s.
Other than last	18	75			
First and second	10	42	0.162	0.687	n.s.
Other than first and second	16	51			
Last and last but one	13	39	1.349	0.245	n.s.
Other than last and second last	13	54			

n.s. : No significant difference , * : p <0.05 , ** : p <0.01

In this experiment, there was no significant difference in any of the conditions. Therefore, it is possible to reduce the influence of the recency effect by voting in the reverse order of the presentations at the time of voting. However, as there is a possibility that there is no significant difference owing to the small sample size, we will maintain this as reference material.

6   Conclusions

In this paper, we discussed the possibility that the response order effect influences the Bibliobattle and analyzed methods to reduce this influence. The response order effect is also a challenge for other communication mechanisms where winning or losing happens by voting. The impact analysis of the order of presentation on Champion Book selection in a Bibliobattle was considered beneficial for the study of other mechanisms.

In addition, in this paper, we investigated the characteristics by gathering information on widely popular mechanisms. This is an era where anyone can transmit information on the Internet, and we think that there is a high possibility that research on the communication mechanism, which was impossible owing to time and manual problems earlier, can now be conducted more easily.

References

1. Taniguchi, T., Kawakami, H., Katai, O.: Bibliobattle: informal community scheme based on book review sessions. In: Proceedings of the 8th International Workshop on Social Intelligence Design (SID 2009), pp. 92–98 (2009)
2. Taniguchi, T.: Bibliobattle. Bungeishunju (2013, in Japanese) 115
3. McGonigal, J.: Reality Is Broken: Why Games Make Us Better and How They Can Change the World. Penguin (2011)
4. Krosnick, J.A.: Survey research. Ann. Rev. Psychol. **50**(1), 537–567 (1999)
5. Akaike, Y., Taniguchi, T.: Designing presentation time of bibliobattle. J. Japan Ind. Manag. Assoc. **65**(3), 157–167 (2014)
6. Oku, K., Taniguchi, T., Akaike, Y.: Evaluation of bibliobattle as recommender systems. J. Hum. Interface Soc. **15**(1–4), 95–106 (2013)
7. Yamaguchi, Y.: Response order effects of answer in social surveys. J. Soc. Stud. Shakaigaku-bu ronshu, J. Fac. Soc. 151–159 (2004)
8. Tsuboi, T.: The role of recall order in serial position effect. Jpn. Psychol. Res. **53**(1), 38–41 (1982)
9. Sudman, S., Bradburn, N.M., Schwarz, N., et al.: Thinking about answers: the application of cognitive processes to survey methodology (1996)
10. Krosnick, J.A., Alwin, D.F.: An evaluation of a cognitive theory of response-order effects in survey measurement. Publ. Opin. Q. **51**(2), 201–219 (1987)

Desertesejo (2000/2014): Notes on the Restoration Process

Gilbertto Prado[1(✉)] and Marcos Cuzziol[2(✉)]

[1] Universidade de São Paulo/Universidade Anhembi Morumbi,
São Paulo, Brazil
gttoprado@gmail.com
[2] Itaú Cultural, São Paulo, Brazil
marcos.cuzziol@itaucultural.org.br

Abstract. The objective of this work is to present and discuss some issues of the Desertesejo project Desertesejo (Gilbertto Prado, 2000, developed at Program New Media Directions - Itaú Cultural, in Sao Paulo) and its restoration occurred in 2014. Desertesejo is an artistic interactive multi-user virtual environment initially developed in VRML. The project is a poetical exploration of geographical extension, the temporary ruptures, the loneliness, the constant reinvention and the proliferation of points of meeting and sharing.

Keywords: Art media · Virtual reality · Poéticas digitais · Digital poetry · Interactive installation

1 Introduction

Since its inauguration in 1987, many of Itaú Cultural Institute's actions have focused on the artistic use of technology. This was the case with the institution's first product, the Computerized Database – which evolved into the current Itaú Cultural Encyclopedia of Brazilian Art and Culture – with the series biennales of art and technology exhibitions – in particular the *Art.ficial* – and the Itaú Cultural Collection of Art and Technology, among other examples.

Gradually and naturally, the specific requirements of digital/technological art exhibitions generated knowledge about the necessary maintenance of such works, from small repairs to complete restorations. We have two examples of restoration works carried out at Itaú Cultural between 2013 and 2014. The first one, *Beabá*, by Waldemar Cordeiro and Giorgio Moscati (1968) and the second, which we will briefly discuss here, *Desertesejo*, by Gilbertto Prado (2000) [1].

The Desertesejo project, by Gilbertto Prado, was selected to be developed in the Itaú Cultural Rumos Novas Mídias program. Proposed as a multiuser 3D virtual environment, Desertesejo provides an interactive experience with the simultaneous presence of a number of participants. The project poetically explores geographic extent, temporal ruptures, solitude, constant reinvention, and proliferation of meeting and sharing points [2–6].

Upon entering the virtual environment, travelers can find a cave from whose roof stones drop gently. Each of them is clickable. After clicking, travelers are transported to

© Springer Nature Switzerland AG 2019
M. Kurosu (Ed.): HCII 2019, LNCS 11568, pp. 239–252, 2019.
https://doi.org/10.1007/978-3-030-22636-7_17

a new environment, where they carry this stone. They can then deposit it in one of the hills (apaicheta) present in different spaces. The stone will mark the passage of this traveler and will be an indication to others that they were there.

Entry into this environment, however, can happen in three different ways. By clicking on a stone in the cave, travelers can be transported as a tiger, a snake or an eagle. That is, they can walk, crawl or fly over the environment, as in a shamanic dream, but they will not know in advance which form they will assume in this new space.

The environments are composed of landscapes, fragments of memories and dreams, being navigable in different routes that intersect and alternate between one another, being linked and composed in several dream paths:

A. Gold This is the zone of silence. In this first room the navigation is lonely, a space without any preordained paths.

B. Viridis This is the space of heaven and colors. Inside it, the traveler will see signs that indicate the presence of other travelers, but won't have any direct contact with them.

C. Plumas (Feathers). This is the axis of dreams and mirages. Within this zone the traveler interacts directly with others, via 3D chat. This is the zone of contact between the avatars of different users.

2 Desertesejo (2000)

Following we carry out a brief exploration of this virtual environment – which could be done online, a guided voyage among many other possibilities [7, 8].

On entering the virtual environment (Fig. 1), the traveler comes across a cave which has rocks falling gently from the ceiling. Any of these rocks can be clicked on. After having clicked on a rock, the traveler is then transported to a new room, in which he or she has to carry the rock selected. The traveler can then place the rock on one of the various heaps (apaicheta) that are found in different locations. The rock will show that this traveler has been through here and will act as a sign of his/her presence to other travelers.

But there are three different ways to enter this room. By clicking on a rock inside the cave, the traveler will be transported as a tiger, a snake or an eagle. In other words: the traveler will be able to walk, slither or fly across the room, as if in a shamanistic dream, but the traveler won't know beforehand what form he/she will take on in this new location. This means that the ways of seeing things, as well as the speed at which they move about, are distinct and related to the creatures in question. The multiplication of points of view allows one to see the world in different ways. As well as this, you do not always land in the same place in this world - you can land in various different locations.

Although this first environment is a multi-user one, the visitor navigates alone within it. He will not meet anyone else, he will be alone and sometimes he will hear the sound of the wind in some open areas. It is a wide-open space of desert and desires that is a place of loneliness, of loss of references and at the same time a place of freedom and possibilities, a flat space without any preordained paths.

The stones that fall from the cave ceiling will be found in the piles of stone spread around at various points in this first virtual environment. I will talk a little bit about their story.

Fig. 1. Desertesejo 2000.

While the artist was carrying out this work, he hiked through various deserts, such as the Atacama one in Chile, as well as in arid sandy regions, such as the Lençois

Maranhenses[1]. When Gilbertto Prado was walking through the desert in Chile, he noticed some of these piles of stones dotted around in that vast space and he wondered what was the purpose of these stones that were piled up and placed close to the paths and trails in the sand. Could it be that they were there to guide someone, so that he would have some sort of reference point in these vast spaces? A native told him that they were special places. When they left home, they used to look for a stone and they would carry it until the moment that they arrived somewhere, which intuition told them was the place where the stone should be deposited together with others. It is a type of offering (Fig. 2).

Fig. 2. Desertesejo 2000. Apaicheta.

Bearing this in mind, the artist transformed these stone mounds (*Apaicheta* in the Aymara language) into presence markers (visitor counter). When one enters this virtual world, and clicks on the first stone, it will be carried until we find a place where we wish to leave it. Prado opted to do this instead of using a conventional counter at the site's entrance in order to give the act of visiting a certain poetic visual element. The visitor receives a stone which he will deposit once and only once in one of the spaces spread out across the various environments. It is a way of saying "this is the place where I want to leave my stone for the others", a way of leaving behind something to mark the fact that you were there, and modify the environment in a subtle way, a trace of this visitor's path for those who will come afterwards. This may only be done once. If he wishes to leave another stone, the visitor will have to enter the site once more and complete the whole course again.

---

[1] It should be remembered that the space is a dreamlike one and is constructed, rather than being a replica of an existing space. Although it contains allusions and references, traced by the sensations, stories and journeys, it is an invented space, made up of fragments and dreams.

The second environment is the "Viridis", a navigation axis which already contains signs of the presence of other visitors, but where it is still not possible to contact them. However, one can see signs of their presence, indicating that there are other navigators in the same environment at that moment.

An example of the Viridis environment is the "five skies room", the walls of which are made up of the colors of the local skies of the last visitors. When the visitor enters the room, the wall in front of him is the color of the sky of Sao Paulo at that moment. As other people enter the Desertesejo site, a CGI allows the system to discover the location of each one of them at that moment and whether it is morning, afternoon or evening where they are. To the extent that the other visitors stay online, they make up the room's four walls.

In other words, the navigator is in a room where the colors of the walls change in accordance with the local color of the sky of those people who are entering the environment. This is one way of transforming the place suffixes of the visitors' e-mails (.br, .uk, .jp, .fr, .es, .de, etc.) into poetic data. The idea is that the visitor knows whether or not someone has come into the room: if the colors of the walls remain the same and the room does not change, then nobody has entered. Whenever the colors change, the visitor knows that someone else is sharing this piece of cyberspace, but he does not who the other person is, what he does, or where he comes from. When someone comes into the environment, the shared presence repositions the visitor within this transformed space. It is possible that the new visitor may have the same color sky as another visitor who is already in the environment. But even if it is another color, another continent, or another time of day, it is the same moment in a sky that involves all of us. Summarizing, it works with the idea of sharing a common space which shelters all of us, (in)dependently of the time zone or places. What you do influences others and is influenced by them, and in one way or another we are all connected.

Lastly, the third axis[2]. In this axis it is possible to have a 3D chat, to meet other people and talk with them through an avatar that was modeled from figures and images of shamanistic flights. Occasionally one of them welcomes the visitor (Fig. 3).

Throughout the whole environment of the Desertesejo project, independently of the zone or axis where the users meet, there are both doorways and communication between these spaces. The portals are semi-transparent cylinders that move about in their own axes. When the visitor clicks on a portal he is transported to another area within the environment.

The different ways of interacting within these spaces, by means of the avatars, helps in the determination, potentiality and perception of the proposed environments. The various speeds and manners of moving around of the avatars that cross each other within the environment, together with the different figures and texts generated by the participants in the chat room in their various languages all reinforces distinct positions and visions of a single world, which is dreamlike and under construction. For example, the speed that is available to the snake avatar is very low, which heightens the sensation

---

[2] In reality, there is no order by which the environments are entered. I am numbering them for the sake of the project's construction and presentation. The one exception is the first world. One always enters through it, although with different angles of vision and in different locations, with this being determined in a random way.

of crawling with difficulty. This is combined with the angle of vision (at floor level) and the observation of the details closest to hand. In the case of the eagle, the flight allows rapid swerves and dives from the tops of mountains, which is coupled with panoramic views of the environment. It is important to underline that this is the space where the real performance takes place, ruled by other laws that allow one to fly, go through walls, put oneself in situations and obtain angles of vision that vary from the very strange indeed to the most commonplace. All those who are on-line at this specific moment are participating in the same space and sharing this moment, interacting, performing an action, creating texts, generating events (whether pre-programmed or otherwise), making new relations and situations of a poetic nature and performance possible within cyberspace.

Fig. 3. Desertesejo 2000. 3D chat room

The artist makes possible a situation in which people can share a world with other people, as well as being able to perceive it in different ways and from new points of view. What is produced is a potentiality, a potential environment and situation in which the visitor may or may not meet other people, and may or may not take part in other actions and performances, or may simply spend his time navigating, exploring and creating his own journeys, within this virtual poetic environment that is shareable.

The visitor is transported to a piece of a desert, which is occupied on-line, at the present moment in which forests that were previously inhabited are spaces visited by avatars. Where previously there was the bottom of the sea or of a river, now there are eagles flying and snakes slithering. Or, at the threshold we have a cybernetic space that is temporarily inhabited. A world like the mist of a desire, the magic of a fleeting encounter and a vision shared over the net of a dreamlike world that can be restarted and is open to participation.

3 Desertesejo (2014): Restoration Process

While in the 1960s, large computers were limited to the printing of paper characters, 30 years later, low-cost personal computers began to exhibit remarkable graphics capabilities on their color video monitors. It became possible in the early 1990 s to simulate the presence of a microcomputer user in navigable virtual environments, constructed by pixels and/or mathematical projections of virtual polygons. The technique already existed a few years prior, that is true, but was until then limited to very expensive graphic stations.

The works that popularized this technology were video games, of which we can cite "Wolfenstein 3D" and "Quake" (id Software, 1992 and 1996, respectively). In turn, one of the first examples of artistic application for 3D virtual environments is Jeffrey Shaw's The Legible City, which had one of its first versions introduced in 1989 using a Silicon Graphics station.

One of the first artists to use this feature in Brazil was Gilbertto Prado, with the Desertesejo project. In the year 2000, the work brought interesting innovations in terms of use of available technology [9, 10]. Virtual environments were able to run on personal computers with a good level of graphic quality (required to create a dreamlike look). In the case in question, the relationship between the graphic quality presented, based on an optimization of the number of polygons and texture, and the filtering of a level of detail of information in the modeling of the environments was worked out. As an example, the largest of the environments – the single user (Gold) – had approximately 2,000 polygons and 380 Kbytes in size (20 × 5 km – relative scale), with a very good level of graphic quality. This was possible after several tests and trials of textures and relative fittings between polygons. This work was long and crucial, the process of construction, modeling and programming of Desertesejo taking about a year.

Consequently, the Gold environment described above was particularly large by the standards of the time but ran with good speed on standard personal computers not in a specific application (as did the main video games of the period), but in a browser plugin, directly embedded in the Internet browsing application. The multiuser feature of the third environment (Plumes), with users from anywhere on the planet being represented by avatars and being able to communicate via text, preceded in three years a very popular application that used a similar browser technology: Second Life, by Linden Lab.

The work received the special mention prize at the 9th Prix Möbius International des Multimédias, held in Beijing, China (2001) and participated in several other exhibitions, including the 25th São Paulo Biennial, Net Arte (2002).

In 2014, Desertesejo was selected to participate in the exhibition Singularidades/ Anotações, by curators Aracy Amaral, Paulo Miyada, and Regina Silveira. Nevertheless, developed in 1999/2000 using a plugin specific to VRML (Virtual Reality Modeling Language) and a 3D chat, the work could no longer be presented. The plugin used 14 years before did not work – it had become obsolete in more recent browsers. How to relive all this in the present time, with other tools and possibilities? How to put the viewer in this dreamlike environment?

The Desertesejo restoration process was the only option so that the work could be presented as originally proposed – as opposed to as a mere video documentation, for example. The work of restoration was intense, as all the environments of the work had to be remodeled in 3D, textures, sounds and lighting recreated, avatars rebuilt, etc. Consequently, even with the creation of new environments developed for different programs, both the looks and experience of the original work were maintained and presented to the public at the 2014 exhibition. The artist's guidance throughout the restoration process was crucial to that the result obtained was as faithful as possible to the original, as well as the various encounters that happened with the 3D modeler in the Unity environment to discuss this new context and the subsequent approval of each stage. For the artist, it was essential that the poetic dimension of the work be preserved, as well as the relationship with the users in the navigable spaces (Figs. 4, 5 and 6).

Fig. 4. Desertesejo, Gilbertto Prado, (2000/2014)

For Karen O'Rourke, the experience proposed by artists in digital art projects beyond the poetic issue also considers a series of composition, reading and practical elements that ensure a better understanding of the project.

"Digital art is part of the temporal development in/through the interfaces. Even if the device cannot be summarized as being the work, it is a not inconsiderable component of the experience. One part of the interface is fixed, while the other depends on choices (i.e., the desires of the viewer) and another is open to randomness of material manipulation (bug, crashes in the material, software aging, etc.). Thus, in each new occurrence and presentation is a time to rethink this relationship." O'ROURKE 2011, p. 137 [11]

Fig. 5. Desertesejo (2000/2014), #Tempo Narrador, 15° Festival de Inverno do Sesc, Petrópolis, Quitandinha, Rio de Janeiro, 2016. Five skies room.

Fig. 6. Desertesejo, Gilbertto Prado (2000/2014). Arte Cibernética - Coleção Itaú Cultural, Museu Nacional do Conjunto Cultural da República, Brasília, 2016.

Fig. 7. Desertesejo, Gilbertto Prado. Views of environments with the Cosmos Player plugin (2000) and the 2014 version.

While there are a number of devices and interfaces that locate us and indicate moments and eras, this does not mean that they cannot be occasionally updated. They are new choices that present themselves and new possible displacements [12, 13].

Fig. 8. Desertesejo, Gilbertto Prado (2000/2014). Circuito Alameda, Claustro Bajo, curatorship Jorge La Ferla, Laboratorio Arte Alameda, Mexico City, 2018.

During the restoration process, which lasted almost a year, issues that were a problem to be worked on in the first version, such as the speed of navigation in the environments, had been transformed14 years later. Computers already allowed much more complex and elaborate environments, as well as a much faster and frantic navigation flow. The initially desired speed of navigation, however, was slow and delicate, not only due to a limitation of the machine, but by a coincident desire also in the poetics.

During the restoration process, in addition to the regular face-to-face meetings, there was an immense correspondence exchange between the team participants. One of the notes shows the artist's intention, assigned to the modeler/programmer, as opposed to the machinic speed possible and desired in the work:

I also remember the "climate" of lethargy, the slow speed of navigation, as if displaced in time, the weight of the environment, the solitude of the solo navigation, as in a space between dream and reality. That sensation the moment you wake up, that you do not know whether you are floating or walking, whether it is cold or hot, the weight of the environment, and the immensity of space. Majestic and lonely, with no way out. (PRADO, project notes)

In another brief comparison between versions, in the environments of the 2000 version show the mouse control of the Cosmo Player navigator, in the environments made in VRML. In 2014, there is no such insertion in the environment using the Unity 3D game engine. Still in 2000, although we already presented the work projected in some occasions, the immersion in the images given was more difficult, given the relative pixelization. The 2000 version provided a better browsing experience on the computer screen itself or in monitors, unlike the new version, which due to the resolution of the images, allowed the exploration through the space and walking using the joypad control in one hand, as opposed to the mouse next to the keyboard (Fig. 7).

In the videos below, we can see an example of navigation in the environments in the different versions:

Desertesejo 2000: https://www.youtube.com/watch?v=1Fov7V32pF8

Desertesejo 2014: https://youtu.be/nzPcC0WJFs8

In 2016, Jonathan Biz Medina and João Amadeu made a version of Desertesejo VR for Oculus Rift.

In 2018, on the occasion of the Paradox(es) of Contemporary Art at the MAC – USP [14], in São Paulo and, simultaneously, the individual exhibition Alameda Circuit, at the Alameda Art Laboratory of Mexico [15], new maintenance and adjustments were made to the 2014 version of Desertesejo, also with the participation of Fernando Oliveira and Felipe Santini (Figs. 8 and 9).

Fig. 9. Desertesejo, Gilbertto Prado (2000/2014). Modos de ver o Brasil: Itaú Cultural 30 anos, OCA – Parque Ibirapuera, São Paulo, 2017; Paradoxo(s) da Arte Contemporânea, curatorship Ana Gonçalves Magalhães and Priscila Arantes, MAC-USP, Sao Paulo, 2018.

We note that the works go beyond the appearances and lines of code and beyond the devices and interfaces and possible enchantments, ensuring the association of complex universes, in an ephemeral approximation and coherence, to bring the tenuity of these incorporations with new insights and conjugations.

Restoring a work of art, and in this case digital art, is more than reconstructing environments: an understanding of the poetics of the work and the subtleties of the work, such as the colors of the spaces, speeds of navigation, possible routes and interactions, etc. is necessary. One cannot generalize what would be a "standard" restoration process for works of art using relatively recent technologies. Such works vary widely between technologies and proposals. There are purely procedural works, virtually independent of the hardware employed, even for those with strong object characteristics, which would be disfigured without specific hardware [16].

The Desertesejo restoration sought to recreate virtual environments that allowed the same interactive experience of the original work. In this case, the technical issue, while obviously important, is secondary. What is it that really matters if Desertesejo is developed for a VRML plugin or a game engine such as Unity 3D? Much more importantly, what must guide any process of restoration of technological/digital works is the poetic aspect. That is what really matters.

Acknowledgements. To the UAM- Universidade Anhembi Morumbi for the research support. To the CNPq – Conselho Nacional de Desenvolvimento Científico e Tecnológico (National Council for Scientific and Technological Development); FAPESP - Fundação de Amparo à Pesquisa do Estado de São Paulo and Itaú Cultural for the support and assistance they have provided in different moments of the projects.

Credits
Gilbertto Prado
Desertesejo (2000/2014)
Production: Rumos Arte e Tecnologia - Novas Mídias 1998–1999
3D Modeling and VRML: Nelson Multari
web-design: Jader Rosa
version 2014
3D Modeling: Jonathan Biz Medina
Technical coordination: Marcos Cuzziol

References

1. Cuzziol, M.: Desertesejo 2000 - Canteiro de Obras. In: Relatoria Coelho, J., Freire, C. (eds.) Arte Contemporânea: Preservar o quê? pp. 161–166. (Org.) MACUSP, São Paulo (2015)
2. Prado, G., Assis, J., Ribemboim, R.: Two recent experiments in multiuser virtual environments in Brazil: Imateriais 99 and Desertesejo. In: Proceedings The Eighth Biennial Symposium on Arts and Technology, Connecticut College, pp. 100–109. New London (2001)
3. Prado, G.: Artistic experiments on telematic nets: recent experiments in multiuser virtual environments in Brazil. Leonardo **37**(4), 297–303 (2004). https://doi.org/10.1162/0024094041724481
4. Machado, A.: O Sujeito na Tela: modos de enunciação no cinema e no ciberespaço. Paulus, São Paulo (2007)
5. Mello, C.: Arte nas Extremidades. In: Machado, A. (ed.) Três Décadas do Vídeo Brasileiro, pp. 143–174. (Org.) Itaú Cultural, São Paulo (2003)

6. Forest, F.: Art et Internet. Editions Cercle d'Art, Paris (2008)
7. Prado, G.: Art et Télématique. In: Les Cahiers du Collège Iconique, Communications et débats, n. XVIII, 2004–2005, pp. 1–39. Inathèque de France - Institut National de l'audiovisuel, Paris (2006)
8. Prado, G.: Arte Telemática: dos intercâmbios pontuais aos ambientes virtuais multiusuário. Itaú Cultural, São Paulo (2003)
9. Couchot, E.: A Tecnologia na Arte: da fotografia à realidade virtual. Editora da UFRGS, Porto Alegre (2003)
10. Prado, G.: Digital art, dialogues and process. In: Magalhães, A., Beiguelman, G. (eds.) Possible Futures: Art, Museums And Digital Archives, pp. 114–128. (Org.) Ed. Peirópolis, São Paulo (2013)
11. O'Rourke, K.: Des Arts-Réseaux auxDérives Programmées: actualité de « l'art comme expérience » . Habilitation à diriger des recherches. Université Paris 1 (2011)
12. Lima, L., Prado, G.: Imagens digitais interativas: do simulacro à imersão. DATJ. Des. Art Technol. 3(2), 43–71 (2018). https://doi.org/10.29147/dat.v3i2.86
13. O'Rourke, K.: Walking and Mapping: Artists as Cartographers. MIT Press, Cambridge (2013)
14. Magalhães, A., Arantes, P.: Paradoxo(s) da Arte Contemporânea. Museu de Arte Contemporânea da Universidade de São Paulo, São Paulo (2018)
15. Prado, G., La Ferla, J.: Circuito Alameda. Instituto Nacional de Bellas Artes, Laboratorio Arte Alameda, Ciudad de México (2018)
16. Cuzziol, M.: Restauração e manutenção de obras digitais: duas experiências no Instituto Itaú Cultural. In: Prado, G., Tavares, M., Arantes, P. (eds.) Diálogos transdisciplinares: arte e pesquisa, pp. 266–273. ECA/USP, São Paulo (2016)

Collaborative Design of Urban Spaces Uses: From the Citizen Idea to the Educational Virtual Development

Monica V. Sanchez-Sepulveda[1] , David Fonseca[1(✉)] ,
Jordi Franquesa[2] , Ernesto Redondo[2] , Fernando Moreira[3] ,
Sergi Villagrasa[1] , Enric Peña[1] , Nuria Martí[1] ,
Xavier Canaleta[1] , and José Antonio Montero[1]

[1] La Salle, Ramon Llull University, 08022 Barcelona, Spain
{monica.sanchez,fonsi,sergiv,enricp,nuria.marti,
xavier.canaleta,joseantonio.montero}@salle.url.edu
[2] Polytechnic University of Catalonia, 08028 Barcelona, Spain
{jordi.franquesa,ernesto.redondo}@upc.edu
[3] Universidade Portucalense, Porto, Portugal
fmoreira@uportu.pt

Abstract. The paper is concerned with the design of virtual environments for collaborative design. The interests of citizens are coming to the forefront nowadays with the awareness that a livable city does not only consist of good infrastructure and sustainable energy supply but also citizen input and feedback. The project consists of a transversal research at the intersection between computer science, the teaching of future architects and multimedia engineers and the urban policies of the cities of the future in which citizen participation is fundamental. The hypothesis is based on demonstrating the following two statement: (1) The implementation of virtual gamified strategies in the field of urban design will generate an improvement in citizen participation by being a more dynamic, real and agile collaborative environment thanks to enhanced visual technologies and immersive. (2) Gamified strategies for the understanding of three-dimensional space improve spatial competencies of students generating greater motivation in their use and a degree of satisfaction high. First, we studied the contemporary student profile and better ways of teaching according to it. Second, rehearse and evaluate the teaching of the urban project incorporating collaborative design, immersive ICTs, gamification and citizen participation. Third, the data obtained from the quantitative assessment, exemplify the role and use of technologies, in the educational processes to improve the students' motivation, involvement and way of learning.

Keywords: Higher education · Information and communication technologies · Architecture schools · User experience · Urban spaces · Virtual reality

© Springer Nature Switzerland AG 2019
M. Kurosu (Ed.): HCII 2019, LNCS 11568, pp. 253–269, 2019.
https://doi.org/10.1007/978-3-030-22636-7_18

1 Introduction

Both, education and the cities in which we live are changing rapidly, presenting the scenery to debate future visions of transformative education and its impact on the city. In order to take advantage of the changes and opportunities offered by the inclusion of digital technologies, an accommodation of the digital transformation into the visualization of Urbanism is required. It is a challenge for Higher Education and society to question the *status quo* and experiment often. This sometimes means walking away from long-standing conventional processes that universities and citizens were built upon, in favor of relatively new practices that are still being defined. The integration of digital transformation in Urbanism consists in balancing the creative act required to generate receptive environments and the social and environmental responsibilities that should be integrated into this act. It is about understanding how knowledge is produced, what the components of that knowledge are and which are the learning processes and social practices that can be used to transmit it.

The main goal of the paper is to present the use of digital transformation in the teaching and processes of urban design and citizenship, through innovative concepts and practical methodologies. The objective is to promote the use of digital technologies, in particular to evaluate the inclusion of virtual reality in various formal and informal teaching environments of collaborative urban design, in order to improve it, speed up and increase its positive social impact. The results will show that it is possible to empower digital transformation, to improve public motivation, implication, and satisfaction in urban decision-making processes.

The paper describes the role and use of technological innovations involving the social re-appropriation of urban spaces and contribute to social inclusion in the city of Barcelona. It is focused on studying the motivation, engagement, and overall experience of the participants (citizenship and the students). The general objectives (or research questions) of this paper is to approach the following topics:

- Combining model with real-scale proposals using Virtual Reality in open spaces makes is it possible to define a new space-participation model, guided, on the local scale, by single citizens, and by a local community.
- It is infer that these initiatives could facilitate public decisions through the social re-evaluation of spaces, real and virtual, in order to respond any needs.
- Organizations can be able to incorporate informal data obtained from citizens, urban and architecture professionals, students, and consequently, designs can be executed with a suitable design, adapted to space and combining the functionality, needs, and interests of all of them.

2 New Generation of Students - Adapting the Profile to Innovative Supporting Technologies

How is the generation of nowadays? This generation is called the Generation Y that comes after the Millennials. This generation are the students that were born in the mid-1990s, early 2000s. They were raised, combined with the school experience, along with their heavy mass media exposure, made them self-confident, extremely social, technologically sophisticated, action bent, goal oriented, service or civic minded, and accustomed to functioning as part of a team, but on the other side, they are also impatient, demanding, stressed out, sheltered, brand oriented, materialistic, and self-centered [1]. This characteristic has a lot to do in the way they perceive the instructor, the institution and education. This generation has an increased use and familiarity with communications, media, and digital technologies, something older generations did not. However, it must be said that the characteristics of this generation do not apply an entire generation but a portion of its members, as the characteristics vary by region, depending on social and economic conditions.

If comparing this generation with past ones, Biggs mention two types of students: the "good" student—intelligent, well prepared, goal oriented, and motivated to master the material, that came to college with solid thinking, writing, and learning skills. This type was about 75% of the students in 1980 and only about 42% are like that today [2]. The 58% are less academically talented, college ready, and motivated to learn, that just wants to get by with the least amount of learning effort, so they can parlay their degree into a decent job. This type of student will rely on memorizing the material rather than reflecting on and constructing it [2]. In different generations, there are the both types of students that Biggs describe. The only thing that change is the percentage.

Over the last decade, European Higher Education Area (EHEA), and institutions have been involved in a transformation process with the aim of creating a common framework for mobility and generating a knowledge-based competitive society [3]. As an objective of the educational reforms, it is promoted in these contexts that: "Higher education institutions should train students to become knowledgeable and deeply motivated citizens with a critical sense and capacity for analyzing the problems of the society, finding solutions for those who oppose to society, applying them and assuming social responsibilities".

In Spain, universities are in the process of redesigning and verifying their qualifications in accordance with the new guidelines established for the EHEA. This change aims to put the student at the center of the teaching-learning process, focusing on the competencies that the new graduate should possess, enhancing students' know-how, initiative and autonomous learning, according to Dublin descriptors [4]. This new scenario creates a suitable context for the use of new ICTs in higher education, key tools in the development of these new competencies. As already predicted [5], the digitalization of information has changed the primordial support of knowledge and with it our habits and customs in relation to knowledge and communication and, in the end, our ways of thinking. In this sense, new ICTs are changing the way to learn and the type of materials [6]. If we analyze the incorporation of ICT in teaching [7, 8], we can observe how universities are increasingly implementing new technologies as support for teaching, but still there is a gap between the potential of ICTs incorporation in classrooms and the unusual renewal of pedagogical processes. This is because the ICTs have been incorporated into our universities are often associated with individual teaching practices and not as a methodical change.

According to EHEA, within the basic competences and training that must be acquired in engineering and architecture degrees, we can identify the "Capacity of spatial vision and knowledge of graphic representation techniques, both by traditional methods of metric geometry and descriptive geometry, such as through computer aided design applications" [9]. In Spain, the academic abilities and competences for the architecture and the urbanism profession were defined by the White Book for Architectural and Building Engineering studies, promoted by the National Agency for Evaluation and Accreditation. The main competences identified to develop are:

- Basic skills in computer use
- Application of graphics procedures in the representation of spaces and objects
- Representation of visual attributes of objects dominating proportion and computer techniques
- Skills with spatial representation systems
- Skills with graphic lifting techniques in all its phases

These competences must be developed in a formal educational context: learning typically provided by an education or a training institution, structured and leading to certification [10]. But in the architectural and urbanism courses is easy to work with a real Project-Based Learning (PBL). Under the guidance of a tutor, students are required to develop a proposal, usually in a given location, in a process that mimics the workflow of an architectural studio. Adding to this training, architects and urban designers learn about their discipline in a continuous and informal way, because the subject of their craft surrounds them almost anywhere and anytime. Under the guidance of a tutor, students are required to develop a proposal, usually in a given location, in a process that mimics the workflow of an architectural studio. Adding to this training, architects and urban designers learn about their discipline in a continuous and informal way (Learning result from daily life activities related to work, family or leisure), because the subject of their craft surrounds them almost anywhere and anytime [11, 12].

2.1 Useful Technologies

In face of the enormous amount of urban (or architectural) data that is needed to develop a proposal, the field of Urbanism (and in a most generic view the Architecture and Building Engineering), is yet to incorporate many sources of information into their workflow, based on the tools developed in the Graphic Expression (GE) framework:

- Basic Digital Applications. The study of spatial geometry is fundamental to enhance the development of reasoning and spatial ability. In this sense we can identify clearly different type of tools:
  - 2Dimensions-3Dimensions CAD (Computer Assisted Design) Systems: The CAD methods allow a quick representation and modelling of the architecture and urban data for developing the spatial skills [13]. The ability in spatial representation capacity requires a learning of spatial perception.
  - GIS (Geographical Information Systems): One of the classical methods in the urban representation that allows linking the graphical elements with alphanumeric information to obtain an expanded analysis of the working area, for example using topologies or thematic maps [14].
  - BIM (Building Information Modelling): BIM applications can apply to the entire process of building construction [15].

- Multimedia Systems: Multimedia and interactive applications have favored the performance and speed of learning as well as personal and intrapersonal skills of students. The contents that are based on these formats are closer to the means of everyday use of students and end-users. For this reason, this type of systems are more attractive, increase the motivation and favor the performance [16]. A few of these examples can be found in the compilation of [17]. The study of matter outside the classroom is promoted through: multimedia systems, interactive tutorials, animation, hypermedia systems, and new visualization methods as for example de Augmented and Virtual Reality (AR/VR) [18–20].
- Social and semantic data: Informal data related to a public space that analyze semantic, temporal and spatial patterns, aspects generally overlooked in traditional approaches, improve the education of future urban designers in order to relate the projects to the main needs of the citizenship [21].
- Videogames/Gamified Systems: Tasks that have a high spatial component (rotate, move, scale, etc.) are present in video games, as well as in serious games applied to the visualization of complex models, where we can find actions in which the user must move the character in a multitude of possible combinations [22, 23].
- Rapid prototyping and real models: Physical models accelerate the spatial learning process as demonstrated by experiences in GE courses. The use of 3D printers for generating rapid prototypes in the classroom reveals that there are students who learn by touching versus traditional methods that are based on the visual aspects [24].

2.2 Technologies Between Citizens and Students

The last decades in urban design research are characterized by a focus on technological aspects of cities [25]. The concerns and interests of citizens are coming to the forefront nowadays with the awareness that a livable city does not only consist of good infrastructure but also citizen input and feedback. The city as an objective reality and as a symbolized image plays a fundamental role in the organization of space. However, the urban phenomenon that completes the urban structure is its representation as a social product, the result of human action [26]. Using new technologies, as for example VR and AR, we can work with defined urban proposals rehearsing various strategies of action in an interactive way and collaboratively evaluate public spaces. Taking into account that the basis of the VR is to create an immersive experience and allow the user to interact with objects [27] (See Fig. 1).

Fig. 1. Gamification for urban design.

Given the approach of the project, it is important to take into account how the VR is a technology, that applied correctly, not only can be a useful teaching tool, but also a tool to involve society and democratize decision making in complex projects, like urban ones. Some studies show that training in a virtual environment in which 3D objects can be manipulated from any angle allows better recognition of objects than if they are taught on paper [28]. By incorporating VR with informal teaching models: citizens generate series of opinions or suggestions, which help students to see different points of view. In this case study the participants are an active element of the project, and the student, will have the ability to learn in real environments and projects (PBL), allowing them to obtain and improve his spatial and social skills in a very optimal way, both formally and informally. This information improves their formal knowledge, as cases were conduct outside an academic environment.

The incorporation of new technologies in education should be considered as part of a global educational policy strategy. In this regard, several important aspects can be mentioned that must be taken into account [29]:

- There is a strong social demand to incorporate the new ICTs to education, often exercised without too much information about the real value of them.
- Strategies related to new technologies require partnerships between the public sector and the private sector, as well as also alliances within the public sector itself.
- Strategies should be considered as a priority to teachers. Relevant studies show that while the majority of teachers show favorable attitudes towards the use of new technologies, there are cultural aspects to which is important to pay attention.
- Given the diversity of situations and the enormous dynamism that exists in this field, political strategies should be based on the development of experiences, innovations and investigations that tend to identify the best paths for universal access to these modalities, which avoids development of new forms of exclusion and marginality.

The active design feedback from a city's inhabitants is an essential way towards a responsive city. We therefore propose a system to merge citizen feedback, which requires a structured evaluation process by the students to integrate for urban design and transmit it to stakeholders and public agencies (See Fig. 2).

Fig. 2. Teaching and management processes of the urban project

This aim is to look and reflect on the urban transformation of public spaces and the built context, from the direct experience with the field of intervention based on virtual reality and the modeling of the project. This direct experience of space in real time allows making more informed and accurate project decisions and guaranteeing much more controlled results.

3 Case Study

The urban project we work on, promoted by the Barcelona Metropolitan Area, aims to generate spaces that are designed to meet the needs of the users. The main intention is to generate spaces that are designed to meet what the users' wants: spacious, pleasant spaces with vegetation, with dynamic uses, spaces for children's games, urban gardens, lighting, recreational and cultural activities, among others.

3.1 Previous Works

A first urban project we work on is in Sant Boi de Llobregat in a short social/urban development of Plaça de la Generalitat. Since it was built in the 70s, the square has been remodeled. Neighbors demanded an intervention on the part of the Administration due to several reasons: the perception of insecurity of the neighborhood, the need to promote the trade of the surroundings and the degradation of the uses in general. The challenge: to design a new place from citizen participation to improve and transform the square according to their needs and desires. In order to gather ideas of improvement on the square, similar to the next projects that will be described, is to (1) Inform and inviting to the participatory process. (2) Know the opinions about the state of the current place and the proposals for improvement. (3) Carry out face-to-face surveys with neighbors. (4) Facilitation of local conferences in order to gather proposals for improvement (See Fig. 3).

Fig. 3. Plaça de la Generalitat neighbors. Collaborative design.

A second project we work on, aims to create a large public space that prioritizes the people of the Example Esquerra District instead of the vehicles [27]. By closing the street to vehicles and allowing it to pedestrians, the program to be situated there is design according to their criteria. Collaboratively, they stated the following conditioners:

- Address the street primarily to pedestrians
- Prevent spaces for stay and neighborhood coexistence
- Increase the low vegetation while maintaining the alignment of trees typical.
- Increase the surface of rainwater catchment on the terrain
- Establish criteria for the location of furniture and services (garbage bins, cargo download, bar terraces…)

3.2   Current Location

The third project we work on is in the area of the Plaça Baró, in Santa Coloma de Gramanet. The base was to produce a collaborative design with a gender perspective from the design phase to the intervention. The aim is to create a specific space adapted to the needs of children between 6 and 12 years old. A participatory process was carried out with students of the 5th grade of the Torre Balldovina School, neighbor of the square, as well as sessions open to the whole neighborhood. The sessions were accompanied by a process of education in architecture and urban planning with a gender perspective for children. All activities have been carried out with approaches that allow children to contribute their realities and needs related to the specific public spaces of action. Consequently, children analyze spaces with a critical eye and can propose improvements with an inclusive perspective and through collective debate and consensus.

In a first phase, neighborhood children participated, in the assignment and distribution of uses to the different parts of the square. In the second phase, the students of the Torre Balldovina School shaped the ideas generated from the different collaborative designs. Finally, the students presented their proposals to the people representing the council. For the realization of the final work, the collage technique on an axonometric was used (See Fig. 4).

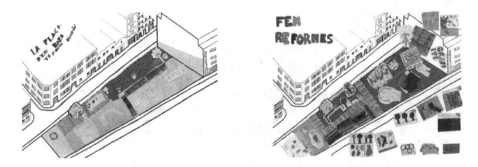

Fig. 4. Work at the Torre Balldovina School.

There have also been sessions for families and careers to share their experiences and needs. The purpose is to detect problems and virtues, a bag of desires and the fabric of the networks. Taking into account that the square is a space for coexistence between different people (age, hobbies and other preferences). Sectors and uses, vegetation and reuse of the existing sources were defined. This is integrated with the uses and requirements of the previous phases. From this premise the most suitable pavements for each of the zones according to their assigned use (color and texture) were chosen, and the different urban elements that could be integrated into the square were imagine and draw in order to decide which of them are necessary to provide service needed and guarantee the comfort of each space.

Broadly speaking, the following areas of activities were defined: rest area and quiet activities (reading, drawing, rest, etc.), low intensity motor activity zone and symbolic game (game structures, free space for games), zone of intense motor activities (such as playing with a ball or as a team) and mediating vertical activities (cartography, chalkboard, basket, fronton…). Finally, the results were presented to the city council.

3.3   From the Citizens to the Architecture Students Education/Implementation

These proposals were passed to the University to digitalize and virtualize them in a three-dimensional way. Students and professors from the universities of the Polytechnic University of Catalonia (UPC) and La Salle - Ramon Llull University (LS-URL), work on the elaboration of taking these spaces to visualize them in real time. The idea is that now the neighbors and the city council can visualize the scale, the textures, the relationship of the uses, the lights and shadows, etc. The persons that has participated using the glasses of virtual reality and through interactive elements, the participants shaped the urban public space. According to their criteria and collaboratively, could again configure the elements. The objective is to bring all citizens the technology of virtual reality so that they can participate in the definition of the uses of the public spaces in the most realistic way before its development (See Fig. 5).

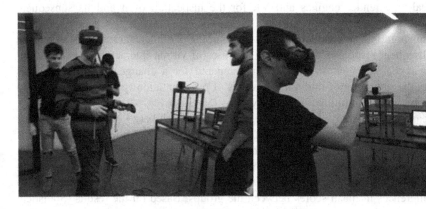

Fig. 5. UPC professors and students.

The virtual reality allowed participants to see in an immersive way the changes and actions that happens in the environment in real time, for example, in the calculation of specific lighting in a space to show a very dynamic and realistic result. Some participants' proposals, inserted into the simulated environment, have the capacity to be in constant interaction by moving and rotating actions (See Fig. 6).

Fig. 6. Work made by the LS-URL.

With the proposals generated in urban participatory processes, based on sketches and work on paper, the students of the degree of architecture passed the project to its development phase. For this phase, we have worked with the subject Architectural Representation III, a teaching unit compulsory with five credits ECTS[1] from Architecture UPC. The main objective of the subject is to develop in the student the aptitude to value and adequately represent the visual attributes of architectural and urban elements. In this way, the concepts of the theory of form and of visual perception in the representation of urban space can be applied in a critical way. The teaching experiment has focused on evaluating the resolution of the visual simulation of the urban scenario as a whole, including all the elements of urban furniture, trees, day and night settings, in a conventional way, using classic render engines or navigating within the model using real-time render engines and VR for the inspection of it and its subsequent adjustment.

At this point, it is important to analyze the profile of students, especially to analyze their subsequent responses to the utility and uses of virtual interactive systems, especially to reveal whether or not they are prepared for a change of paradigm. This meaning, the migration of traditional systems of representation (plans and models), to new interactive and multiplatform 3D systems [30–32].

To carry out the study, we opted for a mixed approach based on the work sample, with 27 students that make one of the groups of the subject. Although the sample is small, it is consistent with the results obtained in previous phases of the project with higher samples of students [27]. We compared the responses of the two groups, using the Student's t-test for assessing the differences, and based on the null hypothesis (H0) of no differences in mean scores between the groups. Based on the results (Statistical significance obtained below the threshold of 0.05, which allows to affirm a guaranteed difference of at least 95%), we can affirm that there is a significance difference between

---

[1] ECTS: European Credit Transfer System.

the student's profile ($p = 0.124$), which discards differences between groups and demonstrates their homogeneity.

The following Figs. 7, 8, and 9, characterize the profile of our current students, separated by gender (although no significant differences are detected: $p = 0.346$), and in an aggregate form:

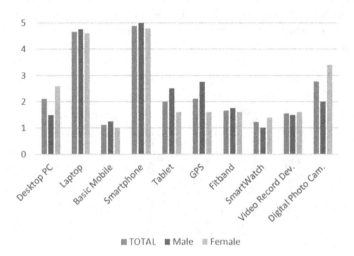

Fig. 7. Devices used daily.

As can be seen, (see Fig. 7), one of the first data that draws the attention is the concentration of use of two clearly predominant the devices: the laptop and the smartphone. This concentration reveals an important fact: the student performs tasks anywhere, and his work is mainly ubiquitous.

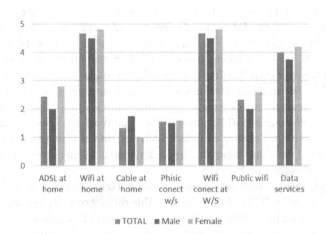

Fig. 8. Type of Internet connection.

In accordance with its ubiquitous work, the main method of connection to the Internet is through Wi-Fi networks and with a data program associated with its contracted rates (see Fig. 8), predominantly the uses centered on Social Networks, listening streaming music and search systems (see Fig. 9). These results are interesting as they predispose the student to little use of visual systems due to the mobile nature of their digital interconnection with the environment that surrounds them. This hypothesis can negatively affect the use and/or perception of utility of the systems more focused on the visual content, which need fixed and stable environments for their use, as it happens with the VR.

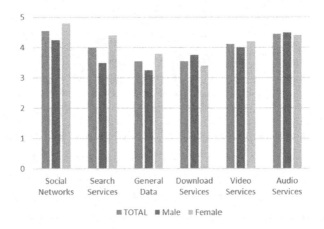

Fig. 9. Daily Internet uses.

Prior to the realization of modeling and representation of the space studied, we conducted a study based on evaluating students' motivation in the use and utility of virtual systems for their training in representation processes using the IMI (Intrinsic Motivation Inventory). The IMI is a multidimensional measurement device intended to assess participants' subjective experience related to a target activity in laboratory experiments [30]. The instrument assesses participants' interest/enjoyment (IMI1), perceived competence (IMI2), effort (IMI3), value/usefulness (IMI4), felt pressure and tension (IMI5), and perceived choice while performing a given activity (IMI6), thus yielding six subscale scores. Recently, a seventh subscale has been added to tap the experiences of relatedness (IMI7), although the validity of this subscale has yet to be established, but we have studied in order to have a general view of the system.

We conducted the same survey to the students and citizens involved in the initial participatory processes (see Fig. 10):

The overall result shows an average of 4.08 (DT: 0.08) of citizen motivation compared to 3.33 (SD: 0.27) of the students. This difference is significant ($p = 0.004$) and comes to explain how while for the end users the use of the VR and the interactive systems are methods that help to the understanding of the urban project, the same thing does not happen for the students. These results are consistent with previous studies carried out on the project [21, 27, 33, 34], and confirm the need for change in the

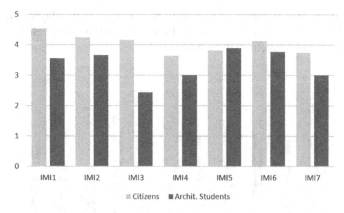

Fig. 10. IMI citizens and students comparison.

introduction of technologies in the classroom in order to improve the students' abilities and therefore society [35].

Historically, in the degree of architecture, the deliveries in subjects of projects and urbanism have focused on panels with photocompositions, sets of plans with different scales and, occasionally, representative models of the space, but without materials, textures or lighting that generate a realistic representation. While these educational systems are accepted and widely implemented, it is not the same in a non-expert environment as that of citizens, which require systems closer to the reality that they want to achieve in order to explain space and for consequently, better understand the proposed changes.

To corroborate the degree of perceived utility on the systems implemented at the educational and professional level, we evaluate the answers of a questionnaire about the perception of virtual, interactive and gamified systems (see Fig. 11). The questions evaluated have been:

- PERC1: Digital 3D visualization of architectural and urban projects is very important to understand the space.
- PERC2: The use of virtual reality (VR) to display projects is useful for understanding.
- PERC3: The use of augmented reality (AR) to display projects is useful for understanding.
- PERC4: I am motivated to use AR7VR during the presentation of projects.
- PERC5: The materials, textures and lighting of a virtual scene must always the most realistic possible.
- PERC6: The environmental sounds must always be the most realistic possible.
- PERC7: The existence of background music satisfies me in the visualization and interaction with virtual spaces.
- PERC8: The visualization device (Smartphone, Tablet, PC, etc....) has a considerable influence in the virtual quality perception.
- GAM1: The use of gamified environment (with missions and achievements) is better than simple free navigation in a virtual space.

- GAM2: In the case of games, I prefer the one-to-one vs. multi-player environments.
- GAM3: I consider that using games in educational environments help to understand the typology and correction of the materials.

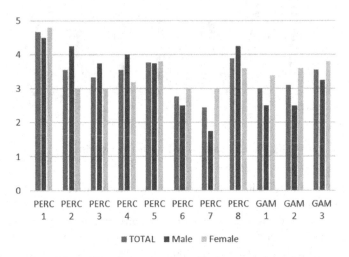

Fig. 11. Perception of the utility of virtual and gamified systems for architecture and urbanism activities.

Overall, there are no significant differences by gender in the results obtained. Likewise, the average on the perception variables stands at 3.44 (SD: 0.68), while for the evaluation of the gamification, it drops to 3.22 (DT: 0.29). The best-valued aspect is the PERC1 that affirms the importance of 3D visualization for the understanding of space (Average 4.67, SD: 0.5). Consistent with this result, the VR systems are slightly better valued (PERC2-Av: 3.56), with respect to the AR (PERC3-Av: 3.33), but the motivation of the students for their use in architectural projects can be defined as low (PERC4-Av: 3.56) [36]. Aspect that is clearly related to the difficulty of use and need to clearly perceive the quality of the model (PERC5-Av: 3.78), in mobile devices with small screens [37]. The perception of the usefulness of sound and the gamification of the interaction are the aspects least valued by the students, and that reflect as there was a lack in the need to take into account other variables of the project in the academic presentations beyond of the visual [38–42]. Just the opposite of users who are not experts in the development or education of architectural or urban projects, an aspect that reflects a gap to be resolved internally in current educational plans.

4 Conclusions: Difficulties and Opportunities

By allowing citizens new ways to co-design public spaces within their city and students to participate in the process of design helping to better visualize and understand physical projects allows to develop both the dimensional and ergonomic relationships between elements as they see their designs come to life in real time. It is understand that virtual reality applied in design and local government contexts, might change the way we conceive the urban development and planning, even thinking in an ecological way.

Based on our hypothesis, we can affirm that the implementation of virtual gamified strategies in the field of urban design will generate an improvement in citizen participation by being a more dynamic, real and agile collaborative environment thanks to enhanced visual technologies and immersive. However, on the other hand, the gamified strategies for the understanding of three-dimensional space improve spatial competencies of students generating greater motivation in their use and a degree of satisfaction is not as high as we expected.

It is necessary to change the way to explain in our educational institutions to reduce the gap between the educational sector and the social sector. This last one seems to be more prepared to incorporate all kinds of technologies, interaction, gamification and different strategies to democratize both visualization and decision making in complex projects. At the educational level, there are few efforts to use these strategies in an active way in the classroom, generating a motivation and perception of low utility in students.

Although the profile of the current students is familiar to the used of technologies to communicate and represent ideas, there still a gap between the potential of ICTs incorporation in classrooms and the renewal of pedagogical processes. Universities are increasingly implementing new technologies as support for teaching, but not as a methodical change. However, their digital profile is fully trained to make a leap in the use of digital methods and systems of last generation in the development and presentation of its architectural and urban projects.

Acknowledgments. This research was supported by the National Program of Research, Development and Innovation, Spain aimed to the Society Challenges with the references BIA2016-77464-C2-1-R & BIA2016-77464-C2-2-R, both of the National Plan for Scientific Research, Development and Technological Innovation 2013–2016, titled "Gamificación para la enseñanza del diseño urbano y la integración en ella de la participación ciudadana (Arch-GAME4CITY)", & "Diseño Gamificado de visualización 3D con sistemas de realidad virtual para el estudio de la mejora de competencias motivacionales, sociales y espaciales del usuario (EduGAME4CITY)". (AEI/FEDER, UE).

References

1. Nilson, L.B.: Teaching at its best (2010)
2. Brabrand, C., Andersen, J., Bucur, D., Thorbek, R.: Teaching teaching & understanding understanding (2006)
3. European Ministers: Towards the European higher education area. Eur. J. Soc. Work. **4**, 320–323 (2001)
4. Initiative, J.Q.: Shared "Dublin" descriptors for short cycle, first cycle, second cycle and third cycle awards. Draft 1, Working Document JQI Meeting, Dublin, pp. 1–5 (2004)

5. Adell, J.: Tendencias en educación en la sociedad de las tecnologías de la información. Edutec. Revista electrónica de tecnología educativa (7), a007. https://doi.org/10.21556/edutec.1997.7.570

6. Negroponte, N.: Being digital (1996)

7. Area Moreira, M., Area-Moreira, M.: Innovación pedagógica con TIC y el desarrollo de las competencias informacionales y digitales. Investig. en la Esc. **64**, 5–18 (2008)

8. Píriz Durán, S., et al.: Universitic 2013: Situación actual de las TIC en el sistema universitario español (2013)

9. Saavedra, M.F.C., Rodríguez, G.G.C.: Competencias TIC Para el Desarrollo Profesional Docente, Ministerio de Educación Nacional (2013)

10. Clark, D.: Formal vs. informal learning. Knowl. Jump. 1–18 (2015)

11. Malcolm, J., Hodkinson, P., Colley, H.: The interrelationships between informal and formal learning. J. Work. Learn. **15**, 313–318 (2003)

12. Bee, R., Analysis, L.N.: The spectrum of learning from formal to informal. Learn. Needs Anal. 87–92 (2003)

13. Bénière, R., Subsol, G., Gesquière, G., Le Breton, F., Puech, W.: A comprehensive process of reverse engineering from 3D meshes to CAD models. CAD Comput. Aided Des. **45**, 1382–1393 (2013)

14. Yeh, A.G.-O.: Urban planning and GIS. In: Geographical Information Systems: Principles, Techniques, Management and Applications, p. 404 (2005)

15. Al Sayed, K., Bew, M., Penn, A., Palmer, D., Broyd, T.: Modelling dependency networks to inform data structures in BIM and smart cities. In: BIM, pp. 1–15 (2016)

16. Martín-Gutiérrez, J., Saorín, J.L., Contero, M., Alcaniz, M.: AR_Dehaes: an educational toolkit based on augmented reality technology for learning engineering graphics. In: 2010 10th IEEE International Conference on Advanced Learning Technologies, pp. 133–137 (2010)

17. García, A.E.: El aprendizaje por proyectos y el trabajo colaborativo, como herramientas de aprendizaje, en la construcción del proceso educativo, de la Unidad de aprendizaje TIC′S. RIDE Rev. Iberoam. para la Investig. y el Desarro. Docente, vol. 3, pp. 1–13 (2015)

18. Campos, B.D.: Realidad Aumentada en la educación. Entorno, vol. 0, pp. 47–53 (2016)

19. Salmerón, H., Rodríguez-Fernández, S., Gutiérrez-Braojos, C.: Metodologías que optimizan la comunicación en entornos de aprendizaje virtual. Comunicar. **17**, 163–171 (2010)

20. Alvarez Rodríguez, S.: Procesos cognitivos de visualizacion espacial y aprendizaje. Rev. Investig. en Educ. 61–71 (2007)

21. Valls, F., Redondo, E., Fonseca, D., Torres-Kompen, R., Villagrasa, S., Martí, N.: Urban data and urban design: a data mining approach to architecture education (2017)

22. Gagnon, D.: Videogames and spatial skills: an exploratory study. Educ. Commun. Technol. **33**, 263–275 (1985)

23. Sedeno, A.: Videogames as cultural devices: development of spatial skills and application in learning. Comunicar **17**, 183–189 (2010)

24. Campbell, I., Bourell, D., Gibson, I.: Additive manufacturing: rapid prototyping comes of age. Rapid Prototyp. J. **18**, 255–258 (2012)

25. Mueller, J., Lu, H., Chirkin, A., Klein, B., Schmitt, G.: Citizen design science: a strategy for crowd-creative urban design, Cities (2018)

26. Sanchez Sepulveda, M.: Building the city from public space: analysis and evaluation tools for the assessment of socio-spatial integration promoting urban typologies. Rev. Urban (2015)

27. Sanchez-Sepulveda, M., Fonseca, D., Franquesa, J., Redondo, E.: Virtual interactive innovations applied for digital urban transformations. Mixed approach. Futur. Gener. Comput. Syst. **91**, 371–381 (2019)

28. James, K.H., Humphrey, G.K., Vilis, T., Corrie, B., Baddour, R., Goodale, M.A.: "Active" and "passive" learning of three-dimensional object structure within an immersive virtual reality environment. Behav. Res. Methods, Instruments, Comput. **34**, 383–390 (2002)

29. Brunner, J.J., Tedesco, J.C.: Nuevas Tecnologias y El Futuro de La Educacion (2005)

30. Deci, E.L., Eghrari, H., Patrick, B.C., Leone, D.: Intrinsic Motivation Inventory (IMI). Intrinsic Motiv. Invent. Scale Descr. **62**, 119–142 (1994)

31. Fonseca, D., Redondo, E.: Are the architecture students prepared for the use of mobile technology in the classroom? In: Proceedings of the First International Conference on Technological Ecosystem for Enhancing Multiculturality - TEEM 2013, pp. 481–487 (2013)

32. Fonseca, D., Martí, N., Redondo, E., Navarro, I., Sánchez, A.: Relationship between student profile, tool use, participation, and academic performance with the use of Augmented Reality technology for visualized architecture models. Comput. Hum. Behav. (2014)

33. Fonseca, D., Valls, F., Redondo, E., Villagrasa, S.: Informal interactions in 3D education: citizenship participation and assessment of virtual urban proposals. Comput. Hum. Behav. **55**, 504–518 (2016)

34. Calvo, X., Fonseca, D., Sánchez-Sepúlveda, M., Amo, D., Llorca, J., Redondo, E.: Programming virtual interactions for gamified educational proposes of urban spaces. In: Zaphiris, P., Ioannou, A. (eds.) LCT 2018. LNCS, vol. 10925, pp. 128–140. Springer, Cham (2018). https://doi.org/10.1007/978-3-319-91152-6_10

35. Fonseca, D., Conde, M.Á., García-Peñalvo, F.J.: Improving the information society skills: is knowledge accessible for all? Univers. Access Inf. Soc. **17**, 229–245 (2018)

36. Fonseca, D., et al.: Student motivation assessment using and learning virtual and gamified urban environments. In: Proceedings of the 5th International Conference on Technological Ecosystems for Enhancing Multiculturality - TEEM 2017, pp. 1–7 (2017)

37. Fonseca, D., Pifarré, M., Redondo, E.: Relationship between perceived quality and emotional affinity of architectonic images depending on display device. Recommendations for teaching purposes. RISTI - Rev. Iber. Sist. e Tecnol. Inf. **11** (2013)

38. Llorca, J., Zapata, H., Redondo, E., Alba, J., Fonseca, D.: Bipolar laddering assessments applied to urban acoustics education. In: Rocha, Á., Adeli, H., Reis, L., Costanzo, S. (eds.) WorldCIST'18 2018. AISC, vol. 747, pp. 287–297. Springer, Cham (2018). https://doi.org/10.1007/978-3-319-77700-9_29

39. Valls, F., Redondo, E., Fonseca, D.: E-learning and serious games: new trends in architectural and urban design education. In: Zaphiris, P., Ioannou, A. (eds.) Learning and Collaboration Technologies, pp. 632–643. Springer, Los Angeles (2015)

40. Valls, F., Redondo, E., Fonseca, D., Garcia-Almirall, P., Subirós, J.: Videogame technology in architecture education. In: Kurosu, M. (ed.) HCI 2016. LNCS, vol. 9733, pp. 436–447. Springer, Cham (2016). https://doi.org/10.1007/978-3-319-39513-5_41

41. Fonseca, D., Villagrasa, S., Navarro, I., Redondo, E., Valls, F., Sánchez, A.: Urban gamification in architecture education. In: Rocha, Á., Correia, A., Adeli, H., Reis, L., Costanzo, S. (eds.) Recent Advances in Information Systems and Technologies. AISC, vol. 571, pp. 335–341. Springer, Cham (2017). https://doi.org/10.1007/978-3-319-56541-5_34

42. Vicent, L., Villagrasa, S., Fonseca, D., Redondo, E.: Virtual learning scenarios for qualitative assessment in higher education 3D arts. J. Univers. Comput. Sci. **21**, 1086–1105 (2015)

Optimizing User Experience in Amusement Parks and Enhancing Their Active Role in Urban Spaces Through New Technology

Eliseo Sciarretta[1]([✉]), Alessandra Carriero[2], and Giada Marinensi[1]

[1] Link Campus University, Rome, Italy
{e.sciarretta, g.marinensi}@unilink.it
[2] Università Degli Studi Della Basilicata, Potenza, Italy
alecarriero1509@gmail.com

Abstract. This paper intends to review the main technological innovations applied to the world of theme parks, with the aim of identifying the strategies that can be planned to guarantee visitors an optimized experience. At the same time, it aims to understand how the new technology can help improving the integration between the fantasy space and the real, urban space. The introduction explains what the challenges for modern parks are and what people are expecting from them. Chapter 2 addresses the use of various kinds of technology within theme parks, in particular virtual and augmented reality, localization and RFID systems to effectively manage the routes of visitors, 3D and multimedia techniques to improve engagement. Before the conclusions, chapter 3 investigates the relationship between the theme park and the spatial context it is built in and how new technology can be used to optimize this relationship and empower people.

Keywords: Theme parks · Amusement parks · New technology · Urban spaces · Virtual Reality · Augmented reality · Social media

1 Introduction

1.1 Amusement and Theme Parks

A theme park, applying themes to provide visitors with interesting experiences different from daily life, is an aggregation of attractions including architecture, landscape, rides, shows, food services, costumed personnel and retail shops (Pearce 1988).

Amusement parks are places where guests, as Walt Disney used to say, "Leave the real world behind and step into a world of fantasy". Still, they are in real world and in real cities and can benefit from this.

Technology has always been crucial in the process to reach this goal and allow visitors to enjoy an exciting and thrilling experience. Parks are always competing to offer higher, faster and more exciting rides.

The amusement park represents an important and historic form of entertainment where mass participation and technological innovation have traditionally worked closely together. The continuing development of ever more exciting visitor experiences

© Springer Nature Switzerland AG 2019
M. Kurosu (Ed.): HCII 2019, LNCS 11568, pp. 270–281, 2019.
https://doi.org/10.1007/978-3-030-22636-7_19

within amusement parks has provided a significant driver for many forms of entertainment technology.

Indeed, we can almost say that, until a couple of decades ago, guests visited theme parks to experience the latest in entertainment and technology.

Whilst the earliest amusement rides were simple manually-operated roundabouts (National Fairground and Circus Archive), modern amusement rides are becoming increasingly dependent upon substantial amounts of computing technology. The use of digital technologies is prominent both during the design process, where simulations of rider experience are often employed before physical prototypes are produced, and during the ride experience, where automated ride control and computer-controlled lighting are becoming commonplace (Worsell 2000).

But with rides reaching physical limits that it is not convenient to overcome, and home entertainment at the highest levels, thanks to digital devices, what can amusement parks do to convince people to leave home and to plan a visit?

This paper intends to review the main technological innovations applied to the world of theme parks, with the aim of identifying the strategies that can be planned to guarantee visitors an optimized experience. At the same time, it aims to understand how the very technology can help improving the integration between the fantasy space and the real, urban space.

Although in this paper the terms amusement parks and theme parks are used as if they were synonymous, they are not exactly the same thing: the former focus on mechanical performance, often associated with increasing levels of thrill, and are increasingly rare; the latter, instead, are characterized by a massive use of storytelling, staged also through multimedia technologies, and constitute a more current line of development.

Multimedia technology and storytelling become inseparable in design to avoid the risk of early obsolescence and ensure a high level of user involvement: in this sense, in fact, multimedia allows a sustainable renewment of the structure of the parks, while storytelling makes it possible to renew the emotional system.

It is therefore necessary to take into account the inclinations and tastes of the visitors, in an attempt to identify new entertainment trends among users, considering that from 2006 to 2015 the park visitors number has increased by 25% in USA and in the rest of the world (Rubin 2016). What do current visitors ask to the amusement parks? A possible answer is provided by the results of a survey conducted by Omnico (Omnico 2017) that lasted two years, based on a sample of 3470 visitors: a widespread use of artificial intelligence is expected from a park, regarding security and reception (92%), while a wide use of Virtual Reality (VR) and Augmented Reality (AR) is hoped for orientation in the park or to reach restaurants and hotels, but also to choose the attractions with apps and finally of course to experience new fun experiences: "visitor expectations are stretching beyond the desire to experience new thrills". The request therefore seems to be a total integration of VR, AR and other technology in every moment of the visit.

Like any other industry, theme parks are now facing severe challenges from other entertainment competitors. To survive in a rapidly changing environment, creating high quality products/services in terms of consumer preference has become a critical issue for theme park managers (Martin 1987).

Anyone who has been at a theme park at least once knows what the main problems people may have during this experience are: long lines, broken rides, high ticket costs, anxieties about losing the kids, weather-related closures.

The goal must therefore be on the one hand to improve more and more attractions, but above all to ensure that the periods in-between the rides are just as immersive and satisfying as the rides, as we are going to address in the next chapter.

Before the conclusions, chapter 3 investigates the relationship between the theme park and the spatial context it is built in and how new technology can be used to optimize this relationship and empower people.

2   Technology and Theme Parks

2.1   Space/Time Management

The main problem in visiting a theme park is guests' time and space management: visitors need to apply an accurate strategy, and use time efficiently in order to visit an amusement park of a certain size. Today mobile apps offer maps of the parks, and through GPS can localize the users and provide them with information about waiting times of nearby attractions and about shortest routes to reach them.

A study by Thinkwell Group shows that 80% of people visiting theme parks have a device on them and they spend part of their time on social media. Through location-based social monitoring, theme parks can have an ear to the mentions and conversations that are taking place, and respond in real-time to guests through social media, or in person if the situation calls for it.

Still, although smartphones provide a lot of utility, it's really important that theme parks are a physical experience. That's why people go there. They want to step into that world and feel like they're a part of it.

So, smartphone isn't the best device in this case and in near future it can be replaced or at least joined by wearable technology.

One of the greatest fears of a parent is, without a doubt, losing sight of their children. In large amusement parks, usually covering an area greater than one square kilometer, locating a child can be a very difficult task.

Especially on high season days, visitors flock to the parks and finding a single child in the middle of the crowd is almost impossible. The consequence is that often the guest service points are stormed, with endless lines of panicked parents looking for their children; the finding process can take several hours and turn into a big security issue that involves both operators and visitors.

In principle, the main instrument used in the case of missing children consists of surveillance records, otherwise operators proceed by asking any witnesses. It is clear that these methods do not guarantee a high success rate, so amusement parks are always looking for further methods. For example, modern location technology, such as GPS, that can track the child's position, is currently used. However, it is necessary for the child to carry a receiver, to make these systems effective. Although nowadays even small children have a smartphone with integrated GPS, this is a limitation to the freedom of movement of the children themselves, and extra care and protection required to prevent damage to the components, can be complicated in an environment like that of theme parks.

Another technology that has been establishing for these purposes in recent years and seems to be much promising is radio frequency identification (RFID), which offers the possibility of low-cost tracking thanks to radio waves. In this case, an integrated tag integrated inside a wristband to be supplied to children records all of their movements inside the park, for example when they enter a ride or pass near checkpoints equipped with RFID readers.

However, there are several challenges facing RFID-based personnel tracking system for amusement parks. Firstly, with the large physical area that must be covered, there will be a large number of RFID readers scattered around the park in order to effectively monitor the entire park due to the limited coverage of RFID radio.

Secondly, security and privacy preservation are of importance to the success of such a tracking system. It is crucial to prevent any adversary from being able to track and/or control children, which could pose security threats to the general public and lead to child abduction (Lin 2010).

For this purpose and in the context of wearable technology, Disney has developed and activated in its parks a system called MyMagic+, based on a wearable RFID bracelet: MagicBand lets guests pay for food and merchandise, be identified, open hotel room doors.

The bracelet links electronically to an encrypted database of visitor information, serve as admission tickets, hotel keys and credit or debit card. It begins when visitors book their hotel and tickets through Disney. After that, they are able to plan every detail on their trip from airport to hotel transportation. Additionally, guests can also schedule when their visit to each theme park is, where they would like to dine for meals. Moreover, users are allowed to pre-order their food. They don't need to endure waiting in a super long line when hungry. Also, the tracking power is extremely important for Disney theme park because it helps Disney determine when to add more staff at ride, what restaurants should serve, what souvenirs should be stocked and how many employees in costume should roam around at any given time.

Another similar example is Accesso Prism, which let the parks schedule ride bookings in advance and reduce queue lines. Accesso Prism is a wearable device that gives theme parks and attractions the power to schedule ride bookings without kiosks or cell phones and connect with visitors in new ways throughout their entire visit. It allows them to have a wait-free experience by reserving their place in line, changing their ride selection and monitoring their ride return time. It also has an integrated smart park system which provides front gate entry, allowing cashless purchases and providing the first interactive wearable that can push notifications or trigger nearby events based on user location.

However, this type of technology is still in its infancy and will evolve in the future through intelligent facial and clothing recognition, that will be used by theme parks to detect individuals and capture their image.

Understanding the spatial and temporal behavior of tourists could enhance the management of attractions and contribute to extending the geographical distribution of tourists and tourist expenditures within regions (Thornton 1997). Knowing which rides have been taken, which shows have been attended and which shops and squares have attracted the attention of tourists, could lead to radical improvement in satisfaction performance.

Beyond this information, however necessary, the visiting sequence is a very important factor that helps visitors complete their trips on time. Without a personalized route suggestion, guests tend to make an inefficient trip or even get lost in the complex theme park environment.

When planning routes, some considerations are to be included: not all visitors have enough time to get around the park in its entirety, so they would like to access a route allowing them to complete their visit in the time they have in mind. This is a fundamental limit to consider, otherwise visitors may not have enough time for their favorite attractions.

Linked to this, we must also consider that every guest, at the beginning of the visit, has a set of "must-play" rides; the suggested route must include these attractions.

Moreover, custom routes do not only have to worry about optimizing visit time, but can get great benefits if they are designed to take account of previous visitors behavior (Tsai 2012).

Finally, quite often in theme parks visitors congregate in certain areas while at the same time other adjacent areas are vacant. If the recommendation system can take the crowd situation into consideration and provide a less congested route, the service quality of the theme parks should be higher (Milman 2001).

Another technology expected to be applied in theme parks is Artificial Intelligence (AI), which offers a way for theme parks to have 'conversations' with guests when people aren't around. By using vast amounts of data, machines can make intelligent recommendations and offer useful information based on a guest's query.

2.2   Virtual Reality and Augmented Reality

The same AI considered in the previous paragraph can also be used in rides, to improve immersivity, combined with Virtual Reality (VR).

It will then tailor the attraction to the needs of the consumer at specific points throughout their journey.

The most common way VR is being used on rides at the moment is that the existing ride simply has a VR experience laid over the top.

People still climb aboard the physical ride and experience all the same twists, turns and acceleration. But they wear a VR headset that enables them to see, and sometimes hear, something completely different to the real-world experience.

The advantages of going VR for theme parks are multiple. It's relatively easy to trick the brain into thinking it's somewhere else, and it's substantially cheaper to create a VR attraction than a traditional coaster or flat ride. These experiences can also be updated quickly (think of a Christmas or Halloween-themed version of an existing offering).

According with our preliminary studies on this topic though, so far rider reactions have been varied. Thrill-seekers want "more story" from these attractions, which suggests that while we rush to embrace flashy technology, we still have an inherent need for narrative—we still want to be told a story. And while many park-goers love the novelty, purists curiously dismiss these VR experiences as "not real".

However, for some industry leaders, VR isn't the silver bullet. Disney's CEO Bob Iger has publicly shunned VR headsets, suggesting they block visitors' view from reality and place them inside a fake digital world. When all visitors see is a VR screen, theme parks lose the value of the physical environments they've spent so much money to create.

But what if parks could put together the best of both worlds and show VR animation in a way that allowed people to keep seeing all that wonderfully themed physical space in the park around them? That's augmented reality, and that might be the next big thing in theme parks.

However, focus should not only be placed on the attractions. These technologies can be applied to a wider level, covering the parks entirely, so that they become fully multimedia. This trend favors an almost total dematerialization of the rides and of the parks, replaced by hybrid environments in which the boundary between park and attraction becomes thinner. Among the most well-fitting examples are: (a) The Void, Virtual Reality Theme Parks where people can experience adventures in augmented reality and in groups, mainly taken from film sagas (such as Star Wars and Ghostbusters), wearing special individual devices; (b) Virtual Reality World USA, huge unthemed "containers" where people can experience dozens of different virtual experiences; and (c) East Science Valley China, one of the first thematic parks entirely based on virtual reality.

VR and AR are rapidly taking off in other areas of hospitality as well, helping users all over the map: from offering instant translation on menus and other signage to enabling wayfinding through interactive wall maps, and even creating virtual, changeable decor.

2.3 Ride Empowerment

The main concern of an amusement park regards the emotions and the adrenaline rush that the rides can trigger.

In the previous paragraph we have already seen how virtual reality and augmented reality can influence this, but there are other technologies to consider.

In particular, an important trend is outlined by the indoor mega dark rides that use integrated systems, sets and 3D projections to immerse guests in a story. The innovations in this area concern both the physical aspects, such as height of attraction, number of falls and air-times that follow the development of the history of dark ride, and the multimedia aspects related to storytelling, as the possibility to include huge screens that allow, given their size, to continue to follow the story of the ride despite the speed.

A particularly intriguing example of project regarding this type of attraction is Pirates of the Future, which aims to lead users into a series of representations of furious battles between the English Navy and a band of outlawed pirates. The most innovative aspect of this attraction, currently at the prototype stage, is that the boats, themed in pirate style, will not sail in a track, but in "open ocean", with their position controlled by a local GPS system. There will also be interactive sections in which users can command a cannon that will trigger explosions in the scenes in front of them. The boats will also have a system that will shake them and tilt them when they are hit or collide with rocks and waves. The scenes will no longer be constructed with the classic animatronics, rather they will present a mix of real sets and 3D images, with life-size holograms. The random combination of all these elements will lead to different experiences conducted by the users themselves.

Digital technology is not used to improve only the integral parts of rides, but also the overall user experience, for example through the production of automatic souvenirs in the form of photos portraying people on the attraction, shot during key moments.

This stratagem is part of a broader strategy applied by the entire entertainment industry, the realization of insights on the experience lived by guests, in order to highlight unusual details that would otherwise be lost, such as the facial expressions of riders. These insights of thrilling individual experiences, obtained through video and audio technologies, are so intriguing that can be shared and enjoyed even by other people who may be unlikely to take part in the activities, perhaps because they are too dangerous or too expensive.

The extension of the experience of rides to watching audience reflects an emerging theme within Human Computer Interaction, it is to say how interaction has to be designed in order to be engaging not only for direct users, but also for spectators as well.

To this extent, telemetry can be used to extend and augment amusement rides to allow the experience to be shared by others and also to be retrospectively enjoyed by riders themselves (Walker 2007).

Static images such as photos, in fact, fail to capture all the emotional and dramatic potential that an adrenaline experience can transmit to the audience, but telemetry can allow a substantial enrichment of the data available.

Furthermore, the same data can be used for a detailed analysis of the experience, which allows designers to understand the precise moments in which an attraction creates an emotion and to understand how people react.

Another possibility is to design future rides that directly adapt to individual riders' preferences or past history, for example tuning their movements in response to telemetry data, providing a more personalized riding experience than is currently possible (Hooper 2005).

Thanks to telemetry, it is possible to design new types of rides focused on users: heart rate monitors, audio inputs and individual touch screens can structure personalized experiences and different levels of thrill. During the ride different sensors measure body reactions to shocks, movements and turns and the route can be recalculated in real time to meet the user's preferences. With audio sensors, words like "stop" can calm the ride; on the contrary, a few seconds of silence will cause the attraction to "engage" to increase the level of thrill. The possibility also to connect this type of ride/experience to the RFID bracelets (an example are the Disney Magicbands, which we have already discussed) also allows the attraction to recognize the user's preferences so as to delineate a tailor-made experience.

3 Amusement Parks in the Urban Context

3.1 Social Parks

Recognition of the tastes and preferences of visitors is a fundamental prerequisite for offering visitors a personalized and interactive experience and the same technologies can be used to improve the relationship between the theme space of the park and the real space of the city surrounding the park, so as to make the transition from one to another as smooth as possible.

Disney's "It's a Small World" ride's automated system recognizes and identifies guests. As they prepare to leave, it tells them good-bye, by name and in the appropriate language.

Disney always knows where guests are. Your favorite Disney character can come up and greet you, personally wishing you a happy birthday or congratulating you on your graduation or marriage. All the data you've fed into the system are available to Disney as they try to deliver an even better theme park experience.

The nice thing about it is that as soon as the guest is identified, the system can immediately present to team members previous information about this guest in a very quick, digestible manner. Team members can respond in a more personalized way rather than having to ask a whole bunch of questions about their day. The team members can see it all on a dashboard.

Otherwise, they get into the parks and they're anonymous to the operators. They're just people coming through.

Theme parks are trying to find ways to incorporate apps and social media into the games and rides, so people will continue the immersive experience even after they've left the park and they're back in the real world. Some rides and theme park experiences allow guests to play game versions of the rides on their phones, or compare their in-game scores to other guests via an app.

There's a social dynamic behind it. At the end of the day, humans are social creatures who get value out of the shared experience. Part of a roller coaster being exciting is the physical senses that you feel, but part of it is also the thrill of having other people around you yelling and screaming.

3.2 Theme Parks and Video-Games

Theme parks can borrow techniques from video-games to improve the dynamic explained in the previous paragraph and allow users to continue the experience at home or in urban space.

The last frontier of video-games is on the one hand a stronger integration with AR and VR technologies, on the other hand the attempt to overcome the boundaries between online and offline, just as the parks are trying to do; proof is the renewed success that in recent years technologically advanced versions of traditional escape rooms and laser games are having.

The video-game is becoming a fundamental tool for the renewal of amusement parks essentially for three reasons:

1. The park can offer a unique and non-replicable context for offline/online integration of video-game experiences: the avatar and the player's body can merge into an all-encompassing experience, capable of involving cognition and sensoriality.
2. Video-games are the most effective "trojan horse" to introduce storytelling strategies within theme parks, since they are capable of transforming attractions based

exclusively on emotions and primary sensations (fear, vertigo, speed, height, etc.) in narrative contexts.
3. Video-games could represent an excellent tool for prolonging the experience beyond the visit to the park and therefore of retain guests. Video-games storyworlds could be built starting inside the park, continuing after the visit on a digital platform, and maybe, at some point, prompting the player to return to the park to finish a field mission.

Although video-games are still slightly used and almost exclusively in their offline-analogical type, the increasingly massive introduction of digital technologies within the parks is almost naturally leading them towards the use of gamification strategies. Examples are the recent VR Park (Dubai and New York) but also the more "traditional" Cinecittà World or Sovereign Hill.

The real keywords are "interactivity" and "immersion". It's not enough to just passively ride an attraction. Thrill seekers want to go fast, watch a 3D movie and shoot zombies at the same time.

3.3   Relationship with the Context

In the seventies Umberto Eco embarked on a trip to the United States in search of confirmations that would support his intuitions concerning the progressive abandonment of reality in favor of fake worlds, reproductions on a 1:1 scale capable of staging improved versions of the world. The result of this trip was the essay Travels in Hyperreality (Eco 1975), in which Eco theorized the concept of hyper-reality associated with the (at that time) growing phenomenon of theme parks. In an essay following Eco's investigation, the anthropologist Marc Augé took up the philosopher's reflections in order to grasp the winning formula of these hyper-worlds, and with regard to Disneyland he stated: "It is to begin a question of scale. Everything is in full size but the worlds that are discovered (Frontierland, Adventureland, Fantasyland, Discoveryland) are miniature worlds. The city, the river, the railway are reduced models. But horses are real horses, cars are real cars, houses are real houses [...]" (Augè 1999).

Since the seventies, the growth of the theme park phenomenon has not stopped, advancing towards continuous updating and improvement of standards. Thinking of the future means managing the obsolescence of traditional mechanical rides as opposed to the potential, in terms of sustainability, updating and experience, of multimedia and ambient intelligence technologies. Eco, at the time of his trip to the United States, said: "Disneyland tells us that technology can give us more reality than nature can ever give".

To create an ever stronger connection with the surrounding territory and the heritage that characterizes it, parks can implement strategies that incorporate the use of technologies we have talked about, such as AR and VR, and at the same time storytelling and gamification mechanisms.

Virtual amusement parks are flourishing, they aggregate activities and shows: from augmented reality to virtual reality, up to hyper-reality. These parks can be categorized into three types, depending on their location and architecture: indoor virtual parks, contained in a building, let user try out various activities such as mad houses or escape rooms; outdoor virtual parks maintain the morphology of traditional synthetic parks, but with a strictly virtual offer; diffused or mixed virtual parks are integrated in multi-functional contexts (malls, outlets, museums, etc.), representing only one section of them.

In this way, theme parks can effectively enter the urban space and no longer be relegated only to its suburbs.

Indoor Virtual Parks. An interesting example is the Virtual Reality World in New York, which is proposed as a place to experiment fifty different virtual performances on the model of digital arts and films, selected among the best practices of VR and AR, with the aim of not circumscribing these technologies exclusively in the sphere of video-games, but exploring different objectives: tests of skills and dexterity like exploding an asteroid before the impact with the Earth, or defusing a robot-bomb, climbing the top of Kilimanjaro or trying culinary skills.

Outdoor virtual parks. In China, the Oriental Science Fiction Valley Theme Park (or East Valley of Science and Fantasy) was recently inaugurated in the city of Guiyang, in the Guinhou province, one of the most depressed in the country. The park, which is totally virtual, will eventually present 35 attractions spread across 330 acres of land. A simil-Transformer giant robot welcomes the public at the entrance, allowing the most reckless to perform bungee jumping. Attractions range from virtual roller coasters, to battle against dragons, or exploration of the galaxy, based on the use of virtual goggles and motion simulators.

Diffused or Mixed Virtual Parks. Adiffused virtual park provides interactive VR shows organized in a public/commercial building or in a reserved wing of the building. The entire Dubai Mall hosts Virtual Reality exhibits with 7D holograms of animals hovering in the crowd of the Mall, or shows with animals in improvised theater spaces. At the same time the VR Park, recently opened in Dubai Mall, uses the storylines of movies and tv series (The Mummy, the zombies of The Walking Dead, the monkeys of Planet of the Apes etc.).

There is a large production of VR machines and systems that can be fitted in every environment: shopping centers, airports, as standalone locations or using an entire space like a train station.

In Dubai, for example, a space in a public building was assigned to a VR room where guests can choose in a screen-menu hung on the wall the virtual reality in which they want to be immersed and the performance they intend to execute: if they choose a fight against the zombies they are equipped with a laser gun to defend themselves. One of the users' most recurrent comment was: "I would like to have it at home", an affirmation that opens up an interesting perspective for home entertainment business.

Another fundamental element to be considered in this analysis is the context, understood not only for its physical and geographical features, but above all from the historical and social point of view. Remarkable is the difference between parks that, like Disneyland Paris, are almost completely unrelated to the place where they are built (Disneyland Paris was in fact built around Paris only as an area easily accessible by the European public) and parks that have instead a relationship between their own narrative universe and the context in which they are inserted (as in the case of Sovereign Hill, Australia).

Thanks to these modalities, the space of the parks tends more and more to merge with the urban and public space: it will never become a desirable substitute for democratic public space, but theme park model can be effectively expanded out of the boundaries of theme parks and transform the public realm as a whole.

Large theme parks are customarily designed, constructed, and operated by thousands of individuals working in multiple, interdisciplinary teams that simultaneously design its presence in the media, the material and immaterial routes that lead people to theme parks, their material environment, and guest experiences alike.

Theme parks exist within the system of urban spaces and that of social relationships, rendering the theme park simultaneously as a spatial and social machine (Mitrasinovic 2006).

4   Conclusions

4.1   The Future of Theme Parks

Theme parks are a form of entertainment that has been intertwined with technological developments since its origins.

In this paper we have therefore analyzed the role of technologies in theme parks and the main innovations that have been recently applied in this area. These innovations aim at guaranteeing visitors a new and enhanced visiting experience. The use of technology in amusement parks is important but it's equally important that technology become invisible, to optimize the experience.

We have seen how, regarding the design of rides, attention has shifted from the pursuit of ever stronger and more extreme physical emotions to the pursuit of involving and exciting storytelling experiences.

In this context, expectations of the insiders are centered on virtual reality and augmented reality, as these technologies are able to foster the engagement and the construction of a consistent narrative universe.

However, a theme park should not be just a set of rides; since most of the visitors' time is spent waiting in between the attractions and idling in the other areas of the park, it is necessary that the technology is used to optimize the user experience even in these situations, so as to provide an efficient management of time, through line-control systems, and space, with personalized routes to go through the park. The application of technologies such as radio frequency identification can serve these purposes and also provide value-added services, like systems to find lost children.

In the final part of the paper, we have focused our attention on the relationship between the themed and fake space of the park and the real space in which it is built. The goal must be to use the technologies to improve this relationship. Actually, in fact, amusement parks are built in liminal areas, set up on purpose in the name of the massification of accesses, thanks to mega-parking lots and structures built ad hoc. In this way, however, theme parks end up becoming non-places, places where people go to spend a funny day but completely disconnected from the urban context and everyday life. Visitors have no motivations to come back, once they leave the park they return to real world and the experience is essentially over.

Thanks to the new technologies that we have discussed, instead, parks can implement strategies to encourage the guests to come back, for example through apps that propose adventures to be continued in daily life, and then be concluded again within the park. Likewise, these technologies make it possible to recover the relationship between city and theme park, and make the latter a space available to citizens, who can access it, paying a reduced price, even just for a walk.

This is, in a way, a return to the origins: in the past, amusement parks were built within the city and became an inseparable part of the urban context, think for example to the case of Tivoli, a park that became a symbol of the city of Copenhagen and that it is one of its main green spots. However, technology can make a significant contribution in this perspective, by retraining spaces that otherwise would be abandoned or underused, for example through the creation of diffused virtual parks. These topics, which are only partially dealt with here, will be the subject of further study in the next works.

References

Augé, M.: Disneyland e altri nonluoghi. Bollati Boringhieri (1999)

Eco, U.: Travels in hyper reality: essays (1975)

Hooper, R.: Just how exciting is it (2005)? http://www.wired.com/news/technology/0,1282,6 6598,00.html

Lin, X., Lu, R., Kwan, D., Shen, X.: REACT: an RFID-based privacy-preserving children tracking scheme for large amusement parks. Comput. Netw. **54**, 2744–2755 (2010)

Martin, W.H., Mason, S.: Social trends and tourism futures. Tourism Manag. **8**(2), 112–114 (1987)

Milman, A.: The future of the theme park and attraction industry: a management perspective. J. Travel Res. **40**(2), 139–147 (2001)

Mitrasinovic, M.: Total Landscape, Theme Parks, Public Space. Routledge, London (2006). https://doi.org/10.4324/9781315236001

National Fairground and Circus Archive. https://www.sheffield.ac.uk/nfca/researchandarticles/fairgrounds

Omnico: The Theme Park Barometer 2 (2017). https://www.omnicogroup.com/wp-content/uploads/2017/07/Omnico-Theme-Park-Barometer-2-June-17.pdf

Pearce, P.L.: The Ulysses Factor: Evaluating Visitors in Tourist Settings. Springer, Heidelberg (1988). https://doi.org/10.1007/978-1-4612-3924-6

Rubin, J.: 2015 theme index: the global attractions attendance report. Themed Entertainment Association/Economics Research Associates (2016). http://www.aecom.com/content/wp-content/uploads/2016/05/2015_Theme_Index__Museum_Index.pdf

Thornton, P.R., Williams, A.M., Shaw, G.: Revisiting time-space diaries: an exploratory case study of tourist behaviour in Cornwall, England. Environ. Plann. A **29**(10), 1847–1867 (1997)

Tsai, C., Chung, S.: A personalized route recommendation service for theme parks using RFID information and tourist behavior. Decis. Support Syst. **52**, 514–527 (2012). https://doi.org/10.1016/j.dss.2011.10.013

Walker, B., et al.: Augmenting amusement rides with telemetry. In: Proceedings of the International Conference on Advances in Computer Entertainment Technology (ACE 2007), pp. 115–122. ACM, New York (2007). http://dx.doi.org/10.1145/1255047.1255070

Worsell, N., Ioannides, A.: Safety integrity levels of fairground ride control systems. UK Health and Safety Executive (2000)

Design for Intelligent Urban Environments

The Semiotics of Toilet Signs

Jun Iio[(✉)]

Chuo University, Shinjuku-Ku, Tokyo 162-8478, Japan
iiojun@tamacc.chuo-u.ac.jp

Abstract. Various types of signs for public restrooms are pervasive in our society. In addition to indicating gender classification, there are cultural differences among regions and communities in the representation of these signs. There have been several studies on toilet signs that possess many aspects of academic investigation, including social study, cognitive analysis, and gender research. To investigate the academic issues surrounding public restroom iconography, - and to understand how the signs convey the designer's intent to citizens, a database of toilet signs has been constructed. More than 550 items are storedin this database, and published on the Internet. They are categorized into several groups by a method similar to a folksonomy. This paper describes the results of an analysis of the database, and what types of toilet sign trends are revealed by the study.

Keywords: Toilet signs · Cultural differences · Consumer-generated database

1 Introduction

Signs for public restrooms are used everywhere in our society, and public toilets are categorized into three types: male, female, and genderless/multipurpose. Thus, each kind of sign represents the gender of that restroom's users. Many toilet signs use human-shaped pictograms to indicate gender. However, various symbols, characters, and other shapes are also used to denote gender. Hence, we can discuss the variety of these representations in order to research impressions of the designs used for public signs. Also, because restroom signs are seen worldwide, there remains room for cultural studies of these signs, as some differences are observable between regions.

2 Related Work

There have been some previous studies on toilet signs. The website Sensemaya analyzed the semiotics of toilet signs[1] in detail. It divided the signs into several groups, according to their representations of gender. Differences in genital and body shapes, comparison of urination poses, and coital metaphors are the critical factors defining

---

[1] Several blog articles describe the existence of an excellent analysis of the semiotics of toilet signs, performed by Sensemaya. However, the report was deleted as of November 2018, and cannot be accessed online.

© Springer Nature Switzerland AG 2019
M. Kurosu (Ed.): HCII 2019, LNCS 11568, pp. 285–294, 2019.
https://doi.org/10.1007/978-3-030-22636-7_20

each group. Genders are indicated by referencing physical possessions, the direct depiction of male and female forms, arbitrary or conventional symbolism, markers of social positions, and, occasionally, photographs.

Chen and Sie [1] argued that the manner in which design factors are employed affects the reaction time for identifying toilet signs. They conducted experiments to understand the factors influencing the speed of translating information from a sign into an appropriate response. This was achieved by displaying 36 toilet signs with modifications to three elements, and measuring the reaction time of all participants.

Johannessen collected Danish toilet signs [2], and Pantouvaki also discussed the social semiotics of toilet signs in Greece [3]. Jie analyzed the application of and problems with bilingual public signs by focusing on toilet signs in China [4].

As these researchers have shown, studies on toilet signs include many standard aspects of academic investigations, including social study, cognitive analysis, and gender research.

3 Toilet Signs Database

To study the topics mentioned above, I started collecting photographs of toilet signs in August 2016. Furthermore, a community of persons wishing to receive efficient information on this topic was established in September 2017. Collected data are published daily, with my brief commentary. Although there are similar websites[2] and public discussion groups on social networking services (SNS)[3], our database has some advantages in that all items are stored in the database, along with my messages. Additionally, much of our data are posted by community members from around the world.

As of January 26, 2019, 612 toilet signs have been collected, and more than 550 signs are available to the public via the Internet. These data are posted from 49 countries and regions. As most group members are Japanese, more than half of the displayed data are toilet signs from Japan. However, some members have frequent opportunities to go abroad for business trips, and sometimes for sightseeing. Therefore, if they find an attractive toilet sign while overseas, they can take a picture and post it via the Internet.

There have been 108 contributors thus far. Although I am the top contributor, approximately two-thirds of items were contributed by other members. Additionally, fifty-three members have provided toilet sign information more than twice. Table 1 shows the top ten contributors.

One of the significant features of our database is that every item utilizes geographical information: for example, the place the photograph was taken, and the name of the facility where the toilet is located. Figure 1 shows the locations of all the signs in our database. The left part of Fig. 2 illustrates a selection of regions throughout Japan,

---

[2] Tweet from the toilet marks: http://1st.geocities.jp/toiletmark/;
TOILETSIGNS: https://toiletsigns.wordpress.com/.

[3] Washroom of the day (Public Facebook group): https://www.facebook.com/groups/washroom.of.the.day/.

Table 1. Top Ten Contributors

Contributor	Number of Items	Contributor	Number of Items
J.I.	164	A.H.	19
T.O.	42	H.S.	17
S.Y.	35	R.S.	16
K.K.	26	M.M.	16
M.K.	23	R.S.	15

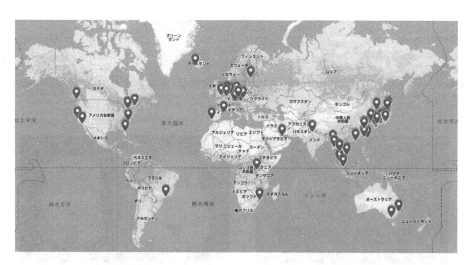

Fig. 1. A world map showing the locations of toilet signs recorded in our database

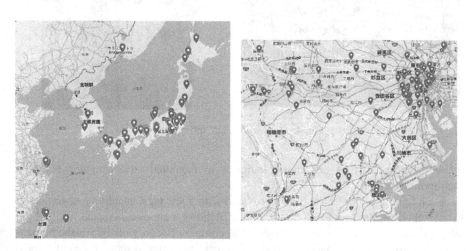

Fig. 2. Left: a selection of regions throughout Japan; Right: a magnified area surrounding the Tokyo metropolitan region

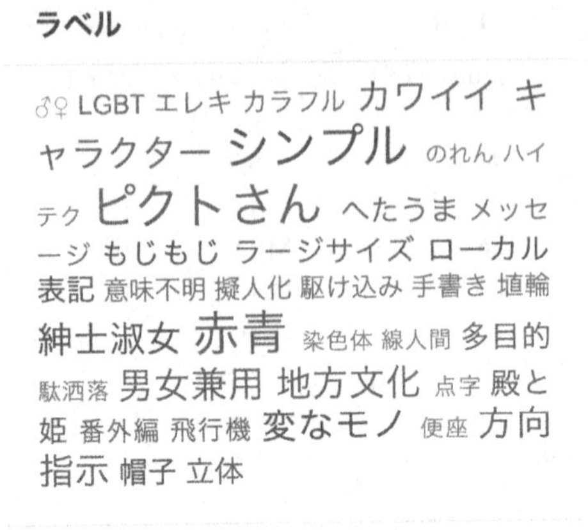

ラベル

♂♀ LGBT エレキ カラフル カワイイ キ
ャラクター シンプル のれん ハイ
テク ピクトさん へたうま メッセ
ージ もじもじ ラージサイズ ローカル
表記 意味不明 擬人化 駆け込み 手書き 埴輪
紳士淑女 赤青 染色体 線人間 多目的
駄洒落 男女兼用 地方文化 点字 殿と
姫 番外編 飛行機 変なモノ 便座 方向
指示 帽子 立体

Fig. 3. A tag-cloud created from all labels in the database, indicating that the most popular category of signs is the human-shaped pictogram

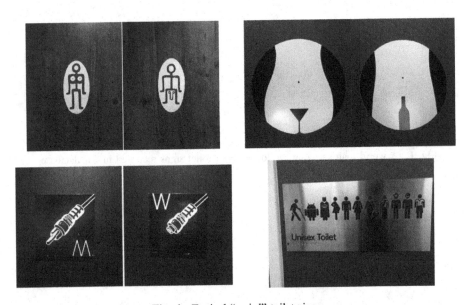

Fig. 4. Typical "weird" toilet signs

while the right part of this figure indicates a magnified area around the Tokyo metropolitan region.

Each item in our database is also provided with a few tags, enabling categorization by a method similar to a folksonomy. Figure 3 shows a tag-cloud created from all the labels in the database, indicating that the most common category of signs is the human-shaped pictogram. An analysis based on access frequency disclosed that the most popular items are those belonging to the category labeled "weird." Figure 4 contains typical signs from this category.

Fig. 5. Typical "squirming" toilet signs

Fig. 6. Typical "large" toilet signs

The signs employing human-shaped pictograms are further divided into several subcategories: squirming, large, electric, and come-here types. Figures 5, 6, 7 and 8 show typical signs belonging to these subcategories.

Fig. 7. Typical "electric" toilet signs

Fig. 8. Typical "come-here" toilet signs

Particularly in Japan and neighboring countries, it is possible recognize the varying colors used to distinguish between the male and female genders. Regularly, blue is used to indicate signs for males, while red is used for females. However, the boundaries between areas where blue and red colors are employed to distinguish the genders, and areas where colors for both genders are identical, are ambiguous.

Specifying genders using blue and red colors is very popular in Japan. Such gender separation by color is also seen in Taiwan, Korea, and China. In Southeast Asia, the frequency of encountering such classifications is decreasing. Furthermore, we seldom see such distinctions in the rest of the world. Discovering the boundaries of areas where genders are separated by color remains a topic for future work.

4 Categorization of Toilet Signs

Figure 9 shows a categorization of toilet signs. They are roughly organized into three major classes: human-shaped, portions, and words. Note that these three classes aren't clearly distinguished: that is, a combination of two or three items from different classes often appears on a single sign.

Fig. 9. A categorization of toilet signs

4.1 Human-Shaped Signs

Human-shaped signs are categorized into three subcategories: simple shapes, characters, and pictograms.

On simple shaped signs, the human form consists of a circle and a triangle, where the circle represents a head, and the triangle represents a body. An interesting thing to note is the direction the triangle faces. In most cases, the combination of a circle and an upward-facing triangle represents a female, and a circle with a downward-facing triangle represents a male (Fig. 10).

Fig. 10. A typical circle-and-triangle toilet sign

The toilet signs represented by certain characters are also divided into several patterns. For instance, if the institution where the toilet is located has some relation to historical or famous persons, such personas are often used as guides to the restroom (Fig. 11).

 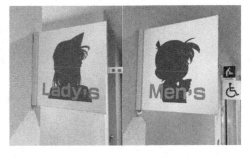

Fig. 11. Typical examples of toilet signs employing local personas Left: a toilet sign utilizing ancient Japanese figures; Right: representative characters from a famous Japanese cartoon.

As mentioned in the previous section, the pictogram signs have several subcategories. Although the figures may be slightly different, these types of toilet signs are quite common all over the world.

4.2   Portion-Type Signs

Several portions of objects indicating gender difference frequently appear in toilet signs. The major subcategories are human body parts, accessories, and combinations of the two.

Genitals are often the typical human body portions placed on toilet signs as a means of distinguishing male and female restrooms. In some cases, they are drawn humorously, as shown in Fig. 4. Furthermore, mustaches and lips are common body parts used to express gender differences (Fig. 12).

Fig. 12. Typical "mustacheandlips" toilet signs

Mustaches and lips are frequently combined with hats or ribbons. The right side of Fig. 12 illustrates such a case. Hats, ribbons, glasses, pearl necklaces, sticks, and umbrellas often appear in toilet signs.

4.3   Words and Messages

In these cases, the location of the toilet is indicated by a written word, or with textual messages. This type of toilet sign is difficult to manage, especially for foreign people who cannot discern the toilet's location if directions are written in only the local language (Fig. 13).

If directions are written in both the local language and in English, few problems would arise. However, especially in very rural areas, many toilet signs are found that lack English notation. This is not only the case in rural areas of Japan, as similar instances can occur anywhere in the world.

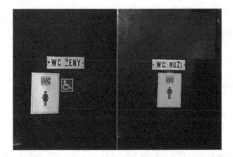

Fig. 13. The directions are written in only the local language ("zeny" and "muzi"). A person would not understand which to enter if signs using standard pictograms were not appended

5 Conclusions and Future Work

This study established a database of toilet signs in collaboration with more than one hundred contributors. They took pictures of toilet signs from all over the world, and sent them to an online community. The result is a collection of over five hundred records.

A unique feature of the database is that it stores not only photographs but also the name of the institution where the sign is located and its exact location. Thus, each record can be added to a world map so that anyone can visit and confirm the information if they wish.

Additionally, hierarchical categories are proposed in this paper. The categories were derived only from the collections in our database. Therefore, confirmation of their adequacy and applicability remains a topic for future work.

References

1. Chen, Y.L., Sie, C.C.: Design factors affecting the reaction time for identifying toilet signs: a preliminary study. Percept. Mot. Skills **122**(2), 636–649 (2016)
2. Johannessen, C.M.: A corpus-based approach to Danish toilet signs. RASK **39**, 149–183 (2013)
3. Pantouvaki, S.: The visual and social semiotics of toilet signs in Greece, In: Drinkwater, M.A. (ed.) Beyond Textual Literacy: Visual Literacy for Creative & Critical Inquiry, pp. 131–139 (2011)
4. Jie, Z.: The analysis of application and problems in bilingual public signs or plates. Sino-US Engl. Teach. **13**(6), 492–498 (2016)

Proposal for Encouraging Tourists to Stroll by Restricting Information Sharing Location to Destinations

Tomoko Izumi[✉] and Koki Takemoto

Faculty of Information Science and Technology, Osaka Institute of Technology,
Hirakata 573-0196, Japan
tomoko.izumi@oit.ac.jp, e1b15060@st.oit.ac.jp

Abstract. In this research, we aim to encourage tourists to take a walk in an area around a final destination, and so propose the restricting timing to share information on sightseeing spots. That is, we give the restriction that the sharing and the browsing of information on sightseeing spots can only be done at spots that are main destinations of tourists. The information shared at destination sightseeing spots is a sightseeing map representing the sightseeing history of a tourist.

In this research, in order to verify the usefulness of our proposal, an evaluation experiment using a prototype system was conducted. In this experiment, the comparison was made between sightseeing using the general electronic map service and the proposed system. Moreover, we compared the sightseeing behaviors between the cases where the information of the tourist maps was browsed before and after sightseeing. We show that making a sightseeing history map during the sightseeing made the participants walked in the wide area, and browsing the shared history maps after the sightseeing encouraged the participants to take a walk around various places in the current and the next sightseeing.

Keywords: Sightseeing support · Sharing information ·
Benefits of Inconvenience · Restriction

1 Introduction

1.1 Background and Motivation

Tourism trend is changing due to development of information technology, especially development of Social Networking Services (SNS) and mobile devices. By using these technologies, users of mobile devices can obtains any information anytime, anywhere. In recent years, word of mouth on SNS is one of the most important sources of sightseeing information tourists obtain: SNS users are able to share their own information about their experience and things they obtained during their sightseeing with photos, movies, and text. Another user is easily

© Springer Nature Switzerland AG 2019
M. Kurosu (Ed.): HCII 2019, LNCS 11568, pp. 295–306, 2019.
https://doi.org/10.1007/978-3-030-22636-7_21

able to obtain information about interesting sightseeing spots from the shared information on SNS and decide spots they visit in advance.

While tourists obtain freely huge amount of and various shared sightseeing information from SNS, however, this situation causes another problem: Since tourists visits sightseeing spots only where they decided to visit in advance based on shared information on SNS, staying time in a sightseeing area becomes short. Tourists may feel that the variety of their sightseeing activities are extended because they obtain a huge amount of sightseeing information and decide their behaviors based on it. However, it can be said that their activities are restricted by the impact of specific influential word of mouth. That is, they visit only specific sightseeing spots, and do not stroll around the spots.

Basically, the purpose of sightseeing is to have an unusual experience and to make a new discovery during interaction with eternal environment outside of daily life zone. However, as mentioned above, giving useful and huge amount of sightseeing information before sightseeing may prevent having opportunities of such an experience and a discovery. From these motivation, we consider an approach to share sightseeing information in order to encourage tourists to take various sightseeing behaviors without the restriction of their activities.

1.2   Our Contributions

In this paper, we propose a process that tourists share their sightseeing information after they arrive at a final destination of sightseeing. That is, tourists share or browse information on sightseeing around the destination only in the restricted area at the destination. This idea are derived from the fact that tourists visit only sightseeing spots which were decided to visit in advance from shared information. By doing this, tourists will stroll spontaneously from what they saw, heard, or felt during their sightseeing until the destination. The information shared at destination sightseeing spots is a sightseeing map representing the sightseeing history of a tourist.

In this research, in order to verify the usefulness of our proposal, an evaluation experiment using a prototype system was conducted. In this experiment, the comparison was made between sightseeing using the general electronic map service and the proposed system. Moreover, we compared the sightseeing behaviors between the cases where the information of the tourist maps was browsed before and after sightseeing. We show that making a sightseeing history map during the sightseeing made the participants walked in the wide area, and browsing the shared history maps after the sightseeing encouraged the participants to take a walk around various places in the current and the next sightseeing.

2   Related Works

The theory of the "Benefits of Inconvenience" (BI) proposed by Kawakami, which suggests that inconvenient things bring benefit in some cases [1]. With advances in information technology, the notion of "anytime, anywhere" is taken for granted in modern society. However, there are benefits that has been over-looked because of too much emphasis on convenience and efficiency. The research group of Kawakami proposed design guidelines of the BI [2]. Our proposal in this paper is included in the framework of the BI because it encourages tourists to take a walk by forcing inconvenience of restricted sharing information.

Also in the research area for sightseeing support, there are some proposals based on the BI. As encouraging tourists to take various sightseeing behaviors, in the research area about navigation systems, there are some studies about restricting provided information, such as detailed map information [3] or information on recommended spots [4].

As research to promote sightseeing behavior by restricting the sharing of information, there is work by Takagi et al. [5]. They proposed a system called "Journey Notes" that can be accessed by tourists only in a restricted area around an access point. Access points are set in sightseeing areas, and users who are about 20 m around the points can upload and read information on the virtual notes. They showed the effect of encouraging users to visit places of access points to obtain information by such the constraints.

Our proposal is very similar to the research by Takagi et al. in terms of restricting places to share information on sightseeing. However, in the existing work, there is no discussion about places to set access points. The purpose of the existing work is to guide tourists to places where they can share information. In our proposal, the location to share information is set to a destination, where tourists will visit. We aim for tourists to take a walk around various places to share valuable information at the destination.

3   Proposal

3.1   Outline of the Proposal

In this research, we aim to encourage tourists to take a walk in an area around a final destination. Currently, tourists can obtain information on sightseeing spots in advance and visit only the spots that they are interested in. So, we propose the sharing information on sightseeing spots after sightseeing. That is, we give the restriction that the sharing and the browsing of information on sightseeing spots can only be done at spots that are main destinations of tourists (see Fig. 1). By doing this, tourists will stroll spontaneously from what they saw, heard, or felt during their sightseeing until the destination. Since they do not receive behavioral constraints from prior information, we expect that tourists take various activities in an area around a destination although restricting the sharing location of information is inconvenient for tourists in terms that information can not be browsed anytime and anywhere.

The information shared at destinations is a sightseeing map representing the sightseeing history of a tourist. In the sightseeing map, tourists record locations, photographs, and their experience on interesting spots. These are information shared as a word of mouth for general SNS. In SNS, it is said that there is a psychology that the "I want to deliver valuable information" or "Information

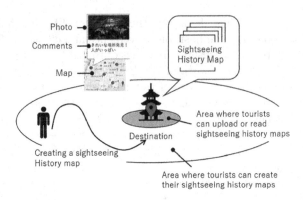

Fig. 1. Outline of our proposal

I delivered has good value" in users who upload words of mouth. Even in this research proposal, we hope that psychology, that tourists wants to provide valuable sightseeing information that they would like to recommend to others, will work. If such psychology works, it is motivated to explore various sightseeing spots before tourists arrive at destinations.

Also, at destinations after sightseeing, tourists can browse sightseeing maps created by others, so they will get information on sightseeing spots that they did not notice during their sightseeings. We expect this will lead to tourists' motivation for sightseeing next time. Masuda et.al. state that producing incomplete sightseeing encourages tourists to visit sightseeing area again [6]. Their work is based on the Zeigarnik effect [7]. The Zeigarnik effect, which is shown by Russian psychologist Zeigarnik, is that "incomplete thinks remember more than that was completed". In the research of Masuda et al., they creates uncompleted feelings by introducing sightseeing spots that tourists passed near but not yet visited, and presenting photos of spots a little different from the time of visit. In our proposal, we also expect that if tourists browse information on interesting sightseeing spots after sightseeing, they can be further promoted their motivation of sightseeing.

3.2   Prototype System

We explain the system constructed based on our proposal described in the previous section. This system was developed as an application running on an Android device. As an electronic map, we used Google Map.

Figure 2 shows the examples of system screens in our system. On the initial screen (Fig. 2(a)), the location of the destination is displayed on the electronic map. An user can create a sightseeing history map for sharing at the destination only within a certain distance away from the destination. This range is assumed to be large enough to stroll. Within this range, the user can register some recommended sightseeing spots on the map. When registering a spot, the

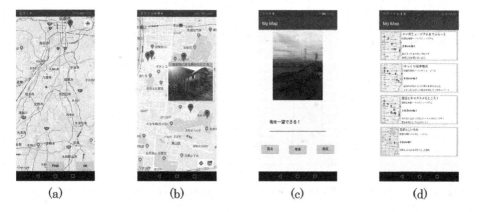

(a)   (b)   (c)   (d)

Fig. 2. Examples of screens of our prototype system

user taps a location to register on the map, takes a picture and inputs a comment for the spot (Fig. 2(c)). Inputting pictures and comments in optional. By repeating the same processes, the user registers multiple sightseeing spots on the map (Fig. 2(b)). When the user enters a range where the sightseeing history map around the destination can be shared, it is possible to share the created map at the destination.

Also within this range, the user can also browse the shared sightseeing maps. At the time of browsing, a list of the thumbnails of the shared sightseeing maps is displayed on the screen (Fig. 2(d)). When the user selects a sightseeing map to be viewed, he/she can see the details of the sightseeing spots registered on the map. The screen of viewing the map is the same as Fig. 2(b).

4   Verification Experiment

4.1   Evaluation Points

The goal of this experiment is to verify the effect of sharing sightseeing history maps at a final destination of sightseeing on behaviors of participants. Concretely, we focused on the following three evaluation points:

1. Does browsing shared history maps before a sightseeing make behavior of a participant restricted?
2. Does making a sightseeing history map during a sightseeing make a participant walked in a wide area?
3. Does browsing shared history maps after a sightseeing encourage participants to take a walk around various places in the next sightseeing?

To investigate these three points, we used two systems: One is an electronic map system (i.e., Google Maps) and the other is our proposal system. Since each participant used these two systems, we set two areas in which participants

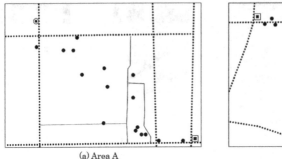 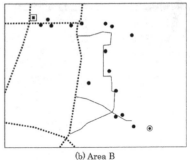

(a) Area A   (b) Area B

Fig. 3. Sightseeing areas for the experiments and the spots shown on the shared history maps.

stroll freely as the experiment area. On the first day of the experiment, a participant strolled in one of the areas using the electronic map system, and after that, he/she strolled in the other area using our system. Moreover, after about a week, he/she strolled in the second area again using our system. We took a log of movement history of each participant, and asked participants to complete a questionnaire after each sightseeing. The questionnaire had the following questions:

1. Did you want to look for and find interesting sightseeing spots? (5 grades)
2. Did you want to walk in an area or along a street where you usually do not walk? (5 grades)
3. Did you walk a lot more than usual sightseeing? (5 grades)
4. Do you want to walk a lot in the next sightseeing? (5 grades)

4.2   Methods

In this research, we set two areas as the experiment area: One is Gion and Sanzyo area (area A) and the other is Gion and Kiyomizu area (area B) in Kyoto. In these areas, there are many streets and sightseeing spots suitable for casual stroll. The final destination spot in the area A is Kyoto International Manga Museum, and one in the area B is Kiyomizu-dera temple. The start position in the both areas are the same point, Gion-Shizyo station. It takes 30 min on foots from the start position of the station to each destination in each area. Figure 3 shows the simple map for each area. In the figures, the bold and dotted lines show the wide streets, and the thin and solid lines show the streets with a lot of sightseeing spots where many tourists stroll. The double circles are the destination spots and the double squares are the start positions.

In this experiment, the participants browsed the shared sightseeing history maps before or after their experiments. We created the shared maps beforehand by taking photos and adding comments for some spots using our system. The number of the shared maps for each area is three. The black circles in the Fig. 3

Table 1. Flow of the experiments for each participant.

	Participant			
	a	b	c	d
The first experiment	Electronic map in the area A	Electronic map in the area A	Electronic map in the area B	Electronic map in the area B
Browse the shared maps		◯		◯
The second experiment	Our system in the area B	Our system in the area B	Our system in the area A	Our system in the area A
Browse the shared maps	◯		◯	
	Share the sightseeing history maps			
Browse the shared maps		◯		◯
The third experiment	Our system in the area B	Our system in the area B	Our system in the area A	Our system in the area A
Browse the shared maps	◯		◯	

shows the registered spots on the shared maps. The area A has some shopping streets, and so the restaurants and the souvenirs were shown in the shared maps. In the area B, there are many temples and shrines. Then in the shared maps for the area B, these temples, shrines, and streets between them were introduced.

We conducted the experiment with 4 participants, who were college students (2 males and 2 female), called participant a, b, c, and d. Table 1 shows the process of the experiments for each participant. In the first day of the experiment, the participant strolled in one of areas using the electronic map system. The system showed only map information and the location of the final destination. Please note that the system did not provide the route information, such as the shortest path to the destination. After that, we conducted the second experiment using our system in the other area on the same day. As explained in the previous section, our system did not also provide the route information to the participants. In the second experiment, the half of the participants browsed the shared history maps using our system before their stroll. So, they could know the information about sightseeing spots in the area (shown in the Fig. 3) by reading the shared maps. The other half did not browse the shared maps before their second stroll, but they checked the shared maps after their strolls at the final destination. Moreover, to verify the behavior of participants in the next sightseeing in the same area, we conducted the same experiments in the same area using our system after about a week. Also in the third experiments, the half of the participants browsed the shared map before their stroll, and the other half did not.

This experiment were approved by the ethics committee of Osaka Institute of Technology. Before the experiments, we explained the purpose and the flow of the experiments, and obtained their consent to participate. After that, we showed and explained how to use the electronic map system and our system. In each of the experiment, we did not set a time for their stroll and the number of spots registered in our system. We asked the participants to stroll freely in the areas, and to arrive at the spots of the final destination. The participants

Table 2. Attribute of the participants.

Questions	Participant			
	a	b	c	d
Use of SNS	Only browsing	Post and browse	Post and browse	Post and browse
Frequency of sightseeing	Once every six months	Once a year	Once every few years	Once every six months
Experience of sightseeing in the experiment areas	No	Several times	Once	Several times

were conducted each of the experiments separately. That is, the days of the experiments are different.

4.3   Results of Movement Histories and Questionnaire

Table 2 shows the attribute of the participants. Three participants except the participant a post and browse the shared information on the SNS. As for the experience of sightseeing, three participants go sightseeing some times every year, and the participant c has low frequency of sightseeing. The participant a and c do not almost visit the sightseeing area in this experiments. On the other hand, the other participants have some experience of sightseeing there.

Figures 4, 5, 6 and 7, show the histories of the movements of the participant a, b, c, and d on the maps in Fig. 3 respectively. In these figures, the solid and bold arrows show the histories of the movements in the first day of the experiments. That is, the movement histories were taken in the first and the second experiment. The dotted and bold arrows show the movement histories taken in the third experiment. In the Fig. 5, there is no dotted arrows. The reason of this is that the participant b walked the same streets in the second and the third experiments. The black stars indicate the locations of spots registered in our system by the participants in the second experiment, and the white stars indicated thats in the third experiment. Table 3 shows the results of the questionnaire. In the questionnaire, we asked each questions in the 5-scale grades, in which 1 corresponds to strongly disagree and 5 corresponds to strongly agree. In this section, we discuss the results of our experiment based on the evaluation points in the Sect. 4.1.

First, we discuss about the effect of browsing the shared history maps before a sightseeing on the restriction of sightseeing behavior. In this experiment, the participants b and d checked the shared maps before their strolls in the second and the third experiments, and the participants a and c did not. As see the Figs. 5(b) and 6(b) , the participant b and d walked along the streets where the many spots registered on the shared maps. Especially, the participant d changed the direction to the registered spots. On the other hand, except the second

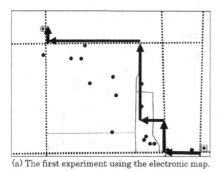
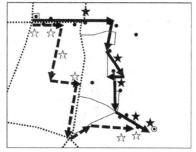

(a) The first experiment using the electronic map.   (b) The second and third experiment using our system.

Fig. 4. The movement histories and the registered spots of sightseeing history map of the participant a.

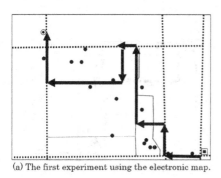
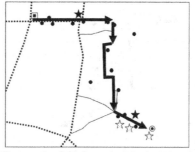

(a) The first experiment using the electronic map.   (b) The second and third experiment using our system.

Fig. 5. The movement histories and the registered spots of sightseeing history map of the participant b. The participant b followed the same streets in the second and the third strolls.

experiment of the participant a, the participant a and c walked different streets from the participant b and d. They walked the narrow lanes and registered the interesting spots on their maps which were not shown on the shared maps. The reason that the participant a followed the almost same streets as the participant b in the second experiment is that these streets are famous and popular streets for tourists and there were many tourists there. From these facts above, it can be said that if the participants browse the shared maps before their sightseeing then they tend to visit the spots registered on the shared maps.

The second evaluation point is whether making a sightseeing history maps during a sightseeing makes the participants walk in a wide area. For this point, we compare the movement histories using the electronic map system and our system in the same areas. In the area A, the participants a and b used the electronic map system. From the Figs. 4(a) and 5(a), it can be seen that they followed the similar streets. As for the participant c and d who used our system in the area A, while the participant d also walked the similar streets to thats of a and b in the second experiment (see Fig. 7(b)), they walked the different

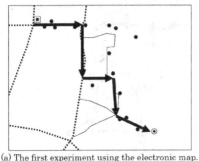
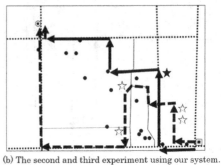

(a) The first experiment using the electronic map.   (b) The second and third experiment using our system.

Fig. 6. The movement histories and the registered spots of sightseeing history map of the participant c.

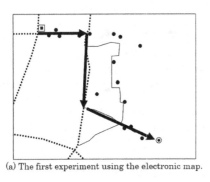
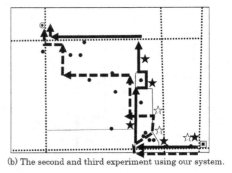

(a) The first experiment using the electronic map.   (b) The second and third experiment using our system.

Fig. 7. The movement histories and the registered spots of sightseeing history map of the participant d.

streets from them in the other three cases. We can see the same tendency for the results in the area B. The participants c and d using the electronic map system in the area B walked along the main streets directly to the destination. On the other hand, the participant a and b walked the different streets from them and walked the narrow streets avoiding the main streets. In the results of the questionnaire (see Table 3), except the answers of the participant b, the other participants answered the better or equal scores for our system to thats for the electronic map system. But note that there are little differences between the answers for the electronic map system and our system in the results of the questionnaire.

To discuss about the last evaluation point, we compare the movement histories in the second and the third experiments. The participant b and d walked the same or the similar streets in that two times. Especially, the participant b followed the completely same route. As mentioned above for the first evaluation point, they walked near the spots shown in the shared maps because they saw these information before their sightseeing. As for the participant a and c who browsed the shared map after their strolls, they walked the different routes in

Table 3. Answers for the questionnaire.

Q1: Did you want to look for and find interesting sightseeing spots?

	a	b	c	d
The first experiment	3	3	3	2
The second experiment	5	3	4	3
The third experiment	4	3	3	3

Q2: Did you want to walk in an area or along a street where you usually do not?

	a	b	c	d
The first experiment	4	3	3	2
The second experiment	4	2	4	3
The third experiment	3	2	4	4

Q3: Did you walk a lot more than usual sightseeing?

	a	b	c	d
The first experiment	2	4	2	2
The second experiment	2	4	2	3
The third experiment	2	3	4	4

Q4: Do you want to walk a lot in the next sightseeing?

	a	b	c	d
The first experiment	4	3	2	3
The second experiment	4	4	3	2
The third experiment	4	3	4	3

that two times. Notice that in the third experiments, they did not pass near the registered spots despite seeing the information about them after their strolls in the second experiments. After their second strolls, they talked about the information about the shared maps such that "there are many spots I have not visited yet" or "I know that some streets also can be good recommended spots to others". From these facts, we consider that they could not remember the details of the information on the shared maps but they had the feeling that there seems to be interesting something. As the results, they followed the different routes in the third experiments from thats in the second experiments.

From the discussion above, it can be said the following results:

1. Browsing shared history maps before a sightseeing makes behavior of a participant restricted.
2. Making a sightseeing history map during a sightseeing makes a participant walked in a wide area.
3. Browsing shared history maps after a sightseeing encourages participants to take a walk around various places in the next sightseeing.

5 Conclusions

In this research, we proposed a system to share information about a sightseeing as a sightseeing history map at a final destination. To verify this proposal, we conducted the experiments with 4 participants. As the results, it was shown that making a sightseeing history map during the sightseeing made the participants walked in the wide area. Moreover, browsing the shared history maps after the sightseeing encouraged the participants to take a walk around various places in the current and the next sightseeing.

Future tasks are to conduct the experiment with more number of participants to obtain a lot of experimental data, and to apply this system to other sightseeing area.

Acknowledgment. This work is supported in part by KAKENHI no18H03483.

References

1. Kawakami, H.: Further benefit of a kind of inconvenience for social information systems. In: Kurosu, M. (ed.) HCI 2013. LNCS, vol. 8006, pp. 301–306. Springer, Heidelberg (2013). https://doi.org/10.1007/978-3-642-39265-8_33
2. Hasebe, Y., Kawakami, H., Hiraoka, T., Nozaki, K.: Guidelines of system design for embodying benefits of inconvenience. SICE J. Control Meas. Syst. Integr. **8**(1), 2–6 (2015)
3. Takagi, S., Izumi, T., Nakatani, Y.: Five sightseeing navigation systems using limited information. In: 2013 Conference on Technologies and Applications of Artificial Intelligence (TAAI 2013) (2013)
4. Hiraishi, Y., Kitamura, T., Izumi, T., Nakatani, Y.: Experimental verification of sightseeing information as a weak trigger to affect tourist behavior. In: Meiselwitz, G. (ed.) SCSM 2018. LNCS, vol. 10913, pp. 303–317. Springer, Cham (2018). https://doi.org/10.1007/978-3-319-91521-0_22
5. Takagi, S., Izumi, T., Nakatani, Y.: Sightseeing assistance via information inheritance with journey note system in sightseeing spots. In: The World Congress on Engineering and Computer Science (WCECS 2013), pp. 764–769 (2013)
6. Masuda, M., Nakatani, Y.: A study of a navigation system that induces tourists to visit sightseeing spots again via a feeling of regret. In: IADIS International Interfaces and Human Computer Interaction 2011 (IHCI 2011), pp. 291–298 (2011)
7. Zeigarnik, B: On finished and unfinished tasks. In: Ellis, W.D. (ed.) A Source Book of Gestalt Psychology, pp. 300–314 (1938)

Proposal of Using Digital Mirror Signage and AR Pictogram for Follow Me Evacuation Guidance

Takayoshi Kitamura, Kazumi Yasui$^{(\boxtimes)}$, and Yoshio Nakatani$^{(\boxtimes)}$

Ritsumeikan University, 1-1-1, Nojihigashi, Kusatsu, Shiga, Japan
ktmr@fc.ritusmei.ac.jp, is0332vk@ed.ritsumei.ac.jp,
nakatani@is.ritsumei.ac.jp

Abstract. There are still many problems with evacuation guidance. After a concert or a game at a stadium, people rush one route, and there are always crowded with people. Of course, the event companies make a guard plan for the event to arrange guards. Nevertheless, there are significant accidents have still occurred. This paper proposes to use digital mirror signage and augmented reality (AR) pictogram animation for Follow Me evacuation guidance. Moreover, the authors designed and evaluated three pictogram animations "Beckoning," "Running," "Pulling" because to discuss how to move pictograms for guidance. The results of using visual analog scale evaluation by nineteen participants, "Running" pictogram animation received high evaluation marks ($p < .05$). Besides, this study has interviewed participants with something felt in time series. After that, participant and we have created the Participant Journey Analysis Map (PaJAMap) which inspired the Trajectory Equifinality Model (TEM). The result of the analysis shows that "Beckoning" can feel antipathy, "Running" was characterized 'Conformity' type of Follow Me moving, "Pulling" had sometimes confused with 'Pushing'.

Keywords: Disaster engineering · Nudge · Stick figure · Beckoning · Agent

1 Introduction

Crowded places present many dangers to people. Mainly when people concentrate on the exit of a building at the time of a disaster or a festival, a concert event, there is no move at all because of congestion, and injured persons occur in some cases. Sugiman et al. [1] propose 'Follow Me method' in which each leader takes only one evacuee to an exit. And Sugiman et al. [1] showed that 'Follow-Me method' is better as compared to 'Follow Directions method,' in which each leader indicates the direction with a loud voice and vigorous gestures. On the other hand, the studies on 'Follow Me methods' using virtual agents using digital signage are not in progress. Signage display is the general name of electronic signage to display digital images, movies, or texts. The number of installed signage display has increased rapidly at stations, airports and large facilities around the world in recent years [2]. Japanese Digital Signage Consortium [3] has developed the contents' guideline to be displayed on the signage display in the disaster. However, the signage display using on disaster currently being studied is

© Springer Nature Switzerland AG 2019
M. Kurosu (Ed.): HCII 2019, LNCS 11568, pp. 307–314, 2019.
https://doi.org/10.1007/978-3-030-22636-7_22

limited to presenting disaster information and attention, evacuation route and direction and so on.

This study proposes to use digital mirror signage and augmented reality (AR) pictogram animation for Follow Me evacuation guidance. Moreover, this study designs and evaluates three pictogram animations "Beckoning," "Running," "Pulling" because to discuss how to move pictograms for guidance.

2 System Proposal

This study proposes the Follow Me system which uses signage display of the station or the stadium when there is not enough staff. Figure 1 shows the image of this system. This system consists of a camera, signage display, and an augmented reality program. When this signage display system displays a passerby like a mirror, a pictogram emerges side of its face and indicating guide staff movement.

Fig. 1. Follow-me system using digital mirror signage.

The authors consider that the proposed system can contribute to the advance improvement of the situation of congestion of people. However, it is not clear what movement is useful for AR pictogram.

3 Evaluation

3.1 Purpose

The purpose of this study is to find out what kind of motion effect for Follow Me evacuation guidance the case of using digital mirror signage. And we proposed three pictogram motions. Figure 2 shows them. Type A is a beckoning motion, type B is a running motion, type C is a pulling motion.

3.2   System

In this evaluation, digital mirror signage system uses Spark AR Studio [4]. Spark AR Studio [4] can create an augmented reality object on the side of the user's face using a web camera. The augmented reality object, three types of pictogram animations (Fig. 2) were made using Stykz [5]. This system uses the projector screen instead of a signage display.

3.3   Participants

Table 1 shows participants' ID and gender. The ID shows the order of participants' experience type A or B or C. The number of males is fifteen and females is four. All participants' age is the early twenties.

3.4   Flow

Figure 3 shows the flow chart of this evaluation. And Fig. 4 shows the walking route of participants which ID is ABCx. After obtaining informed consent, the experimenter instructs a participant to stand at the start point. Participants walk to the screen, and after confirming the pictogram animation (type A), they need to choose right or left root. After that, the participant answer questionnaire and interview. Participants repeat the process of type B and type C.

In the questionnaire, participants answer about a feeling of "I need to choose this root" by drawing a vertical line on a line segment of 10 cm shown in Fig. 4 (visual analog scale) (Fig. 5).

In the interview, experimenter makes Participant Journey Analysis Map (Pa-JAMap) which inspired from Trajectory Equifinality Model (TEM) [6] and customer journey map. As shown in Figs. 7, 8, and 9, the PaJAMap diagram shows the element of how the participants judged by looking at the pictogram and walked the left or the right root. Therefore, those elements become the reasons for the eventually selected or impeded actions.

Type A   Type B   Type C

Fig. 2. Follow Me pictogram animations.

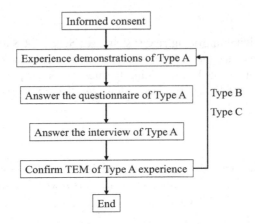

Fig. 3. Flow chart of the evaluation (Pattern of ABC1, ABC2, ABC3).

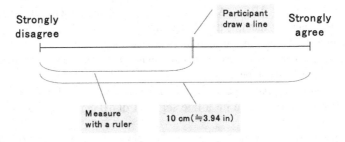

Fig. 4. Visual analog scale.

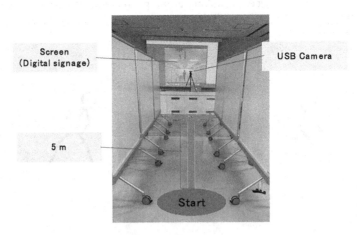

Fig. 5. Walking route for the evaluation.

3.5   Result

Table 1 shows the result of the questionnaire using the visual analog scale. Figure 6 shows the box-and-whisker plot about type A, B, and C. The results from the one-way ANOVA showed the difference is significant (p < .05).

Figures 7, 8, and 9 show the representative PaJAMaps created by type A, B, and C interviews. Figures 7 and 8 indicated that all elements exist in the same direction (up arrow) to the route which was induced by the system. On the other hand, Fig. 9 indicates that some elements push to another route.

3.6   Discussion

In this evaluation, we can find that type B received a high evaluation from participants. However, some participants felt the need to hurry move from type B's running animation (Fig. 8). There may be a possibility of attributed to 'Conformity'. Conformity is the human behavior that follows the usual standards that are expected by a group or society [7]. Therefore, type B has a possibility of useless in the calm behavior requirement.

About type A, some participants had negatively answered because they felt luring customer movement or the action from the top of the eyes. Therefore, it is necessary to discuss deliberately, when we design of beckoning pictogram animation.

About type C, most participants confused because the movement looks like whether pushing and pulling. Hence, this system needs to review the moving design of pulling.

Table 1. Participants' ID, gender, and their results of questionnaire.

ID	Gender	Answer of visual analog scale [cm]		
		Type A	Type B	Type C
ABC1	Male	9.1	9.5	5.1
ABC2	Male	7.6	9.0	4.1
ABC3	Female	8.3	7.2	4.3
ABC4	Male	9.1	7.3	5.9
ACB1	Male	5.4	7.8	4.6
ACB2	Female	8.3	7.3	9.9
ACB3	Male	8.5	7.6	6.1
BAC1	Male	9.6	8.4	6.8
BAC2	Male	5.6	8.2	7.1
BAC3	Male	2.8	8.6	9.3
BCA1	Male	6.5	7.6	2.3
BCA2	Male	8.4	8.4	7.5
BCA3	Male	9.7	8.9	9.5
CAB1	Male	7.3	9.0	7.6
CAB2	Female	9.5	9.4	8.5
CAB3	Male	7.1	6.2	4.1
CBA1	Male	7.4	10	6.9
CBA2	Female	7.4	7.6	7.3
CBA3	Male	7.8	6.3	8.8

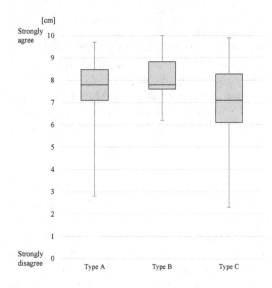

Fig. 6. Box-and-whisker plot.

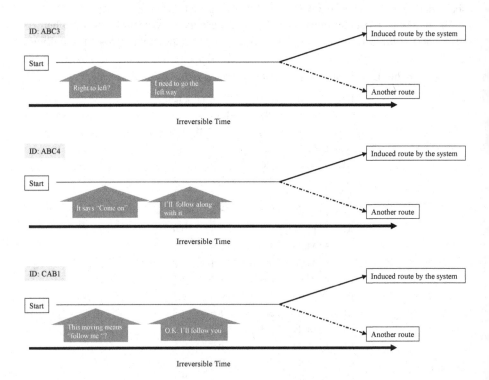

Fig. 7. PaJAMap figures of Type A.

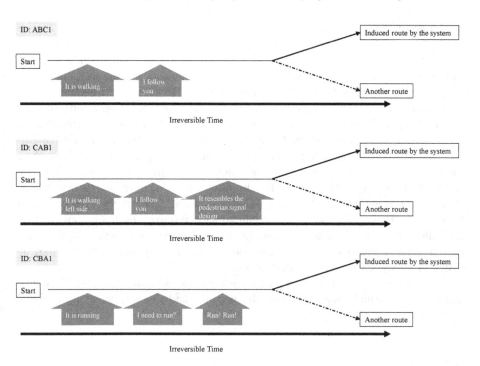

Fig. 8. PaJAMap figures of Type B

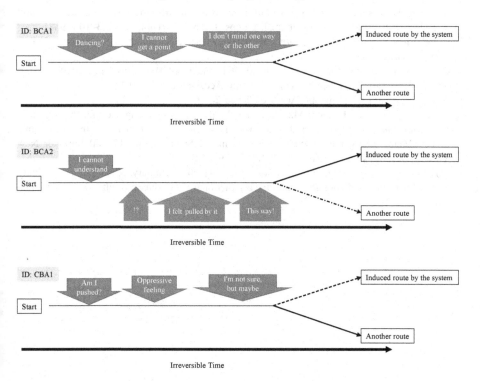

Fig. 9. PaJAMap figures of Type C

4 Conclusion

In this study, the authors proposed to use digital mirror signage and augmented reality (AR) pictogram animation for Follow Me evacuation guidance. Moreover, the authors designed and evaluated three pictogram animations "Beckoning," "Running," "Pulling" because to discuss how to move pictograms for guidance. The results of using visual analog scale evaluation by nineteen participants, "Running" pictogram animation received high evaluation marks ($p < .05$). Besides, the authors interviewed participants with something felt in time series. After that, participant and the authors created the Participant Journey Analysis Map (PaJAMap) which inspired from the Trajectory Equifinality Model (TEM). The result of the analysis shows that "Beckoning" can feel antipathy, "Running" was characterized 'Conformity' type of Follow Me moving, "Pulling" had sometimes confused with 'Pushing.' From the above results, the Follow Me evacuation guidance methods which using digital mirror signage and AR pictograms obtained a certain reputation by the participants. However, moving design of pictogram needs to discuss deliberately.

In the future works, the authors plan to improve AR pictogram design on the digital mirror signage which using "Follow Me method," and to study using multi-digital mirror signage displays.

References

1. Sugiman, T., Misumi, J.: Development of a new evacuationmethod for emergencies: control of collective behavior byemergent small groups. J. Appl. Psychol. **73**(1), 3–10 (1988)
2. Grand View Research, Inc. https://www.grandviewresearch.com/industry-analysis/us-digital-signage-market. Accessed 2 Feb 2019
3. Digital Signage Consortium. https://www.digital-signage.jp/. Accessed 2 Feb 2019
4. Spark AR Studio. https://sparkar.com/ar-studio. Accessed 2 Feb 2019
5. Stykz. https://stykz.softonic.jp/. Accessed 2 Feb 2019
6. Sato, T., Hidaka, T., Fukuda, M.: Depicting the dynamics of living the life: the trajectory equifinality model. In: Valsiner, J., Molenaar, P., Lyra, M., Chaudhary, N. (eds.) Dynamic Process Methodology in the Social and Developmental Sciences, pp. 217–240. Springer, New York (2009). https://doi.org/10.1007/978-0-387-95922-1_10
7. CONFORMITY—meaning in the Cambridge English Dictionary. Cambridge University Press (2019). https://dictionary.cambridge.org/dictionary/english/conformity. Accessed 2 Feb 2019

Verification of a Psychological Effect of Hiding Speedometer when Exceeding a Speed Limit

Tetsuma Konishi[1($\boxtimes$)], Takayoshi Kitamura[2], Tomoko Izumi[3], and Yoshio Nakatani[2]

[1] Graduate School of Science and Engineering, Ritsumeikan University, Kusatsu, Shiga 525-8577, Japan
is0258sv@ed.ritsumei.ac.jp
[2] College of Information Science and Engineering, Ritsumeikan University, Kusatsu, Shiga 525-8577, Japan
ktmr@fc.ritsumei.ac.jp, nakatani@is.ritsumei.ac.jp
[3] College of Information Science and Technology, Osaka Institute of Technology, Hirakata, Osaka 573-0196, Japan
tomoko.izumi@oit.ac.jp

Abstract. On a good road, drivers tend to exceed the legal speed limit because of their sense of security that they are not in danger. However, in some cases, serious accidents are often due to driving at high speed. In this research, to promote safe driving, we propose a natural method to get drivers to slow down by hiding a part of the speedometer. Since the driver cannot see the entire speedometer, they may feel uneasy about driving at an excessive speed. So, to keep their sense of security, the driver may go more slowly. To verify the effectiveness of this system, tests using a motorbike were conducted for 13 participants. Our results show that most participants reduced their speed.

Keywords: Speedometer · Speed control · Anxiety · Benefit of inconvenience

1 Introduction

On good clear roads and highways where cars are driven fast, people drive with the surrounding traffic flow for safety. Hence, they tend to exceed the legal speed. However, serious accidents may be caused by speeding. In recent years, traffic violations and traffic accidents have become common in various places in Japan. The number of traffic violations in 2017 was 6,509,141, and 99% of the drivers were arrested or violating the Road Traffic Act [1]. The most common arrests occur during campaigns to reduce speeding, accounting for about 23% of the total [1]. In addition, the number of traffic accidents in 2017 was 472,165 [1], the most common type being rear-end collisions, of which there were 167,845 cases [2]. Although the number of traffic violations and accidents has tended to decrease year by year, we believe that many people drive without checking their speed.

To prevent accidents and violations, traffic signs and structures can be installed in the road environment, such as traffic enforcement camera (ORBIS), speed limit signs, and speed bumps and humps. However, with modern technology, it is costly to install

© Springer Nature Switzerland AG 2019
M. Kurosu (Ed.): HCII 2019, LNCS 11568, pp. 315–328, 2019.
https://doi.org/10.1007/978-3-030-22636-7_23

these structures on all roads. For this reason, traffic signs and structures are a partial solution, being effective only where they are used. Therefore, it is necessary to modify cars to encourage better driving.

In addition, car companies are automating many aspects of driving to create intelligent transportation systems, such as the Advanced Safety Vehicle (ASV) [3]. Such a vehicle supports safe driving using advanced technology that respects the intentions of the driver. It has three basic principles: the driver is responsible, the driver has confidence in the system, and society understands and accepts the technology. Many auto manufacturers use automatic distance control systems and lane departure warning systems. However, a driver may cause an accident by neglecting to drive responsibly by depending too much on such technology.

In this research, we focus on speed and speedometers to promote safe driving. Subsequently, a part of the speedometer is not shown when the speed exceeds a certain value. Hence, we propose to create anxiety about speed visually, leading the driver to slow down naturally.

2   Related Works

2.1   Benefit of Inconvenience

Problems in producing something convenient are generally solved to produce further convenience. However, this may cause new problems, and the benefit of pursuing improvements in convenience is lost. We can audaciously use the benefit of an inconvenient situation to create a benefit of inconvenience, called "fuben-eki" in Japanese [4]. When designing a benefit of inconvenience, it is important not to inconveniently redesign something convenient but to deliberately use the inconvenience of being time consuming and the allocation of cognitive resources. Hence, we can create advantages that are not possible with convenient things.

In this research, we aim to control driving speed naturally. We propose using an inconvenient speedometer that does not show a part of the display.

2.2   Achieving Sensible Speeds Using Virtual Reality

About 90% of the information obtained when driving a car is visual [5]. Drivers see moving and static objects. Generally, as speed increases, kinetic vision decreases. Therefore, as their speed increases, drivers find it more difficult to see things and their ability to recognize danger greatly diminishes. Hence, there is a significant relationship between visual perception and speed.

Han et al. [6] reproduced a section of a standard two-lane highway—the Shuto Expressway—on a driving simulator. They were able to modify driving behavior by displaying white elliptical dots on the road surface. The frequency of the dots affected the driver's sense of speed.

In addition, Toui et al. [7] suggested using an optical see-through display in a car, rather than displaying the information on road signs. A pattern projected onto the display according to the speed of the car to encourage drivers to control their speed.

Through a simulation using a video of an actual vehicle and an experiment with an actual vehicle in the real world, they confirmed the effectiveness of the virtual pattern on the perception of speed and in controlling speed.

2.3   Using a Mobile Device to Control Speed

Cars are used for many reasons, such as work, hobbies, shopping, and commuting. However, the driver does not always enjoy driving. If the driver is having fun, sometimes the passengers and nearby drivers feel in danger and do not enjoy the experience. Therefore, there has been considerable research on systems with mobile devices that encourage speed control while enhancing driving pleasure.

Nozaki et al. [8] developed seven gimmicks based on the benefit of inconvenience and gamification. They proposed a system in which people drive safely while enjoying the experience.

In addition, Hiraoka et al. [9] focused on gamenics theory which systemizes the know-how of improving the operability and entertainment in game development. Using this theory, they developed a system that naturally encourages people to obey speed limits while enjoying driving.

Such research supports safe driving while enhancing the driver's pleasure. However, there is a possibility that all such systems may be ignored and may make driving more dangerous.

In our research, instead of introducing new equipment, we place a device over the originally installed instrument panel. By doing this, we may be able to get a driver to reduce their speed naturally.

3   Outline of the System Proposal

In this research, we propose a method of hiding a part of the speed displayed by the speedometer when a certain speed is exceeded. We conducted an experiment to verify whether this has the effect of suppressing speed naturally due to visual anxiety. Therefore, we created a speedometer system that does not display the needle and digital display when the speed exceeds a certain value.

We implemented an application for mobile devices, which can easily be fitted to a car or motorbike. This system derives the current location information at regular time intervals using the global positioning system function of a smartphone or tablet. Further, this system employs the location information to obtain the current speed. The speedometer system displays the speed using a needle and a digital display on the tablet. The speed limit is set in advance. If the speed derived from the location information is greater than the limit, the needle and the digital speed are not displayed on the speedometer. Figure 1 shows the speedometer, and Fig. 2 shows when the speedometer is not visible.

Fig. 1. Example of display of speedometer

Fig. 2. Example of hidden speedometer

4 Experiment

4.1 Methods

We conducted the experiment with 13 participants, who were college students (12 males and one female). Participants have a driver's license and have experience of driving since getting a license.

In this experiment, we used two motorbikes. As shown in Fig. 3, a tablet was fitted to one motorbike that a participant rode. The other motorbike was ridden by an experimenter, who acted as a pacemaker. The experimenter compared the speed from the original speedometer with that the experiment, the experimenter intentionally speeds up or slow down, to move closer to or further away from the participant.

Fig. 3. Experimental motorbike fitted with a tablet

The experiment was conducted on a straight section of about 400 m of the road surrounding Biwako-Kusatsu Campus of Ritsumeikan University. Since the speed limit was 30 km/h, we set the speed to 20 km/h, which is lower than this legal limit. For the analysis, we acquired data such as location, speed, and time.

In this experiment, the participants made a total of six round trips (two practice trips plus four experimental trips). In the first two round trips, as shown in Fig. 4, the experimenter went first, and the participant followed. In these practice trips, to allow the participant to get used to the motorbike, the original speedometer was not hidden by the tablet, so that the participant could see their speed at all times.

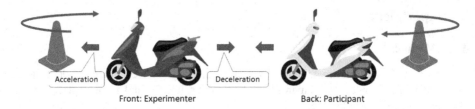

Fig. 4. Experiment method of the two practice trips and the first two round experimental trips

In the next two round trips, as before, the experimenter was followed by the participant. For the final two round trips, as shown in Fig. 5, the participant went first, and the experimenter followed. In these four experimental trips, the participant's speed was concealed when the set speed was exceeded. Before starting the experiment, we said to each participant: "Ride at 20 km/h" and "Be careful with your speed," to make the participants aware of their speed.

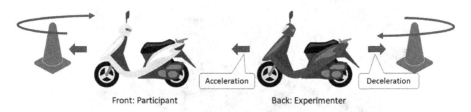

Fig. 5. Experiment method of the last 2 round experimental trips

4.2 Evaluation Points

In this research, we focused on the following two evaluation points:

1. "Did you feel anxious when the speedometer was hidden?": From the questionnaire and the interview conducted after each experiment, we verified that the participants felt anxiety and impatience when the speedometer was hidden due to speeding.
2. "Did you want to slow down when the speedometer was hidden?": The experiment was conducted to investigate whether the participants suppressed their speed naturally as a psychological effect. This was assessed from the speed of the motorbike acquired per second in the experiment and from the questionnaire and interview conducted for each participant.

In this research, to investigate these two points, we asked the participants to complete a questionnaire after the ride. The questionnaire had the following nine questions:

1. "Did you check the speedometer?" (5 grades)
2. "Was it easy to notice when the speedometer was hidden?" (5 grades)
3. "Did you feel anxiety when the speedometer was hidden?" (5 grades)
4. "Did you want to slow down when the speedometer was hidden? "(5 grades)

5. (The first 2 round trips) "Which of the following distances to and speed from the leading car was worried about riding?" ("Speed", "Distance between cars", "Both" and "Not worried" selected one)
6. (The last 2 round trips) "Which of the following distance between the following car and the speed you cared about?" ("Speed", "Distance between cars", "Both" and "Not worried" selected one)
7. "Was the speedometer easy to see?" (5 grades)
8. "Were the words on the speedometer easy to see?" (5 grades)
9. Other opinions (Free description)

4.3 Questionnaire Results

After the experiment, we gave the participants a questionnaire with nine evaluation points and interviewed them to evaluate the speedometer system and its psychological effects. From the data, we found that two of the 13 participants did not exceed the speed limit of 20 km/h and for them, the speedometer was always visible. Therefore, they were excluded from the analysis of the questionnaire data. Table 1 shows the average score for each question for the 11 participants on a scale of 1 to 5 (1 = disagree strongly, 2 = disagree, 3 = neither agree nor disagree, 4 = agree, 5 = agree strongly). It also shows the ratio of 11 participants to the answer. For the first two round trips, the participant was following, and for the second two round trips, the participant was leading.

Table 1. The results of the questionnaire on the consciousness during driving

	Questionnaire	The first 2 round trips	The last 2 round trips
1.	"Did you check the speedometer?"	4.5 (91%)	4.7 (100%)
2.	"Was it easy to notice when the speedometer was hidden?"	4.1 (82%)	4.1 (73%)
3.	"Did you feel anxiety when the speedometer was hidden?"	3.9 (73%)	3.9 (64%)
4.	"Did you want to slow down when the speedometer was hidden?"	4.0 (73%)	3.9 (73%)
5. 6.	"Were you aware of your speed while riding?" ("Speed" + "Both")	73% ("Speed": 27%, "Both": 46%)	91% ("Speed": 82%, "Both": 9%)

Table 1 shows the results for the questions of their awareness during riding (questionnaire items 1 to 6). The score for "Were you aware of your speed while riding?" was higher for the last two round trips than for the first two round trips. In addition, the proportion of participants who were aware of their speed increased significantly between the two sets of trips. On the other hand, the proportion of participants who were conscious of both their speed and the distance between the two bikes decreased significantly. The score for "Did you check the speedometer?" was very high, about 4.5 to 4.7. Moreover, for the last two trips, all the participants checked the speedometer. The score for "Was it easy to notice when the speedometer was hidden?" was high, about 4.1 for both sets of trips. However, the proportion of participants who answered that they noticed that the display had gone decreased. The score for "Did you feel anxiety when the speedometer was hidden?" was 3.9 in both cases. However, the proportion of participants who answered they were anxious decreased. The average score for "Did you want to slow down when the speedometer was hidden?" was slightly different between the two sets of trips. However, the proportion of participants who answered was the same.

Table 2 shows the results for the questions on the system (questionnaire items 7. and 8). Both "Was the speedometer easy to see?" and "Were the words on the speedometer easy to see?" had very high scores.

Table 2. The results of the questionnaire on the system screen

	Questionnaire	Results
7.	"Was the speedometer easy to see?"	4.2 (73%)
8.	"Were the words on the speedometer easy to see?"	4.4 (82%)

As shown in Table 3, in addition to the questionnaire, other opinions and comments were obtained. Their need to see their speed and how they rode depended on the individual.

Table 3. Other opinions and comments

Participants	Comments
B	I thought that the sound of the engine might be faster or slower
D	I was concerned about the reflection of sunlight In the last 2 round trips, I thought rather than the meter rather than the scenery
E	I was concerned about the reflection of sunlight
F	I drove the priority on the surroundings
G	I was concerned about poor meter sensitivity
H	Updating the display of the speedometer when accelerator or brake is applied is slow I felt uneasy when the meter display disappeared
L	I did not care about the distance between two cars in the last 2 round trips In the last 2 round trips, I felt a little impatient when the meter disappeared

4.4   Interviews with Participants and Travel Data

We held an interview individually with each participant at the end of the experiment. Further, we analyzed the speed of each participant. From these data, we look at three participants who were particularly interesting. The orange lines on the graphs in Figs. 6, 7 and 8 are at 20 km/h, which is the speed set for hiding the speedometer.

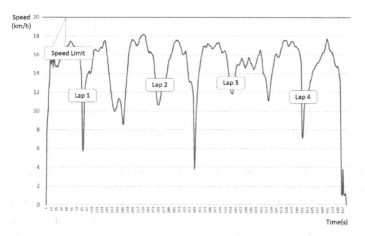

Fig. 6. Transition of speed of experiment participant "C"

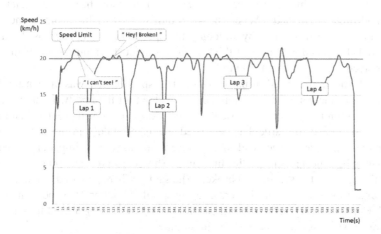

Fig. 7. Transition of speed of experiment participant "I"

Figure 6 shows the speed of participant C. He did not exceed the set speed in the four round trips. Therefore, he did not confirm that the speedometer had disappeared. In the interview, he said, "You said "Ride at 20 km/h," so, I thought that I should not exceed this speed. I tried to keep to 17 to 18 km/h by checking the speedometer."

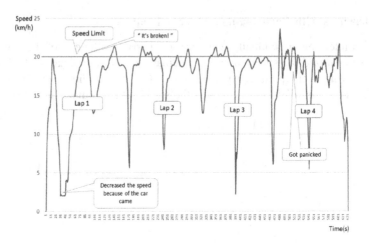

Fig. 8. Transition of speed of experiment participant "J"

Figure 7 shows the speed of participant I. For the four round trips, his speedometer was hidden for a total of 155 s. The lengths of time his speedometer was hidden for the first two round trips and the last two round trips were almost the same. His speed frequently moved up or down around the set speed. When the running speed exceeded 20 km/h at the beginning of the experiment, participant I shouted "I can't see!" and "Broken!" In his interview, he stated that he became anxious and impatient when the speedometer became hidden for the first time. Also, he thought that the tablet or the system had broken. He said, "When the speedometer was visible again, I understood the system. Then, I drove just by watching the speedometer. As soon as the display disappeared, I reduced my speed. I think I was consciously riding, whether my speed was displayed or not, at about 20 km/h."

Figure 8 shows the speed of participant J. Her speedometer was hidden for 128 s. The lengths of time when her speedometer was hidden for the first two round trips and the last two round trips were almost the same. Also, her speed went up and down around the set speed. In particular, her speed fluctuated wildly in the last two round trips. In her interview, she said that she got anxious and impatient when the speedometer became hidden for the first time. She considered stopping because she thought the tablet or the system had broken. She said, "When the speedometer appeared again, I understood the system. I decreased my speed if I noticed the speedometer was hidden." Her speed changes in the last two round trips were to get used to the system. Therefore, it was possible that she was in a panic.

Common opinions of the other participants included: "Results were obtained that the pacemaker was pulled in the first two round trips" and "The second half of the experiment was affected because I got used to what was happening."

4.5 Analysis of Driving Behavior

In our nine-item questionnaire, eight participants answered "I felt anxious," and three participants answered "I didn't feel anxious." In addition, nine participants answered

"I wanted to slow down," and two participants answered "I didn't want to slow down." We compared these results with the driving behavior and personalities of the participants, which were analyzed using the Driving Style Questionnaire (DSQ) and Workload Sensitivity Questionnaire (WSQ) created by Ishibashi et al. [10].

The DSQ investigates driving styles such as attitudes, intention, and ideas during driving, based on the following eight categories:

1. Confident driver
2. Passive driver
3. Impatient driver
4. Scrupulous driver
5. Anticipatory driver
6. Car as a status symbol
7. Unstable driver
8. Anxious driver

The WSQ investigates driving burden, based on the following six categories:

1. Understanding the traffic situation: Involvement with and information about the surrounding traffic
2. Understanding the road conditions: The exterior environment (road, weather, and brightness)
3. Distractions: Considering persons and things inside the vehicle (including yourself)
4. Barriers: Things that prevent you from driving at the pace suited to you
5. Understanding the route: Vehicle position, information about the destination, and positional relationships
6. Awkwardness: The difficulty of manipulating the vehicle's controls

Figure 9 shows the results for the DSQ. Participants who answered "I felt anxious" in the questionnaire got high scores for "Scrupulous driver" and "Anxious driver." In addition, participants who answered "I didn't feel anxious" in the questionnaire got high scores for "Passive driver," "Impatient driver," and "Unstable driver." On the other hand, participants who answered "I wanted to slow down" got high scores for "unstable driver" and "anxious driver." In addition, participants who answered "I didn't want to slow down" in the questionnaire got a high score for "Passive driver" but extremely low scores for "Unstable driver" and "Anxious driver."

Figure 10 shows the results for the WSQ. Participants who answered "I felt anxious" in the questionnaire got a high score for "Understanding the traffic situation." In addition, participants who answered "I didn't feel anxious" in the questionnaire got high scores for "Understanding the route" and "Awkwardness." On the other hand, participants who answered "I wanted to slow down" got high scores for "Distractions." In addition, participants who answered "I didn't want to slow down" in the questionnaire got high scores for "Barriers," "Understanding the route," and "Awkwardness."

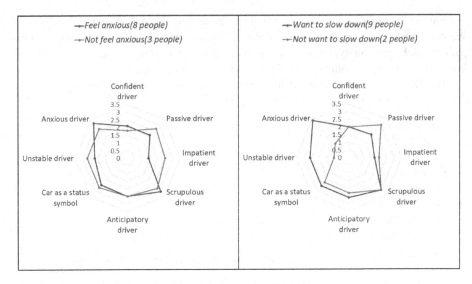

Fig. 9. The results of DSQ

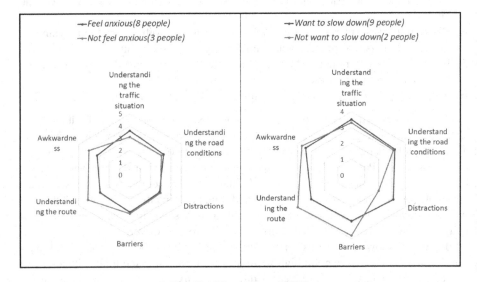

Fig. 10. The results of WSQ

4.6 Consideration

From the results of the questionnaire, the interview, and the analysis of driving behavior, we consider the two evaluation points: "Did you feel anxious when the speedometer was hidden?" and "Did you want to slow down when the speedometer was hidden?" From the questionnaire results, we gave both of these a high score.

From the interviews, we found that most participants felt anxious and wanted to reduce their speed. Thus, hiding the speedometer may be an effective method of preventing speeding.

From the questionnaire (Sect. 4.3), when not hidden, the speedometer was clearly visible. In addition, since the participants were made aware of speed before the experiment, that may have made them decide to speed. However, awareness of the display was low, so it must be improved. For example, it is necessary to get people who do not check the speedometer often to check it more frequently, so they notice it when it is hidden.

From the interview results in Sect. 4.4, we found that there is a possibility that the participant's awareness of a vehicle ahead or behind may be slightly affected by the experimental method. It may be necessary to amend the experimental method such as the running method and the presence or absence of vehicles ahead or behind. Moreover, since the participants got used to the system and some decided that they did not need to check the speedometer, we think that it is necessary to counter this.

Based on the DSQ, the effectiveness of the system was shown for participants who are anxious during driving. On the other hand, the results show that the system is not effective for participants who are passive. This may be because people with a passive nature do not drive at an excess speed more than necessary. Also, for unstable drivers, the effectiveness of the system may change depending on the person's personality.

Based on the WSQ, the effectiveness of the system was shown for participants who have an understanding of the traffic situation. On the other hand, the result shows that the system is not effective for participants who understand the route and are awkward (i.e., clumsy). This is probably because they are easily distracted by the vehicle's controls and find it difficult to grasp the driving conditions, which means they may not have the time to check the speedometer.

5 Conclusions

In this research, we proposed a system to create anxiety about speed by visually concealing a part of the speedometer, leading the driver to slow down naturally. To verify the effectiveness of this system, we ran tests using motorbikes with 13 participants. Overall, all 11 of the 13 participants who broke the speed limit reduced their speed when the speedometer was hidden. Interviews with the participants showed that most of them were anxious and wanted to reduce their speed.

Future tasks include exploring the pattern or hiding the speedometer, how the driver can be made aware of their speed when the speedometer is hidden and improving the experimental method.

References

1. National Police Agency (Japan): White Book on Police (2018). Statistical Data: https://www.npa.go.jp/hakusyo/h30/data.html. Accessed 16 Jan 2019
2. National Police Agency (Japan): Occurrence Situation on Traffic Accident (2017). https://www.npa.go.jp/publications/statistics/koutsuu/H29zennjiko.pdf. Accessed 16 Jan 2019
3. Ministry of Land, Infrastructure, Transport and Tourism: Safety Information on Automobiles: ASV (Advanced Safety Vehicle). http://www.mlit.go.jp/jidosha/anzen/01asv/index.html. Accessed 16 Jan 2019
4. Kawakami, H.: Do set up inconveniences (<special issue> invitation to shikakeology). J. Jpn. Soc. Artif. Intell. **28**(4), 615–620 (2013)
5. Cabinet Office: Agenda for Review Meeting on the Traffic Accident Countermeasure, 3rd edn, Japan (2009)
6. Han, A., et al.: The evaluation of the driving control result by highway sequence design 'optical dots' based on visual-perception information. Seisan Kenkyu **63**(2), 247–252 (2011)
7. Toui, H., Kitahara, I., Kameda, Y., Ohta, Y.: Virtual pattern for affecting the velocity recognition of driver. J. IEICE Trans. Inf. Syst. (Jpn. Ed.) **99**(1), 45–55 (2016)
8. Nozaki, K., Hiraoka, T., Takada, S., Kawakami, H.: Driver-assistance system to enhance driver's motivation for safe driving. In: Proceedings of the Annual Conference of JSAI, 27th Annual Conference, Session ID 1I4-OS-11b-6, vol. JSAI2013, p. 1I4OS11b6 (2013)
9. Takada, S., Hiraoka, T., Saito, A., Fujii, T., An, S.: Experimental study about effectiveness of expressway driving game based on gamenics theory on driver behavior. J. JSCE, Ser. D3 (Infrastruct. Plan. Manag.) **73**(5), 971–980 (2017)
10. Ishibashi, M., Okuwa, M., Akamatsu, M.: Development of driving style questionnaire and workload sensitivity questionnaire for drivers' characteristic identification. Proc. JSAE **55**(2), 9–12 (2002)

Tangible Map: Designing and Assessing Spatial Information Retrieval Through a Tactile Interface

Kimberly Leon, Will Walker, Yihyun Lim$^{(\boxtimes)}$, Scott Penman,
Sara Colombo, and Federico Casalegno

Design Lab, Massachusetts Institute of Technology,
Cambridge, MA 02139, USA
yihyun@mit.edu

Abstract. This paper addresses the design, development and evaluation of an interactive Tangible Map as a way to collect, display, and provide various information about a public space (in this case, a university campus) for easy retrieval and access. Through its ability to (a) display multiple sets of information upon tactile inputs, and (b) encourage interactions through 3D features and visual stimuli, the Tangible Map acts as a bridge between abstract campus data (e.g. classes hours and locations, faculty offices, shuttle hours) and the physical spaces the data refers to. The Map's effectiveness in easing access to information and its potential for encouraging data exploration, compared to existing mediums, is evaluated through a preliminary user study. Results suggest that the map's 3D tangible features and tactile interactions can facilitate information retrieval and can support the exploration of abstract data.

Keywords: Tangible interaction · Information design · User interface design · User experience · Tangible Map

1 Introduction

In today's data-driven world, the abundance of readily available information often goes well beyond users' awareness or understanding. Additionally, the number of viable user interface mediums for an information-based system has grown considerably. Information can be conveyed via a website, app, smart device, installation, or a number of other options. In order to ensure that the intended audience is easily able to access relevant information, the medium in which this information is presented plays a crucial role. The selected medium contributes greatly to the audience's satisfaction with the data they have retrieved, the audience's engagement with the platform used to retrieve the data, the amount of data exploration done, and the efficiency with which the audience obtains the sought out data.

A particular type of data that often needs to be retrieved by users is the one related to the space they live in or they interact with. Users can access different types of interfaces or mediums to retrieve information on their environments, such as private or public buildings, neighborhoods, or cities. Such spatial data can consist in specific

© Springer Nature Switzerland AG 2019
M. Kurosu (Ed.): HCII 2019, LNCS 11568, pp. 329–340, 2019.
https://doi.org/10.1007/978-3-030-22636-7_24

contents (e.g. events on campus, people working in a building, etc.), navigational information (i.e. directions to reach a specific point in space), or transport information, which merge navigational information with the means one can use to reach a specific point, and the time it will take (e.g. a shuttle route and schedule). Representing such data requires a process of abstraction and communication through means that can be textual, such as written or verbal directions, or visual, such as 2D maps.

Concerning space-related data interaction and retrieval, there has been an upsurge in natural language based assistants such as Siri, Google Assistant and Cortana. These systems are able to provide information for multiple tasks and domains including providing weather forecast [1] transportation information, and local and historic information for tourists [2, 3]. The conversational agents at the face of these systems are known as chatbots, and provide an efficient way for users to access a range of information in a friendly, natural way.

Additionally, technologies such as 3D printing and high-resolution displays have made the construction of tangible, 3D interfaces more accessible. However, even with technology's many advancements in the space of automated directions and 3D interfaces over the past few decades, the standard representation remains two-dimensional. This 2D representation uses abstract map symbols, which can make the map a challenge to parse due to the disconnect between flat displays and spatial information.

This paper addresses this issue through the development, implementation, and evaluation of an interactive user interface. This interface comprised an interactive, tactile, digital map display (Tangible Map) constructed with 3D printed physical reproductions of an urban context (the MIT college campus), situated on top of interactive touchscreens, and connected to a native iPad app. The Tangible Map was built with the goal of creating a bridge between abstract campus data and the physical spaces the data represents. The intention behind the map was to provide accessible way of navigating and retrieving information, by allowing a large set of information to be displayed at once, and by offering clarity of the spatial arrangements of the given information through its direct relationship to 3D extrusion of the 2D interactive map.

Figure 1 shows the Tangible Map in its final installation site, the MIT Atlas Center.

Fig. 1. Left: The Tangible Map in its final installation site, the MIT Atlas Center. Right: A building is illuminated and information is displayed on the dynamic touch screen as a user selects a building to explore.

In our preliminary user studies, detailed in Sect. 5, we focus on particular types of information - namely, classes, directions, events, and people collections within the MIT database. We evaluate our Tangible Map against a baseline of existing methods our participants currently use to obtain this information.

In summary, we make the following contributions in this paper:

- We describe the design and implementation of the Tangible Map, a unique tactile, digital representation of an urban setting with interactive touch-points.
- We suggest that information retrieval using the Tangible Map can be easier than using traditional media across a range of information categories, based on the results of a preliminary user study.

2 Background and Related Work

2.1 Tangible Interfaces

Technological advances in the recent past have made affordable hardware technologies that used to be available only to a select few. High-resolution touch screens and 3D printed objects are a few such technologies whose newly found attainability have fostered the development of several new interfaces and applications, including interfaces with tangible interactions. Tangible interaction elements have been shown to attract attention towards a display, provoke curiosity, and encourage engagement of nearby bystanders [4]. Tangible interaction elements have been implemented in the form of tabletops [5], objects atop digital displays [6], and 3D mapped tangible objects [7].

One example of a tangible interaction is Architales, an interactive story table, developed as an experiment in physical/digital co-design. Consisting of an interactive table for shared story engagement, the co-design principles behind this experiment proved successful for this interactive and tangible tabletop [5]. Another example is the T4 (transparent and translucent tangibles on tabletops) design, which enables direct touch of objects underneath, allowing for a stronger connection between the tangible and the screen, as well as more efficient usage of screen space [6]. Furthermore, to enhance user interaction of data, 3D printed maps have been created to act as tangible layers by adapting 2D map data into a printable overlay [7]. These 3D mapped tangible objects have been created by adapting 2-dimensional information into z-axis height or textures.

Our Tangible Map builds off these existing design concepts in order to realize an interactive tangible display that allows for more exploratory user.interactions and facilitate navigation of data gathered from multiple sources.

3   Concept and Design

3.1   Audience

On a day-to-day basis, a variety of individuals access the MIT Atlas Center in order to resolve a variety of different issues. In particular, visitors to the Atlas Center arrive in order to resolve logistical issues concerning their access to various MIT facilities or services. We sourced our participants from this audience, which comprises MIT faculty and students, as well as visitors to the campus otherwise unaffiliated with the university.

3.2   Design Goals

The Tangible Map was designed to encourage exploration and enhance ease of information retrieval, thanks to the variety of information that can be displayed concurrently and its spatial arrangement through the 3-dimensional map. Currently, information of events, classes, and other relevant facts about campus is largely distributed across various websites, physical maps and static public displays. Accessing this information requires users to individually search on its dedicated platforms, and is often a one-way process. Furthermore, location-specific information such as building number or address is difficult to remember and navigate with in real-life context of three-dimensional urban space.

This distribution of resources, and frequent difficulty of access, reflects the difficulty of use that sometimes accompanies smaller scale, 2-dimensional mapping methods. The primary aim of the Tangible Map is to mitigate these difficulties.

Due to the novelty of this medium, we have identified that most of the users of the Tangible Map will have never encountered a similar installation in the past. With this novelty factor, users are interested in being able to explore the Tangible Map and having an organic experience in understanding their surroundings. We wanted the Tangible Map to capitalize on users' inherent interest in engaging with novel, interactive 3D media in order to more easily deliver specific and relevant information. We also hoped this method of interaction would encourage further exploration of information about MIT campus that are otherwise unknown.

4   Implementation

The Tangible Map consists of a touch-sensitive display surface, 3D printed buildings atop this surface, and a connected tablet. Users can either select a building directly and interact with the information that then displays on the touch-sensitive display surface, or search the tablet interface for specific information. The display surface consists of two parts: a section hosting the Tangible Map's 3D printed buildings, and a section that is exposed. The second section forms the information panel for the Tangible Map. The information panel displays information about buildings that have been selected from the Tangible Map and search results that have been selected from the tablet application (Fig. 2).

Fig. 2. The Tangible Map consists of two parts; 3D printed buildings to entice users to touch and to provide visual reference, and an interactive tablet that further displays information about the building selected and vice versa.

4.1 Tangible Map Physical Layout

The Tangible Map's touch-sensitive display surface consists of two LCD displays overlaid with a single capacitive touch input layer. 3D printed campus buildings sit atop this touchscreen. Each building is fitted with a touchpoint containing dual 3 mm diameter aluminum rods connected to a 6 mm circular piece of aluminum foil. When touched, the rods trigger a change in capacitive charge that registers as a finger press on the capacitive touch input layer (Fig. 3).

Fig. 3. Photo of user interacting with Tangible Map via touch. Aluminum rods embedded in the 3D printed buildings allow for digital interaction through capacitive charge.

4.2 Tangible Map Software Layout

The software for the Tangible Map's screen is built using JavaScript for the interactive touch screen site, and Swift for the tablet application. The main website is a Node.js app with MongoDB as the datasource. An important aspect of the Tangible Map's UI design is the use of animations to direct user attention to the appropriate locations in the installation. Directing user attention is an important but difficult task [8, 9], and we use animations to indicate to the user when information is changing and where on the Tangible Map to find relevant information. Pulses of light sweep across the display in order to provide visual feedback immediately after the user selects a component on the screen and to redirect the user's line of vision to the portion of the screen displaying information about the selected component.

5   Preliminary User Study

In order to evaluate the accessibility of data of the designed Tangible Map vis-à-vis other visual interfaces, one preliminary user study was carried out. The study consisted of asking users to retrieve specific bits of information and compare the ease of the task in the designed system versus existing mediums (e.g. the campus website, or web search tools). The study aimed at providing us with preliminary, qualitative results about the effectiveness of the designed tangible interface as well as its potential in terms of generating more engaging user experiences fostering the exploration of the space in a novel way (Fig. 4).

Fig. 4. Participants were asked to retrieve information about campus (location, people, events) using existing medium (web search using mobile devices) as well as the new proposed medium of the Tangible Map.

5.1   Method

Setting. Alt et al. provides a set of guidelines for evaluating public displays [10]. They state that in HCI, controlled lab studies are often carried out, which remove many of the real-world factors present in a public display. For this reason, we conducted our user study in the Tangible Map's final installation site. The participants carried out the tasks asked of them while dozens of other MIT affiliates walked and talked around them, as would be the case if the participant were interacting with the Tangible Map outside of the user study. Performing this study in real-world conditions results in insights applicable to an authentic public display.

Participants. Eleven participants took part in this study. All but one of the participants were current MIT students ranging across departments and years of study, with the final participant being an MIT lab affiliate. This group is largely consistent with that of the projected user population of the medium. Users participated in the study on a voluntary basis.

Process. For each session, a moderator introduced the participant to the Tangible Map, giving a short description of its purpose. The subject was asked to sign a consent form to participate in the study. The moderator then asked the participant to complete the following tasks:

- find information about a building on campus;
- use the shuttle system;
- discover events on campus;
- visualize locations of public artworks/bike racks on campus;
- use the search feature (Fig. 5).

Fig. 5. The interface provides options to look for specific buildings, public art, and location of bike racks on campus. Users can also click on each building to access relevant information.

User study sessions consisted in completing each of the above-mentioned tasks both through the participant's currently favored form of information retrieval (e.g. the campus website) and the Tangible Map. After completing all the tasks, participants were asked to fill out a survey on their experience. The survey was divided into three sections. The first one focused on evaluating current interfaces for information retrieval. Participants used either a web search engine (e.g. Google) or the MIT campus map website (https://whereis.mit.edu) and people finder website (https://web.mit.edu/people.html) through their mobile phones to perform the tasks. This section of the survey was useful to assess the ease of information accessibility through the current digital interfaces, in order to evaluate our hypothesis about the need for tangible interface for more intuitive information retrieval. The second part of the questionnaire explored both the ease of information accessibility and the possibility of encouraging exploration of the space through the Tangible Map compared to current interfaces. Responses were collected through a 3-point Likert scale. The third part of the questionnaire consisted of three open-ended questions investigating advantages of the Tangible Map, the pleasantness of the interactive features and additional comments on the Tangible Map experience (Fig. 6).

Fig. 6. Participants were asked to find information about a building on campus and location of faculty offices using both search features and 3D printed buildings.

5.2 Results

Table 1 shows the results of the first section of the questionnaire. By using current interfaces, finding information about a specific building on campus (i.e. name and address of the building, research groups and faculty members working in the building) and finding relevant events on campus were evaluated as easy tasks by more than half of participants. Making use of the shuttle system was the least easy task to perform by users through current interfaces.

Table 1. Participants were asked to evaluate their current favored type of interface for information retrieval.

Question number	Statement	% Agree	% Undecided	% Disagree
1	It is simple to find information about a building on campus (with current interfaces)	54.55	18.18	27.27
2	I can easily make use of the shuttle system (with current interfaces)	27.27	36.36	36.36
3	I can easily discover relevant events on campus (with current interfaces)	54.55	18.18	27.27

In Sect. 2, we analyzed the user experience with the Tangible Map. The first three questions refer to qualities of the Tangible Map (i.e. how easy it is to retrieve information about a building, how easy and effective the search function is, and how easy it is to find artworks or bike racks on campus). For all these questions, we collected positive responses from the majority of users, with finding information about buildings being the easiest task (Table 2).

Table 2. Participants were asked to compare the Tangible Map vs. other media for effectiveness of information retrieval.

Question number	Statement	% Agree	% Undecided	% Disagree
1	It was simple to find information about a building on the Tangible Map	81.82	18.18	0.00
2	The search feature was simple and effective	63.64	36.36	0.00
3	It was easy to find and use the visualizations of public artwork/bike racks on campus	63.64	27.27	9.09
4	Using the Tangible Map, I can more easily find information about a building on campus	81.82	18.18	0.00
5	Using the Tangible Map, I can more easily make use of the shuttle system	45.45	45.45	9.09
6	Using the Tangible Map, I can more easily discover relevant events on campus	63.64	18.18	18.18
7	Visualizations of locations of public artworks/bike racks are useful for locating resources I might not have been aware of	72.73	18.18	9.09

Questions 4 and 5 specifically ask for a comparison between the Tangible Map and current interfaces. On all accounts, there is an increase in the ease with which participants can find information on buildings and shuttles when using the Tangible Map vs existing mediums.

Questions 6 and 7 investigate the ability of the map to encourage the exploration of the space. Again, most participants found it easier to discover relevant events on campus by interacting with the Tangible Map. Compared to existing interfaces, the map provides the user with building-specific information, which can be retrieved just by touching its 3D representation.

In the last section of the questionnaire, all participants mentioned the tactility of the display as the aspect they liked the most in the Tangible Map. Feedback on the Tangible Map interactive features was positive, and few participants expected to find further responsive features or additional data on the Tangible Map where they did not yet exist.

When participants were left to explore the Tangible Map without specific tasks to complete, they were more explorative and engaged with all touch-enabled parts of the 3D map. Participants touched buildings they were not familiar with in order to learn basic information such as the building's name, and also touched buildings they were very familiar with (i.e. their dorms, the main buildings for their departments) in order to verify information they already knew.

6 Discussion

Results of our preliminary study show that in our area of investigation, the Tangible Map both facilitates information retrieval through ease of access and invites users to explore other information that is not commonly accessed.

Concerning the ease of access to information, it is likely that both the scale and the 3-dimensionality of the Tangible Map played roles in facilitating retrieval. Participants repeatedly reported an increase in ease using the Tangible Map over other mediums, whether it was to retrieve information about a particular building on campus, to acquire real-time data about the MIT shuttle system, or to gather information regarding relevant events on campus.

The Tangible Map's large scale and 3-dimensionality more closely captures and represents users' understanding of real-world conditions. Such a physical map likely leads to faster comprehension of spatial distances, facilitating fast and effortless understanding of buildings location, routes, and travel times across campus, thus easing tasks such as making use of the shuttle system.

Furthermore, since all of the users were affiliated with the university, each came to the map with some form of existing knowledge about the campus' layout; it is likely that the map built upon this existing knowledge to facilitate fast and effortless memory retrieval about reference points on campus. The fact that the Tangible Map consists of 3D-printed buildings, complete with identifying information such as facade detailing, made the buildings more recognizable to users. Where 2D screen-based interfaces are only able to represent building shapes and outlines (and perhaps rough changes in height or massing), a 3D map captures detail much more immediately relevant to typical users. Thus, when users reported an increased ease in building information retrieval, this likely arose from the immediate ability to recognize specific buildings, rather than having to remember their name or building number (as is typically required in alternative search media).

In terms of explorative potential, both the 3-dimensionality and the tactility of the interface, as well as the physicality of the Tangible Map play a significant role. The mere presence of the Tangible Map in the space acts as a trigger for the exploration of campus-related information, by generating curiosity and encouraging interactions. Designed as an interactive table, instead of a vertical display wall, the Tangible Map acts as a place to gather around. These features invite users to walk around and explore the Tangible Map itself, rather than simply use it as a representative tool for information retrieval. Where typical search media have been relegated to objective information retrieval, the Tangible Map invites users to explore and play with the interface in novel ways. Users are not required to approach with any intention of gaining explicit pieces of information; they are free to explore the map out of curiosity, because of its novelty and potential for fun. Participants responded favorably to the existing interactive tangible components of the map, and a few explored the map extensively that they began to expect responsive features where they did not exist, such as on facility buildings that did not have any specific information to display. Novelty and tactility caused users to linger, highly increasing the likelihood that they might discover new and unforeseen information about the space.

Finally, the Tangible Map provided a medium comfortably in between full-scale, real-world conditions and compressed, inaccessible data. Where users might be hesitant to explore further-field campus amenities, due to the time and effort required, and might neglect to investigate databases of information, due to the lack of an engaging interface, the Tangible Map provides an intermediate form of exploration that augments users' ability to easily retrieve interesting information, without requiring too much effort.

The study is qualitative in nature and was aimed at gathering preliminary data about the users' response to the use of tangible interfaces for retrieving spatial information. The main limitations of the research consist in the restricted number of subjects involved in the tests, as well as the limited amount of tasks evaluated. Further analyses will benefit from the evaluation of a larger set of information to display and retrieve.

7 Conclusion

From our specific study, we have shown that large-scale, 3-dimensional, interactive maps facilitate both information retrieval and explorative potential in an urban context. These types of maps can prove especially useful in contexts similar to the MIT campus, where competing sources and scales of information can render traditional mapping methods difficult to use. The Tangible Map allows users to more easily retrieve building-specific information (likely due to building recognition of 3D building forms), understand the shuttle system (likely due to enhance understanding of shuttle times and walking distances), and discover relevant events on campus (likely due to increased exploration of farther-field campus buildings).

Having established that the Tangible Map can serve both an information-retrieval and an exploratory purpose, there are many features that can possibly be added to extend functionality. It is especially exciting to consider how additional features can enhance user engagement, such as the addition of more visual information, alternative forms of touchpoints, or varying forms of animations. Sourcing information from additional databases can enhance the real-time usefulness of the map - from displaying open conference rooms to indicating information about conferences happening on campus, as well as integrating real-time social media data such as Twitter discussion feeds on current events. Overlay of data from various timelines and refreshed user generated contents can aid in keeping the Tangible Map up-to-date and engaging to users. Such additional data will be added to subsequent versions of the Tangible Map, and will be part of more extensive user studies.

References

1. Maragoudakis, M., Thanopoulos, A., Fakotakis, N.: MeteoBayes: effective plan recognition in a weather dialogue system. IEEE Intell. Syst. 22(1), 67–77 (2007). https://doi.org/10.1109/mis.2007.14
2. Kim, S., Banchs, R.E.: R-cube: a dialogue agent for restaurant recommendation and reservation. In: 2014 Asia-Pacific Signal and Information Processing Association Annual Summit and Conference (APSIPA). IEEE (2014). https://doi.org/10.1109/apsipa.2014.7041732

3. Niculescu, A.I., et al.: SARA: Singapore's automated responsive assistant, a multimodal dialogue system for touristic information. In: Awan, I., Younas, M., Franch, X., Quer, C. (eds.) MobiWIS 2014. LNCS, vol. 8640, pp. 153–164. Springer, Cham (2014). https://doi.org/10.1007/978-3-319-10359-4_13

4. Claes, S., Moere, A.V.: The role of tangible interaction in exploring information on public visualization displays. In: Proceedings of the 4th International Symposium on Pervasive Displays - PerDis 2015. ACM Press (2015). https://doi.org/10.1145/2757710.2757733

5. Mazalek, A., Winegarden, C., Al-Haddad, Robinson, S.J., Wu, C.-S.: Architales: physical/digital co-design of an interactive story table. In: Proceedings of the 3rd International Conference on Tangible and Embedded Interaction (TEI 2009), pp. 241–248. ACM, New York (2009). https://doi.org/10.1145/1517664.1517716

6. Büschel, W., Kister, U., Frisch, M., Dachselt, R.: T4 - transparent and translucent tangibles on tabletops. In: Proceedings of the 2014 International Working Conference on Advanced Visual Interfaces (AVI 2014), pp. 81–88. ACM, New York (2014). https://doi.org/10.1145/2598153.2598179

7. Taylor, B., Dey, A., Siewiorek, D., Smailagic, A.: Customizable 3D printed tactile maps as interactive overlays. In: Proceedings of the 18th International ACM SIGACCESS Conference on Computers and Accessibility - ASSETS 2016. ACM Press (2016). https://doi.org/10.1145/2982142.2982167

8. Coenen, J., Wouters, N., Moere, A.V.: Synchronized wayfinding on multiple consecutively situated public displays. In: Proceedings of the 5th ACM International Symposium on Pervasive Displays (PerDis 2016), pp. 182–196. ACM, New York (2016). https://doi.org/10.1145/2914920.2929906

9. Hespanhol, L., Tomitsch, M., Grace, K., Collins, A., Kay, J.: Investigating intuitiveness and effectiveness of gestures for free spatial interaction with large displays. In: Proceedings of the 2012 International Symposium on Pervasive Displays (PerDis 2012), Article ID 6, 6 p. ACM, New York (2012). https://doi.org/10.1145/2307798.2307804

10. Alt, F., Schneegaß, S., Schmidt, A., Müller, J., Memarovic, N.: How to evaluate public displays. In: Proceedings of the 2012 International Symposium on Pervasive Displays (PerDis 2012), Article ID 17, 6 p. ACM, New York (2012)

Directing a Target Person Among Multiple Users Using the Motion Effects of an Image-Based Avatar

Tsubasa Miyauchi[(✉)], Masashi Nishiyama, and Yoshio Iwai

Graduate School of Engineering, Tottori University,
101 Minami 4-chome, Koyama-cho, Tottori 680-8550, Japan
miyauti.tsubasa51@gmail.com

Abstract. We investigate whether an image-based avatar with motion can smoothly direct a target person who has requested guidance. Existing methods that use an avatar generally assume a one-to-one interaction with the user and did not fully consider how the avatar should direct a target person, which is important in interactions with multiple users. When the target person feels that the image-based avatar is facing them and feels that the avatar is directing them, the person judges that the requested guidance has been given. When a nontarget person feels that the image-based avatar is not facing them and also feels that the avatar is not directed towards them, the nontarget person then judges that the requested guidance has not come to them. To direct the target person smoothly, the action-type motion of the image-based avatar and the rotational motion of the video sequence itself relative to the display are important. We performed a subjective assessment of how the target person and the nontarget person feel about the direction by comparing the case where motions were added with the case where motions were not added. The results show that the image-based avatar with the action-type and rotation-type motions is effective for the target person but is not effective for the nontarget person.

Keywords: Image-based avatar · Motion · Direction · Target person · Nontarget person

1 Introduction

We have developed an image-based avatar system [1] that interacts naturally with users. Several image-based avatar systems have been produced over the last decade [2,3]. Specifically, we considered a navigation system that guides a user and consists of an avatar shown on a stationary display. The avatar serves as an alternative to a real guide in an information center located in a public space, e.g., at an airport or in a bus/rail station.

Before describing this system, we consider an actual navigation situation involving people in an information center, where a real guide interacts with

© Springer Nature Switzerland AG 2019
M. Kurosu (Ed.): HCII 2019, LNCS 11568, pp. 341–352, 2019.
https://doi.org/10.1007/978-3-030-22636-7_25

Fig. 1. Navigation situation.

the users waiting around him/her. Figure 1 shows an example of this type of situation. Based on our knowledge of cognitive science [4], the people can be categorized into the following three roles: a guide that provides directions, a participant that receives these directions, and a side participant who is waiting to receive directions from the guide. A side participant becomes a participant when they are given directions by the guide.

Here, we consider how the avatar gives information to a single side participant when multiple side participants are present and waiting to begin interaction with the avatar. First, multiple side participants are waiting around the avatar for directions, as illustrated in Fig. 2(a). In order to provide clear separation of the roles of the multiple side participants, we also newly define the following roles: a target person who is receiving directions and a nontarget person who is not receiving directions, as illustrated in Fig. 2(b). When a target person feels that they are being given directions by the avatar, this person changes from a side participant into a participant, as illustrated in Fig. 2(c). The nontarget person remains in their role as a side participant as long as they do not feel that they are being directed by the avatar. It is important that the avatar only directs the target person in the presence of the nontarget person.

We now discuss how to design a method such that the avatar only directs the target person, even when a nontarget person is present. Existing methods [5–9] have used special displays with embedded motion mechanisms. However, we cannot use this method easily in a stationary display. Caridakis et al. [10] used a stationary display with video sequences that included motion effects when the avatar spoke to the user. We believe that the motion effects provide an important cue when the avatar and the user interact via a stationary display. Therefore, we focused on the use of motion effects in the video sequences for the image-based avatar. However, this method does not sufficiently consider the problem of how to direct a target person when in the presence of a nontarget person.

In this paper, we investigate the use of motion effects in an image-based avatar to enable this avatar to give directions smoothly to a target person in the presence of another nontarget person. To compare methods that add motions to

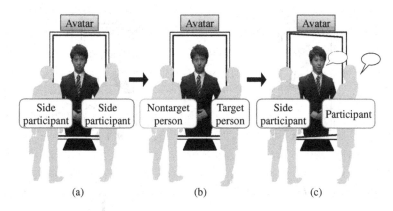

Fig. 2. User role transitions in the proposed navigation system.

the image-based avatar with a method without movement of the image-based avatar, we evaluated the following two hypotheses:

H1: A target person feels that they are facing the image-based avatar. The target person then feels that they are being given directions by the image-based avatar.

H2: A nontarget person does not feel that they are facing the image-based avatar. The nontarget person thus does not feel that they are being given directions by the image-based avatar.

We evaluated the effects of an action-type motion (where the face and body of the avatar move to face the target person) and a rotational motion (where the display rotates to face the target person).

2 Navigation Situation

We assume a situation in which the side participants stand on the right and left sides of the participant in the information center. Figure 3 shows the flow that occurs in this situation. At t_1, a participant is guided by an image-based avatar. At t_2, a side participant who wants to use the image-based avatar arrives the information center and stands in an empty space at the side of the participant. At t_3, another side participant arrives at the information center and stands on the empty side opposite the first side participant. At t_4, the participant leaves the information center after receiving the image-based avatar's guidance. At this point, the side participants stand on the right and left sides of the position that had been occupied by the participant. To direct the target person only, we add motion effects to the image-based avatar in this situation.

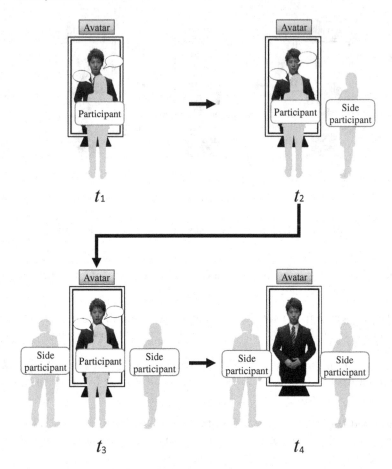

Fig. 3. Flow of the situation that we consider in this paper.

3   Motion Effects

3.1   Overview

To direct a target person only, we must consider what motion must be added to the image-based avatar. Because the image-based avatar resembles the appearance of a person, the image-based avatar is then expected to interact like a person. However, the image-based avatar is also expected to produce an interaction like that between a person and a machine because the image-based avatar is displayed on a display. We therefore added a guide motion and a rotating display to the image-based avatar. We describe the details of each motion below.

First, we explain how a guide moves to direct a target person only. A guide talks to a target person after facing that target person. It is important that the guide faces the target person. Figure 4 shows the way in which a guide moves to direct the target person only. The target person feels that they are facing a guide

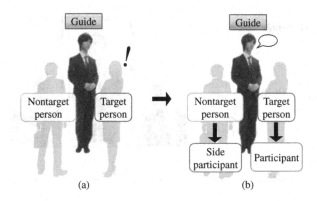

Fig. 4. How the guide moves to direct the target person only.

because that guide is facing them (Fig. 4(a)). Furthermore, the target person feels that they are being given directions because that guide is talking to them (Fig. 4(b)). In contrast, the nontarget person does not feel that they are facing the guide because that guide is facing the target person (Fig. 4(a)). Furthermore, the nontarget person does not feel that they are being given directions by that guide because the guide is talking to the target person (Fig. 4(b)). There are motions in the face, the body and the eyes in the case where the guide faces the target person.

Below, we consider addition of the motions of a guide to the image-based avatar. When using a video sequence for an image-based avatar, we must consider the Mona Lisa effect [11,12], which occurs whenever users see an avatar that is displayed on a flat panel. This effect causes the users to feel that an avatar who is facing the camera is actually gazing directly at them. If the avatar faces the camera, then both the target person and the nontarget person will feel that they are facing the avatar simultaneously. To alleviate the Mona Lisa effect, our method uses the fact that the avatar rotates both its face and its body while gazing at the camera. When an image-based avatar talks to a target person after

Fig. 5. Angle parameter θ_b for an action-type motion.

Fig. 6. Angle parameter θ_f for a rotational motion

rotating its face and body, the target person then feels that they are being given directions by the image-based avatar.

Next, we explain how to move a rotating display to direct a target person only. The display rotates towards the target person. It is important that the rotating display faces the target person. In this paper, we represent the physical frame of the rotating display in the video sequence of the image-based avatar. We can change the appearance of the region of the frame in which the avatar is located using projective transformation of the video sequence. As a result, the target person feels that they are facing an image-based avatar. When the image-based avatar talks to a target person after the projective transformation, the target person then feels that they are being given directions by the image-based avatar.

3.2   Action-Type Motion

Action-type motion is used to describe the scenario where the image-based avatar has a guiding motion added to the video sequence. In this case, the image-based avatar rotates its face and body while its gaze remains fixed towards the camera. Note that the image-based avatar rotates its face and body in conjunction because rotation of its face and body individually would occur only rarely in the information center. Figure 5 shows the angle parameter θ_b for an action-type motion. θ_b is the angle of the rotating body. θ_b sets the front direction to 0°. When the target person is standing on the right side of the avatar, θ_b has a positive value. When the target person is standing on the left side of the avatar, θ_b has a negative value.

3.3   Rotational Motion

Rotational motion is used to describe the situation where the motion of a rotating display is added to the image-based avatar in the video sequence. Changes in the appearance of the subject region in the frame and the frame itself are expressed by projective transformation. Figure 6 shows the angle parameter θ_f of the rotational motion. θ_f is the angle of the rotating frame. θ_f sets the front direction to $0°$. When the target person is standing on the right side of the avatar, θ_f has a positive value. When the target person is standing on the left side of the avatar, θ_f has a negative value.

3.4 Combination of an Action-Type Motion with a Rotational Motion

Next, we need to consider combination of an action-type motion with a rotational motion. A rotational motion is added to an image-based avatar during an action-type motion. This combination of the action-type motion and the rotational motion has an angle parameter composed of θ_b' and θ_f'. We set $\theta_b' = \theta_b/2$ and $\theta_f' = \theta_f/2$.

4 Subjective Assessment

4.1 Experimental Conditions

We performed a subjective assessment to investigate the hypotheses described in Sect. 1. In addition, we performed another subjective assessment to investigate the impression that is made by the image-based avatar. Twenty subjects (17 males and 3 females, with an average age of 22.2 ± 1.1 years) participated in this assessment. We compared the following four motion methods for the image-based avatar:

M1: No motion effects
M2: Action-type motion
M3: Rotational motion
M4: Both motion types

Figure 7 shows examples of these methods.

The 20 subjects were split randomly into pairs to view a video sequence of an image-based avatar for each method. One subject was assigned the role of the target person and the other subject was assigned the nontarget person role. The two subjects then stood to the side of the display. Figure 4 shows the standing positions of the two subjects. After viewing the video sequence, the subjects then answered the following questions:

Q1: Did you feel that you faced an image-based avatar?
Q2: Did you feel that you were given directions by an image-based avatar?
Q3: Did you feel that you interacted smoothly with the image-based avatar?
Q4: Did you feel that the image-based avatar interacted politely with you?
Q5: Did you feel that the image-based avatar interacted nicely with you?

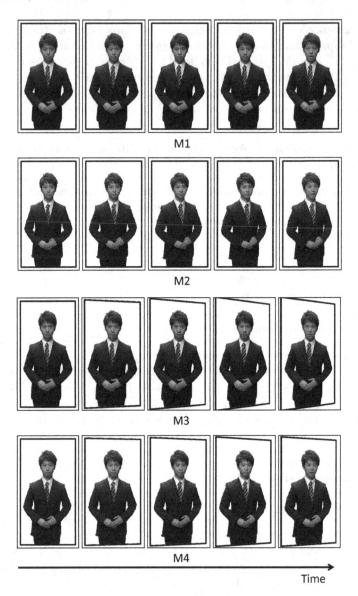

Fig. 7. Image-based avatars M1 to M4 with and without motion effects for the subjective assessment.

Each subject provided a rated score using four response levels (-1.5: disagreeable; -0.5: slightly disagreeable; 0.5: fairly agreeable; 1.5: agreeable) for each question. We also asked the reverse questions to Q1 to Q4. We set $\theta_b = 15[\deg]$ and $\theta_f = 15[\deg]$. We used two-way analysis of variance (ANOVA) and the Wilcoxon signed-rank test to evaluate the test results.

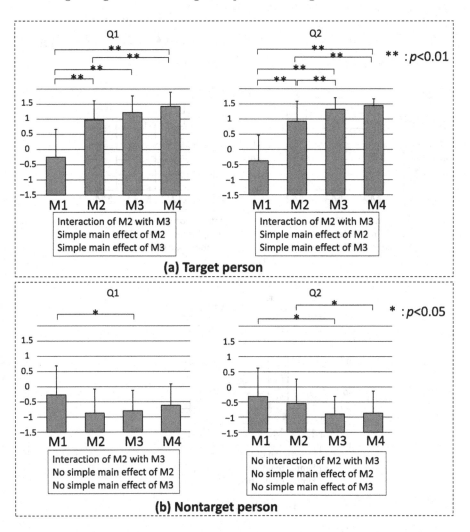

Fig. 8. Results of subjective assessments of Q1 and Q2.

4.2   Results of Subjective Assessment

Figure 8(a) shows the subjective scores for Q1 and Q2 for the target persons. The high subjective scores indicate agreement among the target persons. Additionally, there are significant differences among M1 and the other three methods. Therefore, we can claim that H1, as described in Sect. 1, is valid under the condition that motion effects were used. Figure 8(b) shows the subjective scores for Q1 and Q2 for the nontarget persons. The low subjective scores also indicate agreement among the nontarget persons. There were no significant differences among M1 and the other three methods. Therefore, we cannot claim that H2, as described in Sect. 1, was valid under the condition that motion effects are used.

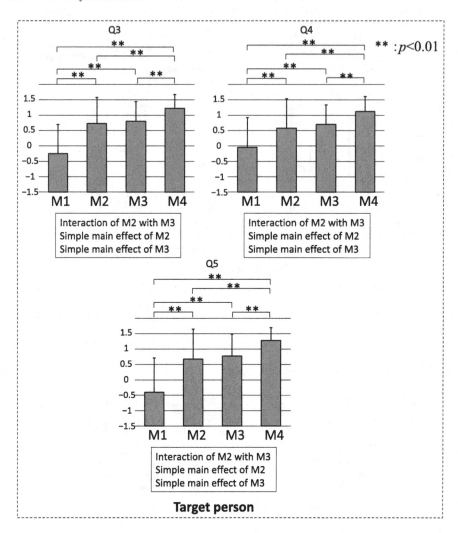

Fig. 9. Results of subjective assessments of Q3 to Q5 for the target persons.

Figure 9 shows the subjective scores for Q3 to Q5 for the target persons. The high subjective scores again indicate agreement among the target persons. Additionally, there are significant differences among M1 and the other three methods. Therefore, we can claim that the image-based avatar made a good impression under the conditions where motion effects were used. Figure 10 shows the subjective scores for Q3 and Q5 for the nontarget persons. The low subjective scores also indicate agreement among the nontarget persons. There were no significant differences in this case among M1 and the other three methods. Therefore, we cannot claim that the image-based avatar made a good impression under the conditions where motion effects were used.

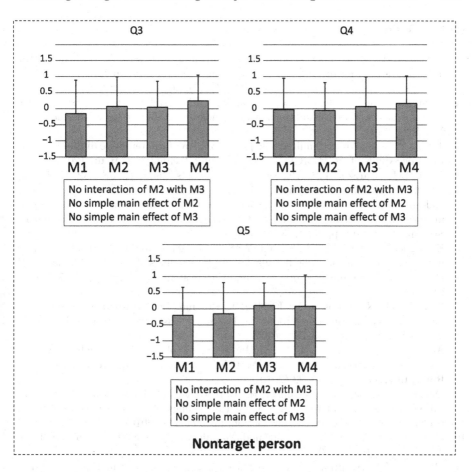

Fig. 10. Results of subjective assessments of Q3 to Q5 for the nontarget persons.

5 Conclusions

We have proposed a method to ensure that an image-based avatar only directs a specific target person. We added an action effect and a rotation effect to an image-based avatar. We then performed a subjective assessment to compare the methods that add the effects to the image-based avatar with a method without movement in the image-based avatar. The results of a subjective assessment showed that a target person feels that they are being given directions by the image-based avatar when the motion effects are used. In addition, the image-based avatar also made a good impression on the target person during the use of motion effects. However, the results of the subjective assessment did not show that the nontarget person did not feel that they were being given directions by the image-based avatar. In future work, we will consider motion effects in another situation in an information center, and we will also compare motion effects and special displays.

References

1. Miyauchi, T., Ono, A., Yoshimura, H., Nishiyama, M., Iwai, Y.: Embedding the awareness state and response state in an image-based avatar to start natural user interaction. IEICE Trans. Inf. Syst. **E100-D**(12), 3045–3049 (2017)
2. Artstein, R., et al.: Time-offset interaction with a Holocaust survivor. In: Proceedings of the 19th International Conference on Intelligent User Interfaces, pp. 163–168 (2014)
3. Jones, A., et al.: An automultiscopic projector array for interactive digital humans. In: Proceedings of ACM SIGGRAPH Emerging Technologies, p. 6:1 (2015)
4. Clark, H.H., Carlson, T.B.: Hearers and speech acts. Language **58**, 332–373 (1982)
5. Otsuki, M., Kawano, T., Maruyama, K., Kuzuoka, H., Suzuki, Y.: ThirdEye: simple add-on display to represent remote participant's gaze direction in video communication. In: Proceedings of the CHI Conference on Human Factors in Computing Systems, CHI 2017, pp. 5307–5312 (2017)
6. Kawaguchi, I., Kuzuoka, H., Suzuki, Y.: Study on gaze direction perception of face image displayed on rotatable flat display. In: Proceedings of the 33rd Annual ACM Conference on Human Factors in Computing Systems, CHI 2015, pp. 1729–1737 (2015)
7. Yankelovich, N., Simpson, N., Kaplan, J., Provino, J.: Porta-person: telepresence for the connected conference room. In: Extended Abstracts on Human Factors in Computing Systems, CHI 2007 (2007)
8. Adalgeirsson, S.O., Breazeal, C.: MeBot: a robotic platform for socially embodied presence. In: Proceedings of 5th ACM/IEEE International Conference on Human-Robot Interaction, pp. 15–22 (2010)
9. Onishi, Y., Tanaka, K., Nakanishi, H.: Embodiment of video-mediated communication enhances social telepresence. In: Proceedings of the Fourth International Conference on Human Agent Interaction, pp. 171–178 (2016)
10. Caridakis, G.: Virtual agent multimodal mimicry of humans. Lang. Resour. Eval. **41**(3–4), 367–388 (2007)
11. Masame, K.: Perception of where a person is looking: overestimation and understimation of gaze direction. Tohoku Psychologica Folia **49**, 33–41 (1990)
12. Kendon, A.: Some functions of gaze-direction in social interaction. Acta Psychologica **26**, 22–63 (1967)

Analyzing Social Impact Evaluation Tools Applied to Design Thinking: A Proposal for Improving User Experience in Urban Spaces Through Social Innovation

Valentina Volpi[(✉)], Antonio Opromolla, and Carlo Maria Medaglia

Link Campus University, Via del Casale di San Pio V 44, 00165 Rome, Italy
{v.volpi,a.opromolla,c.medaglia}@unilink.it

Abstract. The digital and social transformation we are facing affects also the urban spaces by redirecting the attention and the efforts of different stakeholders towards a renewed interest for the human aspect of the city and for behaviors more aware of their possible impacts at a systemic level on society and environment. The human-centered design approach and the design thinking provide specific tools and methodologies which allow to consider the 'human' point of view during the different stages of the design process. However, some limitations arise: in details, most of these methodologies do not take into adequate consideration the social, environmental and economic impact of the designed solutions. For this reason, the research on design should identify the most suitable tools for measuring and assessing the impact of the project during and after its implementation, in order to find solutions really desirable from the social point of view, feasible from the organizational and technical perspective and economically viable. This contribution intends to discuss these issues by suggesting an increasing use of social impact evaluation tools in the design frameworks for urban environment.

Keywords: Social impact · Human-centered design · Design thinking · Urban spaces · Social innovation

1 Introduction

Cities have been transforming by the integration in the urban spaces of digital technologies supporting information and communication exchanges. Of course, this transformation is not only technological, but also social, as the creation of blended spaces of interaction fosters new social uses and behaviors. In details, the expression 'blended spaces' has been provided by Benyon [1] who uses it to indicate the urban spaces in which digital and physical elements are integrated one with each other. This blend increases the level of complexity in the spaces and modifies the urban experience of people. In this regard, one of the most challenging topics emerging in academic and non-academic research is the 'urban interaction design', an expression which indicates a complex research area focusing on three elements, i.e. urban spaces, people and technologies, whose main objective is investigating how people can interact in a more

© Springer Nature Switzerland AG 2019
M. Kurosu (Ed.): HCII 2019, LNCS 11568, pp. 353–361, 2019.
https://doi.org/10.1007/978-3-030-22636-7_26

efficient and effective way in and with an urban environment more and more 'hybrid', by focusing on people and their needs [2].

Indeed, any innovative intervention in urban spaces should consider the mutual process occurring between people and technology in socio-technical distributed systems of interaction [3]. In this sense, in order to make cities more livable, the improvement of the user experience became a key element in all the sectors and fields of action regarding the city.

At the same time, the widespread of sharing approaches in private and public life, have been boosted a renewed interest towards the creation and the exploitation of shared public spaces in everyday life for activities that enhance the common good [4].

These two processes are strictly intertwined and lead to the adoption of approaches focusing on the human aspect and the sustainability of the smart city, in our vision a model of city that use smartness, both computer-based and human, to seize opportunities and to effectively and efficiently adapt itself to the needs and contingencies that arise. That means putting together social, cultural, economic, environmental, and technological issues. In effect, in our network society the resolution of problems, but also the management of many daily activities, depends on complexity and on a wider ecosystem of relations and interactions. In this context, the collaboration of all the involved stakeholders, up to the whole society, is needed. The social aspect, increasingly supported by the widespread of new information and communication technologies, especially social networking and mobile technologies and data mining, has been gaining importance in fostering innovation processes and in tackling emerging global challenges. Therefore the 'social innovation' term has been assuming a wide range of conceptual variants and its use has been stressed everywhere. Indeed, social innovation can be seen as 'a potentially powerful force for positive change and a new way of responding to the challenges confronting us' [5]. According to some of the most popular and convincing definitions, social innovation concerns new ideas (products, services and models) created with the intention of addressing a social need in a positive or beneficial way and that are social in their means and in their ends, as they engage and mobilize beneficiaries and enhance society's capacity to act [6–8].

So, along with the improvement of the personal user experience, another key element for making cities more livable places is the definition of shared goals towards which cities and communities must actively steer, in order to assure equal and accessible-by-everyone benefits for society. The major intervention in this direction are the Sustainable Development Goals (SDGs) set by the United Nations General Assembly in 2015 [9]. These goals set global challenges, imposing to reflect on the impact that the solutions we design have on a social level and to define clear responsibilities towards the society and the environment. Cities are included among the key points on which to intervene. In detail, the 11th goals concern sustainable cities and communities and around one third of SDGs indicators have an urban component. Although many interventions aiming at adequately fulfilling these ambitious objectives have been already implemented, it is a relatively new and open field for research and experimentation, especially regarding the identification of effective and sustainable tools for intervention.

So, this paper focuses on these two elements: on the one side, the focus on human perspective in urban spaces; on the other side, the need of identifying shared objectives towards cities which consider social, economic and environmental variables. In detail, starting from the identification of the characteristics of the human-centered design and design thinking approaches in urban space, it intends to study the existing connections and the gaps between the social impact evaluation tools and models and the design thinking ones, suggesting that they should be better integrated and organized in the design of user experience in urban spaces from a social innovation perspective.

2 Human-Centered Design Applied to Digital and Social Transformation of Urban Spaces

The starting point of this process is the identification of the main characteristics of the human-centered design approach. Generally, it is based on the active involvement of people we are designing for in creating different kinds of (digital and non-digital) solutions: this action allows not only to consider final users as partners of the design activities, by involving them in participatory processes, but also to find solutions which integrate the emotional and human point of view. These elements increasingly characterize also the design of services and solutions for the urban environment. The aim is to create a more direct relation between citizens and Institutions, in order to improve the mutual trust and increase responsibilities.

According to that, Manzini [10] focuses on the importance to consider design for urban environment not as a prerogative of 'expert' designers, but as a process more and more open to 'non-expert' people, who can carry out design activities by using their basic and common human skills and abilities. In particular, he gives importance to take into account the point of view of the different stakeholders as a fundamental driver for the identification of effective solutions to the complex problems which characterize the cities.

In fact, the latter can be considered as complex systems, since they consist in a set of different and unpredictable elements, characterized by uncertain links that are not easily recognizable. In this sense, only the application of a human-centered approach, as described above, gives the possibility to consider the different possible facets of a problem and designing solutions which include all the different desires and needs. In effect, an organizational model based on collaboration and communication among different disciplines allows to establish a formative and educational paradigm which, by reducing risks and conflicts, let emerge the best solution, which is not only desirable from the social point of view, but also feasible from the organizational and technical perspective and viable from the economic point of view [11].

One of the most know approaches of the human-centered design is the design thinking [12]. Its peculiarity is that it allows the application of different tools which foster creativity and the continuous reformulation of the problem space (a fundamental element which allows to deal with the complexity of the urban environment), creating an increasing value for people. Moreover, the nature of this approach follows a non-linear path for problem-solving and for the creation of shared value. In fact, if the design thinking consists of the six different stages (listed below), they need to be considered following an iterative path, which requires to continuously return to the same stages in order to evaluate that needs and requirements are opportunely met.

Following, a short description of the six stages of the design thinking. The focus of this section is not providing an exhaustive description of tools and methodologies used in the single stage, but only identifying the general elements which characterize the mentioned approach.

1. Empathize. It consists in identifying behaviors, general approaches, physical and emotional needs of people we are designing for in the specific context in which they live. The value of this stage is to identify non-obvious findings, which allow to define really innovative solution. For this reason, it is important that people are not only observed but also listen and actively engaged.
2. Define. It consists in extracting useful information from the data collected in the previous stage. The output is the identification of the specific problem to face. Different tools and techniques are used in this stage to better focus the problem and to continuously question what has been identified, in order to meet the most significant need.
3. Ideate. It focuses on the idea generation. Creativity and imagination are the basic elements to use in this stage. The general approach is that in the ideation phase no idea should be discarded and people should be left free to share ideas; in fact, the best idea will probably emerge from an optimization of the single shared contributions.
4. Prototype. It consists in building prototypes of the solution, in order to evaluate the efficiency and effectiveness of the interaction, before the implementation. Prototype is a term that can be applied both to digital solution and non-digital ones: its aim is to effectively communicate the project.
5. Test. During this stage specific feedbacks from people who will use the solution will be collected, by encouraging them to interact with the built prototype.
6. Implementation. It consists in the specific development of the designed, realized and tested solution.

During their work experience, the authors of this contribution have carried out many workshops, organized and conducted following the design thinking approach. Most of these workshops have focused on the design for urban environment. Generally, they have been organized considering the following main elements:

1. The focus is around a specific topic. People are encouraged to focus on specific scenarios which describe the main elements which characterize the urban area of interest. This provides participants the possibility to have a description of the urban context to reflect on. In fact, starting from this point, the participants to the workshop are involved in brainstorming and in defining a more specific issue to face;
2. The identification of one persona (or more than one) is realized. Generally, we ask participants to identify the categories of people who live in the specific urban area, by identifying their most common habits, needs, desires and difficulties;
3. The participants are given cards, each of which representing some of the technologies used in the urban environment. These cards represent a useful tool, since it encourages also non-expert participants in defining how specific technologies work. A very important element is that participants are led to think the represented technologies not as proper solutions, but only as tools that need to be combined one

with each other in order to imagine more complex and exhaustive services. To do that, participants are generally asked to identify some moments of interaction of target people with the imagined service, in order to imagine the technological solution from the human point of view;

4. The identification of a solution map, which represents the main elements of a concept solution (in particular the objective to reach and the main features of the solution).

The elements above described consist in the main stages of a co-design process aiming to the design of a specific solution for the urban environment, according to the general approach followed by the authors of this contribution. The next steps concern the detailed design of the solution, its implementation and the test with the potential final users, following an iterative approach.

However, without emphasizing these stages, for the aims of this paper, it is fundamental to focus on the fact that, for better highlighting the purpose of making changes in society, it might be useful to strengthen tools and models for evaluating the social impact generated by the designed solutions, already from the beginning of the design cycle. Next section will focus on the tools for social impact evaluation currently available for creating a link with the design thinking methodologies.

3   Social Impact Evaluation Tools and Design Thinking

Nowadays, the chain of events that can be summarized with the expression of 'digital and social transformation' have been causing overflowing changes in all sectors of human life. In front of this epochal shift, the social aspect of each human activity has been arising as a crucial parameter for the evaluation of the positive impact produced in a specific context by such activity. So, evaluating the social impacts of projects and human activities, is more and more becoming a required action to gain sustain from the main stakeholders in society, such as Institutions, but also (and more importantly) local civic communities. There are many social impact evaluation tools, each one proposing a specific model for a sustainable development [13, 14]. The aim of this paper is not to evaluate their performance, but to reflect on the role that design thinking and human-centered design tools have within these models.

Some of the most diffused social impact evaluation tools include some tools also applied and very used by the human-centered design. For example, one of the main steps of the SIA (Social Impact Assessment) in measuring the social impact is the identification of the value proposition of the social impact through the theory of change. These tools are generally applied in human-centered design when the aim is to define more in depth the motivations and the objectives of the project.

By the authors' point of view, social impact evaluation tools present some common approaches regarding the different aspects of a project. The first one is the analysis of the context affected by the project (already existing or proposed) and the kinds of changes that the project aims to bring in it. The second one concerns the management of the project and the evaluation of the effective outputs and outcomes produced by the project. The last one is the financial part, integrated with the social indicators that allow to evaluate the effective social impact of a solution. It is certainly a generalization, but it is useful to identify some points of intervention for human-centered design activities, such as those described into the second section of this paper. In this regard, although also the financial aspect is fundamental for the success of a project by having a central part in defining the success of an idea or project (as shown by the business model canvas method [15]), the other two aspects appear to be closer to the kind of interventions that design thinking and human-centered design usually deal with. In effect, the third one appears to be more distant from the attitude generally attributable to the design methodologies, as it is more like a monitoring approach. However, it can be very useful also in the design process for the definition of KPIs, especially social ones.

In general, the authors of this paper argue that the role of design thinking and human-centered design can be more preeminent when coming to define the social impact of a specific solution or human activity. In the view of creating more interdisciplinary and collaborative frameworks for the definition of more sustainable projects, the creative and generative tools usually applied in design field can gain a larger diffusion also in this instance, i.e. the entrepreneurial field, as demonstrated by some contribution as the Sprint [16] and the Lean design method [17]. At the same time, the interest towards the social impact produced by a project or organization can be extended far beyond the management and business fields. In this sense, until now the focus of social impact evaluation approaches has been more oriented towards social enterprises, than towards a wider range of projects. On the contrary, a greater part of the design process should be oriented towards the definition of the possible social impact produced and the sustainable goals addressed by the project, not only for projects of social development, but for any project locating the person in the center. Although the satisfaction of social needs and the sustainability were key principles in the human-centered design process, there is not a very structured process with specific instruments specifically oriented towards the design of social impact. Or at least, the fragmented landscape of the research on social impact opens new possibilities of intersection with the design thinking approach that should be explored for improving the user experience in urban spaces through social innovation. Some examples can be found in some toolkits used in the field of the design practice that are going to be analyzed in the next section.

4 Design-Centered Tools Oriented Towards the Creation of Social Impact

The design research and the design practice of these last decades have been widely putting a focus on the social aspect of the design, especially referring to the different human-centered approaches. Indeed, according to these methods the capacity of the designed solution of effectively meeting the people's needs is a fundamental parameter to recognize the success and the goodness of that solution. Moreover, we can observe a widespread rethinking on what is the role of design, as it assumes a strong social connotation [7, 10]. This include also the tools used by designers, and potentially extended to non-expert designers, that are continuously improved through the practice and the collaboration of different actors. In this sense, because of the increasing importance given to the social impacts generated by the design of new solutions, a more structured intervention in order to establish good practices in this direction is needed.

In this paper the authors selected three specific toolkit that are seen as aiming to systematize the instruments for creating a social impact through design: the DIY Toolkit [18], the Digital Social Innovation Toolkit [19] and the Social Impact Design Toolkit [20]. This is not a complete list of toolkits addressed to the design of social impact projects, since here the aim is not to evaluate the single technique or method, but to identify some elements useful for a systematization of social impact tools, in order to apply them in a urban interaction design context.

In general, all these toolkits are open and adaptable to the different needs of designers, that can select methods and activities, and even processes, or letting be inspired by the toolkit.

The DIY Toolkit (Development Impact & You) is a collection of well documented and largely applied tools for inventing, adopting and adapting ideas that can deliver better results, especially in development. It has been selected by the authors of this paper because of its potential in empowering people and stimulating active behaviors. Moreover, it is social in its purpose, as it gathers practical tools to trigger and support social innovation, such as the 'theory of change' tool.

The Digital Social Innovation Toolkit refers to open approaches of innovation, such as open hardware, open knowledge, open networks and open data, that develop inspiring digital solutions to social challenges. The toolkit gathers the different experiences (case studies, tool, etc.) in the Digital and Social Innovation landscape arisen from an European project aimed to support new ways of creating social impact in different fields as healthcare, education, democracy, environment, transport and housing. This tool aims to empower people by providing them instruments to create social impact, especially thanks to digital innovations. In detail, it proposes an open design method focusing on collaborative tools to solve societal issues, in order to support the sustainable growth of Digital Social Innovation. So, it goes beyond the mere release of a project and values the benefits derived from the social nature of the open processes and practices implemented for developing the solution.

Lastly, the Social Impact Design (SID) Toolkit is explicitly addressed to the design of solutions aiming at producing a social impact: physical and social changes, any intervention leading to social impacts, and social issues. It gathers several approaches, activities and methods from design thinking, participatory planning and strategic design. The toolkit suggested perspectives and roles to designers and planners encouraged to create positive effects in the urban environment. The aim is to minimize negative social and economic impacts of urban regeneration projects on 'place' and 'people'. In details, it identifies three main phases of the design process: Research Process to Discover Problems, Empathy and Negotiation Based Participation Process, and Solution Based Strategic Design Process. The SID Toolkit is addressed to pre-determine the possible impacts of a project beforehand and to develop design principles to minimize negative effects by applying human centered and participatory processes and by creating models for economic alternatives. Along with the Social Impact Design, other two actions referred to the 'social impact' theme are considered, i.e. Social Impact Assessment and Social Impact Programs. In conclusion, the vision at the basis of the SID Toolkit opens to a wide panorama of design interventions, as 'social impact refers to the changes that results from any intervention in life and physical environment of people' [20]. For developing social impact design, however, some important actions are required, like redefining the physical and social considerations and approaches of design thinking and developing new methodologies to strengthen empathy between designers and affected people.

5 Conclusions

In this paper the authors made a reflection on the necessity of focusing more in depth on the implementation of social impact evaluation and design tools, by better integrating these two perspectives. In fact, on the one hand the design approaches are generally applied with a focus on user-centered design tools, without considering a more complete identification of the social impacts generated by the designed solutions. While, on the other hand, the focus of social impact evaluation approaches is more oriented towards the social enterprises, than towards a wider range of projects.

However, some good examples regarding the evaluation of social impacts in design can be found both in the principles at the basis of Human-Centered Design and Design Thinking and in some toolkit addressed to social innovators. For instance, approaches aiming at creating a positive social impact refer to the fundamental principle of the Human-Centered Design approaches of taking inspiration by people for developing solutions and generating change on various scales and levels. In details, in this paper the authors analyzed some features of social impact evaluation tools and three design toolkits oriented towards the creation of social impact. Certainly, they are not exhaustive of all work on the topic, but they give important insights for improving user experience in urban spaces through social innovation.

First of all, design approaches aiming at social impacts should in the first place gain in-depth understanding of the dynamics occurring among the different stakeholder of an ecosystem, by fostering an active participation and an open collaboration of all the various actors affected by the impacts generated through a project. Moreover, beside the design process, it is important to consider assessment and planning process, too.

So, in the end, the purpose of this paper is to highlight how it is possible to develop a better user experience in urban spaces starting by the consideration of how the designed solutions can produce positive social, environmental and economic outcomes, how they can reach the identified project's outputs and finally solve the city needs. In order to reach this objective, it is fundamental to consolidate methods that improve the effectiveness of the solution. For this reason, the research on design needs to strengthen methodologies which, starting from the definition of a specific outcome to reach, identifies the most suitable tools for the measurement of the social, environmental and economic impacts. It includes not only the identification of specific indicators, but also the definition of the metrics for the impact assessment during the realization of the project and after its implementation.

In concluding, this is only the first step of a wider research activity on the topic that would be conducted on the field, by ideating, prototyping and testing methods and tools with designers and the affected people.

References

1. Benyon, D.R.: Spaces of Interaction, Places for Experience. Morgan and Claypool Publishers, San Rafael (2014)
2. UrbanIxD: From urban space to future place. Book Sprints for ICT Research (2013)
3. Elzen, B., Geels, F., Green, K.: System Innovation and the Transition to Sustainability: Theory, Evidence and Policy. Edward Elgar Publishing, Cheltenham (2004)
4. McLaren, D., Agyeman, J.: Sharing Cities: A Case for Truly Smart and Sustainable Cities. The MIT Press, Cambridge (2015)
5. Harris, M., Aldbury, D.: The Innovation Imperative. NESTA, London (2009)
6. TEPSIE: Social Innovation Theory and Research: A Guide for Researchers. A deliverable of the project: "The theoretical, empirical and policy foundations for building social innovation in Europe" (TEPSIE). European Commission – 7th Framework Programme, Brussels: European Commission, DG Research. http://www.transitsocialinnovation.eu/resource-hub/social-innovation-theory-and-research–a-guide-for-researchers
7. Murray, R., Caulier-Grice, J., Mulgan, G.: The Open Book of Social Innovation. The Young Foundation, London (2010)
8. Phills, J.A., Deiglmeier, K., Miller, D.T.: Rediscovering social innovation. Stanford Soc. Innov. Rev. 6(4), 34–43 (2008)
9. United Nations: Transforming our world: the 2030 Agenda for Sustainable Development. United Nations – Sustainable Development knowledge platform. https://sustainabledevelopment.un.org/post2015/transformingourworld
10. Manzini, E.: Design When Everybody Designs: An Introduction to Design for Social Innovation. The MIT Press, Cambridge (2015)
11. IDEO.org: The Field Guide to Human-Centered Design. IDEO.org/Design Kit (2015)
12. Hasso Plattner Institute of Design at Stanford: An Introduction to Design Thinking PROCESS GUIDE. Institute of Design at Stanford (2010)
13. Zamagni, S., Venturi, P., Rago, S.: Valutare l'impatto sociale. La questione della misurazione nelle imprese sociali. Impresa Sociale 6, 77–97 (2015)
14. Rawhouser, H., Cummings, M., Newbert, S.L.: Social impact measurement: current approaches and future directions for social entrepreneurship research. Entrep. Theory Pract. 43(1), 82–115 (2019). https://doi.org/10.1177/1042258717727718
15. Osterwalder, A.: Business Model Generation: A Handbook for Visionaries, Game Changers, and Challengers. Wiley, New York (2010)
16. Knapp, J., Zeratsky, J., Kowitz, B.: Sprint: How to Solve Big Problems and Test New Ideas in Just Five Days. Simon & Schuster, New York (2016)
17. Ries, E.: The Lean Startup: How Constant Innovation Creates Radically Successful Businesses: How Relentless Change Creates Radically Successful Businesses. Portfolio Penguin, London (2011)
18. NESTA: Development Impact & You. Practical Tools to Trigger & Support Social Innovation. NESTA, London (2014). https://diytoolkit.org/
19. Cangiano, S., Romano, Z. (eds.): Digital Social Innovation Toolkit. DSI4EU, Nesta, Waag society, SUPSI (2017). https://dsi4eu.github.io/toolkit/
20. Kentsel Strateji: Social Impact Design (SID) Toolkit. Kentsel Strateji (2015). https://kentselstrateji.com/en/proje/social-impact-design-toolkit/

Preliminary Comparison of a Curved Public Display vs a Flat Public Display

Junichiro Yamashita[1($\boxtimes$)], Kazuo Isoda[1], Riyoko Ashida[1],
Ichiro Hisanaga[1], and Junko Ichino[2]

[1] Dai Nippon Printing Co., Ltd., Tokyo, Japan
{Yamashita-j4,Isoda-k,Hirabayashi-R,
Hisanaga-I}@mail.dnp.co.jp
[2] Tokyo City University, Yokohama, Kanagawa, Japan
ichino@tcu.ac.jp

Abstract. In this paper, we describe how passers-by are affected by a curved public display compared to a flat public display. Through observing social behaviors of people around a curved public display, we found that firstly more people tend to stop in front of a curved display than a flat display. Secondly, a certain number of audience members viewed the public display at the nearest distance, and audience members at closer dwelling positions to the display tended to dwell longer than those who stay farther from the display. Furthermore, our observations reveal that, for both the curved display and the flat display, more passers-by were attracted and stopped to view the display when there was already an audience standing in front of the display, which is known as the honeypot effect. However, these audience members have shorter dwelling times than those of other audience members.

Keywords: Public display · Social behavior · Field study · Non-flat display · OLED · OEL display · Curved display

1 Introduction

Public displays that show digital content using various displays are currently installed in public spaces such as airports, stations, commercial facilities, and buildings. Recently, display panels have been improved so that they can be installed in various shapes. Consequently, displays with different shapes have become available in addition to large displays. Furthermore, non-flat displays can now be used in various situations and spaces, and so the use of non-planar display panels is increasing dramatically and will continue to grow.

On the other hand, research studies on non-planar public displays have just started. In particular, very few research results on non-planar, large-size public displays are available. As use of public displays that need to be in harmony with the surroundings is becoming more and more important and is practically required, it is necessary to understand what effects and characteristics are specific to non-planar large-size public displays for better space design. Curved type displays are typically important when considering installing large-size displays in public spaces, because they are easily

© Springer Nature Switzerland AG 2019
M. Kurosu (Ed.): HCII 2019, LNCS 11568, pp. 362–373, 2019.
https://doi.org/10.1007/978-3-030-22636-7_27

installed into or on a wall or ceiling. Therefore, we launched our study focusing on a curved public display.

This research aims to clarify the characteristics of curved displays through observation of people's social behaviors in front of displays. In this paper, we will introduce the preliminary observed social behaviors of passers-by for a giant non-planar, arch-shaped public display (hereinafter called a "curved public display") installed at a station concourse. With our observation results, we will discuss the characteristics of the curved public display and differences from a general, flat-shaped public display (hereinafter called a "flat public display").

2 Related Work

Due to the thinning of display panels and the narrowing of bezels, there are many existing research studies focusing on using and connecting multiple displays into one screen. Some studies were carried out on these types of displays, and typical research studies are introduced in [1–4]. Koppel et al. [1] introduced a constructed system called a "Chained Display", which connects flat, hexagonal or concave type displays, and found the influences on users with the different types. From these kinds of studies, it is known that the "honeypot effect" [5] of hexagonal and concave Chained Displays is lower than flat type public displays [1].

Recently, studies have been performed by creating a cylindrical public display with a non-planar display panel. According to these research studies, cylindrical public displays are more adoptable for moving audience members. Meanwhile, it is also known that fewer users stopped compared with a planar type, and their viewing time of public displays was shorter [2, 3].

Previous in-the-wild studies that evaluated behavior of people around public displays were conducted in different contexts: museums [6–11], urban public spaces [12–14], aquariums [15], public transportation [16], construction sites [17], universities [18].

However, these research studies were not carried out with large-sized displays exceeding human height, so these research results are insufficient for large-size displays that need to be designed and installed in harmony with the surroundings.

3 Research Questions

Based on a prior study [6], we established the following two research questions.

3.1 Attractiveness

How strongly does a curved public display attract passers-by? That is, how many passers-by will view the display or stop to view the display? Are there any differences in attractiveness between a curved public display and a flat display?

If there is an audience in front of a curved public display, how will it influence the attractiveness to passers-by? For example, will the honeypot effect appear? If yes, are there differences in the honeypot effect compared to a flat display?

3.2 Engagement

How much are passers-by engaged by a curved public display? To answer this research question, answers to the following questions need to be made clear. How far do most audience members view a display? How long is their dwelling time? Are there any differences in engagement between a curved public display and a flat display? Is dwelling time influenced by the dwelling position?

4 Field Observations

In this study, we carried out two observations. In one, we observed and collected data with our target curved public display installed at a terminal station concourse as shown in Fig. 1. In the other, we observed and collected data with a flat public display installed at a subway station concourse for comparison.

Fig. 1. Overview of the curved public display. This arch-shaped display has a total of 36 (6 × 6) 55-in. OLED curved display panels made by LG.

4.1 Environment

The curved public display was installed on the ground floor of a station concourse in Fukuoka city in Japan and was 4 m in height and 7 m in width, as shown in Fig. 1. About 124,000 railway passengers pass through per day, and the curved public display is visible from a wide range on the concourse.

The flat public display was installed in a subway concourse in Sapporo city in Japan and was 2 m in height and 3.2 m in width, as shown in Fig. 3. About 80,000 railway passengers pass through per day. The flat public display was also visible from a wide range on the concourse. As shown in Figs. 2 and 3, there was enough space around both displays so that audience members could stop easily in front of the displays to view them (Table 1).

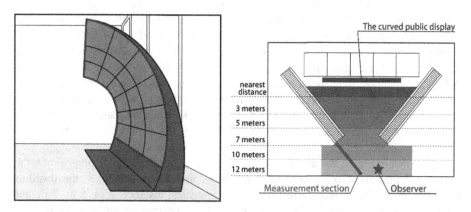

Fig. 2. Installation location of the curved public display.

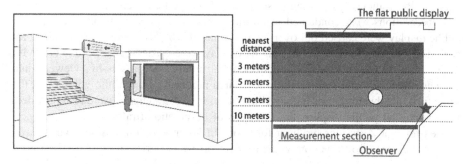

Fig. 3. Installation location of the flat public display.

Table 1. Installation locations of the curved public display and flat public display.

	Curved public display	Flat public display
Display size	7 × 4 m	3.2 × 2 m
Location	Fukuoka City, Japan Terminal Station Railway passers-by: 124,000/day	Sapporo City, Japan Subway Station Railway passers-by: 80,000/day
Display panel	LG OLED (Curved type)	Flat LED
Observation period	June 14–16, 2018 (3 days)	July 10, 2018 (1 day)
Observation time	9:30–17:00 Total: 650 min	15:00–17:00 Total: 110 min
Observed passers-by	5,492	778

4.2   Data Collection

In this study, people passing through the measurement sections shown in Figs. 2 and 3 were observed and called "passers-by". As shown in Fig. 4, we define two specific types of passers-by. One is defined as a "viewer" who walked through and looked at the display or stopped to view the display for fewer than 10 s. The other is defined as an "audience member" who stopped to view the display more than 10 s. Also, in order to observe the behaviors affected by the honeypot, we defined "prior audience" as an audience already in front of the display. In order to evaluate Attractiveness, percentages of viewers and audience members out of all people that passed by were adopted. A larger percentage indicates a more attractive display. At the same time, to evaluate Engagement, the distance (hereinafter called the "dwelling position") from the display where the audience stopped, and the time period (hereinafter called the "dwelling time") from when the audience member started to view the display to when they started to leave were adopted.

As shown in Fig. 2, the dwelling positions for the curved public display were set as follows: nearest distance, 3 m, 5 m, 7 m, 10 m, and 12 m. In Fig. 3, the dwelling positions for the flat display were set as follows: nearest distance, 3 m, 5 m, 7 m, and 10 m. One of the authors, as the observer, stood at a position about 10 to 12 m away from the public display. The observer inferred from the directions of the viewer's face, eyes, body and so on whether the screen of the public display was viewed. Simultaneously, the audience's dwelling position and dwelling time were recorded manually.

Observations were conducted in 10-min sessions. All observations of the curved public display were carried out over 3 days (June 14–16, 2018) from 9:30 to 17:00 for each day. Observations of the flat public display were carried out on 1 day (July 10, 2018) from 15:00 to 17:00. We collected the number of passers-by, viewers, and audience members and summarized these three numbers as the traffic volume. At the same time, the dwelling time and dwelling position of the audience were also recorded. For the curved public display, the first type of observation (traffic volume) was performed for 1 or 2 sessions per hour for a total of 20 observation sessions over 3 days. The second type of observation (audience behavior) was carried out for 3 or 4 sessions

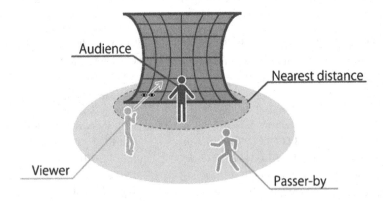

Fig. 4. Definitions of passer-by, viewer, and audience in our study.

Table 2. Definitions.

Passer-by	Person who passed through the "Measurement section" close to the display
Viewer	A passer-by who watched the display while working or stopped to view the display for less than 10 s
Audience	A passer-by who stopped to view the display for longer than 10 s
Prior audience	A person who was viewing a display earlier in front of the display
Dwelling time	Time from when the person stopped to watch until the person started to leave
Dwelling position	Position while viewing the display. Set at nearest distance, 3 m, 5 m, 7 m, 10 m, and 12 m from the display

per hour for a total of 45 sessions. For the flat public display, similar observations were carried out in one day. Observations for traffic volume were held for 1 session per hour, for a total of 2 sessions. Observations for audience behavior were carried out for 3 or 4 sessions per hour, for a total of 9 sessions. For the curved public display, we collected the number of audience members and their dwelling positions and dwelling time under two situations, one with a prior audience and one without a prior audience (Table 2).

5   Results and Discussion

5.1   Attractiveness

Figure 5 illustrates the percentages of audience members out of passers-by for the curved public displays and flat public displays. It's clear that 842 viewers out of 5,208 passers-by (16.1%) viewed the curved public display as viewers, and 140 people (2.6%) were recognized as audience members. Regarding the flat public display, of the 756 people who passed by, 113 people (14.9%) viewed the display as viewers, and 8 people (1.0%) were audience members. The ratio of audience members is slightly higher for the curved public display than for the flat public display. Also, more passers-by tend to stop. In other words, more viewers were observed in the case of the curved public display.

Figure 6 shows the number of audience members in two situations: with or without prior audience members. For the curved display, the average number of passers-by per session of the curved public display was 260.2 people. The average number of audience members was 5.8 people (2.2%) without prior audience members and 7.5 people (2.8%) with prior audience members. For the flat public display, the number of passers-by per session was 378.0 people. The average number of audience members was 1.3 people (0.4%) without prior audience members and 4.3 people (1.1%) with prior audience members.

Furthermore, Fig. 7 illustrates the ratio of audience members at different dwelling times for both the curved display and the flat display. For the curved display, without a prior audience, 23.8% of audience members had a dwelling time longer than 120 s. However, with a prior audience, only 8.4% of audience members had a dwelling time

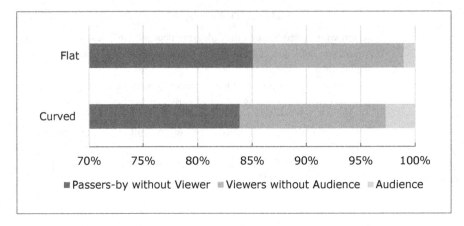

Fig. 5. Percentages of viewers and audience members of passers-by.

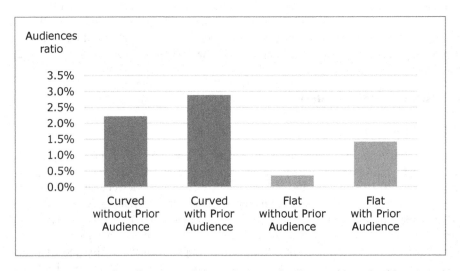

Fig. 6. Percentages of audience members under two situations: with and without a prior audience.

longer than 120 s. For the flat display, without a prior audience, 30.8% of audience members had a dwelling time longer than 120 s. However, with a prior audience, 11.1% of audience members had a dwelling time longer than 120 s. Thus, it's clear that for both displays, the number of audience members with long dwelling times was lower with a prior audience.

Regarding Attractiveness, Figs. 5 and 6 suggest that more passers-by tended to stop in front of the curved public display than the flat public display. At the same time, it's clear that for both displays, the proportion of audience members is higher when there is a prior audience, which proves very well the honeypot effect.

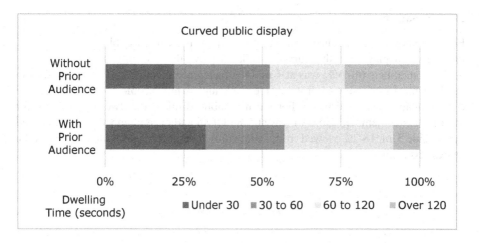

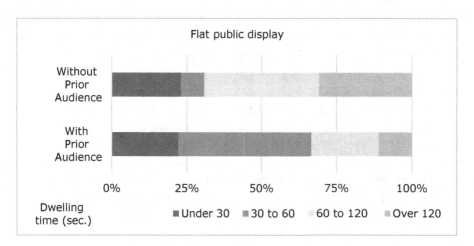

Fig. 7. Differences in dwelling time with and without a prior audience

Figure 7 indicates that there was no difference between the curved public display and flat public display under both situations with and without a prior audience. However, for both displays, audience members dwelled for a shorter time, and the number of audience members who viewed for a long time was lower with a prior audience. Traditional research studies on the honeypot effect often discuss the effect of attracting passers-by. However, our results indicate that audience members attracted by the honeypot effect tended to have shorter dwelling times than other people. This is one of our most important findings and is valuable information regarding general public displays.

5.2   Engagement

Figure 8 shows the audience dwelling positions of the curved public display and the flat public display. For the curved public display, the dwelling position for most audience members (40.5%) was at 7 m. Of all audience members, 43.8% viewed from inside 5 m, 18.0% viewed from inside 3 m, and a few people (6.3%) viewed the display at the nearest distance. For the flat public display, the dwelling position for most audience members (50.0%) was at 5 m. Of all audience members, 68.0% viewed from inside 5 m, 18.2% viewed from inside 3 m, and nobody viewed the display at the nearest distance.

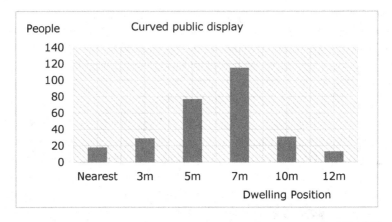

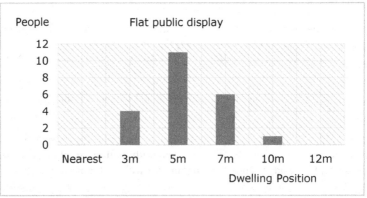

Fig. 8. Dwelling position for curved and flat displays

Comparing the data for the curved public display and flat display, we can see that despite the large size of the curved public display, many people viewed it from within 3 m. This phenomenon did not appear for the flat public display, even though it is smaller. Therefore, it can be said that people prefer to view a curved public display over a flat public display at a close dwelling position, which in this case was less than 3 m.

Figure 9 shows the relationships between audience's dwelling position and dwelling time. For the curved public display, when the dwelling position was closer than 7 m, the dwelling time increases the closer people stand. The results were similar for the flat public display.

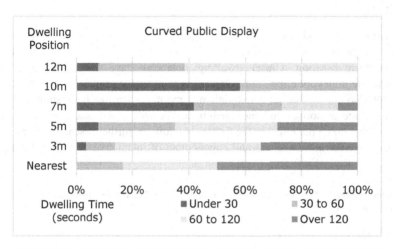

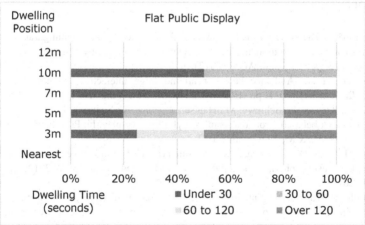

Fig. 9. Relationships between audience dwelling position and dwelling time.

With these results, we can say firstly more audience members viewed the curved public display and had a longer dwelling time. Secondly, audience members tended to view the curved public display at a close dwelling position.

5.3 Discussion

One of the known problems of large-size displays is how to attract people to come and stop right in front of the display in order to make a display interactive. Our field studies indicate that people moved much closer to the curved display than the flat display. Also, the honeypot effect occurred with the curved display to the same extent as the flat display. These findings will be further studied for large-size and interactive displays.

6 Conclusion

In this study, we found that the curved public display tended to be more attractive to people than the flat public display. Also, people prefer to view a curved display at a close dwelling position. Closer dwelling positions have longer dwelling times. Regarding the honeypot effect, our collected data not only proves its known attraction effect, but also shows that attracted audience members tend to have shorter dwelling times compared to normal audience members. We will investigate these new characteristics of this honeypot effect in the future. In addition, further research will be carried out to improve the attractiveness and engagement of interactive curved and flat public displays.

Acknowledgements. We sincerely thank the JR Kyushu Agency for their great contribution to the field case study.

References

1. Koppel, M.T., Bailly, G., Muller, J., Walter, R.: Chained displays: configurations of public displays can be used to influence actor-, audience-, and passer-by behavior. In: Proceedings of CHI 2012, pp. 317–326. ACM (2012)
2. Beyer, G., et al.: Audience behavior around large interactive cylindrical screens. In: Proceedings of CHI 2011, pp. 1021–1030. ACM, New York (2011)
3. Beyer, G., Kottner, F., Schiewe, M., Haulsen, I., Butz, A.: Squaring the circle: how framing influences user behavior around a seamless cylindrical display. In: Proceedings of CHI 2013, pp. 1729–1738. ACM, New York (2013)
4. Bolton, J., Kim, K., Vertegaal, R.: A comparison of competitive and cooperative task performance using spherical and flat displays. In: Proceedings of CSCW 2012, pp. 529–538. ACM (2012)
5. Brignull, H., Rogers, Y.: Enticing people to interact with large public displays in public spaces. In: Proceedings of the Ninth IFIP TC13 International Conference on Human-Computer Interaction (INTERACT 2003), pp. 17–24. IOS Press (2003)
6. Ichino, J., Isoda, K., Ueda, T., Satoh, R.: Effects of the display angle on social behaviors of the people around the display: a field study at a museum. In: Proceedings of CSCW 2016, pp. 26–37. ACM (2016)
7. Horn, M., et al.: Of BATs and APEs: an interactive tabletop game for natural history museums. In: Proceedings of the SIGCHI Conference on Human Factors in Computing Systems (2012)
8. Block, F., et al.: Fluid grouping: quantifying group engagement around interactive tabletop exhibits in the wild. In: Proceedings of the 33rd Annual ACM Conference on Human Factors in Computing Systems (2015)

9. Roberts, J., Banerjee, A., Hong, A., McGee, S., Horn, M., Matcuk, M.: Digital exhibit labels in museums: promoting visitor engagement with cultural artifacts. In: Proceedings of ACM SIGCHI Conference on Human Factors in Computing Systems, p. 623. ACM (2018)

10. Vom Lehn, D.: Withdrawing from exhibits: the interactional organisation of museum visits. In: Haddington, P., Mondada, L., Nevile, M. (eds.) Interaction and Mobility: Language and the Body in Motion, vol. 20, pp. 65–90. Linguae & litterae, Aldine de Gruyter, Berlin (2013)

11. Vom Lehn, D., Heath, C.: Action at the exhibit face: video and the analysis of social interaction in museums and galleries. J. Mark. Manag. 32(15–16), 1441–1457 (2016)

12. Memarovic, N., Fatah gen Schieck, A., Schnädelbach, H.M., Kostopoulou, E., North, S., Ye, L.: Capture the moment: "In the Wild" longitudinal case study of situated snapshots captured through an urban screen in a community setting. In: Proceedings of the 18th ACM Conference on Computer Supported Cooperative Work & Social Computing, CSCW 2015, pp. 242–253. ACM, New York (2015)

13. Müller, J., Walter, R., Bailly, G., Nischt, M., Alt, F.: Looking glass: a field study on noticing interactivity of a shop window. In: Proceedings of CHI 2012, pp. 297–306. ACM (2012)

14. Peltonen, P., et al.: It's Mine, Don't Touch!: interactions at a large multi-touch display in a city centre. In: Proceedings of the SIGCHI Conference on Human Factors in Computing Systems (2008)

15. Hinrichs, U., Carpendale, S.: Gestures in the wild: studying multi-touch gesture sequences on interactive tabletop exhibits. In: Proceedings of the SIGCHI Conference on Human Factors in Computing Systems (2011)

16. Alt, F., Vehns, J.: Opportunistic deployments: challenges and opportunities of conducting public display research at an airport. In: Proceedings of the 5th ACM International Symposium on Pervasive Displays (PerDis 2016), pp. 106–117. ACM, New York (2016)

17. Memarovic, N.: Construction on display: exploring the use of public displays on construction sites. In: Proceedings of the 4th International Symposium on Pervasive Displays (PerDis 2015), pp. 155–162. ACM, New York (2015)

18. Müller, J., Eberle, D., Tollmar, K.: Communiplay: a field study of a public display media space. In: Proceedings of the SIGCHI Conference on Human Factors in Computing Systems (CHI 2014), pp. 1415–1424. ACM New York (2014)

Research on Innovative Design of Urban Smart Lighting Equipment Based on User Experience

Junnan Ye, Jianxin Cheng, Dadi An, Chaoxiang Yang[✉], Sihui Shen,
and Junzhe Lu

School of Art Design and Media ECUST, M.BOX 286, No. 130 Meilong Road,
Xuhui District, Shanghai 200237, China
yejunnan971108@qq.com, 13901633292@163.com,
61915633@qq.com, yangchaoxiang@qq.com,
1042106594@qq.com, 994710097@qq.com

Abstract. Since the beginning of the 21st century, with the development and maturity of the Internet of Things, sensor, processing and software technology, products are no longer a single product, but will digitize machines (computers), agents, sensors, information data in the network system, and then connect with people, devices and business processes to realize complex system products with collective consciousness and thinking. Smart city is a large-scale system with thorough perception, comprehensive interconnection and in-depth intelligence. As terminal and carrier of smart city system, urban street lamp implements important technology in the perspectives of perception, network and application, which will play a tremendous role in the construction of future smart city.

Firstly, through document retrieval, market research and the requirements analysis of User experience, this paper analyzes the background, meaning and development status of urban smart lighting equipment (USLE), summarizes the construction of USLE and the intelligent functions that have been achieved, and teases out the relationship between USLE and smart city project application with the combination of the content of "13th Five-Year plan" for smart city construction in Shanghai. On this basis, the general framework of the emotional design and evaluation system of USLE form under user experience is put forward, which includes Five parts: (1) Users' three levels of emotional needs for products; (2) the demand evaluation of product perceptual image; (3) the perception evaluation of design prototype; (4) the perception evaluation of design model; (5) product use and interaction experience. After that, the specific implementation contents of the five parts are analyzed and discussed in depth. Finally, taking study of PRONA Smart Lighting Design in Shanghai, China for instance, it is proved that the general framework has strong feasibility and application value, which can provide pattern references for government, enterprises and designers to carry out innovative design and development of urban smart lighting equipment in the future.

Keywords: Innovative design · Urban smart lighting equipment ·
User experience · Design method · Smart city

© Springer Nature Switzerland AG 2019
M. Kurosu (Ed.): HCII 2019, LNCS 11568, pp. 374–386, 2019.
https://doi.org/10.1007/978-3-030-22636-7_28

1   Introduction

1.1   Urban Smart Lighting Equipment (Hereinafter Referred to as USLE) Will Become a Comprehensive Solution for the Renewal and Construction of Smart Cities

Smart city is a large system with thorough perception, comprehensive interconnection and deep intelligence. Its core is to connect the physical, information, social and commercial infrastructures in modern cities by using information and digital technologies such as the Internet, cloud computing, big data, and the Internet of Things to respond intelligently and quickly to the various demands of people's livelihood, environmental protection, transportation, public safety, urban services, industrial and commercial activities and so on generated in the city, improve urban operational efficiency on the basis of energy conservation, and achieve urban green sustainable development of cities, and create a better life for urban residents [1, 2].

The street lamp is one of the important public facilities in the city. Through research, it is found that urban street lamps naturally exist in the three levels of perception, network and application in the smart city system, which is the most economical, the most environmentally friendly and the most rapid comprehensive solution to arrange the functions of each subsystem of the smart city. Its main advantages include the following aspects:

Street Lamps Are Regularly Distributed in the Urban Road Network
The design and construction of urban street lamps are carried out in accordance with the "Urban Road Lighting Design Standards", so that the street lamps are regularly distributed along the urban roads according to the prescribed distance standards. With the deepening of the urbanization process, street lamps also extend to all corners of the city along with road construction.

Street Lamps Provide Precise Geographical Coordinates
According to the regularity and extensiveness of street lamps along urban roads, the precise positioning function of street lamps can be realized as long as the positioning device is installed on the street lamps, which makes it easier to realize intelligent traffic, security alarm, visual management and other functions in smart cities.

Street Lamps Have the Best Urban Communication Location
Street lamps are basically set up along both sides of urban roads, providing excellent urban communication positions. According to their own wireless network needs, communication operators can easily realize urban wireless network communication functions by installing mobile communication devices such as micro-base stations at the top of lamp posts in areas requiring network coverage.

Street Lamps Have an Existing Power Supply Network
The power supply lines between street lamps form a huge power supply network in the city. As the node of power supply network, street lamp is often used as the power access point of surrounding billboards, bus stop signs, road landscape and so on. Therefore, in the future, street lamp base can be fully used as car charging station. And

a communication network installed along the power supply line can easily form an Internet of things road covering the whole city.

Street Lamp Has Better Design and Development Function

By integrating solar panels, video probes, micro-base stations, multimedia advertising screens, information interactive screens, detection instruments, charging stations and other hardware on the existing street lamps, it is easy to realize the perception and services of urban environment, traffic, lighting, life and other aspects, so as to quickly realize the multi-directional intelligent services and management of municipal administration, people's livelihood and industry.

1.2 The Design and Development of USLE Will Play an Important Role in the Construction of Smart Cities

USLE will be an important application carrier to realize the renewal and construction of smart city. It will play a significant role in the following aspects.

USLE Construction Can Achieve Energy Saving and Emission Reduction in Cities

USLE construction is the need for smart cities to save energy and reduce emissions. In January 2017, the State Council of China issued a notice on the "13th Five-Year Plan" for energy conservation and emission reduction, in which the green lighting project was clearly defined in the key energy conservation projects [3]. The USLE can combine smart city street lamps with LED lighting to reduce the use of electricity, the consumption of coal and other fuels in power plants, and the emission of harmful gases such as carbon dioxide. In addition, photovoltaic solar panels, wind power generation and other power generation equipment can be installed on the top of the base terminal to increase the power supply. Moreover, visual management can be realized through the intelligent control system, and energy regulation and control can be carried out through the Internet of things according to actual demand, so as to achieve the goal of urban energy conservation and emission reduction.

USLE Construction Can Enhance the Image of the City

As the name card of a beautiful city, USLE reflects the scale of urban development, economic strength, management level, cultural positioning and other information. Its form is designed and developed according to the urban public environment, cultural landscape, historical relics, landmarks and other morphological elements, which can accurately express the urban material culture, spiritual culture and regional cultural concepts [4]. Moreover, the comprehensive utilization of lamp post is one of the important carriers to change the urban appearance and improve the urban image and connotation.

USLE Construction Can Make Full Use of Urban Resources to Achieve Sustainable Development

USLE can be connected to a variety of urban Internet of things information sensing equipment, such as: air quality, humidity, temperature and other weather detection equipment; traffic monitoring equipment such as cameras, infrared monitoring and alarm points; wireless communication equipment, like WIFI, and micro-base station;

road signs, billboards, parking fees and other public service equipment. Therefore, functions such as environmental monitoring, traffic detection, intelligent charging station, scenic spot information and convenient services can be realized through the Internet of things. And USLE can make full use of all kinds of urban resources and realize the green and sustainable development of the city.

1.3   Product Design Based on User Experience

With the development of society and the continuous progress of science and technology, functional structural products designed and developed by the producer can no longer meet the personalized experience of users. In order to gain higher market competitiveness and better product revenue, more and more enterprises have begun to fully study the user experience of products and design products that conform to the user experience. Therefore, user-experience-oriented product design has become one of the important means for the development of design innovation and business activities in today's society and enterprises, attracting more and more attention from the society and enterprises.

The design philosophy of user-experience-oriented originated from the concept of User-Center-Design (UCD) in Donald Arthur Norman's book *User Centered System Design: New Perspectives on Human-Computer Interaction* that published in the late 1980s [5]. This is a design concept for a product, system or service that places the user in an important position in product development and design. The concept has been widely used in industrial design, interaction design, service design and ergonomics. User-oriented design requires designers to conduct in-depth analysis and research on user psychology, behavioral habits, and usage environments during product design, development, and maintenance. In addition, the designer needs to work from the user experience to the various stages of product design, and combine the influence of social and cultural aspects to finally design a product that meets the user experience.

2   The Concept, Application Scope and Content of USLE

2.1   The Basic Concept of USLE

The basic concepts of USLE can be summarized as follows: on the basis of LED energy-saving lighting function of urban street lamps, by integrating high-definition cameras, micro base station, wireless radio, LED electronic screen, electronic interactive screen, charging station, GPS positioning system, the environmental information acquisition sensor, alarm, photovoltaic panels and other hardware equipment, using advanced information technology such as Internet of things, Internet, big data, cloud computing, it is a set of technical terminal equipment, which transmits the collected data and information to the "USLE Information Management System" and makes immediate response and decision processing to realize smart city functions, such as intelligent control, energy-saving lighting, electric vehicle charging, information release and interaction, smart transportation, wireless city, environmental monitoring, voice broadcasting, and one-click calling for help under the interactive environment of big data [6].

2.2 The Application Scope of USLE

In September 2016, the Shanghai Municipal People's Government promulgated the "13th Five-Year Plan for Promoting the Construction of Smart Cities in Shanghai" [7]. The following will be combined with the overall framework of the 13th Five-Year Plan for Smart City Construction in Shanghai, China to illustrate the application area of USLE, as shown in Fig. 1.

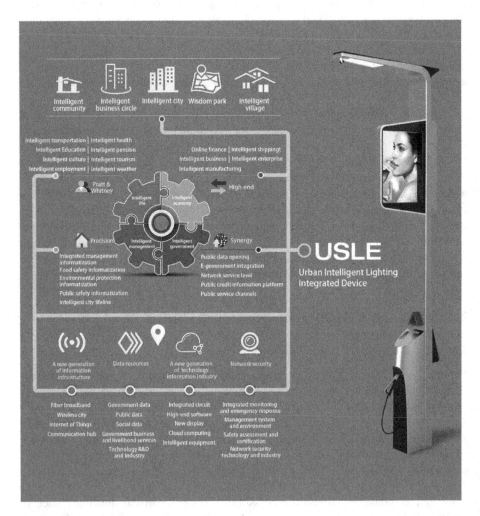

Fig. 1. The relationship diagrams of USLE and the smart city project to promote construction in the 13th five-year plan of Shanghai, China

USLE Can Be Widely Used in Smart City Demonstration Areas to Improve the Image of Urban Areas

Shanghai mainly focuses on the five demonstration areas of smart community, smart village, smart business circle, smart park and smart new district, and promotes innovation pilot and application demonstration. As a terminal product developed on the basis of intelligent street light, USLE also has the advantages of street light, that is, it is ubiquitous in every corner of smart city area along with road network. Meanwhile, through the modeling design of USLE in different areas, the image of urban area can be further improved.

USLE Can Become an Important Technology Terminal Product of Smart Life, Smart Economy, Smart Governance and Smart Government Affair

The smart city in Shanghai will be specifically applied in the four aspects of smart life, smart economy, smart governance and smart government affair. Intelligent life includes eight aspects, which are intelligent transportation, intelligent health, intelligent education, intelligent endowment, intelligent culture, intelligent tourism, intelligent employment and intelligent weather. Smart economy includes Internet finance, smart shipping, smart business, smart enterprise and smart manufacturing. There are five sections included in smart governance, which are comprehensive management informatization, food safety informatization, environmental protection informatization, public safety informatization, and smart city lifeline. Smart government affair includes five platforms: the opening of public data, the integration of e-government, the upgrading of network services, public credit information, and public service channels. It can be found that these smart applications can be more or less implemented on the USLE. For example, the information interactive screen installed at the bottom of the lamp post can provide residents with information services such as social security, medical health, transportation, meteorological information, cultural entertainment, public utilities and intelligent security; the full coverage of the wireless communication network can be achieved through the micro-base station installed on the USLE lamp post, which can provide hardware support for the urban public information service platform, medical information system and other intelligent systems; also through the high-definition video camera installed on the top of the lamp post, traffic information collection and processing can be carried out, and the safety monitoring of urban road violations can be conducted, thus the visual management of urban traffic and public safety can be realized finally.

USLE Can Provide Basic and Affordable Information Network for Information Infrastructure

The foundation of promoting the construction of smart city is to accelerate the construction of new-generation information infrastructure. The original street lamp and wire network of USLE can provide basic and affordable information network for urban fiber broadband, wireless network, Internet of things and communication hub, thus further promoting the construction of smart city.

USLE Can Provide Data Collection and Security Monitoring Services for Data Resources, Information Technology Industry and Network Security

Another important basis for realizing urban intellectualization is to collect all kinds of data in the city through various sensors, and make a positive response to urban problems by timely processing data. And USLE is the best data acquisition terminal.

2.3 Analysis of the Extended Application Content and Technology of USLE

Cities at home and abroad have gradually begun to promote the construction of USLE. Through market research and literature retrieval analysis, according to incomplete statistics of USLE construction in domestic and foreign cities as of August 2018, the realized USLE smart application contents currently include smart control, energy-saving lighting, charging pile and other functions, as shown in Table 1.

Table 1. By August 2018, the application content of USLE in domestic and foreign cities (incomplete statistics)

Serial number	Contents of app	Content description
1	Intelligent control	Adaptive regulation of street lighting can be realized according to the road traffic vehicles, traffic flow, weather and environmental changes. And intelligent control and maintenance and management can be achieved by using intelligent lighting control system
2	Energy saving lighting	Through the installation of solar panels, LED lighting to achieve the energy saving and lighting of city lamps
3	Charging station	It can charge communication devices such as electric cars, e-bikes and mobile phones
4	LED electronic information screen	High resolution LED electronic information screen will achieve commercial outdoor advertising, urban information bulletin, video broadcast and other functions
5	Electronic interactive screen	Through access to the Internet and the Internet of things, it is possible to understand, interact with and push urban public information, such as printing and downloading coupons, paying for urban life, and consulting public information
6	HD video monitoring	Through the collection and processing of traffic information, the safety monitoring of urban road violations, and so on, the visual management of urban traffic and public safety can be finally realized
7	One-click calling for help	Immediate help for road traffic accidents, fires, urban road crimes can be realized
8	WIFI (micro-base station)	A micro-base station is installed in the lamp post to realize the function of urban wireless network
9	Environment monitoring	By installing corresponding environmental sensors, the monitoring of environmental air quality (PM2.5), temperature, humidity, weather and wind force can be realized
10	Atmosphere lamp	Through the design of the shape of USLE, it becomes the atmosphere lamp of the city road

(continued)

Table 1. (*continued*)

Serial number	Contents of app	Content description
11	Voice broadcast	In order to realize the broadcast of city emergency, traffic, weather and other information, wireless radio is installed in the lamp post
12	Management of the road cover	The management and maintenance of the road cover are realized through the detection of the road cover by video
13	Underground pipe network monitoring	To manage and maintain underground power lines, cables, sewers, water pipes and other urban underground pipe network facilities
14	Parking fee	Realize the function of parking charge in the public area of the city

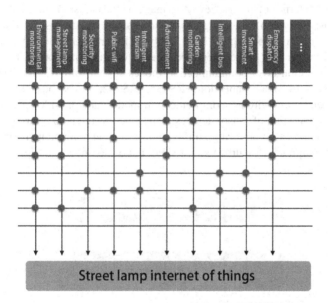

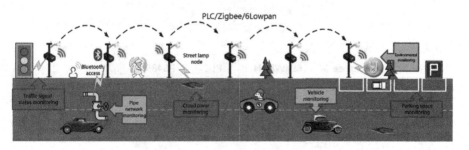

Fig. 2. The function application of internet of things about USLE

As an important infrastructure of a smart city, urban smart street lamps cover all traffic networks in the city [8]. By adopting high-tech such as Internet of things and cloud computing, and then combining the accessible sensors with urban smart street lamps, the integrated sensing platform of unified intelligent street lamps Internet of things can be established in order to realize the sharing of sensing device resources in various application fields, the sharing of information resources collected by sensing terminals, the sharing of basic and comprehensive sensing network resources of smart street lamps Internet of things, and the application of various fields in smart cities, such as environmental monitoring and street lamp management, notice, Wi-Fi, advertisement, emergency dispatch and other cooperative work, as shown in Fig. 2.

The technical architecture of the integrated device of urban smart street lamp is mainly composed of five parts: smart city application, integrated Internet of things platform, multi-protocol gateway, integration of multiple perception-layer communication modes and sensor access. Among them, smart city application refers to the specific smart function application combined with urban smart street lamp. The integrated Internet of things platform provides a unified interface of the standard system to achieve unified Internet of things device management, data storage, data mining and other functions. The multi-protocol gateway adapts and transforms a variety of interfaces and protocols in the perception layer, supports Ethernet/GPRS/3G/WIFI and other modes, and transmits data to the integrated Internet of things platform. The integration of multiple perception-layer communication modes support 6LoWPAN, Zigbee wireless sensor network interconnection, RS485, RS232, CAN bus, power carrier, GPRSCDMA and other wireless communication modes, and provide open interface to support arbitrary addition of sensor devices. Sensor access refers to a variety of sensors, such as environmental monitoring, traffic monitoring and municipal pipe network monitoring, are supported by urban smart street lamps, as shown in Fig. 3.

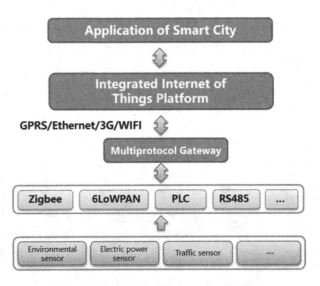

Fig. 3. The technical framework of USLE

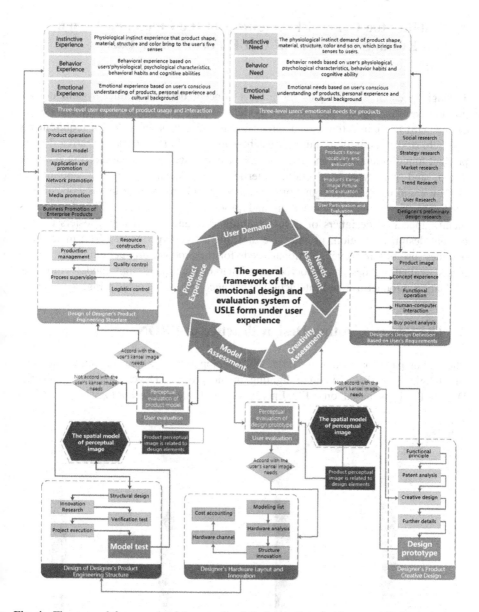

Fig. 4. The general framework of the emotional design and evaluation system of USLE form based on user experience.

3   Building the General Framework of the Emotional Design and Evaluation System of USLE Form Under User Experience

Through research and analysis of product concept design, product system design, product coordination design, product modular design and product intelligent system design, USLE's innovative design process can include: product design requirements research, design definition and goal establishment, product program creative design, product function hardware analysis and cost accounting, product engineering structure design and prototype production, enterprise manufacturing, product commercial operation and use [9, 10]. In this process, users mainly participate in the work of user needs, perceptual design evaluation and product use experience. Therefore, users mainly appear as designers of design requirements and design ideas, testers of perceptual design evaluation, product use and interactive experiencers. The main work includes: users' three-level emotional needs for the product, product emotional image needs evaluation, design prototype emotional evaluation, design model emotional evaluation, product use and interaction experience, etc., as shown in Fig. 4.

4   The Smart Lighting Design Practice of PRONA

The author participated in the design and development of Shanghai multi-functional smart lighting – PRONA smart lighting in the project "Development of Industrial Design Products based on LED Energy-saving Lighting Technology", which is a

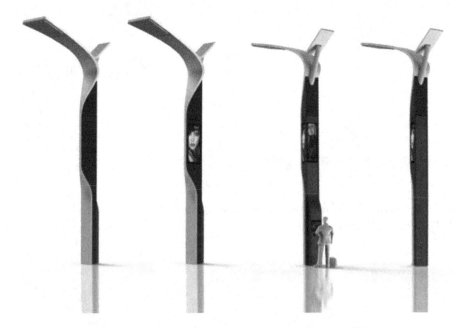

Fig. 5. PRONA Smart Lighting Design in Shanghai, China

financial support fund project of promoting the development of cultural and creative industries in Shanghai. PRONA intelligent lighting is designed through the general framework of the emotional design and evaluation system of USLE form under user experience, as shown in Fig. 5. Finally, through the user satisfaction survey, it was found that the average satisfaction of the designed PRONA was 8.7 (10 points in total), with high user satisfaction.

5 Conclusion

USLE is becoming a critical application carrier in reconstructing smart cities, playing a significant role in implementing energy conservation and emission reduction, enhancing urban image, utilizing urban resources, and promoting sustainable development. Through document retrieval, market research and the requirements analysis of User experience, this paper analyzes the background, meaning and development status of USLE, summarizes the construction of USLE and the intelligent functions that have been achieved, and teases out the relationship between USLE and smart city project application with the combination of the content of "13th Five-Year plan" for smart city construction in Shanghai. On this basis, the general framework of the emotional design and evaluation system of USLE form under user experience is put forward, which includes Five parts: (1) Users' three levels of emotional needs for products; (2) the demand evaluation of product perceptual image; (3) the perception evaluation of design prototype; (4) the perception evaluation of design model; (5) product use and interaction experience. Finally, taking study of PRONA Smart Lighting Design in Shanghai, China for instance, it is proved that the general framework has strong feasibility and application value, which can provide pattern references for government, enterprises and designers to carry out innovative design and development of urban smart lighting equipment in the future.

Funding. This research was supported by open fund project of research on art engineering and modern service design supported by shanghai summit discipline in design (Granted No. DA18303).

References

1. Tao, X.: Smart city in the context of big data. Mob. Commun. **21**, 14–18 (2014)
2. Badii, C., Bellini, P., Cenni, D., et al.: Analysis and assessment of a knowledge based smart city architecture providing service APIs. Future Gener. Comput. Syst. **75**, 14–29 (2017)
3. The central people's government of the People's Republic of China. The state council issued a notice on the "13th five-year" comprehensive work plan for energy conservation and emission reduction [EB/OL]. http://www.gov.cn/zhengce/content/2017-01/05/content_5156789.htm. Accessed 05 Jan 2017/29 Apr 2018
4. Jin, H.: Research on the role of street lights in shaping the image of the city. Art Des. **06**, 81–83 (2011)
5. Norman, D.A.: Emotional Design, Why We Love (or Hate) Everyday Things. Basic Books, New York (2003)

6. Ye, J., Cheng, J., Yang, C., Zhang, Z., Yang, X., Yao, L.: Research on the construction of the hierarchical classification model of the urban intelligent lighting appliance (UILA) based on user needs. In: Karwowski, W., Ahram, T. (eds.) IHSI 2018. AISC, vol. 722, pp. 315–320. Springer, Cham (2018). https://doi.org/10.1007/978-3-319-73888-8_49

7. Shanghai municipal people's government. The Shanghai municipal people's government has issued a notice on the "13th five-year plan of Shanghai for promoting smart city construction" [EB/OL]. http://www.shanghai.gov.cn/nw2/nw2314/nw2319/nw12344/u26aw50147.html. Accessed 19 Sept 2016/07 Aug 2017

8. Ye, J., Cheng, J., Yang, C., et al.: Construction and application of functional requirement model of the urban intelligent lighting appliance (UILA) based on the users' need. Adv. Transdisc. Eng. **5**, 925–932 (2017)

9. Xiang, W.: Product System Design - Product Design 2. China Light Industry Press, Beijing (2000)

10. Wang, Y.: Design practice and research on urban public facilities system. China Academy of Fine Arts (2014)

Design and Evaluation Case Studies

The Relationship Between Technology Self-Efficacy Beliefs and User Satisfaction – User Experience Perspective

Hasna Agourram[1][✉], Juliana Alvarez[1], Sylvain Sénécal[1],
Sylvie Lachize[2], Julie Gagné[2], and Pierre-Majorique Léger[1]

[1] Tech3Lab, HEC Montréal, 3000 Chemin de la Côte-Sainte-Catherine,
Montréal, QC H3T 2A7, Canada
hasna.agourram@hec.ca
[2] Vidéotron, 612 Rue St-Jacques, Montréal, QC H3C 1C8, Canada

Abstract. Scholars and researchers are becoming more interested in research that focus on the users' interaction with mobile technology as information technology providers are striving to develop innovative devices to attract more users. User self-efficacy and specifically Technology Self-Efficacy (TSE) has been largely used to predict user's task success and user's acceptance of technology. In other words, we assume that users who report high TSE are likely to succeed technology-based tasks and are likely to accept and use technology. However, little research investigates the relationship between pre- and posts-task self-perceived TSE and its relationship with user satisfaction. Based on the theory on self-perception, we aim to fill in this gap. First, we explore the relationship between TSE and user satisfaction. Second, we investigate on one hand the relationship between satisfaction and individuals whose TSE increase after the user test, and on the other hand, the relationship between satisfaction and individuals whose TSE decrease at the end of the user test. Theoretical contributions to HCI literature and practical implications to HCI practitioners are discussed.

Keywords: User experience · Satisfaction · Self-efficacy ·
Technology Self-Efficacy

1 Introduction

Self-efficacy is defined as people's beliefs in their capabilities to produce desired effects by their own actions [1]. One type of self-efficacy is Technology Self-Efficacy (TSE), which has been defined as "an individual's belief in his or her ability to use a computer effectively" [1]. The TSE construct has been used extensively to predict users' task effectiveness and technology acceptance [2]. The rationale is that when an individual believes he has the ability to successfully perform a task using a technology (High TSE), he will engage and make all efforts to successfully complete the task using the technology. He considers failures as challenges and believes that failures are usually dues to lack of experience and technological knowledge or skills that can be accessed or acquired easily [4].

© Springer Nature Switzerland AG 2019
M. Kurosu (Ed.): HCII 2019, LNCS 11568, pp. 389–397, 2019.
https://doi.org/10.1007/978-3-030-22636-7_29

Over the past decades, TSE has gained prominence in the social science literature, particularly in Information Systems (IS) and Human Computer Interaction (HCI) research as scholars use it as a predictor of users' responses (e.g., attitude and behaviors) towards a technology (p. 190) [5]. However, no or very little research has been conducted to investigate relationship between TSE and user satisfaction. Understanding this relationship leads to many managerial implications. For example, when a specific technology is deployed in an organization, managers are more concerned with the outcomes (users' satisfaction) towards the technology and are rarely concerned with why some users are more satisfied with the technology than others. If the TSE and satisfaction are correlated, then managers might want to explore ways to enhance TSE for low TSE users.

In order to address this gap in the literature, an experiment involving twenty-six users was performed. Prior to the experimental task, users reported their TSE. Then, they performed a task, which consisted of interacting with an electronic device. Finally, they were asked to report their post-task TSE. Results suggest that users with high TSE are more satisfied than users with low TSE.

Our findings add knowledge to existing research on user experience by exploring the relationship between user Technology Self-Efficacy and satisfaction. Technology Self-Efficacy can be added as a determinant to user satisfaction in IT implementation, acceptance and success models. Our findings may help these organizations ensure a high degree of user satisfaction in regards to the new technology.

2   Theoretical Background and Hypotheses

2.1   Satisfaction

From psychology perspective, user satisfaction "has been considered as the sum of one's feelings or attitudes toward a variety of factors affecting the situation" (p. 192) [6]. From an information technology perspective, user satisfaction is considered as one of the most important measure of IS success [7]. It is one of the essential factors, which researchers need to take into consideration when studying technology usage [7]. Delone and MacLean included user satisfaction as a major construct in their updated model of IS success [9]. DeLone and MacLean argue that when users are satisfied with a technology, this technology is considered to be beneficial and therefore leads to some success [9]. Sharma and Baoku added that the understanding of user satisfaction is vital to the success of business on the Web [10].

2.2   Self-perception, Self-efficacy, and Technology Self-Efficacy

Self-efficacy is defined as people's beliefs in their capabilities to produce desired effects by their own actions [1]. It is the expression of beliefs of individuals related to their own capability to perform a certain behavior [4, 11]. Bandura argues that people with high self-efficacy consider tasks as challenges [12]. The more challenging the task is, the more they get engaged. Bandura also argues that these people not only complete their task, but they also ensure the task is completed with a high degree of effectiveness [12].

Self-Efficacy is also fueled by the degree of skills of the individual who can be either low in self-efficacy or high in self-efficacy in specific disciplined. The self-efficacy scale developed by Bandura is a psychometric tool often deployed in UX testing. The Self-efficacy scale is assessed based on two concepts: the capacity and the confidence personally perceived by the user – the "I can do" [13] which influence a third construct, the motivation – the "I will do" [14]. Moreover, according to the self-efficacy literature, user's dissatisfaction occurs when the user lack confidence about the goal he wishes to attain [15, 16].

We have noticed a strong interest of IT researchers towards TSE [17–23]. The Technology Self-efficacy is defined as "an individual's belief in his or her ability to use a computer effectively" (p.101) [2]. The concept has been used extensively to predict user's use and acceptance of technology (024; 025; 03). The idea is that when an individual believes he or she has the ability in successfully perform a task using a technology, he or she will engage and makes all efforts to successfully complete the task. He or she sees failures as challenges and believes that failure is usually due to lack of experience and skills that can be easily acquired.

Moreover, Bem's [26] theory on self-perception suggests that people can infer their attitudes and self-perceptions by observing their own behaviours. This theory adds much to our understanding of how people learn from their own experiences and the consequences of this learning on their perceptions [25]. Bem [26] claims that individuals come to "know" their own attitudes, emotions, and other internal states partially by inferring them from observations of their own overt behaviours and/or the circumstances in which these behaviours occur [25]. Based on this theory and by using Technology Self-Efficacy as an example of self-perception, we are interested in user technology self-efficacy before the task (Pre-TSE) and user Technology Self- Efficacy after the task (Post-TSE).

We develop two hypotheses to investigate the relationship between pre- and posts-task self-perceived TSE particularly in relation to user satisfaction. The first hypothesis focuses on investigating the overall relationship between users Post-TSE and satisfaction. We argue that users with high Post-TSE are more likely to express a high degree of satisfaction after completing the task than users with low Post-TSE. Furthermore, this study goes deeper than just exploring the relationship between user TSE beliefs and satisfaction. The second hypothesis is based on Bem's [26] theory. The author claims that self-perception is likely to be altered by the experience (task). We focus this time on the variation process of user's TSE and argue that when users' TSE goes up (from Pre-TSE to Post-TSE), they are likely to be satisfied and when TSE decreases (from Pre-TSE to Post-TSE), the users are not likely to be satisfied.

We hence posit that:

Hypothesis 1: Users with high Post-TSE will likely be more satisfied than users with low Post-TSE.

Hypothesis 2: Users whose Post-TSE is greater than the Pre-TSE are likely be more satisfied than those whose Post-TSE decrease from the Pre-TSE.

3   Method

To test our hypothesis, we conducted a home device configuration study. Subjects were asked to setup a new version of a home entertainment system to a TV in an experimental living room. The Ethics Committee of our institution approved this study and each participant received a gift card to participate in this study.

3.1   Participants

During the recruitment of participant, several criteria were considered. All individuals wishing to participate in the study were asked to answer a short self-completed questionnaire so that the research team could learn about their skills and knowledge of electronic and audio-visual devices. The objective of this recruitment was to have participants whose ages ranged from 20 to 70 years, a balance between genders (13 men and 13 women) as well as between participant's IT knowledge and skills; Are the participants able to install or configure their devices on their own, on their own but with some help, do someone else around them doing it for them or are they request a technician to do it for themselves? The sample was selected to ensure that we could include and test different potential user profiles; thirteen participants with low TSE, who do not possess experience in using information technology-based tasks and thirteen participants with high TSE, who have good experience with IT. Herewith, we wanted to create some variance among the participants according to the user's ability to use technologies.

3.2   Procedure

The experiment room has been installed to reproduce a living room. The participants sat in a chair facing a television. They had at their disposal a table with all the materials that could help them complete the required configuration tasks: i.e. a spouse's note (contextualization), a remote control, a leaflet that referred to a website or an application as well as a computer or a smartphone.

In general, the basic configuration of common devices that we use on a day-to-day basis, such as an audio-visual material, are perceived as being unambiguous and easily achievable by most people. However, configuring tasks may affect a wide range of people. For this reason, in the experimental protocol, we select different tasks, which were likely to vary in their difficult to achieve across our sample. Each participant was asked to configure a smart device by performing four different configuring tasks: (1) tuning; (2) synchronization of the remote control with the device; (3) remote commands execution, and (4) search and launch of device content.

3.3   Apparatus and Psychometric Measures

As part of the user test, in total, participants were asked to complete pre and post questionnaires including the Pre-TSE and Post-TSE. Finally, in order to measure user satisfaction, we used a validated measurement scales to assess the participants' satisfaction towards the technology used. This post-questionnaire allowed participant to evaluate the usability of the technology in relation to their degree of satisfaction.

4   Results

4.1   Satisfaction Level According to User's Self-efficacy

The first objective of this research was to explore the relationship between TSE and user satisfaction. In order to analyze the effects of satisfaction on the users' Post-TSE and test the first hypothesis, we did a logistic regression with mixed model (2-tailed p-value). When crossing the results between users' satisfaction scores and their self-efficacy reported measures, results show a significant difference in the satisfaction level between users having a low Post-TSE and users with a high Post-TSE, with a p-value of <.0001. In other words, the results shown in Table 1 indicate that users with high Post-TSE seem to be more satisfied about their experience than users with low Post-TSE when completing configuration-tasks. Thus, H1 is validated. Users with high Post-TSE were more satisfied than users who reported low Post-TSE.

Table 1. User's satisfaction according to their post-reported TSE.

Dependent Variable	Effect	Nbr Obs	Estimate	StdErr	DF	T_Value	P-value	HSE_Pre	HSE_Post
Satisfaction	HSE_Pre	56	1.0317	0.2022	78	5.1	<.0001	1	
Satisfaction	HSE_Post	56	1.0833	0.1996	78	5.43	<.0001		1

In the second objective, which was based on Bem's theory (1972), we focused on the variation process of user's TSE. In order to analyze the variation of users' Pre- and Post-TSE with regard to satisfaction and to test the second hypothesis, we used the Wilcoxon signed-rank test (one-tailed p-value) and found a statistically significant result with a p-value of 0.047. When comparing users whose Technology Self-Efficacy (TSE) goes up (i.e., 17 participants) to those whose TSE goes down (i.e., 4 participants), the results shown in Table 2, indicate that participants whose TSE goes up (i.e., higher Post-TSE than Pre-TSE), report a higher degree of satisfaction than those whose TSE goes down. Thus, our second hypothesis is validated.

Table 2. Sample means and median of satisfaction (p = 0.047)

TSE variation	Number of participants	Means	Median
Down	4	4.75	4.8333
Up	17	6.5490	6.6667

5   Discussion

In summary, this research aims to investigate how self-efficacy is related to the user satisfaction. The first objective of this research was to explore the relationship between TSE and user satisfaction. Our results suggest that users with high Post-TSE are more satisfied than those with low Post-TSE. Thus, our first hypothesis is validated. The second objective of this research is to explore the relationship between the variation of the degree of TSE from Pre- and Post-TSE and Satisfaction We found out that a high number of participants whose TSE increase from Pre-TSE to Post-TSE are more satisfied than those whose TSE decrease from Pre-TSE to Post-TSE.

As we mentioned earlier, satisfaction is the expression of the sum of many feelings. A very high number of participants who have high TSE have expressed satisfaction after completing the task. This result can be explained by many factors. First, the participants associate their satisfaction with their ability to complete the task regardless of the task itself. These people express pride and satisfaction because they prove their ability to succeeding the task. The beauty of the TSE belief is that when the task is easy to use and user friendly, the task might take less time to complete but satisfaction will always maintain high. On the other hand, when the task is complex and not user friendly, according to Brandon people with high TSE challenge themselves and make all possible efforts to bypass the task complexity and obstacles in order to complete the task [27]. At the same time, these people feel again satisfied with their work.

The task simplicity is a major factor that can explain the second result. As a matter of facts, when people found out that the task was simple and did not require much effort to complete, they felt confident on their ability to succeed IT-based tasks and this has been translated in their degree of satisfaction. On the other hand, people who found out that the task was complex have lost confidence on their ability to handle IT tasks.

5.1   Theoretical Implications

Our findings contribute to knowledge in IT and HCI [28–32] by exploring the relationship between user's Technology Self-Efficacy and user satisfaction. We found out that Technology Self-Efficacy could be added as a determinant to user satisfaction in IT implementation, acceptance and success models. The results support a correlation between Task Simplicity and TSE as well [33, 34]. The more simple the task is the higher TSE becomes.

5.2   Managerial Implications

Our results bring many managerial implications. First, from marketing perspectives and in an effort to reduce operating costs or servicing customers, many organizations turn to self-service. Self-Service Technology (SST) is defined as "technological interfaces that enable customers to produce a service independent of direct service employee involvement" (p. 50) [35]. In other words, organizations try to convince their customers to use this type of technology as an alternative to service representative service [36]. Our results bring support to these organizations and suggest that these organizations may offer customer SST only to customers who have high TSE. The use of SST aims to meet the need for greater autonomy issued by customers. Practically speaking, they can distribute TSE questionnaires to all their customers and select only those who rank high in TSE. It would be a waste of time to offer technology to people who have low to very low TSE.

Second, organizations that develop business information systems are always faced with the challenge to motivate their employees to use the new systems and technology.

There may be employees who have high TSE and others who have low TSE. The fact that High TSE leads to satisfaction is a good reason to make these organizations think of ways to enhance TSE to those who have low TSE. The higher the TSE the more satisfied users would be and the more users are satisfied the more likely they would accept and use the system.

5.3   Limitations and Future Research

This research presents limits and opportunities for future research. First, the control variables of the recruitment process, such as user IT experience, could have been further explore. In fact, since we have chosen to collect information on only two groups of people, users with high TSE and users with low TSE, we did not consider users with average TSE beliefs; users who are neither high nor low in TSE. We encourage further research to consider these individuals in order to find a trend in between these three categories and meaningful relationships. Second, in this research we measured user satisfaction only once after completing the user test. We wish we could have measured user satisfaction after completing each of the four tasks. This way, we would have investigated the impact or the relationship between the task itself and user satisfaction.

References

1. Bandura, A.: Self-efficacy in Changing Societies. Cambridge University Press, Cambridge (1997)
2. Simmering, M., Posey, C., Piccoli, G.: Computer self-efficacy and motivation to learn in a self-directed online course. Decis. Sci. J. Innov. Educ. **7**, 99–121 (2009)
3. Chen, Y.: A study on student self-efficacy and technology acceptance model within an online task-based learning environment. J. Comput. **9**, 34–43 (2014)
4. Bandura, A.: Self-efficacy: toward a unifying theory of behavioral change. Psychol. Rev. **84**, 191–215 (1977)
5. Compeau, D., Higgins, C.: Computer self-efficacy: development of a measure and initial test. MIS Q. **19**, 189 (1995)
6. Legris, P., Ingham, J., Collerette, P.: Why do people use information technology? A critical review of the technology acceptance model. Inf. Manag. **40**, 191–204 (2003)
7. Urbach, N., Müller, B.: The updated DeLone and McLean model of information systems success. In: Information Systems Theory, pp. 1–18 (2011)
8. Isaac, O., Abdullah, Z., Ramayah, T., Mutahar, A.: Internet usage, user satisfaction, task-technology fit, and performance impact among public sector employees in Yemen. Int. J. Inf. Learn. Technol. **34**, 210–241 (2017)
9. Delone, W., McLean, E.: The DeLone and McLean model of information systems success: a ten-year update. J. Manag. Inf. Syst. **19**, 9–30 (2003)
10. Sharma, G., Baoku, L.: Customer satisfaction in Web 2.0 and information technology development. Inf. Technol. People **26**, 347–367 (2013)
11. Gençtürk, E., Gökçek, T., Güneş, G.: Reliability and validity study of the technology proficiency self-assessment scale. Proc. - Soc. Behav. Sci. **2**, 2863–2867 (2010)
12. Bandura, A.: Self-efficacy. In: Encyclopedia of Human Behaviour, pp. 71–81. Academic Press, NY (1994)

13. Bandura, A.: Self-Efficacy Beliefs of Adolescents, pp. 307–337. Information Age Publishing, Greenwich (2006)
14. Bandura, A.: Reflections on self-efficacy. Adv. Behav. Res. Ther. 1, 237–269 (1978)
15. Locke, E.: Social foundations of thought and action: a social-cognitive view. Acad. Manag. Rev. 12, 169–171 (1987). Bandura, A.: Social Foundations of Thought and Action: A Social-Cognitive, 617 p. Prentice-Hall, Englewood Cliffs (1986)
16. Latham, G., Brown, T.: The effect of learning vs. outcome goals on self-efficacy, satisfaction and performance in an MBA program. Appl. Psychol. 55, 606–623 (2006)
17. Feng, W., Tu, R., Lu, T., Zhou, Z.: Understanding forced adoption of self-service technology: the impacts of users' psychological reactance. Behav. Inf. Technol. 1–13 (2018)
18. Gan, C., Balakrishnan, V.: Mobile technology in the classroom: what drives student-lecturer interactions? Int. J. Hum.-Comput. Interact. 34, 666–679 (2017)
19. Hwang, Y., Lee, Y., Shin, D.: The role of goal awareness and information technology self-efficacy on job satisfaction of healthcare system users. Behav. Inf. Technol. 35, 548–558 (2016)
20. Kitchens, B., Dobolyi, D., Li, J., Abbasi, A.: Advanced customer analytics: strategic value through integration of relationship-oriented big data. J. Manag. Inf. Syst. 35, 540–574 (2018)
21. Nguyen, Q., Ta, A., Prybutok, V.: An integrated model of voice-user interface continuance intention: the gender effect. Int. J. Hum.-Comput. Interact. 1–16 (2018)
22. Peñarroja, V., Sánchez, J., Gamero, N., Orengo, V., Zornoza, A.: The influence of organisational facilitating conditions and technology acceptance factors on the effectiveness of virtual communities of practice. Behav. Inf. Technol. 1–13 (2019)
23. Shu, Q., Tu, Q., Wang, K.: The impact of computer self-efficacy and technology dependence on computer-related technostress: a social cognitive theory perspective. Int. J. Hum.-Comput. Interact. 27, 923–939 (2011)
24. Davis, F.: Perceived usefulness, perceived ease of use, and user acceptance of information technology. MIS Q. 13, 319 (1989)
25. Laver, K., George, S., Ratcliffe, J., Crotty, M.: Measuring technology self efficacy: reliability and construct validity of a modified computer self efficacy scale in a clinical rehabilitation setting. Disabil. Rehabil. 34, 220–227 (2011)
26. Bem, D.J.: Self-perception theory. Adv. Exp. Soc. Psychol. 6, 1–62 (1972)
27. Salyzyn, B.: How teachers' experience, attitudes, and self-efficacy concerning technology influence its use in the classroom. http://dspace.library.uvic.ca:8080/bitstream/handle/1828/9251/Salyzyn_Brandon_MEd_2018.pdf?sequence=3&isAllowed=y
28. Birk, M., Mandryk, R., Miller, M., Gerling, K.: How self-esteem shapes our interactions with play technologies. In: Proceedings of the 2015 Annual Symposium on Computer-Human Interaction in Play - CHI PLAY 2015 (2015)
29. John, P.: Influence of computer self-efficacy on information technology adoption. Int. J. Inf. Technol. 19, 1–13 (2013)
30. Yi, M., Hwang, Y.: Predicting the use of web-based information systems: self-efficacy, enjoyment, learning goal orientation, and the technology acceptance model. Int. J. Hum Comput Stud. 59, 431–449 (2003)
31. Kujala, S., Roto, V., Väänänen-Vainio-Mattila, K., Karapanos, E., Sinnelä, A.: UX Curve: a method for evaluating long-term user experience. Interact. Comput. 23, 473–483 (2011)
32. Rajeswari, K., Anantharaman, R.: Role of human-computer interaction factors as moderators of occupational stress and work exhaustion. Int. J. Hum.-Comput. Interact. 19, 137–154 (2005)
33. Oppewal, H., Klabbers, M.: Compromising between information completeness and task simplicity: a comparison of self-explicated, hierarchical information integration, and full-profile conjoint methods. Adv. Consum. Res. 30, 298–304 (2003)

34. Ben-Gurion, E., Tractinsky, N.: The Paradox of simplicity: effects of user interface design on perceptions and preference of interactive systems. In: Proceedings Mediterranean Conference on Information Systems - MCIS (2010)
35. Meuter, M.L., Ostrom, A.L., Roudtree, R.I., Bitner, M.J.: Self-service technologies: understanding customer satisfaction with technology-based service encounters. J. Mark. **64**, 50–64 (2000)
36. Considine, E., Cormican, K.: Self-service technology adoption: an analysis of customer to technology interactions. Proc. Comput. Sci. **100**, 103–109 (2016)

A Digital Twin-Based Multi-modal UI Adaptation Framework for Assistance Systems in Industry 4.0

Klementina Josifovska[(✉)], Enes Yigitbas, and Gregor Engels

Paderborn University, Paderborn, Germany
{klementina.josifovska,enes.yigitbas,gregor.engels}@uni-paderborn.de

Abstract. As a consequence of digital transformation many aspects related to the industrial manufacturing processes are facing changes. In terms of Human-Machine Interaction, the User Interface (UI) plays the most important role as a mediator between the human and certain assistance systems. In traditional industrial environments, the UIs are usually designed to handle a unimodal input command (via touch screen, keyboard or mouse) and to present a feedback in a visual way. However, due to the nature of the tasks there is a need for the human workers to easily shift tasks and acquire new skills. For this reason, in the UI adaptation process the personal abilities and preferences of the human workers should be taken into consideration. In this paper, we present a novel reference model for multi-modal adaptive UIs for assistance systems in manufacturing processes. Our approach provides a solution framework for adaptation of assistance systems in manufacturing processes not only based on the environmental conditions, but also based on the personal characteristics and abilities of the human workers, obtained by a personalized Digital Twin.

Keywords: Adaptive user interface · Digital Twin · Industry 4.0

1 Introduction

In recent years, many governments and industrial associations in the world introduced various initiatives oriented towards the new industrial revolution, including Industry 4.0. The vision of these initiatives is incorporating technological changes and advancements in different industrial applications, which subsequently will induce changes in the nature of the tasks and the demands for the human workers. Each individual worker in context of Industry 4.0 will face variety of challenges and problems to solve, mostly related to high cognitive activities [1]. To address this problem, one of the visions is to ensure that the machines and the humans interact and work collaboratively, such that the machines assist the humans. In terms of the Human-Machine Interaction, the User Interface (UI) plays the most important role as a mediator between the human and a

© Springer Nature Switzerland AG 2019
M. Kurosu (Ed.): HCII 2019, LNCS 11568, pp. 398–409, 2019.
https://doi.org/10.1007/978-3-030-22636-7_30

certain machine. Traditional industrial UIs are usually designed to handle a uni-modal input and to present visual feedback. However, in a dynamically context-changing environment, the possibility for having a unimodal interaction represents a big constraint for the human workers. Therefore, there is an emerging need for providing multi-modal UIs which adapt to the current context, personal abilities and preferences of the human workers. In order to tackle this problem, in our paper, we introduce a solution approach for providing multi-modal adaptive UIs for assistance systems in context of industrial manufacturing processes. For this purpose, we extend our existing model-based reference framework for adaptive UIs [2] by incorporation of a *Digital Twin* of a human in order to define a structure which models in a systematic and fine-grained way specific human abilities, characteristics and preferences. We use this structure as a source for providing personalized information, based on which the UIs of assistance systems can adapt. The rest of the paper is structured in the following way: in Sect. 2 we elaborate two example scenarios which describe the problem space. Section 3 presents the related work in respect to topics related to adaptive UIs and the concept of a digital twin. Our solution approach is elaborated in Sect. 4 and in Sect. 5 we evaluate our approach based on two case studies. Section 6 concludes this paper and provides outlook for the future work.

2   Example Scenarios

In this section, we present two example scenarios in order to illustrate the problem in respect to assistance systems in manufacturing processes. The first example scenario is related to manual assembly of an Electrical Cabinet (E-cabinet), while the second scenario represents the process of manual assembly of a concrete product in a Smart Factory. With these example scenarios we intend to illustrate more precisely the problem domain and the current challenges. These example scenarios are derived from the results of our interdisciplinary study, realized by conduction of semi-structured interviews with experts from different research fields: Psychology, Sociology, Didactic, Economics, Computer Science, Electrical and Mechanical Engineering. The main objective of the study was investigation of the requirements and needs of the human workers in the industrial sector and development of a solution to meet these requirements.

2.1   Example Scenario 1: Manual Assembly of E-Cabinet

Figure 1 illustrates an example scenario by emphasizing the challenges which the human worker (electrician) is facing by performing an assembly task for an E-cabinet with help of an assistance system - tablet. As we can observe in Fig. 1, there are six different situations depicting the current challenges. According to *Situation 2*, the electrician faces problems due to the brightness of the tablet and has to stop assembling in order to re-configure it. In *Situation 3*, he has to perform actions in the back side of the E-Cabinet and he can't carry the tablet with him. He has to go several times back and forth to finish connecting some cables. *Situation 4* shows that even in vocal mode, the adaptation is not appropriately personalized - the interfering noise from other machines around and the speed of the voice instructions are too fast for a 60 year old worker.

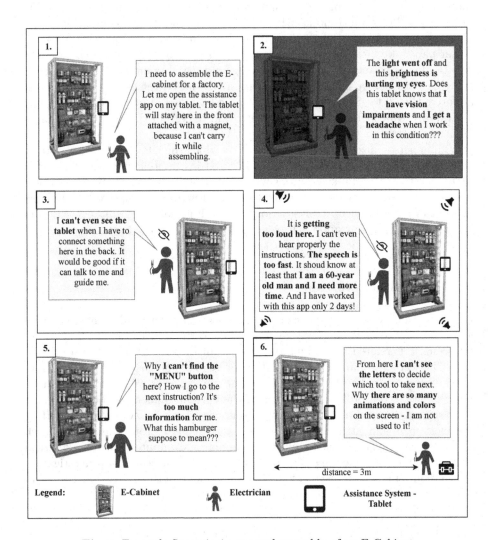

Fig. 1. Example Scenario 1 - manual assembly of an E-Cabinet

In *Situation 5*, we can observe that he has difficulties in terms of the navigation and dealing with the information presentation on the graphical UI, since he doesn't have advanced user experience. Furthermore, as presented in *Situation 6*, when attempting to perform an action from a longer distance, the electrician faces problems in recognition of the layout and the size of the UI elements.

2.2 Example Scenario 2: Manual Assembly of a Product in a Smart Factory

This scenario demonstrates the challenges which the human worker faces during manual assembly of a product (LEGO car) in a Smart Factory. As Fig. 2 depicts, the working environment consists of an *Assembly Station*, a *Tool Kit* and an *Assistance System - Tablet* (on the left side, fixed). According to *Situation 1*, the worker opens the interactive guide and starts with the assembly instructions, which are visually presented on the screen. In *Situation 2*, the worker has to use gloves for operating with a tool and therefore he can not give commands by touch. It takes him a lot of time to stop and set back the instructions while removing the gloves several times.

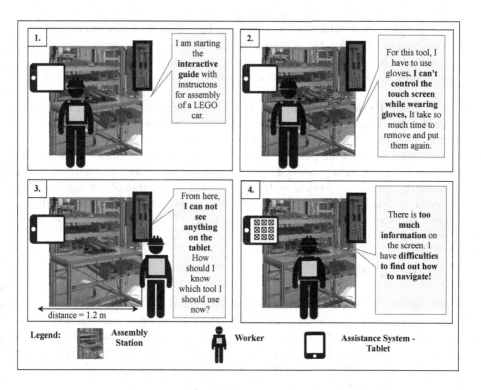

Fig. 2. Example Scenario 2 - manual assembly of a product in Smart Factory

In *Situation 3*, the worker switches to the next assembly step, for which he has to use a specific tool and it is practically impossible to follow the instructions while searching for the tool in the *Tool Kit* placed on the right side. This situation requires that the worker again moves several times until he identifies the desired tool. In *Situation 4*, the worker finds difficulties in recognizing a concrete assembly piece of the product. He is confused, because he sees many details on the screen, which de-focus him. He needs more precise details about the concrete piece, since the assembly piece looks very similar to some of the previous ones. For this, the worker invests much time in navigating and orienting on the graphical UI.

From these two scenarios, we can observe that both human workers experience several challenges during interaction with an assistance system due to context-changing conditions, as well as their personal abilities and characteristics. Based on the concrete example scenarios, we can identify several main challenges for supporting the development of smart assistance systems:

- **C1: Monitoring the context of use.** This aspect refers to uncontrollable contextual and environmental changes during the working process and domain-specific constraints, such as change in the lighting condition, noise interference or distance and location variability.
- **C2: Lack of UI adaptation features in existing assistance systems.** This aspect addresses the problem that existing assistance systems lack capabilities to adapt the UI based on the current contextual conditions, such as switching to vocal mode, adapting the navigation or adapting the presentation.
- **C3: User Experience improvement through analysis of interaction patterns.** This aspect targets the need for personalization and knowledge from past user experiences. Currently, there is no approach in the context of assistance systems for manufacturing processes which includes these factors in the UI adaptation process. From the example scenarios, we can observe the necessity for the assistance systems to obtain knowledge about the workers' personal characteristics (e.g. age, vision impairments, cognitive capabilities, etc.) and the past user experiences (e.g. usage of certain devices, apps, interaction styles, etc.)

3   Related Work

In this section, we provide an overview of the related work in respect to the concepts associated to adaptive UI and digital twin. In terms of assistance systems, the study of Gorecky [1] provides an overview of the possibilities for human-machine interaction in Industry 4.0, with indication that the interaction in the industrial environments in the future will be mostly based on intelligent mobile assistance systems, such as tablets and mobile phones.

3.1   Adaptive UI

Currently, various research approaches address specific aspects of the UI adaptation process. An overview of the variety of adaptation techniques is presented in the studies of Oppermann [3] and Brusilovsky [4]. Furthermore, in our existing work [2,5–7], we have established a model-driven engineering approach for generating context-specific adaptive UIs which support the modeling, transformation and execution of adaptive UIs. Our model-driven engineering approach was applied for different application domains like cross-channel banking applications or library management applications. In addition, we elaborate the aspect of model-driven context management in our work presented in [8], with focus on contextual parameters which effect the adaptation process of the UIs. However, these approaches do not focus on UI adaptation in terms of incorporating a fine-grained human model for accurate personalization of the adaptive UIs.

3.2 Digital Twin

Nowadays, the *Digital Twin* framework is frequently mentioned as one of the main enablers for digital transformation. The term *Digital Twin* was first introduced in 2002 by Grieves [9] in context of product lifecycle management. In the context of Industry 4.0, the *Digital Twin* is introduced as a framework for mirroring certain aspects of the underlying physical entities in the manufacturing processes. The high-level goal of using a *Digital Twin* framework is to ensure certain type of process optimization [10–13]. However, in respect of integrating the human factor, still, one of the biggest challenges requires establishing a relevant knowledge and comprehensive information model of the human worker. This knowledge can be used for various purposes such as for UI adaptation processes or in recommender systems.

4   Digital Twin-Based Multi-modal UI Adaptation Framework

In order to tackle the defined challenges, we have developed a *Digital Twin-Based Multi-Modal UI Adaptation Framework* for assistance systems in the context of manufacturing processes. As depicted in Fig. 3, our solution extends the existing MAPE-K paradigm for self-adaptive software systems [14] and it consists of three main components: *Context Manager, Adaptation Manager* and *Self-adaptive UI*.

The *Context Manager* addresses challenge C1 and is responsible for storing context of use data and providing contextual information to the *Adaptation Manager*. The *Context Manager* consists of three models: *Platform Model, Environment Model* and a *Digital Twin of a Human Model*.

The *Platform Model* defines the characteristics of the underlying interaction platform. It includes the *Operating System* and various properties of the underlying *Device*, such as: *Battery Level, Network Connection, Screen*, as well as various types of *Sensors*. In addition, the *Context Manager* contains the *Environment Model* which specifies the environmental characteristics and include the current *Time, Date, Noise Level, Movement Status, Weather* and *Location*. Furthermore, the *Digital Twin of a Human Model* provides a fine grained representation of the human worker, by considering numerous human characteristics including: *Personal and Demographic Data, Physical Abilities, Sensory Abilities, Communication Preferences, Skills, Social and Personal Characteristics, Health Data* and *Cognitive Abilities*. The development of the *Digital Twin of a Human Model* is based on an interdisciplinary study by conduction of semi-structured interviews with experts engaged in various research fields. By incorporation of the *Digital Twin of a Human Model* we include the personalization factor as an additional context information for adaptation of the UIs.

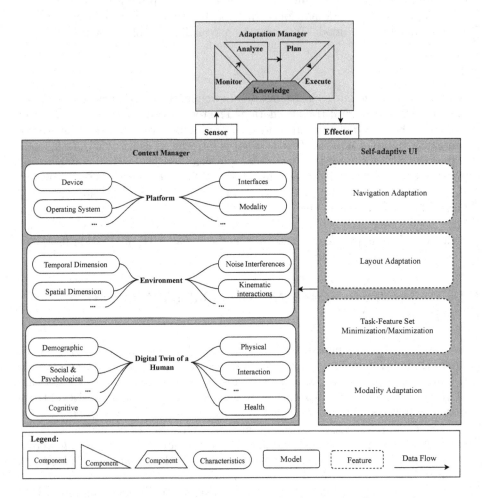

Fig. 3. Digital Twin-Based Multi-modal UI Adaptation Framework

The *Adaptation Manager* follows the MAPE-K paradigm [14] and it is responsible for *Monitoring* the context of use provided by the *Context Manager*, *Analyzing* and *Planning* which adaptation rules will be triggered and finally *Executing* the adaption operations on the *Self-adaptive UI*. The *Adaptation Manager* supports four different layers of adaptation rules for the adaptive UIs: *Navigation, Layout, Task-Feature Set Minimization/Maximization* and *Modality* adaptation which are explained in the following paragraph. The adaptation rules are specified based on the *ECA (Event-Condition-Action)* paradigm and the *Context*

Model. By establishing a *Knowledge* component in the *Adaptation Manager* we address challenge C3 since it is possible to store log data about previous context information and adaptation changes. This is achieved due to the *Self-adaptive UI* which informs the *Context Manager* about previously executed adaptation information.

The *Self-adaptive UI* component addresses the challenge C2 and provides a solution for this requirement by establishment of adaptation features which allow the UIs to be adapted. The adaptation features include: *Navigation, Layout, Task-Feature Set Minimization/Maximization* and *Modality* adaptation. The *Navigation* adaptation deals with changes in the navigation flow and adapting the navigation links, while the *Layout* adaptation ensures proper adaptation of the *Font, Font Size, Color Theme*, etc. Furthermore, the *Task-Feature Set Minimization/Maximization* adaptation allows changes based on the current context where the amount of information presented to the user is minimized or maximized. The *Modality* adaptation allows change in the interaction modality with the user. When certain conditions are detected, the graphical UI can change to a vocal UI and the user can interact by providing and receiving voice commands.

5   Case Studies

In this section, we demonstrate and apply our solution approach for two case studies related to the example scenarios presented in Sect. 2. We describe the solution based on the *Digital Twin-Based Multi-Modal UI Adaptation Framework*. Besides the variety of sensors which are monitoring the environment, the framework incorporates a fine-grained *Digital Twin of a Human Model* for providing personalized adaption of the UI.

5.1   Case Study 1: Solution Approach for Manual Assembly of E-Cabinet

In this case study, we apply our model-based solution framework for Example Scenario 1, which is depicted in Fig. 1. In order to tackle the challenge in *Situation 2*, the *Digital Twin* provides information about *Vision Impairment* of the worker. In addition, the *Ambient Light Sensor* detects the *Brightness* decrease in the room and based on these two parameters, the brightness of the tablet is adapted appropriately. In respect to *Situation 3*, we can refer to the excerpt from the *Object Diagram of the Context Model* presented in Fig. 4. The *Proximity Sensor* detects that, despite the *Movement Status*, the *Distance* between the worker and the tablet is too big (80 cm) and this is the condition which triggers adaptation of the UI *Modality* into vocal. Figure 5, depicts this concrete adaptation rule and the underlying parameters for adapting the modality from visual to vocal.

However, in *Situation 4*, the speed and the sound level of the voice instructions are too high for the worker. Based on the personalized information from the *Digital Twin*, such as *Usage Time, Age* and previous *Interaction Data*, the UI is adapted, such that the *Speed* and the *Sound Volume* of the instructions fit to the personal abilities of the human worker. In Fig. 6, we can observe the underlying parameters for triggering the adaptation rule for *Situation 4*.

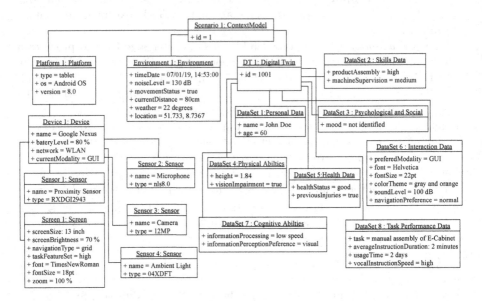

Fig. 4. Excerpt from the Object Diagram of the Context Model for Example Scenario 1 - Situation 3

In Situation 5, the worker faces a problem with the navigation and the content presentation. The *Digital Twin* provides information that the worker has used the app only 2 days. Based on additional information from the *Digital Twin* the navigation is adapted to a grid navigation and the amount of content presented on the UI is decreased. The worker can now navigate more intuitively though the app. In *Situation 6*, the distance among the worker and the tablet increases again.

Event	Environment.CurrentDistance = 80 cm AND Environment.MovementStatus = true
Condition	Environment.CurrentDistance > 50 cm AND Device.CurrentModality != vocal
Action	ChangeModalityOfUI (vocal);

Fig. 5. Adaptation rule for adapting to vocal modality (Example Scenario 1 - Situation 3)

In this case, the *Digital Twin* provides information about his preferences for *Font, Font Size and Theme Color* when he works on longer distance. Therefore, the *Font Size* increases and the *Color Theme* changes, such that the worker can clearly follow the visual content presentation.

Event	Environment.NoiseLevel = 130 dB AND TaskPerformanceData.VocalInstructionSpeed = high
Condition	Environment.NoiseLevel > 100 dB AND TaskPerformanceData.VocalInstructionSpeed = high AND PersonalData.Age > 50 AND TaskPerformanceData.UsageTime < 1 month
Action	ChangeSoundLevel (100 dB); ChangeInstructionDuration (4 minutes); ChangeVocalInstructionSpeed (medium);

Fig. 6. Adaptation rule for adapting vocal preferences (Example Scenario 1 - Situation 4)

5.2 Case Study 2: Solution Approach for Manual Assembly of a Product in a Smart Factory

In the following, we elaborate the solution approach for Example Scenario 2 presented in this paper. As we can observe from Fig. 2, the worker starts to use the interactive visual guide for instructions. However, in *Situation 2* he has to use gloves for operating a tool and the visual UI modality is not appropriate anymore.

Similarly as in Example Scenario 1, the *Context Model* provides information from the past user experience about preferred interaction modality when using a concrete tool and the UI modality is switched to vocal. Furthermore, the *Digital Twin* provides personalized information about the vocal interaction preferences of the user - for the adaptation process in *Situation 2*.

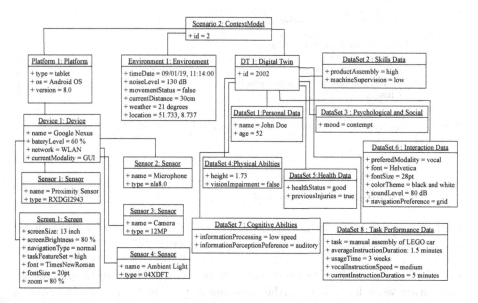

Fig. 7. Excerpt from the Object Diagram of the Context Model for Example Scenario 2 - Situation 4

After the UI is adapted back to visual modality, the current distance among the assistance system and the worker increases (1.2 m) and this condition triggers again vocal adaptation of the UI - *Situation 3*.

Furthermore, *Situation 4* illustrates a challenge where the worker is having difficulties in recognizing a concrete piece needed for assembling the product. The *Context Manager* detects that the worker needs much time regarding a concrete instruction (5 min), but at the same time there is no *Movement Status* detected. This event triggers the UI adaptation process and for this purpose several conditions are checked. The *Digital Twin* informs that the *Mood* of the worker changed from normal to contempt. In addition, the *Usage Time, Current Distance, Navigation Type, Navigation Preferences, Information Processing Preferences* and *Task Feature Set* are evaluated. As a result of the conditions check, the layout of the graphical UI is adapted. This includes adaptation to a grid navigation and reduction of the amount of information shown on the screen. In addition, the *Font Size* is increased and the underlying *Color Theme* is adapted. Figure 7 presents an excerpt from the *Object Diagram of the Context Model for Example Scenario 2* in respect to *Situation 4*, while Fig. 8 depicts the adaptation rule for *Situation 4*.

Event	TaskPerformanceData.CurrentInstructionDuration = 5 minutes AND Environment.MovementStatus = false
Condition	PsychologicalAndSocial.Mood = contempt AND Environment.CurrentDistance < 50 cm AND CognitiveAbilities.InformationPerceptionPreference = auditory AND Screen.NavigationType = normal AND InteractionData.NavigationPreferences = grid AND Screen.TaskFeatureSet = high
Action	ChangeNavigationType (grid); ChangeTaskFeatureSet (minimized); ChangeFont (helvetica); ChangeFontSize (28 pt); ChangeColorTheme (black and white); ChangeZoom (100 %);

Fig. 8. Adaptation rule for adapting the graphical UI layout (Example Scenario 2 - Situation 4)

6   Conclusion and Outlook

With our solution approach, we provide a novel reference model for multi-modal adaptive UIs in the context of manufacturing processes. We have demonstrated the benefit and application of our *Digital Twin-Based Multi-Modal UI Adaptation Framework* based on two case studies in the context of smart manufacturing. Our future work focuses on further development of the framework in terms of refinement of the *Digital Twin of a Human Model*, development of novel adaptation features and adaptation rules to fit into the domain of smart manufacturing.

References

1. Gorecky, D., Schmitt, M., Loskyll, M., Zühlke, D.: Human-machine-interaction in the industry 4.0 era. In: 2014 12th IEEE International Conference on Industrial Informatics (INDIN), pp. 289–294. IEEE (2014)
2. Yigitbas, E., Sauer, S., Engels, G.: A model-based framework for multi-adaptive migratory user interfaces. In: Kurosu, M. (ed.) HCI 2015. LNCS, vol. 9170, pp. 563–572. Springer, Cham (2015). https://doi.org/10.1007/978-3-319-20916-6_52
3. Oppermann, R.: Individualisierte systemnutzung. In: Paul, M. (ed.) GI—19. Jahrestagung I. Informatik-Fachberichte, vol. 222, pp. 131–145. Springer, Heidelberg (1989). https://doi.org/10.1007/978-3-642-75177-6_11
4. Brusilovsky, P.: Adaptive educational hypermedia. In: International PEG Conference, vol. 10, pp. 8–12 (2001)
5. Yigitbas, E., Sauer, S.: Engineering context-adaptive uis for task-continuous cross-channel applications. In: Bogdan, C., Gulliksen, J., Sauer, S., Forbrig, P., Winckler, M., Johnson, C., Palanque, P., Bernhaupt, R., Kis, F. (eds.) HCSE/HESSD -2016. LNCS, vol. 9856, pp. 281–300. Springer, Cham (2016). https://doi.org/10.1007/978-3-319-44902-9_18
6. Yigitbas, E., Sauer, S., Engels, G.: Adapt-UI: An IDE supporting model-driven development of self-adaptive UIs. In: Proceedings of the 9th ACM SIGCHI Symposium on Engineering Interactive Computing Systems, EICS 2017, pp. 99–104. ACM (2017)
7. Yigitbas, E., Stahl, H., Sauer, S., Engels, G.: Self-adaptive UIs: integrated model-driven development of UIs and their adaptations. In: Anjorin, A., Espinoza, H. (eds.) ECMFA 2017. LNCS, vol. 10376, pp. 126–141. Springer, Cham (2017). https://doi.org/10.1007/978-3-319-61482-3_8
8. Yigitbas, E., Grün, S., Sauer, S., Engels, G.: Model-driven context management for self-adaptive user interfaces. In: Ochoa, S.F., Singh, P., Bravo, J. (eds.) UCAmI 2017. LNCS, vol. 10586, pp. 624–635. Springer, Cham (2017). https://doi.org/10.1007/978-3-319-67585-5_61
9. Grieves, M., Vickers, J.: Digital twin: mitigating unpredictable, undesirable emergent behavior in complex systems. In: Kahlen, F.-J., Flumerfelt, S., Alves, A. (eds.) Transdisciplinary Perspectives on Complex Systems, pp. 85–113. Springer, Cham (2017). https://doi.org/10.1007/978-3-319-38756-7_4
10. Tao, F., et al.: Digital twin-driven product design framework. Int. J. Prod. Res. (2018). https://doi.org/10.1080/00207543.2018.1443229
11. Tao, F., Zhang, M.: Digital twin shop-floor: a new shop-floor paradigm towards smart manufacturing. IEEE Access 5, 20418–20427 (2017)
12. Uhlemann, T.H.J., Lehmann, C., Steinhilper, R.: The digital twin: Realizing the cyber-physical production system for industry 4.0. Proc. CIRP 61, 335–340 (2017)
13. Vachálek, J., Bartalský, L., Rovný, O., Šišmišová, D., Morháč, M., Lokšík, M.: The digital twin of an industrial production line within the industry 4.0 concept. In: 2017 21st International Conference on Process Control (PC), pp. 258–262. IEEE (2017)
14. Kephart, J.O., Chess, D.M.: The vision of autonomic computing. Computer 36(1), 41–50 (2003)

Preliminary Experiment for Navigation on Tactile Display Using DC Motor

Yusuke Komatsu[✉] and Makio Ishihara

Fukuoka Institute of Technology,
3-30-1 Wajiro-higashi, Higashi-ku, Fukuoka 811-0295, Japan
mfm18104@bene.fit.ac.jp, m-ishihara@fit.ac.jp,
http://www.fit.ac.jp/~m-ishihara/Lab/

Abstract. In this paper, as a preliminary experiment for walking navigation, conduct experiments of the pseudo force sense using four different waveforms when holding the DC motor with three fingers. In addition, two types of the DC motors with different rotation per minute or RPM and torque, are used to examine an impact of those properties of motors on the pseudo force sense. As a result, it is found that people would feel the pseudo force sense in the direction of the weak rotational acceleration. And There can also be a tendency for people to perceive the pseudo force more easily in the extending direction of the wrist. Moreover, by comparing results from two type of motors with different RPM and torques, it is found that the motor with higher RPM and torque would cause people to feel easily pseudo force.

Keywords: Pseudo force sense · DC motor · Walking navigation

1 Introduction

In recent years, tactile presentation using vibration has been discussed in the field of human computer interaction. Tomohiro et al. [3] proposed a walking navigation system with traction force illusion which is presented by a mechanism that converts the constant rotation into the translational periodic motion. This mechanism however prevents its device size from downsizing. Yem et al. [5] showed that a pseudo force sense occurs by presenting an asymmetric rotation to a DC motor. By putting two DC motors on the thumb and index finger, people would feel the pseudo force so that the fingers are spreading out or pinching in. Their device uses just only a DC motor so that it could become small enough for people to carry. When it comes back to walking navigation, it is still unclear if the pseudo force sense DC motors manages to display the specific direction. In this manuscript, we focus on walking navigation with a single DC motor and report some properties of the pseudo force sense when people grasp the DC motor with the thumb, index finger and middle one. Specifically two types of DC motors with different velocity of rotation per minute or RPM and torque are used to examine an impact of those types of motors on the pseudo force sense.

© Springer Nature Switzerland AG 2019
M. Kurosu (Ed.): HCII 2019, LNCS 11568, pp. 410–419, 2019.
https://doi.org/10.1007/978-3-030-22636-7_31

2   Previous Work

The previous studies [1,5] discuss a pseudo force sense for the case when a DC motor is attached to the index fingertip in such a way that the output shaft of the motor is held horizontally and orthogonally shown in Fig. 1, and two types of voltage change: the sawtooth wave and the reverse sawtooth wave shown in Fig. 2, are fed. In Fig. 2, the direction in which the gradient of the voltage change is comparatively steep is referred to as the direction of strong rotational acceleration and the direction in which the gradient is comparatively gentle is referred to as the direction of weak rotational acceleration. The result shows that people feel more pseudo force sense in a stronger rotational acceleration direction of the output shaft and they also feel the pseudo force sense easily in the bending direction of the finger. Their system focuses on a way of providing people with the feel of touching and holding an virtual object in a virtual space. This manuscript focuses on a way of providing them with the feel of traction force in a specified direction.

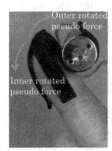  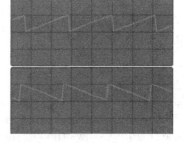

Fig. 1. A DC motor attached on the index fingertip. (cited from [5], p. 49)

Fig. 2. A sawtooth wave (upper) and reverse sawtooth wave (lower). (cited from [1], p. 594)

Another research related to walking navigation using the pseudo force sense is done by Takeshi et al. [2] and it shows that an asymmetric vibration is given on the belly of the finger and if the user grips the vibration speaker then he/she would perceive translational force. Although this device has the advantage of providing translation force to the user, it emits noise due to the vibration speaker. Yuki et al. [6] built a walking navigation system with a hanger reflex. A hanger reflex is a reflection where the head rotates sideways regardless of his intention by attaching the wire hanger to the head so as to sandwich the temporal head. Although their way has the advantage of hands-free device, the device is cumbersome because it needs to be worn around the head. In comparison with these previous devices, the DC motors is compact and small enough to carry, and also works quietly.

3   Experiment

The aim of this experiment is to verify three hypotheses about pseudo force sense.

3.1   Research Hypothesis

In the previous study [5], a DC motor was attached to the fingertip to investigate pseudo force sense for the purpose of providing people with the feel of grasping objects in a virtual space. This manuscript investigates properties of the pseudo force sense when a DC motor is held with the three fingers, aiming for walking navigation. Holding the similarity with the properties of pseudo force sense mentioned in [5], the following three hypotheses are defined in order to show properties of the pseudo force sense in our approach.

H1: People feel pseudo force sense in the direction of strong rotational acceleration of sawtooth wave.

H2: People perceive easily pseudo force sense in the bending direction of the wrist.

H3: People recognize more easily pseudo force sense for a DC motor with a higher RPM and torque value.

3.2   Preparation

In this experiment, two types of DC motors with different RPM and torque, are used to examine an impact of those properties of DC motors on pseudo force sense. Figure 3 shows the DC motors and Table 1 shows their mechanical specifications. Figure 4 shows the user's hand holding the DC motor with three fingers (the thumb, index finger and middle one), and Table 2 shows four different waveforms of voltage (Duty Cycle) change.

Table 1. Specifications of two DC motors used in the experiment.

Item	3254 E_0	3261 E_0
Motor type	DC motor with encoder	DC motor with encoder
Output power (mechanical)	590 mW	2.9 W
Maximum speed at rated voltage	230 RPM	1080 RPM
Rated torque	200 g-cm	240 g-cm
Stall torque	1 kg-cm	1.3 kg-cm

The left is a DC motor of Phidgets Inc.-3254 E_0 and the right is the other DC motor of Phidgets Inc.-3261 E_0. The right DC motor has higher RPM and torque value than the left one. The rounded part at the top is the weight of 17 g and it is attached to the tip of the output shaft of the DC motor. The weight makes the pseudo force sense more easily recognizable.

Fig. 3. Two types of DC motors (Left:3254 E_0, Right:3261 E_0) and a their weight.

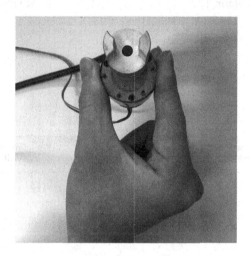

Fig. 4. The user is holding a DC motor with the thumb, index finger and middle one.

The direction of rotation (clockwise or counterclockwise) of the shaft of the DC motor is defined as follows. The clockwise direction is the extending direction and the counterclockwise one is the bending direction of the wrist. The DC motor rotates in the clockwise direction when the duty cycle is a positive value and in the counterclockwise direction when the duty cycle is a negative value.

In Table 2, the rotational acceleration means that the rotation speed (Duty Cycle) is added until it reaches 100 or -100 and it changes to the opposite rotational acceleration. The duty cycle of 100 is roughly 230 RPM (3254 E_0) and 1080 RPM (3261 E_0). The performance obtained from 3254E_0 where the corresponding waveform is fed into, is shown in Fig. 5, and those for 3261E_0 is shown in Fig. 6.

For example, the performance in the top left corner in Fig. 5 is obtained when the waveform 1 in Table 2 is fed to the motor 3254E_0. Since the clockwise rotational acceleration is 1000 (%Duty Cycle/s), it reaches from 0 Duty Cycle to

Table 2. Four experiment conditions of waveforms presented to the motor.

Item	Clockwise rotational acceleration (%Duty Cycle/s)	Counterclockwise rotational acceleration (%Duty Cycle/s)
Waveform 1 (Sawtooth wave)	1000	−10000
Waveform 2 (Reverse sawtooth wave)	10000	−1000
Waveform 3	1000	−1000
Waveform 4	10000	−10000

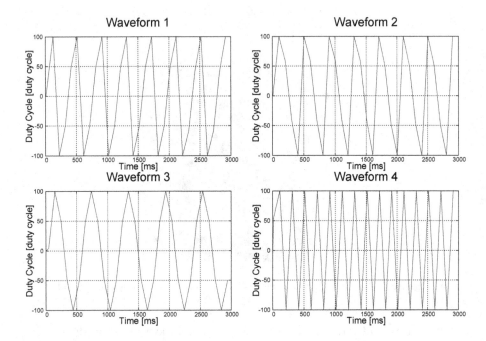

Fig. 5. The performance obtained from 3254E_0.

100 Duty Cycle in about 0.1 s and it reaches from 100 Duty Cycle to −100 Duty Cycle in about 0.02 s since the counterclockwise acceleration is −10000 (%Duty Cycle/s).

3.3   Subjects

There are seven subjects and they are all students (Male: 6, Female: 1) aged from 21 to 26 years old. They are also all right-handed.

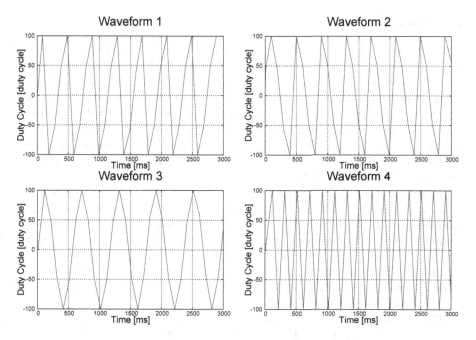

Fig. 6. The performance obtained from 3261E_0.

3.4 Procedure

They are asked to hold either DC motor (Phidgets Inc.-3254 E_0) or (Phidgets Inc.-3261 E_0) with three fingers of the dominant hand (the thumb finger, index finger and middle finger), so that the output shaft is in the vertical direction. Next, one of the four waveforms is presented to the DC motor with the presentation duration of 15 s. After the presentation, they are asked to answer a questionnaire on pseudo force sense. The questionnaire asks the subject to evaluate the direction in which they have felt the pseudo force sense and the reliability of the answer they made with 11 scales of 0 (low confident) to 10 (high confident). This is repeated with the other three waveforms in a random order.

During the presentation, they are instructed not to contact the desk with the hand holding the DC motor.

During the experiment, the subject puts on a headphone equipped with noise canceling function to block unwanted noise from the DC motor and he/she is instructed not to look directly at the DC motor. As regards unwanted noise, Yamada et al. [4] shows that auditory information alters tactile information, that is people perceive the weight of a thing differently depending on types of collision sounds.

3.5   Results

Figure 7 shows the questionnaire results for 3254E_0 and Fig. 8 shows for 3261E_0. They show histograms of direction of pseudo force sense that the subject perceived (left column) and its reliability that he/she answered (right column). From Fig. 7, when the waveform 1 was fed to the DC motor, six subjects felt the pseudo force clockwise, and when the waveform 2 was fed six subjects felt the pseudo force counterclockwise. There could be a tendency for people to feel the pseudo force sense in the direction of weak rotational acceleration. This tendency holds for the other DC motor 3261E_0 shown in Fig. 8. This result does not support the hypothesis H1.

As regards the reliability of the answer, by comparing the waveform 1 and 2, the former seems to be easier for people to perceive the pseudo force because the histogram for the former at the answer "clockwise" is condensed between 7 and 10 while it is scattered over from 3 to 10 for the latter at the answer "counterclockwise". There could also be a tendency for people to perceive the pseudo force more easily in the extending direction of the wrist. This tendency holds for the other DC motor 3261E_0 shown in Fig. 8. This result does not support the hypothesis H2.

The average of histogram values of reliability at the answer "clockwise" for the waveform 1 is 9.00 for 3254E_0 and 9.29 for 3261E_0. The average of histogram values of reliability at the answer "counterclockwise" for the waveform 2 is 7.17 for 3254E_0 and 8.50 for 3261E_0. Therefore the DC motor of 3261E_0 gives the subject much more pseudo force sense. This result supports the hypothesis H3. For the waveforms 3 and 4, their reliability is low to some extent.

3.6   Discussions

The hypothesis H1 seems incorrect. The previous study [5] says that people would feel a pseudo force sense in the strong acceleration direction of the saw-tooth wave. The result from our experiment is the reverse of the previous one and says that people would feel a pseudo force sense in the weak acceleration direction. It could stem from that this would be influenced by how to hold the DC motor by mounting on the fingertip or holding with the fingers. Since the mass of the fingertip is smaller than the hand size, when the DC motor is attached to the fingertip, the reaction force is large against the acceleration of rotation of the DC motor. However, since the mass of the hand is larger than the fingertip, when the DC motor is held with your fingers, a small reaction force will be added against the acceleration of rotation of the DC motor. It seems that the result was reversed by this.

The hypothesis H2 seems incorrect. The previous study [1] says that people would feel the pseudo force sense easily in the bending direction of the finger. The result from our experiment is the reverse of the previous one and says that people would feel it easily in the extending direction of the wrist. This is also considered to be reversed for the same reason as H1.

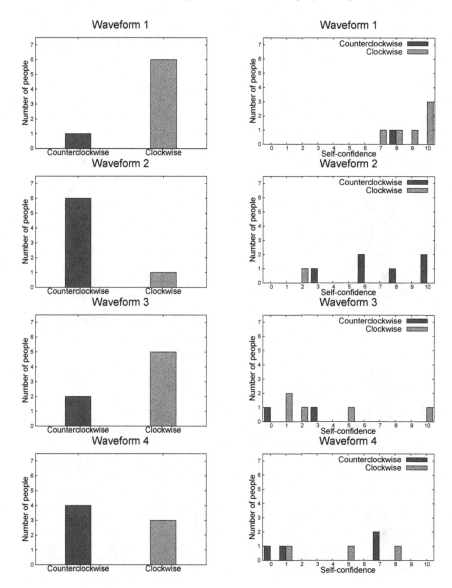

Fig. 7. Results from 3254E_0.

The hypothesis H3 seems correct. The hypothesis states that people recognize more easily the pseudo force sense for a DC motor with a higher RPM and torque value. This is because even when the duty cycle reaches 100 or −100, the DC motor with the higher RPM value is rotating much more than the DC motor with the lower RPM value. It needs a stronger reaction force to reverse the rotation of the motor. As a result, the pseudo force sense could be more recognizable for the DC motor with higher RPM and torque values.

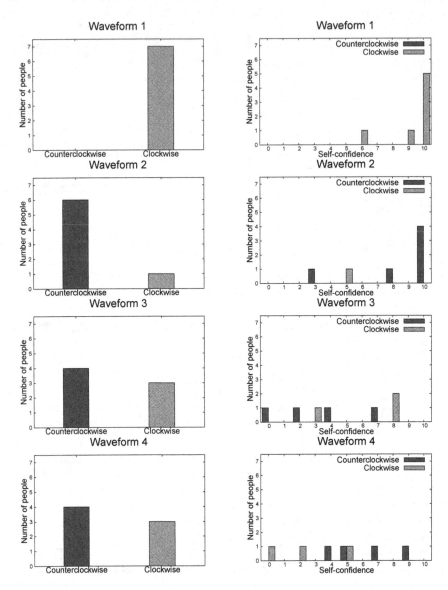

Fig. 8. Results from 3261E_0.

4   Conclusions

This manuscript discussed properties of pseudo force sense when people hold a DC motor with three fingers of the thumb, index finger and middle finger, and conducted an experiment using two types of DC motors and four different waveforms of voltage change that are fed to the DC motors. As a result, it was found that people would feel the pseudo force sense in the direction of the weak rotational acceleration. And there could also be a tendency for people to perceive the pseudo force more easily in the extending direction of the wrist. Moreover, by comparing the results from two types of motors it was found that the motor with higher RPM and torque would cause people to feel easily pseudo force.

References

1. Rei, S., Yem, V., Hiroyuki, K.: Pseudo force sense presentation to multiple fingers by asymmetric rotation using a motor: consideration in grasping posture. In: INTERACTION 2017, pp. 593–596 (2017)
2. Takeshi, T., Hiroaki, Y., Iwata, H.: Non-grounded translational force and torque display using two vibration speakers. Trans. Virtual Real. Soc. Japan **22**(1), 125–134 (2017)
3. Tomohiro, A., Hiroaki, G.: Pedestrian navigation system utilizing effectiveness of dynamic exploration for force direction perception. In: The IEICE Transactions, pp. 260–269 (2014)
4. Yamada, T., Shibata, F., Kimura, A.: Analysis of the R-V dynamics illusion behavior in terms of auditory stimulation. In: Proceedings of the 24th ACM Symposium on Virtual Reality Software and Technology, VRST 2018, pp. 70:1–70:2. ACM, New York (2018). https://doi.org/10.1145/3281505.3281595
5. Yem, V., Okazaki, R., Kajimoto, H.: Vibrotactile and pseudo force presentation using motor rotational acceleration. In: 2016 IEEE Haptics Symposium (HAPTICS), pp. 47–51, April 2016
6. Yuki, K., Takuto, N., Kajimoto, H.: Effect of hanger reflex on walking. Trans. Virtual Real. Soc. Japan **21**(4), 565–573 (2016)

Analysis of a Programming Process Sharing the Card-Type Programming Tool "Pro-Tan"

Tatsuo Motoyoshi[✉], Kei Sawai, Hiroyuki Masuta, Takumi Tamamoto, Ken'ichi Koyanagi, and Toru Oshima

Toyama Prefectural University, 5180 Kurokawa, Imizu, Toyama, Japan
{motoyosh,k_381,masuta,tamamoto,koyanagi,oshima}@pu-toyama.ac.jp
https://www.pu-toyama.ac.jp/english/eindex.html

Abstract. We have been developing a tangible programming tool called "Pro-tan" which has a card-type interface. This paper reports the system configuration of Pro-tan and analysis of the usefulness when two users share Pro-tan. We conducted an experiment comparing Pro-tan with the programming software "Studuino", which has an interface suitable for operation by children. We evaluated the usefulness of Pro-tan in a collaborative learning process in which two users share the same system.

Keywords: Tangible user interfaces · Programming education · Fuben-eki

1 Introduction

We have been developing a card-type programming tool called "Pro-Tan" which uses a tangible user interface (TUI) [1]. Since operating Pro-Tan involves attaching cards onto a panel, Pro-Tan is a user-friendly tool for creating a program. Some programming tools exist which use a TUI [3–5]. It is easy for multiple people at the same time to handle tools using TUI. We consider TUI tools to have the merit of collaborative learning, although this has not been verified.

We attempted an experiment which records the time required for the programming training, and test scores which assess the depth of understanding of a program structure. The framework of this paper is as follows. Section 2 presents Pro-tan. Consideration of collaborative learning evaluation is described in Sect. 3. Section 4 presents a discussion and conclusion.

2 Pro-Tan

Pro-Tan is a card-type programming tool which consists of a program panel, programming cards, and a PC for data transfer. Users can create programs simply by placing RFID tag-equipped programming cards on the program panel.

M. Kurosu (Ed.): HCII 2019, LNCS 11568, pp. 420–429, 2019.
https://doi.org/10.1007/978-3-030-22636-7_32

2.1   System Configuration

Figure 2 shows the concept of Pro-Tan. A user can create a program for controlling a controlled object by attaching programming cards onto the program panel. There are four types of programming cards: Motion, Timer, IF, and LOOP. Figure 1 shows programming card types. Each type of card corresponds to various programming elements, such as the controlled object's system behavior, a while loop, or a sequential branch of the sensors. Pro-Tan is intended to help users learn the fundamental programming structures (sequences, branches, and loops).

Programming Cards. There are four types of programming cards: Motion, Timer, IF, and LOOP1. Information indicating the card type is incorporated into the surface of the card, and a stainless-steel sheet and an RFID tag are set into the back surface.

Motion cards have one RFID tag on the face and instruct the controlled object to light upor to sound a buzzer. A timer card sets the movement duration of the controlled object on a scale of one to four. Users have to set timer blocks next to motion blocks. IF cards correspond to the IF functions of a touch sensor and a light sensor on the controlled object. Loop cards correspond to the LOOP functions, which repeat the program operation indefinitely. Using these control cards, the user can create conditional branch programs.

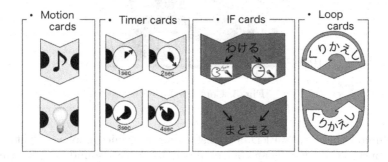

Fig. 1. Card types.

Program Panel. The program panel has 10 RFID readers under each cell. The information of the programming card type is obtained from the RFID tags of the programming cards and is transmitted by the PC. A magnetic sheet is attached by magnetic force to the surface or the panel for holding program cards.

2.2   Controlled Object

We produced a prototype controlled object for the evaluation experiment. Figure 3 shows the controlled object. This system consists of seven components:

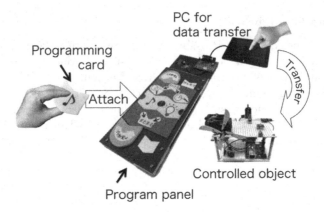

Fig. 2. Overview of the system.

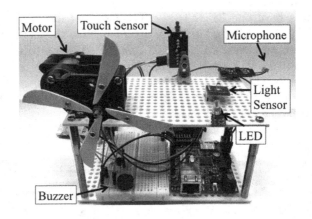

Fig. 3. Controlled object.

an Arduino Ethernet, an LED, a buzzer, a motor, a microphone, a light sensor, and a touch sensor. Users can control an LED, a buzzer sound, and the turning of a propeller by creating a program using Pro-Tan.

3   Collaborative Learning Experiment

We conducted an experiment to analyze the programming process when two users shared the programming tool. In the experiment, we prepared three programming tools, Pro-Tan, Studuino software [7], and Arduino IDE [8]. Subjects were shown how to create a program using Pro-Tan or Studuino. After the instruction, subjects were told to try one programming task using Arduino IDE. Figure 4 shows Studuino software and Arduino IDE.

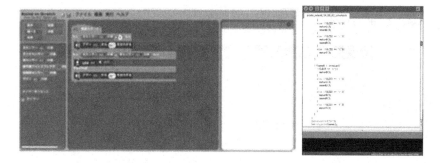

Fig. 4. Studuino software & Arduino IDE.

3.1 Flow of the Experiment

We set 10 programming tasks in the experiment. The first term is the collaborative learning term, which contains Tasks 1–5. Pairs of subjects were instructed to learn the operation and program structures using Pro-Tan or Studuino. The second term is the personal learning term, which contains Tasks 6–11. In Tasks 6–10, subjects were instructed to solve programming tasks by themselves using the same programming tools from Tasks 1–5. In Task 11, they were instructed to solve a programming task by themselves using Arduino IDE. Subjects were divided into two groups by the type of a programming tool used during Tasks 1–10 (Figs. 5 and 6).

Tasks The contents of Tasks 1–11 are as follows.

Task 1 Light up the LED for a defined period of time.
Task 2 Light up the LED for a defined period of time. Then, buzz the buzzer for a defined period of time.
Task 3 Repeat the sequence of Task 2 indefinitely.
Task 4 Buzz the buzzer if a sound is heard; otherwise, light up the LED.

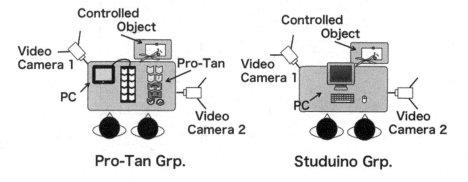

Fig. 5. Layout of the experiment.

424   T. Motoyoshi et al.

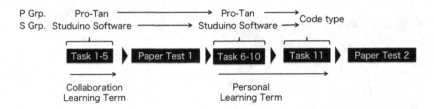

Fig. 6. Flow of experiment

Task 5 Light up the LED if a touch sensor is pushed; otherwise, buzz the buzzer.

Task 6 Light up the LED for two seconds. Then, buzz the buzzer for one second. Then, turn the propeller for four seconds.

Task 7 Turn the propeller for three seconds. Then, light up the LED for one second. Then, buzz the buzzer for two seconds. Repeat the sequence.

Task 8 Light up the LED if a sound is heard.

Task 9 Light up the LED if a room is dark; otherwise, buzz the buzzer.

Task 10 Turn the propeller if a button is pushed; otherwise, light up the LED.

Task 11 The contents of this task are the same as those of Task 10. Subjects are instructed to use Arduino IDE [8], which is a code-type programming application.

Paper Tests. All subjects were instructed to take paper Test 1 after Task 5, and paper Test 2 after Task 11. The number of exercises in Test 1 is 19. Subjects were checked for comprehension of a program, such as imagining an operation flow or

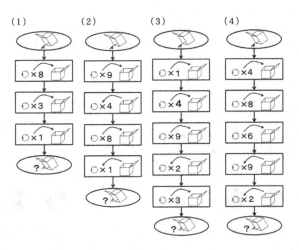

Fig. 7. Example of an exercise - Test 1.

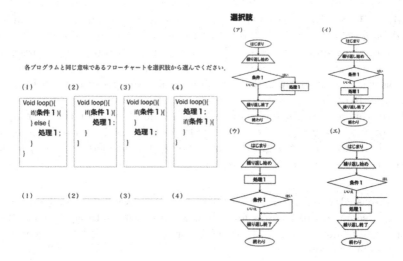

Fig. 8. Example of an exercise - Test 2.

a structure of a program. The number of exercises in Test 2 is 20. Figure 7 shows an example of an exercise in Test 1. Figure 8 shows an example of an exercise in Test 2 (Table 1).

3.2 Subjects

Sixteen subjects inexperienced in programming who were between 19 and 24 years old participated in the experiment. They were separated into a P group (using Pro-Tan at Tasks 1–10) and an S group (using Scratch at Tasks 1–10). They were instructed to form pairs and to share the programming tools.

3.3 Results

Table 1. Subject

Subject(P.Grp.)	Tool	Subject(S.Grp.)	Tool
P_{11}	Pro-Tan	S_{11}	Studuino software
P_{12}		S_{12}	
P_{21}		S_{21}	
P_{22}		S_{22}	
P_{31}		S_{31}	
P_{32}		S_{32}	
P_{41}		S_{41}	
P_{42}		S_{42}	

Required Time for Tasks. We recorded the required time for programming tasks during the experiment. All required times are shown in Tables 2 and 3. The averages of the required times for Tasks 1–5 of the P group were shorter than those of the S group. There were significant differences ($p < 0.05$) for Tasks 2 and 5 between the P group and the S group. The averages of the required times for Tasks 6–10 of the P group were shorter than those of the S group. There were significant differences ($p < 0.05$) for Tasks 6, 7, and 10 between the P group and the S group. The averages of the required times for Task 11 of the P group were shorter than those of the S group. There was a significant difference ($p < 0.05$) between the P group and the S group.

Test Scores. We recorded the number of right answers to Test 1 and Test 2 as the test score. All test scores for subjects are shown in Tables 4 and 5. There were no significant differences ($p < 0.05$) for Test 1 and Test 2 between the P group and the S group.

3.4   Discussion

We recorded the operation duration for subjects handling the programming tool using motion capture (OptiTrack V120:Trio). Table 6 shows the operation time ratio between members of the pair. The average ratio of the subjects who handled Pro-Tan the least of the subjects in the pair, P_{i2}, was 14.5%, and that of the subjects who handled Studuino the least of the subjects in the pair, S_{i2}, was 5.0%. These results show that the user who is not the main operator of the tool has more opportunities to handle Pro-Tan than Studuino.

Subjects using Pro-Tan completed Tasks 2, 5, 6, 7, and 10 More quickly than subjects using Studuino. Furthermore, subjects using Pro-Tan for the collaborative learning term were able to complete Task 11 more quickly than subjects using Studuino. We consider these results to indicate that Pro-Tan created less

Table 2. Completion times of Tasks 1–5

Subjects	Task 1[s]	Task 2[s]	Task 3[s]	Task 4[s]	Task 5[s]
P_{11} & P_{12}	103	39	33	398	23
P_{21} & P_{22}	70	46	100	413	30
P_{31} & P_{32}	36	29	120	294	41
P_{41} & P_{42}	24	42	36	269	30
Ave. (P)	58	39	72	344	31
S_{11} & S_{12}	73	62	68	681	63
S_{21} & S_{22}	276	87	60	1548	73
S_{31} & S_{32}	294	85	53	421	66
S_{41} & S_{42}	173	58	118	2004	52
Ave. (S)	204	73	75	1164	64

Table 3. Completion times of Tasks 6–11

Subject	Task 6[s]	Task 7[s]	Task 8[s]	Task 9[s]	Task 10[s]	Task 11[s]
P_{11}	48	33	63	78	42	227
P_{12}	42	31	64	32	29	220
P_{21}	30	37	66	47	30	212
P_{22}	33	35	30	27	25	128
P_{31}	37	55	83	38	27	176
P_{32}	44	55	94	35	34	139
P_{41}	33	34	37	29	49	194
P_{42}	34	47	66	37	29	337
Ave.(P)	38	41	63	40	33	204
S_{11}	96	56	72	233	83	240
S_{12}	147	85	190	186	97	474
S_{21}	109	56	108	113	116	436
S_{22}	149	62	215	104	82	247
S_{31}	199	82	941	374	362	536
S_{32}	130	68	284	1118	113	328
S_{41}	189	80	127	114	103	344
S_{42}	139	63	176	122	170	299
Ave.(S)	145	69	264	295	141	363

Table 4. Scores for paper Test 1

Subject	Score	Subject	Score
P_{s11}	23	S_{s11}	21
P_{s12}	22	S_{s12}	25
P_{s21}	19	S_{s21}	22
P_{s22}	20	S_{s22}	23
P_{ns11}	13	S_{ns11}	17
P_{ns12}	23	S_{ns12}	25
P_{ns21}	20	S_{ns21}	23
P_{ns22}	24	S_{ns22}	21
Ave.(P_s)	21	Ave.(S_s)	23
Ave.(P_{ns})	20	Ave.(S_{ns})	22
Ave.(P)	21	Ave.(S)	22

Table 5. Scores for paper Test 2

Subject	Score	Subject	Score
P_{s11}	19	S_{s11}	20
P_{s12}	20	S_{s12}	20
P_{s21}	16	S_{s21}	16
P_{s22}	21	S_{s22}	17
P_{ns11}	20	S_{ns11}	20
P_{ns12}	22	S_{ns12}	20
P_{ns21}	19	S_{ns21}	19
P_{ns22}	20	S_{ns22}	17
Ave.(P_s)	19	Ave.(S_s)	18
Ave.(P_{ns})	20	Ave.(S_{ns})	19
Ave.(P)	20	Ave.(S)	19

Table 6. Operation time ratio

Subject	%	Subject	%
P_{11}	88	S_{11}	92
P_{12}	12	S_{12}	8
P_{21}	91	S_{21}	100
P_{22}	9	S_{22}	0
P_{31}	92	S_{31}	89
P_{32}	8	S_{32}	11
P_{41}	71	S_{41}	99
P_{42}	29	S_{42}	1
Ave.P_{i2}	14.5	Ave. of S_{i2}	5.0

difference in operation duration in the collaborative learning process than did Studuino, and suggest that Pro-Tan is suitable for collaborative learning.

4   Discussion and Conclusion

We developed a prototype of a card-type programming tool called "Pro-Tan" which uses a tangible user interface (TUI) [1]. We conducted an experiment to analyze the programming process when two users shared the programming tool. In the experiment, we prepared two programming tools, Pro-Tan and Studuino software, as training tools for subjects, and instructed all subjects to use Arduino IDE as the final task. Subjects using Pro-Tan completed Tasks 2, 5, 6, 7, 10, and 11 more quickly than subjects using Studuino. Furthermore, we recorded the operation duration for subjects handling the programming tool, and compared the possession times of subjects in the operating process. The results show that the user who is not the main operator of the tool has more opportunities to handle Pro-Tan than Studuino. We consider that these results show that Pro-Tan created less difference in the operation duration than did Studuino in the collaborative learning process, and suggest that Pro-Tan is suitable for collaborative learning.

In future work, we will compare the test scores and required times for tests for the subjects who are the main users of the programming tool in the pair. We will analyze the association the inconvenience in the process of copying and the learning effectiveness from the point of view of Fuben-eki.

Acknowledgment. This work was supported by JSPS KAKENHI Grant Number 18K02902. The authors would like to thank the Pastel Studio staff at Toyama Prefectural University.

References

1. Ishi, H., Ulmer, B.: Tangible bit: toward seamless interface between people, bits, and atoms. In: Proceedings of Conference on Human Factors in Computing Systems & CHI 1997, pp. 234–241 (1997)
2. Motoyoshi, T., Tetsumura, N., Masuta, H., Koyanagi, K., Oshima, T., Kawakami, H.: Tangible programming Gimmick using RFID systems considering the use of visually impairments. In: Miesenberger, K., Bühler, C., Penaz, P. (eds.) Computers Helping People with Special Needs, ICCHP 2016. Lecture Notes in Computer Science, vol. 9758, pp. 51–58. Springer, Cham (2016). https://doi.org/10.1007/978-3-319-41264-1_7
3. Wang, D., Zhang, Y., Chen, S.: E-Block: a tangible programming tool with graphical blocks. In: Proceedings of Mathematical Problems in Engineering & MPE 2013, vol. 2013 (2013). Article ID 598547
4. Suzuki, H., Kato, H.: Interaction-level support for collaborative learning: AlgoBlock An open programming language. In: Proceedings of the First International Conference on Computer Support for Collaborative Learning & CSCL 1995, pp. 349–355 (1995)
5. Horn, M.S., Solovey, E.T., Crouser, R.J., Jacob, R.J.K.: Comparing the use of tangible and graphical programming languages for informal science education. In: Proceedings of the SIGCHI Conference on Human Factors in Computing Systems & CHI 2009, pp. 975–984 (2009)
6. Tetsumura, N., Oshima, T., Koyanagi, K., Masuta, H., Motoyoshi, T., Kawakami, H.: Interface design proposal of card-type programming tool. In: Kubota, N., Kiguchi, K., Liu, H., Obo, T. (eds.) ICIRA 2016. LNCS (LNAI), vol. 9835, pp. 71–77. Springer, Cham (2016). https://doi.org/10.1007/978-3-319-43518-3_7
7. Studuino. http://www.artec-kk.co.jp/studuino/en/
8. Aruduino. http://www.arduino.cc

Study on Career Education for the Age of Computerization with Benefit of Inconvenience

Kiyohisa Nishiyama[1](✉) and Manabu Sawaguchi[2]

[1] Nagoya University, Furo-cho, Chikusa-ku, Nagoya-shi, Aichi 484-8603, Japan
nishiyama.kiyohisa@e.mbox.nagoya-u.ac.jp
[2] Ritsumeikan University, Osaka Ibaraki Campus 2-150 Iwakura-cho,
Ibaraki, Osaka 567-8570, Japan

Abstract. This paper aims to introduces a challenge in career education for university students then further argues about the possibility of next generation career development methodology assuming the future Human Computer Interaction. The career education utilizes innovation methodology based on Benefit of Inconvenience (BI), which is called "Fubeneki" in Japanese. In this research, we analyzed the sample ideas of BI systems submitted by participant students in lectures and workshops in which BI concept was introduced and then, recognized typical misunderstandings of BI. In addition, we explored the results of a survey conducted on the students and business persons. The survey results of the participant students were compared with those of the business persons to argue expected connection between the innovation with BI and future methodology for career education.

Keywords: Benefit of inconvenience · Career education · Idea generation

1 Research Back Ground

In the long history of technological evolution, innovations have mainly focused on eliminating time consumption and other physical burdens spent for achieving intended objectives; so, the meaning of innovation may have been equivalent to developing a new convenient system. In fact, human beings, so far, have successfully reduced their physical burden by replacing manual labor operations by automated machines since the Industrial Revolution. Management techniques such as Industrial Engineering and Quality Control also have greatly contributed to improvement of productivity in mass production. In addition, the recent evolution of Information Technology based on computer is reducing even intellectual burdens on human beings. The word, IOT (Internet of Things), has become popular since a few years ago; one may feel that many sorts of things are starting to be interactively connected thorough computer network and our society is rapidly becoming more convenient.

Excessively convenient society, however, may be exposed to various problems, while the technological evolution has realized many conveniences. Carl Benedikt Frey and Michael A. Osborne evaluated occupations that may disappear in near future at

M. Kurosu (Ed.): HCII 2019, LNCS 11568, pp. 430–444, 2019.
https://doi.org/10.1007/978-3-030-22636-7_33

higher possibility being replaced by machines equipped with AI (Artificial Intelligence) and pointed that workers engaged in these occupations may lose their jobs [1]. Operations in the occupations at higher risk of disappearing seems to be composed by tasks that may be easily standardized, and some have already started to be replaced by computerized machines. As other examples, human abilities may be worsened by excessive dependence on the convenient machines and excessively convenient society may be stressful by making our lives more hectic.

The university career education, which is the main agenda of this paper, is an important issue for providing guidelines with the students to proactively design their future life plans. In general, typical contents of university career education includes lecture talks given by successful business persons, introduction to certain industries and occupations, and others. Individuals each, however, may be further required to proactively challenge to create new values that contributes future society for progressive career development. In near future, human beings will be more surrounded by computerized machines equipped with ultimately optimized capabilities in certain designated tasks, where manual routine task generates extremely lower additive values.

The authors are focusing on an innovation methodology that exploits Benefit of Inconvenience (BI) mainly associating with the value creation in excessively convenient society. This methodology intentionally add inconvenience for value creation, while conventional innovation methodologies aims to eliminate time consumption and other physical burdens for value creation. The authors and the other members, so far, have formed BI Research Group, which is organized by Society of Japanese Value Engineering, and developed a methodology for systematic innovation by using BI through analysis on successful innovations based on BI [2].

2 Research Objective

This research aims to apply the innovation methodology that exploits BI to lectures and workshops that can be associated with career development and argue about new university career education contents for next working trend. This paper introduces systematic procedures for generating BI systems implemented in workshops and lectures provided by the first author. The lecture participant students, so far, submitted many sample ideas of BI systems based on the instruction. Then the samples have been analyzed to evaluate the understanding of participant students on the concept of BI system through the lectures and workshops for future challenges. In addition, we explored the results of a survey conducted on the students and business persons who have strong interest on Value Engineering [3], a world-widely popular management technique. The survey results of the lecture participant students were compared with those of the business persons to argue expected connection between the innovation with BI and future methodology for career education.

3 Research Methodology

In the workshops and lectures, the author firstly provided systematic procedures for generating systems that exploits BI, which is the concept of BI system, with participant students. Then, the students tried to generate original BI systems with respect to the procedure. The students were asked to record and submit detailed idea generation process. As analysis on the samples, we observed the submitted BI systems and their generation processes to define their ideation and misunderstanding patterns. In addition, we asked the participant students, who has experienced the explanation about the BI system above, to voluntarily join questionnaire survey and investigated the students' awareness on value creation. The following part of this paper will illustrate the systematic procedures for generating BI system provided in the workshops and lectures followed by the details of the questionnaire analysis.

3.1 Systematic Procedure for Generating BI System

The systematic procedures for generating BI system developed by the BI Research Group has assumed that its users are familiar with function analysis, a fundamental method of VE. One may predict that the participant students without enough knowledge about function analysis take time to generate BI system following the procedure. Then, the authors have simplified the instruction to the procedure by exploiting the concept of the technology evolution proposed by Theory of Inventive Problem Solving (TRIZ) [4] as well as a problem model developed by the first author [5]. The instruction focuses on visually clarifying the difference between conventional value creations and those exploiting the concept of BI by using schematics.

3.1.1 Conventional Value Creations

The procedure proposed by the BI Research Group firstly requires its users to define detailed functions of a system, which is an artificial object or service designed to achieve certain purpose, by using function analysis to BI potential essence for effectively develop BI system. On the contrast, the instruction in the author's lectures and workshop, requires the participant students to grab the definition of a system with a problem; A system generates "Positive State", in which the purpose of the system is achieved, at the same time "Negative State" is generated as shown in Fig. 1. Here, the "Negative State" is a state in which costs such as time, labor, resource, energy, environmental burden, and others are generated. This concept is based on the definition of a conflict introduced in TRIZ [4].

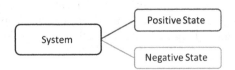

Fig. 1. System and its conflict

Figure 2 shows the major trend of innovations in the 20th century. The main interest of the innovations was mass production of systems that realizes the "Positive State", which is commonly desired by the public, and reduction of its "Negative State". One may notice that many systems are still evolving following the trend.

Automobile may be a typical example of this evolution. Humans used horse and carriage as a mean for traveling before automobile was put into practical use. The system of "horse and carriage" may have required a lot of labor to take care of the horse, and the horse itself would have been so expensive that anyone could not purchase. This is "Negative State" generated from the horse and carriage system. Then, automobile powered by engine were invented, and then, the "Negative States" have been greatly reduced. The system of automobile continues to evolve for reducing other "Negative States" such as lowering prices, reducing failures, increasing fuel efficiency and others.

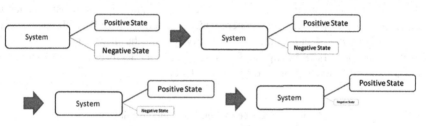

Fig. 2. System evolution in 20th century

Harmful Effects of an Excessively Convenient System
However, the situation may be eventually recognized as too convenient and, therefore, harmful, when this evolution reaches excessive. An example is that many workers are under the risk of unemployment because they may be replaced by machines equipped with Artificial Intelligence in near future. So, people may be concerned by such situation and start arguments on the relationship between human beings and highly evolved computers (Fig. 3).

Fig. 3. System with excessive convenience

Automobile may also be an example of harmfulness due to excessively convenient system. Old fashioned automobiles have been fixed by owners familiar with its simple mechanism. Present automobiles, however, uses electronic control units, which operates with unknown complex mechanism, for various functions. So, it is almost impossible for the user to fully understand the operation mechanism of an automobile. Automobile technology is still remarkably evolving; some owners, who know old fashioned automobiles, may feel anxious about this situation. In addition, practical application of automatic driving system may cause further trend shifts of mobility deteriorating human physical functions.

Benefit of Inconvenience

Benefit of Inconvenience (BI), which is called "Fubeneki" in Japanese, is the concept of creating new benefits by intentionally adding inconvenience to a system. Harmfulness in an excessively convenient system may be observed in many fields, when technological evolutions for convenience exceeds their limits. The examples may include not only replacement of working operations by AI but also other cases in various fields. This recognition is our motivation to focus on the BI system as a concept of new value creation and to apply the concept to university career education.

Hiroshi Kawakami has introduced the essences included in BI systems shown in Table 1, "12 inconvenience types that generate benefit" and "8 benefit types generated from inconvenience" [6]. One may generate ideas associated with BI with respect to the ideation cards of Fig. 4 enhancing one's creativity with the inspiring illustrations [7]. The author introduced the examples of each essence in the lectures and workshops, and shared the example ideas proposed by the students.

Table 1. Essence of Benefit of Inconvenience

(a) 12 types of inconvenience for BI	(b) 8 types of BI
Enlargement	Prevent downskilling
Increase of number of operations	Improve
Time consumption	Devise ways
Constraint	Feel at ease, feel reliability
Continuity (Analog)	Enhance awareness
Fatigue	Understand system
Increase of amount of operations	Make original
Less information	Personalization
Stimulation	
Danger	
Disorder	
Degradation	

BI System Generation Based on 4 System Categories

As shown in Fig. 5, BI Research Group categorizes all systems, such as product and services, into four categories, "A: Harmful and Inconvenient (HI system)", "B: Beneficial and Convenient system (BC system)", "C: Harmful and Convenient system (HC system)", and "D: Beneficial and Inconvenient System (BI system)". The "convenient" and "inconvenient" depend on the amount of time, labor, resources, energy and others consumed to achieve the system purpose, while the "beneficial" and "harmful"

(a) 12 types of inconvenience for BI   (b) 8 types of BI

Fig. 4. Inspiration card for idea generation with BI

		How much resource is spent for realizing the "Positive State"	
		Inconvenient	Convenient
Individual Perception	Beneficial	D	B
	Harmful	A	C

Fig. 5. Four system categories

somehow depend on individual subjective perception. Following the idea, one may recognize that innovations in the 20th century mentioned in Sect. 3.1.1 have modified Harmful and Inconvenient systems to be Beneficial and Convenient systems, which is equivalent to shifting systems from "A: HI system to B: BC system".

BI Research Group proposes BI system generation procedure from the viewpoint, how to evolve a system in each of the 4 system categories into a BI system as shown in Fig. 6. So, the BI system generation procedure can be classified into the 4 types of category shift: "A: HI system to D: BI system", "B: BC system to D: BI system", "C: HC system to D: BI system" and "D: BI system to D: BI system". The BI system may be developed by intentionally adding the essence of inconvenience by using the ideation cards following the procedure. This concept is also applied in the author's simplified explanation in the lectures and workshops. The following sections illustrates the detailed explanation about the procedure to shift systems into the category of D: BI system.

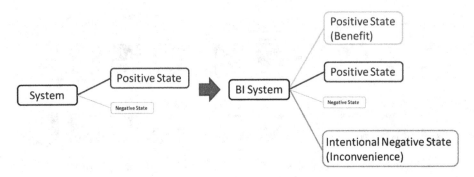

Fig. 6. Schematic of BI system development

A: HI System to D: BI System
This idea generation procedure is extracting potential BI elements from an existing HI system and, then, recognizing it as a BI system as shown in Fig. 7. For example, majority of current automobiles are equipped with automatic transmission, while previously manual transmission was more common. Automatic transmission is obviously a convenient system because it reduces burden on drivers, but one may also feel the fear of uncontrollable situation caused by unpredictable system failures in which drivers cannot do anything. On the contrast, automobiles equipped with manual transmission, drivers may notice a secure feeling that is originated from actual engagement with mechanics. One may notice that this is a BI system, which exploits the inconvenience of manual transmission to obtain the feeling of security, and it should be clearly distinguished from nostalgic feeling on old fashioned system.

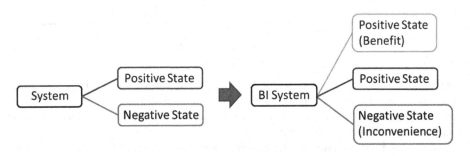

Fig. 7. A: HI system to D: BI system

No product and service that exists in the world is perfect; this thinking procedure is equivalent to defining BI that has not been recognized so far associating with inconvenience in arbitrary systems. In this category shift, one may firstly select a product or service and confirm recognizable inconveniences, then, generate BI ideas exploiting them with respect the ideation cards.

B: BC System to D: BI System
As shown in Fig. 8, this idea generation procedure is creating a BI system by adding inconveniences to an existing BC system. An application example of this procedure is an automobile equipped with special automatic transmission that has a special control mode similar to manual transmission style. BBQ restaurant, as another example, allows customers partially engaged in the cooking process, room for devising, providing opportunity for cooking skill improvement and accomplishment feeling.

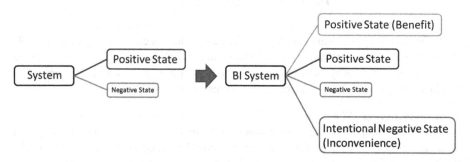

Fig. 8. B: BC system to D: BI system

Our predecessors have invented products and services that exist in the world pursuing certain conveniences. So, in this category shift, one may again firstly select a product or service, and select potential inconveniences with respect to the ideation cards, then, generate BI ideas exploiting the added inconveniences.

C: HC System to D: BI System
As shown in Fig. 9, this idea generation procedure aims to cancel the "Negative State" caused by convenience in a HC system by intentionally adding inconveniences to the system. As mentioned above, excessive pursuit of convenience may cause harmfulness resulting in an HC system. For example, the development of IT has enabled us to easily send messages through e-mail or SNS. However, this development has accompanied "Negative State" caused by excessive convenience such as overlooking important mails, lack of organic communication and others. As another example, too much dependence on electronic calculator may increase the number of people who do not understand the fundamental calculation theory. One may develop a BI system by adding small inconvenience to the HC system to cancel the harmfulness caused by excessive convenience.

In Japan, like other advanced countries, the population of elderly people is increasing and the future importance of elder care services is often stressed. Some elder care services may focus on eliminating the burden in the life of elderly people, which is equivalent to pursuit of convenience. However, it may result in deteriorating the physical function of the elderly people. So, in aging society, one may have potential opportunities for new value creation exploiting the category shift of "C: HC system to D: BI system". Therefore, it may be advantageous for university students to take the new category of value creation, BI concept, for their effective career development.

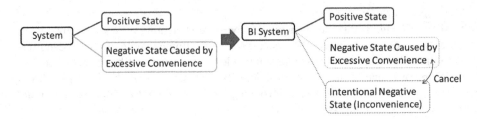

Fig. 9. C: HC system to D: BI system

In this category shift, one may firstly select a system that can be recognized as a HC system or a system that has potential to be a future HC system and select candidate inconveniences that may be intentionally added to the system for BI generation to cancel the "Negative State" caused by the excessive convenience.

D: BI System to D: BI System
As shown in Fig. 10, this idea generation procedure aims to develop a new BI system by transferring the essence of already recognized BI to another system. For example, BBQ restaurant provides the guests with the opportunity to devise and sense of accomplishment through the self-service of cooking. This concept can also be applied to other restaurants dealing serving other cuisines.

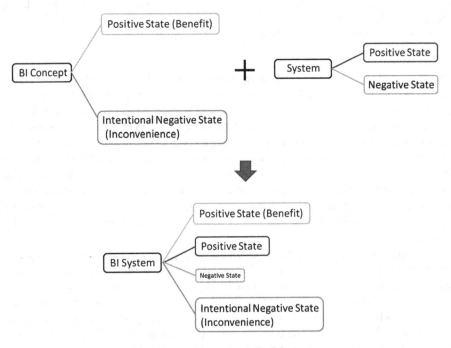

Fig. 10. D: BI system to D: BI system

In this category shift, one may start with recognizing a BI essence in a BI system that has been already invented, and by transferring it to another system for generating new BI system concept.

3.2 Questionnaire Survey

The authors have performed questionnaire survey, which aims to confirm the perception on BI, with voluntary cooperation of participant students in the lectures and workshops. The questionnaire survey has already been performed on business persons who has interest on VE by Society of Japanese Value Engineering [8]. The questions focused in this research were, *Q1: "Do you think that there are some benefits (value) that come from an inconvenient situation"*, *Q2: "If your answer to the previous question is "Yes", do you think that there is a function which may intentionally realize some benefits from an inconvenient situation?"*. The answers to these questions are "Yes", "No" and "Yes or No". The results from the business person and the students were compared to argue about the application of BI to university career education.

4   Results

This section shows the results of the lectures and workshops about BI focusing on the submitted BI systems as well as the questionnaire survey performed on the business persons and the participant students.

4.1   BI Systems Generated Through Idea Generation Procedure

So far, 81 ideas of BI system have been submitted through the workshops and lectures. These BI systems were generated based on the idea generation procedure introduced above, but some ideas seemed to be generated with misunderstanding about the BI concept. Here, Table 2 shows the number of BI systems based on each idea generation procedure with the number of ideas that seemed to include misunderstanding.

Table 2. Sample ideas of BI

	Number of submitted BI systems	Number of BI systems with misunderstanding
A: HI system to D: BI system	25	5
B: BC system to D: BI system	25	8
C: HC system to D: BI system	12	3
D: BI system to D: BI system	16	3

4.2 Questionnaire Survey

In total, 83 business persons and 22 students have answered to the questionnaire survey. "Yes" was selected by 59 business persons and 20 students selected in *Q1: "Do you think that there are some benefits (value) that come from an inconvenient situation?"*. Then, 67 business persons and 22 students joined *Q2: "If your answer to the previous question is "Yes", do you think that there is a function which may intentionally realize some benefits from an inconvenient situation?"*. "Yes" was selected by 52 business persons and 15 students in Q2. Figure 11(a) and (b) illustrates the breakdown of the answers made by the business persons and the students respectively. The sample numbers for Q2 is smaller than those for Q1, because only those who answer "Yes" to Q1 join Q2.

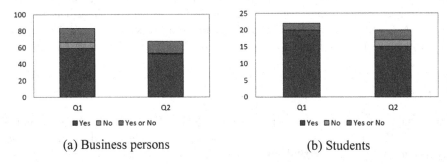

(a) Business persons   (b) Students

Fig. 11. Survey results

5   Discussions

This section firstly performs discussions about the BI systems submitted by the participant students in the lectures and workshops. The discussions focus on each of the four idea generation procedures, "A: HI system to D: BI system", "B: BC system to D: BI system", "C: HC system to D: BI system" and "D: BI system to D: BI system". In addition, the results of the questionnaire survey conducted on the business persons and the students are compared to consider the meanings of learning the concept of BI for the students' career development.

5.1   BI Systems Submitted by the Participant Students

A: HI System to D: BI System
Typical BI systems proposed by the category shift of "A: HI system to D: BI system" included flea market services such as auction, street stalls and others. The inconvenience here is time consumption required for negotiating directly with the product sellers or producers, while one may be possible to confirm the personality of them as the BI of "Feel at ease", "Reliability" and "Understand System". Other opinions of BI essences were "Make original" and "Devise ways" because one may customize own

services through the negotiation. Another typical BI system proposal was festivals and ceremonies. Festivals and ceremonies require the inconvenience of time and effort for preparation, while they promote the understanding one's own society culture as the BI of "Enhance awareness" and further tighten family ties as "Feel at ease". Festivals and ceremonies may also include "Make original" and "Devise way" because various creativities are required in their planning phase. Other BI systems, which may have been inspired by the examples shown in the instruction, were products and services related to DIY (Do it yourself), such as hot pot restaurant, BBQ, self-made furniture. Instead of the inconvenience of time and effort spent on DIY, these systems improve skills for each task as the BI of "Improve", provide rooms for creativity as "Devise ways" and provide opportunity to understand their production processes as "Understand system".

Some BI systems proposed by international students included traditional foods and cultures in their country. In addition, their proposals also included BI essences originated from everyday lives in their home country, which has been firstly recognized through convenient life and relatively temperate climate in Japan. So, career education with BI concept may also be applicable for fostering international perspective.

Meanwhile, some ideas indicated that some students generated BI system with misunderstandings because the fundamental BI concept may not have been properly transmitted through the instruction. For example, some were trying to increase self-satisfaction instead of inconveniencing others. Others generated ideas of BI systems that seemed to be intending to "improve" situation. The BI essence of "Improve", however, should contribute to improvement of certain skills.

B: BC System to D: BI System
Some BI systems generated through the category shift of "B: BC system to D: BI system" was added with randomness to gamify ordinary products or services as the inconvenience of "Disorder" to generate the BI of "Improve" and "Enhance awareness". Other systems realized the BI of "Prevent downskilling" by introducing restriction to a human action that should be unconsciously done, posture for example, as an inconvenience. Other interesting examples include providing an opportunity to

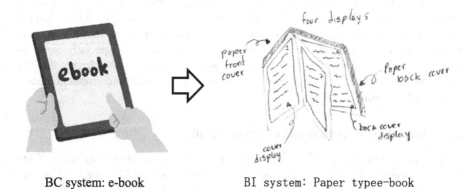

BC system: e-book   BI system: Paper typee-book

Fig. 12. Paper type e-book

appreciate beautiful scenery by riding on slow-speed vehicles, providing special experiences at travel destinations by limiting certain services, and providing a new type of e-book which has multiple displays that simulates to be a paper book as shown in Fig. 12.

Especially in this process, the participant students were required to generate a new system that does not currently exist, but some of them exploited the sample examples of BI systems, such as DIY, without thorough consideration. So, as a future challenge, we may limit the topic of idea generation in order to promote more creative and practical ideas.

Some examples presented here indicated that some participant students misunderstood about BI. Some proposed systems that transfer inconveniences on a certain products and services to others just for their own convenience. Others presented systems that require inconveniences in order to achieve certain purposes. These systems, however, should be considered as either HI system or HC system. Although these system evolutions may include ethical problems, the instruction should have more clearly stressed that these system evolutions are not about BI systems but only transition from HI system to BC system.

C: HC System to D: BI System

In this category shift, the participant students mentioned the following systems as the examples of HC system. It is convenient to have convenience stores that open 24 h anywhere in Japan, but sometimes people waste time by popping into there without clear items to buy. E-mail and SNS are convenient to send messages anywhere at any time, but one may not reply to all messages in a hectic situation and, in addition, organic interactions among people have been lost. Search engines are convenient tool to obtain necessary information anywhere at any time, but too much dependence may deteriorate memory ability.

The participant students have suggested BI system against the harmfulness by adding the inconvenience of restriction on the usage of convenience store, search engine, e-mail and SNS. Some proposed, which is based on misunderstanding about BI, to use previous system with inconvenience to avoid harmfulness in HC system.

D: BI System to D: BI System

For effective idea generation by exploiting this category shift may be just recognizing unknown potential BI essences sooner than others. So, the BI system in this category shift may have been easier process for innovating new systems. Many proposals, however, were only pointing the essence of existing BI systems. Especially, some BI systems, which are similar to existing systems, were generated by transferring the DIY factors to another system. Some proposed previous systems with inconvenience based on misunderstanding about BI.

5.2   Discussion on Questionnaire Survey Result

In order to confirm the statistical significance of the questionnaire survey result, Z-test was performed on the ratio of the respondents who chose "Yes" to the total respondents. The null hypothesis for the Z-test was "The probability that a questionnaire respondent chooses "Yes" is 1/2.". The calculated Z-value were 3.8, on business person who answered "Yes" to Q1, 4.5, on business person who answered "Yes" to Q2, 3.8, on students who answered "Yes" to Q1 and 2.2, on students who answered "Yes" to Q2. Hence, the null hypothesis is rejected for all the respondent types at the significance level of 5%. The results of the Z-test indicate that larger number of both the business persons and the students who have been exposed to BI concept recognized potential value in BI and intentional addition of inconveniences works as a strategic BI generation.

Especially recognizing the category shift of "C: HC system to D: BI system" probably contributes the career development of the participant students, in which various tasks are replaced by machines equipped with computers and the students may be required to create values exploiting BI system rather than pursuing convenience. Future works on this research should develop more practical contents such as discussions engaging companies that deal with products and services engaged in this category shift seeking the possibility of application of BI.

6 Conclusion

Innovations have mainly focused on eliminating time consumption and other physical burdens spent for achieving intended purposes; so, the meaning of innovation may have been equivalent to developing a new convenient system. Excessively convenient society, however, may be exposed to various problems, while the technological evolution has realized many conveniences. The authors, then, focus on applying an innovation methodology that exploits BI associating with the value creation in excessively convenient society to university career education as an important guideline for university students to proactively design their future life plans. This research has introduced our challenges on lectures and workshops, where innovation methodology with BI was introduced and associated with career development. The BI systems submitted by the lecture participant students were analyzed to recognize the students' understandings on the BI concept. In addition, we explored the results of a survey conducted on the students and business persons who have strong interest on Value Engineering to indicate possible connection between the innovation with BI and future methodology for career education.

References

1. Frey, C.B., Osborne, M.A.: The Future of Employment: How Susceptible are Jobs to Computerization? Oxford University (2013)
2. Sawaguchi, M., Kawakami, H., Matsuzawa, I., Nishiyama, K., Miyata, N.: Study of VE/VM method sustainable for social growth period-introduction of the third-function named "Fubeneki". In: 2018 Value Summit Conference Proceeding (2018)
3. Tsuchiya, H.: Shin VE no Kihon (New Basic VE in English). The SANNO Institute of Management Press (1998). (in Japanese)
4. Fey, V., Rivin, E.: Innovation on Demand: New Product Development Using TRIZ. Cambridge University Press, Cambridge (2005)

5. Nishiyama, K., Emanuel, L.: Development of checklist for systematic research communication in multidisciplinary fields. In: 2018 IEEE Global Engineering Education Conference (EDUCON), pp. 427–436. IEEE, Spain (2018)
6. Kawakami, H., Sawaguchi, M., Matsuzawa, I., He, X.: Value engineering introducing value of Fubeneki. Value Eng. (294), 10–15 (2016). (in Japanese)
7. Further Benefit of a Kind of Inconvenience System Laboratory. http://fuben-eki.jp/. Accessed 31 Jan 2019
8. Society of Japanese Value Engineering. https://www.sjve.org/eng/eng-home. Accessed 31 Jan 2019

User Experience and Perceived Usability of Traditional and Multimodal Interfaces for Scientific Information Seeking

Patrik Pluchino[1(✉)], Luciano Gamberini[1], and Giulio Jacucci[2]

[1] Human Inspired Technology (HIT) Research Centre,
University of Padova, Padua, Italy
patrik.pluchino@unipd.it
[2] Helsinki Institute for Information Technology (HIIT),
Department of Computer Science, University of Helsinki, Helsinki, Finland

Abstract. The current study was carried out to investigate users' preferences for different input modalities (i.e., mouse or gaze) when involved in scientific information-seeking tasks. According to the task that they had to perform (i.e., abstract opening, gaze bookmarking, or keyword highlighting), participants were randomly assigned to three different conditions. They had to carry out the same task twice with both means of interaction (i.e., mouse or gaze); input modalities were counterbalanced across participants. The findings showed that users were faster and perceived the system as more pleasant when they performed the tasks using their gaze. However, when participants controlled the system with a more familiar mouse interface, they perceived the system as more accurate, easy to use, and efficient. Future studies will evaluate how increasing users' familiarity with alternative input modalities (i.e., gaze) can affect their perception of accuracy, easiness, and efficiency.

Keywords: Multimodal interface · Eye tracking · Facial expressions · Emotions · Arousal

1 Introduction

The term Multimodal Human-Computer Interaction (MMHCI) refers to an emerging field of research that bonds together various domains, such as cognitive psychology, artificial intelligence, computer vision, and many others (Jaimes and Sebe 2007; Turk 2014). The general aim is to create computers that are more usable and that can positively enhance the user experience. Particular consideration has been given to the user, the technological device, and their interaction. In traditional human-computer interaction, users control a system/application using conventional input modalities such as a mouse and/or keyboard. In the context of MMHCI, instead, several different means of control are considered: gestures (Pavlovic et al. 1997), voice (Van der Kamp and Sundstedt 2011), eye tracking, and related indices (Grauman et al. 2003; Penkar et al. 2012). An additional crucial point regarding MMHCI is that, similarly to human-human interaction, communication involves a combination of different means (e.g., voice, body and hand gestures, gaze, etc.). Perceptual interfaces (PUIs; Turk and

© Springer Nature Switzerland AG 2019
M. Kurosu (Ed.): HCII 2019, LNCS 11568, pp. 445–458, 2019.
https://doi.org/10.1007/978-3-030-22636-7_34

Robertson 2000) are specific systems that aim at providing interaction exploiting non-conventional human-computer interaction input modalities. The latter are more natural and similar to the ones utilized in the real world. Thus, computers that are capable of exploiting these channels of communication can support users in performing various tasks. These machines can implement actions on the basis of users' gaze position on the screen, or they can modify their functioning in accordance with the emotions that users' faces show. Jaimes and Sebe (2007) characterized MMHCI in three categories according to the different parts of the human body involved: body movements, hand gestures, and gaze. The first category is related to technological systems that aim at interpreting general body posture and motion in order to change their operating behavior. The second category refers to devices that are able to adapt their functioning based on codified essential actions (e.g., pointing at specific objects) or on more complex ones (e.g., actions that convey feelings). The third category concerns the exploitation of eye-related indices and is based on the eye-mind hypothesis (Just and Carpenter 1976), which states that the spatial position of the gaze reflects what the participant is currently processing. This latter category is the more suitable in the context of utilization and evaluation of desktop interfaces. One key feature of the eye-tracking methodology is that it permits tracing of cognitive processing in an unobtrusive way. Different types of data (e.g., fixation and saccade durations, dwell time, etc.) can be collected while participants are dealing with different kinds of stimuli (e.g., texts, images, visual search, scene perception; Rayner 1998, 2009). Nevertheless, the eye tracker can also be exploited as a means of control. Indeed, it is possible to acquire eye-related data in real time, and computers can utilize this information to implement simple actions (e.g., selecting a button on the screen). Duchowski (2017) described such tools as selective interactive systems when changes that occur on the display are the consequence of an intentional gaze pattern. Indeed, in these conditions, the gaze is utilized to operate the systems instead of traditional controllers such as a mouse, a joystick, and/or a keyboard. Several studies have focused on disabled users (Levine 1984; Bates et al. 2007; Donegan et al. 2009), but eye tracking can also be adopted as a means of interaction for non-disabled people (Hyrskykari et al. 2005; Drewes 2010). Moreover, it is important to bear in mind that there could be constraints, for instance, that the visual modality in such conditions will be utilized for both perceiving the stimuli and controlling the interface/system. For this reason, the implementation of such a means of control has to be capable of discriminating between situations of "casual looking" and intentional viewing. The purpose is to prevent the "Midas touch" issue that concerns the selection of items that are randomly fixated on and not just the ones relevant to the current task that has to be accomplished (Jacob 1991; Majaranta and Bulling 2014).

The current experiment aimed at comparing, in terms of performance and user experience, the gaze input modality with a more conventional type of control, namely the mouse, while users performed different information-seeking tasks. Moreover, users' experienced emotions and level of general activation (arousal) were monitored during the interaction.

2 Method

2.1 Participants

Fifty-nine students from the University of Padua took part in the experiment on a voluntary basis. Eight participants were excluded as outliers due to the following: long temporal session duration, poor quality of the video recordings, and the impossibility of using the recordings to analyze participants' emotions and arousal. Fifty-one students (F = 23) with a mean age of 27.05 years (*SD* = 3.87) were considered for the analyses. All participants presented normal or corrected-to-normal vision. Seventeen participants were randomly assigned to each of the three experimental conditions (see *Experimental conditions and tasks* section for details).

2.2 Materials

Stimuli. The interface was developed in C++. Each screen presented a query field at the top left; an *orbitarium* at the center, where scientific keywords were graphically presented using polar coordinates; and finally, a set of abstract papers on the right side (see Fig. 1). The interface is described in detail by Serim and collaborators (Serim et al. 2017). When a/more word/s was/were inserted in the query field, a search iteration could be started by pressing the enter key. Thus, a pool of abstracts was selected from the interface database. This database retrieved over 50 million scientific documents from the Web of Science prepared by Thomson Reuters, Inc., and from the Digital Libraries of the Association of Computing Machinery (ACM), the Institute of Electrical and Electronics Engineers (IEEE), and Springer. Simultaneously, from among all the keywords that belonged to these selected abstracts, the more relevant keywords were shown inside the *orbitarium*. Furthermore, the relative positions of the keywords determined their relevance (i.e., more relevant keywords were located closer to the center).

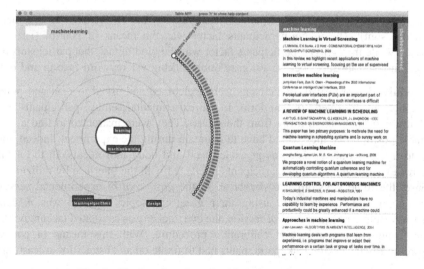

Fig. 1. The interface for scientific information seeking.

Experimental Conditions and Tasks. Regardless of the experimental condition, participants performed the same task twice utilizing the mouse and their gaze as means of control. The order was counterbalanced across participants. In each condition, the experimenter entered a topic keyword in the query field that started the first search iteration. On the basis of the resulting screen, participants had to, respectively, open 7 abstracts (*abstract opening* condition); bookmark 7 abstracts (*gaze bookmarking* condition); or access all the keywords that were linked to 7 abstracts (*fade in and out* condition). In all conditions, participants had to choose a set of abstracts that were relevant to the initial topic keyword. Participants could scroll up/down the list of abstracts in both experimental sessions (mouse and gaze-controlled).

Equipment. Several devices were adopted in the present experiment (Fig. 2). A RED500 (SMI) remote eye tracker with a sampling frequency of 500 Hz was utilized to collect the eye-tracking data. The software iViewX v. 2.8 (SMI), which was installed on a Dell Latitude E6530 notebook, was utilized to store the eye-tracking data. The software Experiment Center v. 3.6 (SMI), which was installed on a Dell desktop computer, was utilized to perform and validate the calibration of the eye tracker. The interface for scientific information seeking was installed on a MacPro that was connected to a 22" Dell monitor (1680 × 1050 pixels) under which the eye tracker was placed. Participants' faces were video recorded during the experimental sessions. The quality of the videos was enhanced utilizing two halogen bulb lights (60 W) that were located at both ends of the screen. Finally, utilizing the FaceReader software (Noldus), the recorded videos were analyzed to compute the proportion of different participants' emotions and arousal levels. The software is capable of automatically analyzing six basic facial expressions (i.e., happiness, sadness, fear, disgust, surprise, and anger) and a neutral state. Furthermore, FaceReader provides the opportunity to measure the emotional valence (pleasant = 1, unpleasant = −1) and the arousal level (active = 1, inactive = 0). All the computers were connected through a TL-SF1005D Ethernet switch. Thus, data regarding the gaze positions, collected by iView X, were sent to the C++ interface to enable the participants to accomplish the tasks using their eyes.

Experimental Design. The independent manipulation of two factors was considered (mixed-design): The *within*-participants factor was the means of control (gaze vs. mouse), while the *between*-participants factor was the kind of task that participants had to accomplish (abstract opening vs. gaze bookmarking vs. keyword fade in and out).

Procedure. Upon arrival, participants were welcomed and asked to read and potentially sign an informed consent form. In the experimental setting, participants were seated around 60–70 cm away from the screen. They were instructed to find a comfortable position that they would have to maintain during the experiment. Indeed, they had to try to avoid, as much as possible, head and body movements. In the *mouse control* experimental session, participants interacted with the interface by utilizing the mouse; the topic keyword was *database*. In the *gaze control* experimental session, users controlled the interface using their gaze; the topic keyword was *machine learning*. Before the *gaze control* session, the eye tracker was calibrated (accuracy: 0.5° visual angle) using a 5-point calibration procedure. With this means of control, according to the specific task, participants had to fixate on an abstract for at least three

Fig. 2. Experimental setup.

seconds (non-cumulative) in order to open it (*abstract opening* condition, Fig. 3a); fixate on an abstract for at least 5 s (non-cumulative) in order to bookmark it (*gaze bookmarking* condition, Fig. 3b); or fixate on an abstract for a non-specified amount of time to make the correspondent keywords appear (*fade in and out* condition, Fig. 3c). A training session preceded both experimental sessions. The aim was to give participants the opportunity to become familiar with the interface and its controls. In the training phases, the topic keywords were *EEG* and *ERPs*. At the end of both

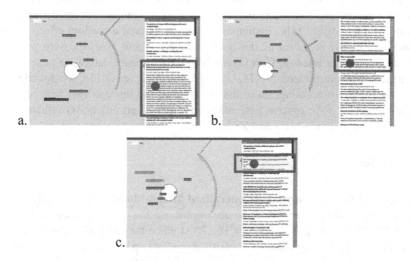

Fig. 3. Experimental tasks: (a) *abstract opening*, (b) *gaze bookmarking*, and (c) *fade in and out* utilizing the gaze (the red dot corresponds to the gaze position; it is shown for clarity and was not presented to the participants). (Color figure online)

experimental sessions, participants were administered an electronic questionnaire regarding the interface evaluation. Then, participants were debriefed about the study aims. Both experimental sessions together lasted 25 min.

Measures. Several metrics were collected during and after the experimental sessions:

- *Experimental session duration.* The total time (sec) needed to perform a task.
- *Experienced emotions.* The percentage of positive and negative emotions experienced during each experimental session.
- *Emotional valence.* The maximal level of emotional valence (range: -1 to 1) reached during each experimental session.
- *Arousal.* The maximal level of arousal (range: 0 to 1) reached during each experimental session.
- *System evaluation.* An ad hoc 20-item user experience questionnaire was administered (10 items of evaluation regarding each means of control). Usability (easiness, efficiency, fatigue, clarity, speed, fluidity, intuitiveness), pleasantness, perceived utility, and accuracy of the interface were evaluated using a 5-point scale (1 = not at all; 5 = very; see Appendix for detailed information about the items).

3   Data Analyses

The interquartile range (IQR) procedure (i.e., all values falling outside 1.5 IQR from the extremes of the IQR box were considered outliers) was adopted to exclude participants that were outliers in terms of total duration in at least one of the two experimental sessions. Some of the following analyses were conducted by means of mixed models (generalized in accordance with non-normal distribution of the data). The considered fixed effects were the task (abstract opening vs. gaze bookmarking vs. keyword fade in and out) and the type of control (mouse vs. gaze) utilized to accomplish the assigned task. Participants were considered a random effect. Abstract opening and mouse were set as the contrast levels. These analyses were performed using the R package lme4 (R Core Team 2015). FaceReader data were pre-processed utilizing a set of customized MATLAB functions (Release 2015a, Mathworks Inc.). Following the pre-processing, these data were analyzed through two beta regression analyses (positive and negative percentage of experienced emotions) utilizing the R package betareg (Cribari-Neto and Zeileis 2010).

3.1   Results

Experimental Session Duration (Generalized Mixed-Models). A main effect of task type emerged. Users were faster in accomplishing the abstract bookmarking task ($b = -0.82$, $t = -4.05$, $p < .001$; $M = 165.76$ s) when they had to access all the keywords of the selected abstracts ($b = -0.49$, $t = -2.41$, $p < .05$; $M = 244.67$ s) compared to when they had to open the abstracts ($M = 373.07$ s; see Fig. 4).

Moreover, a main effect of the means of control was found ($b = -0.15$, $t = -2.15$, $p < .05$). Users in general needed a shorter amount of time to perform the various tasks

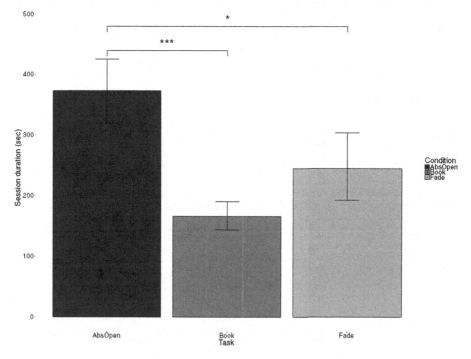

Fig. 4. Mean duration of an experimental session as a function of task.

utilizing their gaze (M = 247.34 s) compared to when they interacted with the system using the mouse (M = 274.99 s; Fig. 5). No significant interaction emerged.

Experienced Emotions (Beta Regressions). No main effect emerged considering either the positive or the negative emotions. Similar percentages were shown despite both the main effect of task type and of means of control (see Table 1 for positive emotions and Table 2 for negative emotions).

Emotional Valence. A main effect of the means of control on the maximal level of emotional valence emerged (b = 0.07, t = 2.80, p < .05; see Fig. 6). This value was higher when participants were controlling the interface with their gaze (M = 0.83) compared to when they utilized the mouse (M = 0.73). No significant main effect emerged considering the main effect of task type.

Arousal. No main effect emerged considering the maximal arousal level insofar as it was similar despite the main effect of both the task type and the means of control (see Table 3).

System Evaluation. A series of Kruskal-Wallis tests were performed considering delta values to evaluate the main effect of the task. Delta values were computed for each pair of scores regarding the same item (e.g., pleasantness: mouse score − gaze score). No differences emerged.

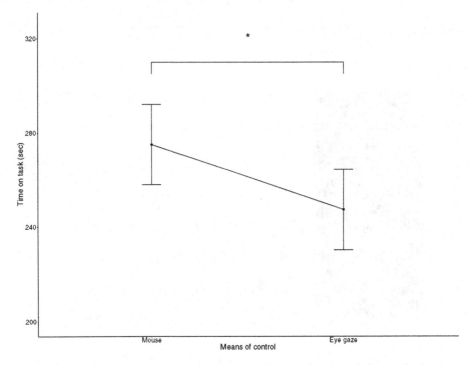

Fig. 5. Average duration of an experimental session as a function of means of control.

Table 1. Percentage of positive emotions as a function of task and means of control.

Tasks	Controls	
	Mouse	Eye gaze
	M(SD)	M(SD)
Abs opening	13.59(17.40)	14.40(18.33)
Bookmarking	9.52(10.93)	12.38(15.78)
Fade in/out	17.61(18.63)	14.68(17.32)

Table 2. Percentage of negative emotions as a function of task and means of control.

Tasks	Controls	
	Mouse	Eye gaze
	M(SD)	M(SD)
Abs opening	42.64(24.09)	37.95(22.16)
Bookmarking	53.54(32.93)	47.12(34.81)
Fade in/out	30.70(24.56)	36.43(29.05)

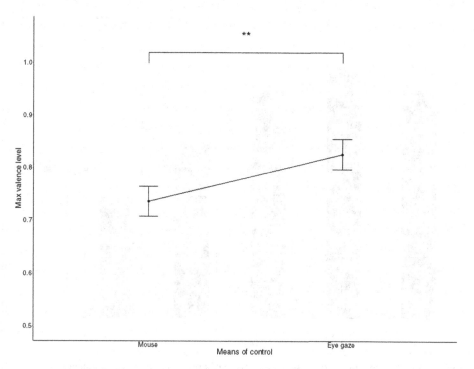

Fig. 6. Maximal emotional valence level as a function of means of control.

Table 3. Maximal arousal level as a function of task and means of control.

Tasks	Controls	
	Mouse	Eye gaze
	M(SD)	M(SD)
Abs opening	0.66(0.13)	0.60(0.13)
Bookmarking	0.59(0.13)	0.56(0.16)
Fade in/out	0.59(0.12)	0.58(0.13)

Furthermore, a series of Wilcoxon tests were conducted to evaluate the main effect of the means of control. Some differences in the questionnaire scores emerged (Fig. 7). Users perceived the interface as more accurate (W = 1743, p < .01), more efficient (W = 1697, p < .05), easier (W = 1626.5, p < .05), and less tiresome (W = 868.5, p < .001) when they interacted with it utilizing the mouse. In contrast, participants experienced a more pleasant interaction (W = 725, p < .001) when the means of control was the gaze.

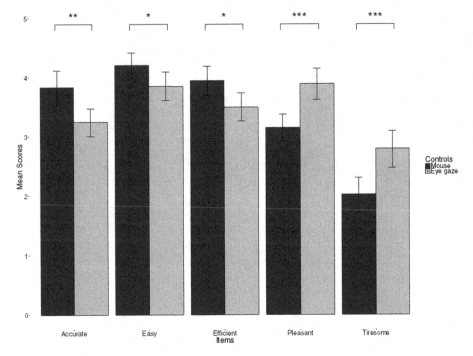

Fig. 7. Mean scores for the questionnaire items that showed differences as a function of means of control.

4 General Discussion

The aim of the study was to investigate how the input modality (mouse vs. gaze) could influence the performance and user experience of participants, as well as their emotions, when they were performing information-seeking tasks.

The results in terms of performance (i.e., time needed to accomplish a task) showed that participants were faster in carrying out the various tasks when they were utilizing their gaze as a means of control. These outcomes are in agreement with the idea that eye-related input is quicker than other forms of input, such as mechanical pointing devices (Jacob and Karn 2003). Another study showed that the action of pointing using the eyes was almost 10 times faster than utilizing a joystick in an immersive projection display (Asai et al. 2000). The authors stated that an eye-pointing task was not influenced by participants' experience when it was performed using the eyes. Indeed, individuals could easily and similarly (in terms of time on task) point using their eyes in the absence of specific training. In contrast, the large variability of time needed when utilizing the joystick was related to the participants' level of practice. Moreover, Jacob (1991) found a decrease of 30% in the time needed to accomplish a selection task utilizing the eyes compared to the mouse. Likewise, Tanriverdi and Jacob (2000) showed an advantage of gaze, compared to the hand, in terms of speed in carrying out a selection task. Moreover, any hand-controlled input tool could implement a specific action (e.g., mouse cursor movement) just on the basis of the previous eye movements made on the destination of this specific goal-oriented action.

Regarding the emotions experienced, no differences emerged for positive or for negative emotions. These results could be expected because the interface proposed had, per se, a low emotional valence. The same applies to the outcomes of the analysis concerning the maximal arousal level. To support the accuracy in collecting data on arousal level of participants utilizing the FaceReader software, the utilization of surface electrodes for monitoring the electrodermal activity could be considered. A difference emerged concerning the maximal level of emotional valence. Results showed that participants experienced a higher peak of positive emotions when they were interacting with the interface through their gaze. Considered together with the higher level of perceived pleasantness of the interface, in the gaze control experimental sessions, this occurrence confirmed the idea that the eye tracker could be exploited as a means of interaction and not only as a tool that records eye-related data in a passive way. Indeed, participants considered positively interacting through this alternative means of control at both the quantitative (maximal valence) and subjective level (evaluation in terms of pleasantness).

The findings about the user experience underlined issues related to the fact the participants are not accustomed to interfaces that can be controlled with their eyes (Jacob and Karn 2003). Compared to a traditional input modality (i.e., mouse) that gives constant visual feedback to the users regarding the actual position of the cursor on the screen, gaze control does not provide such information. This could explain why participants perceived the interface as less accurate, efficient, easy to use, and tiresome. Indeed, users did not know where their gaze was precisely located at any time, and this uncertainty led them to subjectively perceive the interface functioning in a negative way, in accordance with previous works (Serim et al. 2017). The interface only provided raw feedback about gaze data availability. Indeed, the color of the interface background slightly changes from the original grey when the eye tracker is not properly collecting gaze data (i.e., overly extensive head/body movements outside of the so-called head box; Serim et al. 2017). No actual point of gaze indicator was continuously shown. The authors made this choice with the aim of keeping the interaction as natural as possible, in line with previous findings (Slobodenyuk 2016). Indeed, the cursor would hamper the task accomplishment insofar as it would partially hide the information at which the participant was looking. Nevertheless, to experience the so-called oculomotor agency, which Slobodenyuk (2016) defined as "an experience of control over eye movements that involves perception of gaze-related causality and correspondence of the outcome to intention," the presence of a cursor that indicates the actual gaze point is necessary. This is in accordance with a literature study that demonstrated how the self-agency of participants was very low when the cursor was absent (Wang et al. 2012). Participants could not explicitly experience the sense of gaze agency, which occurrence is reflected in the negative perception of the interface. Moreover, eyes are characterized by continuous small movements, even during a fixation (i.e., microsaccades, tremors, and drifts) that can be additional factors of gaze-location instability. Finally, individuals are not familiar with real-world objects that respond to their eye movements. The only exception is when they are interacting with other people (Jacob and Karn 2003).

In general, a pivotal aspect could be clarifying the eye tracker functioning insofar as head and body movements adversely affect its tracking accuracy. Morimoto and Mimica (2005) pointed out how such issues impact the usability and, as a consequence, wider uptake of gaze-based interactive systems. During the *gaze control* experimental sessions, participants might forget this constraint. Thus, the potential decrease in tracking accuracy could cause them to negatively perceive the interface responsiveness. In contrast, the interface was perceived as more pleasant when users performed the task by means of their gaze. The interface could be perceived as capable of understanding participants' intentions before they actually express them (Jacob 1991). Moreover, this could mean that the implicit feature of this technique (the participants do not continuously pay attention to the fact that the eye tracker is working) can positively affect the user experience evaluation.

Considering the overall findings, it is possible to speculate on the opportunity to control interfaces by adopting a MMHCI approach combining, for instance, a traditional modality (i.e., mouse and keyboard) with one or more alternative modalities of interaction (e.g., gaze). Nevertheless, it is crucial to bear in mind that the interfaces or the target applications have to be conceived on the basis of the alternative modalities' characteristics. In a multimodal interface/system that exploits the eye direction as an alternative input modality, the size of the gaze-interactive item (e.g., button or menu) has to be large enough to allow a fluid interaction. This constraint could force, for instance, creation of menus and submenus, which are well-known factors that can reduce the interaction flow. Differently, the size of the mouse-interactive items (e.g., scroll bar) does not need to be changed. This kind of advanced interface has to show a display that contains a combination of stimuli that show *gaze*-friendly features and stimuli that show *mouse*-friendly characteristics. This could ensure full exploitation of the strength points of both input modalities. Moreover, the outcomes regarding the higher perceived pleasantness of the gaze-controlled version of the interface could be exploited. Users should be provided with full information about the issues that can adversely affect the eye-tracking accuracy and should be trained on how to avoid them. An expected consequence will be better evaluation of the gaze-based component of these envisioned multi-modal interfaces in terms of accuracy, efficiency, and ease of use. In these cutting-edge interfaces, the combination of different input modalities will lead to more effective human-computer communication that will resemble human-human communication (Jaimes and Sebe 2007).

Acknowledgements. This work was supported by the European Commission (Symbiotic Mind Computer Interaction for Information Seeking, MindSee FP7-ICT; Grant Agreement #611570).

Appendix

User Experience Questionnaire

Considering the situation in which you control the interface utilizing mouse/gaze control, please indicate using a 5-point scale (1 = not at all; 5 = very):

1. ...to what extent you believe the interface to be easy
2. ...to what extent you believe the interface to be intuitive
3. ...to what extent you believe the interface to be pleasant
4. ...to what extent you believe the interface to be useful
5. ...to what extent you believe the interface to be tiresome
6. ...to what extent you believe the interface to be fluid
7. ...to what extent you believe the interface to be accurate
8. ...to what extent you believe the interface to be efficient
9. ...to what extent you believe the interface to be clear
10. ...to what extent you believe the interface to be fast.

References

Asai, K., et al.: Eye mark pointer in immersive projection display. Proc. IEEE Virtual Reality **2000**, 125–132 (2000)

Bates, R., Donegan, M., Istance, H.O., Hansen, J.P., Räihä, K.J.: Introducing COGAIN: communication by gaze interaction. Univ. Access Inf. Soc. **6**(2), 159–166 (2007)

Cribari-Neto, F., Zeileis, A.: Beta regression in R. J. Stat. Softw. **34**(2), 1–24 (2010)

Donegan, M., et al.: Understanding users and their needs. Univ. Access Inf. Soc. **8**(4), 259 (2009)

Drewes, H.: Eye gaze tracking for human computer interaction (Doctoral dissertation, LMU) (2010)

Duchowski, A.T.: Eye Tracking Methodology: Theory and Practice, p. 366. Springer, Heidelberg (2017). https://doi.org/10.1007/978-3-319-57883-5

Grauman, K., Betke, M., Lombardi, J., Gips, J., Bradski, G.R.: Communication via eye blinks and eyebrow raises: video-based human-computer interfaces. Univ. Access Inf. Soc. **2**(4), 359–373 (2003)

Hyrskykari, A., Majaranta, P., Räihä, K.J.: From gaze control to attentive interfaces. In: Proceedings of HCII, vol. 2, July 2005

Jaimes, A., Sebe, N.: Multimodal human–computer interaction: a survey. Comput. Vis. Image Understand. **108**(1), 116–134 (2007)

Jacob, R.J.: The use of eye movements in human-computer interaction techniques: what you look at is what you get. ACM Trans. Inf. Syst. (TOIS) **9**(2), 152–169 (1991)

Jacob, R.J., Karn, K.S.: Eye tracking in human-computer interaction and usability research: ready to deliver the promises. In: Hyönä, J., Radach, R., Deubel, H. (eds.) The Mind's Eye: Cognitive and Applied Aspects of Eye Movement Research, pp. 573–605. Elsevier Science, Amsterdam (2003)

Just, M.A., Carpenter, P.A.: Eye fixations and cognitive processes. Cogn. Psychol. **8**(4), 441–480 (1976)

Levine, J.L.: Performance of an eye tracker for office use. Comput. Biol. Med. **14**(1), 77–89 (1984)

Majaranta, P., Bulling, A.: Eye tracking and eye-based human–computer interaction. In: Fairclough, S.H., Gilleade, K. (eds.) Advances in Physiological Computing. HIS, pp. 39–65. Springer, London (2014). https://doi.org/10.1007/978-1-4471-6392-3_3

Morimoto, C.H., Mimica, M.R.: Eye gaze tracking techniques for interactive applications. Comput. Vis. Image Understand. **98**(1), 4–24 (2005)

Pavlovic, V.I., Sharma, R., Huang, T.S.: Visual interpretation of hand gestures for human-computer interaction: a review. IEEE Trans. Pattern Anal. Mach. Intell. **7**, 677–695 (1997)

Penkar, A.M., Lutteroth, C., Weber, G.: Designing for the eye: design parameters for dwell in gaze interaction. In: Proceedings of the 24th Australian Computer-Human Interaction Conference, pp. 479–488. ACM, November 2012

Rayner, K.: Eye movements in reading and information processing: 20 years of research. Psychol. Bull. **124**(3), 372 (1998)

Rayner, K.: Eye movements and attention in reading, scene perception, and visual search. Q. J. Exp. Psychol. **62**(8), 1457–1506 (2009)

R Core Team: R: A language and environment for statistical computing. R Foundation for Statistical Computing, Vienna, Austria (2015). http://www.R-project.org/

Serim, B., Chech, L., Vasilieva, M., Papa, L., Gamberini, L., Jacucci, G.: Exploring gaze-adaptive features for interacting with multi-document visualizations. In: Proceedings of the 10th International Symposium on Visual Information Communication and Interaction, pp. 85–92. ACM, August 2017

Slobodenyuk, N.: Towards cognitively grounded gaze-controlled interfaces. Pers. Ubiquit. Comput. **20**(6), 1035–1047 (2016)

Tanriverdi, V., Jacob, R.J.: Interacting with eye movements in virtual environments. In: Proceedings of the SIGCHI Conference on Human Factors in Computing Systems, pp. 265–272. ACM, April 2000

Turk, M., Robertson, G.: Perceptual user interfaces (introduction). Commun. ACM **43**(3), 32–34 (2000)

Turk, M.: Multimodal interaction: a review. Pattern Recogn. Lett. **36**, 189–195 (2014)

Van der Kamp, J., Sundstedt, V.: Gaze and voice controlled drawing. In: Proceedings of the 1st Conference on Novel Gaze-Controlled Applications, p. 9. ACM, May 2011

Wang, Q., Bolhuis, J., Rothkopf, C.A., Kolling, T., Knopf, M., Triesch, J.: Infants in control: rapid anticipation of action outcomes in a gaze-contingent paradigm. PLoS ONE **7**(2), e30884 (2012)

Participatory Design of System Messages in Petroleum Fields Management Software

Pedro Alan T. Ramos[1,2], Julio Cesar dos Reis[1(✉)],
Antonio Alberto de Souza dos Santos[2], and Denis José Schiozer[2]

[1] Institute of Computing, UNICAMP, Campinas, SP, Brazil
{palan,jreis}@ic.unicamp.br
[2] Center for Petroleum Studies, UNICAMP, Campinas, SP, Brazil
{alberto,denis}@cepetro.unicamp.br

Abstract. Users face difficulties in understanding the progress of simulation tasks in oil reservoirs. It is necessary to turn clear to users when some task suffers errors because this is time consuming. In this paper, we propose the use of participatory design to conceive Application System Messages (ASMs) in software tools implemented to support studies related to Numerical Simulation and Management of Petroleum Reservoirs. We explored braindrawing and brainwriting techniques to acquire early concepts for a redesign of the ASMs' presentation and content. Our obtained results indicate that the use of participatory practices is useful to improve the redesign of ASMs in our study context.

Keywords: Participatory design · Reservoir simulations ·
Braindrawing · Brainwriting · Scientific software ·
Application System Messages

1 Introduction

Deciding whether an oil reservoir is worth exploring requires an expensive and scrutinizing process that is essential for reservoir engineers. Not only the field's infrastructure and future production is a deciding factor, but which process of extraction was used to maximize profit, given the various uncertainties related to this process [14]. Usually, reservoir simulations are used to help answering these questions. They are the most reliable method that can predict reservoirs' behavior when using a certain method of extraction [8,13].

Understanding the results of simulation tasks in oil reservoirs requires interactive software environments to enhance user's experience. The massive amount of data and parameters hamper procedures required by domain experts. In this context, the software MERO is a framework with a collection of tools implemented to support studies related to Numerical Simulation and Management of

© Springer Nature Switzerland AG 2019
M. Kurosu (Ed.): HCII 2019, LNCS 11568, pp. 459–475, 2019.
https://doi.org/10.1007/978-3-030-22636-7_35

Petroleum Reservoirs. The system's purpose is to provide flexible and powerful tools that help reservoir engineers and researchers with the automation of certain tasks.

This context of MERO's usage and implementation enables us to categorize it as a scientific software (SS) [4], meaning that usability was not the focus on development. SS usually are very effective in achieving their required results, given that they are generally implemented by field experts [4,7]. For this reason, SS development cycle focuses more on balancing between software sustainability and performance than on its usability and users' appeal [7].

As a direct result, despite having different technological backgrounds, MERO's users have been experiencing some disadvantages with the way the system communicates with them. Previous investigations have shown that most of MERO's users do not find utility in most system messages [11]. Results indicated that some users did not even pay attention to the interface's log section due to the difficulties in interpreting it. They reported only looking at it when some relevant error occurred. Moreover, sometimes, the error messages were not even helpful, with some cases being too technical or being just a stack trace. As a consequence, users need to contact the support staff for every issue that they cannot resolve. This current state of MERO's messages hampers users to smoothly perform some key activities in the software. In addition, attempts of interface-redesign activities become difficult due to the MERO's scientific nature.

Existing studies have shown that Application System Messages (ASMs), such as the ones presented in MERO's log system, imply in a significant impact on user frustration and can severely hinder their overall task performance [3,5,6,15]. In this context, literature has shown that User-Centered Design (UCD) [2] applied to SS can achieve promising results for improving their usability [7,12,16].

In this paper, we analyze if Participatory Design [9] techniques usage on ASMs of a scientific software reduces user's frustration and improve overall research-related task performance. Participatory Design enables the active participation of stakeholders in the design process and can better reflect their perspectives and necessities. Our goal is to propose a redesign to improve users understanding of the system's current status and enhance their interaction experience and usability.

First, we conducted semi-structured interviews to obtain an in-depth understanding of the impact of MERO's log system on users. After further analysis, we traced the most common use-cases of MERO's tools and set apart the most problematic ones in relation to log messages. Based on that information, we searched for these occurrences in MERO's source code and bracketed each one of them into two groups: their presentation and content.

After gathering the most common occurrences of user's frustration, we conducted braindrawing and brainwriting sessions with the participation of MERO's users. As a result of the braindrawing session, we acquired early concepts for a redesign of the ASMs' presentation. From the brainwriting session, we found insights into how improving the messages' content. Our findings show adequate design solutions involving the stakeholders. Obtained results indicate that the redesign of MERO interface for ASMs presentation and content can potentially better help users to interpret the simulations tasks and system status.

This paper is structured as follows: Sect. 2 describes the literature review and the theoretical background. Section 3 presents the research methodology. Section 4 reports on the obtained results. Whereas Sect. 5 discusses the achieved findings, Sect. 6 presents the conclusions and future work.

2   Foundations and Related Work

In this section, we explain the definition of Application System Messages used in this paper, their current situation on MERO and related work linking ASMs to user frustration (Subsect. 2.1). Subsection 2.2 describes the basis for Participatory Design and the techniques explored in this investigation.

2.1   Application System Messages

This work deals with issues related to MERO's Application System Messages. Within a software application, Application System Messages (ASMs) can be defined as messages displayed to the user, such as error messages, alerts or reminders. Shneiderman [15] proposed a set of guidelines for these messages that are still useful to this day. The author states that ASMs should not be wordy, negative in tone or too general. Instead these messages should be brief, positive and constructive. Nowadays, MERO's system messages are represented only by a textual log section that is rarely considered useful by users when dealing with a problem.

This ineffectiveness is not MERO's exclusivity. ASMs can have an impact on user affective responses, going as far as causing user frustration if implemented carelessly. Jones *et al.* [5] conducted an study to understand the impact of these types of messages on the usability of four different healthcare software applications. More than half of the study's participants indicated that the application they were using lacked ASMs with constructive advice. Almost half of the participants declared that the message's improper delivery caused interruption of their work. Lazar *et al.* [6] defines that frustration occurs when "there is an inhibiting condition that interferes with or stops the realization of a goal". We can assume that some of Jones' study participants [5] were experiencing frustration, due to being interrupted on their task. Lazar *et al.* investigated what were the main causes for workplace users' frustration, finding users lost 40% of their time due to frustration. Ceaparu *et al.* [3] also concerned users' frustations and their work concluded similar observations as those from Lazar *et al.*. In this sense, it is essential to handle the ineffectiveness of ASMs due to the effects on user frustration, which in consequence, can result in loss of time and productivity.

In this paper, we organize ASMs into their presentation and their content. Message presentation is here defined as the way or interactive mechanism in which the message is presented to the user. Message content refers to the message or text itself. Pop-ups, notifications, new windows or even SMS are examples of different forms of message presentation and what is being presented on them is the message's content. Therefore, our objective is to improve MERO's messages' content and presentation as a way to reduce user frustration and increase productivity. We used a Participatory Design approach to achieve this goal.

2.2 Participatory Design

Participatory Design (PD) is an approach to design where there is an attempt to involve all stakeholders in the design process. This approach helps designers obtain a result that meets stakeholders' needs and expectations. When dealing with improving software's usability, this means that users work together with designers to determine the best solutions to their problems. In this context, the designer's job is of a facilitator, adhering to the core concepts of Human-Computer Interaction, defining the best tools and methods suited to the problem and applying them in a well-constructed process.

Participatory Design presents a relationship with User-Centered Design (UCD). We assume that UCD can provide several benefits when applied to scientific software. UCD is a practice of designing and developing software focusing on user's needs throughout the software's lifecycle [10]. However, this does not necessarily mean that users participate in the process, as only a team of designers could generate solutions based on user needs (without their explicit participation in the design process). PD in our context is user-centered because it focuses entirely on end-users' (stakeholders) interests while still enabling them to participate in the process (act as co-designers).

Consequently, we argue that the results of UCD applied to scientific software, for instance, the studies conducted by Macaulay et al. [7] and Sultanum et al. [16], can be achieved by a PD approach and be more sensitive in considering user's needs. These studies focused more on understanding users' needs first, then providing a fitting solution. In this investigation, we hypothesize that if MERO's stakeholders actually participate in the redesign process, further results regarding the quality of the design can be achieved.

There are many techniques in PD that help to generate ideas for a redesign. One of these techniques is Braindrawing, which is a type of brainstorming in which participants collaboratively sketch their ideas for designs or other solutions, instead of just saying them [9]. The only resources needed are paper and pens for each participant. They start their sketch on a paper and, after a short period of time, they switch papers counterclockwise with another participant. Later, after a discussion about the best aspects of each drawing, the result is a fusion of all participants bests ideas [9]. Another tool with a similar concept is Brainwriting, in which instead of drawings, only text is allowed. Both techniques were used in this study, as they benefit from low cost, few resources needed and high throughput of ideas.

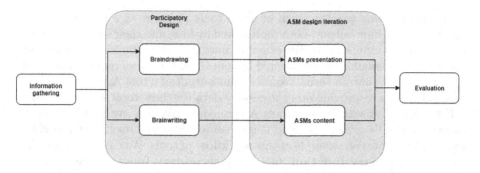

Fig. 1. Research methodology designed in this study.

3   Design of the Study

Our methodology consisted of three activities. First, we gathered information about MERO's current ASMs and asserted to which extent they present issues concerning their effectiveness. Afterwards, we carried out braindrawing sessions to get ideas for different ASMs presentations or mechanisms and brainwriting sessions to bring together the structure and vocabulary of ASM content according to the stakeholders' view. Finally, with these results, we achieved a first iteration of design for MERO's ASMs. Figure 1 presents each activities' role in our methodology.

The remainder of this section is organized as follows: Subsect. 3.1 details how MERO works and the usability issues it has been facing; Subsect. 3.2 explains how we gathered relevant information about MERO; Subsect. 3.3 describes the braindrawing and brainwriting participants profiles; Subsects. 3.4 and 3.5 describes how the brainwriting and brainwriting sessions were both elaborated and performed, respectively; Finally, Subsect. 3.6 describes how we evaluated the first iteration of a ASM design based on the brainwriting and braindrawing results.

3.1   MERO

MERO refers to a collection of tools implemented to support studies related to Numerical Simulation and Management of Petroleum Reservoirs. Its development team is comprised of a research group, called UNISIM, located at the Center of Petroleum Studies (CEPETRO) in the University of Campinas (Unicamp), Brazil. MERO's objective is to provide to oil reservoir engineers, researchers and students a powerful and flexible tool to assist them in automating tasks related to the decision analysis process in the development and management of oil reservoirs [17]. MERO does not run reservoir simulations by itself, but it helps managing the process and interface with commercial simulators. These simulation runs are performed by clusters located at CEPETRO. In general, MERO's tools applications can vary from generating a combination of certain variables needed for another tool to calling the simulations with the required settings.

Deepening this concept, each of these tools operates as a function, taking input and returning output, both represented by files, and their sequential execution performs automatically. For example, imagine a situation where a researcher needs to run a simulation represented by tool C, and this tool requires some output of a tool B, that, in turns, requires some output of a tool A. In this case, the user only needs to provide other necessary data for these tools and indicates to MERO that they want to run tools A through C. We can say that this practicality is MERO's cornerstone and is represented by a tool itself called **WKFL**. Figure 2 illustrates an example of this **workflow** of tools. We can determine that tool A is a **primary function**, tool B is a **secondary function** and so on.

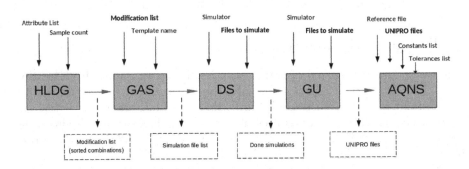

Fig. 2. Example of a workflow of tools HLDG, GAS, DS, GU, AQNS. Inputs are indicated by black arrows and outputs by red arrows. Each output description is indicated by a dashed arrow followed by a dashed rectangle. Inputs that are outputs of another tool are in bold. A simple call to WKFL describing this sequence of tools and providing the non-bold input would generate this workflow. (Color figure online)

Due to its relative simplicity and development environment, MERO's usability was never the main focus, as this is a common characteristic of Scientific Software [7]. Despite MERO acting only as a sort of "compiler" of its tools, users have been experiencing problems related to its usability. Our previous studies have shown that users face problems with the way MERO communicates with them [11]. They expressed that documentation was not easily accessible, nor "to the point", and that error messages were not very clear, resulting in a dependence of contact with the support team to continue their tasks. Our investigation showed not only the dissatisfaction with MERO's communication, but also how users most commonly use the software [11].

3.2   Study Context

Aiming to improve MERO's communication with its users, we first collected data about its current messages and the way they are presented. This was performed by interacting with the development team and analyzing the source code. After gathering this data, we analyzed the ASMs to discover patterns.

Without going any further, as Sect. 4 provides additional findings, three important details came from these interactions and analysis. First, MERO indeed presents problematic messages, in that "problematic" means they do not follow ASMs guidelines (*cf.* Sect. 2). Second, ASMs in this software are only presented via a log portion visible on the interface, without any prominence between two different kind of messages. Finally, it was discovered that each one of MERO's tool can undergo either a syntactic exception or a semantic exception. **Syntactic exceptions** generally mean that there is something wrong with the input files that can be identified prior to execution. **Semantic exceptions** are errors that can only be identified while executing certain tool. These three concepts were essential to the elaboration of our subsequent methodology steps.

3.3 Participants

There were 5 participants of the braindrawing and brainwriting sessions which age ranged between 25 and 28 years old. This group was comprised by 4 developers and 1 researcher at CEPETRO. Despite the majority of the group being developers, we must remember that in a scientific software context the concepts of users (researchers) and developers sometimes end up mixed together [7]. Users' scientific discoveries are implemented on the scientific software, and SS tools assist users with their research. This is also the case for MERO, in which developers use MERO at the workplace and even have the same frustrations as non-developers users [11]. So it is safe to assume that, being given total liberty about their ideas for the ASMs presentation, we can achieve similar results as if the group was comprised only by researchers. These participants were also contacted to evaluate our first ASM design iteration later on.

3.4 Braindrawing

Relying on the information gathered, We chose two different and representative scenarios for each activity. The scenarios presented to the participants of the braindrawing session were as follows:

1. You are using a MERO's tool that takes a considerable amount of time to finish. Some unknown error occurred during this tool's execution. How MERO should report this incident to you?
2. You are going to execute a tool or a workflow of tools. MERO detected an issue with one of your input files and could not perform this task. How should MERO warn you about this occurrence?

Considering the concepts of semantic and syntactic exceptions explained, we can say that item 1 is more closely related to semantic exceptions. This scenario can happen if MERO founds out that some input does not makes sense much later on execution. Taking into context that tools related with simulation usually deal with enormous amount of data, as simulations of oil reservoirs often are, the task can go wrong hours after its beginning. In this sense, as stated by some users, it is safe to assume that the user in Scenario 1 might not be interacting with MERO's interface when this occurs. Therefore, our goal with this scenario was to find a design that does not relies on the current log portion of MERO's interface to present an ASM for an error of a "long-duration" tool. However, an important point to be addressed is that this scenario does not limit the cause of this type of error, despite one of the possibilities being a semantic exception. It is possible that a network or memory failure occurred midway through execution, causing MERO to report the issue.

Scenario 2, on the other hand, is more closely related with syntactic exceptions. In this situation, there is something wrong with the input file and MERO can identify it right away. The cause could be that some keyword cannot be identified, a value was missing, or even the file itself was not found. Also, we can safely assume that the user might be interacting with MERO's interface when this happens. Therefore, our goal with this scenario was to reach a design that improve how MERO alert its users when something went wrong shortly after first executing a tool or workflow.

After explaining in detail each scenario, the participants were given two minutes to draw for the first round and one minute for the others. The rounds for each scenario ended when the participant passed on their first drawing for the second time. This last round was made to give participants a chance to add to their first drawing a second time, now that their initial sketch had been filled with new ideas.

3.5   Brainwriting

After we finished the two scenarios for the braindrawing session, the brainwriting session begun right away. Now, instead of thinking about which mechanism or how the ASMs could be presented, we were interested in ideas on what would be the content of these ASMs. We chose brainwriting because generally the contents of ASMs are textual, and our objective consisted of picking vocabulary and general ideas of the textual structure of these ASMs.

Moreover, the reason why these two activities were conducted on after another was to reach a consistent design for MERO's ASMs. It is important to state that participants were not tied to create textual content for a particular message mechanism. However, there was no problem if while thinking about a textual design, they wanted to suggest content for previously seen ideas at the braindrawing session. For that reason, we reach a general ASM design that conciliates their presentation and content.

The brainwriting session consisted of the same participants as the braindrawing session and also consisted of two scenarios similar to the braindrawing ones. They covered semantic exceptions or misfortunes during long-duration tools and syntactic problems that happen right after some tool is executed. The only difference was that here we asked for textual representation of ideas. We describe the two scenarios as follows:

1. You are using a MERO's tool that takes a considerable amount of time to finish. Some unknown error occurred during this tool's execution. How MERO should report this incident to you (textually)?
2. You are going to execute a tool or a workflow of tools. MERO detected an issue with one of your input files and could not perform this task. How should MERO warn you about this occurrence (textually)?

The braindrawing and brainwriting sessions were followed by a debriefing session to help us consolidating the design ideas.

3.6   Evaluation

Following the braindrawing and brainwriting sessions, a first mockup of a design for MERO was created. After that, some of the ideas and corrections for new iterations were discussed informally between researchers and MERO's developers, some of which also participated in the sessions. The mockup focused more on the results from the braindrawing, that is, only visual ideas were taken into account for it. Actually, only visual ideas for MERO's actual user interface were used for the mockup. Other types of propositions were only discussed, such as suggesting other types of interactions that require other channels of communication and ideas regarding textual content. Feedback from these conversations were used to give a more complete picture of what MERO's users want to turn its ASMs effective.

4   Results

We present the results regarding the understanding of MERO's ASMs (Subsect. 4.1) followed by the findings related to the braindrawing (Subsect. 4.2), brainwriting (Subsect. 4.3) and evaluation (Subsect. 4.4).

4.1   Understanding MERO's ASMs

We made contact with MERO development team to gather information about how MERO's ASMs were currently implemented and whether they have issues. We were given access to the source code and had conversations with its team to obtain the results.

MERO is implemented mostly in Java and the development team work in a Eclipse environment. Because we were mostly interested in details about how the ASMs worked, our research covered the most important Java classes and packages. Each MERO's tool is represented in the source code as being an implementation of the *AbstractCommand* abstract class. As expected, the *AbstractCommand* class covers common behavior to all tools, such as being able to read the input file, or setting the required log "level", as MERO gives the user or programmer the option to set which types of messages they want to see in the log section. The most important method of this abstract class is called *execute()*

as it basically does all the steps required by all tools, such as checking for file existence or selecting the appropriate parser. Parsers in this context are classes responsible for checking any **syntactic exceptions** when reading an input file, that is, any invalid inputs or data structures.

One of the most important relationships to our understanding of MERO's ASMs is between its parsers and the SLF4J [1] abstraction for logging frameworks, the one currently in use. MERO's usage of SLF4J allows it to quickly call for log messages when needed. After called they appear either at the log section of MERO graphical interface or at the console terminal, if the user is using it. SLF4J allows an easy way of using tags and the required message formats, with the *java.MessageFormat* package, for instance. As a consequence, one common use that we found is that after every "parser checking", if something goes wrong, the logger is immediately called.

However, this is not the only way the logger messages can be called. As stated by MERO's developers, each tool implements their execution differently in some way. So it is possible that other types of exceptions arise after initial validation. In this paper, we used the term **semantic exceptions** for these occurrences.

As for the messages themselves, they can be either be hardcoded directly at the logger call or be called from a "properties" file, the most appropriate way. Due to MERO's code complexity, we focus on messages contained in those properties files, as we can already analyse some issues with them. These files are located at the "messages" package and are divided into the "parser" package and the "command" package. The former represent messages used by parsers that

Gerais para todos os comandos	shared-command-messages.properties	
Tag	**Português**	**Inglês**
input_arg_description	Caminho do arquivo de entrada	Input File Path
help_arg_description	Mostra as opcoes de uso	Display this help and exit
log_arg_description	Nivel de log. Opcoes (do menos para o mais detalhado): error (ou 0), warn (ou 1), info (ou 2), debug (ou 3), trace (ou 4). Default: info (2)	Level of the log provided. Options: error (or 0), warn (or 1), info (or 2), debug (or 3), trace (or 4). Default: info (2)
log_arg_conversion_failed	[{0}] nao e um nivel de log valido	[{0}] is not a valid log level
start_of_run_info	Inicio da Execucao	Start of Run
end_of_run_info	Fim da Execucao	End of Run
unexpected_error_message	Ocorreu um erro inesperado. Por favor entre em contato com o suporte UNISIM e forneca os seguintes dados:\	An unexpected error occured. Please contact UNISIM Support and provide the following data:\
seconds_unit	segundos	seconds

Fig. 3. Excerpt of messages used to analyze MERO's current ASMs. This represents the messages and text used by all of MERO's tools. From left to right, each box's column represent the messages' tag, its content in Portuguese and in English (Manual translation from the authors), respectively. Messages that were not clear or had other issues are highlighted.

check general aspects of every tool regarding data syntax. The latter represent messages related specifically to syntax of each tool. We showcase only a few examples of these messages in Fig. 3[1].

4.2   Braindrawing

We performed the braindrawing for two scenarios. Scenario 1 was about a tool running for a long time that suffered from a semantic exception or other misfortune. We had as a result a total of five different drawings for a design that represented how MERO should communicate with its users when that happened. Figure 4 presents a scan of one of the sketches that represents the most accurate depiction of the best ideas of each drawing.

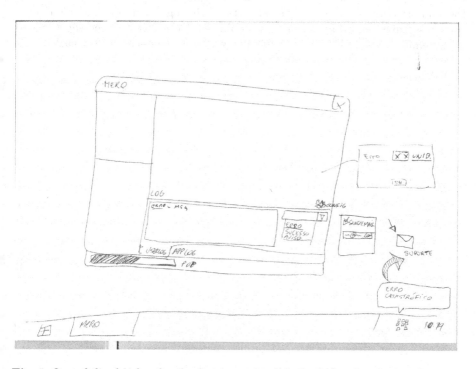

Fig. 4. One of the sketches for the first scenario of the braindrawing session. It represents the ideas for a progress bar for each tool, pop-up notifications both when MERO is in focus as when out of focus; and some sort of configuration for sending alerts via email and filtering through tags.

One of the ideas it showcases is of **pop-up notifications** appearing both when MERO's is in the operational system focus and when not. In this case, appearing as a speech bubble. This was a feature present in both scenarios, but

---

[1] We kept the original messages in Portuguese Language.

with more emphasis in this one. Another idea presented was a **progress bar** for the whole process. This concept appeared in two drawings, but was agreed upon as a good idea by all participants after later discussion. Other variations of this concept included different colors for each type of message and different bars for each tool, when running a workflow. Other drawings depicted different alert symbols at the side of the bar, when something out of ordinary occurred, but MERO continued the tool's execution. Also, a type of progress bar for memory usage was a suggestion, as some MERO's tools end up using a lot of memory and could fail execution if they reach the computer's limit.

External communication was the most present concept among all drawings. Either via email or phone messages, participants expressed they wanted to know if their long-time simulations were successful or not even if they were not near the computer running them. Other related concepts included contacting the support team automatically sending them the log file, and being able to customize settings regarding when they would like to receive this messages. Some participants argued that they would like to receive messages after each tool's

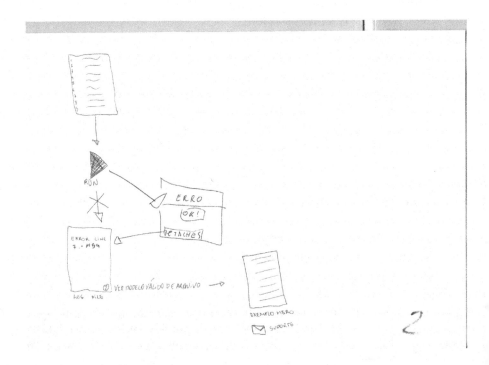

Fig. 5. One of the sketches for the second scenario of the braindrawing session. It showcases a sequence of events after a syntactic exception occurrence. First, we have the file input of the tool, then the user presses the "run" button. After the error occurs, a pop-up message window appears providing additional information. A direct way of accessing a sample file input is also mentioned.

step was completed, where others said that they would only like to receive this messages when the tool succeeded.

Figure 5 represents one of the sketches made for Scenario 2, that was related to the situation where a syntactic exception occurred shortly after running the tool. This sketch comprises most of the concepts that were prevalent among all drawing for this scenario.

One of key propositions in this sketch was of **pop-up notifications** showing up at the screen. There were ideas of allowing these notifications to show detailed information about the exception on them, suggesting that the participants were not interested in looking through the log section to find where the exception was mentioned. Another suggestion was to provide a quick access to a sample file input for that tool to help novice users if they had difficulty with the files expected syntax.

In this scenario, the participants represented more their ideas through text, even if advised not to do so. Therefore, ideas about the ASMs content happened to appear before their intended appearance at the brainwriting session. As these ideas were also addressed later, we discuss them more in the following subsection.

4.3 Brainwriting

In the two scenarios, there was little difference regarding how the messages should be, generally. For both scenarios, examples of participants' propositions for the ASMs' content were: *"Ser mais direto nas mensagens de erro. Mensagens do MERO são muito genéricas"*[2], *"Texto descritivo com sugestão de correção"*[3] and *"A linguagem deve estar mais próxima do usuário"*[4]. These examples represent the participants' ideas that the error messages should be always "to the point", should be written with terms that the users could easily understand and that they should always suggest a course of action.

According to the brainwriting results, the main difference between the messages for the two scenarios is that in the second one, the ASM should highlight where the exception occurred. This highlight could be done directly at the file or indirectly, at the message. Also, if the error was related to some wrong typing of a keyword, MERO should suggest valid keywords for that specific tool.

4.4 Evaluation

After the braindrawing and brainwriting sessions, a first mockup of a design for MERO was created. Our wireframe proposition refers to a medium-fidelity prototype and contain some sort of interaction based on links. The log section

---

[2] In English language (manual translation from the authors): "Be more direct on the error messages".

[3] In English language (manual translation from the authors): "Descriptive text with correction suggestion".

[4] In English language (manual translation from the authors): "The language should be clearer for the user".

in Fig. 6 has two tabs. One represents the actual log with some alterations and the other presents progress bars for each tool. If the user clicks on one of these tabs, the wireframe takes them to the page linked to them. Figure 6 represents MERO screen when the user clicks on the "Progress" tab of the log, when some workflow is being executed.

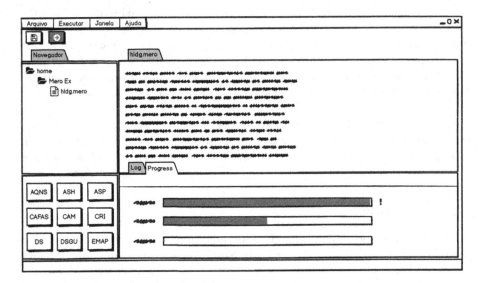

Fig. 6. One page of the first mockup made based on the results from the braindrawing. This screen represents mostly MERO's actual first screen but with a difference on the log section.

This wireframe, in conjunction with other ideas from previous activities was discussed with some of MERO's developers. Their reaction was mostly positive, given that most of them participated in the braindrawing and brainwriting session and had at least one idea represented in the mockup.

5   Discussion

The design of system messages in petroleum fields management software is not a trivial task. In this paper, we proposed the use of participatory design to address the difficulties in this context. We found that one of the most interesting results that came from the braindrawing and brainwriting sessions was that most of the suggestions given by the participants regarding semantic errors required other communication channels, such as e-mail or SMS. This was somewhat expected due to this being a scenario where the user is not in front of the screen. Even so, it is interesting to observe that the participants were not bound to MERO's current interface when thinking about how improving its ASMs, somewhat validating our approach rooted in participatory design.

Another important finding is that the participants mostly suggested some sort of pop-up notifications, despite the general idea that we should avoid using them in favor of a more non-invasive solution. Perhaps when dealing with scientific software, users tend to want to be alerted about the task progress. This is specially true if we consider the nature of the environment itself. MERO's users generally use MERO as a way to get some result important to their research. As simulations require a considerable amount of time of their research time, they want to optimize MERO's use, so any errors should be dealt with as soon as possible.

Given that we lacked more time with MERO end-users only, we were not capable of observing the long-time effects of the suggested changes of MERO's ASMs to user's frustration. Future work should focus on implementing these changes and seeing its effects on MERO's users affective responses when seeing an error. Moreover, future research on this topic should improve the ASMs content based on feedback from multiple users, given that we had a limited amount of users to better identify how the text would be on these ASMs. Our preliminary user evaluation indicated some minor corrections in the prototype. By taking into account the implementation of these improvements, we can achieve a more faithful design solution.

Our investigation concludes that the use of participatory practices can be useful to improve the redesign of SS for the management of petroleum fields management. We plan the evaluation of high-fidelity prototypes already integrated into the system as a result of the participatory activities to provide and improve user experience.

6   Conclusion

The reduction of user frustration related to Application System Messages requires appropriate interaction design. In this study, we conducted a case study with MERO, a scientific software supporting activities in the petroleum fields management. We employed a participatory design approach to obtain design solutions in this context. Our methodology performed three activities. We first analyzed MERO's current messages and had a deeper understanding of how they work. We found that some of the messages lacked clarity and only a few stated a course of action for the user to solve the problem. We classified MERO's exceptions either as syntactic or semantic. Syntactic errors were related to wrong data formatting or invalid inputs and can be detected soon after execution, whereas semantic errors can only be detected later after calculations and are related to some data discrepancy. Based on these concepts, we conducted braindrawing and brainwriting sessions to reach a design for the ASMs' presentation and content, respectively. Some of the key concepts suggested for presentation were progress bars for the tools execution, pop-up notifications both outside and inside MERO and external notification via email or SMS. As for suggestions of ASM's content, participants valued concise statements using user's jargons and proposed a course of action to solve the problem. In both presentation and content, users suggested that MERO should point to working input examples if something went wrong with their input. Future work will focus on developing further prototypes based on these ideas and validate them with a participatory design approach.

Acknowledgments. We appreciate the support from the following institutions: Petrobras; Energi Simulation inside of the R&D of ANP; Institute of Computing at UNICAMP; Center for Petroleum Studies (CEPETRO-UNICAMP); Energy Department (DE-FEM-UNICAMP); and from the Research Group of Simulations and Management of Petroleum Reservoirs (UNISIM-UNICAMP) at CEPETRO.

References

1. SLF4J user manual. https://www.slf4j.org/manual.html
2. Abras, C., Maloney-Krichmar, D., Preece, J.: User-centered design. In: Bainbridge, W. (ed.) Encyclopedia of Human-Computer Interaction, vol. 37, no. 4, pp. 445–456. Sage Publications, Thousand Oaks (2004)
3. Ceaparu, I., Lazar, J., Bessiere, K., Robinson, J., Shneiderman, B.: Determining causes and severity of end-user frustration. Int. J. Hum.-Comput. Interact. **17**(3), 333–356 (2004)
4. Hannay, J.E., MacLeod, C., Singer, J., Langtangen, H.P., Pfahl, D., Wilson, G.: How do scientists develop and use scientific software? In: Proceedings of the 2009 ICSE workshop on Software Engineering for Computational Science and Engineering, pp. 1–8. IEEE Computer Society (2009)
5. Jones, S., Keane, A., Stawiarski, A., Fatus, R., Kane, B.: The impact of application system messages on the usability of healthcare software applications. In: 2016 IEEE 29th International Symposium on Computer-Based Medical Systems (CBMS), pp. 306–311. IEEE (2016)
6. Lazar, J., Jones, A., Shneiderman, B.: Workplace user frustration with computers: an exploratory investigation of the causes and severity. Behav. Inf. Technol. **25**(03), 239–251 (2006)
7. Macaulay, C., et al.: Usability and user-centered design in scientific software development. IEEE Softw. **1**, 96–102 (2009)
8. Mattax, C.C., Dalton, R.L., et al.: Reservoir simulation (includes associated papers 21606 and 21620). J. Pet. Technol. **42**(06), 692–695 (1990)
9. Muller, M.J., Haslwanter, J.H., Dayton, T.: Participatory practices in the software lifecycle. In: Handbook of Human-Computer Interaction, 2nd edn, pp. 255–297. Elsevier (1997)
10. Norman, D.A., Draper, S.W.: User Centered System Design: New Perspectives on Human-Computer Interaction. L. Erlbaum Associates Inc., Hillsdale (1986)
11. Ramos, P.A.T., dos Reis, J.C., Schiozer, D.J., de Souza dos Santos, A.A.: Estudando as dificuldades de interação em software para gerenciamento de campos de petróleo. In: Anais Estendidos do XVII Simpósio Brasileiro sobre Fatores Humanos em Sistemas Computacionais. SBC, Porto Alegre, Brazil (2018). https://doi.org/10.5753/ihc.2018.4179
12. Rampersad, L., Blyth, S., Elson, E., Kuttel, M.M.: Improving the usability of scientific software with participatory design: a new interface design for radio astronomy visualisation software. In: Proceedings of the South African Institute of Computer Scientists and Information Technologists, p. 29. ACM (2017)

13. Schiozer, D.J., Santos, A.A.S., Drumond, P.S., et al.: Integrated model based decision analysis in twelve steps applied to petroleum fields development and management. In: EUROPEC 2015. Society of Petroleum Engineers (2015)
14. Schiozer, D., Ligero, E., Santos, J.: Risk assessment for reservoir development under uncertainty. J. Braz. Soc. Mech. Sci. Eng. **26**(2), 213–217 (2004)
15. Shneiderman, B.: Designing computer system messages. Commun. ACM **25**(9), 610–611 (1982)
16. Sultanum, N., Somanath, S., Sharlin, E., Sousa, M.C.: Point it, split it, peel it, view it: techniques for interactive reservoir visualization on tabletops. In: Proceedings of the ACM International Conference on Interactive Tabletops and Surfaces, pp. 192–201. ACM (2011)
17. UNISIM: MERO, Manual do Usuário. UNISIM-CEPETRO

Workstations of the Future for Transformational Gains in Solving Complex Problems

Rukman Senanayake$^{(\boxtimes)}$ and Grit Denker$^{(\boxtimes)}$

SRI International, 333 Ravenswood Avenue, Menlo Park, CA 94025, USA
{rukman.senanayake,grit.denker}@sri.com

Abstract. This paper describes fundamental concepts of future workstations that will achieve transformational gains in problem solving for end users. The results are based on 7 years of Human-Computer Interaction (HCI) research on the bRIGHT platform. bRIGHT already incorporates solutions for modeling and understanding end-user contexts/intent and employs these to design algorithms for task automation, context filtering, and contextual auto-fill to support end users in complex tasks. bRIGHT also includes solutions for collaborative problem solving. We summarize insights gained from conducting user experiments and describe the technical capabilities required of future workstations to ensure a leap of performance when groups of users can jointly solve complex problems.

Keywords: Intelligent interfaces · Contextual modeling · Context filtering · Task automation · Adaptive interfaces · Collaboration

1 Introduction

bRIGHT [1, 37]—a Human-Computer Interaction (HCI) research framework and workstation developed at SRI over the last 7 years—is the basis for the HCI innovations and concepts we discuss in this paper. The objective of this technology is to develop and experiment with visualization and interaction modalities that will yield revolutionary insight into demands placed on the end user's cognitive load and contextual processing when solving complex problems in domains such as cyber security, intelligence analysis, disaster recovery, or Battle Management Command and Control (BM2C). Our research in the last few years has allowed us to gain insights on techniques for accurately modeling user context, predicting and tracking user interest, as well as identifying workflows and learning procedures by demonstration. The bRIGHT research framework was also developed to support distributed real-time collaboration among geographically disparate teams. The system architecture and its back-end server were designed based on Massively Multi-player Online Role Player games (MMORPG) such as World of Warcraft and League of Legends to support problem solving in collaborative contexts. Because our framework will scale to large user bases, one can imagine a new scale of *collaborative complex problem solving* in the future.

Current research in HCI and Artificial Intelligence (AI) seldom achieves the prediction accuracy needed to pro-actively support the end user because researchers are

© Springer Nature Switzerland AG 2019
M. Kurosu (Ed.): HCII 2019, LNCS 11568, pp. 476–488, 2019.
https://doi.org/10.1007/978-3-030-22636-7_36

not able to access the user's context. Improved interface modalities, such as voice, gaze, or gesture, provide some enhancement to user input processes. However, they cannot address fundamental challenges in big data manipulation, such as mitigating cognitive overload caused by the speed and volume of new information or supporting human-human and human-machine collaboration. Achieving higher performance and productivity will require novel approaches. Three fundamental challenges face decision makers and operators handling large data sets; they must:

(a) Enhance the cognitive performance of users by reducing the overwhelming influx of data. This involves accurately filtering information based on the users' contexts, goals, and needs, and providing only highly relevant information at the right time and in the right amount and format;

(b) Enable users to rapidly execute decision processes and actions through task automation and adaptive interfaces. This involves anticipating user needs and putting the necessary, context-specific execution controls at their fingertips (e.g., using dynamic interaction models such as proximity detection for context-specific placement of user interface [UI] controls); and

(c) Encourage effective collaboration by sharing users' contexts so that individual actions are informed by, and contribute to, collective knowledge across an entire team that may be geographically disparate (Fig. 1).

Fig. 1. A 3rd-generation bRIGHT device being used at SRI International's Menlo Park Campus in defense against a cyber attack.

Based on our findings in the last 6 years of research, we believe future workstations used by knowledge workers should be supported with a wide array of design considerations and features (both hardware and software). This paper is organized into five main sections. In the Sect. 2, we review research and development work and describe important hardware- and software-related advances. Section 3 covers our objectives in developing bRIGHT, and the design considerations and features for an ideal end-to-end future workstation framework are discussed in Sect. 4. In Sect. 5, we present the lessons we have learned, new research avenues we propose, and the future goals of the bRIGHT project.

2   Related Work

We have been keenly aware of the significance of Cognitive Task Analysis (CTA) in terms of gaining insight [44] into the issues related to cognitive load, workflows, skills, skill acquisition, and task automation for some time. Historically, CTA has been used with great success to design applications and systems for human interaction [34–36]. In a sense, bRIGHT is an extension to the typical CTA processes because it enables us to capture and analyze with improved accuracy a broader range of factors that contribute to HCI bottlenecks and cognitive load. bRIGHT utilizes semantic interaction and visualization models to capture the end user's context in a very rich fashion, see [1, 37] for a detailed discussion on how this is achieved.

CTA is also quite useful in helping us develop predictive models of human performance and understanding application models [38–40]. In our research, we identified the need for such predictive modeling early on (due to client requirements). To successfully implement contextual filtering, predictive task automation, contextual autofill, and UI control pre-positioning, we needed to leverage work done in developing such models [34, 41, 42]. Typically, such work has historically been carried out by two communities: The Human Factors Engineering Community and The Cognitive Psychology Research Community. We investigated the approaches taken by both communities to deepen our understanding of pertinent techniques and help us develop the theoretically unified architecture that is the basis of the HCI testing framework for bRIGHT.

The cognitive demand of most jobs has increased rapidly during the information age [44]. bRIGHT's ability to play a key role in identifying skills and skills development and its use in evaluating effectiveness of training depends on building an HCI framework that can leverage applied cognitive analysis in such situations. We also studied various cognitive engineering approaches [43] to help us understand the implications of human factors methods on the design and engineering of the system.

To gain insight into the user's engagement with the system, we added gaze-tracking support to the bRIGHT systems [1, 3]. Gaze tracking (GT) is the process of detecting gaze coordinates on a display to indicate what a person is looking at. Recently, GT has proven useful in conventional HCI research [3–5] as well as in studies of human cognition [6–11]. Many explorations of nonintrusive [12–21] and intrusive GT techniques [21–24] have been made to aid development of accurate, efficient, and user-friendly systems. Nonintrusive methods are preferred because they have the potential to increase a user's GT comfort level.

bRIGHT is an extensible multimodal input system. We developed a workstation design in which new input modalities can be added as needed as determined by evaluating end-user context. The systems contextual modeling and other features can dynamically adapt to such novel input modalities. Indeed, the user benefits of multi-modal input include flexibility and reliability the ability to meet the needs of a variety of operators [25–27]. Such systems improve efficiency, allow alternate interaction techniques, and accommodate individual differences, such as those associated with permanent or temporary handicaps [28–33].

3 Objectives

bRIGHT was initially conceived as a platform or framework for HCI research. Our main objective at the time was to develop new interaction models based on emerging sensor technology so that we could increase the input bandwidth from end users to a computer system. Over last 6 years, the R&D has evolved and we are now building an experimental platform that enables us to test hypotheses regarding task automation and extrapolate them across large-scale collaborative teams.

We soon learned that capturing the user's context with a high degree of accuracy was invaluable as we designed future research. As such, we enhanced traditional application modeling with interaction models and semantic visualization models (see below and [1]) to accurately capture users' contexts. Even so, we came to understand a great deal of basic science still needed to be unraveled. For example, we needed to identify and track the evolution of the user's interest over time by examining the things that populated her contextual model. We addressed this challenge by developing a rule-based contextual model that highlights user interest and dynamically changes over time. This contextual user model is now the central component of bRIGHT and is the basis for developing solutions to meet our other technical objectives. We propose to:

- Develop a mechanism to identify and extract user workflows from the user's contextual model and understand its evolution over time.
- Establish metrics based on the user context to identify opportunities to apply contextual filtering.
- Increase the accuracy and robustness of the contextual auto-fill mechanism that aides manual input.
- Experiment with large teams of end users to improve the contextual modeling approach with regard to collaborative user groups and develop a 'hive-mind' model to reflect the group's overall context and its dynamics.
- Investigate technical approaches that could conceivably be used to build a con-textual desktop that accurately reflects the user's current mental model.

4   Methodology

The bRIGHT approach is based on the development of solutions for semantic inter-action modeling and semantic markup tools (see below for details on the approach). We semantically enhance selected software that is used by our clients and develop an HCI experimentation platform by incorporating the semantically enhanced software within the bRIGHT framework. bRIGHT includes data and reporting capabilities that allow us to identify key areas in end users' context models and understand how to improve their workflows. We then design and conduct HCI experiments to develop contextual and cognitive models of decision makers or system end users. These models form the basis for developing algorithms for task automation, contextual filtering, and context-based recommendation, and for learning by observation and user interface (UI) control pre-positioning using proximity detection, measures of effectiveness, and error reduction.

4.1   Semantic User Interaction Modeling

Semantic User Interaction Modeling involves two parts: (a) instrumenting software applications with semantically meaningful data to report how users interact with the application (i.e., what actions users perform) and (b) instrumenting the end users' environments with touch, gaze, and proximity sensors to report what information users looked at. Correlating the information from the application instrumentation with that from the user's environment allows us to create a semantically meaningful record of what the user did and perceived, and that forms the basis for contextual and cognitive modeling. While the user's action model is highly accurate, the semantic interaction model accounts for uncertainty due to inaccuracies in gaze tracking fidelity: it is not possible to model gaze interactions to a degree such that we can say with absolute certainty that the user has read an onscreen construct.

4.2   Semantic Markup Tools

Instrumenting applications can be time-consuming depending on the complexity of the application. We have designed a methodology and protocols to instrument software when the source code is available and can be extended and recompiled. Since this is not often the case, we now propose to develop tools that will allow a person proficient with the application and the end user's context to add semantic markup to applications through onscreen markup techniques that highlight essential elements of information or context relevant to the modeling. This will eliminate the need for recompilation of source code.

4.3   Highly Accurate Contextual Models

Accurate user context needs to be modeled to reflect the user's reasoning and decision-making value system. Given the central role of decision making in any HCI-related research, it is critical to have a framework that allows for experimentation and iterative improvement of cognitive and contextual modeling so that the results of such experiments can be incorporated into future versions of the system. To accomplish this, we design experiments to estimate and predict user interest and intent; determine the effect of contextual filtering on cognitive load; detect skill acquisition and measures of proficiency and effectiveness; and identify collaboration during task performance and decision making using contextual indexing [1].

4.4   Active Authentication

Using multi-factor authentication (typically face recognition), our bRIGHT system is designed to continuously authenticate the user and digitally stamp every atomic action he performs. Presently, this can be done using face-recognition or iris recognition. There are some very critical advantages of active authentication:

- It significantly increases security of the system
- Continuously auditing user action creates an electronic trail of each performed action. Such audit trails can be used to better understand causes for errors and improve end-user training. They can also help us design systems that prevent user fatigue (or other issues) that can cause users to claim they did not see an instruction.
- If invoking certain execution logic requires active authentication, then network-based attacks may become less effective against such a system in the future.

4.5   Platform Handler

Most users utilize a multitude of devices with varying form factors throughout their work day. These can range from large-screen workstations with support for multi-touch to smartphones. Depending on the type of hardware employed by the user, bRIGHT adapts the way information is rendered on screen and the types of interaction offered to the end user.

We will develop a platform handler to recognize the capabilities of the hardware available to the user and, accordingly, will design how the contextual desktop is rendered, and which interaction models are provided. The benefit is that end users will experience a seamless management of their context by the system, irrespective of the hardware they use. The platform handler is enabled by programmable interaction models that will be specifically tailored to different hardware platforms. For example, the conventional mouse and keyboard will constitute one such interaction model, though with lots of limits in terms of the dynamicity (e.g., the position, appearance, or size of keys cannot be dynamically adjusted to the user context as would be possible for digital versions of such interaction models). For workstations such as bRIGHT or smart-phones/tablets, we can introduce programmable interaction models. This will enable us to offer several interaction models to users so they can select a suitable hardware platform. To effectively implement the platform handler, the hardware platforms will need to support declarative implementations of their capabilities.

4.6   MMORPG-Based Backend Design

MMORPGs such as World of Warcraft have solved some very challenging engineering issues to manage extremely complex world state information that is simultaneously being changed by tens of thousands of players. We believe future workstations should be modeled after this engineering approach.

The main reason for the success of these games is the paradigm shift in the system design that allows multiple users. Instead of building a system to be used by a single person, we must build a system that can model the 'world state' of a collective of users and then manage how they all change that world's state together. This will enable design of an engineering foundation for truly collaborative systems.

Introducing the notion of a world state to the proposed system means the entire set of system users will effect change and also be affected by those changes. Each end user renders his world state based on interests, goals, role, etc. This is similar to how MMORPG systems parse the game's user interface to different classes of players depending on the play character class. Obviously more than just the user's role can be used to customize the subset of the world state being rendered. Such a system can also address major engineering challenges such as load balancing and synchronizing extremely high rates of updates to the world state.

4.7   UI Paradigm Shift

To truly benefit from the improvements to the backend and middleware, the top-layer interaction technology needs to evolve as well. We are proposing a paradigm shift in fundamental interaction modalities. For example, using proximity detection we can position the controls user's needs depending on current context directly under his hands on the primary interaction surface ('controls to your hands'). This can be further improved by 'gaze-based locking' in which the control construct under the hand is filtered by the location of the user's gaze on screen. For example, if the user is looking at a link on a web browser, then wherever he touches the primary interaction surface we can interpret that as a 'click' on the link and pass that interaction to the browser to load the relevant content. It does not matter what kind of screen construct is under the user's hand, because the interpretation of the user's action (click on screen) is contextually interpreted (i.e., determined by what is the user looking at).

The UI paradigm shift is inspired by graphics accelerators that have been used for several decades to achieve transformative output acceleration in rendering (and, more recently, for physics modeling and some AI reasoning). We flip this paradigm and imagine an input accelerator in which the entire focus is to achieve transformative gains in user input to the system. This could be done using contextual filtering that predicts with extreme accuracy the user's next input needs (thus, minimizing the task of user input so the user can simply approve the top-predicted next input). Transformative gains could also be achieved through task automation that allows multiple parallel workflows to be executed proactively so that the user is presented with automation results and can pick a completed (or possibly partially completed) workflow.

5 Future Work

In this section, we describe key ideas based on the research discussed above and detail the work we plan to explore in the future.

5.1 Self-describing Systems

In the future, all of the system components—hardware and software—should describe their own functionality, requirements, and limitations. This will enable the system to develop an operational picture about its own abilities and reason about them. The description should include things such as: how the component should be rendered on screen, where it should be rendered in the operational picture, which controls are required to manipulate the construct, which interactions are associated with those controls, what mandatory inputs are needed and their type information and possible origins of such information. Such capability is critical when it comes to determining what hardware or software components are needed to automate certain tasks. This information is also critical in developing a composite contextual desktop that reflects the user's current mental state. Assuming self-describing systems, each system component can then be intelligently arranged and managed by the system to fit into the current contextual 'picture' the user is manipulating to achieve the current goal.

5.2 Self-aware Systems

Our approach to self-aware systems does not mean we require sentient AI. What we propose is a significantly lower threshold of awareness than sentient AI. The system should be able to understand its role in relationship to the end user. That is, it should be able to identify the goals that are typically significant to the end user and ascertain the factors that relate to these goals. The system needs to identify behavior patterns of the user and how those relate to goals, and it needs to identify user's typical workflows and which triggers can be associated with these workflows. Furthermore, the system should be actively reasoning about its own role in relationship to the user as the user engages with the system. This is akin to a pro-active human assistant who develops a deep understanding of the user over the course of a long observation period. The system should be able to observe and learn by observation the goals, workflows, and triggers of each user. In addition, the system should be able to reason effectively in real time given the nature of its role in terms of achieving typical user wants amid the current context.

5.3 Built-in OODA Loop

In complex problem-solving scenarios such as defending against a cyber-attack or conducting a large-scale battle management training exercise, the typical warfighter interaction loop is characterized as an Observe-Orient-Decide-Act (OODA) loop. The OODA loops should be built into the future workstation in two different ways: (1) The system should itself have a built-in OODA cycle in which it observes the user, orients itself based on the reasoning conclusions in the observation stage, decides which actions to take to support the user, executes those actions, then observes the user's reaction to those actions, and starts the loop again. This will allow us to design and model the system as another class of user, maybe as an assistant that reflects the user's goals. (2) The second version of the OODA loop should be based on the observation and learning abilities of the system. This OODA loop is purely a reflection of the user and her engagements with the system, allowing us to characterize such actions into the different states in the OODA loop and study the state transitions. This is useful in developing assistive technology closely tied to various state transitions in the OODA loop.

5.4 Hierarchy of Contextual/Cognitive Models

Complex problems are not typically solved by a single individual working in isolation. In most real-life scenarios, groups of people from various levels of an organizational hierarchy (with differing roles) collaborate in solving critically important and complex problems. Capturing the nature of such collaboration and reflecting it as a hierarchical contextual model cluster will assist in achieving transformative progress in collaborative groups. Such a system can effectively detect and track 'emergent collaboration', that is the moment when end users naturally gravitate to work together to solve a complex problem. Identifying such patterns allows us to reason beyond a single user's goals. This will enable the system to reason about the organizational goals at a strategic level. The system can then associate its knowledge of each person's roles, skills, and goals to match that higher-level knowledge. This in turn will enable the development of technologies that can accelerate group-level interactions and collaborative task performance. The hive-mind hierarchy will also allow the system to track goals and directives being passed from top-to-bottom as well as results and feedback that flow in the reverse. These will allow the system to understand operational or decision-making bottle-necks so that tasking and role management can be improved.

5.5 Contextual Desktop

Our understanding of the nature and complexity of the contextual models has evolved over the last few years. We hypothesize it may be possible to transform such a contextual model into a 'contextual desktop' that is a visualization and a direct reflection of the user's current mental model of the problem space she is addressing. To successfully achieve such a goal, it may be necessary to revamp the application modeling approaches used in today's software engineering. Instead of writing individual pieces of software that separately (and in a monolithic fashion) solve independent problems, we suggest building software to harmoniously co-exist and yield a common operational picture.

The main idea is to create a single operational picture that accurately reflects the user's mental model and provide her with the tools to effectively and efficiently manipulate it to achieve her goals. Parts of the operational picture will be generated by different pieces of software and the tools to manipulate this may be provided by the same (or other) software. All such software will be combined into a single cohesive contextual desktop in which the user can execute tasks that chain multiple different types of software without the need to switch from one monolithic application to another. This may also eliminate the need to copy and paste data from one application to another since the system should be able to create wiring to get the data to seamlessly flow from one application to another. This will eliminate the minutiae of data manipulation that nowadays consumes a great deal of end-user time and cognitive capital.

The main reason to develop a singular operational picture as the contextual desktop is to permanently eliminate the sustained cognitive load of end users known to conventional systems. In such systems, end users always struggle to semantically map the state and context of the system they are using to their own mental models of the problems they are trying to solve. We believe our approach will radically reduce: the sustained cognitive load of operators; the manual input errors (by several orders of magnitude); and the tactical as well as strategic level reasoning errors made by users due to less cognitive strain. It will also simplify workflows by eliminating manual data manipulation to a significant degree and allow better collaboration because it will be easier to understand others' contexts and workflows.

We face significant challenges in successfully achieving a singular operational picture as the contextual desktop. The application modeling paradigms will need to be revamped to support application integration into a singular contextual desktop. This means most software will depend on features provided by other parts of the system or afforded by other software. Although this is very different from today's approach to application software, it is not an unprecedented method. Indeed, very complex software systems often feature a plug-in framework that enables independent development of new capabilities that can then be seamlessly added to the system. We propose to essentially elevate that practice to the bRIGHT framework's layer so any software that runs on the system would be a plug-in to the bRIGHT framework that develops the singular, cohesive operational picture for the user.

Combining various independently developed software components and their rendered user interfaces into a meaningful and manageable singular construct will be particularly challenging. At present, each piece of software we execute generates its own monolithic user interface and control set. We must abandon that approach and create a declarative user interface and interaction model that can be intelligently merged into the contextual desktop. The UI and interaction model need to be declarative because the operating system (or some component that manages the contextual desktop) has to be able to quickly reason how the software fits into the current context of the user and then position it accordingly.

Adopting large and complex software that has been developed to solve a problem—often with a uniform look and feel and a cohesive workflow—will be challenging. Such software exists as windowed user interfaces with a monolithic execution model, which will not integrate well with a common operational picture-based system. If the system needs to be retrofitted into the contextual desktop, that may be difficult. On the other hand, if a system is developed from scratch, a collection of plug-ins can likely be used to cohesively integrate it with the contextual desktop.

6 Discussion

Our research in client labs has demonstrated the impact our work can have in contexts such as Battle Management and Command and Control. Given our ability to generate highly accurate contextual models that can be used to identify user's interests and skills, skill acquisition during training, and how it evolves under operational circumstances, we are starting to see exciting possibilities using this technology. The approach seems to be broadly applicable for use in various domains in which the end user is routinely handling a large influx of data and making decisions at a rapid rate, and when collaboration is necessary to achieve a solution. While the context model development is the basis of the key features that increase a user's throughput in interacting with the system, we also believe it can reveal important insights into inter-relationships between cognitive load and error rates, decision-making, the volume of data consumed by a user, and the evolution of skills based on operational situations. We are currently using our technology in client's labs to evaluate the cognitive load of operators solving complex problems in the BM2C domain, and we expect to gain more insight about the factors and parameters that affect end-user performance and skill acquisition in such scenarios. We are also improving the robustness of our systems so they can be used effectively with others, and are developing tools that reduce the risk and engineering effort required to extend third-party applications to engage with a bRIGHT system. This will make the base technology accessible to a wider audience, hopefully beyond the military domain.

References

1. Senanayake, R., Denker, G.: Towards more effective cyber operator interfaces through semantic modeling of user context. In: Nicholson, D. (ed.) Advances in Human Factors in Cybersecurity. AISC, vol. 501, pp. 19–31. Springer, Cham (2016). https://doi.org/10.1007/978-3-319-41932-9_3
2. Han, J.Y.: Low-cost multi-touch sensing through frustrated total internal reflection. In: Proceedings of the 18th Annual ACM Symposium on User Interface Software and Technology. ACM (2015)
3. Bulling, A., Gellersen, H.: Toward mobile eye-based human computer interaction. IEEE Pervasive Comput. 9(4), 8–12 (2010)
4. Rantanen, V., et al.: A wearable, wireless gaze tracker with integrated selection command source for human-computer interaction. IEEE Trans. Inf Technol. Biomed. 15(5), 795–801 (2011)
5. Corcoran, P.M., Nanu, F., Petrescu, S., Bigioi, P.: Real-time eye gaze tracking for gaming design and consumer electronics systems. IEEE Trans. Consum. Electron. 58(2), 347–355 (2012)
6. Bolmont, M., Cacioppo, J.T., Cacioppo, S.: Love is in the gaze: an eyetracking study of love and sexual desire. Psychol. Sci. 25, 1748–1756 (2014)
7. Judd, T., Ehinger, K., Torralba, A.: Learning to predict where humans look. In: ICCV, pp. 2106–2113 (2009)
8. Senju, A., Johnson, M.H.: The eye contact effect: mechanisms and development. Trends Cogn. Sci. 13(3), 127–134 (2009)

9. Tylén, K., Allen, M., Hunter, B.K., Roepstorff, A.: Interaction vs. observation: distinctive modes of social cognition in human brain and behavior? A combined fMRI and eye-tracking study. Front. Hum. Neurosci. 6(December), 331 (2012)

10. Kochukhova, O., Gredeba, G.: Preverbal infants anticipate that food will be brought to the mouth: an eye tracking study of manual feeding and flying spoons. Child Dev. 81(6), 1729–1738 (2010)

11. Kano, F., Tomonaga, M.: How chimpanzees look at pictures: a comparative eye-tracking study. Proc. Biol. Sci. 276(1664), 1949–1955 (2009)

12. Bergasa, L.M., Member, A., Nuevo, J., Sotelo, M.A., Barea, R., Lopez, M.E.: Real-time system for monitoring driver vigilance. IEEE Trans. Intell. Transp. Syst. 7(1), 63–77 (2006)

13. Qi, Y., Wang, Z., Huang, Y.: A non-contact eye-gaze tracking system for human computer interaction. In: 2007 International Conference on Wavelet Analysis Pattern Recognition, pp. 68–72, November 2007

14. Iqbal, N., Lee, H., Lee, S.-Y.: Smart user interface for mobile consumer devices using model-based eye-gaze estimation. IEEE Trans. Consum. Electron. 59(1), 161–166 (2013)

15. Guestrin, E.D., Eizenman, M.: General theory of remote gaze estimation using the pupil center and corneal reflections. IEEE Trans. Biomed. Eng. 53(6), 1124–1133 (2006)

16. Hennessey, C., Noureddin, B., Lawrence, P.: Fixation precision in highspeed noncontact eye-gaze tracking. IEEE Trans. Syst. Man Cybern. B (Cybern.) 38(2), 289–298 (2008)

17. Nawaz, T., Mian, M., Habib, H.: Infotainment devices control by eye gaze and gesture recognition fusion. IEEE Trans. Consum. Electron. 54(2), 277–282 (2008)

18. Asteriadis, S., Karpouzis, K., Kollias, S.: Visual focus of attention in noncalibrated environments using gaze estimation. Int. J. Comput. Vis. 107(3), 293–316 (2013)

19. Zhu, Z., Ji, Q.: Novel eye gaze tracking techniques under natural head movement. IEEE Trans. Biomed. Eng. 54(12), 2246–2260 (2007)

20. Xia, D., Ruan, Z.: IR image based eye gaze estimation. In: Eighth ACIS International Conference on Software Engineering, Artificial Intelligence, Parallel/Distributed Computer (SNPD 2007), vol. 1, pp. 220–224, July 2007

21. Nguyen, Q.X., Jo, S.: Electric wheelchair control using head pose free eyegaze tracker. Electron. Lett. 48(13), 750 (2012)

22. Rae, J.P., Steptoe, W., Roberts, D.J.: Some implications of eye gaze behavior and perception for the design of immersive telecommunication systems. In: 2011 IEEE/ACM 15th International Symposium on Distributed Simulation and Real Time Applications, pp. 108–114, September 2011

23. Panwar, P., Sarcar, S., Samanta, D.: EyeBoard: a fast and accurate eye gazebased text entry system. In: 2012 4th International Conference on Intelligent Human Computer Interaction, pp. 1–8, December 2012

24. Qiang, J., Zhu, Z.: Eye and gaze tracking for interactive graphic display. In: Proceedings of the 2nd International Symposium on Smart Graphics. ACM (2002)

25. Dahlback, N., Jönsson, A., Ahrenberg, L.: Wizard of Oz studies - why and how. Knowl.-Based Syst.ms 6(4), 258–266 (1993)

26. Cohen, P., Johnston, M., McGee, D., Oviatt, S.: The efficiency of multimodal interaction: a case study. In: International Conference on Spoken Language Processing (ICSLP), Sydney, Australia (1998)

27. Oviatt, S., Lunsford, R., Coulston, R.: Individual differences in multimodal integration patterns: what are they and why do they exist? In: Conference on Human Factors in Computing Systems (CHI), New York, USA (2005)

28. Ruiz, N., Chen, F., Oviatt, S.: Multimodal input. In: Thiran, J.-P., Marques, F., Bourlard, H. (eds.) Multimodal Signal Processing, Chap. 12, pp. 231–255 (2010)

29. Turk, M.: Multimodal interaction: a review. Pattern Recogn. Lett. 36, 189–195 (2014)

30. Perzylo, A., Somani, N., Profanter, S., Rickert, M., Knoll, A.: Toward efficient robot teach-in and semantic process descriptions for small lot sizes. In: Robotics: Science and Systems (RSS), Workshop on Combining AI Reasoning and Cognitive Science with Robotics, Rome Italy (2015)

31. Akan, B., Ameri, A., Cürüklü, B., Asplund, L.: Intuitive industrial robot programming through incremental multimodal language and augmented reality. In: International Conference on Robotics and Automation (ICRA), Shanghai, China (2011)

32. Stenmark, M., Nugues, P.: Natural language programming of industrial robots. In: International Symposium on Robotics (ISR), Seoul, Korea (2013)

33. Stenmark, M., Malec, J.: Describing constraint-based assembly tasks in unstructured natural language. In: World Congress of the International Federation of Automatic Control (IFAC) (2014)

34. Seamster, T.L., Redding, R.E., Kaempf, G.L.: A skill-based cognitive task analysis framework. Cogn. Task Anal. 135–146 (2000)

35. Ormerod, T.C.: Using task analysis as a primary design method: the SGT approach. Cogn. Task Anal. 181–200 (2000)

36. Kieras, D.E., Meyer, D.E.: The role of cognitive task analysis in the application of predictive models of human performance. Cogn. Task Anal. 237–260 (2000)

37. Senanayake, R., Denker, G., Lincoln, P.: bRIGHT – workstations of the future and leveraging contextual models. In: Yamamoto, S., Mori, H. (eds.) HIMI 2018. LNCS, vol. 10904, pp. 346–357. Springer, Cham (2018). https://doi.org/10.1007/978-3-319-92043-6_29

38. Gray, W.D., Boehm-Davis, D.A.: Milliseconds matter: an introduction to microstrategies and to their use in describing and predicting interactive behavior. J. Exp. Psychol.: Appl. **6** (4), 322 (2000)

39. Kieras, D.E., Meyer, D.E., Ballas, J.A., Lauber, E.J.: Modern computational perspectives on executive mental processes and cognitive control: where to from here. In: Control of Cognitive Processes: Attention and Performance XVIII, pp. 681–712 (2000)

40. Gray, W.D., Fu, W.T.: Soft constraints in interactive behavior: the case of ignoring perfect knowledge in-the-world for imperfect knowledge in-the-head. Cogn. Sci. **28**(3), 359–382 (2004)

41. Kieras, D.: Model-based evaluation. In: The Human-Computer Interaction: Development Process, pp. 294–310 (2009)

42. Howes, A., Lewis, R.L., Vera, A.: Rational adaptation under task and processing constraints: implications for testing theories of cognition and action. Psychol. Rev. **116**(4), 717 (2009)

43. Bonaceto, C., Burns, K.: A survey of the methods and uses of cognitive engineering. In: Expertise out of Context: Proceedings of the Sixth International Conference on Naturalistic Decision Making, pp. 29–75. Psychology Press (2007)

44. Chipman, S.F., Schraagen, J.M., Shalin, V.L.: Introduction to cognitive task analysis. Cogn. Task Anal. 3–23 (2000)

VujaDessin: A Sketch Learning Support System Using a Blurred Motif Object

Kentaro Takashima$^{(\boxtimes)}$, Ryuichi Tsuchiya, and Kazushi Nishimoto

Japan Advanced Institute of Science and Technology, Nomi, Ishikawa, Japan
ktaka@jaist.ac.jp

Abstract. Sketch is a creative activity that anybody can start casually and often used as training to begin a full-fledged painting. Since beginners sometimes feel difficulty to draw accurate sketch, various tutoring systems of sketch have been developed. However, some problems about seeing motif object have not been solved. First, they often have difficulty to grasp the entirety of the object and fail to draw balanced sketch. Second, they have difficulty to draw exactly what they saw due to labeling of conceptual meaning. We assumed that these problems are caused by their inappropriate way of seeing motif object: an excessive focus on detail of specific part. In order to solve these problems, we proposed sketch learning support system VujaDessin. This system prompts users to see the entirety of the motif object by blurring motif image when focus on detail parts is detected. We conducted user study of the system targeting two subjects to evaluate the system effectiveness. While the system did not provide positive effect to quality of outcome, we confirmed generated blur changed users seeing behavior. The system possibly encouraged users to see entire motif object including peripheral parts in a more exploratory way. Further system development and study is required in order to support beginners who strongly feel they are not good at drawing and confirm the long-term learning effect.

Keywords: Creativity support · Sketch support · Support by disturbance · Benefits of inconvenience

1 Introduction

1.1 Sketch and Sketch Support

A sketch is a drawing act where one roughly depicts objects such as a person and a landscape. Since anybody can start sketch if they only have paper and pen, it becomes a widely-practiced creative activity. Digital sketch also has become popular, along with a spread of high-performance smart devices with large screen. Since it is one of the basic skills in painting, sketching is often adopted as a training task for beginners.

Up to now, various sketch learning support systems for beginners have been studied and developed. Most of these systems provide users "tutorials and guides" according to typical drawing procedures. By using them, beginners can learn basic procedures to depict the object. For example, Fernquist et al. [1] developed a comprehensive sketch tutorial and assistance system that provides drawing step navigation, stroke guidance, stroke feedback, and automatic tutorial generation function. Soga et al.

© Springer Nature Switzerland AG 2019
M. Kurosu (Ed.): HCII 2019, LNCS 11568, pp. 489–500, 2019.
https://doi.org/10.1007/978-3-030-22636-7_37

[2] developed a system that provides advices annotated in sketch area in advance according to user's pen position. Soga et al. [3] also proposed a system to support drawing appropriate rough composition in the sketch process. This system requests users to draw circumscribed rectangle of motifs' view on a paper and diagnoses its location, size, and aspect ratio. Similarly, Takagi et al. [4] proposed a system that compares completed user's sketch image with motif data set by using feature extraction and diagnosing the balance. Nishizawa [5] proposed a support system to draw a balanced portrait based on correct understanding of the human body structure by providing overlaid semi-transparent skeleton model. Xie et al. [6] developed a system that automatically adjusts both outlines and shading strokes in real-time based on important features of a motif portrait image. Several studies proposed an environment for learners on which users can generate tips for learning by themselves. For example, Huang et al. [7] developed a system that users can practice drawing and share drawing process with other learners. They proposed a reflection workflow that allows learners to append annotation of learning points on shared drawing process before or after short practice.

1.2   Problems in Beginners' Sketch

While various support systems had been proposed, few studies focused on the fundamental problems into which beginners often fall. In the training of sketch, an important issue for beginners is to learn how to see the motif object and draw it as they see, before learning the procedure to depict it. Beginners often see motif object inappropriately and face following problems.

The first problem is a difficulty to grasp the entirety of the object. Beginners often attempt to draw the specific part of object as accurate as possible from the beginning of the sketch [8]. As a result, the balance of the entire sketch often collapses. In the beginning of the sketch, it is necessary to roughly see the entire shape of the object to grasp its entire proportion, rather than focusing on the details of the parts.

The second problem is a difficulty to draw exactly what they saw caused by labeling of conceptual meaning to focused part. Beginners often draw the object as "what they know," instead of "what they see." Edwards [9] suggested two types of mode of human cognition; L-mode and R-mode. L-mode manages verbal, symbolic, and analytic thought while R-mode manages nonverbal, actual, and spatial thought. Edwards pointed out that L-mode is usually activated since our thought is often associated with language, and it frequently interferes drawing sketch. For example, when beginners draw sketch of person's figure, L-mode expects to see motif based on conceptual human figure that they are familiar with. To be released from the curse of L-mode, a method to see a person's figure upside down has been often employed. By using this method, they become able to see the figure as unfamiliar aggregate of lines, and they become able to draw it as they see it.

We assumed these problems are caused by beginners' subjective way of seeing, i.e. excessive focus on detail of specific parts of motif object. In order to solve these problems, we propose a sketch learning support system VujaDessin. The system supports beginners to see the entirety of motif object and to draw sketch as they see it by showing a blurred motif object image. We conducted user studies and evaluated the effectiveness of the system.

2   Method and System

2.1   Proposed Method

We propose a novel method for beginners to experience how they should see the motif object. Two problems mentioned in previous chapter are caused by the fact that beginners can see all parts of motif object in detail. To avoid it, we propose an approach that artificially and temporarily deteriorates the beginners' eyesight. Since they have good eyesight, they unintentionally focus on the details and ignore entirety. If that is the case, by deteriorating their eyesight, they become unable to unintentionally (and also intentionally) look at them. Our method disturbs beginners to see the details of the object when it is unnecessary and unpreferable.

In our proposed method, the motif objects are blurred when beginner focused on the detail, while those are always clearly shown in the conventional methods. Beginners can hardly draw a detail part and remember that they have to consider the balance of the whole motif object. Accordingly, they are led into experts' procedure in which they start drawing from the whole so as to prevent them from losing entire balance. Also, since blurring might prevent them from understanding what they see, it becomes difficult for them to label conceptual meaning to each part of the motif object. It might help them concentrate on drawing sketch of what they see without unconscious interference of L-mode. To substantiate this idea, automatic detection of focus on detail and adjustment of the degree of blur are required. Since we aim at improving balance and accuracy of the sketch, we consider only contour line; other sophisticated expressions such as shadows and texture are out of the scope of this research.

2.2   Developed System - VujaDessin

Based on the proposed method described in previous section, a sketch learning support system VujaDessin (VJD) was developed. The name "VujaDessin" is a coined word that combines the word "Vuja DE" which means observing familiar object as if they see it for the first time, and the word "Dessin".

Figure 1 shows user interface of the system. Image of motif object is displayed on the left area of screen (motif object display area). A user performs sketch drawing on the right area (sketch drawing area) while seeing the motif object on the left area.

We assumed that the user will bring his/her face closer to the screen to gaze at the motif object when they pay attention to the detail parts. The system makes the image of the motif object blur when his/her face gets closer to the screen. In the most intense blur condition, the user cannot see any detail parts but can identify only whole contour of the motif object.

Figure 2 shows the overview of the structure of the system. The system includes several key modules: a focus monitoring module and a blur generation module. The focus monitoring module determines how much the user pay attention to the detail parts according to a distance between the face and the screen. The distance is estimated by the face size captured by a web camera. Then, the blurred motif image generation module decides the degree of blur of the motif object according to the degree of user's attention and focus on the detail parts, and generates a blurred image.

motif object display area   sketch drawing area

Fig. 1. User interface of the system.

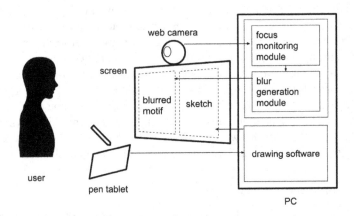

Fig. 2. Overview of the system

A pen tablet and a drawing software allow the users to draw sketch while seeing the image of the motif object. We adopted XP-Pen Deco 03 for the pen tablet device and Microsoft Paint for the drawing software. In order to simplify experimental condition, advanced functions (e.g. a layer function and a zoom function) were inactivated, and only pen, eraser, and undo functions were permitted to use.

Figure 3 shows a relationship between the user's face position, i.e. distance between eye position and screen, and degree of blur. Adjustment of the degree of blur was conducted in the preliminary calibration by the second author. In the calibration, we determined a standard distance between the user's face and the screen as 70 cm: the system applied minute blur on motif object image at this position to notify users that the system is working. User can identify detail parts easily in this condition. As the distance decreases, the system applies stronger blur. We set the shortest distance as 40 cm where the second author put his face to see the detail parts of the motif during the calibration. At this position, the most intense blur is applied: the users cannot identify any detail parts. We applied gaussian blur algorithm and dynamically changed width and height values of kernel. Both modules were implemented by using OpenCV.

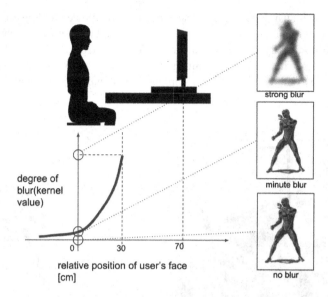

Fig. 3. Relationship of user's face position and degree of blur

3   User Study

In order to investigate how the blurring affects the user's behavior, we conducted a user study with VujaDessin. The purpose of this user study is to evaluate the direct effect of the system that is how much the seeing behavior and outcomes (sketches) were improved by the system. Concretely, the system was evaluated according to following two viewpoints.

(1)   Can the system help users grasp the entirety of the object without excessively focusing on the detail in the drawing process?

(2)   Can the system help users draw a well-balanced sketch as a result?

In order to evaluate the first point, we recorded eye movement for seeing the motif object by using an eye tracking device (Tobii X120 Eye Tracker). Movement and retention of point-of-regard on the motif object image were quantitatively recorded and analyzed. Moreover, after the sketching was completed, an interview was conducted in order to ask how users drew sketches.

In order to evaluate the second point, the sketches were evaluated by a questionnaire. Subjects were asked to evaluate balance of the sketches by using five-point Likert scale. To evaluate comprehensive quality of the sketches, they were also asked to answer its accuracy.

In this user study, we employed two subjects and requested them to draw the sketches of a human model. Both subjects are master course students of the authors' institute in their 20's who do not have experience of receiving higher education of drawing. Subjects were asked to draw sketches in two conditions. In the first condition, they drew a sketch without using the system. In the second condition, they were asked to draw sketch with using the system. The subjects were allowed to draw their sketch in their own ways without any constraints or time limit. Figure 4 shows appearance of the setting of the user study. As shown in Fig. 5, We adopted the picture of the human body model as the motif object (the image was quoted from Posemaniacs.com [10]). Recorded data of both conditions were compared and analyzed to reveal effects of the system.

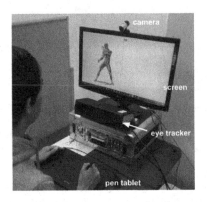

Fig. 4. Setting of user study

Fig. 5. Motif object image

4   Results and Analysis

Both subjects could complete their sketches in two conditions. Table 1 summarizes total spent time for completing the sketches. Table 2 shows outcomes (sketches) of each condition of both subjects. Figures 6 and 7 shows chronological shift of degree of blur in the drawing process in the second condition (with VJD).

Figures 6 and 7 show that degree of blur changed throughout the drawing processes of both subjects. Especially, subject A periodically got closed to the screen, which caused the strong blur. He reported he was curious about the blur and his seeing behavior was influenced. As for subject B, relatively strong blur was generated at the later phase of the drawing process while she reported she did not care about the blur.

While both subjects moved their face position in this user study, we also have to note that other two users did not get closed to the screen in preliminary tests that were conducted before this user study. They retained straight posture and the degree of blur hardly changed. The way of system usage possibly depends on user's drawing style. Some users could focus on the detail parts without changing their face position. We can improve focus detection module to acquire point-of-regard retention from the eye tracking device directly. Another possible factor is the effect of the eye tracking device. The subjects could unconsciously keep their face position to maintain eye tacking accuracy. We thought wearable camera type eye tacking devices would be more suitable for the user study of this system.

Table 1. Total spent time to complete sketch of each condition

	Subject A	Subject B
First condition	24 min 3 s	28 min 11 s
Second condition (with VJD)	30 min 20 s	15 min 34 s

Table 2. Motif object and outcomes of each condition

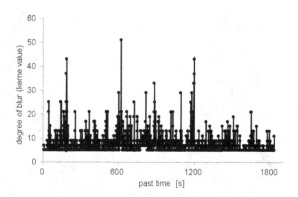

	Motif object	Subject A	Subject B
First condition			
Second condition (with VJD)			

Fig. 6. Degree of blur in drawing process (subject A)

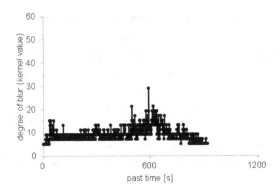

Fig. 7. Degree of blur in drawing process (subject B)

4.1 System Effect on the Way of Seeing

We analyzed eye tracking data in order to explore the user's seeing behavior in the drawing process. Figures 8 and 9 are heatmaps that express total fixation time on each part in their drawing process. Red means longer total fixation time.

Figure 8 shows that subject A spent longer time on the head part of the human model in the second condition with using the system. In addition, he also spent relatively longer time to both legs, foots, and toes parts that are the peripheral parts of the motif object in the second condition, comparing to the first condition. It suggests that expected effect was partly verified; subject A payed attention to whole of the motif object while bias to the head part was also observed. He reported that the blur made him become more conscious for outer contour of the human model image. He also reported he could be conscious of "thickness" of each parts without being aware of detailed inside lines.

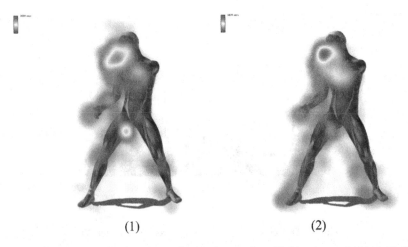

(1)   (2)

Fig. 8. Duration of stay of point-of-regard on each part of motif object image (subject A), (1) fist condition and (2) second condition with VJD

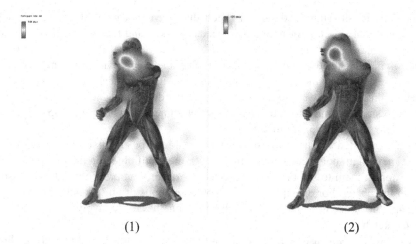

(1)   (2)

Fig. 9. Duration of stay of point-of-regard on each part of motif object image (subject B), (1) fist condition and (2) second condition with VJD

Figure 9 shows, on the other hand, that it is difficult to conclude that the system provided expected effect to subject B. Subject B also saw the head part for longer time in the second condition, but did not pay enough attention to the lower body parts including both legs, foots and toes parts.

Table 3 summarized the results of quantitative analysis of seeing behaviors of both subjects. Velocity and total moving distance of point-of-regards, number and average duration of fixation were calculated. Threshold value of fixation was 60 ms. Subject A spent longer time for seeing at motif object (and also drawing area) in the second condition compared with the first condition. Total moving distance and number of fixations were increased, and it was implied subject A took exploratory seeing behavior. Since the average duration of one fixation was slightly declined, degree of focus on specific parts was not intensive in the second condition. On the other hand, subject B less saw the motif object display area in the second condition, explored smaller distance, and more concentrated during one fixation.

Table 3. Summary of analysis of seeing behavior and fixation

	Subject A		Subject B	
	First condition	Second condition	First condition	Second condition
Total duration of seeing motif object display area	7 min 43 s	8 min 29 s	5 min 18 s	3 s 36 min
Average velocity of point-of-regard [px/ms]	1.95	2.02	3.72	2.6
Total moving distance of point-of-regard [px]	872220	996101	1068041	541643
Number of fixations	1197	1323	353	361
Average duration of each fixation [ms]	248.4	245.9	135.2	140.6

Interview results suggested subject B felt that she is not good at drawing sketch. She reported that she did not notice that system worked and blur was generated, thus she saw the motif object in the same way. She would not carefully observe the motif object compared with the case of subject A. She spent approximately only five and three minutes to see the motif object display area and its percentage in the total duration of seeing screen was 24% and 27% in the first condition and the second condition. They were smaller time and ratio than those of subject A who spent approximately seven (39%) and eight (32%) minutes.

It was suggested that the proposed system would not be effective to very beginners because they might not spend enough time to see the motif object in the first place. We should support them to see the motif object itself rather than preventing the excessive focus on the object. For example, the blur could be applied to the sketch drawing area to prompt the users to see the motif object when they excessively concentrate on drawing sketch.

By the way, in this user study, we did not take user's learning and mastering effect into account. Experiment in more strict condition is a future issue.

4.2   System Effect for Quality of Outcome

Table 4 shows results of answers of questionnaires about self-evaluation of the outcomes and comments.

Table 4. Evaluation for outcomes according to five-point Likert scale (1: poor ~ 5: excellent) and comments.

	Subject A		Subject B	
	First condition	Second condition	First condition	Second condition
Balance of outcome	4	2	1	1
Accuracy of outcome	3	1	2	1
Comments	-I failed to draw a good sketch in second condition. -I could not understand the rule of blur generation. Way of blur generation can be improved to reduce user's mental burden		-I am not good at drawing sketches. -The system did not give my outcomes any influence	

It suggests the usage of the system did not contribute to subjective quality of outcomes. As for subject A, he talked the sketch in the second condition was poor compared with the first condition. Although he reported he paid more attention to whole contour than detailed parts of the motif object, the score for balance was declined. Drawing environment with VJD was unusual for subject A and it might provide some stress and anxiety in drawing process. He also reported that he felt difficulty when he drew the detail parts and it causes the decline of the score for accuracy. On the other hand, subject B gave low evaluation for all her outcomes regardless of the system.

Those results show that seeing behavior for grasping entirety in the process is not a sufficient condition and did not always directly improve the quality of outcomes. Many factors such as drawing skills also effects on quality of outcome. Subject's comments gave us hints to consider approaches to improve the system. One possible approach is to improve the system to restrain unintended negative effect for other aspects (e.g. drawing behavior) in drawing process. We could let users understand how the system works and reduce their stress. Also, the degree of blur should be reduced when the users started to draw details after they completed rough contours. Another approach is to regard the system as an enlightenment material for appropriate seeing rather than a support system. Current system gives a message about the importance of grasping entirety of motif object to the users. We have to evaluate long-term learning effect of the system in future study.

5 Conclusion

Excessive focus on the specific detail parts of the motif object is a common problem of beginner's sketch drawing and it might result in collapse of the balance of outcome. In this study, we proposed a sketch learning support system VujaDessin (VJD), which prompts the users to see the entirety of the motif object by blurring the motif object image when excessive focusing on the detail parts is detected. We conducted user study of the system targeting two beginners to evaluate the effectiveness; whether the system can help users grasp the entirety of the object and draw a well-balanced sketch. Although it did not bring positive effect to quality of outcome, we confirmed the blur changed users seeing behaviors in drawing process. Subject paid more attention to the peripheral parts of the motif object and spent longer time to explore the motif object display area. Several suggestions for improving the system were obtained. Another type of support such as support to pay attention to the motif object itself is required in order to help very beginners who strongly feel they are not good at drawing sketch. If we develop this system as an immediate support system in drawing process, the system should be improved to avoid negative effects e.g., user's stress and difficulty of drawing detail parts in finalization phase. We also need to explore its long-term learning and enlightenment effect in the future study.

Acknowledgement. This work was supported by JSPS KAKENHI Grant Number JP18H03483.

References

1. Fernquist, J., Grossman, T., Fitzmaurice, G.: Sketch-sketch revolution: an engaging tutorial system for guided sketching and application learning. In: Proceedings of the 24th Annual ACM Symposium on User Interface Software and Technology, pp. 373–382. ACM, Santa Barbara (2011)
2. Soga, M., Matsuda, N., Taki, H.: A sketch learning support environment that gives area-dependent advice during drawing the Sketch. Trans. Jpn. Soc. Artif. Intell. **23**(3), 96–104 (2008). (in Japanese)

3. Soga, M., Kuriyama, S., Taki, H.: Sketch learning environment with diagnosis and drawing guidance from rough form to detailed contour form. In: Pan, Z., Cheok, A.D., Müller, W., Chang, M. (eds.) ISVC 2013. LNCS, vol. 5670, p. 109. Springer, Heidelberg (2009). https://doi.org/10.1007/978-3-642-03364-3_14

4. Takagi, S., Matsuda, N., Soga, M., Taki, H., Shima, T., Yoshimoto, F.: A learning support system for beginners in pencil drawing. In: Proceedings of the 1st International Conference on Computer Graphics and Interactive Techniques in Australasia and South East Asia (GRAPHITE 2003), pp. 281–282. ACM, New York (2003)

5. Nishizawa, H., Ura, M., Miyata, K.: A self-learning support system for drawing actual human body model by pose estimation. ITE Tech. Rep. **42**(12), 87–90 (2018). (in Japanese)

6. Xie, J., Hertzmann, A., Li, W., Winnemöller, H.: PortraitSketch: face sketching assistance for novices. In: Proceedings of the 27th Annual ACM Symposium on User Interface Software and Technology, pp. 407–417. ACM, Honolulu (2014)

7. Huang, Y.C., Chan, J.Y.H., Hsu, J.: Reflection before/after practice: learnersourcing for drawing support. In: Extended Abstracts of the 2018 CHI Conference on Human Factors in Computing Systems, LBW059. ACM, New York (2018)

8. Takarai, Y., Watanabe, N., Kubomura, C., Kameda, H.: Construction of proportional perspective model learning support system based on the person skilled in the line of sight for sketch. The Japanese Society for Artificial Intelligence Report, SIG-KST-026-05 (2015). (in Japanese)

9. Edwards, B.: Drawing on the Right Side of the Brain: The Definitive. Penguin, London (2012)

10. Posemaniacs.com. http://www.posemaniacs.com/

Tool UTAUT Applied to Measure Interaction Experience with NAO Robot

Adrián Vega$^{(\boxtimes)}$, Kryscia Ramírez-Benavidez$^{(\boxtimes)}$, and Luis A. Guerrero$^{(\boxtimes)}$

Universidad de Costa Rica, San José, Costa Rica
adrian.vegavega@ucr.ac.cr, {kryscia.ramirez, luis.guerrero}@ecci.ucr.ac.cr

Abstract. This research described the utilization of the Unified Theory of Acceptance and Use of Technology (UTAUT) to evaluate a high-level interactive scenario of using Nao Robot in the role of co-presenting in an educative context. Describing the registered result of construct such as Intention of Use, Perceived Enjoyment (PE), Perceived Sociability (PS), and Trust.

The study also describes the process of elaboration of this interaction. Multiple User-Centered Design techniques applied to the Human Interaction Robot field. Also, describes how the interaction of the robot with the participant was accomplished by using Wizard of Oz techniques.

Keywords: Human and computer interaction · User Centered Design · User Experience · Unified Theory of Acceptance and Use of Technology · Wizard of OZ · Nao robot

1 Introduction

Developments in robotics can be explained as a long process of historical evolution [1]. Starting from the methods which humans interact with objects and the control we get over them. Since ancient civilizations such as Egyptian and Roman exist records of art sample of human simulations represented by puppets, paintings, and statues. Alongside this process are the records of mechanical devices created to simplify human tasks. A long evolution of technologies such as hydraulic, steam, oils, electric… was required to integrate kinesthetic functions to what might be described as "human automation." Those basic devices bring about basic functions, but they were more related to the entertainment industry and science fiction. It is until the development of the last 50 years that it was allowed the automation of complex cognitive and physical functions. Currently, there are plenty of examples of robotic devices competing with people in activities such as manufacturing, sports, data analysis, among many others.

Nowadays, the robotics field is even growing its application coverage. However, additional challenges have been added besides the functionality, aesthetics, and complexity of the robots. One of the main current challenges is related to find more emphatic ways the people interact naturally with the robots in everyday environments. Thus, developing social engaging interactions with robots.

© Springer Nature Switzerland AG 2019
M. Kurosu (Ed.): HCII 2019, LNCS 11568, pp. 501–512, 2019.
https://doi.org/10.1007/978-3-030-22636-7_38

Robotics has proven to have diverse application in areas such as education [2–4], relate [5], health [6, 7], among others. Many research described different elements to consider in the design of interactions with socially intelligent robots [7–10]. Theory of "Social Intelligent Robots" [7] describes that the interaction with a robot must meet four different criteria. *Socially evocative* rely on anthropomorphizing and capitalize on feelings evoked. *Socially Situated* able to react to other social agents and object in the environment. *Sociable* proactively engage with humans to satisfy internal social aims. *Socially Intelligent* shows deep models of human cognition and social competence during robot interaction.

Many different requirements needed to be considered in the design of more Social Intelligent Robots. The Human-Robot Interaction (HRI) uses different techniques to improve the design and evaluation of effective interactions. One frequent sample of interaction technique in HRI, especially over early stages of development, is the Wizard of Oz (WoZ). Meanwhile, a sample of HRI evaluation technique is the Unified Theory of Acceptance and Use of Technology (UTAUT).

About the design of the interaction, one of the most current approaches is User-Centered Design (UCD). Through this approach, it has been possible to design meaningful interactions [2] with robots further than the current state of the technology. The UCD propose focus design of technologies on how people use those technologies instead of just technology itself. It is by integrating knowledge and techniques from different fields such as Design, Anthropology, Psychology, Robotics, Engineering, among others, that UCD shifts the focus of technology development cycle in the interaction with the users. Tools such as prototyping, scripts, and pilot testing are every day more frequently used in designing desktop software, mobile apps, websites, and currently robotics interactions. Despite the technologic limitations or budget resources, the UCD allows the validation of the next required stages of technology to accomplish users' expectations and requirements.

The current research contains the design of a presentation using the Robot Nao as a co-presenter during a presentation. The presentation was designed by using UCD techniques with the goal to generate awareness about the risks of using weapons in the resolution of conflicts. The presentation was presented to four groups of secondary students using the WoZ technique and evaluated by using UTAUT constructs. The objectives of this research aim to (1) Evaluate the use and acceptance of the robot during the activity. (2) Evaluate the context in which the presentation is carried out. (3) Evaluate the impact of the activity on the population.

2 Theoretical Framework

In the HRI, we find multiple designs and evaluation techniques. The WoZ is one of the most frequently utilized techniques in the design of interactive prototype due its flexibility and adaptability. Meanwhile, the UTAUT offers solid theoretical support to create an evaluation of interaction among different technologies.

2.1   Wizard of Oz (WoZ)

The Woz [11] is utilized in multiple areas of the design of technologies, especially under development. It is especially useful in cases where the implementation has a high cost, or the technology is still emerging.

In HRI the WoZ technique [12] involves simulating the end state of the technology operating through the assistance of people operating the robot. This simulation creates the illusion that the robot works autonomously. The operator of the robot works as part of the design group. They are managing the robot in a way that cannot be perceived for the study participant. Usually, the operator controls the robot remotely using robot sensors or cameras to interact with the participants.

Through the advantages of using this technique are [11, 12] that you can create interactions to be ready on the early stages of the project. Also, it is possible to evaluate the multiples iteration of the same project since its design stage. Finally, it is an effective way to evaluate participant responses identifying possible future problems without complex developments.

Some points that might consider when applying this technique are [11, 12] you will require to train the operator of the robot. Also, adding additional costs on ad extended stages of the design process. Moreover, because of being a technique based on the natural interaction with the participant, it can be challenging to be consistent in the application with different groups. Finally, it is pointed out that there is a risk of designing interaction beyond current technology capabilities.

2.2   Unified Theory of Acceptance and Use of Technology (UTAUT)

UTAUT [13] is a theoretical framework to evaluate the acceptance and usage of technologies. The main advantage of this framework is that it can be applied to different types of technologies. Founded in the Model of Technology Acceptance (TAM) [14], it integrates elements of other theories such as Theory of the reasoned Action, Motivation Model, Theory of Social Cognition, Innovation Diffusion Theory, among others.

The surveys developed from this theory consist of multiple questions grouped by constructs. Each question is elaborated in the format of Likert scales sorted in a random order to bring reliability to the different constructs.

Previous research [14] have evaluated the application of these constructs in cross-cultural scenarios and languages. These evaluations support the reliability and validity of the constructs among six different countries. Also, this framework has been previously applied in the robotics field, in samples such as the evaluation of the acceptance of assistive social robot by older adults [15].

Among the available constructs in this framework are use/usage, trust, anxiety, facilitating conditions, intention to use, perceived enjoyment, perceived sociability, social presence, among others [15]. Because in this study the only direct interaction of the participant with the robot is through dialoging during the presentation, constructs such as anxiety, facilitating conditions, or usage were not included in the evaluation.

3 Methodology

The current research consists of the design of a presentation using the Robot Nao as a co-presenter during a presentation. The presentation was designed by using UCD techniques with the goal to generate awareness about the risks of using weapons to solve violent situations. The presentation was presented to four groups of secondary students under the same conditions. In was applied the WoZ technique for interacting with the robot. The presentation was executed between a presenter and the robot using a script during the presentation. At the end of the presentation, the participant interacted directly with the robot by asking questions about the presented topic. The evaluation of the activity was fulfilled by mainly using UTAUT constructs.

The objectives of this research are to (1) Evaluate the use and acceptance of the robot during the activity. (2) Evaluate the context in which the presentation is carried out. (3) Evaluate the impact of the activity on the population.

The data collection was made in collaboration with the Social Program of the Universidad de Costa Rica and Fundación Fundamentes. In these programs, the university offers robotics workshops and trains in specific topics to the community. The Foundation raised the need to promote awareness about the danger of using weapons in the resolution of conflicts.

Two questionnaires were applied before and after the presentation to collect the data. The process begins with the first questionnaire, which consisted of a single question evaluating the perception of using weapons in the resolution of conflicts. After the first questionnaire, the person participates different activities such as workshops, tours inside the university facilities, and others. Finally, the participants participated in the presentation related to the risk of using weapons in the resolution of conflicts. There is 3 h difference between each questionnaire application.

The second questionnaire contained an evaluation of the interaction with the robot during the presentation. Multiple questions based on the UTAUT framework were implemented to evaluate this interaction. Also, designed additional questions to assess the presenter and content of the presentation. The final question evaluated any change in the perception of using weapons in the resolution of conflicts (Table 1).

Table 1. Activities table.

Questionnaire I	Intrusive tasks	Presentation	Questionnaire II
Evaluation of the topic	Tour in the University and workshop	Presentation with the robot Nao	Evaluation of the robot, presenter, and topic

3.1   Nao Robot

We used the Robot Model Nao of SoftBank Robotics. Among its main characteristics of this robot are: the ability to move, limited manipulation of objects, verbal communication capacity, and humanoid appeal (Fig. 1).

3.2   Population

The population was composed of four groups of high school students attending 7, 8 and 9 levels. Students ages were between 12 and 17 years old. These groups

Fig. 1. Imagen del Robot NAO

were pre-selected by Fundación Fundamentes from high schools at social risk they supported.

Participation in the experiment was anonymous and voluntary. For this reason, no records were kept of the identity of any of the participants. All students participated in the first questionnaire. Only the students who attended the presentation participated in the second survey. So, 100% of the students participated in the first questionnaire, while only 77% of the population participated in the second questionnaire. The average age of the population of the first questionnaire was 13.53 years. Meanwhile, in the second questionnaire, it was 13.59 years old (Table 2).

Table 2. Groups by Gender (F = Female, M = Male, and O = Other).

	G 1	G 2	G 3	G 4	Total
Questionnaire I	T = 24	T = 30	T = 19	T = 28	T = 101
	F = 14	F = 13	F = 5	F = 17	F = 49
	M = 9	M = 17	M = 14	M = 11	M = 51
	O = 1				O = 1
Questionnaire II	T = 16	T = 28	T = 15	T = 18	T = 77
	F = 11	F = 13	F = 5	F = 12	F = 41
	M = 5	M = 15	M = 10	M = 6	M = 36

3.3   Design of the Presentation

Different types of resources were utilized to design the presentation. Utilized concepts and methods of Human and Robot Interactive (HRI), User-Centered Design (UCD) and User Experience (UX). To support the interaction with the robot, we included visual resources such as powerpoint slides and the collaboration of a presenter.

By the collaboration of multidisciplinary groups of HCI specialist, Psychologists and Engineers the presentation script was created. Selecting the dialogues and behaviors of the robot during the presentation. This process was done by adapting Storytelling and Sketching techniques to the interaction with Nao robots. Two different testing groups evaluated the prototypes of the script. Creating a script capable of present the topic and that could be consistently shared between the different groups (Fig. 2).

Fig. 2. Sketch of the script of the presentation

In this stage, some issues were identified as needing attention. The first need identified was creating alternative ways of representing the robot's emotions at different moments of the presentation. It was required due to the limitations of the Nao robot with facial expressions and voice accents – especially in Spanish -. During the presentations to the test groups, they pointed out the need highlighting the emotions of the robot to achieve empathy with the stories presented. The solution included adding slides in the presentation representing the internal emotions of the robot during the presentation.

The second requirement identified was including a human presenter with the robot. At initial stages of the project, it was expected to have two Nao robots along interacting during the presentation. However, cause limitations such as the speaking speed of the robots, it was difficult to keep the attention of the public for a long time. Moreover, it was risking having two people coordinating the interaction of two different robots at the same time with the current resources.

3.4   Robot Script and the WoZ

This process required the application of mixed techniques during the script and open questions of the presentation. For this reason, the technical team implemented an interface that would allow movement and dialogues pre-programmed for NAO during the presentation, as well as independent movements and dialogs in order to freely and spontaneously interact with the participants.

To make the presentation consistent among the different groups, it was necessary that both the presenter and the robot presented the contents in the same way on each group. For this reason, the script was created. Both movements and dialogs of the presenter and robot were predefined and coordinated using the script as the reference in multiple rehearsals.

Finally, in order to provide the sensation of spontaneity and direct interaction of the participants with the robot. At the end of the presentation, there was a space of open questions regarding the subject presented. In this space, the participants could ask random questions to the robot controlled by using the WoZ technique (Fig. 3).

Fig. 3. Robot Nao and presenter during a presentation

4 Evaluation

As mentioned before, one of the central evaluations was based on the UTAUT framework. It is a broad model that seeks to encompass the evaluation of different types of interactions with technologies. For this reason, the required construct should be selected according to the specific technology and interaction required.

According to the scope of this research, four fundamental constructs were selected [15]. *Intention of Use* (IU) which evaluates the intent to use the technology for an extended time This is especially important to know if the contribution of the robot in the presentation must be maintained over time. *Perceived Enjoyment* (PE) which consists in the perception of pleasure felt by the user while using the technology. It is contributing to evaluating if users enjoyed their interaction with the robot. *Perceived Sociability* (PS) refers to the ability of the system to develop social behaviors. It is very important to evaluate its relationship with the perception of the robot as socially intelligent. Finally, *Trust* (T) refers to the reliability and security that the interaction with technology transmits. In the case of the robot, it is important to verify that the information presented is reliably when presented by the robot (Table 3).

Table 3. English to Spanish translation of the constructs selected to replicate from the research of Heerink et al. [15]

Variable	English	Spanish
IU	I'm planning to use the robot during the next few days	Consideraría participar con robots similares si tuviera la oportunidad
IU	I think I'll use the robot during the next few days	Recomendaría seguir utilizando al robot en actividades similares
IU	I am certain to use the robot during the next few days	Quisiera ver más robots como este en diferentes actividades
PE	I enjoy the robot talking to me	Disfruté hablando con el robot
PE	I find the robot fascinating	Encontré al robot fascinante
PE	I find the robot enjoyable	Encontré al robot agradable
PE	I enjoy doing things with the robot	Disfruté interactuando con el robot
PE	I find the robot boring	Pienso que el robot NO es aburrido
PS	I feel the robot understands me	Siento que el robot me ha entendido
PS	I consider the robot a pleasant conversational partner	Pienso que este robot ha sido un presentador agradable
PS	I think the robot is nice	Pienso que el robot ha sido amable
PS	I find the robot pleasant to interact with	Encuentro que la interacción con el robot ha sido satisfactoria
T	I would follow the advice the robot gives me	Estoy dispuesto(a) a seguir los consejos que el robot pudiera darme
T	I would trust the robot if it gave me advice	Confiaría en el robot si me brindara algún consejo

In addition to the UTAUT constructs, we also evaluated. The information presented, resources utilized and presenter attitude. It is also required to evaluate the context where the presentation is applied.

5 Results

5.1 UTAUT

Analyzed the preselected constructs previously mentioned identified Perception of Enjoyment (PE), Perception of Sociability (PS), Intention to Use (IU) y Trust (T), using variance analysis sorted by group, gender, and age.

Table 4. UTAUT Cronbach Alpha

Variable	Cronbach Alpha	Items
PE	.77	5
PS	.67	4
IU	.74	3
T	.73	2

Table 5. UTAUT descriptive analysis

Variable	N	Mean	S.E.	Std Dev
PE	77	1.59	.05	.43
PS	77	1.68	.05	.42
IU	77	1.72	.05	.42
T	77	1.29	.08	.74

In order to know the reliability of the four constructs (PE, PS, IU, and T) utilized a Cronbach Alpha Analysis. As described the Table 4, the result of this analysis shows acceptable reliability in all constructs.

To analyze the data utilized a Likert scale with the parameters between −2 to 2. Considering 2 as the higher value. The different constructs describe a positive perception of the interaction with the Nao. According to Table 5, the higher value identified was IU (M = 1.72, SD = .42), follow by a high PS (M = 1.68, SD = .42), PE (M = 1.59, SD = .43), and a consistent T (M = 1.29, SD .74).

The lower mean identified in T requires future research to identify the causes in the decrease of this value. It is also important to consider if the topic presented matched the Nao appeal and the relationship of T when the robot presents mature topics such as the risks of using weapons (Table 6).

Table 6. Anova analysis UTAUT x Group X Gender X Age

		PE	PS	IU	T
Groups	Levene	**.002**	.626	.951	.262
	Anova	F(3,73) = 2.9 p = **.041**	F(3,73) = .94 p = .427	F(3,73) = .26 p = .853	F(3,73) = .53 p = .662
Gender	Levene	.131	.081	.194	.378
	Anova	F(1,75) = .92 p = .341	F(1,75) = .62 p = .432	F(1,75) = .45 p = .506	F(1,75) = 1.33 p = .253
Age	Levene	.344	**.042**	.489	.090
	Anova	F(4,72) = 1.59 p = .186	F(4,72) = 1.66 p = .170	F(4,72) = .86 p = .495	F(4,72) = .44 P = .781

Alpha = .05

According to the variance analysis, the perception of the robot among groups was not significant. This value is important to be considered in the evaluation of consistence of the information presented among the four groups. As mentioned before, one of the main challenges of the research was creating a script consistent to be present among all four groups. According to the variance analysis, the only significant difference identified among groups was PE (F (3, 73) = 2.9 p = .041). Future research is required to identify if the context elements might have impacted this value. However, the post-hoc analysis of each group criteria revealed no significant relationships identified. Finally, no significant difference of gender or age was identified between the constructs of the experiment.

5.2   Context

To evaluate other elements of the context where the robot performed, we also evaluated: the attitude of the presenter, accessibility of the information presented, and utility of the information presented. Using parameters between −2 to 2, considering 2 as the higher value. Table 7 describes the performance of each variable:

Table 7. Context analysis

Variable	N	Mean	S.E.	Std Dev
Affordability of the information	77	1.74	.06	.52
Presenter Attitude	77	1.69	.05	.47
Usability of the information in daily life	77	1.56	.08	.66

The usability of the presented information evaluated as M = 1.74, SD = .52. The presenter attitude performed a M = 1.69, SD = .47. Finally, the usability of the presented information in everyday life registered a M = 1.56, SD = .66. It might be possible to consider evaluating element to increase the utility of the information presented in the context of everyday life.

5.3   Topic

A one-tailed two-sample independent means t-test, equal variance assumed, revealed that after the presentation the topic impact recorded (M = 1.7, SD = .54), it was not significantly higher without the presentation value (M = 1.54, SD = .81), F(3, 73) = 2.06, p = .113. Even though it was detected an increase in the attitude to lower the use of violence and weapons in our society, that increment was not significant enough to reject the null hypothesis.

6   Conclusion

Using methodologies such as Sketching, and Story Telling from the User-Centered Design applied to the Human Interaction Robot it is possible to offer a higher quality of interactive experience with the robot. Identifying alternatives to possible improvement areas of robots such as NAO. For example, it was essential to evaluate the need to create alternative solutions that highlight the emotional expressions in the limited facial and oral expression in the NAO robot. Using these techniques brought more positive feedback in the testing groups, and participants of the experiment PE, PS, IU, and T.

The applied research demonstrated a functional application of the UTAUT framework in the evaluation of HRI. By using UTAUT constructs, UCD design techniques, and WoZ interaction, we could design an appealing interaction of using the Nao robot as co-presenter of information. It was also possible to evaluate how consistent was the interaction among the different groups—elaborating an interaction inclusive in factors such as age and gender. Also, by using UTAUT constructs simplified the evaluation process by making the constructs more reliable and confiable. It is required a deeper evaluation in future research of the impact on the perception of T in the interaction with robots. It might require to study the different levels of T using robots to present information. Identifying the effect in T of the presence of the robot in the presentation and the topic.

About the impact of the presentation, it is necessary to mention that no statistically significant variability was identified. However, an increased mean can be observed in the population during the evaluation. The high value in the mean presented in the assessment before the presentation shows high awareness of the participants regarding the issue of the risks of the use of weapons. This element might be considered in order to evaluate the effectiveness of the presentation.

Finally, it is required to highlight the positive perception of the interaction with the robot perceived among the groups in the context of assisting the presentation of information.

Acknowledgments. This work was supported by ECCI-UCR (*Escuela de Ciencias de la Computación e Informática*) and by CITIC-UCR (*Centro de Investigaciones en Tecnologías de la Información y Comunicación*) both at Universidad de Costa Rica (UCR). Grand No. 834-B7-267. Additionally, thanks to the User Interaction Group (USING) for providing ideas to refine and complete the research. Finally, thanks to the Fundación Fundamentes for the collaboration collection the data.

References

1. Oh, C.G., Park, J.: From mechanical metamorphosis to empathic interaction: a historical overview of robotic creatures. J. Hum.-Robot Interact. **331**(10) (2014)
2. Ramírez-Benavides, K., López, G., Guerrero, L.A.: Designing tools that allows children in the early childhood to program robots. In: Zaphiris, P., Ioannou, A. (eds.) LCT 2017. LNCS, vol. 10296, pp. 71–89. Springer, Cham (2017). https://doi.org/10.1007/978-3-319-58515-4_7
3. Bravo, F.A., González, A.M., González, E.: Interactive drama with robots for teaching non-technical subjects. J. Hum.-Robot Interact. **6**(2), 48–69 (2017)
4. Baxter, P., Ashurst, E., Read, R., Kennedy, J., Belpaeme, T.: Robot education peers in a situated primary school study: Personalisation promotes child learning. PLoS ONE **12**(5), 1–23 (2017)
5. Torta, E., Oberzaucher, J., Werner, F., Cuijpers, R.H., Juola, J.F.: Attitudes Towards Socially Assistive Robots in Intelligent Homes: Results From Laboratory Studies and Field Trials. J. Human-Robot Interact. **1**(2), 76–99 (2013)
6. Wood, L.J., Dautenhahn, K., Rainer, A., Robins, B., Lehmann, H., Syrdal, D.S.: Robot-mediated interviews - how effective is a humanoid robot as a tool for interviewing young children? PLoS ONE **8**(3), e59448 (2013)
7. Dautenhahn, K.: Socially intelligent robots: dimensions of human-robot interaction. Philos. Trans. R. Soc. Lond. B Biol. Sci. **362**(1480), 679–704 (2007)
8. Fortunati, L.: Social robots from a human perspective. Soc. Robot Hum. Perspect. **73**, 1–144 (2015)
9. Dautenhahn, K.: Roles and functions of robots in human society: implications from research in autism therapy. Robotica **21**(4), S0263574703004922 (2003)

10. Vlachos, E., Jochum, E., Demers, L.-P.: The effects of exposure to different social robots on attitudes toward preferences. Interact. Stud. **17**(3), 390–404 (2016)
11. Usability Body of Knowledge, "Wizard of Oz" (2012). http://www.usabilitybok.org/wizard-of-oz. Accessed 13 Apr 2017
12. Riek, L.D.: Wizard of Oz studies in HRI: a systematic review and new reporting guidelines. J. Hum.-Robot Interact. **1**(1), 119–136 (2012)
13. Heerink, M., Kröse, B., Evers, V., Wielinga, B.: Measuring acceptance of an assistive social robot: a suggested toolkit. In: Proceedings of IEEE International Symposium on Robot and Human Interactive Communication, pp. 528–533 (2009)
14. Oshlyansky, L., Cairns, P., Thimbleby, H.: Validating the Unified Theory of Acceptance and Use of Technology (UTAUT) Tool Cross-Culturally
15. Heerink, M., Kröse, B., Evers, V., Wielinga, B.: Assessing acceptance of assistive social agent technology by older adults: the almere model. Int. J. Soc. Robot. **2**(4), 361–375 (2010)
16. Fundamentes, "¿Quienes somos?—Fundamentes" (2019). http://www.fundamentes.or.cr/es/content/quienes-somos. Accessed 11 Feb 2019

Keep System Status Visible: Impact of Notifications on the Perception of Personal Data Transparency

Lucia Vilela Leite Filgueiras[1](✉) , Adriano da Silva Ferreira Leal[1],
Thiago Adriano Coleti[1,3] , Marcelo Morandini[2] ,
Pedro Luiz Pizzigatti Correa[1] , and Solange N. Alves-Souza[1,3]

[1] Escola Politécnica, Universidade de São Paulo, São Paulo, SP, Brazil
lfilguei@usp.br
[2] Escola de Artes, Ciências e Humanidades, Universidade de São Paulo,
São Paulo, SP, Brazil
[3] Centro de Ciências Tecnológicas, Universidade Estadual do Norte do Paraná,
Jacarezinho, PR, Brazil

Abstract. Personal Data Transparency (PDT) requires that companies provide information for subjects about activities performed in their personal data such as collecting, processing, disseminating and sharing. Recent regulations on personal data have addressed the improvement of subjects' capability in giving consent to controllers/processors, ensuring that data collection and usage policies are presented to the subject in an intelligible and easily accessible form, using clear and plain language. However, the objective of ensuring that people have more control over their personal data presumes that they are conscious on the value of their personal data, understand the concept of privacy, and are aware of risks, consequences and safeguards concerned and their rights in relation to the processing of personal data. This conscience should be complete in the moment of consent. Wisely, regulators have been cautious and included the right to withdraw the consent and the right of having personal data "forgotten". However, a person's conscience of risks comes with experience brought by the exposition to the facts, whether good or adverse, that happen after consent is given. Users frequently accept all terms without fully agreeing with them because they are motivated to access a service or product. In this paper, we report and discuss the results of an experiment showing that instantaneous notification of data collection to smartphone users' increases significantly their awareness of transparency. Based on this discussion, we advocate that feedback should be enforced in the transparency regulations.

Keywords: Feedback · Personal Data Transparency ·
Data Protection Regulation

1 Introduction

Data driven systems and services have boosted the need for data collection and data processing, whether proprietary or third-party data. Within collected data, personal data has a special importance both for controllers/processors (companies that collect and

© Springer Nature Switzerland AG 2019
M. Kurosu (Ed.): HCII 2019, LNCS 11568, pp. 513–529, 2019.
https://doi.org/10.1007/978-3-030-22636-7_39

process data) and for data subjects (owners of data). Personal data is any information relating to an identified or identifiable natural person [1] (European Union, 2016).

The interest in data produced by individuals or communities is so evident that it is currently unlikely that a digital service or application operates without collecting personal data or without using information produced through personal data.

Aspects of ethics regarding personal data have been receiving attention from the academic and professional communities in the new research area of Human-Data Interaction [2] (Mortier *et al.*, no date).

One of the biggest challenges in this area is the study of Personal Data Transparency (PDT). PDT occurs when the individuals affected by the data collection and processing are aware of the complete flow concerning their personal data, from collection, transformation, processing, to their availability and use - not by deduction or supposition, but because the flow is well documented and exposed in an intelligible way to the users of a certain service or product. In the past decade, the concerns about PDT became more significant due to the reason that the use of personal data also increased for several commercial and non-commercial reasons.

Recent regulations on personal data protection like European General Data Protection Regulation - GDPR [1] have improved clarity and understandability of privacy policies and usage terms and conditions are presented to the user. This regulation determines that service providers state how and when user data will be collected and used, warranting the users important rights (such as the right to be forgotten) and avoiding leakage of personal information to unauthorized companies.

Mortier and colleagues [2] associate the concepts of transparency and intelligibility to legibility. According to the authors, "(p)remised on the recognition that interactions with data flows and data processes are often opaque, legibility is concerned with making data and analytic algorithms both transparent and comprehensible to users." In this paper, we use the term legibility as a quality associated to the user's perception of transparency, that is, the degree with which a system, product or service communicates its transparency to their users.

It is interesting to notice that, according to Oliver [3], in the context of public policies and governance, the term transparency used to mean "letting the truth available for others to see if they so choose", that implies that observers of transparency may not want to look, or may not have the means to look, or may not have the ability to see the truth. In modern organizations and governments, this form of passive transparency is giving place to active disclosure, in which controllers have the responsibility of releasing clear and updated information to stakeholders so that they can manage risk effectively.

In fact, the motivation for this work stems from the observation that users of digital services may not want to look or may not have the means to look or may not have the ability to see the truth regarding their data. These users, from now on in this paper referred to as "data subjects", are often aware of data collection and processing, but they do not know when, how or where they happen, and they do not give due importance to examining terms of use and privacy policies of digital services before consenting.

Among other reasons for this careless behaviour is the fact that data subjects are requested to examine privacy policies and usage terms and conditions at the time they are contracting a desired service and under the self-imposed pressure for beginning to use, with little or no power of negotiation.

Tasks performed upon personal data are often opaque for subjects, even though they may have a strong relationship with people's privacy, security and agency. Even though data subjects have the intellectual and legal ability to decide and to take risks, as with every new technology, the implications of personal data usage are yet to be discovered. In this situation, capable adults may be as a vulnerable as a child. Regulators have been wise to include the right to revoke the consent and the right of deletion of a person's data, given that many consequences of usage of personal data are not yet possible of identification.

One of the most relevant design rules for human-computer interaction is "visibility of system status". This rule is explained by Nielsen and Norman: "The system should always keep users informed about what is going on, through appropriate feedback within reasonable time." [4]. Visibility of system status requires the system to always give users prompt and unambiguous feedback so that they can diagnose the state the system is in and whether an action produced any changes in this state. Lack of visibility of system status has been a contributing factor in many industrial accidents in history and is still the cause of many usability problems in different systems, from critical systems [5] to wearables [6].

We show, in this paper, that instantaneous notification to a data subject of data collection can improve legibility. We advocate that requirements of feedback should be addressed and enforced because of its great potential to educate users towards conscious consent.

In order to discuss this issue, we organize the paper as follows. In Sect. 2, we present the concept of feedback and the heuristic of visibility of system status in the context of designing usable systems. In Sect. 3, we analyse GDPR to show how the regulation addresses legibility and feedback. In Sect. 4, we describe our active disclosure experiment to assess the impact of feedback on users' data collection on their perception of transparency. Section 5 details the results, based on which, in Sect. 6, we discuss how recent regulations should address users' awareness of personal data collection and propose changes in the regulation text to enforce the development of notifications.

2 Feedback and Visibility of System Status

Feedback is the reaction to a process/activity, or the information obtained from a given action. For HCI community, the term feedback means the communication of the result of any interaction and should be easily visible and understandable by humans.

According to Harley [7], communicating the current state of the system allows users to feel in control, take appropriate actions, and thus feel more confident. This communication or feedback contributes to transparency about system behaviour and results in better decision making. It's not hard to find simple, ordinary examples of feedback, such as the smartphone battery alert, warning of unread emails in your inbox, and even an elevator signalling your current floor. Harley further states that system state visibility refers to how well the current state of the system is passed on to users, and ideally systems should always keep users informed of what is happening through feedback at an appropriate time.

Feedback can assume two forms regarding the time moment that it is issued. While final feedback signals the completion of a given activity and the change in system state, instantaneous feedback informs on the ongoing activities of a system. For instance, in a train control system, the operator could see a railroad switch icon as a blinking icon while the physical object is in movement between two stable states. In file transfers, the dynamic filling bar reports that the operation is being carried on. Both forms of feedback are important to keep users aware of system state.

Information on system status helps build users' trust in the system, because users can keep a mental model of the system logic thus anticipating consequences of their actions.

3   GDPR and Legibility

The General Data Protection Regulation (GDPR) was created to protect European citizens regarding the processing of personal data and to establish rules to provide a sound base for movement of personal data within the member states.

The initiative has promoted important changes in personal data collection and processing, by imposing measures of privacy and data protection. The text was published in the Official Journal of the European Union on May 4, 2016 and provided a two-year adaptation time. Since May 25, 2018, the regulation is effective in all member states. Regulation, as its name implies, dictates obligations of companies providing services on the processing of personal data and privacy of citizens of the European Union. Failure to comply with the rules imposes sanctions on companies, and fines may reach 4% of annual revenues up to 20 million euros if the violations are serious.

The regulation is organized in Chapters that address General provisions, Principles, Rights of the data subject, Controller and processor, Transfers of personal data to third countries or international organisations, Independent supervisory authorities, Cooperation and consistency, Provisions relating to specific processing situations, Delegated acts and implementing acts and Final provisions. The regulation has 99 articles and 173 recitals. A recital is part of the legal text that explains the context and purpose for many articles, disclosing how the regulation is interpreted by Data Protection Authorities.

GDPR grants subjects several rights regarding their personal data, from the right to request information on whether personal data concerning them are being processed to the right of being forgotten. In this work, we have scrutinized GDPR to capture the general understanding of transparency and legibility. Articles that address this matter are concentrated in the first three chapters the regulation and in some of its recitals. We group in the following paragraphs citations of the regulation that express provisions for subjects' awareness of their rights, even though the regulation has not as primary motivation to educate citizens on their rights but to protect these rights.

1. Consent must be informed. GDPR states that collection and processing personal data depend on data subjects giving consent for every purpose. Consent is a freely given affirmative action, either by a statement or by a clear action, that must be

specific to the purpose of processing. In order to consent be informed, GDPR requires that any information and communication relating to the processing of personal data must be easily accessible and easy to understand. Clear and plain language must be used to communicate.

2. Access request to controller information. In article 15, GDPR states the right of access by data subjects to obtain from the controller confirmation as to whether personal data concerning them are being processed, as well as:

- the purposes of the processing;
- the categories of personal data concerned;
- the recipients or categories of recipient to whom the personal data have been or will be disclosed, in particular recipients in third countries or international organisations;
- where possible, the envisaged period for which the personal data will be stored, or, if not possible, the criteria used to determine that period;
- the existence of the right to request from the controller rectification or erasure of personal data or restriction of processing of personal data concerning the data subject or to object to such processing;
- the right to lodge a complaint with a supervisory authority;
- where the personal data are not collected from the data subject, any available information as to their source;
- the existence of automated decision-making, including profiling, and, at least in those cases, meaningful information about the logic involved, as well as the significance and the envisaged consequences of such processing for the data subject.

3. Details of processing operations and standardized icons. Recital 60 states that the data subject must be informed on details of processing operations and that standardized icons can be used to give in an easily visible, intelligible and clearly legible manner, a meaningful overview of the intended processing:

- existence of the processing operation
- its purposes
- specific circumstances and context in which the personal data are processed
- existence of profiling and the consequences of such profiling
- whether the subject is obliged to provide the personal data and of the consequences, where he or she does not provide such data.

4. Agency regarding subjects' rights. Recital 59 states that controllers must provide **modalities** [emphasis added] for facilitating the exercise of the data subject's rights including mechanisms to request, obtain access to personal data, rectifying, erasing and objecting to processing. This statement improves the quality of agency of data subjects regarding their rights to manage their personal data.

5. Data subjects "should be made aware of risks, rules, safeguards and rights in relation to the processing of personal data and how to exercise their rights in relation to such processing." (Recital 39).

We are also interested in the provisions in GDPR regarding the timing involved in collection, processing and notifying subjects about the collection and processing of data.

Feedback, as a design solution to provide visibility of system status, must be close in time to the events that cause change in system status to be understood as such and allow users to predict system behaviour. However, in case a data subject requires information from a controller, the response from the controller may take one month, with two months more of allowed extension.

Article 13 of GDPR makes a statement about the moment in time when information should be provided by controllers to subjects: "1. Where personal data relating to a data subject are collected from the data subject, the controller shall, at the time when personal data are obtained [emphasis added], provide the data subject with all of the following information [list of information follows]".

This moment in time is hard to define. The emphasized expression can mean that the information should be provided before data is collected, as usual in informed consents, but it can be interpreted as the availability of that information at the precise time that data is collected, notifying the subject of collection and processing.

4   Experimenting Active Disclosure

This section describes the experiment we have performed to assess the impact of feedback on data subjects' perception of transparency. Our hypothesis was that a continued experience of active disclosure would change the subjects' perception regarding data collection and processing policies.

The experiment consisted in collecting subjects' opinion on transparency issues and identifying their attitude towards analysing terms of usage and privacy policies, before and after the usage of an Android application that monitored data upload activity.

Our application presented a notification when data uploaded reached a given amount. The notification was designed to be minimally intrusive as the user could receive many instances of the notification during the day.

Mobile applications were preferred to desktop applications as the data-driven target services because (1) people carry their smartphones with them, thus the instantaneous notification had the chance of being be noticed; (2) the process of installing applications is frequent, thus there is a chance that the person has been exposed to the need to evaluate service policies.

4.1   Research Question

We proposed the following research question: "does notification of data collection activity (feedback) change the subjects' attitude towards data policies?

4.2   Limits of Validity

The following facts limited the validity of the experiment.

- The experiment was performed only with mobile digital services
- The notification expresses the amount of data uploaded, not the *personal* data upload.
- The number of participants was too small to allow generalization of findings.

4.3   Description of the Experiment

The experiment was organized in two phases. In the first phase, the objective was to understand participants' perception regarding PDT. In the second phase, the participants were invited to use an application that notifies them on data collection, after which they were invited to assess the change in their perception of PDT.

First phase: survey about perception of PDT

The first survey intended to collect participants' perception about PDT. Participants were invited to participate of the study by messages widely disseminated in social networks. The survey was prepared with Google Forms, in five sections:

1. Title and explanation of the terms of use of the research, stating the objective and the rights of the participants according to Brazilian ethical procedures related to Research with Humans in the Social Sciences [8];
2. Demographics: age, monthly income and education level;
3. Technological profile: time of usage of smartphones; frequency of usage of popular applications (Google Maps, Waze, Facebook, Twitter, Instagram, WhatsApp and email);
4. Participant's perception about personal data and their applications installed on their devices, further explained;
5. Invitation to participate in the second phase (requiring the provision of the participant's e-mail address).

The questions on the perception of personal data were preceded by this explanation, in equivalent Portuguese:

> *"Currently, many companies that provide digital services collect personal data from users, stating that this action is essential to improve users' experience with their products.*
> *Personal data means data relating to a person that can identify the person, either alone or together with other data. Examples of personal data are: CPF, personal characteristics, behavior, preferences, relationships, health information.*
> *The usage terms and privacy policies of these digital services should state what data is collected, the frequency of collection, and how this data is used."*

Subsequently, participants were asked to rate their experience with PDT, answering the following questions:

- Do you remember any application on your smartphone informing you that it collects and/or shares your personal data during its use? (*Answers: Yes|No*)
- How often do you read the terms of use and privacy policies of an application? (*Answers: Never|Rarely|Frequently|Always*)

- If you answered something other than "always" in the previous question, explain why you do not read the terms of use and privacy policies. Select the alternative that best explains your attitude. (*Answers could be one of the following options or an open answer:*
  - *The policy texts are too long.*
  - *The terms of the policies are difficult to understand.*
  - *I do not know where to find the policies in the applications.*
  - *It's no use reading because the policies protect the rights of who makes the application and not mine.*
  - *It's no use reading because if I do not agree I will not be able to change anything.*
- Has some application you installed on your smartphone given you the opportunity to choose which of your personal data you authorize to collect? (*Answers: Yes|No*)
- Has some application you installed on your smartphone allowed you to select which forms of usage you authorize the app to apply to your data? (*Answers: Yes|No*)
- Please comment on the two previous questions. Do you remember which app and your answer? (*Open answer*)
- Would you stop to use an app or website if you found out that it collects and/or shares your personal data? (*Answers: I would certainly stop using| I would probably stop using| I would not stop using*).
- Please explain your choice in the previous question. (*Open answer*)

The first phase was run for one week with Brazilian participants, in June 14-21, 2018, a few days after GDPR became enforceable in Europe. We obtained 130 responses.

Second phase: installation and usage of the feedback application
Participants who expressed their interest in participating in further steps of our research provided a contact e-mail in the first phase survey form. 72 participants agreed to participate.

On June 21 2018, we sent these participants an e-mail containing the feedback application in *apk* format, the procedures for installation, operation and uninstallation. They were asked to install the app and use it for at least one day.

The application is detailed further.

Second phase: survey about changes in the perception of PDT
After 1 week of sending the application, a questionnaire was sent to all participants who consented in using the application. The intention of this questionnaire was to identify changes in user attitude towards PDT.

The questionnaire also used Google Forms in one single section, in which the following questions were presented:

- Please fill in your email so that we can relate the answers to the first part of the survey. (*Open answer*)
- How surprised you felt with the data collection feedback presented by our prototype? Consider "1" as little surprised and "5" as extremely surprised. (*Answer: 1|2|3|4|5*)
- How much has your experience with data collection feedback changed your awareness of your personal data? Consider "1" as no change and "5" as a complete change. (*Answer: 1|2|3|4|5*)

- Based on your experience with the prototype, how often will you read the terms of use and privacy policies of an application? (*Answer: Never|Rarely|Frequently| Always*)
- Based on your experience with the prototype, would you stop to use an app or website if you found out that it collects and/or shares your personal data? (*Answers: I would certainly stop using| I would probably stop using| I would not stop using*).

The last survey was run for 11 days, from June 25 to July 4,2018. As expected, many participants did not engage with the last phase. Only 23 of the 72 participants that were originally interested in participating installed the application and sent their answers.

4.4   Description of the Feedback Application

In order to provide the instantaneous feedback on data collection, we developed an Android application that met the following functional requirements:

1. The app monitors the amount of data uploaded;
2. The app notifies the user every 2Mbytes of data uploaded by issuing a continuous, 2-sec long vibratory signal;
3. Upon users' request, the app displays the total amount of data uploaded since the app activation;
4. User can turn the application on/off;

Also, the app met the following non-functional requirements:

5. Notification is minimally intrusive but non-negligible;
6. Notification is distinguishable from other applications' notifications;
7. The app does not collect or process any personal data;
8. The app runs in the Android platform (chosen because of its large market share in Brazil;
9. The app does not require root access to the user's smartphone;
10. The app installs with no need of user interaction apart from the acceptance of the installation process;
11. The app uninstalls with no traces left.

It is important to notice that the feedback app does not identify which application is responsible for data upload. While this seemed to be an interesting information to be presented to the user, the implementation of this feature would require the user granting permission in installation. We discarded this option because of the risk of mistrust.

The final version is an application that runs as a service (in background), continuously monitoring the network activity. Notification is generated whenever 2 MB of data is uploaded, by vibrating the device for 2 s and displaying a notification icon in the status bar. Also, if the user opens the notification drawer, the application displays a screen that shows the amount of uploaded data in megabytes and time since when the app started to run.

The intended usage scenario is the following: "Carmela received the app by email this morning, together with the instructions for installation and uninstallation. She installed it easily while having breakfast. In the first hour of app operation, Carmela did not notice any difference in her smartphone, as she drove to work. In the parking lot, however, the phone vibrated for 2 s, which was unusual. She looked at the screen with strangeness, but soon recognized that the vibration was the app notification that her applications had uploaded 2Mbytes. In fact, that was exactly the displayed information she found when she clicked the app icon. During the morning, as she worked, the 2-s vibration happened again for three times. As she had not accessed any application in her smartphone in that period, she wondered which application was uploading data. During lunchtime she accessed Facebook and Twitter, as well as her email, and the app presented a more frequent notification pattern that was compatible with her activity. Good, she thought, this makes sense. In the afternoon, again she left her phone resting in her table, and now and then the vibrating notification sounded. During dinner, she talked to her husband about privacy and personal data collection, while uninstalling the app. She said, I wonder what these applications were talking about me!"

Figure 1 shows the screens that informs total uploaded data.

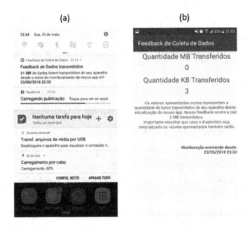

Fig. 1. Screenshots of feedback application. (a) brief notification (drawer) with totals from monitoring start time. (b) full display with information on data uploaded.

For monitoring uploaded data, we used the "getTotalTxBytes" method of the "TrafficStats" class, available from API 8 of the Android SDK [9]. This version is supported by many devices. According to the Android documentation, this method "returns the number of bytes transmitted since device boot. It counts packets across all network interfaces, increasing monotonically since device boot. Statistics are measured at the network layer, so they include both TCP and UDP usage"

The application code is available at https://drive.google.com/file/d/1gWwrtBygelf YOz3ancFsptc05hRBBzeR/view?usp=sharing.

5 Results

In this section, we present the results obtained in the three phases of the experiment.

5.1 Demographics

130 people participated of the first phase, from which 23 participated also in the second. Figure 2 describes age and Fig. 3 describes educational level of participants.

Participants age is from 17 to 68 y-o, with median of 31 y-o in phase 1. In phase 2, participants' age is from 17 to 65, with median of 28 y-o.

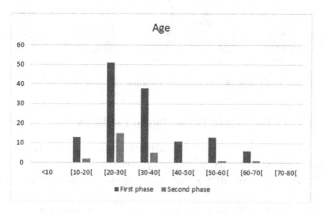

Fig. 2. Demographic profile of participants: age

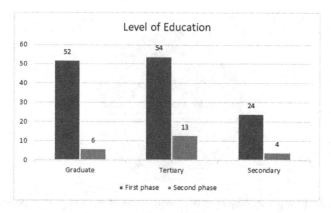

Fig. 3. Demographic profile of participants: level of education

5.2   Technological Profile

Technology profile intended to discriminate participants according to their technological expertise and frequency of usage of common mobile applications. Figure 4 shows the usage of technology.

Quais apps você costuma usar e com que frequência?

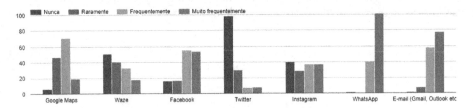

Fig. 4. Phase 1, technological profile

5.3   Perception of PDT Before Exposition to Feedback

The first phase survey showed, in general, that participants are aware of data collection but do not pay attention to terms of use and privacy policies.

74% of participants remember some application informing that it collects/shares personal data.

86% of participants declared never or rarely read an application terms of use or privacy policies. Figure 5 presents the distribution of answers.

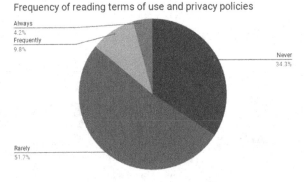

Fig. 5. First phase, frequency of reading terms of use and privacy policies

The main reason for not reading the terms is because they are too long. Table 1 shows other answers, considering that participants were requested to mark only the reason that apply in most cases.

Table 1. Reasons for not reading policies (participants marked only one)

Reasons for not reading policies	%
The policy texts are too long	47,7
The terms of the policies are difficult to understand	6,2
I do not know where to find the policies in the applications	0
It's no use reading because policies protect the rights of who makes the application and not mine	4,6
It's no use reading because if I do not agree I will not be able to change anything	27,7
Other reasons	6,1
No answer	7,7

Other reasons mentioned include carelessness, lack of time, trust in the company that uses the data, similarity between texts and herd behaviour.

Most participants were unsure whether they would cease or not to use an app or service if they found that their personal data was collected and/or shared, as shown in Fig. 6.

Those who would certainly stop using justify their decision based on the perception of privacy ("I value the right of being anonymous, especially in internet. I am not comfortable when I find out that a company is selling my personal data. I don't agree with this, but I know it's very common nowadays"), ownership of data ("Nobody has the right to use my data without my consent", "My data is my data"), perception of personal risk ("The risk of having my data explored makes me protect myself ceasing to use the application", "Certainly my data will not be used to my benefit!").

Would you stop to use an app or website if you found out that it collects and/or shares your personal data?

● I would certainly stop using
● I would prob-ably stop using
● I would not stop using

20,3%
26,6%
53,1%

Fig. 6. Attitude towards ceasing to use an application after evidence that it collects or shares personal data

Participants that declared they would keep on using the applications justified their opinion based on service utility ("If I denied my data I would not be able to use it and I need it badly", "I choose the services based on their functionality.", "They make my life much easier"), on the feeling of helplessness because data is already public ("Our personal data are already in the internet, there is nothing we can do about that.", "I use my smartphone for such a long time, everybody has my data", "I have nothing to hide"), the perception that the data is a fair price for free services and recommendation ("The company must make some money, so they sell my data; and doing that they send me advertisements that I may like."). Some participants say they select the data they consent in sharing ("I control myself regarding what I share in these tools").

Participants that stated they would probably stop using the application justified their answers based on several dependencies: on perceived necessity of the service, on sensitiveness and intimacy of data, on the potential of damage to the person, on companies sharing data, on the type of information collected. As for the latter, some protect specific data: they are not willing to share location, access to camera and contacts.

5.4 Change in Attitude After Exposition to Feedback

The number of participants who answered the second questionnaire is too limited to allow quantitative results (23 out of 130) however, they indicate a behaviour that can be further explored in more extensive studies.

10 out of the 23 participants of the second phase rated their surprise with the collection of data after the experience of feedback as extreme, as Fig. 7 shows.

Analysing the answers of the population that participated in both phases of this research, we observe that there is a change towards more attention to terms of usage and privacy policies of services. If we associate the answers never/rarely/frequently/always as a linear scale, Fig. 8 shows that most participants changed at least one point towards being more careful with reading these terms.

Finally, Fig. 9 shows that participants did not reject the usage of the applications when they learn that they collect and/or share users' personal data. Instead, all participants either maintained their attitude or became more tolerant to usage of personal data. This finding suggests that awareness is not a determinant factor for acceptance or rejection of a data-based service of application.

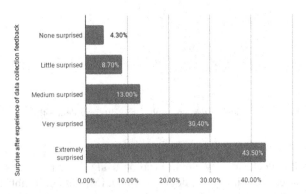

Fig. 7. Participants' feeling of surprise after experience of data collection feedback

Changes in atitude after using the feedback app

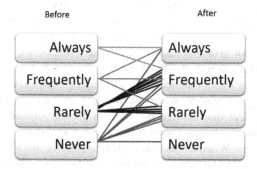

Fig. 8. Change in attitude towards reading policies, after usage of feedback application, subjects participating in both questionnaires

Changes in atitude towards stop using app

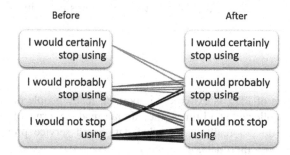

Fig. 9. Changes in attitude towards ceasing to use an application after evidence that it collects or shares personal data

6 Discussion

The analysis of participants' opinion, although not statistically significative, indicates that:

- The presentation of terms of usage and privacy policies do not stimulate users to read and understand them;
- Most participants are not interested in reading long texts prior to start using the services;
- Their attitude towards reading the policies change of they become continuously aware that their data is being collected.
- Their attitude towards ceasing to use an application that collects data does not change or tend to be more tolerant after they become aware that their data is being collected.

Because of the lack of interest in understanding the policies, we can discuss that the present form of transparency is equivalent to the passive transparency discussed by Oliver – the information may be available, but it depends on the will of the user to disclose the information. A large part of the research population is aware of data collection, but does not give due importance to the terms of use or privacy policies.

We advocate that continuous feedback is relevant to prepare users to understand the collection, but also the flow of subjects' data through processes. Continuous feedback moves the time displacement between the moment that the subject's conscience is formed and the moment that consent is given. In present situation, the moment that subjects are required to consent (prior to usage) is too distant from the moment in which awareness arises. When subjects are asked to consent in data collection, they are pressed against their own will to use the service. Reading text, whether long or short, in legalese or plain language, is not subjects' intention at that moment.

Of course, consent must be given prior to usage; it would not be fair otherwise. We argue that the instrument of revoking the consent will be used properly only if data collection and processing is actively disclosed. During usage, active feedback reminds subjects that data being uploaded comes at a price (sometimes minimally associated to subjects' consumption of their data allowance) and brings curiosity on what is being uploaded.

7   Conclusion

Although the theme of PDT is extremely important, many people do not realize that their data is being collected at all times; they do not read the terms of use and privacy policies, and thus do not really know what data-based service providers and data controllers can do with their data.

In this paper, we have reported our findings with an experiment of giving feedback of data collection on perception of transparency.

This work, despite having a simple proposal of feedback to inform the user when their data is being collected shows the users were surprised with the fact of the collection of data and that they had their perceptions changed regarding PDT, especially when it comes to reading the privacy policies of a service.

These findings suggest that visibility of the state of the system for the data collection collaborates to system legibility. Systems thus need not only to be transparent about personal data, but to promote active disclosure of data usage.

It is important to notice that in our experiment, the feedback given to our subjects was not associated to personal data upload, but any data. They were free to envisage the association between their behaviour using applications and the uploaded data. That is, the intention of the application was not to inform on the fact that personal data was being uploaded, but to create the conscience that data, whatever its nature, was being uploaded.

Because our research was carried on close to the GDPR enforcement, we believe that many subjects were not yet familiar with the discussion that came afterwards. Two participants in the first survey have asked researchers to try the application after the research was closed. Both informed that they remembered the invitation after having contact with the PDT issue.

Data collection feedback aims to change the way subjects understand their personal data, raising more importance to this concept, educating them not to disregard the terms of use and privacy policies, understanding their rights, and even questioning whether the use of a digital service is worth, if your personal data must be given in.

We expect this work to contribute to companies, in order to motivate them to perceive the trend of subjects' behaviour change after the experience of feedback. Companies that collect, distribute or consume personal data from users can exploit feedback to increase user trust in their services and even improve their image to the market. Finally, we expect to contribute the evolution of policies, showing the importance of active disclosure on collection, distribution and consumption of their personal data, in an instant and continuous manner.

References

1. European Union: Regulation 2016/679 of the European Parliament and the Council of the European Union of 27 April 2016 on the protection of natural person
2. Mortier, R., Haddadi, H., Henderson, T., Mcauley, J.: Human-data interaction. In: Soegaard, M., Friis Dam, R. (eds.) The Encyclopedia of Human-Computer Interaction, 2nd ed. The Interaction Design Foundation
3. Oliver, R.: What is Transparency?. McGraw-Hill, New York (2004)
4. Nielsen, J.: 10 Usability Heuristics for User Interface Design, https://www.nngroup.com/articles/ten-usability-heuristics/. Accessed 14 Feb 2019
5. Johnston, J., Eloff, J., Labuschagne, L.: Security and human computer interfaces. Comput. Secur. **22**(8), 675–684 (2003)
6. Mackinlay, M.: Phases of accuracy diagnosis: (in)visibility of system status in the Fitbit. Intersect: Stanf. J. Sci. Technol. Soc. **6**(2), 1–9 (2013)
7. Harley, A.: Visibility of system status. https://www.nngroup.com/articles/visibility-system-status/?lm=match-system-real-world&pt=article. Accessed 14 Feb 2019
8. Brasil. Conselho Nacional de Saúde. Resolução 510 (2016)
9. Google Developers documentation on TrafficStats class. https://developer.android.com/reference/kotlin/android/net/TrafficStats. Accessed 14 Feb 2019

Author Index

Printed in the United States
By Bookmasters